Sports Illustrated For Kids

YEAR IN SPORTS 2006

from the Editors of SPORTS ILLUSTRATED FOR KIDS

SCHOLASTIC REFERENCE

AN IMPRINT OF

SCHOLASTIC

Cover photography credits
Tom Brady: Rich Kane/Icon SMI
Michelle Kwan: John Amis/AP
Tracy McGrady: Bill Baptist/NBAE/Getty Images
Freddy Adu: John Todd
Hannah Teter: Jed Jacobsohn/Getty Images
Allyson Felix: Jamie Squire/Getty Images
Manny Ramirez: Ezra Shaw/Getty Images

Back-cover photography credits
Roger Federer: Simon Bruty/Sports Illustrated
Matt Leinart: Kirby Lee/WireImage.com
Lisa Leslie: Barry Gossage/Getty Images

SPORTS ILLUSTRATED FOR KIDS Year in Sports 2006 is a production of SPORTS ILLUSTRATED FOR KIDS and SPORTS ILLUSTRATED FOR KIDS Books: Erin Egan, Senior Editor/Editorial Projects; Beth Power Bugler, Creative Director; Edward Duarte, Designer; Ryan Schick, Photo Editor; Nick Friedman, Ellen C. Labrecque, Justin Tejada, Senior Editors; Sachin Shenolikar, Chief of Reporters; André Carter, Davin Coburn, Gary Gramling, Ted Keith, Shawn Nicholls, Craig Usiak, Reporters; John Kreiser, Copy Chief; Howard Gotfryd, Editorial Production Manager; Steve Chanin, Page Makeup Deputy; Rena Gross, Roy White, Data Entry

Scholastic Reference staff: Kenneth Wright, Editorial Director; Mary Varilla Jones, Editor; Brenda Murray, Assistant Editor; Karyn Browne, Managing Editor; Melinda Weigel, Production Editor; Nancy Sabato, Art Director; Kirk Howle, Manufacturing Coordinator

0-439-75516-6

10 9 8 7 6 5 4 3 2   05 06 07 08 09

Printed in the U.S.A. 23
First printing, December 2005

The story of the 2004 NFL season was the continued control of one team over the rest of the league. The New England Patriots became just the second team in NFL history to win three Super Bowls in four seasons by beating the Philadelphia Eagles, 24–21, in Super Bowl XXXIX. The Patriots joined the Dallas Cowboys, who won three Super Bowls from 1992-95.

The Pats also became the seventh team to win back-to-back Super Bowls. Patriot wide receiver Deion Branch tied Cincinnati tight end Dan Ross and San Francisco wide receiver Jerry Rice for the Super Bowl single-game reception record (11) and was named MVP of the game.

Some of the best single-season quarterback performances in recent NFL history occurred in 2004.

Five quarterbacks passed for more than 4,000 yards, and another seven passed for more than 3,500 yards. Peyton Manning of the Indianapolis Colts threw 49 touchdown passes to break Dan Marino's single-season record. Manning also passed for a career-high 4,557 yards and set an NFL record for highest passer rating (121.1). Daunte Culpepper of the Minnesota Vikings led all quarterbacks in passing yards (4,717). Donovan McNabb of the Eagles established career highs in passing yards (3,875), touchdown passes (31), passer rating (104.7), and completion percentage (64 percent).

The NFL's all-time leading rusher, Emmitt Smith, of the Dallas Cowboys and Arizona Cardinals, retired. Smith finished his 15-year career with 18,355 rushing yards. The title of leading active NFL rusher now belongs to Curtis Martin of the New York Jets. At the start of the 2005 season, Martin was fourth on the all-time rushing list, with 13,366 yards. In 2004, at age 31, he became the oldest running back to win the regular-season rushing title. Martin (1,697 yards) edged Shaun Alexander of the Seattle Seahawks for the title by one yard.

Quarterback Tom Brady led the New England Patriots to their third Super Bowl victory in four seasons.

BOB ROSATO/SPORTS ILLUSTRATED

AFC TEAMS

Baltimore Ravens
Buffalo Bills
Cincinnati Bengals
Cleveland Browns
Denver Broncos
Houston Texans
Indianapolis Colts
Jacksonville Jaguars
Kansas City Chiefs
Miami Dolphins
New England Patriots
New York Jets
Oakland Raiders
Pittsburgh Steelers
San Diego Chargers
Tennessee Titans

CONTENTS

Patriot wide receiver Deion Branch tied a Super Bowl record with 11 receptions.

Wide receiver Terrell Owens of the Eagles came back from a broken ankle to catch 9 passes in the big game.

NFC TEAMS

Arizona Cardinals
Atlanta Falcons
Carolina Panthers
Chicago Bears
Dallas Cowboys
Detroit Lions
Green Bay Packers
Minnesota Vikings
New Orleans Saints
New York Giants
Philadelphia Eagles
San Francisco 49ers
Seattle Seahawks
St. Louis Rams
Tampa Bay Buccaneers
Washington Redskins

2004 NFL FINAL STANDINGS

AFC EAST							NFC EAST					
TEAM	W	L	T	PCT	PF	PA	TEAM	W	L	T	PCT	PF	PA
yz-Patriots	14	2	0	.875	437	260	*yz-Eagles	13	3	0	.812	386	260
Jets	10	6	0	.625	333	261	Giants	6	10	0	.375	303	347
Bills	9	7	0	.562	395	284	Cowboys	6	10	0	.375	293	405
Dolphins	4	12	0	.250	275	354	Redskins	6	10	0	.375	240	265

AFC NORTH							NFC NORTH					
TEAM	W	L	T	PCT	PF	PA	TEAM	W	L	T	PCT	PF	PA
*yz-Steelers	15	1	0	.938	372	251	y-Packers	10	6	0	.625	424	380
Ravens	9	7	0	.562	317	268	x-Vikings	8	8	0	.500	405	395
Bengals	8	8	0	.500	374	372	Lions	6	10	0	.375	296	350
Browns	4	12	0	.250	276	390	Bears	5	11	0	.312	231	331

AFC SOUTH							NFC SOUTH					
TEAM	W	L	T	PCT	PF	PA	TEAM	W	L	T	PCT	PF	PA
y-Colts	12	4	0	.750	522	351	yz-Falcons	11	5	0	.688	340	337
Jaguars	9	7	0	.562	261	280	Saints	8	8	0	.500	348	405
Texans	7	9	0	.438	309	339	Panthers	7	9	0	.438	355	339
Titans	5	11	0	.312	344	439	Buccaneers	5	11	0	.312	301	304

AFC WEST							NFC WEST					
TEAM	W	L	T	PCT	PF	PA	TEAM	W	L	T	PCT	PF	PA
y-Chargers	12	4	0	.750	446	313	y-Seahawks	9	7	0	.562	371	373
x-Broncos	10	6	0	.625	381	304	x-Rams	8	8	0	.500	319	392
Chiefs	7	9	0	.438	483	435	Cardinals	6	10	0	.375	284	322
Raiders	5	11	0	.312	320	442	49ers	2	14	0	.125	259	452

x-clinched playoff berth y-clinched division title z-clinched first-round bye *clinched home-field advantage

KEY — W=win; L=loss; T=tie; PCT=winning percentage; PF=points for; PA=points against

2004 NFL PLAYOFFS

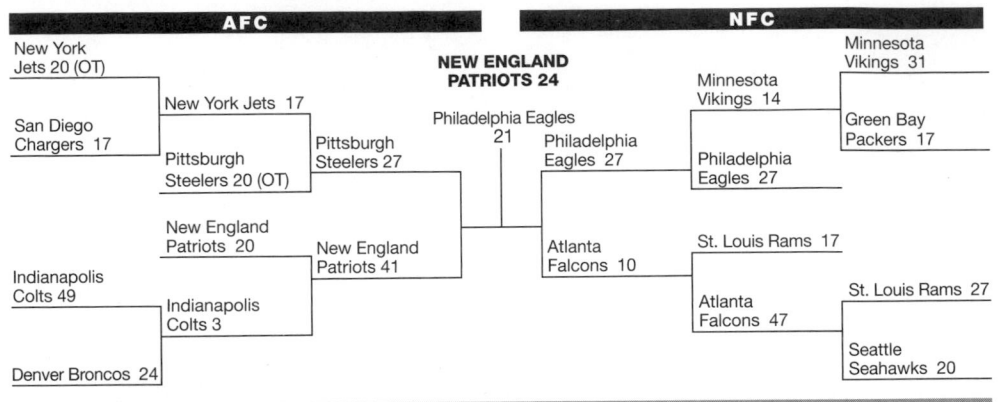

| AFC | | | | | | | | NFC | | |

New York
Jets 20 (OT)

New York Jets 17

San Diego
Chargers 17

Pittsburgh
Steelers 20 (OT)

Pittsburgh
Steelers 27

**NEW ENGLAND
PATRIOTS 24**

Philadelphia Eagles
21

New England
Patriots 20

New England
Patriots 41

Indianapolis
Colts 49

Indianapolis
Colts 3

Denver Broncos 24

Minnesota
Vikings 31

Minnesota
Vikings 14

Green Bay
Packers 17

Philadelphia
Eagles 27

Philadelphia
Eagles 27

Atlanta
Falcons 10

St. Louis Rams 17

Atlanta
Falcons 47

St. Louis Rams 27

Seattle
Seahawks 20

| WILD CARD | DIV. PLAYOFF | CONF. CHAMPIONSHIP | CONF. CHAMPIONSHIP | DIV. PLAYOFF | WILD CARD |

AFC WILD-CARD GAMES

NEW YORK JETS 20
SAN DIEGO CHARGERS 17 (OT)

	1Q	2Q	3Q	4Q	OT	T
JETS	0	7	10	0	3	20
CHARGERS	0	7	0	10	0	17

1ST QUARTER
None
2ND QUARTER
TD SD: Keenan McCardell, 26-yard pass from Drew Brees
(Nate Kaeding, extra point), 9:26. Drive: 13 plays, 88 yards
in 8:25.
TD NY: Anthony Becht, 13-yard pass from Chad Pennington
(Doug Brien, extra point), 2:54. Drive: 5 plays, 37 yards
in 2:19.
3RD QUARTER
TD NY: Santana Moss, 47-yard pass from Chad Pennington
(Doug Brien, extra point), 10:29. Drive: 5 plays, 75 yards
in 2:31.
FG NY: Doug Brien, 42 yards, 1:23. Drive: 8 plays, 42 yards
in 5:31.
4TH QUARTER
FG SD: Nate Kaeding, 35 yards, 10:43. Drive: 12 plays,
54 yards in 5:40.
TD SD: Antonio Gates, 1-yard pass from Drew Brees (Nate
Kaeding, extra point), 0:11. Drive: 10 plays, 80 yards in 4:35.
OVERTIME
FG NY: Doug Brien, 28 yards, 0:05. Drive: 8 plays, 60 yards
in 4:14.

■ *Fast Fact:* The Dallas Cowboys
have scored the most points (1,281)
and allowed the most points (1,008) in
post-season history.

INDIANAPOLIS COLTS 49
DENVER BRONCOS 24

	1Q	2Q	3Q	4Q	T
BRONCOS	0	3	14	7	24
COLTS	14	21	0	14	49

1ST QUARTER
TD Ind: James Mungro, 2-yard pass from Peyton Manning
(Mike Vanderjagt, extra point), 7:23. Drive: 9 plays, 76 yards
in 3:43.
TD Ind: Edgerrin James, 1-yard run (Mike Vanderjagt, extra
point), 0:38. Drive: 8 plays, 87 yards in 4:59.
2ND QUARTER
TD Ind: Dallas Clark, 19-yard pass from Peyton Manning
(Mike Vanderjagt, extra point), 8:11. Drive: 4 plays, 52 yards
in 1:42.
FG Den: Jason Elam, 33 yards, 5:19. Drive: 7 plays,
51 yards in 2:52.
TD Ind: Reggie Wayne, 35-yard pass from Peyton Manning
(Mike Vanderjagt, extra point), 4:29. Drive: 2 plays, 40 yards
in 0:50.
TD Ind: Peyton Manning, 1-yard run (Mike Vanderjagt, extra
point), 0:06. Drive: 8 plays, 75 yards in 3:07.
3RD QUARTER
TD Den: Rod Smith, 9-yard pass from Jake Plummer (Jason
Elam, extra point), 9:01. Drive: 10 plays, 71 yards in 5:59.
TD Den: Jeb Putzier, 35-yard pass from Jake Plummer
(Jason Elam, extra point), 1:10. Drive: 9 plays, 85 yards
in 5:39.
4TH QUARTER
TD Ind: Reggie Wayne, 43-yard pass from Peyton Manning
(Mike Vanderjagt, extra point), 12:48. Drive: 6 plays, 80 yards
in 3:22.
TD Den: Tatum Bell, 1-yard run (Jason Elam, extra point),
7:45. Drive: 10 plays, 57 yards in 5:03.
TD Ind: Dominic Rhodes, 2-yard run (Mike Vanderjagt, extra
point), 2:02. Drive: 9 plays, 45 yards in 5:43.

NFC WILD-CARD GAMES

MINNESOTA VIKINGS 31
GREEN BAY PACKERS 17

	1Q	2Q	3Q	4Q	T
VIKINGS	17	7	0	7	31
PACKERS	3	7	0	7	17

1ST QUARTER
TD Minn: Moe Williams, 68-yard pass from Daunte Culpepper (Morten Andersen, extra point), 13:20. Drive: 3 plays, 76 yards in 1:40.
TD Minn: Randy Moss, 20-yard pass from Daunte Culpepper (Morten Andersen, extra point), 9:50. Drive: 4 plays, 55 yards in 1:55.
FG Minn: Morten Andersen, 35 yards, 6:06. Drive: 6 plays, 40 yards in 2:38.
FG GB: Ryan Longwell, 43 yards, 2:42. Drive: 8 plays, 37 yards in 3:24.
2ND QUARTER
TD GB: Bubba Franks, 4-yard pass from Brett Favre (Ryan Longwell, extra point), 10:24. Drive: 10 plays, 57 yards in 6:14.
TD Minn: Nate Burleson, 19-yard pass from Daunte Culpepper (Morten Andersen, extra point), 6:33. Drive: 2 plays, 28 yards.
3RD QUARTER
None
4TH QUARTER
TD Minn: Najeh Davenport, 1-yard run (Ryan Longwell, extra point), 13:37. Drive: 9 plays, 78 yards in 4:16.
TD Minn: Randy Moss, 34-yard pass from Daunte Culpepper (Morten Andersen, extra point), 10:18. Drive: 6 plays, 66 yards in 3:19

ST. LOUIS RAMS 27
SEATTLE SEAHAWKS 20

	1Q	2Q	3Q	4Q	T
RAMS	7	7	3	10	27
SEAHAWKS	3	7	3	7	20

1ST QUARTER
TD StL: Torry Holt, 15-yard pass from Marc Bulger (Jeff Wilkins, extra point), 11:33. Drive: 6 plays, 75 yards in 3:27.
FG Sea: Josh Brown, 47 yards, 2:05. Drive: 9 plays, 46 yards in 4:30.
2ND QUARTER
TD StL: Marshall Faulk, 1-yard run (Jeff Wilkins, extra point), 13:32. Drive: 6 plays, 75 yards in 3:33.
TD Sea: Bobby Engram, 19-yard pass from Matt Hasselbeck (Josh Brown, extra point), 8:18. Drive: 9 plays, 84 yards in 5:14.
3RD QUARTER
FG Sea: Josh Brown, 30 yards, 8:52. Drive: 14 plays, 64 yards in 6:08.
FG StL: Jeff Wilkins, 38 yards, 2:35. Drive: 12 plays, 48 yards in 6:17.
4TH QUARTER
TD Sea: Darrell Jackson, 23-yard pass from Matt Hasselbeck (Josh Brown, extra point), 13:43. Drive: 7 plays, 76 yards in 3:52.
FG StL: Jeff Wilkins, 27 yards, 8:07. Drive: 11 plays, 60 yards in 5:36.
TD StL: Cameron Cleeland, 17-yard pass from Marc Bulger (Jeff Wilkins, extra point), 2:11. Drive: 7 plays, 76 yards in 3:31.

AFC DIVISIONAL GAMES

PITTSBURGH STEELERS 20 (OT)
NEW YORK JETS 17

	1Q	2Q	3Q	4Q	OT	T
JETS	0	10	7	0	0	17
STEELERS	10	0	0	7	3	20

1ST QUARTER
FG Pitt: Jeff Reed, 45 yards, 5:18. Drive: 7 plays, 37 yards in 3:20.
TD Pitt: Jerome Bettis, 3-yard run (Jeff Reed, extra point), 1:58. Drive: 5 plays, 25 yards in 2:18.
2ND QUARTER
FG NY: Doug Brien, 42 yards, 10:33. Drive: 11 plays, 38 yards in 6:25.
TD NY: Santana Moss, 75-yard punt return (Doug Brien, extra point), 3:00.
3RD QUARTER
TD NY: Reggie Tongue, 86-yard interception return (Doug Brien, extra point), 3:52.
4TH QUARTER
TD Pitt: Hines Ward, 4-yard pass from Ben Roethlisberger (Jeff Reed, extra point), 6:00. Drive: 12 plays, 66 yards in 6:41.
OVERTIME
FG Pitt: Jeff Reed, 33 yards, 0:50. Drive: 14 plays, 72 yards in 8:19.

NEW ENGLAND PATRIOTS 20
INDIANAPOLIS COLTS 3

	1Q	2Q	3Q	4Q	T
COLTS	0	3	0	0	3
PATRIOTS	0	6	7	7	20

1ST QUARTER
None
2ND QUARTER
FG NE: Adam Vinatieri, 24 yards, 10:40. Drive: 16 plays, 78 yards in 9:07.
FG NE: Adam Vinatieri, 31 yards, 7:56. Drive: 6 plays, 48 yards in 1:26.
FG Ind: Mike Vanderjagt, 23 yards, 0:00. Drive: 11 plays, 67 yards in 1:52.
3RD QUARTER
TD NE: David Givens, 5-yard pass from Tom Brady (Adam Vinatieri, extra point), 1:30. Drive: 15 plays, 87 yards in 8:16.
4TH QUARTER
TD NE: Tom Brady, 1-yard run (Adam Vinatieri, extra point), 7:10. Drive: 14 plays, 94 yards in 7:24.

TRIVIA CHALLENGE

How many cities have had a Super Bowl champion and a World Series champion in the same season?

Three: Boston (Patriots and Red Sox in 2004), Pittsburgh (Steelers and Pirates in 1979), and New York (Jets and Mets in 1969).

NFC DIVISIONAL GAMES

PHILADELPHIA EAGLES 27
MINNESOTA VIKINGS 14

	1Q	2Q	3Q	4Q	T
VIKINGS	0	7	0	7	14
EAGLES	7	14	0	6	27

1ST QUARTER
TD Phi: Freddie Mitchell, 2-yard pass from Donovan McNabb (David Akers, extra point), 6:18. Drive: 7 plays, 92 yards in 3:57.
2ND QUARTER
TD Phi: Brian Westbrook, 7-yard pass from Donovan McNabb (David Akers, extra point), 14:16. Drive: 7 plays, 92 yards in 3:57.
TD Minn: Daunte Culpepper, 7-yard run (Morten Andersen, extra point), 10:37. Drive: 6 plays, 58 yards in 3:39.
TD Phi: Freddie Mitchell, 0-yard fumble return (David Akers, extra point), 10:08. Drive: 2 plays, 46 yards in 0:29.
3RD QUARTER
None
4TH QUARTER
FG Phi: David Akers, 21 yards, 13:20. Drive: 6 plays, 66 yards in 2:24.
FG Phi: David Akers, 23 yards, 6:39. Drive: 10 plays, 55 yards in 5:36.
TD Minn: Marcus Robinson, 32-yard pass from Daunte Culpepper (Morten Andersen, extra point), 1:59. Drive: 12 plays, 80 yards in 4:40.

ATLANTA FALCONS 47
ST. LOUIS RAMS 17

	1Q	2Q	3Q	4Q	T
RAMS	7	10	0	0	17
FALCONS	14	14	10	9	47

1ST QUARTER
TD Atl: Alge Crumpler, 18-yard pass from Michael Vick (Jay Feely, extra point), 12:00. Drive: 5 plays, 76 yards in 3:00.
TD StL: Kevin Curtis, 57-yard pass from Marc Bulger (Jeff Wilkins, extra point), 9:14. Drive: 5 plays, 81 yards in 2:46.
TD Atl: Warrick Dunn, 62-yard run (Jay Feely, extra point), 7:52. Drive: 4 plays, 80 yards in 1:22.
2ND QUARTER
TD Atl: Warrick Dunn, 19-yard run (Jay Feely, extra point), 9:58. Drive: 13 plays, 80 yards in 8:18.
TD StL: Torry Holt, 28-yard pass from Marc Bulger (Jeff Wilkins, extra point), 5:26. Drive: 8 plays, 75 yards in 4:32.
TD Atl: Allen Rossum, 68-yard punt return (Jay Feely, extra point), 0:59.
FG StL: Jeff Wilkins, 55 yards, 0:00. Drive: 9 plays, 43 yards in 0:59.
3RD QUARTER
TD Atl: Peerless Price, 6-yard pass from Michael Vick (Jay Feely, extra point), 10:05. Drive: 6 plays, 32 yards in 3:15.
FG Atl: Jay Feely, 38 yards, 5:54. Drive: 4 plays, -7 yards in 2:02.
4TH QUARTER
SAFETY Atl: Brady Smith, 11:39.
TD Atl: T.J. Duckett, 4-yard run (Jay Feely, extra point), 1:54. Drive: 15 plays, 58 yards in 9:45.

AFC CONFERENCE CHAMPIONSHIP

NEW ENGLAND PATRIOTS 41
PITTSBURGH STEELERS 27

	1Q	2Q	3Q	4Q	T
PATRIOTS	10	14	7	10	41
STEELERS	3	0	14	10	27

1ST QUARTER
FG NE: Adam Vinatieri, 48 yards, 11:20. Drive: 5 plays, 18 yards in 2:13.
TD NE: Deion Branch, 60-yard pass from Tom Brady (Adam Vinatieri, extra point), 6:49. Drive: 1 play, 60 yards in 0:09.
FG Pitt: Jeff Reed, 43 yards, 1:22. Drive: 5 plays, 23 yards in 2:10.
2ND QUARTER
TD NE: David Givens, 9-yard pass from Tom Brady (Adam Vinatieri, extra point), 7:08. Drive: 5 plays, 70 yards in 2:52.
TD NE: Rodney Harrison, 87-yard interception return (Adam Vinatieri, extra point), 2:14.
3RD QUARTER
TD Pitt: Jerome Bettis, 5-yard run (Jeff Reed, extra point), 10:54. Drive: 5 plays, 56 yards in 2:39.
TD NE: Corey Dillon, 25-yard run (Adam Vinatieri, extra point), 7:27. Drive: 7 plays, 69 yards in 3:27.
TD Pitt: Hines Ward, 30-yard pass from Ben Roethlisberger (Jeff Reed, extra point), 2:35. Drive: 10 plays, 60 yards in 4:52.
4TH QUARTER
FG Pitt: Jeff Reed, 20 yards, 13:29. Drive: 6 plays, 53 yards in 2:14.
FG NE: Adam Vinatieri, 31 yards, 8:03. Drive: 10 plays, 49 yards in 5:26.
TD NE: Deion Branch, 23-yard run (Adam Vinatieri, extra point), 2:23. Drive: 10 plays, 55 yards in 5:06.
TD Pitt: Plaxico Burress, 7-yard pass from Ben Roethlisberger (Jeff Reed, extra point), 0:52. Drive: 6 plays, 61 yards in 1:31.

NFC CONFERENCE CHAMPIONSHIP

PHILADELPHIA EAGLES 27
ATLANTA FALCONS 10

	1Q	2Q	3Q	4Q	T
FALCONS	0	10	0	0	10
EAGLES	7	7	6	7	27

1ST QUARTER
TD Phi: Dorsey Levens, 4-yard run (David Akers, extra point), 4:16. Drive: 6 plays, 70 yards in 3:09.
2ND QUARTER
FG Atl: Jay Feely, 23 yards, 10:19. Drive: 17 plays, 64 yards in 8:57.
TD Phi: Chad Lewis, 3-yard pass from Donovan McNabb (David Akers, extra point), 4:58. Drive: 9 plays, 72 yards in 5:21.
TD Atl: Warrick Dunn, 10-yard run (Jay Feely, extra point), 2:02. Drive: 5 plays, 70 yards in 2:56.
3RD QUARTER
FG Phi: David Akers, 31 yards, 8:55. Drive: 11 plays, 60 yards in 6:05.
FG Phi: David Akers, 34 yards, 2:00. Drive: 4 plays, -5 yards in 0:56.
4TH QUARTER
TD Phi: Chad Lewis, 2-yard pass from Donovan McNabb (David Akers, extra point), 3:21. Drive: 11 plays, 65 yards in 6:53.

SUPER BOWL XXXIX

NEW ENGLAND PATRIOTS 24
PHILADELPHIA EAGLES 21

FEBRUARY 6, 2005
ALLTELL STADIUM, JACKSONVILLE, FLORIDA

	1Q	2Q	3Q	4Q	T
PATRIOTS	0	7	7	10	24
EAGLES	0	7	7	7	21

1ST QUARTER
None
2ND QUARTER
TD Phi: L.J. Smith, 6-yard pass from Donovan McNabb (David Akers, extra point), 9:55. Drive: 9 plays, 81 yards in 4:36.

TD NE: David Givens, 4-yard pass from Tom Brady (Adam Vinatieri, extra point), 1:10. Drive: 7 plays, 37 yards in 3:15.
3RD QUARTER
TD NE: Mike Vrabel, 2-yard pass from Tom Brady (Adam Vinatieri, extra point), 11:04. Drive: 9 plays, 69 yards in 3:56.
TD Phi: Brian Westbrook, 10-yard pass from Donovan McNabb (David Akers, extra point), 3:35. Drive: 10 plays, 74 yards in 4:17.
4TH QUARTER
TD NE: Corey Dillon, 2-yard run (Adam Vinatieri, extra point), 13:44. Drive: 9 plays, 66 yards in 4:51.
FG NE: Adam Vinatieri, 22 yards, 8:40. Drive: 8 plays, 43 yards in 3:49.
TD Phi: Greg Lewis, 30-yard pass from Donovan McNabb (David Akers, extra point), 1:48. Drive: 13 plays, 79 yards in 3:52.

LEGENDS

Eric Dickerson gained more than 1,000 yards in each of his first four NFL seasons.

PETER READ MILLER/SPORTS ILLUSTRATED

■ **Eric Dickerson, running back,** b. November 2, 1960, Sealy, Texas. Dickerson ranks sixth on the NFL's career rushing list (13,259 yards). He led the NFL in rushing four times (1983, 1984, 1986, and 1988). As a Los Angeles Ram, Dickerson had the NFL's greatest individual rushing season (2,105 yards) in 1984. He ran for 100 or more yards 64 times during his 11-season career. Dickerson was inducted into the Pro Football Hall of Fame in 1999.

■ **Alan C. Page, defensive tackle,** b. August 7, 1945, Canton, Ohio. Page had 148.5 quarterback sacks during his 15-season career with the Minnesota Vikings and Chicago Bears. He also blocked 28 kicks and recovered 23 fumbles by opponents. In 1971, Page became the first defensive player to be named the NFL's MVP. He was the NFC Defensive Player of the Year four times. Page was inducted into the Pro Football Hall of Fame in 1988. He now serves as a judge on the Minnesota Supreme Court, the first African American to do so.

■ **Barry Sanders, running back,** b. July 16, 1968, Wichita, Kansas. Sanders retired from the Detroit Lions in 1998 after 10 NFL seasons. He was 31 years old. Sanders ranks third on the NFL's career rushing list (15,269 yards). He became the third player to break the 2,000-yard barrier when he rushed for 2,053 yards in 1997. Sanders holds NFL rushing records for most 1,500-yard rushing seasons in a career (5), consecutive 1,500-yard rushing seasons (4), single-season 100-yard rushing games (14), and career touchdown runs of 50 or more yards (15). He was inducted into the Pro Football Hall of Fame in 2004.

SUPER BOWL XXXIX (cont.)

TEAM STATS

	PATRIOTS	EAGLES
First Downs	21	24
Rushing	6	4
Passing	14	18
Penalty	1	2
3rd-Down Conversions	4-12	9-16
4th-Down Conversions	0-0	0-0
Total Net Yards	331	369
Total Plays	63	72
Average Gain	5.3	5.1
Net Yards Rushing	112	45
Rushes	28	17
Avg. Per Rush	4.0	2.6

	PATRIOTS	EAGLES
Net Yards Passing	219	324
Comp.-Att.	23-33	30-51
Yards Per Pass	6.3	5.9
Sacked-Yards Lost	2-17	4-33
Had Intercepted	0	3
Punts-Average	7-45.1	5-42.8
Return Yards	92	133
Punts-Returns	4-26	3-19
Kickoffs-Returns	3-61	5-114
Int.-Returns	3-5	0-0
Penalties-Yards	7-47	3-35
Fumbles-Lost	1-1	2-1
Time of Pos.	31:37	28:23

PLAYER STATISTICS: PATRIOTS

OFFENSE

PASSING	COMP-ATT	YDS	TD	INT
T. Brady	23-33	236	2	0

RUSHING	ATT	YDS	TD	LG
C. Dillon	18	75	1	25
K. Faulk	8	38	0	12
P. Pass	1	0	0	0
T. Brady	1	-1	0	-1

RECEIVING	REC	YDS	TD	LG
D. Branch	11	133	0	27
C. Dillon	3	31	0	16
K. Faulk	2	27	0	14
D. Givens	3	19	1	13
T. Brown	2	17	0	12
D. Graham	1	7	0	7
M. Vrabel	1	2	1	2

DEFENSE	T-A	SCK	INT	FF
R. Gay	10-0	0	0	0
R. Harrison	7-0	1	2	0
T. Bruschi	6-1	1	1	0
A. Samuel	4-0	0	0	0
R. Phifer	3-0	0	0	0
D. Reid	3-0	0	0	0
E. Wilson	3-0	0	0	0
M. Chatham	2-0	0	0	0
T. Johnson	2-1	0	0	0
W. McGinest	2-0	0	0	0
R. Seymour	2-0	1	0	0
M. Vrabel	2-2	1	0	0
R. Abdullah	1-0	0	0	0
R. Colvin	1-0	0	0	0
L. Izzo	1-0	0	0	0
H. Poteat	1-0	0	0	0
K. Traylor	1-0	0	0	0
T. Warren	1-0	0	0	0

PLAYER STATISTICS: EAGLES

OFFENSE

PASSING	COMP-ATT	YDS	TD	INT
D. McNabb	30-51	357	3	3

RUSHING	ATT	YDS	TD	LG
B. Westbrook	15	44	0	22
D. Levens	1	1	0	1
D. McNabb	1	0	0	0

RECEIVING	REC	YDS	TD	LG
T. Owens	9	122	0	36
T. Pinkston	4	82	0	40
B. Westbrook	7	60	1	15
G. Lewis	4	53	1	30
L. Smith	4	27	1	9
F. Mitchell	1	11	0	11
J. Parry	1	2	0	2

DEFENSE	T-A	SCK	INT	FF
M. Lewis	5-1	0	0	0
K. Adams	4-1	0	0	0
B. Dawkins	4-1	0	0	0
J. Trotter	4-0	0	0	0
M. Ware	4-0	0	0	0
S. Brown	3-1	0	0	0
D. Burgess	3-1	1	0	0
R. Hood	3-0	0	0	0
D. Jones	2-0	0	0	0
M. Labinjo	2-0	0	0	0
G. Lewis	2-0	0	0	0
S. Rayburn	2-0	0	0	0
I. Reese	2-0	0	0	0
L. Sheppard	2-1	0	0	0
M. Simoneau	2-0	0	0	0
D. Walker	2-1	0	0	0
J. Kearse	1-1	0	0	0
J. Mayberry	1-0	0	0	0
Q. Mikell	1-0	0	0	0
F. Mitchell	1-0	0	0	0
T. Owens	1-0	0	0	0
J. Reed	1-0	0	0	0
C. Simon	1-0	0	0	0
H. Thomas	1-2	0	0	0
J. Thomason	1-0	0	0	0

KEY COMP-ATT=completions-attempts; YDS=yards; TD=touchdowns; INT=interceptions; ATT=attempts; LG=long; REC=receptions; T-A=tackles-assists; SCK=sacks; FF=forced fumbles

THE ASSOCIATED PRESS 2004 ALL-PRO TEAM

OFFENSE

QUARTERBACK Peyton Manning, Indianapolis Colts

RUNNING BACKS Curtis Martin, New York Jets; LaDainian Tomlinson, San Diego Chargers

FULLBACK William Henderson, Green Bay Packers

TIGHT END Antonio Gates, San Diego Chargers

WIDE RECEIVERS Terrell Owens, Philadelphia Eagles; Muhsin Muhammad, Carolina Panthers

TACKLES Walter Jones, Seattle Seahawks; William Roaf, Kansas City Chiefs; Willie Anderson, Cincinnati Bengals

GUARDS Alan Faneca, Pittsburgh Steelers; Brian Waters, Kansas City Chiefs

CENTER Jeff Hartings, Pittsburgh Steelers

KICKER Adam Vinatieri, New England Patriots

KICK RETURNER Eddie Drummond, Detroit Lions

Curtis Martin,
New York Jets

DEFENSE

ENDS Dwight Freeney, Indianapolis Colts; Julius Peppers, Carolina Panthers

TACKLES Kevin Williams, Minnesota Vikings; Richard Seymour, New England Patriots

OUTSIDE LINEBACKERS Takeo Spikes, Buffalo Bills; Derrick Brooks, Tampa Bay Buccaneers

INSIDE LINEBACKERS James Farrior, Pittsburgh Steelers; Ray Lewis, Baltimore Ravens

CORNERBACKS Ronde Barber, Tampa Bay Buccaneers; Champ Bailey, Denver Broncos; Lito Sheppard, Philadelphia Eagles

SAFETIES Ed Reed, Baltimore Ravens; Brian Dawkins, Philadelphia Eagles

PUNTER Shane Lechler, Oakland Raiders

2004 REGULAR-SEASON RESULTS — AFC

BALTIMORE RAVENS

WEEK	OPPONENT	SCORE	W/L/T
1	at Browns	3–20	L
2	STEELERS	30–13	W
3	at Bengals	23–9	W
4	CHIEFS	24–27	L
5	at Redskins	17–10	W
6	BYE WEEK	—	—
7	BILLS	20–6	W
8	at Eagles	10–15	L
9	BROWNS	27–13	W
10	at Jets	20–17	W
11	COWBOYS	30–10	W
12	at Patriots	3–24	L
13	BENGALS	26–27	L
14	GIANTS	37–14	W
15	at Colts	10–20	L
16	at Steelers	7–20	L
17	DOLPHINS	30–23	W

BUFFALO BILLS

WEEK	OPPONENT	SCORE	W/L/T
1	JAGUARS	10–13	L
2	at Raiders	10–13	L
3	BYE WEEK	—	—
4	PATRIOTS	17–31	L
5	at Jets	14–16	L
6	DOLPHINS	20–13	W
7	at Ravens	6–20	L
8	CARDINALS	38–14	W
9	JETS	22–17	W
10	at Patriots	6–29	L
11	RAMS	37–17	W
12	at Seahawks	38–9	W
13	at Dolphins	42–32	W
14	BROWNS	37–7	W
15	at Bengals	33–17	W
16	at 49ers	41–7	W
17	STEELERS	24–29	L

CINCINNATI BENGALS

WEEK	OPPONENT	SCORE	W/L/T
1	at Jets	24–31	L
2	DOLPHINS	16–13	W
3	RAVENS	9–23	L
4	at Steelers	17–28	L
5	BYE WEEK	—	—
6	at Browns	17–34	L
7	BRONCOS	23–10	W
8	at Titans	20–27	L
9	COWBOYS	26–3	W
10	at Redskins	17–10	W
11	STEELERS	14–19	L
12	BROWNS	58–48	W
13	at Ravens	27–26	W
14	at Patriots	28–35	L
15	BILLS	17–33	L
16	GIANTS	23–22	W
17	at Eagles	38–10	W

CLEVELAND BROWNS

WEEK	OPPONENT	SCORE	W/L/T
1	RAVENS	20–3	W
2	at Cowboys	12–19	L
3	at Giants	10–27	L
4	REDSKINS	17–13	W
5	at Steelers	23–34	L
6	BENGALS	34–17	W
7	EAGLES	31–34	L
8	BYE WEEK	—	—
9	at Ravens	13–27	L
10	STEELERS	10–24	L
11	JETS	7–10	L
12	at Bengals	48–58	L
13	PATRIOTS	15–42	L
14	at Bills	7–37	L
15	CHARGERS	0–21	L
16	at Dolphins	7–10	L
17	at Texans	22–14	W

Note: Home games are capitalized.

2004 REGULAR-SEASON RESULTS — AFC (cont.)

DENVER BRONCOS

WEEK	OPPONENT	SCORE	W/L/T
1	CHIEFS	34–24	W
2	at Jaguars	6–7	L
3	CHARGERS	23–13	W
4	at Buccaneers	16–13	W
5	PANTHERS	20–17	W
6	at Raiders	31–3	W
7	at Bengals	10–23	L
8	FALCONS	28–41	L
9	TEXANS	31–13	W
10	BYE WEEK	—	—
11	at Saints	34–13	W
12	RAIDERS	24–25	L
13	at Chargers	17–20	L
14	DOLPHINS	20–17	W
15	at Chiefs	17–45	L
16	at Titans	37–16	W
17	COLTS	33–14	W

HOUSTON TEXANS

WEEK	OPPONENT	SCORE	W/L/T
1	CHARGERS	20–27	L
2	at Lions	16–28	L
3	at Chiefs	24–21	W
4	RAIDERS	30–17	W
5	VIKINGS	28–34	L
6	at Titans	20–10	W
7	BYE WEEK	—	—
8	JAGUARS	20–6	W
9	at Broncos	13–31	L
10	at Colts	14–49	L
11	PACKERS	13–16	L
12	TITANS	31–21	W
13	at Jets	7–29	L
14	COLTS	14–23	L
15	at Bears	24–5	W
16	at Jaguars	21–0	W
17	BROWNS	14–22	L

INDIANAPOLIS COLTS

WEEK	OPPONENT	SCORE	W/L/T
1	at Patriots	24–27	L
2	at Titans	31–7	W
3	PACKERS	45–31	W
4	at Jaguars	24–17	W
5	RAIDERS	35–14	W
6	BYE WEEK	—	—
7	JAGUARS	24–27	L
8	at Chiefs	35–45	L
9	VIKINGS	31–28	W
10	TEXANS	49–14	W
11	at Bears	41–10	W
12	at Lions	41–9	W
13	TITANS	51–24	W
14	at Texans	23–14	W
15	RAVENS	20–10	W
16	CHARGERS	34–31	W
17	at Broncos	14–33	L

JACKSONVILLE JAGUARS

WEEK	OPPONENT	SCORE	W/L/T
1	at Bills	13–10	W
2	BRONCOS	7–6	W
3	at Titans	15–12	W
4	COLTS	17–24	L
5	at Chargers	21–34	L
6	CHIEFS	22–16	W
7	at Colts	27–24	W
8	at Texans	6–20	L
9	BYE WEEK	—	—
10	LIONS	23–17	W
11	TITANS	15–18	L
12	at Vikings	16–27	L
13	STEELERS	16–17	L
14	BEARS	22–3	W
15	at Packers	28–25	W
16	TEXANS	0–21	L
17	at Raiders	13–6	W

KANSAS CITY CHIEFS

WEEK	OPPONENT	SCORE	W/L/T
1	at Broncos	24–34	L
2	PANTHERS	17–28	L
3	TEXANS	21–24	L
4	at Ravens	27–24	W
5	BYE WEEK	—	—
6	at Jaguars	16–22	L
7	FALCONS	56–10	W
8	COLTS	45–35	W
9	at Buccaneers	31–34	L
10	at Saints	20–27	L
11	PATRIOTS	19–27	L
12	CHARGERS	31–34	L
13	at Raiders	34–27	W
14	at Titans	49–38	W
15	BRONCOS	45–17	W
16	RAIDERS	31–30	W
17	at Chargers	17–24	L

MIAMI DOLPHINS

WEEK	OPPONENT	SCORE	W/L/T
1	TITANS	7–17	L
2	at Bengals	13–16	L
3	STEELERS	3–13	L
4	JETS	9–17	L
5	at Patriots	10–24	L
6	at Bills	13–20	L
7	RAMS	31–14	W
8	at Jets	14–41	L
9	CARDINALS	23–24	L
10	BYE WEEK	—	—
11	at Seahawks	17–24	L
12	at 49ers	24–17	W
13	BILLS	32–42	L
14	at Broncos	17–20	L
15	PATRIOTS	29–28	W
16	BROWNS	10–7	W
17	at Ravens	23–30	L

NEW ENGLAND PATRIOTS

WEEK	OPPONENT	SCORE	W/L/T
1	COLTS	27–24	W
2	at Cardinals	23–12	W
3	BYE WEEK	—	—
4	at Bills	31–17	W
5	DOLPHINS	24–10	W
6	SEAHAWKS	30–20	W
7	JETS	13–7	W
8	at Steelers	20–34	L
9	at Rams	40–22	W
10	BILLS	29–6	W
11	at Chiefs	27–19	W
12	RAVENS	24–3	W
13	at Browns	42–15	W
14	BENGALS	35–28	W
15	at Dolphins	28–29	L
16	at Jets	23–7	W
17	49ERS	21–7	W

NEW YORK JETS

WEEK	OPPONENT	SCORE	W/L/T
1	BENGALS	31–24	W
2	at Chargers	34–28	W
3	BYE WEEK	—	—
4	at Dolphins	17–9	W
5	BILLS	16–14	W
6	49ERS	22–14	W
7	at Patriots	7–13	L
8	DOLPHINS	41–14	W
9	at Bills	17–22	L
10	RAVENS	17–20	L
11	at Browns	10–7	W
12	at Cardinals	13–3	W
13	TEXANS	29–7	W
14	at Steelers	6–17	L
15	SEAHAWKS	37–14	W
16	PATRIOTS	7–23	L
17	at Rams	29–32	L

OAKLAND RAIDERS

WEEK	OPPONENT	SCORE	W/L/T
1	at Steelers	21–24	L
2	BILLS	13–10	W
3	BUCCANEERS	30–20	W
4	at Texans	17–30	L
5	at Colts	14–35	L
6	BRONCOS	3–31	L
7	SAINTS	26–31	L
8	at Chargers	14–42	L
9	at Panthers	27–24	W
10	BYE WEEK	—	—
11	CHARGERS	17–23	L
12	at Broncos	25–24	W
13	CHIEFS	27–34	L
14	at Falcons	10–35	L
15	TITANS	40–35	W
16	at Chiefs	30–31	L
17	JAGUARS	6–13	L

PITTSBURGH STEELERS

WEEK	OPPONENT	SCORE	W/L/T
1	RAIDERS	24–21	W
2	at Ravens	13–30	L
3	at Dolphins	13–3	W
4	BENGALS	28–17	W
5	BROWNS	34–23	W
6	at Cowboys	24–20	W
7	BYE WEEK	—	—
8	PATRIOTS	34–20	W
9	EAGLES	27–3	W
10	at Browns	24–10	W
11	at Bengals	19–14	W
12	REDSKINS	16–7	W
13	at Jaguars	17–16	W
14	JETS	17–6	W
15	at Giants	33–30	W
16	RAVENS	20–7	W
17	at Bills	29–24	W

SAN DIEGO CHARGERS

WEEK	OPPONENT	SCORE	W/L/T
1	at Texans	27–20	W
2	JETS	28–34	L
3	at Broncos	13–23	L
4	TITANS	38–17	W
5	JAGUARS	34–21	W
6	at Falcons	20–21	L
7	at Panthers	17–6	W
8	RAIDERS	42–14	W
9	SAINTS	43–17	W
10	BYE WEEK	—	—
11	at Raiders	23–17	W
12	at Chiefs	34–31	W
13	BRONCOS	20–17	W
14	BUCCANEERS	31–24	W
15	at Browns	21–0	W
16	at Colts	31–34	L
17	CHIEFS	24–17	W

TENNESSEE TITANS

WEEK	OPPONENT	SCORE	W/L/T
1	at Dolphins	17–7	W
2	COLTS	17–31	L
3	JAGUARS	12–15	L
4	at Chargers	17–38	L
5	at Packers	48–27	W
6	TEXANS	10–20	L
7	at Vikings	3–20	L
8	BENGALS	27–20	W
9	BYE WEEK	—	—
10	BEARS	17–19	L
11	at Jaguars	18–15	W
12	at Texans	21–31	L
13	at Colts	24–51	L
14	CHIEFS	38–49	L
15	at Raiders	35–40	L
16	BRONCOS	16–37	L
17	LIONS	24–19	W

2004 REGULAR-SEASON RESULTS — NFC

ARIZONA CARDINALS

WEEK	OPPONENT	SCORE	W/L/T
1	at Rams	10–17	L
2	PATRIOTS	12–23	L
3	at Falcons	3–6	L
4	SAINTS	34–10	W
5	at 49ers	28–31	L
6	BYE WEEK	—	—
7	SEAHAWKS	25–17	W
8	at Bills	14–38	L
9	at Dolphins	24–23	W
10	GIANTS	17–14	W
11	at Panthers	10–35	L
12	JETS	3–13	L
13	at Lions	12–26	L
14	49ERS	28–31	L
15	RAMS	31–7	W
16	at Seahawks	21–24	L
17	BUCCANEERS	12–7	W

DID YOU KNOW?

Eight NFL teams have never appeared in the Super Bowl: the Arizona Cardinals, Cleveland Browns, Detroit Lions, Houston Texans, Indianapolis Colts, Jacksonville Jaguars, New Orleans Saints, and Seattle Seahawks. (The Colts played in Super Bowl III and V when the franchise was located in Baltimore.)

■ **Fast Fact:** On the opening weekend of the 2004 season, the NFL had 200 players from California on its rosters, the most from any state.

TODAY'S STARS

■ **Ben Roethlisberger, quarterback,** b. March 2, 1982, Findlay, Ohio. Roethlisberger was The Associated Press 2004 Offensive Rookie of the Year and the NFL's Rookie of the Year. The Pittsburgh Steeler became the first quarterback in NFL history to go 13–0 in a season. He broke two of Hall of Famer Dan Marino's rookie records: passer rating (98.1) and completion percentage (66.4). In the post-season, Roethlisberger led the Steelers to the AFC Championship Game, where they lost to the New England Patriots.

■ **LaDainian Tomlinson, running back,** b. June 23, 1979, Rosebud, Texas. Tomlinson is one of only nine players in NFL history to rush for at least 1,000 yards in each of his first four seasons. In 2004, the San Diego Charger joined Eric Dickerson and Earl Campbell as the only players in NFL history to rush for 10 or more touchdowns in each of their first four seasons. In 2003, Tomlinson became the first NFL player to rush for 1,000 yards and catch 100 passes in one season.

Ben Roethlisberger is the first quarterback to win the AP Offensive Rookie of the Year Award.

BOB ROSATO/SPORTS ILLUSTRATED

■ **Tom Brady, quarterback,** b. August 3, 1977, San Mateo, California. In 2004, Brady became the first quarterback in NFL history to start and win three Super Bowls before turning 28. The New England Patriot is also just the fourth player to be named Super Bowl MVP twice. After leading the Pats to victory in Super Bowl XXXIX, Brady has a 9–0 career post-season record. That ties him with Green Bay Packer legend Bart Starr for most consecutive playoff victories by a quarterback.

2004 REGULAR-SEASON RESULTS — NFC (cont.)

ATLANTA FALCONS

WEEK	OPPONENT	SCORE	W/L/T
1	at 49ers	21–19	W
2	RAMS	34–17	W
3	CARDINALS	6–3	W
4	at Panthers	27–10	W
5	LIONS	10–17	L
6	CHARGERS	21–20	W
7	at Chiefs	10–56	L
8	at Broncos	41–28	W
9	BYE WEEK	—	—
10	BUCCANEERS	24–14	W
11	at Giants	14–10	W
12	SAINTS	24–21	W
13	at Buccaneers	0–27	L
14	RAIDERS	35–10	W
15	PANTHERS	34–31	W
16	at Saints	13–26	L
17	at Seahawks	26–28	L

CAROLINA PANTHERS

WEEK	OPPONENT	SCORE	W/L/T
1	PACKERS	14–24	L
2	at Chiefs	28–17	W
3	BYE WEEK	—	—
4	FALCONS	10–27	L
5	at Broncos	17–20	L
6	at Eagles	8–30	L
7	CHARGERS	6–17	L
8	at Seahawks	17–23	L
9	RAIDERS	24–27	L
10	at 49ers	37–27	W
11	CARDINALS	35–10	W
12	BUCCANEERS	21–14	W
13	at Saints	32–21	W
14	RAMS	20–7	W
15	at Falcons	31–34	L
16	at Buccaneers	37–20	W
17	SAINTS	18–21	L

CHICAGO BEARS

WEEK	OPPONENT	SCORE	W/L/T
1	LIONS	16–20	L
2	at Packers	21–10	W
3	at Vikings	22–27	L
4	EAGLES	9–19	L
5	BYE WEEK	—	—
6	REDSKINS	10–13	L
7	at Buccaneers	7–19	L
8	49ERS	23–13	W
9	at Giants	28–21	W
10	at Titans	19–17	W
11	COLTS	10–41	L
12	at Cowboys	7–21	L
13	VIKINGS	24–14	W
14	at Jaguars	3–22	L
15	TEXANS	5–24	L
16	at Lions	13–19	L
17	PACKERS	14–31	L

DALLAS COWBOYS

WEEK	OPPONENT	SCORE	W/L/T
1	at Vikings	17–35	L
2	BROWNS	19–12	W
3	at Redskins	21–18	W
4	BYE WEEK	—	—
5	GIANTS	10–26	L
6	STEELERS	20–24	L
7	at Packers	20–41	L
8	LIONS	31–21	W
9	at Bengals	3–20	L
10	EAGLES	21–49	L
11	at Ravens	10–30	L
12	BEARS	21–7	W
13	at Seahawks	43–39	W
14	SAINTS	13–27	L
15	at Eagles	7–12	L
16	REDSKINS	13–10	W
17	at Giants	24–28	L

DETROIT LIONS

WEEK	OPPONENT	SCORE	W/L/T
1	at Bears	20–16	W
2	TEXANS	28–16	W
3	EAGLES	13–30	L
4	BYE WEEK	—	—
5	at Falcons	17–10	W
6	PACKERS	10–38	L
7	at Giants	28–13	W
8	at Cowboys	21–31	L
9	REDSKINS	10–17	L
10	at Jaguars	17–23	L
11	at Vikings	19–22	L
12	COLTS	9–41	L
13	CARDINALS	26–12	W
14	at Packers	13–16	L
15	VIKINGS	27–28	L
16	BEARS	19–13	W
17	at Titans	19–24	L

GREEN BAY PACKERS

WEEK	OPPONENT	SCORE	W/L/T
1	at Panthers	24–14	W
2	BEARS	10–21	L
3	at Colts	31–45	L
4	GIANTS	7–14	L
5	TITANS	27–48	L
6	at Lions	38–10	W
7	COWBOYS	41–20	W
8	at Redskins	28–14	W
9	BYE WEEK	—	—
10	VIKINGS	34–31	W
11	at Texans	16–13	W
12	RAMS	45–17	W
13	at Eagles	17–47	L
14	LIONS	16–13	W
15	JAGUARS	25–28	L
16	at Vikings	34–31	W
17	at Bears	31–14	W

Note: Home games are capitalized.

2004 REGULAR-SEASON RESULTS — NFC (cont.)

MINNESOTA VIKINGS

WEEK	OPPONENT	SCORE	W/L/T
1	COWBOYS	35–17	W
2	at Eagles	16–27	L
3	BEARS	27–22	W
4	BYE WEEK	—	—
5	at Texans	34–28	W
6	at Saints	38–31	W
7	TITANS	20–3	W
8	GIANTS	13–34	L
9	at Colts	28–31	L
10	at Packers	31–34	L
11	LIONS	22–19	W
12	JAGUARS	27–16	W
13	at Bears	14–24	L
14	SEAHAWKS	23–27	L
15	at Lions	28–27	W
16	PACKERS	31–34	L
17	at Redskins	18–21	L

NEW ORLEANS SAINTS

WEEK	OPPONENT	SCORE	W/L/T
1	SEAHAWKS	7–21	L
2	49ERS	30–27	W
3	at Rams	28–25	W
4	at Cardinals	10–34	L
5	BUCCANEERS	17–20	L
6	VIKINGS	31–38	L
7	at Raiders	31–26	W
8	BYE WEEK	—	—
9	at Chargers	17–43	L
10	CHIEFS	27–20	W
11	BRONCOS	13–34	L
12	at Falcons	21–24	L
13	PANTHERS	21–32	L
14	at Cowboys	27–13	W
15	at Buccaneers	21–17	W
16	FALCONS	26–13	W
17	at Panthers	21–18	W

NEW YORK GIANTS

WEEK	OPPONENT	SCORE	W/L/T
1	at Eagles	17–31	L
2	REDSKINS	20–14	W
3	BROWNS	27–10	W
4	at Packers	14–7	W
5	at Cowboys	26–10	W
6	BYE WEEK	—	—
7	LIONS	13–28	L
8	at Vikings	34–13	W
9	BEARS	21–28	L
10	at Cardinals	14–17	L
11	FALCONS	10–14	L
12	EAGLES	6–27	L
13	at Redskins	7–31	L
14	at Ravens	14–37	L
15	STEELERS	30–33	L
16	at Bengals	22–23	L
17	COWBOYS	28–24	W

PHILADELPHIA EAGLES

WEEK	OPPONENT	SCORE	W/L/T
1	GIANTS	31–17	W
2	VIKINGS	27–16	W
3	at Lions	30–13	W
4	at Bears	19–9	W
5	BYE WEEK	—	—
6	PANTHERS	30–8	W
7	at Browns	34–31	W
8	RAVENS	15–10	W
9	at Steelers	3–27	L
10	at Cowboys	49–21	W
11	REDSKINS	28–6	W
12	at Giants	27–6	W
13	PACKERS	47–17	W
14	at Redskins	17–14	W
15	COWBOYS	12–7	W
16	at Rams	7–20	L
17	BENGALS	10–38	L

SAN FRANCISCO 49ERS

WEEK	OPPONENT	SCORE	W/L/T
1	FALCONS	19–21	L
2	at Saints	27–30	L
3	at Seahawks	0–34	L
4	RAMS	14–24	L
5	CARDINALS	31–28	W
6	at Jets	14–22	L
7	BYE WEEK	—	—
8	at Bears	13–23	L
9	SEAHAWKS	27–42	L
10	PANTHERS	27–37	L
11	at Buccaneers	3–35	L
12	DOLPHINS	17–24	L
13	at Rams	6–16	L
14	at Cardinals	31–28	W
15	REDSKINS	16–26	L
16	BILLS	7–41	L
17	at Patriots	7–21	L

SEATTLE SEAHAWKS

WEEK	OPPONENT	SCORE	W/L/T
1	at Saints	21–7	W
2	at Buccaneers	10–6	W
3	49ERS	34–0	W
4	BYE WEEK	—	
5	RAMS	27–33	L
6	at Patriots	20–30	L
7	at Cardinals	17–25	L
8	PANTHERS	23–17	W
9	at 49ers	42–27	W
10	at Rams	12–23	L
11	DOLPHINS	24–17	W
12	BILLS	9–38	L
13	COWBOYS	39–43	L
14	at Vikings	27–23	W
15	at Jets	14–37	L
16	CARDINALS	24–21	W
17	FALCONS	28–26	W

2004 REGULAR-SEASON RESULTS — NFC (cont.)

ST. LOUIS RAMS

WEEK	OPPONENT	SCORE	W/L/T
1	CARDINALS	17–10	W
2	at Falcons	17–34	L
3	SAINTS	25–28	L
4	at 49ers	24–14	W
5	at Seahawks	33–27	W
6	BUCCANEERS	28–21	W
7	at Dolphins	14–31	L
8	BYE WEEK	—	—
9	PATRIOTS	22–40	L
10	SEAHAWKS	23–12	W
11	at Bills	17–37	L
12	at Packers	17–45	L
13	49ERS	16–6	W
14	at Panthers	7–20	L
15	at Cardinals	7–31	L
16	EAGLES	20–7	W
17	JETS	32–29	W

TAMPA BAY BUCCANEERS

WEEK	OPPONENT	SCORE	W/L/T
1	at Redskins	10–16	L
2	SEAHAWKS	6–10	L
3	at Raiders	20–30	L
4	BRONCOS	13–16	L
5	at Saints	20–17	W
6	at Rams	21–28	L
7	BEARS	19–7	W
8	BYE WEEK	—	—
9	CHIEFS	34–31	W
10	at Falcons	14–24	L
11	49ERS	35–3	W
12	at Panthers	14–21	L
13	FALCONS	27–0	W
14	at Chargers	24–31	L
15	SAINTS	17–21	L
16	PANTHERS	20–37	L
17	at Cardinals	7–12	L

WASHINGTON REDSKINS

WEEK	OPPONENT	SCORE	W/L/T
1	BUCCANEERS	16–10	W
2	at Giants	14–20	L
3	COWBOYS	18–21	L
4	at Browns	13–17	L
5	RAVENS	10–17	L
6	at Bears	13–10	W
7	BYE WEEK	—	—
8	PACKERS	14–28	L
9	at Lions	17–10	W
10	BENGALS	10–17	L
11	at Eagles	6–28	L
12	at Steelers	7–16	L
13	GIANTS	31–7	W
14	EAGLES	14–17	L
15	at 49ers	26–16	W
16	at Cowboys	10–13	L
17	VIKINGS	21–18	W

> ### DID YOU KNOW?
> Tom Brady is the NFL career leader among quarterbacks in overtime wins without a defeat (7–0).

2004 INDIVIDUAL LEADERS — AFC

TOUCHDOWNS	TEAM	TD	RSH	REC	RET	PTS
LaDainian Tomlinson	SD	18	17	1	0	108
Marvin Harrison	IND	15	0	15	0	90
Priest Holmes	KC	15	14	1	0	90
Curtis Martin	NYJ	14	12	2	0	84
Domanick Davis	HOU	14	13	1	0	84
Willis McGahee	BUF	13	13	0	0	78
Corey Dillon	NE	13	12	1	0	78
Jerome Bettis	PIT	13	13	0	0	78
Antonio Gates	SD	13	0	13	0	78
Reggie Wayne	IND	12	0	12	0	72
Rudi Johnson	CIN	12	12	0	0	72
Drew Bennett	TEN	11	0	11	0	66
Larry Johnson	KC	11	9	2	0	66

KEY TD=touchdowns; RSH=rushing touchdowns; REC=receiving touchdowns; RET=returns; PTS=points

2004 INDIVIDUAL LEADERS — AFC (cont.)

KICKING	TEAM	FGM	FGA	LONG	XPM	XPA	PTS
Adam Vinatieri	NE	31	33	48	48	48	141
Matt Stover	BAL	29	32	50	30	30	117
Jason Elam	DEN	29	34	52	42	42	129
Jeff Reed	PIT	28	33	51	40	40	124
Shayne Graham	CIN	27	31	53	41	41	122
Sebastian Janikowski	OAK	25	28	52	31	32	106
Rian Lindell	BUF	24	28	43	45	45	117
Doug Brien	NYJ	24	29	53	33	34	105
Phil Dawson	CLE	24	29	50	28	28	100
Josh Scobee	JAC	24	31	53	21	21	93

PASSER RATING	TEAM	YDS	ATT	COMP	TD	INT	LONG	RATING
Peyton Manning	IND	4,557	497	336	49	10	80	121.1
Drew Brees	SD	3,159	400	262	27	7	79	104.8
Ben Roethlisberger	PIT	2,621	295	196	17	11	58	98.1
Trent Green	KC	4,591	556	369	27	17	70	95.2
Tom Brady	NE	3,692	474	288	28	14	50	92.6
Chad Pennington	NYJ	2,673	370	242	16	9	48	91.0
Billy Volek	TEN	2,486	357	218	18	10	48	87.1
Jake Plummer	DEN	4,089	521	303	27	20	85	84.5
David Carr	HOU	3,531	466	285	16	14	69	83.5
Byron Leftwich	JAC	2,941	441	267	15	10	65	82.2

**Tony Gonzalez,
Kansas City Chiefs**

RECEPTIONS	TEAM	REC	YDS	AVG	TD	LONG
Tony Gonzalez	KC	102	1,258	12.3	7	32
Derrick Mason	TEN	96	1,168	12.2	7	37
Chad Johnson	CIN	95	1,274	13.4	9	53
Eric Moulds	BUF	88	1,043	11.9	5	49
Marvin Harrison	IND	86	1,113	12.9	15	59
Antonio Gates	SD	81	964	11.9	13	72
Hines Ward	PIT	80	1,004	12.6	4	58
Drew Bennett	TEN	80	1,247	15.6	11	48
Rod Smith	DEN	79	1,144	14.5	7	85
Andre Johnson	HOU	79	1,142	14.5	7	54

RECEIVING YARDS	TEAM	REC	YDS	AVG	TD	LONG
Chad Johnson	CIN	95	1,274	13.4	9	53
Tony Gonzalez	KC	102	1,258	12.3	7	32
Drew Bennett	TEN	80	1,247	15.6	11	48
Reggie Wayne	IND	77	1,210	15.7	12	71
Jimmy Smith	JAC	74	1,172	15.8	6	65
Derrick Mason	TEN	96	1,168	12.2	7	37
Rod Smith	DEN	79	1,144	14.5	7	85
Andre Johnson	HOU	79	1,142	14.5	6	54
Marvin Harrison	IND	86	1,113	12.9	15	59
Eddie Kennison	KC	62	1,086	17.5	8	70

KEY FGM=field goals made; FGA=field goals attempted; XPM=extra points made; XPA=extra points attempted; PTS=points; YDS=yards; ATT=attempts; COMP=completions; TD=touchdowns; INT=interceptions; REC=receptions; AVG=average

2004 INDIVIDUAL LEADERS — AFC (cont.)

RUSHING	TEAM	YDS	ATT	AVG	TD	LONG
Curtis Martin	NYJ	1,697	371	4.6	12	25
Corey Dillon	NE	1,635	345	4.7	12	44
Edgerrin James	IND	1,548	334	4.6	9	40
Rudi Johnson	CIN	1,454	361	4.0	12	52
LaDainian Tomlinson	SD	1,335	339	3.9	17	42
Reuben Droughns	DEN	1,240	275	4.5	6	51
Fred Taylor	JAC	1,224	260	4.7	2	46
Domanick Davis	HOU	1,188	302	3.9	13	44
Willis McGahee	BUF	1,128	284	4.0	13	41
Chris Brown	TEN	1,067	220	4.9	6	52
Jamal Lewis	BAL	1,006	235	4.3	7	75

Dwight Freeney, Indianapolis Colts

INTERCEPTIONS	TEAM	INT	YDS	TD	LONG
Ed Reed	BAL	9	358	1	106
Tory James	CIN	8	66	0	23
Nate Clements	BUF	6	77	1	35
Andre Dyson	TEN	6	135	0	44
Dunta Robinson	HOU	6	146	0	61
Takeo Spikes	BUF	5	122	2	62
Donovin Darius	JAC	5	80	0	37
Hashean Mathis	JAC	5	42	0	21
Troy Polamalu	PIT	5	58	1	26
Donnie Edwards	SD	5	49	1	30
Aaron Glenn	HOU	5	40	0	23

SACKS	TEAM	SACKS	TACKLES
Dwight Freeney	IND	16.0	34
Shaun Ellis	NYJ	11.0	57
Robert Mathis	IND	10.5	36
Terrell Suggs	BAL	10.5	80
Reggie Hayward	DEN	10.5	43
Steve Foley	SD	10.0	64
Jason Taylor	MIA	9.5	67
Willie McGinest	NE	9.5	51
John Abraham	NYJ	9.5	48
Jared Allen	KC	9.0	31

PUNTING	TEAM	NO.	YDS	AVG	NAVG	LG	TB	BLK	IN 20	RET	RET AVG	RET TD
Shane Lechler	OAK	73	3,409	46.7	37.2	67	14	0	22	35	11.8	0
Hunter Smith	IND	54	2,443	45.2	36.8	62	3	0	21	29	13.6	1
Brian Moorman	BUF	77	3,325	43.2	36.8	80	9	0	17	37	6.5	0
Mike Scifres	SD	69	2,974	43.1	38.4	60	8	0	29	23	7.1	0
Chris Gardocki	PIT	67	2,879	43.0	37.4	61	6	0	24	34	7.4	0
Chris Hanson	JAC	84	3,592	42.8	35.5	69	9	0	28	38	11.3	2
Craig Hentrich	TEN	73	3,117	42.7	38.0	64	8	0	20	29	6.3	1
Kyle Larson	CIN	83	3,499	42.2	35.5	66	7	0	21	51	7.4	0
Josh Miller	NE	56	2,350	42.0	33.7	69	5	0	19	31	11.8	1
Matt Turk	MIA	98	4,088	41.7	37.2	67	10	0	29	44	5.5	0

2004 INDIVIDUAL LEADERS — NFC

TOUCHDOWNS	TEAM	TD	RSH	REC	RET	PTS
Shaun Alexander	SEA	20	16	4	0	120
Muhsin Muhammad	CAR	16	0	16	0	96
Tiki Barber	NYG	15	13	2	0	90
Terrell Owens	PHI	14	0	14	0	84
Randy Moss	MIN	13	0	13	0	78
Javon Walker	GB	12	0	12	0	72
Joe Horn	NO	11	0	11	0	66
Michael Pittman	TB	10	7	3	0	60
Nate Burleson	MIN	10	0	9	1	60
Torry Holt	STL	10	0	10	0	60

KEY NO.=number; NAVG=net average; LG=long; TB=touchback; BLK=blocked; IN 20=inside 20-yard line; RET=returned; RET AVG=return average; RET TD=returned for a touchdown

2004 INDIVIDUAL LEADERS — NFC (cont.)

KICKING	TEAM	FGM	FGA	LONG	XPM	XPA	PTS
David Akers	PHI	27	32	51	41	42	122
Ryan Longwell	GB	24	28	53	48	48	120
Jason Hanson	DET	24	28	48	28	28	100
Josh Brown	SEA	23	25	54	40	40	109
John Carney	NO	22	27	53	38	38	104
Steve Christie	NYG	22	28	53	33	33	99
Neil Rackers	ARI	22	29	55	28	28	94
Billy Cundiff	DAL	20	26	49	31	31	91
Jeff Wilkins	STL	19	24	53	32	32	89
John Kasay	CAR	19	22	54	27	28	84

PASSER RATING	TEAM	YDS	ATT	COMP	TD	INT	LONG	RATING
Daunte Culpepper	MIN	4,717	548	379	39	11	82	110.9
Donovan McNabb	PHI	3,875	469	300	31	8	80	104.7
Brian Griese	TB	2,632	336	233	20	12	68	97.5
Marc Bulger	STL	3,964	485	321	21	14	56	93.7
Brett Favre	GB	4,088	540	346	30	17	79	92.4
Jake Delhomme	CAR	3,886	533	310	29	15	63	87.3
Kurt Warner	NYG	2,054	277	174	6	4	62	86.5
Matt Hasselbeck	SEA	3,382	474	279	22	15	60	83.1
Aaron Brooks	NO	3,810	542	309	21	16	57	79.5
Tim Rattay	SF	2,169	325	198	10	10	65	78.1
Michael Vick	ATL	2,313	321	181	14	12	62	78.1

**Daunte Culpepper,
Minnesota Vikings**

RECEPTIONS	TEAM	REC	YDS	AVG	TD	LONG
Joe Horn	NO	94	1,399	14.9	11	57
Torry Holt	STL	94	1,372	14.6	10	75
Muhsin Muhammad	CAR	93	1,405	15.1	16	51
Laveranues Coles	WAS	90	950	10.6	1	45
Javon Walker	GB	89	1,382	15.5	12	79
Isaac Bruce	STL	89	1,292	14.5	6	56
Darrell Jackson	SEA	87	1,199	13.8	7	56
Jason Witten	DAL	87	980	11.3	6	42
Donald Driver	GB	84	1,208	14.4	9	50
Eric Johnson	SF	82	825	10.1	2	25

RECEIVING YARDS	TEAM	REC	YDS	AVG	TD	LONG
Muhsin Muhammad	CAR	93	1,405	15.1	16	51
Joe Horn	NO	94	1,399	14.9	11	57
Javon Walker	GB	89	1,382	15.5	12	79
Torry Holt	STL	94	1,372	14.6	10	75
Isaac Bruce	STL	89	1,292	14.5	6	56
Donald Driver	GB	84	1,208	14.4	9	50
Terrell Owens	PHI	77	1,200	15.6	14	59
Darrell Jackson	SEA	87	1,199	13.8	7	56
Michael Clayton	TB	80	1,193	14.9	7	75
Nate Burleson	MIN	68	1,006	14.8	9	68

2004 INDIVIDUAL LEADERS — NFC (cont.)

RUSHING	TEAM	YDS	ATT	AVG	TD	LONG
Shaun Alexander	SEA	1,696	353	4.8	16	44
Tiki Barber	NYG	1,518	322	4.7	13	72
Clinton Portis	WAS	1,315	343	3.8	5	64
Ahman Green	GB	1,163	259	4.5	7	90
Kevin Jones	DET	1,133	241	4.7	5	74
Warrick Dunn	ATL	1,106	265	4.2	9	60
Deuce McAllister	NO	1,074	269	4.0	9	71
Thomas Jones	CHI	948	240	4.0	7	54
Emmitt Smith	ARI	937	267	3.5	9	29
Michael Pittman	TB	926	219	4.2	7	78

Ken Lucas,
Seattle Seahawks

INTERCEPTIONS	TEAM	INT	YDS	TD	LONG
Ken Lucas	SEA	6	46	1	25
Chris Gamble	CAR	6	15	0	13
Michael Boulware	SEA	5	69	1	63
Marcus Trufant	SEA	5	141	0	58
Lito Sheppard	PHI	5	172	2	101
Shawn Springs	WAS	5	117	0	38
Nathan Vasher	CHI	5	177	1	71
Mike McKenzie	NO	5	19	0	14
Jerametrius Butler	STL	5	15	0	10

SACKS	TEAM	SACKS	TACKLES
Bertrand Berry	ARI	14.5	49
Kabeer Gbaja-Biamila	GB	13.5	47
Patrick Kerney	ATL	13.0	66
Simeon Rice	TB	12.0	40
Kevin Williams	MIN	12.0	70
James Hall	DET	11.5	48
Rod Coleman	ATL	11.5	40
Lance Johnstone	MIN	11.0	31
Darren Howard	NO	11.0	46
Julius Peppers	CAR	11.0	64

TRIVIA CHALLENGE

True or false: Built in 1957, Green Bay's
Lambeau Field is the oldest stadium in
the NFL.

False. Chicago's Soldier Field was built in 1923,
though it was remodeled before the 2004 season.

PUNTING	TEAM	NO.	YDS	AVG	NAVG	LG	TB	BLK	IN 20	RET	RET AVG	RET TD
Tom Tupa	WAS	103	4,544	44.1	35.2	61	8	0	30	65	11.2	1
Todd Sauerbrun	CAR	76	3,351	44.1	37.5	65	8	0	25	38	8.0	0
Mitch Berger	NO	85	3,704	43.6	39.0	63	4	0	28	43	7.2	1
Sean Landeta	STL	40	1,733	43.3	35.2	63	3	0	9	24	15.5	1
Scott Player	ARI	98	4,230	43.2	36.4	57	7	0	32	56	8.7	1
Brad Maynard	CHI	108	4,638	42.9	38.7	58	5	0	34	55	6.6	0
Mat McBriar	DAL	75	3,182	42.4	35.1	68	7	0	22	39	10.5	0
Josh Bidwell	TB	82	3,472	42.3	36.8	60	7	0	23	31	9.0	0
Dirk Johnson	PHI	72	3,032	42.1	37.4	62	6	0	20	34	6.5	0
Andy Lee	SF	96	3,990	41.6	35.3	81	8	0	25	51	8.7	0

TEAM-BY-TEAM STATS — AFC

BALTIMORE RAVENS

PASSING

PLAYER	ATT	COMP	YDS	PCT COMP	YDS/ATT	TD	INT	RATING
Kyle Boller	464	258	2,559	55.6	5.5	13	11	70.9

RUSHING

PLAYER	NO.	YDS	AVG	LG	TD
Jamal Lewis	235	1,006	4.3	75	7
Chester Taylor	160	714	4.5	47	2
Kyle Boller	53	189	3.6	19	1
Jamel White	14	62	4.4	16	0
Musa Smith	12	48	4.0	13	0
Alan Ricard	10	36	3.6	14	0
B.J. Sams	4	19	4.8	8	1

RECEIVING

PLAYER	NO.	YDS	AVG	LG	TD
Travis Taylor	34	421	12.4	47	0
Kevin Johnson	35	373	10.7	35	1
Randy Hymes	26	323	12.4	57	2
Todd Heap	27	303	11.2	37	3
Clarence Moore	24	293	12.2	52	4
Daniel Wilcox	25	219	8.8	20	1
Chester Taylor	30	184	6.1	23	0
Terry Jones	20	152	7.6	19	1

KICKING

PLAYER	FGM	FGA	PCT	XPM	XPA
Matt Stover	29	32	90.6	30	30

PUNTING

PLAYER	NO.	AVG	NET AVG	TB	IN 20	LG	BLK
Dave Zastudil	73	40.4	34.6	12	26	61	0
Nick Murphy	18	43.2	36.6	2	6	54	0

INTERCEPTIONS Ed Reed, 9   SACKS Terrell Suggs, 10.5

BUFFALO BILLS

PASSING

PLAYER	ATT	COMP	YDS	PCT COMP	YDS/ATT	TD	INT	RATING
Drew Bledsoe	450	256	2,932	56.9	6.5	20	16	76.6

RUSHING

PLAYER	NO.	YDS	AVG	LG	TD
Willis McGahee	284	1,128	4.0	41	13
Travis Henry	94	326	3.5	19	0
Shaud Williams	42	167	4.0	27	2
Lee Evans	5	85	17.0	48	0
Joe Burns	20	73	3.7	21	0

RECEIVING

PLAYER	NO.	YDS	AVG	LG	TD
Eric Moulds	88	1,043	11.9	49	5
Lee Evans	48	843	17.6	69	9
Mark Campbell	17	203	11.9	27	5
Willis McGahee	22	169	7.7	16	0
Josh Reed	16	153	9.6	20	0
Sam Aiken	11	148	13.5	54	0
Daimon Shelton	17	114	6.7	24	0
Tim Euhus	11	98	8.9	17	2

KICKING

PLAYER	FGM	FGA	PCT	XPM	XPA
Rian Lindell	24	28	85.7	45	45

PUNTING

PLAYER	NO.	AVG	NET AVG	TB	IN 20	LG	BLK
Brian Moorman	77	43.2	36.8	9	17	80	0

INTERCEPTIONS Nate Clements, 6   SACKS Aaron Schobel, 8

KEY ATT=attempts; COMP=completions; YDS=yards; PCT COMP=completion percentage; YDS/ATT=yards per attempt; TD=touchdowns; INT=interceptions; NO.=number; AVG=average; LG=long; FGM=field goals made; FGA=field goals attempted; PCT=percentage; XPM=extra points made; XPA=extra points attempted; NET AVG=net average; TB=touchbacks; IN 20=inside 20-yard line; BLK=blocked

CINCINNATI BENGALS

PASSING

PLAYER	ATT	COMP	YDS	PCT COMP	YDS/ATT	TD	INT	RATING
Carson Palmer	432	263	2,897	60.9	6.7	18	18	77.3
Jon Kitna	104	61	623	58.7	6.0	5	4	75.9

RUSHING

PLAYER	NO.	YDS	AVG	LG	TD
Rudi Johnson	361	1,454	4.0	52	12
Kenny Watson	26	161	6.2	25	0
T.J. Houshmandzadeh	6	51	8.5	16	0
Carson Palmer	18	47	2.6	14	1
Jon Kitna	10	42	4.2	15	0
Chad Johnson	4	39	9.8	18	0

RECEIVING

PLAYER	NO.	YDS	AVG	LG	TD
Chad Johnson	95	1,274	13.4	53	9
T.J. Houshmandzadeh	73	978	13.4	62	4
Kelley Washington	31	378	12.2	28	3
Matt Schobel	21	201	9.6	76	4
Kenny Watson	25	171	6.8	21	1
Peter Warrick	11	127	11.5	30	0
Reggie Kelly	15	85	5.7	14	0

KICKING

PLAYER	FGM	FGA	PCT	XPM	XPA
Shayne Graham	27	31	87.1	41	41

PUNTING

PLAYER	NO.	AVG	NET AVG	TB	IN 20	LG	BLK
Kyle Larson	83	42.2	35.5	7	21	66	0

INTERCEPTIONS Tory James, 8   **SACKS** Justin Smith, 8

CLEVELAND BROWNS

PASSING

PLAYER	ATT	COMP	YDS	PCT COMP	YDS/ATT	TD	INT	RATING
Jeff Garcia	252	144	1,731	57.1	6.9	10	9	76.7
Kelly Holcomb	87	59	737	67.8	8.5	7	5	96.8
Luke McCown	98	48	608	49.0	6.2	4	7	52.6

RUSHING

PLAYER	NO.	YDS	AVG	LG	TD
Lee Suggs	199	744	3.7	39	2
William Green	163	585	3.6	46	2
Jeff Garcia	35	169	4.8	21	2
James Jackson	12	81	6.8	38	0
Luke McCown	6	25	4.2	11	0
Adimchinobe Echemandu	8	25	3.1	6	0

RECEIVING

PLAYER	NO.	YDS	AVG	LG	TD
Dennis Northcutt	55	806	14.7	58	2
Antonio Bryant	42	546	13.0	55	4
Andre Davis	16	416	26.0	99	2
Steve Heiden	28	287	10.3	30	5
Aaron Shea	26	252	9.7	35	4
Lee Suggs	20	178	8.9	59	1
Frisman Jackson	13	168	12.9	24	0
Quincy Morgan	9	144	16.0	46	3

KICKING

PLAYER	FGM	FGA	PCT	XPM	XPA
Phil Dawson	24	29	82.8	28	28

PUNTING

PLAYER	NO.	AVG	NET AVG	TB	IN 20	LG	BLK
Derrick Frost	85	40.0	35.4	4	24	54	0

INTERCEPTIONS Anthony Henry, 4   **SACKS** Ebenezer Ekuban, 8

DENVER BRONCOS

PASSING

PLAYER	ATT	COMP	YDS	PCT COMP	YDS/ATT	TD	INT	RATING
Jake Plummer	521	303	4,089	58.2	7.8	27	20	84.5

RUSHING

PLAYER	NO.	YDS	AVG	LG	TD
Reuben Droughns	275	1,240	4.5	51	6
Tatum Bell	75	396	5.3	29	3
Quentin Griffin	85	311	3.7	47	2
Jake Plummer	62	202	3.3	22	1
Garrison Hearst	20	81	4.1	11	1

RECEIVING

PLAYER	NO.	YDS	AVG	LG	TD
Rod Smith	79	1,144	14.5	85	7
Ashley Lelie	54	1,084	20.1	58	7
Jeb Putzier	36	572	15.9	39	2
Darius Watts	31	385	12.4	28	1
Reuben Droughns	32	241	7.5	23	2
Dwayne Carswell	22	198	9.0	20	1
Kyle Johnson	9	126	14.0	31	2
Tatum Bell	5	80	16.0	58	0
Nate Jackson	8	73	9.1	20	0

KICKING

PLAYER	FGM	FGA	PCT	XPM	XPA
Jason Elam	29	34	85.3	42	42

PUNTING

PLAYER	NO.	AVG	NET AVG	TB	IN 20	LG	BLK
Micah Knorr	54	41.5	34.2	6	12	66	0
Jason Baker	15	39.4	34.4	1	7	48	0

INTERCEPTIONS Champ Bailey, 3   **SACKS** Reggie Hayward, 10.5

HOUSTON TEXANS

PASSING

PLAYER	ATT	COMP	YDS	PCT COMP	YDS/ATT	TD	INT	RATING
David Carr	466	285	3,531	61.2	7.6	16	14	83.5

RUSHING

PLAYER	NO.	YDS	AVG	LG	TD
Domanick Davis	302	1,188	3.9	44	13
Jonathan Wells	82	299	3.6	14	3
David Carr	73	299	4.1	24	0
Tony Hollings	11	47	4.3	13	0

RECEIVING

PLAYER	NO.	YDS	AVG	LG	TD
Andre Johnson	79	1,142	14.5	54	6
Jabar Gaffney	41	632	15.4	69	2
Domanick Davis	68	588	8.6	38	1
Derick Armstrong	29	415	14.3	44	1
Corey Bradford	27	399	14.8	47	3
Billy Miller	17	178	10.5	27	1
Jonathan Wells	11	79	7.2	28	2

KICKING

PLAYER	FGM	FGA	PCT	XPM	XPA
Kris Brown	17	24	70.8	34	34

PUNTING

PLAYER	NO.	AVG	NET AVG	TB	IN 20	LG	BLK
Chad Stanley	73	41.2	35.7	7	19	57	0

INTERCEPTIONS Dunta Robinson, 6   **SACKS** Kailee Wong, 5.5

INDIANAPOLIS COLTS

PASSING

PLAYER	ATT	COMP	YDS	PCT COMP	YDS/ATT	TD	INT	RATING
Peyton Manning	497	336	4,557	67.6	9.2	49	10	121.1

RUSHING

PLAYER	NO.	YDS	AVG	LG	TD
Edgerrin James	334	1,548	4.6	40	9
Dominic Rhodes	53	254	4.8	55	1
Peyton Manning	25	38	1.5	19	0
James Mungro	5	19	3.8	8	0

RECEIVING

PLAYER	NO.	YDS	AVG	LG	TD
Reggie Wayne	77	1,210	15.7	71	12
Marvin Harrison	86	1,113	12.9	59	15
Brandon Stokley	68	1,077	15.8	69	10
Edgerrin James	51	483	9.5	56	0
Dallas Clark	25	423	16.9	80	5
Marcus Pollard	29	309	10.7	31	6
James Mungro	7	36	5.1	16	3
Ben Hartsock	4	33	8.3	17	0

KICKING

PLAYER	FGM	FGA	PCT	XPM	XPA
Mike Vanderjagt	20	25	80.0	59	60

PUNTING

PLAYER	NO.	AVG	NET AVG	TB	IN 20	LG	BLK
Hunter Smith	54	45.2	36.8	3	21	62	0

INTERCEPTIONS Jason David, 4   **SACKS** Dwight Freeney, 16

JACKSONVILLE JAGUARS

PASSING

PLAYER	ATT	COMP	YDS	PCT COMP	YDS/ATT	TD	INT	RATING
Byron Leftwich	441	267	2,941	60.5	6.7	15	10	82.2
David Garrard	72	38	374	52.8	5.2	2	1	71.2

RUSHING

PLAYER	NO.	YDS	AVG	LG	TD
Fred Taylor	260	1,224	4.7	46	2
LaBrandon Toefield	51	169	3.3	16	0
Greg Jones	62	162	2.6	12	3
Byron Leftwich	39	148	3.8	17	2
David Garrard	12	76	6.3	12	1
Chris Fuamatu-Ma'afala	20	69	3.5	10	1

RECEIVING

PLAYER	NO.	YDS	AVG	LG	TD
Jimmy Smith	74	1,172	15.8	65	6
Troy Edwards	50	533	10.7	36	1
Fred Taylor	36	345	9.6	64	1
Ernest Wilford	19	271	14.3	46	2
Reggie Williams	27	268	9.9	26	1
Todd Yoder	14	157	11.2	56	0
LaBrandon Toefield	28	151	5.4	16	1
Kyle Brady	14	103	7.4	21	1
Brian Jones	6	87	14.5	26	1
Cortez Hankton	9	81	9.0	14	2
George Wrighster	10	69	6.9	12	1

KICKING

PLAYER	FGM	FGA	PCT	XPM	XPA
Josh Scobee	24	31	77.4	21	21

PUNTING

PLAYER	NO.	AVG	NET AVG	TB	IN 20	LG	BLK
Chris Hanson	84	42.8	35.5	9	28	69	0

INTERCEPTIONS Rashean Mathis, Donovin Darius, 5   **SACKS** John Henderson, Greg Favors, 5.5

KANSAS CITY CHIEFS

PASSING

PLAYER	ATT	COMP	YDS	PCT COMP	YDS/ATT	TD	INT	RATING
Trent Green	556	369	4,591	66.4	8.3	27	17	95.2

RUSHING

PLAYER	NO.	YDS	AVG	LG	TD
Priest Holmes	196	892	4.6	33	14
Larry Johnson	120	581	4.8	46	9
Derrick Blaylock	118	539	4.6	24	8
Trent Green	25	85	3.4	13	0
Tony Richardson	12	56	4.7	13	0
Dante Hall	8	56	7.0	17	0

RECEIVING

PLAYER	NO.	YDS	AVG	LG	TD
Tony Gonzalez	102	1,258	12.3	32	7
Eddie Kennison	62	1,086	17.5	70	8
Johnnie Morton	55	795	14.5	52	3
Larry Johnson	22	278	12.6	40	2
Derrick Blaylock	25	246	9.8	30	1
Dante Hall	25	230	9.2	22	0
Priest Holmes	19	187	9.8	52	1
Chris Horn	15	178	11.9	30	1

KICKING

PLAYER	FGM	FGA	PCT	XPM	XPA
Lawrence Tynes	17	23	73.9	58	60

PUNTING

PLAYER	NO.	AVG	NET AVG	TB	IN 20	LG	BLK
Steve Cheek	42	39.1	31.6	6	8	55	0
Jason Baker	9	37.8	26.9	0	3	52	0
Nick Murphy	4	47.3	40.8	1	1	58	0

INTERCEPTIONS Eric Warfield, Greg Wesley, 4   **SACKS** Jared Allen, 9

MIAMI DOLPHINS

PASSING

PLAYER	ATT	COMP	YDS	PCT COMP	YDS/ATT	TD	INT	RATING
A.J. Feeley	356	191	1,893	53.7	5.3	11	15	61.7
Jay Fiedler	190	101	1,186	53.2	6.2	7	8	67.1

RUSHING

PLAYER	NO.	YDS	AVG	LG	TD
Sammy Morris	132	523	4.0	35	6
Travis Minor	109	388	3.6	34	3
Leonard Henry	46	141	3.1	53	0
Chris Chambers	9	76	8.4	24	0

RECEIVING

PLAYER	NO.	YDS	AVG	LG	TD
Chris Chambers	69	898	13.0	76	7
Randy McMichael	73	791	10.8	42	4
Marty Booker	50	638	12.8	45	1
Derrius Thompson	23	359	15.6	36	4
Bryan Gilmore	15	206	13.7	37	1
Sammy Morris	22	124	5.6	24	0
Donald Lee	13	110	8.5	15	1

KICKING

PLAYER	FGM	FGA	PCT	XPM	XPA
Olindo Mare	12	16	75.0	18	18
Bill Gramatica	3	3	100.0	0	1
Matt Bryant	3	4	75.0	12	12
Wes Welker	1	1	100.0	1	1

PUNTING

PLAYER	NO.	AVG	NET AVG	TB	IN 20	LG	BLK
Matt Turk	98	41.7	37.2	10	29	67	0

INTERCEPTIONS Sammy Knight, Patrick Surtain, Arturo Freeman, 4   **SACKS** Jason Taylor, 9.5

NEW ENGLAND PATRIOTS

PASSING

PLAYER	ATT	COMP	YDS	PCT COMP	YDS/ATT	TD	INT	RATING
Tom Brady	474	288	3,692	60.8	7.8	28	14	92.6

RUSHING

PLAYER	NO.	YDS	AVG	LG	TD
Corey Dillon	345	1,635	4.7	44	12
Kevin Faulk	54	255	4.7	20	2
Patrick Pass	39	141	3.6	19	0
Cedric Cobbs	22	50	2.3	13	0
Tom Brady	43	28	0.7	10	0
Rabih Abdullah	13	13	1.0	5	1

RECEIVING

PLAYER	NO.	YDS	AVG	LG	TD
David Givens	56	874	15.6	50	3
David Patten	44	800	18.2	48	7
Deion Branch	35	454	13.0	26	4
Daniel Graham	30	364	12.1	48	7
Kevin Faulk	26	248	9.5	31	1
Patrick Pass	28	215	7.7	22	0
Christian Fauria	16	195	12.2	25	2
Troy Brown	17	184	10.8	22	1
Bethel Johnson	10	174	17.4	48	1
Corey Dillon	15	103	6.9	20	1

KICKING

PLAYER	FGM	FGA	PCT	XPM	XPA
Adam Vinatieri	31	33	93.9	48	48

PUNTING

PLAYER	NO.	AVG	NET AVG	TB	IN 20	LG	BLK
Josh Miller	56	42.0	33.7	5	19	69	0

INTERCEPTIONS Eugene Wilson, 4

SACKS Willie McGinest, 9.5

NEW YORK JETS

PASSING

PLAYER	ATT	COMP	YDS	PCT COMP	YDS/ATT	TD	INT	RATING
Chad Pennington	370	242	2,673	65.4	7.2	16	9	91.0
Quincy Carter	58	35	498	60.3	8.6	3	1	98.2

RUSHING

PLAYER	NO.	YDS	AVG	LG	TD
Curtis Martin	371	1,697	4.6	25	12
LaMont Jordan	93	479	5.2	33	2
Chad Pennington	34	126	3.7	16	1
Jerald Sowell	2	28	14.0	19	0

RECEIVING

PLAYER	NO.	YDS	AVG	LG	TD
Santana Moss	45	838	18.6	69	5
Justin McCareins	56	770	13.8	43	4
Wayne Chrebet	31	397	12.8	35	1
Jerald Sowell	45	342	7.6	34	1
Curtis Martin	41	245	6.0	22	2
Chris Baker	18	182	10.1	23	4
Jonathan Carter	10	173	17.3	46	1

KICKING

PLAYER	FGM	FGA	PCT	XPM	XPA
Doug Brien	24	29	82.8	33	34

PUNTING

PLAYER	NO.	AVG	NET AVG	TB	IN 20	LG	BLK
Toby Gowin	80	38.2	33.5	8	22	58	0

INTERCEPTIONS Erik Coleman, 4

SACKS Shaun Ellis, 11

OAKLAND RAIDERS

PASSING

PLAYER	ATT	COMP	YDS	PCT COMP	YDS/ATT	TD	INT	RATING
Kerry Collins	513	289	3,495	56.3	6.8	21	20	74.8
Rich Gannon	68	41	524	60.3	7.7	3	2	86.9

RUSHING

PLAYER	NO.	YDS	AVG	LG	TD
Amos Zereoue	112	425	3.8	55	3
Tyrone Wheatley	85	327	3.8	60	4
Zack Crockett	49	232	4.7	47	2
Justin Fargas	35	126	3.6	15	1
J.R. Redmond	21	119	5.7	18	0

RECEIVING

PLAYER	NO.	YDS	AVG	LG	TD
Jerry Porter	64	998	15.6	52	9
Ronald Curry	50	679	13.6	63	6
Doug Gabriel	33	551	16.7	58	2
Doug Jolley	27	313	11.6	34	2
Amos Zereoue	39	284	7.3	13	0
J.R. Redmond	32	233	7.3	22	0
Alvis Whitted	9	227	25.2	57	2
Courtney Anderson	13	175	13.5	28	1
Teyo Johnson	9	131	14.6	25	2

KICKING

PLAYER	FGM	FGA	PCT	XPM	XPA
Sebastian Janikowski	25	28	89.3	31	32

PUNTING

PLAYER	NO.	AVG	NET AVG	TB	IN 20	LG	BLK
Shane Lechler	73	46.7	37.2	14	22	67	0

INTERCEPTIONS Phillip Buchanon, 3   **SACKS** Tommy Kelly, 4

PITTSBURGH STEELERS

PASSING

PLAYER	ATT	COMP	YDS	PCT COMP	YDS/ATT	TD	INT	RATING
Ben Roethlisberger	295	196	2,621	66.4	8.9	17	11	98.1
Tommy Maddox	60	30	329	50.0	5.5	1	2	58.3

RUSHING

PLAYER	NO.	YDS	AVG	LG	TD
Jerome Bettis	250	941	3.8	29	13
Duce Staley	192	830	4.3	38	1
Verron Hayes	55	272	4.9	18	0
Willie Parker	32	186	5.8	58	0
Ben Roethlisberger	56	144	2.6	20	1
Antwaan Randle El	8	34	4.3	12	0
Hines Ward	7	25	3.6	16	1

RECEIVING

PLAYER	NO.	YDS	AVG	LG	TD
Hines Ward	80	1,004	12.6	58	4
Plaxico Burress	35	698	19.9	48	5
Antwaan Randle El	43	601	14.0	39	3
Verron Hayes	18	142	7.9	26	2
Lee Mays	9	137	15.2	46	0
Jerame Tuman	9	89	9.9	26	3
Jay Riemersma	7	82	11.7	26	2
Dan Kreider	10	75	7.5	13	1

KICKING

PLAYER	FGM	FGA	PCT	XPM	XPA
Jeff Reed	28	33	84.8	40	40

PUNTING

PLAYER	NO.	AVG	NET AVG	TB	IN 20	LG	BLK
Chris Gardocki	67	43.0	37.4	6	24	61	0

INTERCEPTIONS Troy Polamalu, 5   **SACKS** Aaron Smith, 8

SAN DIEGO CHARGERS

PASSING

PLAYER	ATT	COMP	YDS	PCT COMP	YDS/ATT	TD	INT	RATING
Drew Brees	400	262	3,159	65.5	7.9	27	7	104.8
Doug Flutie	38	20	276	52.6	7.3	1	0	85.0

RUSHING

PLAYER	NO.	YDS	AVG	LG	TD
LaDainian Tomlinson	339	1,335	3.9	42	17
Jesse Chatman	65	392	6.0	52	3
Michael Turner	20	104	5.2	30	0
Drew Brees	53	85	1.6	22	2
Tim Dwight	4	54	13.5	48	0

RECEIVING

PLAYER	NO.	YDS	AVG	LG	TD
Antonio Gates	81	964	11.9	72	13
Eric Parker	47	690	14.7	79	4
LaDainian Tomlinson	53	441	8.3	74	1
Keenan McCardell	31	393	12.7	31	1
Reche Caldwell	18	310	17.2	58	3
Kassim Osgood	15	308	20.5	65	2
Justin Peelle	10	84	8.4	17	2
Ryan Krause	5	81	16.2	29	1

KICKING

PLAYER	FGM	FGA	PCT	XPM	XPA
Nate Kaeding	20	25	80.0	54	55

PUNTING

PLAYER	NO.	AVG	NET AVG	TB	IN 20	LG	BLK
Mike Scifres	69	43.1	38.4	8	29	60	0

INTERCEPTIONS Donnie Edwards, 5   SACKS Steve Foley, 10

TENNESSEE TITANS

PASSING

PLAYER	ATT	COMP	YDS	PCT COMP	YDS/ATT	TD	INT	RATING
Billy Volek	357	210	2,490	61.1	7.0	18	10	87.1
Steve McNair	215	129	1,343	60.0	6.2	8	9	73.1

RUSHING

PLAYER	NO.	YDS	AVG	LG	TD
Chris Brown	220	1,067	4.9	52	6
Antowain Smith	137	509	3.7	43	4
Steve McNair	23	128	5.6	23	1
Robert Holcombe	17	62	3.6	20	0
Billy Volek	11	50	4.5	14	1

RECEIVING

PLAYER	NO.	YDS	AVG	LG	TD
Drew Bennett	80	1,247	15.6	48	11
Derrick Mason	96	1,168	12.2	37	7
Ben Troupe	33	329	10.0	33	1
Eddie Berlin	20	278	13.9	31	1
Erron Kinney	25	193	7.7	21	3
Antowain Smith	22	169	7.7	31	3
Troy Fleming	19	164	8.6	37	2
Chris Brown	20	147	7.4	21	0
Shad Meier	25	127	5.1	29	2

KICKING

PLAYER	FGM	FGA	PCT	XPM	XPA
Gary Anderson	17	22	77.3	37	37

PUNTING

PLAYER	NO.	AVG	NET AVG	TB	IN 20	LG	BLK
Craig Hentrich	73	42.7	38.0	8	20	64	0

INTERCEPTIONS Andre Dyson, 6   SACKS Kevin Carter, 6

TEAM-BY-TEAM STATS — NFC

ARIZONA CARDINALS

PASSING

PLAYER	ATT	COMP	YDS	PCT COMP	YDS/ATT	TD	INT	RATING
Josh McCown	408	233	2,511	57.1	6.2	11	10	74.1
Shaun King	84	47	502	56.0	6.0	1	4	57.7

RUSHING

PLAYER	NO.	YDS	AVG	LG	TD
Emmitt Smith	267	937	3.5	29	9
Troy Hambrick	63	283	4.5	62	1
Obafemi Ayanbadejo	30	122	4.1	23	3
Josh McCown	36	112	3.1	12	2
Josh Scobey	27	89	3.3	10	0

RECEIVING

PLAYER	NO.	YDS	AVG	LG	TD
Larry Fitzgerald	58	780	13.4	48	8
Anquan Boldin	56	623	11.1	31	1
Bryant Johnson	49	537	11.0	40	1
Freddie Jones	45	426	9.5	40	2
Karl Williams	18	197	10.9	33	0
Josh Scobey	18	191	10.6	42	0
Obafemi Ayanbadejo	19	171	9.0	21	1
Emmitt Smith	15	105	7.0	18	0

KICKING

PLAYER	FGM	FGA	PCT	XPM	XPA
Neil Rackers	22	29	75.9	28	28

PUNTING

PLAYER	NO.	AVG	NET AVG	TB	IN 20	LG	BLK
Scott Player	98	43.2	36.4	7	32	57	0

INTERCEPTIONS David Macklin, 4   **SACKS** Bertrand Berry, 14.5

ATLANTA FALCONS

PASSING

PLAYER	ATT	COMP	YDS	PCT COMP	YDS/ATT	TD	INT	RATING
Michael Vick	321	181	2,313	56.4	7.2	14	12	78.1
Matt Schaub	70	33	329	47.1	4.7	1	4	41.9

RUSHING

PLAYER	NO.	YDS	AVG	LG	TD
Warrick Dunn	265	1,106	4.2	60	9
Michael Vick	120	902	7.5	58	3
T.J. Duckett	104	509	4.9	35	8

RECEIVING

PLAYER	NO.	YDS	AVG	LG	TD
Alge Crumpler	48	774	16.1	49	6
Peerless Price	45	575	12.8	50	3
Dez White	30	370	12.3	54	2
Warrick Dunn	29	293	10.1	59	0
Brian Finneran	23	258	11.2	26	2
Justin Griffith	22	220	10.0	62	1
Michael Jenkins	7	119	17.0	46	0

KICKING

PLAYER	FGM	FGA	PCT	XPM	XPA
Jay Feely	18	23	78.3	40	40

PUNTING

PLAYER	NO.	AVG	NET AVG	TB	IN 20	LG	BLK
Chris Mohr	76	40.6	36.9	7	19	56	0

INTERCEPTIONS Aaron Beasley, 4   **SACKS** Patrick Kerney, 13

CAROLINA PANTHERS

PASSING

PLAYER	ATT	COMP	YDS	PCT COMP	YDS/ATT	TD	INT	RATING
Jake Delhomme	533	310	3,886	58.2	7.3	29	15	87.3

RUSHING

PLAYER	NO.	YDS	AVG	LG	TD
Nick Goings	217	821	3.8	57	6
DeShaun Foster	59	255	4.3	71	2
Brad Hoover	68	246	3.6	16	0
Stephen Davis	24	92	3.8	12	0
Jake Delhomme	25	71	2.8	13	1

RECEIVING

PLAYER	NO.	YDS	AVG	LG	TD
Muhsin Muhammad	93	1,405	15.1	51	16
Keary Colbert	47	754	16.0	63	5
Ricky Proehl	34	497	14.6	34	0
Nick Goings	45	394	8.8	37	1
Kris Mangum	34	323	9.5	26	3
Brad Hoover	21	161	7.7	34	2
Mike Seidman	13	123	9.5	27	2

KICKING

PLAYER	FGM	FGA	PCT	XPM	XPA
John Kasay	19	22	86.4	27	28
Todd Sauerbrun	1	1	100.0	4	4

PUNTING

PLAYER	NO.	AVG	NET AVG	TB	IN 20	LG	BLK
Todd Sauerbrun	76	44.1	37.5	8	25	65	0

INTERCEPTIONS Chris Gamble, 6   **SACKS** Julius Peppers, 11

CHICAGO BEARS

PASSING

PLAYER	ATT	COMP	YDS	PCT COMP	YDS/ATT	TD	INT	RATING
Chad Hutchinson	161	92	903	57.1	5.6	4	3	73.6
Craig Krenzel	127	59	718	46.5	5.7	3	6	52.5
Rex Grossman	84	47	607	56.0	7.2	1	3	67.9
Jonathan Quinn	98	51	413	52.0	4.2	1	3	53.7

RUSHING

PLAYER	NO.	YDS	AVG	LG	TD
Thomas Jones	240	948	4.0	54	7
Anthony Thomas	122	404	3.3	41	2
Bobby Wade	12	76	6.3	14	0
Rex Grossman	11	48	4.4	8	1
Craig Krenzel	18	41	2.3	12	0

RECEIVING

PLAYER	NO.	YDS	AVG	LG	TD
David Terrell	42	699	16.6	63	1
Bobby Wade	42	481	11.5	40	0
Thomas Jones	56	427	7.6	45	0
Desmond Clark	24	282	11.8	31	1
Bernard Berrian	15	225	15.0	49	2
Justin Gage	12	156	13.0	32	0

KICKING

PLAYER	FGM	FGA	PCT	XPM	XPA
Paul Edinger	15	24	62.5	22	22

PUNTING

PLAYER	NO.	AVG	NET AVG	TB	IN 20	LG	BLK
Brad Maynard	108	42.9	38.7	5	34	58	0

INTERCEPTIONS Nathan Vasher, 5   **SACKS** Alex Brown, 6

DALLAS COWBOYS

PASSING

PLAYER	ATT	COMP	YDS	PCT COMP	YDS/ATT	TD	INT	RATING
Vinny Testaverde	495	297	3,532	60.0	7.1	17	20	76.4

RUSHING

PLAYER	NO.	YDS	AVG	LG	TD
Julius Jones	197	819	4.2	53	7
Eddie George	132	432	3.3	24	4
Richie Anderson	57	246	4.3	27	1
ReShard Lee	27	128	4.7	14	1
Vinny Testaverde	20	42	2.1	10	1

RECEIVING

PLAYER	NO.	YDS	AVG	LG	TD
Keyshawn Johnson	70	981	14.0	39	6
Jason Witten	87	980	11.3	42	6
Terry Glenn	24	400	16.7	48	2
Antonio Bryant	16	266	16.6	48	2
Quincy Morgan	22	260	11.8	53	0
Richie Anderson	26	207	8.0	28	0
Patrick Crayton	12	162	13.5	39	1

KICKING

PLAYER	FGM	FGA	PCT	XPM	XPA
Billy Cundiff	20	26	76.9	31	31

PUNTING

PLAYER	NO.	AVG	NET AVG	TB	IN 20	LG	BLK
Mat McBriar	75	42.4	35.1	7	22	68	0

INTERCEPTIONS Terence Newman, 4   **SACKS** Greg Ellis, 9

DETROIT LIONS

PASSING

PLAYER	ATT	COMP	YDS	PCT COMP	YDS/ATT	TD	INT	RATING
Joey Harrington	489	274	3,047	56.0	6.2	19	12	77.5
Mike McMahon	15	11	77	73.3	5.1	0	1	56.8

RUSHING

PLAYER	NO.	YDS	AVG	LG	TD
Kevin Jones	241	1,133	4.7	74	5
Shawn Bryson	50	264	5.3	28	0
Joey Harrington	48	175	3.6	17	0
Artose Pinner	57	174	3.1	14	2

RECEIVING

PLAYER	NO.	YDS	AVG	LG	TD
Roy Williams	54	817	15.1	46	8
Az-Zahir Hakim	31	533	17.2	39	3
Stephen Alexander	41	377	9.2	30	1
Shawn Bryson	44	322	7.3	30	0
Tai Streets	28	260	9.3	22	1
Reggie Swinton	18	213	11.8	28	1
Kevin Jones	28	180	6.4	34	1
Casey Fitzsimmons	10	103	10.3	27	0
Cory Schlesinger	10	91	9.1	30	3

KICKING

PLAYER	FGM	FGA	PCT	XPM	XPA
Jason Hanson	24	28	85.7	28	28

PUNTING

PLAYER	NO.	AVG	NET AVG	TB	IN 20	LG	BLK
Nick Harris	92	40.9	34.2	7	32	60	0

INTERCEPTIONS Dre' Bly, 4   **SACKS** James Hall, 11.5

GREEN BAY PACKERS

PASSING

PLAYER	ATT	COMP	YDS	PCT COMP	YDS/ATT	TD	INT	RATING
Brett Favre	540	346	4,088	64.1	7.6	30	17	92.4
Craig Nall	33	23	314	69.7	9.5	4	0	139.4

RUSHING

PLAYER	NO.	YDS	AVG	LG	TD
Ahman Green	259	1,163	4.5	90	7
Najeh Davenport	71	359	5.1	40	2
Tony Fisher	65	224	3.4	24	0

RECEIVING

PLAYER	NO.	YDS	AVG	LG	TD
Javon Walker	89	1,382	15.5	79	12
Donald Driver	84	1,208	14.4	50	9
Robert Ferguson	24	367	15.3	48	1
Bubba Franks	34	361	10.6	29	7
Tony Fisher	38	277	7.3	25	2
Ahman Green	40	275	6.9	48	1
Antonio Chatman	22	246	11.2	21	1
William Henderson	34	239	7.0	38	3

KICKING

PLAYER	FGM	FGA	PCT	XPM	XPA
Ryan Longwell	24	28	85.7	48	48

PUNTING

PLAYER	NO.	AVG	NET AVG	TB	IN 20	LG	BLK
Bryan Barker	66	40.1	33.4	7	16	64	0

INTERCEPTIONS Darren Sharper, 4   **SACKS** Kabeer Gbaja-Biamila, 13.5

MINNESOTA VIKINGS

PASSING

PLAYER	ATT	COMP	YDS	PCT COMP	YDS/ATT	TD	INT	RATING
Daunte Culpepper	548	379	4,711	69.2	8.6	39	11	110.9

RUSHING

PLAYER	NO.	YDS	AVG	LG	TD
Onterrio Smith	124	544	4.4	38	2
Daunte Culpepper	88	406	4.6	16	2
Mewelde Moore	65	379	5.8	33	0
Michael Bennett	70	276	3.9	25	1
Moe Williams	30	161	5.4	49	3

RECEIVING

PLAYER	NO.	YDS	AVG	LG	TD
Nate Burleson	68	1,006	14.8	68	9
Randy Moss	49	767	15.7	82	13
Jermaine Wiggins	71	705	9.9	39	4
Marcus Robinson	47	657	14.0	50	8
Onterrio Smith	36	394	10.9	63	2
Kelly Campbell	19	364	19.2	61	1
Mewelde Moore	27	238	8.8	26	0
Moe Williams	21	233	11.1	28	1
Michael Bennett	21	207	9.9	38	1

KICKING

PLAYER	FGM	FGA	PCT	XPM	XPA
Morten Andersen	18	22	81.8	45	45

PUNTING

PLAYER	NO.	AVG	NET AVG	TB	IN 20	LG	BLK
Darren Bennett	57	39.3	35.3	3	18	61	0

INTERCEPTIONS Antoine Winfield, 3   **SACKS** Kevin Williams, 12

NEW ORLEANS SAINTS

PASSING

PLAYER	ATT	COMP	YDS	PCT COMP	YDS/ATT	TD	INT	RATING
Aaron Brooks	542	309	3,810	57.0	7.0	21	16	79.5

RUSHING

PLAYER	NO.	YDS	AVG	LG	TD
Deuce McAllister	269	1,047	4.0	71	9
Aaron Stecker	58	244	4.2	42	2
Aaron Brooks	58	173	3.0	15	4

RECEIVING

PLAYER	NO.	YDS	AVG	LG	TD
Joe Horn	94	1,399	14.9	57	11
Donte' Stallworth	58	767	13.2	45	5
Jerome Pathon	34	581	17.1	38	1
Boo Williams	33	362	11.0	22	2
Deuce McAllister	34	228	6.7	20	0
Aaron Stecker	29	174	6.0	26	0
Michael Lewis	8	127	15.9	30	0
Ernie Conwell	10	102	10.2	28	1

KICKING

PLAYER	FGM	FGA	PCT	XPM	XPA
John Carney	22	27	81.5	38	38

PUNTING

PLAYER	NO.	AVG	NET AVG	TB	IN 20	LG	BLK
Mitch Berger	85	43.6	39.0	4	28	63	0

INTERCEPTIONS Mike McKenzie, 5   **SACKS** Darren Howard, 11

NEW YORK GIANTS

PASSING

PLAYER	ATT	COMP	YDS	PCT COMP	YDS/ATT	TD	INT	RATING
Kurt Warner	277	174	2,054	62.8	7.4	6	4	86.5
Eli Manning	197	95	1,043	48.2	5.3	6	9	55.4

RUSHING

PLAYER	NO.	YDS	AVG	LG	TD
Tiki Barber	322	1,518	4.7	72	13
Ron Dayne	52	179	3.4	15	1
Mike Cloud	21	90	4.3	26	3

RECEIVING

PLAYER	NO.	YDS	AVG	LG	TD
Amani Toomer	51	747	14.6	48	0
Jeremy Shockey	61	666	10.9	38	6
Tiki Barber	52	578	11.1	62	2
Ike Hilliard	49	437	8.9	43	0
Tim Carter	12	182	15.2	38	1
David Tyree	10	155	15.5	49	1
Jamaar Taylor	6	146	24.3	52	0

KICKING

PLAYER	FGM	FGA	PCT	XPM	XPA
Steve Christie	22	28	78.6	33	33

PUNTING

PLAYER	NO.	AVG	NET AVG	TB	IN 20	LG	BLK
Jeff Feagles	74	41.5	34.6	4	23	55	0

INTERCEPTIONS Gibril Wilson, Brent Alexander, 3   **SACKS** Osi Umenyiora, 7

PHILADELPHIA EAGLES

PASSING

PLAYER	ATT	COMP	YDS	PCT COMP	YDS/ATT	TD	INT	RATING
Donovan McNabb	469	300	3,875	60.4	8.3	31	8	104.7

RUSHING

PLAYER	NO.	YDS	AVG	LG	TD
Brian Westbrook	177	812	4.6	50	3
Dorsey Levens	94	410	4.4	45	4
Donovan McNabb	41	220	5.4	28	3
Reno Mahe	23	91	4.0	22	0
Eric McCoo	9	54	6.0	12	0

RECEIVING

PLAYER	NO.	YDS	AVG	LG	TD
Terrell Owens	77	1,200	15.6	59	14
Brian Westbrook	73	703	9.6	50	6
Todd Pinkston	36	676	18.8	80	1
Freddie Mitchell	22	377	17.1	60	2
L.J. Smith	34	377	11.1	31	5
Chad Lewis	29	267	9.2	21	3
Greg Lewis	17	183	10.8	25	0
Reno Mahe	14	123	8.8	30	0

KICKING

PLAYER	FGM	FGA	PCT	XPM	XPA
David Akers	27	32	84.4	41	42

PUNTING

PLAYER	NO.	AVG	NET AVG	TB	IN 20	LG	BLK
Dirk Johnson	72	42.1	37.4	6	20	62	0

INTERCEPTIONS Lito Sheppard, 5   **SACKS** Jevon Kearse, 7.5

SAN FRANCISCO 49ERS

PASSING

PLAYER	ATT	COMP	YDS	PCT COMP	YDS/ATT	TD	INT	RATING
Tim Rattay	325	198	2,169	60.9	6.7	10	10	78.1
Ken Dorsey	226	123	1,231	54.4	5.4	6	9	62.4

RUSHING

PLAYER	NO.	YDS	AVG	LG	TD
Kevan Barlow	244	822	3.4	60	7
Maurice Hicks	96	362	3.8	35	2
Terry Jackson	26	101	3.9	13	0
Jamal Robertson	16	71	4.4	16	1

RECEIVING

PLAYER	NO.	YDS	AVG	LG	TD
Eric Johnson	82	825	10.1	25	2
Cedrick Wilson	47	641	13.6	39	3
Brandon Lloyd	43	565	13.1	52	6
Curtis Conway	38	403	10.6	37	3
Kevan Barlow	35	212	6.1	15	0
Rashaun Woods	7	160	22.9	59	1
Maurice Hicks	16	154	9.6	19	0
Arnaz Battle	8	143	17.9	65	0
Terry Jackson	21	139	6.6	22	0

KICKING

PLAYER	FGM	FGA	PCT	XPM	XPA
Todd Peterson	18	22	81.8	23	23

PUNTING

PLAYER	NO.	AVG	NET AVG	TB	IN 20	LG	BLK
Andy Lee	96	41.6	35.3	8	25	81	0

INTERCEPTIONS Tony Parrish, 4   **SACKS** John Engelberger, 6

SEATTLE SEAHAWKS

PASSING

PLAYER	ATT	COMP	YDS	PCT COMP	YDS/ATT	TD	INT	RATING
Matt Hasselbeck	474	279	3,382	58.9	7.1	22	15	83.1
Trent Dilfer	58	25	333	43.1	5.7	1	3	46.1

RUSHING

PLAYER	NO.	YDS	AVG	LG	TD
Shaun Alexander	353	1,696	4.8	44	16
Mack Strong	36	131	3.6	11	0
Maurice Morris	30	126	4.2	12	0
Matt Hasselbeck	27	90	3.3	19	1

RECEIVING

PLAYER	NO.	YDS	AVG	LG	TD
Darrell Jackson	87	1,199	13.8	56	7
Bobby Engram	36	499	13.9	60	2
Koren Robinson	31	495	16.0	33	2
Jerry Rice	25	362	14.5	56	3
Jerramy Stevens	31	349	11.3	32	3
Itula Mili	23	240	10.4	20	1
Shaun Alexander	23	170	7.4	24	4
Jerheme Urban	6	117	19.5	33	1

KICKING

PLAYER	FGM	FGA	PCT	XPM	XPA
Josh Brown	23	25	92.0	40	40

PUNTING

PLAYER	NO.	AVG	NET AVG	TB	IN 20	LG	BLK
Donnie Jones	26	38.0	32.2	2	6	51	0
Tom Rouen	26	42.0	37.8	1	10	60	0
Ken Walter	24	38.3	33.0	1	4	50	0

INTERCEPTIONS Ken Lucas, 6

SACKS Chike Okeafor, 8.5

ST. LOUIS RAMS

PASSING

PLAYER	ATT	COMP	YDS	PCT COMP	YDS/ATT	TD	INT	RATING
Marc Bulger	485	321	3,964	66.2	8.2	21	14	93.7
Chris Chandler	62	35	463	56.5	7.5	2	8	51.4

RUSHING

PLAYER	NO.	YDS	AVG	LG	TD
Marshall Faulk	195	774	4.0	40	3
Steven Jackson	134	673	5.0	48	4
Marc Bulger	19	89	4.7	19	3
Arlen Harris	20	63	3.2	14	0

RECEIVING

PLAYER	NO.	YDS	AVG	LG	TD
Torry Holt	94	1,372	14.6	75	10
Isaac Bruce	89	1,292	14.5	56	6
Shaun McDonald	37	494	13.4	52	3
Kevin Curtis	32	421	13.2	41	2
Marshall Faulk	50	310	6.2	25	1
Steven Jackson	19	189	9.9	28	0
Dane Looker	13	183	14.1	29	0
Brandon Manumaleuna	15	174	11.6	48	1

KICKING

PLAYER	FGM	FGA	PCT	XPM	XPA
Jeff Wilkins	19	24	79.2	32	32

PUNTING

PLAYER	NO.	AVG	NET AVG	TB	IN 20	LG	BLK
Sean Landeta	40	43.3	32.5	3	9	63	0
Kevin Stemke	28	39.8	36.1	3	12	56	0

INTERCEPTIONS Jerametrius Butler, 5

SACKS Bryce Fisher, 8.5

TAMPA BAY BUCCANEERS

PASSING

PLAYER	ATT	COMP	YDS	PCT COMP	YDS/ATT	TD	INT	RATING
Brian Griese	336	233	2,632	69.3	7.8	20	12	97.5
Brad Johnson	103	65	674	63.1	6.5	3	3	79.5
Chris Simms	73	42	467	57.5	6.4	1	3	64.1

RUSHING

PLAYER	NO.	YDS	AVG	LG	TD
Michael Pittman	219	926	4.2	78	7
Mike Alstott	67	230	3.4	32	2
Charlie Garner	30	111	3.7	25	0
Earnest Graham	13	73	5.6	13	0
Michael Clayton	5	30	6.0	15	0

RECEIVING

PLAYER	NO.	YDS	AVG	LG	TD
Michael Clayton	80	1,193	14.9	75	7
Joey Galloway	33	416	12.6	36	5
Michael Pittman	41	391	9.5	68	3
Ken Dilger	39	345	8.8	45	3
Joe Jurevicius	27	333	12.3	42	2
Charles Lee	15	207	13.8	35	0
Mike Alstott	29	202	7.0	20	0
Tim Brown	24	200	8.3	21	1
Bill Schroeder	7	156	22.3	54	1
Will Heller	12	98	8.2	22	1

KICKING

PLAYER	FGM	FGA	PCT	XPM	XPA
Martin Gramatica	11	19	57.9	21	22
Jay Taylor	4	5	80.0	11	11

PUNTING

PLAYER	NO.	AVG	NET AVG	TB	IN 20	LG	BLK
Josh Bidwell	82	42.3	36.8	7	23	60	0

INTERCEPTIONS Brian Kelly, 4   **SACKS** Simeon Rice, 12

WASHINGTON REDSKINS

PASSING

PLAYER	ATT	COMP	YDS	PCT COMP	YDS/ATT	TD	INT	RATING
Patrick Ramsey	272	169	1,665	62.1	6.1	10	11	74.8
Mark Brunell	237	118	1,194	49.8	5.0	7	6	63.9

RUSHING

PLAYER	NO.	YDS	AVG	LG	TD
Clinton Portis	343	1,315	3.8	64	5
Ladell Betts	90	371	4.1	27	1
Mark Brunell	19	62	3.3	21	0
Patrick Ramsey	10	19	1.9	17	0
Rod Gardner	3	7	2.3	11	0

RECEIVING

PLAYER	NO.	YDS	AVG	LG	TD
Laveranues Coles	90	950	10.6	45	1
Rod Gardner	51	650	12.7	51	5
Chris Cooley	37	314	8.5	31	6
Clinton Portis	40	235	5.9	18	2
James Thrash	17	203	11.9	31	0
Taylor Jacobs	16	178	11.1	45	0
Ladell Betts	15	108	7.2	20	0

KICKING

PLAYER	FGM	FGA	PCT	XPM	XPA
John Hall	8	11	72.7	13	13
Ola Kimrin	6	10	60.0	6	6
Jeff Chandler	5	8	62.5	14	14

PUNTING

PLAYER	NO.	AVG	NET AVG	TB	IN 20	LG	BLK
Tom Tupa	103	44.1	35.2	8	30	61	0

INTERCEPTIONS Shawn Springs, 5   **SACKS** Shawn Springs, Cornelius Griffin, 6

SUPER BOWL RESULTS

SUPER BOWL	DATE	WINNER	LOSER	SCORE	SITE	ATTENDANCE
XXXIX	2-6-05	Patriots	Eagles	24–21	Jacksonville, FL	78,125
XXXVIII	2-1-04	Patriots	Panthers	32–29	Houston, TX	71,525
XXXVII	1-26-03	Buccaneers	Raiders	48–21	San Diego, CA	67,603
XXXVI	2-3-02	Patriots	Rams	20–17	New Orleans, LA	72,922
XXXV	1-28-01	Ravens	Giants	34–7	Tampa, FL	71,921
XXXIV	1-30-00	Rams	Titans	23–16	Atlanta, GA	72,625
XXXIII	1-31-99	Broncos	Falcons	34–19	Miami, FL	74,803
XXXII	1-25-98	Broncos	Packers	31–24	San Diego, CA	68,912
XXXI	1-26-97	Packers	Patriots	35–21	New Orleans, LA	72,301
XXX	1-28-96	Cowboys	Steelers	27–17	Tempe, AZ	76,347
XXIX	1-29-95	49ers	Chargers	49–26	Miami, FL	74,107
XXVIII	1-30-94	Cowboys	Bills	30–13	Atlanta, GA	72,817
XXVII	1-31-93	Cowboys	Bills	52–17	Pasadena, CA	98,374
XXVI	1-26-92	Redskins	Bills	37–24	Minneapolis, MN	63,130
XXV	1-27-91	Giants	Bills	20–19	Tampa, FL	73,813
XXIV	1-28-90	49ers	Broncos	55–10	New Orleans, LA	72,919
XXIII	1-22-89	49ers	Bengals	20–16	Miami, FL	75,129
XXII	1-31-88	Redskins	Broncos	42–10	San Diego, CA	73,302
XXI	1-25-87	Giants	Broncos	39–20	Pasadena, CA	101,063
XX	1-26-86	Bears	Patriots	46–10	New Orleans, LA	73,818
XIX	1-20-85	49ers	Dolphins	38–16	Stanford, CA	84,059
XVIII	1-22-84	Raiders	Redskins	38–9	Tampa, FL	72,920
XVII	1-30-83	Redskins	Dolphins	27–17	Pasadena, CA	103,667
XVI	1-24-82	49ers	Bengals	26–21	Pontiac, MI	81,270
XV	1-25-81	Raiders	Eagles	27–10	New Orleans, LA	76,135
XIV	1-20-80	Steelers	Rams	31–19	Pasadena, CA	103,985
XIII	1-21-79	Steelers	Cowboys	35–31	Miami, FL	79,484
XII	1-15-78	Cowboys	Broncos	27–10	New Orleans, LA	76,400
XI	1-9-77	Raiders	Vikings	32–14	Pasadena, CA	103,438
X	1-18-76	Steelers	Cowboys	21–17	Miami, FL	80,187
IX	1-12-75	Steelers	Vikings	16–6	New Orleans, LA	80,997
VIII	1-13-74	Dolphins	Vikings	24–7	Houston, TX	71,882
VII	1-14-73	Dolphins	Redskins	14–7	Los Angeles, CA	90,182
VI	1-16-72	Cowboys	Dolphins	24–3	New Orleans, LA	81,023
V	1-17-71	Colts	Cowboys	16–13	Miami, FL	79,204
IV	1-11-70	Chiefs	Vikings	23–7	New Orleans, LA	80,562
III	1-12-69	Jets	Colts	16–7	Miami, FL	75,389
II	1-14-68	Packers	Raiders	33–14	Miami, FL	75,546
I	1-15-67	Packers	Chiefs	35–10	Los Angeles, CA	61,946

SUPER BOWL MVPS

SUPER BOWL	PLAYER/TEAM	POSITION	SUPER BOWL	PLAYER/TEAM	POSITION
XXXIX	Deion Branch, Patriots	WR	XVIII	Marcus Allen, Raiders	RB
XXXVIII	Tom Brady, Patriots	QB	XVII	John Riggins, Redskins	RB
XXXVII	Dexter Jackson, Buccaneers	S	XVI	Joe Montana, 49ers	QB
XXXVI	Tom Brady, Patriots	QB	XV	Jim Plunkett, Raiders	QB
XXXV	Ray Lewis, Ravens	LB	XIV	Terry Bradshaw, Steelers	QB
XXXIV	Kurt Warner, Rams	QB	XIII	Terry Bradshaw, Steelers	QB
XXXIII	John Elway, Broncos	QB	XII (tie)	Randy White, Cowboys	DT
XXXII	Terrell Davis, Broncos	RB		Harvey Martin, Cowboys	DE
XXXI	Desmond Howard, Packers	KR	XI	Fred Biletnikoff, Raiders	WR
XXX	Larry Brown, Cowboys	DB	X	Lynn Swann, Steelers	WR
XXIX	Steve Young, 49ers	QB	IX	Franco Harris, Steelers	RB
XXVIII	Emmitt Smith, Cowboys	RB	VIII	Larry Csonka, Dolphins	RB
XXVII	Troy Aikman, Cowboys	QB	VII	Jake Scott, Dolphins	S
XXVI	Mark Rypien, Redskins	QB	VI	Roger Staubach, Cowboys	QB
XXV	Ottis Anderson, Giants	RB	V	Chuck Howley, Cowboys	LB
XXIV	Joe Montana, 49ers	QB	IV	Len Dawson, Chiefs	QB
XXIII	Jerry Rice, 49ers	WR	III	Joe Namath, Jets	QB
XXII	Doug Williams, Redskins	QB	II	Bart Starr, Packers	QB
XXI	Phil Simms, Giants	QB	I	Bart Starr, Packers	QB
XX	Richard Dent, Bears	DE			
XIX	Joe Montana, 49ers	QB			

KEY QB=quarterback; S=safety; LB=linebacker; RB=running back; KR=kick returner; DB=defensive back; WR=wide receiver; DE=defensive end; DT=defensive tackle

2004-05 TIME LINE

■ **April 24, 2004:** Quarterback Eli Manning of the University of Mississippi is drafted by the San Diego Chargers as the Number 1 overall pick in the 2004 NFL Draft. About an hour later, Manning is traded to the New York Giants.

■ **September 9, 2004:** The 85th NFL season kicks off with a Thursday night game featuring a rematch of the 2003 AFC Championship Game. The defending Super Bowl champion New England Patriots defeat the Indianapolis Colts, 27-24.

■ **September 12, 2004:** Three-time Super Bowl winner Joe Gibbs returns to the sideline as head coach of the Washington Redskins for the first time since retiring in 1992. The Redskins defeat the Tampa Bay Buccaneers, 16-10, in his debut.

■ **December 26, 2004:** Quarterback Peyton Manning of the Indianapolis Colts throws his 49th touchdown pass of the season, breaking the record set by former Miami Dolphin quarterback Dan Marino.

■ **December 26, 2004:** Former defensive end Reggie White dies of a respiratory ailment at age 43. White played for the Eagles, Packers, and Panthers and is second on the NFL's career sack list (198).

■ **January 23, 2005:** After losing three straight NFC Championship Games (2001-03), the Philadelphia Eagles defeat the Atlanta Falcons, 27–10, and advance to the Super Bowl for the first time in 24 years.

■ **February 0, 2005:** Emmitt Smith, the NFL's career rushing leader, announces his retirement after 15 seasons with the Dallas Cowboys and Arizona Cardinals.

■ **February 6, 2005:** The New England Patriots defeat the Philadelphia Eagles, 24-21, in Super Bowl XXXIX.

■ **April 23, 2005:** Quarterback Alex Smith of Utah is chosen by the San Francisco 49ers as the first pick in the 2005 NFL Draft.

ALL-TIME NFL INDIVIDUAL
STATISTICAL LEADERS — CAREER LEADERS

Emmitt Smith,
Arizona Cardinals

PAUL CONNORS/AP

SCORING

PLAYER	YRS	TD	FG	PAT	PTS
†Morten Andersen	23	0	520	798	2,358
†Gary Anderson	22	0	521	783	2,346
George Blanda	26	9	335	942	2,002
Norm Johnson	18	0	366	638	1,736
Nick Lowery	18	0	383	562	1,711
Jan Stenerud	19	0	373	580	1,699
Eddie Murray	19	0	352	538	1,594
Al Del Greco	17	0	347	543	1,584
†John Carney	17	4	365	442	1,537
†Matt Stover	14	3	350	431	1,481
†Steve Christie	15	6	336	468	1,476
Pat Leahy	18	0	304	558	1,470
†Jason Elam	12	5	317	491	1,442
Jim Turner	16	1	304	521	1,439
Matt Bahr	17	0	300	522	1,422
Mark Moseley	16	0	300	482	1,382
Jim Bakken	17	0	282	534	1,380
Fred Cox	15	0	282	519	1,365
Lou Groza	17	1	234	641	1,349
Jim Breech	14	0	243	517	1,246

RUSHING

PLAYER	YRS	ATT	YDS	AVG	LG	TD
†Emmitt Smith	15	4,409	18,355	4.2	75	164
Walter Payton	13	3,838	16,726	4.4	76	110
Barry Sanders	10	3,062	15,269	5.0	85	99
†Curtis Martin	10	3,298	13,366	4.1	70	85
†Jerome Bettis	12	3,369	13,294	3.9	71	82
Eric Dickerson	11	2,996	13,259	4.4	85	90
Tony Dorsett	12	2,936	12,739	4.3	99	77
Jim Brown	9	2,359	12,312	5.2	80	106
Marcus Allen	16	3,022	12,243	4.1	61	123
Franco Harris	13	2,949	12,120	4.1	75	91
Thurman Thomas	13	2,877	12,074	4.2	80	65
†Marshall Faulk	11	2,771	11,987	4.3	71	100
John Riggins	14	2,916	11,352	3.9	66	104
Ricky Watters	12	2,622	10,643	4.1	57	78
O.J. Simpson	11	2,223	10,539	4.9	94	59
†Eddie George	9	2,865	10,441	3.6	76	68
Ottis Anderson	14	2,562	10,273	4.0	76	81
Earl Campbell	8	2,187	9,407	4.3	81	74
Terry Allen	11	2,152	8,614	4.0	55	73
Jim Taylor	10	1,941	8,597	4.4	84	83

TOUCHDOWNS

PLAYER	YRS	RUSH	REC	RET	TD
†Jerry Rice	20	10	197	0	207
†Emmitt Smith	15	164	11	0	175
Marcus Allen	16	123	21	1	145
†Marshall Faulk	11	100	35	0	135
Cris Carter	16	0	130	1	131
Jim Brown	9	106	20	0	126
Walter Payton	13	110	15	0	125
John Riggins	14	104	12	0	116
Lenny Moore	12	63	48	2	113
Barry Sanders	10	99	10	0	109

PLAYER	YRS	RUSH	REC	RET	TD
Don Hutson	11	3	99	3	105
†Tim Brown	17	1	100	4	105
Steve Largent	14	1	100	0	101
Franco Harris	13	91	9	0	100
Eric Dickerson	11	90	6	0	96
Jim Taylor	10	83	10	0	93
Tony Dorsett	12	77	13	1	91
Bobby Mitchell	11	18	65	8	91
Ricky Watters	11	78	13	0	91

PASSING — EFFICIENCY*

PLAYER	YRS	ATT	COMP	PCT COMP	YDS	YDS/ATT	TD	INT	RATING
Steve Young	15	4,149	2,667	64.3	33,124	7.98	232	107	96.8
†Kurt Warner	7	1,965	1,295	65.9	16,501	8.40	108	69	95.7
†Daunte Culpepper	6	2,391	1,539	64.4	18,598	7.78	129	74	93.2
Joe Montana	15	5,391	3,409	63.2	40,551	7.52	273	139	92.3
†Peyton Manning	7	3,880	2,464	63.5	29,442	7.59	216	120	92.3
†Trent Green	12	2,822	1,705	60.4	21,607	7.66	133	82	87.9
†Tom Brady	5	2,018	1,243	61.6	13,925	6.90	97	52	87.5
†Brett Favre	14	7,004	4,306	61.5	49,734	7.10	376	226	87.4
†Jeff Garcia	6	2,612	1,593	61.0	18,139	6.94	123	65	87.2
Dan Marino	17	8,358	4,967	59.4	61,361	7.34	420	252	86.4

PASSING — YARDS

PLAYER	YRS	ATT	COMP	PCT COMP	YDS
Dan Marino	17	8,358	4,967	59.4	61,361
John Elway	16	7,250	4,123	56.9	51,475
†Brett Favre	14	7,004	4,306	61.5	49,734
Warren Moon	17	6,823	3,988	58.4	49,325
Fran Tarkenton	18	6,467	3,686	57.0	47,003
†Vinny Testaverde	18	6,420	3,631	56.6	44,475

PLAYER	YRS	ATT	COMP	PCT COMP	YDS
Dan Fouts	15	5,604	3,297	58.8	43,040
Joe Montana	15	5,391	3,409	63.2	40,551
Johnny Unitas	18	5,186	2,830	54.6	40,239
Dave Krieg	19	5,311	3,105	58.5	38,147
Boomer Esiason	14	5,205	2,969	57.0	37,920
Jim Kelly	11	4,779	2,874	60.1	35,467

*1,500 or more attempts. The passer ratings are based on performance standards established for completion percentage, interception percentage,
touchdown percentage, and average gain. Passers are allocated points according to how their marks compare with those standards.
†Active in 2004

KEY | YRS=years; TD=touchdowns; FG=field goals; PAT=extra points; PTS=points; ATT=attempts; AVG=average; LG=long; RUSH=rushing; REC=receiving;
RET=returns; COMP=completions; PCT COMP=completion percentage; YDS/ATT=yards per attempt; INT=interceptions; COMP YDS=completion yards

ALL-TIME NFL INDIVIDUAL STATISTICAL LEADERS (cont.)

PASSING — TOUCHDOWNS

PLAYER	TD
Dan Marino	420
†Brett Favre	376
Fran Tarkenton	342
John Elway	300
Warren Moon	291
Johnny Unitas	290
Joe Montana	273
†Vinny Testaverde	268
Dave Krieg	261
Sonny Jurgensen	255
Dan Fouts	254
Boomer Esiason	247
Jim Kelly	237
Steve Young	232
John Brodie	214
Terry Bradshaw	212
Y.A. Tittle	212

SACKS

PLAYER	SACKS
Bruce Smith	200.0
Reggie White	198.0
Kevin Greene	160.0
Chris Doleman	150.5
Richard Dent	137.5

Note: Officially compiled since 1982

Jerry Rice, Seattle Seahawks

INTERCEPTIONS

PLAYER	YRS	NO.	YDS	AVG	LG	TD
Paul Krause	16	81	1,185	14.6	81	3
Emlen Tunnell	14	79	1,282	16.2	55	4
Rod Woodson	17	71	1,483	20.9	98	12
Dick "Night Train" Lane	14	68	1,207	17.8	80	5
Ronnie Lott	14	63	730	11.6	83	5

RECEIVING — RECEPTIONS

PLAYER	YRS	NO.	YDS	AVG	LG	TD
†Jerry Rice	20	1,549	22,895	14.8	96	197
Cris Carter	16	1,101	13,899	12.6	80	130
†Tim Brown	17	1,094	14,934	13.7	80	100
Andre Reed	16	951	13,198	13.9	83	87
Art Monk	16	940	12,721	13.5	79	68
Irving Fryar	17	851	12,785	15.0	80	84
†Marvin Harrison	9	845	11,185	13.2	79	98
Larry Centers	14	827	6,797	8.2	54	28
Steve Largent	14	819	13,089	16.0	74	100
Shannon Sharpe	14	815	10,060	12.3	82	62
Henry Ellard	16	814	13,777	16.9	81	65
James Lofton	16	764	14,004	18.3	80	75

RECEIVING — YARDS

PLAYER	YDS
†Jerry Rice	22,895
†Tim Brown	14,934
James Lofton	14,004
Cris Carter	13,899
Henry Ellard	13,777
Andre Reed	13,198
Steve Largent	13,089
Irving Fryar	12,785
Art Monk	12,721
Charlie Joiner	12,146

† Active in 2004

SINGLE-SEASON LEADERS

SCORING — POINTS

PLAYER	YEAR	TD	PAT	FG	PTS
Paul Hornung, Packers	1960	15	41	15	176
Gary Anderson, Vikings	1998	0	59	35	164
Jeff Wilkins, Rams	2003	0	46	39	163
Priest Holmes, Chiefs	2003	27	0	0	162
Mark Moseley, Redskins	1983	0	62	33	161
Marshall Faulk, Rams	2000	26	0	0	160
Gino Cappelletti, Patriots	1964	7	36	25	155
Emmitt Smith, Cowboys	1995	25	0	0	150
Chip Lohmiller, Redskins	1991	0	56	31	149
Gino Cappelletti, Patriots	1961	8	48	17	147

Note: Cappelletti's 1964 total includes a 2-point conversion.

TOUCHDOWNS

PLAYER	YEAR	RUSH	REC	RET	TOTAL
Priest Holmes, Chiefs	2003	27	0	0	27
Marshall Faulk, Rams	2000	18	8	0	26
Emmitt Smith, Cowboys	1995	25	0	0	25
John Riggins, Redskins	1983	24	0	0	24
Priest Holmes, Chiefs	2002	21	3	0	24
O.J. Simpson, Bills	1975	16	7	0	23
Jerry Rice, 49ers	1987	1	22	0	23
Terrell Davis, Broncos	1998	21	2	0	23

Three tied with 22.

FIELD GOALS

PLAYER	YEAR	ATT	NO.
Jeff Wilkins, Rams	2003	42	39
Olindo Mare, Dolphins	1999	46	39
John Kasay, Panthers	1996	45	37
Mike Vanderjagt, Colts	2003	37	37
Cary Blanchard, Colts	1996	40	36
Al Del Greco, Titans	1998	39	36

Four tied with 35.

RUSHING — YARDS GAINED

PLAYER	YEAR	ATT	YDS	AVG
Eric Dickerson, Rams	1984	379	2,105	5.6
Jamal Lewis, Ravens	2003	387	2,066	5.3
Barry Sanders, Lions	1997	335	2,053	6.1
Terrell Davis, Broncos	1998	392	2,008	5.1
O.J. Simpson, Bills	1973	332	2,003	6.0
Earl Campbell, Oilers	1980	373	1,934	5.2
Jim Brown, Browns	1963	291	1,863	6.4
Barry Sanders, Lions	1994	331	1,883	5.7
Ahman Green, Packers	2003	355	1,883	5.3
Ricky Williams, Dolphins	2002	383	1,853	4.8
Walter Payton, Bears	1977	339	1,852	5.5

SINGLE-SEASON LEADERS (cont.)

RUSHING — AVERAGE GAIN

PLAYER	YEAR	AVG
Beattie Feathers, Bears	1934	8.44
Randall Cunningham, Eagles	1990	7.98
Michael Vick, Falcons	2002	6.88
Bobby Douglass, Bears	1972	6.87

Minimum 100 attempts.

RUSHING — TOUCHDOWNS

PLAYER	YEAR	NO.
Priest Holmes, Chiefs	2003	27
Emmitt Smith, Cowboys	1995	25
John Riggins, Redskins	1983	24

Five tied with 21.

PASSING — YARDS GAINED

PLAYER	YEAR	ATT	COMP	PCT	YDS
Dan Marino, Dolphins	1984	564	362	64.2	5,084
Kurt Warner, Rams	2001	546	375	68.7	4,830
Dan Fouts, Chargers	1981	609	360	59.1	4,802
Dan Marino, Dolphins	1986	623	378	60.7	4,746
Daunte Culpepper, Vikings	2004	548	379	69.2	4,717
Dan Fouts, Chargers	1980	589	348	59.1	4,715
Warren Moon, Oilers	1991	655	404	61.7	4,690
Warren Moon, Oilers	1990	584	362	62.0	4,689
Rich Gannon, Raiders	2002	618	418	67.6	4,689
Neil Lomax, Cardinals	1984	560	345	61.6	4,614
Peyton Manning, Colts	2004	497	336	67.6	4,557

PASSER RATING

PLAYER	YEAR	RATING
Peyton Manning, Colts	2004	121.1
Steve Young, 49ers	1994	112.8
Joe Montana, 49ers	1989	112.4
Daunte Culpepper, Vikings	2004	110.9
Milt Plum, Browns	1960	110.4
Sammy Baugh, Redskins	1945	109.9
Kurt Warner, Rams	1999	109.2

PASSING — TOUCHDOWNS

PLAYER	YEAR	NO.
Peyton Manning, Colts	2004	49
Dan Marino, Dolphins	1984	48
Dan Marino, Dolphins	1986	44
Kurt Warner, Rams	1999	41
Brett Favre, Packers	1996	39
Daunte Culpepper, Vikings	2004	39

Four tied with 36.

RECEIVING — RECEPTIONS

PLAYER	YEAR	NO.	YDS
Marvin Harrison, Colts	2002	143	1,722
Herman Moore, Lions	1995	123	1,686
Cris Carter, Vikings	1994	122	1,256
Jerry Rice, 49ers	1995	122	1,848
Cris Carter, Vikings	1995	122	1,371
Isaac Bruce, Rams	1995	119	1,781
Torry Holt, Rams	2003	117	1,696
Jimmy Smith, Jaguars	1999	116	1,636
Marvin Harrison, Colts	1999	115	1,663
Rod Smith, Broncos	2001	113	1,343

Four tied with 112.

RECEIVING — YARDS GAINED

PLAYER	YEAR	YDS
Jerry Rice, 49ers	1995	1,848
Isaac Bruce, Rams	1995	1,781
Charley Hennigan, Oilers	1961	1,746
Marvin Harrison, Colts	2002	1,722
Torry Holt, Lions	2003	1,696
Herman Moore, Lions	1995	1,686

RECEIVING — TOUCHDOWNS

PLAYER	YEAR	NO.
Jerry Rice, 49ers	1987	22
Mark Clayton, Dolphins	1984	18
Sterling Sharpe, Packers	1994	18

Eight tied with 17.

INTERCEPTIONS

PLAYER	YEAR	NO.
Dick "Night Train" Lane, Rams	1952	14
Dan Sandifer, Redskins	1948	13
Spec Sanders, N.Y. Yankees	1950	13
Lester Hayes, Raiders	1980	13

Nine tied with 12.

SACKS

PLAYER	YEAR	NO.
Michael Strahan, N.Y. Giants	2001	22.5
Mark Gastineau, Jets	1984	22.0
Reggie White, Eagles	1987	21.0
Chris Doleman, Vikings	1989	21.0
Lawrence Taylor, N.Y. Giants	1986	20.5

PRO BOWL RESULTS

DATE	RESULT	DATE	RESULT	DATE	RESULT
2-13-05	AFC 38, NFC 27	2-2-97	AFC 26, NFC 23	1-29-89	NFC 34, AFC 3
2-8-04	NFC 55, AFC 52	2-4-96	NFC 20, AFC 13	2-7-88	AFC 15, NFC 6
2-2-03	AFC 45, NFC 20	2-5-95	AFC 41, NFC 13	2-1-87	AFC 10, NFC 6
2-9-02	AFC 38, NFC 30	2-6-94	NFC 17, AFC 3	2-2-86	NFC 28, AFC 24
2-4-01	AFC 38, NFC 17	2-7-93	AFC 23, NFC 20	1-27-85	AFC 22, NFC 14
2-6-00	NFC 51, AFC 31	2-2-92	NFC 21, AFC 15	1-29-84	NFC 45, AFC 3
2-7-99	AFC 23, NFC 10	2-3-91	AFC 23, NFC 21	2-6-83	NFC 20, AFC 19
2-1-98	AFC 29, NFC 24	2-4-90	NFC 27, AFC 21	1-31-82	AFC 16, NFC 13

PRO BOWL RESULTS (cont.)

DATE	RESULT	DATE	RESULT	DATE	RESULT
2-1-81	NFC 21, AFC 7	1-22-67	NFL East 20, West 10	1-15-56	East 31, West 30
1-27-80	NFC 37, AFC 27	1-21-67	AFL East 30, West 23	1-16-55	West 26, East 19
1-29-79	NFC 13, AFC 7	1-15-66	NFL East 36, West 7	1-17-54	East 20, West 9
1-23-78	NFC 14, AFC 13	1-15-66	AFL All-Stars 30, Buffalo 19	1-10-53	N. Conf. 27, A. Conf. 7
1-17-77	AFC 24, NFC 14	1-16-65	AFL West 38, East 14	1-12-52	N. Conf. 30, A. Conf. 13
1-26-76	NFC 23, AFC 20	1-10-65	NFL West 34, East 14	1-14-51	A. Conf. 28, N. Conf. 27
1-20-75	NFC 17, AFC 10	1-19-64	AFL West 27, East 24	12-27-42	NFL All-Stars 17,
1-20-74	AFC 15, NFC 13	1-12-64	NFL West 31, East 17		Washington 14
1-21-73	AFC 33, NFC 28	1-13-63	NFL East 30, West 20	1-4-42	Chi. Bears 35,
1-23-72	AFC 26, NFC 13	1-13-63	AFL West 21, East 14		NFL All-Stars 24
1-24-71	NFC 27, AFC 6	1-14-62	NFL West 31, East 30	12-29-40	Chi. Bears 28,
1-18-70	NFL West 16, East 13	1-7-62	AFL West 47, East 27		NFL All-Stars 14
1-17-70	AFL West 26, East 3	1-15-61	West 35, East 31	1-14-40	Green Bay 16,
1-19-69	NFL West 10, East 7	1-17 60	West 38, East 21		NFL All-Stars 7
1-19-69	AFL West 38, East 25	1-11-59	East 28, West 21	1-15-39	N.Y. Giants 13,
1-21-68	NFL West 38, East 20	1-12-58	West 26, East 7		Pro All-Stars 10
1-21-68	AFL East 25, West 24	1-13-57	West 19, East 10		

2005 NFL DRAFT — FIRST ROUND   April 23-24, 2005, New York, NY

PICK	TEAM	PLAYER	POS.	HT.	WT.	SCHOOL
1	San Francisco	Alex Smith	QB	6-4	212	Utah
2	Miami	Ronnie Brown	RB	6-0	233	Auburn
3	Cleveland	Braylon Edwards	WR	6-3	211	Michigan
4	Chicago	Cedric Benson	RB	5-10	222	Texas
5	Tampa Bay	Carnell Williams	RB	5-11	217	Auburn
6	Tennessee	Adam Jones	CB	5-11	187	West Virginia
7	Minnesota (from Oakland)	Troy Williamson	WR	6-1	203	South Carolina
8	Arizona	Antrel Rolle	CB	6-0	202	Miami (Florida)
9	Washington	Carlos Rogers	CB	6-0	199	Auburn
10	Detroit	Mike Williams	WR	6-5	229	Southern California
11	Dallas	Demarcus Ware	DE	6-4	247	Troy State
12	San Diego (from N.Y. Giants)	Shawne Merriman	OLB	6-4	253	Maryland
13	New Orleans (from Houston)	Jammal Brown	OT	6-6	313	Oklahoma
14	Carolina	Thomas Davis	FS	6-1	231	Georgia
15	Kansas City	Derrick Johnson	OLB	6-3	234	Texas
16	Houston (from New Orleans)	Travis Johnson	DT	6-4	290	Florida State
17	Cincinnati	David Pollack	DE	6-2	261	Georgia
18	Minnesota	Erasmus James	DE	6-4	263	Wisconsin
19	St. Louis	Alex Barron	OT	6-7	320	Florida State
20	Dallas (from Buffalo)	Marcus Spears	DE	6-4	298	Louisiana State
21	Jacksonville	Matt Jones	WR	6-6	242	Arkansas
22	Baltimore	Mark Clayton	WR	5-10	193	Oklahoma
23	Oakland (from Seattle)	Fabian Washington	CB	5-10	183	Nebraska
24	Green Bay	Aaron Rodgers	QB	6-2	223	California
25	Washington (from Denver)	Jason Campbell	QB	6-4	223	Auburn
26	Seattle (from N.Y. Jets through Oakland)	Chris Spencer	C	6-3	309	Mississippi
27	Atlanta	Sharod White	WR	6-1	201	Alabama-Birmingham
28	San Diego	Luis Castillo	DT	6-3	306	Northwestern
29	Indianapolis	Marlin Jackson	CB	6-0	196	Michigan
30	Pittsburgh	Heath Miller	TE	6-5	265	Virginia
31	Philadelphia	Mike Patterson	DT	5-11	292	Southern California
32	New England	Logan Mankins	G	6-4	307	Fresno State

KEY QB=quarterback; RB=running back; WR=wide receiver; CB=cornerback; DE=defensive end; OLB=outside linebacker; OT=offensive tackle; FS=free safety; DT=defensive tackle; C=center; TE=tight end; G=guard

In many ways, the 2004 college football season was a repeat of 2003: The Southern California Trojans were named national champion (they were co-national champs in 2003), there was controversy over which teams should play in the title game, and quarterback Jason White of Oklahoma was a finalist for the Heisman Trophy. He won the award in 2003. This time, however, junior quarterback Matt Leinart of USC won the Heisman.

Four teams finished the 2004 regular season unbeaten. USC, Oklahoma, and Auburn all were a perfect 12–0. Utah was 11–0. Division I-A football relies on a computer-based system called the Bowl Championship Series (BCS) to determine which two teams play in the BCS national championship game.

Controversy swirled as the BCS decided which of these undefeated teams deserved to play in the Orange Bowl, the title game. The end result was that USC met Oklahoma because the two teams were ranked Number 1 and 2, respectively, in The Associated Press and ESPN/USA Today Coaches polls at the end of the season, giving them an edge over Auburn and Utah in the BCS rating system. The other two unbeaten teams stayed that way by winning their bowl games: Auburn defeated Virginia Tech, 16–13, in the Sugar Bowl, and Utah clobbered Pittsburgh, 35–7, in the Fiesta Bowl.

In the national title game, Oklahoma proved to be no match for USC. The Trojans trounced the Sooners, 55–19. USC's Leinart tossed an Orange Bowl–record five touchdowns. He completed 18 of 35 passes for 332 yards.

When the final polls came out, USC was ranked Number 1, even though Auburn and Utah were also undefeated. The Trojans were declared the undisputed national champs.

When post-season awards were handed out, Derrick Johnson of Texas was a double winner. The senior linebacker won the Bronko Nagurski Trophy as the nation's best defensive player and the Butkus Award as the nation's best linebacker.

Once the season was over, the college football world waited to see if Leinart would return to school for his senior season or opt to enter the NFL Draft, where he was likely to be the Number 1 pick. On January 14, 2005, Leinart announced that he would stay in school and go for a third consecutive national title.

Quarterback Matt Leinart led USC to its second straight national championship in 2004.

JOHN W. McDONOUGH/SPORTS ILLUSTRATED

FINAL 2004 COLLEGE FOOTBALL POLLS

THE ASSOCIATED PRESS

	TEAM	RECORD	POINTS
1.	USC	13–0	1,622
2.	Auburn	13–0	1,559
3.	Oklahoma	12–1	1,454
4.	Utah	12–0	1,438
5.	Texas	11–1	1,391
6.	Louisville	11–1	1,261
7.	Georgia	10–2	1,204
8.	Iowa	10–2	1,111
9.	California	10–2	1,060
10.	Virginia Tech	10–3	996
11.	Miami (Florida)	9–3	917
12.	Boise State	11–1	888
13.	Tennessee	10–3	868
14.	Michigan	9–3	842
15.	Florida State	9–3	754
16.	LSU	9–3	711
17.	Wisconsin	9–3	482
18.	Texas Tech	8–4	476
19.	Arizona State	9–3	463
20.	Ohio State	8–4	423
21.	Boston College	9–3	314
22.	Fresno State	9–3	203
23.	Virginia	8–4	157
24.	Navy	10–2	126
25.	Pittsburgh	8–4	99

ESPN/USA TODAY COACHES

	TEAM	RECORD	POINTS
1.	USC	13–0	1,525
2.	Auburn	13–0	1,460
3.	Oklahoma	12–1	1,366
4.	Texas	11–1	1,324
5.	Utah	12–0	1,300
6.	Georgia	10–2	1,191
7.	Louisville	11–1	1,166
8.	Iowa	10–2	1,022
9.	California	10–2	937
10.	Virginia Tech	10–3	906
11.	Miami (Florida)	9–3	903
12.	Michigan	9–3	802
13.	Boise State	11–1	792
14.	Florida State	9–3	776
15.	Tennessee	10–3	771
16.	LSU	9–3	693
17.	Texas Tech	8–4	478
18.	Wisconsin	9–3	449
19.	Ohio State	8–4	430
20.	Arizona State	9–3	377
21.	Boston College	9–3	245
22.	Fresno State	9–3	206
23.	Virginia	8–4	157
24.	Navy	10–2	129
25.	Florida	7–5	101

2004–05 COLLEGE BOWL AND PLAYOFF RESULTS

BOWL GAME	DATE	SITE	RESULT
ORANGE	Jan. 4	Miami, Florida	USC 55, Oklahoma 19
SUGAR	Jan. 3	New Orleans, Louisiana	Auburn 16, Virginia Tech 13
FIESTA	Jan. 1	Tempe, Arizona	Utah 35, Pittsburgh 7
COTTON	Jan. 1	Dallas, Texas	Tennessee 38, Texas A&M 7
ROSE	Jan. 1	Pasadena, California	Texas 38, Michigan 37
CAPITAL ONE	Jan. 1	Orlando, Florida	Iowa 30, LSU 25
GATOR	Jan. 1	Jacksonville, Florida	Florida State 30, West Virginia 18
OUTBACK	Jan. 1	Tampa, Florida	Georgia 24, Wisconsin 21
PEACH	Dec. 31	Atlanta, Georgia	Miami 27, Florida 10
LIBERTY	Dec. 31	Memphis, Tennessee	Louisville 44, Boise State 40
SUN	Dec. 31	El Paso, Texas	Arizona State 27, Purdue 23
MUSIC CITY	Dec. 31	Nashville, Tennessee	Minnesota 20, Alabama 16
SILICON VALLEY CLASSIC	Dec. 30	San Jose, California	Northern Illinois 34, Troy 21
HOLIDAY	Dec. 30	San Diego, California	Texas Tech 45, California 31
EMERALD	Dec. 30	San Francisco, California	Navy 34, New Mexico 19
CONTINENTAL TIRE	Dec. 30	Charlotte, North Carolina	Boston College 37, North Carolina 24
ALAMO	Dec. 29	San Antonio, Texas	Ohio State 33, Oklahoma State 7
HOUSTON	Dec. 29	Houston, Texas	Colorado 33, Texas-El Paso 28
INDEPENDENCE	Dec. 28	Shreveport, Louisiana	Iowa State 17, Miami (Ohio) 13
INSIGHT	Dec. 28	Phoenix, Arizona	Oregon State 38, Notre Dame 21
MOTOR CITY	Dec. 27	Pontiac, Michigan	Connecticut 39, Toledo 10
MPC COMPUTERS	Dec. 27	Boise, Idaho	Fresno State 37, Virginia 34
HAWAII	Dec. 24	Honolulu, Hawaii	Hawaii 59, Alabama-Birmingham 40
LAS VEGAS	Dec. 23	Las Vegas, Nevada	Wyoming 24, UCLA 21
FORT WORTH	Dec. 23	Fort Worth, Texas	Cincinnati 32, Marshall 14
GMAC	Dec. 22	Mobile, Alabama	Bowling Green 52, Memphis 35
CHAMPS SPORTS	Dec. 21	Orlando, Florida	Georgia Tech 51, Syracuse 14
NEW ORLEANS	Dec. 14	New Orleans, Louisiana	Southern Mississippi 31, North Texas 10

Matt Leinart is the sixth USC player to win the Heisman.

2004 HEISMAN VOTING

PLAYER, SCHOOL	POSITION	1ST	2ND	3RD	TOTAL
Matt Leinart, USC	QB	267	211	102	1,325
Adrian Peterson, Oklahoma	RB	154	180	175	997
Jason White, Oklahoma	QB	171	149	146	957
Alex Smith, Utah	QB	98	112	117	635
Reggie Bush, USC	RB	118	80	83	597
Cedric Benson, Texas	RB	12	41	69	187
Jason Campbell, Auburn	QB	21	24	51	162
J.J. Arrington, California	RB	10	33	19	115
Aaron Rodgers, California	QB	8	14	15	67
Braylon Edwards, Michigan	WR	3	13	27	62

2004 AP ALL-AMERICA TEAM

OFFENSE

QB Matt Leinart, USC, junior
RB Adrian Peterson, Oklahoma, freshman
    J.J. Arrington, California, senior
WR Braylon Edwards, Michigan, senior
    Taylor Stubblefield, Purdue, senior
TE Heath Miller, Virginia, junior
C David Baas, Michigan, senior
OL Jammal Brown, Oklahoma, senior
    Alex Barron, Florida State, senior
    Elton Brown, Virginia, senior
    Michael Munoz, Tennessee, senior
K Mike Nugent, Ohio State, senior
AP Reggie Bush, USC, sophomore

DEFENSE

DL Erasmus James, Wisconsin, senior
    David Pollack, Georgia, senior
    Shaun Cody, USC, senior
    Marcus Spears, LSU, senior
LB Derrick Johnson, Texas, senior
    Matt Grootegoed, USC, senior
    A.J. Hawk, Ohio State, senior
DB Carlos Rogers, Auburn, senior
    Antrel Rolle, Miami (Florida), senior
    Marlin Jackson, Michigan, senior
    Ernest Shazor, Michigan, senior
P Brandon Fields, Michigan State, sophomore

■ **Fast Fact:** Penn State's football team set a program record with 50 players on the squad who finished the 2004 fall semester with at least a B average.

KEY QB=quarterback; RB=running back; WR=wide receiver; TE=tight end; C=center; OL=offensive lineman; K=kicker; DL=defensive lineman; LB=linebacker; DB=defensive back; P=punter; AP=all purpose

2004 NCAA DIVISION I-A CONFERENCE STANDINGS

Atlantic Coast Conference

TEAM	CONFERENCE				OVERALL			
	W	L	PF	PA	W	L	PF	PA
Virginia Tech	7	1	230	114	10	2	387	151
Florida State	6	2	208	111	8	3	272	151
Miami (Florida)	5	3	226	143	8	3	353	194
Virginia	5	3	203	151	8	3	329	175
North Carolina	5	3	230	227	6	5	295	345
Georgia Tech	4	4	142	177	6	5	213	213
Clemson	4	4	166	189	6	5	236	229
North Carolina State	3	5	156	182	5	6	264	218
Maryland	3	5	111	159	5	6	195	220
Wake Forest	1	7	140	219	4	7	230	253
Duke	1	7	123	263	2	9	183	322

Big East Conference

TEAM	CONFERENCE				OVERALL			
	W	L	PF	PA	W	L	PF	PA
Boston College	4	2	152	114	8	3	259	179
Pittsburgh	4	2	152	136	8	3	318	253
West Virginia	4	2	165	128	8	3	343	216
Syracuse	4	2	194	170	6	5	273	293
Connecticut	3	3	171	183	7	4	324	250
Rutgers	1	5	139	185	4	7	269	343
Temple	1	5	131	188	2	9	238	399

KEY W=win; L=loss; PF=points for; PA=points against

Big Ten Conference

TEAM	CONFERENCE				OVERALL			
	W	L	PF	PA	W	L	PF	PA
Michigan	7	1	246	182	9	2	333	241
Iowa	7	1	199	125	9	2	262	186
Wisconsin	6	2	167	145	9	2	228	161
Northwestern	5	3	168	198	6	6	295	342
Purdue	4	4	207	156	7	4	358	179
Ohio State	4	4	184	171	7	4	257	212
Michigan State	4	4	253	228	5	7	353	326
Minnesota	3	5	207	199	6	5	341	257
Penn State	2	6	103	124	4	7	195	168
Illinois	1	7	141	248	3	8	240	323
Indiana	1	7	159	258	3	8	262	343

Big 12 Conference (North)

TEAM	CONFERENCE				OVERALL			
	W	L	PF	PA	W	L	PF	PA
Colorado	4	4	169	205	7	5	271	304
Iowa State	4	4	148	188	6	5	229	246
Missouri	3	5	142	171	5	6	256	215
Nebraska	3	5	178	243	5	6	275	298
Kansas	2	6	161	108	4	7	262	235
Kansas State	2	6	238	259	4	7	326	337

Big 12 Conference (South)

TEAM	CONFERENCE				OVERALL			
	W	L	PF	PA	W	L	PF	PA
Oklahoma	8	0	257	117	12	0	433	164
Texas	7	1	263	145	10	1	385	178
Texas Tech	5	3	268	208	7	4	389	283
Texas A&M	5	3	255	207	7	4	334	254
Oklahoma State	4	4	252	220	7	4	380	268
Baylor	1	7	149	319	3	8	224	406

Conference USA

TEAM	CONFERENCE				OVERALL			
	W	L	PF	PA	W	L	PF	PA
Louisville	8	0	453	155	10	1	553	196
Memphis	5	3	276	254	8	3	395	323
Alabama-Birmingham	5	3	242	231	7	4	332	292
Cincinnati	5	3	254	234	6	5	312	306
Southern Mississippi	5	3	238	218	6	5	278	288
Texas Christian University (TCU)	3	5	235	258	5	6	362	373
Tulane	3	5	212	304	5	6	300	361
South Florida	3	5	233	267	4	7	271	351
Houston	3	5	197	243	3	8	230	354
Army	2	6	222	275	2	9	260	388
East Carolina	2	6	177	300	2	9	231	439

Mid-American Conference (East)

TEAM	CONFERENCE				OVERALL			
	W	L	PF	PA	W	L	PF	PA
Miami (Ohio)	7	1	282	158	8	4	394	281
Marshall	6	2	238	180	6	5	277	234
Akron	6	2	237	217	6	5	271	347
Kent State	4	4	269	186	5	6	335	264
Ohio	2	6	148	217	4	7	221	271
Buffalo	2	6	167	247	2	9	197	351
University of Central Florida (UCF)	0	8	136	246	0	11	175	362

Mid-American Conference (West)

TEAM	CONFERENCE				OVERALL			
	W	L	PF	PA	W	L	PF	PA
Toledo	7	1	307	195	9	3	422	365
Northern Illinois	7	1	303	190	8	3	387	283
Bowling Green	6	2	337	181	8	3	480	247
Eastern Michigan	4	4	249	333	4	7	328	458
Central Michigan	3	5	199	286	4	7	260	378
Ball State	2	6	207	279	2	9	225	405
Western Michigan	0	8	179	343	1	10	248	436

2004 NCAA DIVISION I-A CONFERENCE STANDINGS (cont.)

Mountain West Conference

TEAM	CONFERENCE				OVERALL			
	W	L	PF	PA	W	L	PF	PA
Utah	7	0	351	178	11	0	509	227
New Mexico	5	2	136	125	7	4	225	190
Brigham Young University (BYU)	4	3	200	171	5	6	267	295
Wyoming	3	4	173	196	6	5	283	284
Air Force	3	4	218	220	5	6	326	342
Colorado State	3	4	182	201	4	7	261	325
San Diego State	2	5	138	194	4	7	234	282
University of Nevada-Las Vegas (UNLV)	1	6	140	253	2	9	229	357

Pacific-Ten Conference

TEAM	CONFERENCE				OVERALL			
	W	L	PF	PA	W	L	PF	PA
University of Southern California (USC)	8	0	285	117	12	0	441	150
California	7	1	287	103	10	1	410	147
Arizona State	5	3	216	234	8	3	331	271
Oregon State	5	3	210	191	6	5	282	273
University of California-Los Angeles (UCLA)	4	4	252	227	6	5	340	285
Oregon	4	4	203	211	5	6	282	282
Washington State	3	5	193	262	5	6	275	307
Stanford	2	6	147	197	4	7	242	233
Arizona	2	6	130	240	3	8	164	275
Washington	0	8	114	255	1	10	154	334

Southeastern Conference (East)

TEAM	CONFERENCE				OVERALL			
	W	L	PF	PA	W	L	PF	PA
Tennessee	7	1	215	199	9	3	340	288
Georgia	6	2	231	133	9	2	311	177
Florida	4	4	251	187	7	4	372	226
South Carolina	4	4	185	190	6	5	243	229
Kentucky	1	7	106	253	2	9	173	341
Vanderbilt	1	7	133	213	2	9	212	286

Southeastern Conference (West)

TEAM	CONFERENCE				OVERALL			
	W	L	PF	PA	W	L	PF	PA
Auburn	8	0	247	96	12	0	401	134
Louisiana State University (LSU)	6	2	220	131	9	2	319	175
Alabama	3	5	152	149	6	5	279	169
Arkansas	3	5	196	215	5	6	328	270
Mississippi	3	5	142	200	4	7	215	278
Mississippi State	2	6	125	237	3	8	173	280

Sun Belt Conference

TEAM	CONFERENCE				OVERALL			
	W	L	PF	PA	W	L	PF	PA
North Texas	7	0	251	153	7	4	299	327
Troy	5	2	197	96	7	4	265	166
New Mexico State	4	3	187	182	5	6	273	355
Louisiana-Monroe	4	3	153	172	5	6	211	303
Middle Tennessee State	4	4	202	190	5	6	269	293
Arkansas State	3	4	136	185	3	8	215	365
Louisiana-Lafayette	2	5	145	167	4	7	242	272
Utah State	2	5	124	181	3	8	184	333
Idaho	2	5	154	218	3	9	245	473

Western Athletic Conference

TEAM	CONFERENCE				OVERALL			
	W	L	PF	PA	W	L	PF	PA
Boise State	8	0	401	196	11	0	547	264
Texas-El Paso	6	2	315	227	8	3	401	268
Fresno State	5	3	338	158	8	3	445	212
Louisiana Tech	5	3	260	220	6	6	308	382
Hawaii	4	4	238	324	7	5	408	459
Nevada	3	5	236	318	5	7	356	413
Tulsa	3	5	272	303	4	8	345	398
Southern Methodist University (SMU)	3	5	182	290	3	8	202	420
Rice	2	6	236	321	3	8	272	377
San Jose State	1	7	256	377	2	9	312	469

Independents

TEAM	OVERALL			
	W	L	PF	PA
Navy	9	2	300	219
Notre Dame	6	5	268	251

Atlantic 10 Conference (North)

TEAM	CONFERENCE				OVERALL			
	W	L	PF	PA	W	L	PF	PA
New Hampshire	6	2	278	200	10	0	420	339
Massachusetts	4	4	191	207	6	5	279	256
Northeastern	4	4	246	207	5	6	355	276
Maine	3	5	254	262	5	6	321	296
Hofstra	3	5	272	241	5	6	401	303
Rhode Island	2	6	176	292	4	7	265	355

Atlantic 10 Conference (South)

TEAM	CONFERENCE				OVERALL			
	W	L	PF	PA	W	L	PF	PA
James Madison	7	1	201	125	12	2	390	247
William & Mary	7	1	249	180	11	3	488	373
Delaware	7	1	213	178	9	4	344	300
Villanova	3	5	272	205	6	5	330	248
Richmond	2	6	148	227	3	8	198	297
Towson	0	8	99	275	3	8	195	306

Big Sky Conference

TEAM	CONFERENCE				OVERALL			
	W	L	PF	PA	W	L	PF	PA
Montana	6	1	253	171	12	2	514	308
Eastern Washington	6	1	308	149	9	4	488	323
Portland State	4	3	207	161	7	4	335	223
Montana State	4	3	222	195	6	5	296	285
Northern Arizona	3	4	169	210	4	7	244	314
Sacramento State	2	5	124	223	3	8	190	415
Idaho State	2	5	145	197	3	8	266	357
Weber State	1	6	125	247	1	10	202	375

Big South Conference

TEAM	CONFERENCE				OVERALL			
	W	L	PF	PA	W	L	PF	PA
Coastal Carolina	4	0	141	67	10	1	413	176
Liberty	3	1	95	65	6	5	280	275
Gardner-Webb	2	2	74	65	5	6	282	335
Charleston Southern	1	3	59	132	5	5	262	212
Virginia Military Institute	0	4	72	112	0	11	137	327

2004 NCAA DIVISION I-AA CONFERENCE STANDINGS (cont.)

Gateway Conference

TEAM	CONFERENCE				OVERALL			
	W	L	PF	PA	W	L	PF	PA
Southern Illinois	7	0	308	88	10	2	511	158
Western Kentucky	6	1	199	124	9	3	350	227
Northern Iowa	5	2	245	130	7	4	351	198
Southwest Missouri State	3	4	179	218	6	5	295	324
Western Illinois	2	5	136	275	4	7	309	409
Youngstown State	2	5	172	194	4	7	270	270
Illinois State	2	6	182	270	4	7	282	352
Indiana State	1	6	141	291	4	7	243	415

Great West Conference

TEAM	CONFERENCE				OVERALL			
	W	L	PF	PA	W	L	PF	PA
California Polytechnic	4	1	115	70	9	2	336	183
California-Davis	3	2	140	97	6	4	323	211
North Dakota State	2	3	96	80	8	3	338	150
South Dakota State	2	3	62	117	6	5	245	263
Southern Utah	2	3	87	125	6	5	294	248
Northern Colorado	2	3	84	95	2	9	186	294

Ivy League

TEAM	CONFERENCE				OVERALL			
	W	L	PF	PA	W	L	PF	PA
Harvard	7	0	225	97	10	0	339	134
Pennsylvania	6	1	132	86	8	2	238	145
Cornell	4	3	141	135	4	6	167	181
Brown	3	4	145	154	6	4	227	194
Yale	3	4	100	132	5	5	179	207
Princeton	3	4	126	143	5	5	211	207
Columbia	1	6	99	171	1	9	140	265
Dartmouth	1	6	69	119	1	9	108	205

Metro Atlantic Athletic Conference

TEAM	CONFERENCE				OVERALL			
	W	L	PF	PA	W	L	PF	PA
Duquesne	4	0	139	60	7	3	319	212
Marist	3	1	107	76	3	6	163	262
Saint Peter's	1	3	78	100	3	7	154	260
La Salle	1	3	135	166	3	7	297	327
Iona	1	3	84	141	2	8	182	349

Mid-Eastern Athletic Conference

TEAM	CONFERENCE				OVERALL			
	W	L	PF	PA	W	L	PF	PA
Hampton	6	1	304	166	10	2	523	279
South Carolina State	6	1	226	173	9	2	384	230
Bethune-Cookman	4	3	222	119	6	4	330	209
Delaware State	4	3	168	177	4	7	204	352
Howard	3	4	143	175	6	5	249	225
Morgan State	3	4	248	264	5	6	403	423
North Carolina A&T	1	6	129	213	3	8	180	302
Norfolk State	1	6	127	280	1	8	168	338
Florida A&M	0	0	0	0	3	8	253	408

Northeast Conference

TEAM	CONFERENCE				OVERALL			
	W	L	PF	PA	W	L	PF	PA
Monmouth (New Jersey)	6	1	154	140	10	1	299	182
Central Connecticut	6	1	196	125	8	2	261	192
Albany (New York)	4	3	177	142	4	7	198	280
Sacred Heart	3	4	142	175	6	4	276	206
Wagner	3	4	137	151	6	5	241	241
Robert Morris	3	4	161	148	6	5	277	213
Stony Brook	2	5	178	176	3	7	246	275
Saint Francis (Pennsylvania)	1	6	136	224	3	8	207	322

2004 NCAA DIVISION I-AA CONFERENCE STANDINGS (cont.)

Ohio Valley Conference

TEAM	CONFERENCE				OVERALL			
	W	L	PF	PA	W	L	PF	PA
Jacksonville State	7	1	315	148	9	2	412	233
Murray State	6	2	196	137	7	4	287	220
Eastern Kentucky	6	2	254	150	6	5	290	239
Eastern Illinois	4	4	199	227	5	6	291	323
Tennessee Tech	3	4	183	174	6	5	290	265
Samford	3	5	233	266	4	7	284	359
Southeast Missouri State	3	5	216	269	3	8	256	404
Tennessee State	2	5	187	233	4	7	278	311
Tennessee-Martin	1	7	118	297	2	9	173	394

Patriot League

TEAM	CONFERENCE				OVERALL			
	W	L	PF	PA	W	L	PF	PA
Lehigh	5	1	183	101	9	3	345	193
Lafayette	5	1	165	91	8	4	324	229
Bucknell	4	2	170	127	7	4	296	221
Colgate	4	2	157	117	7	4	261	225
Fordham	2	4	160	158	5	6	288	270
Holy Cross	1	5	134	251	3	8	240	367
Georgetown	0	6	77	201	3	8	174	280

Pioneer Football League (North)

TEAM	CONFERENCE				OVERALL			
	W	L	PF	PA	W	L	PF	PA
Drake	4	0	134	60	10	2	365	200
San Diego	3	1	166	102	7	4	397	266
Dayton	2	2	128	68	7	3	325	140
Valparaiso	1	3	62	150	5	6	250	300
Butler	0	4	54	164	1	10	118	344

Pioneer Football League (South)

TEAM	CONFERENCE				OVERALL			
	W	L	PF	PA	W	L	PF	PA
Morehead State	2	1	66	42	6	6	235	231
Jacksonville (Florida)	2	1	74	68	3	7	188	345
Davidson	1	2	57	59	2	7	102	254
Austin Peay	1	2	48	76	2	9	161	313

Southern Conference

TEAM	CONFERENCE				OVERALL			
	W	L	PF	PA	W	L	PF	PA
Furman	6	1	214	131	10	3	449	216
Georgia Southern	6	1	313	104	9	3	564	221
Wofford	4	3	191	190	8	3	339	247
Appalachian State	4	3	234	210	6	5	374	347
Western Carolina	2	5	120	162	4	7	245	254
Citadel	2	5	120	189	3	7	162	250
Elon	2	5	100	194	3	8	196	287
Tennessee-Chattanooga	2	5	205	317	2	9	320	529

Southland Conference

TEAM	CONFERENCE				OVERALL			
	W	L	PF	PA	W	L	PF	PA
Northwestern State	4	0	173	67	8	3	387	242
Sam Houston State	4	1	175	139	11	3	518	338
Texas State University	3	2	122	124	5	6	283	285
Nicholls State	1	3	72	126	4	5	193	223
Stephen F. Austin	1	4	136	133	6	5	284	256
McNeese State	1	4	128	217	4	7	262	423

2004 NCAA DIVISION I-AA CONFERENCE STANDINGS (cont.)

Southwestern Athletic Conference (East)

TEAM	CONFERENCE				OVERALL			
	W	L	PF	PA	W	L	PF	PA
Alabama State	6	1	260	120	10	2	407	228
Alabama A&M	5	2	166	116	7	4	269	200
Alcorn State	4	3	160	158	7	4	244	230
Jackson State	3	4	138	185	4	7	242	300
Mississippi Valley State	1	6	127	191	3	8	248	314

Southwestern Athletic Conference (West)

TEAM	CONFERENCE				OVERALL			
	W	L	PF	PA	W	L	PF	PA
Southern	6	1	226	128	8	4	369	265
Arkansas-Pine Bluff	5	2	229	132	6	3	291	193
Grambling	3	4	182	188	6	5	294	295
Prairie View	1	6	133	236	3	8	246	349
Texas Southern	0	7	35	230	0	11	82	355

Independents

TEAM	OVERALL			
	W	L	PF	PA
Florida Atlantic	9	3	299	207
Southeastern Louisiana	7	4	425	271
Florida International	3	7	261	325
Savannah State	2	8	194	414

2004 NCAA INDIVIDUAL LEADERS: DIVISION I-A

SCORING

	TD	PTS
DeAngelo Williams, Memphis	23	138
Chad Owens, Hawaii	22	132
P.J. Pope, Bowling Green	21	126
Garrett Wolfe, Northern Illinois	21	126
Eric Shelton, Louisville	20	120
Cedric Benson, Texas	20	120
Ryan Moats, Louisiana Tech	19	114
Taurean Henderson, Texas Tech	18	108
Carlton Jones, Army	17	104*

*Includes one 2-point conversion

TRIVIA CHALLENGE

Which of these teams played in the Atlantic Coast Conference for the first time in 2004: North Carolina State, Clemson, or Virginia Tech?

Virginia Tech, along with Miami (Florida), joined the ACC for the first time in 2004. Both schools were previously in the Big East.

FIELD GOALS

	FGM	FGA	PCT
Mike Nugent, Ohio State	24	27	88.9
Tyler Jones, Boise State	24	27	88.9
Mason Crosby, Colorado	23	29	79.3
Dave Rayner, Michigan State	22	31	71.0
Kyle Schlicher, Iowa	21	26	80.8
Brandon Pace, Virginia Tech	21	27	77.8
Andrew Wellock, Eastern Michigan	21	23	91.3

RUSHING

	G	CARRIES	YDS	AVG	TD
J.J. Arrington, California	12	289	2,018	7.0	15
DeAngelo Williams, Memphis	12	313	1,948	6.2	22
Adrian Peterson, Oklahoma	13	339	1,925	5.7	15
Cedric Benson, Texas	12	326	1,834	5.6	19
Jamario Thomas, North Texas	10	285	1,801	6.3	17
Ryan Moats, Louisiana Tech	12	288	1,774	6.2	18
Garrett Wolfe, Northern Illinois	11	256	1,656	6.5	18
Vernand Morency, Oklahoma State	11	258	1,474	5.7	12
Mike Hart, Michigan	11	282	1,455	5.2	9

KEY TD=touchdowns; PTS=points; FGM=field goals made; FGA=field goals attempted; PCT=percentage; G=games; YDS=yards; AVG=average; TD=touchdowns

TODAY'S STARS

Adrian Peterson set an NCAA freshman record for most 100-yard games (11) in 2004.

■ **Adrian Peterson, running back,** b. March 21, 1985, Palestine, Texas. Peterson proved to be one of the best freshmen running backs in college football history. The Oklahoma Sooner rushed for an NCAA freshman-record 1,925 yards (second in the nation) in 2004. He also led the nation in rushing attempts (339). The bulldozer of a back became the first Sooner freshman to be named an All-America. He also finished second in the Heisman Trophy voting, behind USC quarterback Matt Leinart.

■ **Reggie Bush, running back,** b. March 2, 1985, Spring Valley, California. Bush is one of the fastest running backs in college football. Coming off the bench for USC in 2004, the sophomore ran for 908 yards and six touchdowns. He finished fifth in the Heisman Trophy race. Bush ran for 521 yards and three touchdowns as a freshman in 2003.

■ **Chris Leak, quarterback,** b. May 3, 1985, Charlotte, North Carolina. Leak threw for 3,197 yards and 29 touchdowns as a sophomore in 2004. In 2003, he led the Florida Gators to a 6–3 record, the highest winning percentage of any freshman quarterback in the country. He was named to the Southeastern Conference All-Freshman team after throwing for 2,435 yards and 16 touchdowns. At Independence High School in Charlotte, North Carolina, Leak led his team to three consecutive state championships (2000-02) and threw for 185 touchdowns, a national high school record.

2004 NCAA INDIVIDUAL LEADERS: DIVISION I-A (cont.)

PASSING EFFICIENCY	ATTS	COMP PCT	YDS	INT	TD	RATING
Stefan LeFors, Louisville	257	73.5	2,596	3	20	181.7
Alex Smith, Utah	317	67.5	2,952	4	32	176.5
Jason Campbell, Auburn	270	69.6	2,700	7	20	172.9
Omar Jacobs, Bowling Green	462	66.9	4,002	4	41	167.2
Bruce Gradkowski, Toledo	399	70.2	3,518	8	27	162.6
Jason White, Oklahoma	390	65.4	3,205	9	35	159.4
Matt Leinart, USC	412	65.3	3,322	6	33	156.5
Aaron Rodgers, California	316	66.1	2,566	8	24	154.3
Lester Ricard, Tulane	231	61.9	1,881	9	21	152.5
Kyle Orton, Purdue	389	60.7	3,090	5	31	151.1

KEY ATTS=attempts; COMP PCT=completion percentage; YDS=yards; INT=interceptions; TD=touchdowns

■ *Fast Fact:* The Boise State Broncos own the nation's longest active home winning streak. They won their 21st straight game at home when they beat Louisiana Tech, 55–14, on November 20, 2004.

JOHN W. McDONOUGH/SPORTS ILLUSTRATED

2004 NCAA INDIVIDUAL LEADERS: DIVISION I-A (cont.)

RECEIVING	G	REC	YDS	YDS/G	TD
Roddy White, Alabama-Birmingham	12	71	1,452	121.0	14
Dante Ridgeway, Ball State	11	105	1,399	127.1	8
Mike Hass, Oregon State	12	86	1,379	114.9	7
Braylon Edwards, Michigan	12	97	1,330	110.8	15
Greg Lee, Pittsburgh	12	68	1,297	108.0	10
Chad Owens, Hawaii	13	102	1,290	99.2	17
Eric Deslauriers, Eastern Michigan	11	84	1,257	114.2	13
Derek Hagan, Arizona State	12	83	1,248	104.0	10
Lance Moore, Toledo	13	90	1,189	91.4	14
Jarrett Hicks, Texas Tech	12	76	1,177	98.0	13

INTERCEPTIONS	INT	YDS	TD
Chris Harris, Louisiana-Monroe	7	11	0
Charles Gordon, Kansas	7	52	0
Ko Simpson, South Carolina	6	94	1
Ray Henderson, Boston College	6	52	0
Kerry Rhodes, Louisville	6	56	1
Junior Rosegreen, Auburn	6	48	0
Mitch Meeuwsen, Oregon State	6	12	0
Brandon Payne, New Mexico	6	69	0
Morgan Scalley, Utah	6	79	0
Keon Newson, Bowling Green	6	107	2
Chris Royal, Marshall	6	103	1

Chris Harris (above) and Charles Gordon (left) tied for most interceptions (7) in 2004.

2004 NCAA INDIVIDUAL LEADERS: DIVISION I-AA

SCORING	TD	PTS
Chaz Williams, Georgia Southern	25	152
Eric Kimble, Eastern Washington	21	128
Oscar Bonds, Jacksonville State	19	114
Evan Harney, San Diego	19	114
Brandon Jacobs, Southern Illinois	19	114
Bradshaw Littlejohn, Morgan State	18	112*
Clifton Dawson, Harvard	18	108

*Includes two 2-point conversions

FIELD GOALS	FGM	FGA	PCT
Mike Myers, Florida Atlantic	20	28	71.4
Greg Kuehn, William & Mary	19	28	67.9
Dan Carpenter, Montana	18	29	62.1
Joe Johnson, Weber State	17	22	77.3
Lance Garner, Sam Houston	16	21	76.2
Andrew Paterini, Hampton	16	22	72.7
Kyle Hooper, Indiana State	16	20	80.0

RUSHING	G	CARRIES	YDS	AVG	TD
Charles Anthony, Tennessee State	11	306	1,739	158.1	14
Sean Mayers, St. Peter's	10	270	1,546	154.6	8
Scott Phaydavong, Drake	12	234	1,539	128.3	9
Ed Pricolo, Sacred Heart	9	209	1,339	148.8	14
Evan Harney, San Diego	11	303	1,334	121.4	18
Clifton Dawson, Harvard	10	248	1,302	130.2	17
Oscar Bonds, Jacksonville State	11	203	1,263	114.8	19
Nick Hartigan, Brown	10	323	1,263	126.3	17
C.J. Hudson, Eastern Kentucky	11	266	1,212	110.2	8
Joe McCourt, Lafayette	12	250	1,193	99.4	16

TRIVIA CHALLENGE

True or False: The national championship game is always the Orange Bowl.

False. The national championship game rotates every year among the four BCS bowls: Rose, Sugar, Fiesta, and Orange. The Rose Bowl will be the title game for the 2005 season.

KEY G=games; REC=receptions; YDS=yards; YDS/G=yards per game; TD=touchdowns; INT=interceptions; PTS=points; FGM=field goals made; FGA=field goals attempted; PCT=percentage; AVG=average

PASSING EFFICIENCY

	ATTS	COMP PCT	YDS	INT	TD	RATING
Erik Meyer, Eastern Washington	382	67.8	3,707	9	31	171.4
Joel Sambursky, Southern Illinois	234	60.7	2,224	5	19	163.0
Craig Ochs, Montana	450	68.7	3,807	8	33	160.4
Lang Campbell, William & Mary	455	65.5	3,988	5	30	158.7
Richie Williams, Appalachian State	350	66.9	3,109	10	24	158.4
Princeton Shepherd, Hampton	200	54.0	1,890	7	18	156.1
Dustin Long, Sam Houston	531	62.7	4,588	18	39	152.7
Ingle Martin, Furman	320	61.9	2,792	9	22	152.2
Mark Borda, Lehigh	330	62.1	2,682	6	24	150.8
Martin Hankins, Southeastern Louisiana	540	66.1	4,240	12	35	149.0

JOHN BETHUNE

RECEIVING

	G	REC	YDS	YDS/G	TD
DaVon Fowlkes, Appalachian State	11	103	1,618	147.1	14
Dominique Thompson, William & Mary	14	79	1,585	113.2	13
David Ball, New Hampshire	12	86	1,504	124.6	17
Eric Kimble, Eastern Washington	13	83	1,453	111.3	19
Jarrod Fuller, Sam Houston	14	99	1,383	98.8	8
Vincent Jackson, Northern Colorado	11	80	1,382	125.6	11
Jason Mathenia, Sam Houston	14	74	1,357	96.9	13
Felton Huggins, Southeastern Louisiana	11	84	1,313	119.4	13
Jefferson Heidelberger, Montana	14	80	1,240	88.6	10
Fred Amey, Sacramento State	11	76	1,186	107.8	6

INTERCEPTIONS

	INT	YDS	TD
Ahmad Trueado, Southern	9	166	1
Shannon James, Massachusetts	8	110	0
Tad Kornegay, Fordham	8	103	0
Allante Harrison, Towson	7	128	2
Kenny Chicoine, California Polytechnic	7	157	1
Onsha Whitaker, Murray State	7	-1	0
Darren Barnett, Southwest Missouri State	7	41	0
Antonio Thomas, Western Kentucky	7	15	0

DID YOU KNOW?

Nebraska finished the 2004 season with a 5-6 record, ending the Cornhuskers' streak of 42 non-losing seasons.

NATIONAL CHAMPIONSHIPS

YEAR	CHAMPION	RECORD	HEAD COACH	YEAR	CHAMPION	RECORD	HEAD COACH
2004	USC	13–0	Pete Carroll	1982	Penn St.	11–1–0	Joe Paterno
2003	USC	12–1	Pete Carroll	1981	Clemson	12–0–0	Danny Ford
(split)	LSU	13–1	Nick Saban	1980	Georgia	12–0–0	Vince Dooley
2002	Ohio St.	14–0	Jim Tressel	1979	Alabama	12–0–0	Bear Bryant
2001	Miami (Florida)	12–0	Larry Coker	1978	Alabama	11–1–0	Bear Bryant
2000	Oklahoma	13–0	Bob Stoops	(split)	USC (UPI)	12–1–0	John Robinson
1999	Florida St.	12–0	Bobby Bowden	1977	Notre Dame	11–1–0	Dan Devine
1998	Tennessee	13–0	Phillip Fulmer	1976	Pittsburgh	12–0–0	Johnny Majors
1997	Michigan	12–0	Lloyd Carr	1975	Oklahoma	11–1–0	Barry Switzer
(split)	Nebraska (ESPN)	13–0	Tom Osborne	1974	Oklahoma (AP)	11–0–0	Barry Switzer
1996	Florida	12–1	Steve Spurrier	(split)	USC (UPI)	10–1–1	John McKay
1995	Nebraska	12–0–0	Tom Osborne	1973	Notre Dame	11–0–0	Ara Parseghian
1994	Nebraska	13–0–0	Tom Osborne	(split)	Alabama (UPI)	11–1–0	Bear Bryant
1993	Florida St.	12–1–0	Bobby Bowden	1972	USC	12–0–0	John McKay
1992	Alabama	13–0–0	Gene Stallings	1971	Nebraska	13–0–0	Bob Devaney
1991	Miami (Florida)	12–0–0	Dennis Erickson	1970	Nebraska	11–0–1	Bob Devaney
(split)	Washington (CNN)	12–0–0	Don James	(split)	Texas (UPI)	10–1–0	Darrell Royal
1990	Colorado	11–1–1	Bill McCartney	1969	Texas	11–0–0	Darrell Royal
(split)	Georgia Tech (UPI)	11–0–1	Bobby Ross	1968	Ohio St.	10–0–0	Woody Hayes
1989	Miami (Florida)	11–1–0	Dennis Erickson	1967	USC	10–1–0	John McKay
1988	Notre Dame	12–0–0	Lou Holtz	1966	Notre Dame	9–0–1	Ara Parseghian
1987	Miami (Florida)	12–0–0	Jimmy Johnson	1965	Alabama	9–1–1	Bear Bryant
1986	Penn St.	12–0–0	Joe Paterno	(split)	Michigan St. (UPI)	10–1–0	Duffy Daugherty
1985	Oklahoma	11–1–0	Barry Switzer	1964	Alabama	10–1–0	Bear Bryant
1984	Brigham Young	13–0–0	LaVell Edwards	1963	Texas	11–0–0	Darrell Royal
1983	Miami (Florida)	11–1–0	Howard Schnellenberger				

Note: National Champion selectors: Helms Athletic Foundation (H), 1883–1935; The Dickinson System (D), 1924–40; The Associated Press (AP), 1936–present; United Press International (UPI), 1958–90; *USA Today*/CNN (CNN), 1991–96; *USA Today*/ESPN (ESPN), 1997–present. In 1996, the NCAA introduced overtime to break ties.

NATIONAL CHAMPIONSHIPS (cont.)

YEAR	CHAMPION	RECORD	HEAD COACH
1962	USC	11–0–0	John McKay
1961	Alabama	11–0–0	Bear Bryant
1960	Minnesota	8–2–0	Murray Warmath
1959	Syracuse	11–0–0	Ben Schwartzwalder
1958	Louisiana St.	11–0–0	Paul Dietzel
1957	Auburn	10–0–0	Shug Jordan
(split)	Ohio St. (UPI)	9–1–0	Woody Hayes
1956	Oklahoma	10–0–0	Bud Wilkinson
1955	Oklahoma	11–0–0	Bud Wilkinson
1954	Ohio St.	10–0–0	Woody Hayes
(split)	UCLA (UPI)	9–0–0	Red Sanders
1953	Maryland	10–1–0	Jim Tatum
1952	Michigan St.	9–0–0	Biggie Munn
1951	Tennessee	10–1–0	Robert Neyland
1950	Oklahoma	10–1–0	Bud Wilkinson
1949	Notre Dame	10–0–0	Frank Leahy
1948	Michigan	9–0–0	Bennie Oosterbaan
1947	Notre Dame	9–0–0	Frank Leahy
(split)	Michigan	10–0–0	Fritz Crisler
1946	Notre Dame	8–0–1	Frank Leahy
1945	Army	9–0–0	Red Blaik
1944	Army	9–0–0	Red Blaik
1943	Notre Dame	9–1–0	Frank Leahy
1942	Ohio St.	9–1–0	Paul Brown
1941	Minnesota	8–0–0	Bernie Bierman
1940	Minnesota	8–0–0	Bernie Bierman
1939	Texas A&M (AP)	11–0–0	Homer Norton
(split)	USC (D)	8–0–2	Howard Jones
1938	TCU (AP)	11–0–0	Dutch Meyer
(split)	Notre Dame (D)	8–1–0	Elmer Layden
1937	Pittsburgh	9–0–1	Jock Sutherland
1936	Minnesota	7–1–0	Bernie Bierman
1935	Minnesota (H)	8–0–0	Bernie Bierman
(split)	SMU (D)	12–1–0	Matty Bell
1934	Minnesota	8–0–0	Bernie Bierman
1933	Michigan	8–0–0	Harry Kipke
1932	USC (H)	10–0–0	Howard Jones
(split)	Michigan (D)	8–0–0	Harry Kipke
1931	USC	10–1–0	Howard Jones
1930	Notre Dame	10–0–0	Knute Rockne
1929	Notre Dame	9–0–0	Knute Rockne
1928	Georgia Tech (H)	10–0–0	Bill Alexander
(split)	USC (D)	9–0–1	Howard Jones
1927	Illinois	7–0–1	Bob Zuppke
1926	Alabama (H)	9–0–1	Wallace Wade
(split)	Stanford (D)(H)	10–0–1	Pop Warner
1925	Alabama (H)	10–0–0	Wallace Wade
(split)	Dartmouth (D)	8–0–0	Jesse Hawley
1924	Notre Dame	10–0–0	Knute Rockne
1923	Illinois	8–0–0	Bob Zuppke
1922	Cornell	8–0–0	Gil Dobie
1921	Cornell	8–0–0	Gil Dobie
1920	California	9–0–0	Andy Smith
1919	Harvard	9–0–1	Bob Fisher
1918	Pittsburgh	4–1–0	Pop Warner
1917	Georgia Tech	9–0–0	John Heisman
1916	Pittsburgh	8–0–0	Pop Warner
1915	Cornell	9–0–0	Al Sharpe
1914	Army	9–0–0	Charley Daly
1913	Harvard	9–0–0	Percy Haughton
1912	Harvard	9–0–0	Percy Haughton
1911	Princeton	8–0–2	Bill Roper
1910	Harvard	8–0–1	Percy Haughton
1909	Yale	10–0–0	Howard Jones
1908	Pennsylvania	11–0–1	Sol Metzger
1907	Yale	9–0–1	Bill Knox
1906	Princeton	9–0–1	Bill Roper
1905	Chicago	10–0–0	Amos Alonzo Stagg
1904	Pennsylvania	12–0–0	Carl Williams
1903	Princeton	11–0–0	Art Hillebrand
1902	Michigan	11–0–0	Fielding Yost
1901	Michigan	11–0–0	Fielding Yost
1900	Yale	12–0–0	Malcolm McBride
1899	Harvard	10–0–1	Benjamin H. Dibblee
1898	Harvard	11–0–0	W. Cameron Forbes
1897	Pennsylvania	15–0–0	George W. Woodruff
1896	Princeton	10–0–1	Garrett Cochran
1895	Pennsylvania	14–0–0	George W. Woodruff
1894	Yale	16–0–0	William C. Rhodes
1893	Princeton	11–0–0	Tom Trenchard
1892	Yale	13–0–0	Walter Camp
1891	Yale	13–0–0	Walter Camp
1890	Harvard	11–0–0	G. Stewart/G.Adams
1889	Princeton	10–0–0	Edgar Poe
1888	Yale	13–0–0	Walter Camp
1887	Yale	9–0–0	Harry W. Beecher
1886	Yale	9–0–1	Robert N. Corwin
1885	Princeton	9–0–0	Charles DeCamp
1884	Yale	8–0–1	Eugene L. Richards
1883	Yale	8–0–0	Ray Tompkins

MAJOR BOWL GAME RESULTS

ROSE BOWL

DATE	RESULT
2005	Texas 38, Michigan 37
2004	USC 28, Michigan 14
2003	Oklahoma 34, Washington St. 14
2002	Miami 37, Nebraska 14
2001	Washington 34, Purdue 24
2000	Wisconsin 17, Stanford 9
1999	Wisconsin 38, UCLA 31
1998	Michigan 21, Washington St. 16
1997	Ohio St. 20, Arizona St. 17
1996	USC 41, Northwestern 32
1995	Penn St. 38, Oregon 20
1994	Wisconsin 21, UCLA 16
1993	Michigan 38, Washington 31
1992	Washington 34, Michigan 14
1991	Washington 46, Iowa 34
1990	USC 17, Michigan 10

DATE	RESULT
1989	Michigan 22, USC 14
1988	Michigan St. 20, USC 17
1987	Arizona St. 22, Michigan 15
1986	UCLA 45, Iowa 28
1985	USC 20, Ohio St. 17
1984	UCLA 45, Illinois 9
1983	UCLA 24, Michigan 14
1982	Washington 28, Iowa 0
1981	Michigan 23, Washington 6
1980	USC 17, Ohio St. 16
1979	USC 17, Michigan 10
1978	Washington 27, Michigan 20
1977	USC 14, Michigan 6
1976	UCLA 23, Ohio St. 10
1975	USC 18, Ohio St. 17
1974	Ohio St. 42, USC 21

ROSE BOWL (cont.)

DATE	RESULT	DATE	RESULT
1973	USC 42, Ohio St. 17	1943	Georgia 9, UCLA 0
1972	Stanford 13, Michigan 12	1942	Oregon St. 20, Duke 16
1971	Stanford 27, Ohio St. 17	1941	Stanford 21, Nebraska 13
1970	USC 10, Michigan 3	1940	USC 14, Tennessee 0
1969	Ohio St. 27, USC 16	1939	USC 7, Duke 3
1968	USC 14, Indiana 3	1938	California 13, Alabama 0
1967	Purdue 14, USC 13	1937	Pittsburgh 21, Washington 0
1966	UCLA 14, Michigan St. 12	1936	Stanford 7, SMU 0
1965	Michigan 34, Oregon St. 7	1935	Alabama 29, Stanford 13
1964	Illinois 17, Washington 7	1934	Columbia 7, Stanford 0
1963	USC 42, Wisconsin 37	1933	USC 35, Pittsburgh 0
1962	Minnesota 21, UCLA 3	1932	USC 21, Tulane 12
1961	Washington 17, Minnesota 7	1931	Alabama 24, Washington St. 0
1960	Washington 44, Wisconsin 8	1930	USC 47, Pittsburgh 14
1959	Iowa 38, California 12	1929	Georgia Tech 8, California 7
1958	Ohio St. 10, Oregon 7	1928	Stanford 7, Pittsburgh 6
1957	Iowa 35, Oregon St. 19	1927	Stanford 7, Alabama 7
1956	Michigan St. 17, UCLA 14	1926	Alabama 20, Washington 10
1955	Ohio St. 20, USC 7	1925	Notre Dame 27, Stanford 10
1954	Michigan St. 28, UCLA 20	1924	Washington 14, Navy 14
1953	USC 7, Wisconsin 0	1923	USC 14, Penn St. 3
1952	Illinois 40, Stanford 7	1922	California 0, Washington & Jefferson 0
1951	Michigan 14, California 6	1921	California 28, Ohio St. 0
1950	Ohio St. 17, California 14	1920	Harvard 7, Oregon 6
1949	Northwestern 20, California 14	1919	Great Lakes 17, Mare Island 0
1948	Michigan 49, USC 0	1918	Mare Island 19, Camp Lewis 7
1947	Illinois 45, UCLA 14	1917	Oregon 14, Pennsylvania 0
1946	Alabama 34, USC 14	1916	Washington St. 14, Brown 0
1945	USC 25, Tennessee 0	1902	Michigan 49, Stanford 0
1944	USC 29, Washington 0		

Note: From 1903–15, no Rose Bowl football game was held. In 1903, polo replaced football. From 1904–1915, chariot races were held. Football returned in 1916.

ORANGE BOWL

DATE	RESULT	DATE	RESULT
January 4, 2005	USC 55, Oklahoma 19	January 1, 1975	Notre Dame 13, Alabama 11
January 1, 2004	Miami (Florida) 16, Florida St. 14	January 1, 1974	Penn St. 16, LSU 9
January 2, 2003	USC 38, Iowa 17	January 1, 1973	Nebraska 40, Notre Dame 6
January 2, 2002	Florida 56, Maryland 23	January 1, 1972	Nebraska 38, Alabama 6
January 3, 2001	Oklahoma 13, Florida St. 2	January 1, 1971	Nebraska 17, LSU 12
January 1, 2000	Michigan 35, Alabama 34 (OT)	January 1, 1970	Penn St. 10, Missouri 3
January 2, 1999	Florida 31, Syracuse 10	January 1, 1969	Penn St. 15, Kansas 14
January 2, 1998	Nebraska 42, Tennessee 17	January 1, 1968	Oklahoma 26, Tennessee 24
December 31, 1996	Nebraska 41, Virginia Tech 21	January 2, 1967	Florida 27, Georgia Tech 12
January 1, 1996	Florida St. 31, Notre Dame 26	January 1, 1966	Alabama 39, Nebraska 28
January 1, 1995	Nebraska 24, Miami (Florida) 17	January 1, 1965	Texas 21, Alabama 17
January 1, 1994	Florida St. 18, Nebraska 16	January 1, 1964	Nebraska 13, Auburn 7
January 1, 1993	Florida St. 27, Nebraska 14	January 1, 1963	Alabama 17, Oklahoma 0
January 1, 1992	Miami (Florida) 22, Nebraska 0	January 1, 1962	LSU 25, Colorado 7
January 1, 1991	Colorado 10, Notre Dame 9	January 2, 1961	Missouri 21, Navy 14
January 1, 1990	Notre Dame 21, Colorado 6	January 1, 1960	Georgia 14, Missouri 0
January 2, 1989	Miami (Florida) 23, Nebraska 3	January 1, 1959	Oklahoma 21, Syracuse 6
January 1, 1988	Miami (Florida) 20, Oklahoma 14	January 1, 1958	Oklahoma 48, Duke 21
January 1, 1987	Oklahoma 42, Arkansas 8	January 1, 1957	Colorado 27, Clemson 21
January 1, 1986	Oklahoma 25, Penn St. 10	January 2, 1956	Oklahoma 20, Maryland 6
January 1, 1985	Washington 28, Oklahoma 17	January 1, 1955	Duke 34, Nebraska 7
January 2, 1984	Miami (Florida) 31, Nebraska 30	January 1, 1954	Oklahoma 7, Maryland 0
January 1, 1983	Nebraska 21, LSU 20	January 1, 1953	Alabama 61, Syracuse 6
January 1, 1982	Clemson 22, Nebraska 15	January 1, 1952	Georgia Tech 17, Baylor 14
January 1, 1981	Oklahoma 18, Florida St. 17	January 1, 1951	Clemson 15, Miami (Florida) 14
January 1, 1980	Oklahoma 24, Florida St. 7	January 2, 1950	Santa Clara 21, Kentucky 13
January 1, 1979	Oklahoma 31, Nebraska 24	January 1, 1949	Texas 41, Georgia 28
January 2, 1978	Arkansas 31, Oklahoma 6	January 1, 1948	Georgia Tech 20, Kansas 14
January 1, 1977	Ohio St. 27, Colorado 10	January 1, 1947	Rice 8, Tennessee 0
January 1, 1976	Oklahoma 14, Michigan 6	January 1, 1946	Miami (Florida) 13, Holy Cross 6

MAJOR BOWL GAME RESULTS (cont.)

ORANGE BOWL (cont.)

DATE	RESULT
January 1, 1945	Tulsa 26, Georgia Tech 12
January 1, 1944	LSU 19, Texas A&M 14
January 1, 1943	Alabama 37, Boston College 21
January 1, 1942	Georgia 40, TCU 26
January 1, 1941	Mississippi St. 14, Georgetown 7
January 1, 1940	Georgia Tech 21, Missouri 7

DATE	RESULT
January 2, 1939	Tennessee 17, Oklahoma 0
January 1, 1938	Auburn 6, Michigan St. 0
January 1, 1937	Duquesne 13, Mississippi St. 12
January 1, 1936	Catholic 20, Mississippi 19
January 1, 1935	Bucknell 26, Miami (Florida) 0

SUGAR BOWL

DATE	RESULT
January 3, 2005	Auburn 16, Virginia Tech 13
January 4, 2004	LSU 21, Oklahoma 14
January 1, 2003	Georgia 26, Florida St. 13
January 1, 2002	LSU 47, Illinois 34
January 2, 2001	Miami (Florida) 37, Florida 20
January 4, 2000	Florida St. 46, Virginia Tech 29
January 1, 1999	Ohio St. 24, Texas A&M 14
January 1, 1998	Florida St. 31, Ohio St. 14
January 2, 1997	Florida 52, Florida St. 20
December 31, 1995	Virginia Tech 28, Texas 10
January 2, 1995	Florida St. 23, Florida 17
January 1, 1994	Florida 41, West Virginia 7
January 1, 1993	Alabama 34, Miami (Florida) 13
January 1, 1992	Notre Dame 39, Florida 28
January 1, 1991	Tennessee 23, Virginia 22
January 1, 1990	Miami (Florida) 33, Alabama 25
January 2, 1989	Florida St. 13, Auburn 7
January 1, 1988	Auburn 16, Syracuse 16
January 1, 1987	Nebraska 30, LSU 15
January 1, 1986	Tennessee 35, Miami (Florida) 7
January 1, 1985	Nebraska 28, LSU 10
January 2, 1984	Auburn 9, Michigan 7
January 1, 1983	Penn St. 27, Georgia 23
January 1, 1982	Pittsburgh 24, Georgia 20
January 1, 1981	Georgia 17, Notre Dame 10
January 1, 1980	Alabama 24, Arkansas 9
January 1, 1979	Alabama 14, Penn St. 7
January 2, 1978	Alabama 35, Ohio St. 6
January 1, 1977	Pittsburgh 27, Georgia 3
December 31, 1975	Alabama 13, Penn St. 6
December 31, 1974	Nebraska 13, Florida 10
December 31, 1973	Notre Dame 24, Alabama 23
December 31, 1972	Oklahoma 14, Penn St. 0
January 1, 1972	Oklahoma 40, Auburn 22
January 1, 1971	Tennessee 34, Air Force 13
January 1, 1970	Mississippi 27, Arkansas 22

DATE	RESULT
January 1, 1969	Arkansas 16, Georgia 2
January 1, 1968	LSU 20, Wyoming 13
January 2, 1967	Alabama 34, Nebraska 7
January 1, 1966	Missouri 20, Florida 18
January 1, 1965	LSU 13, Syracuse 10
January 1, 1964	Alabama 12, Mississippi 7
January 1, 1963	Mississippi 17, Arkansas 13
January 1, 1962	Alabama 10, Arkansas 3
January 2, 1961	Mississippi 14, Rice 6
January 1, 1960	Mississippi 21, LSU 0
January 1, 1959	LSU 7, Clemson 0
January 1, 1958	Mississippi 39, Texas 7
January 1, 1957	Baylor 13, Tennessee 7
January 2, 1956	Georgia Tech 7, Pittsburgh 0
January 1, 1955	Navy 21, Mississippi 0
January 1, 1954	Georgia Tech 42, West Virginia 19
January 1, 1953	Georgia Tech 24, Mississippi 7
January 1, 1952	Maryland 28, Tennessee 13
January 1, 1951	Kentucky 13, Oklahoma 7
January 2, 1950	Oklahoma 35, LSU 0
January 1, 1949	Oklahoma 14, North Carolina 6
January 1, 1948	Texas 27, Alabama 7
January 1, 1947	Georgia 20, North Carolina 10
January 1, 1946	Oklahoma St. 33, Saint Mary's (Colorado) 13
January 1, 1945	Duke 29, Alabama 26
January 1, 1944	Georgia Tech 20, Tulsa 18
January 1, 1943	Tennessee 14, Tulsa 7
January 1, 1942	Fordham 2, Missouri 0
January 1, 1941	Boston College 19, Tennessee 13
January 1, 1940	Texas A&M 14, Tulane 13
January 2, 1939	TCU 15, Carnegie Mellon 7
January 1, 1938	Santa Clara 6, LSU 0
January 1, 1937	Santa Clara 21, LSU 14
January 1, 1936	TCU 3, LSU 2
January 1, 1935	Tulane 20, Temple 14

COTTON BOWL

DATE	RESULT
January 1, 2005	Tennessee 38, Texas A&M 7
January 2, 2004	Mississippi 31, Oklahoma St. 28
January 1, 2003	Texas 35, LSU 20
January 1, 2002	Oklahoma 10, Arkansas 3
January 1, 2001	Kansas St. 35, Tennessee 21
January 1, 2000	Arkansas 27, Texas 6
January 1, 1999	Texas 38, Mississippi St. 11
January 1, 1998	UCLA 29, Texas A&M 23
January 1, 1997	BYU 19, Kansas St. 15
January 1, 1996	Colorado 38, Oregon 6
January 2, 1995	USC 55, Texas Tech 14
January 1, 1994	Notre Dame 24, Texas A&M 21
January 1, 1993	Notre Dame 28, Texas A&M 3
January 1, 1992	Florida St. 10, Texas A&M 2

DATE	RESULT
January 1, 1991	Miami (Florida) 46, Texas 3
January 1, 1990	Tennessee 31, Arkansas 27
January 2, 1989	UCLA 17, Arkansas 3
January 1, 1988	Texas A&M 35, Notre Dame 10
January 1, 1987	Ohio St. 28, Texas A&M 12
January 1, 1986	Texas A&M 36, Auburn 16
January 1, 1985	Boston College 45, Houston 28
January 2, 1984	Georgia 10, Texas 9
January 1, 1983	SMU 7, Pittsburgh 3
January 1, 1982	Texas 14, Alabama 12
January 1, 1981	Alabama 30, Baylor 2
January 1, 1980	Houston 17, Nebraska 14
January 1, 1979	Notre Dame 35, Houston 34
January 2, 1978	Notre Dame 38, Texas 10

LEGENDS

Roger Staubach served in Vietnam after playing for Navy.

■ **Roger Staubach, quarterback,** b. February 5, 1942, Cincinnati, Ohio. During three varsity seasons at the U.S. Naval Academy (1962–64), Staubach completed 292 of 463 pass attempts — an amazing 63 percent completion rate. He threw just 19 interceptions during his college career and won the Heisman Trophy in 1963. Staubach served four years in the navy before joining the NFL in 1969. He played for the Dallas Cowboys from 1969-79. Staubach won two Super Bowls (1972 and 1978) and was named the NFL MVP in 1971. He was inducted into the College Football Hall of Fame in 1981 and the Pro Football Hall of Fame in 1985.

■ **Billy Sims, running back,** b. September 18, 1955, St. Louis, Missouri. The super-fast Sims led the nation in rushing yards and touchdowns as a junior and a senior at Oklahoma. In 1978, the 6-foot, 205-pound junior had 1,762 yards and 20 touchdowns, tops in the country. He rushed for 1,500 yards and 22 touchdowns as a senior in 1979. Sims won the Heisman Trophy in 1978 and was the runner-up the next year. He played five seasons in the NFL with the Detroit Lions (1980-84), before retiring because of a knee injury. He was inducted into the College Football Hall of Fame in 1995.

■ **Earl Campbell, running back,** b. March 29, 1955, Tyler, Texas. At 5' 11", 220 pounds, Campbell ran over defenders like a steamroller. In four seasons at Texas (1974-77), he rumbled for 4,443 yards (the fifth-highest total at the time) and was named an All-America as a sophomore and a senior. As a senior, he ran for 1,744 yards to lead the nation in rushing and win the Heisman Trophy. Campbell was chosen by the Houston Oilers as the Number 1 pick in the 1978 NFL Draft. As a rookie, he led the league in rushing yards (1,450) and was named the NFL's Most Valuable Player. Campbell was named to the Pro Bowl five times in his first six NFL seasons. He retired after the 1985 season and was inducted into the College Football Hall of Fame in 1990 and the Pro Football Hall of Fame in 1991.

MAJOR BOWL GAME RESULTS (cont.)

COTTON BOWL (cont.)

DATE	RESULT	DATE	RESULT
January 1, 1977	Houston 30, Maryland 21	January 1, 1962	Texas 12, Mississippi 7
January 1, 1976	Arkansas 31, Georgia 10	January 2, 1961	Duke 7, Arkansas 6
January 1, 1975	Penn St. 41, Baylor 20	January 1, 1960	Syracuse 23, Texas 14
January 1, 1974	Nebraska 19, Texas 3	January 1, 1959	TCU 0, Air Force 0
January 1, 1973	Texas 17, Alabama 13	January 1, 1958	Navy 20, Rice 7
January 1, 1972	Penn St. 30, Texas 6	January 1, 1957	TCU 28, Syracuse 27
January 1, 1971	Notre Dame 24, Texas 11	January 2, 1956	Mississippi 14, TCU 13
January 1, 1970	Texas 21, Notre Dame 17	January 1, 1955	Georgia Tech 14, Arkansas 6
January 1, 1969	Texas 36, Tennessee 13	January 1, 1954	Rice 28, Alabama 6
January 1, 1968	Texas A&M 20, Alabama 16	January 1, 1953	Texas 16, Tennessee 0
December 31, 1966	Georgia 24, SMU 9	January 1, 1952	Kentucky 20, TCU 7
January 1, 1966	LSU 14, Arkansas 7	January 1, 1951	Tennessee 20, Texas 14
January 1, 1965	Arkansas 10, Nebraska 7	January 2, 1950	Rice 27, North Carolina 13
January 1, 1964	Texas 28, Navy 6	January 1, 1949	SMU 21, Oregon 13
January 1, 1963	LSU 13, Texas 0	January 1, 1948	SMU 13, Penn St. 13

MAJOR BOWL GAME RESULTS (cont.)

COTTON BOWL (cont.)

DATE	RESULT	DATE	RESULT
January 1, 1947	Arkansas 0, LSU 0	January 1, 1941	Texas A&M 13, Fordham 12
January 1, 1946	Texas 40, Missouri 27	January 1, 1940	Clemson 6, Boston College 3
January 1, 1945	Oklahoma St. 34, TCU 0	January 2, 1939	St. Mary's (Calif.) 20, Texas Tech 13
January 1, 1944	Texas 7, Randolph Field 7	January 1, 1938	Rice 28, Colorado 14
January 1, 1943	Texas 14, Georgia Tech 7	January 1, 1937	TCU 16, Marquette 6
January 1, 1942	Alabama 29, Texas A&M 21		

FIESTA BOWL

DATE	RESULT	DATE	RESULT
January 1, 2005	Utah 35, Pittsburgh 7	January 1, 1988	Florida St. 31, Nebraska 28
January 2, 2004	Ohio St. 35, Kansas St. 28	January 2, 1987	Penn St. 14, Miami (Florida) 10
January 3, 2003	Ohio St. 31, Miami (Florida) 24 (2OT)	January 1, 1986	Michigan 27, Nebraska 23
January 1, 2002	Oregon 38, Colorado 16	January 1, 1985	UCLA 39, Miami (Florida) 37
January 1, 2001	Oregon St. 41, Notre Dame 9	January 2, 1984	Ohio St. 28, Pittsburgh 23
January 2, 2000	Nebraska 31, Tennessee 21	January 1, 1983	Arizona St. 32, Oklahoma 21
January 4, 1999	Tennessee 23, Florida St. 16	January 1, 1982	Penn St. 26, USC 10
December 31, 1997	Kansas St. 35, Syracuse 18	December 26, 1980	Penn St. 31, Ohio St. 19
January 1, 1997	Penn St. 38, Texas 15	December 25, 1979	Pittsburgh 16, Arizona 10
January 2, 1996	Nebraska 62, Florida 24	December 25, 1978	Arkansas 10, UCLA 10
January 2, 1995	Colorado 41, Notre Dame 24	December 25, 1977	Penn St. 42, Arizona St. 30
January 1, 1994	Arizona 29, Miami (Florida) 0	December 25, 1976	Oklahoma 41, Wyoming 7
January 1, 1993	Syracuse 26, Colorado 22	December 26, 1975	Arizona St. 17, Nebraska 14
January 1, 1992	Penn St. 42, Tennessee 17	December 28, 1974	Oklahoma St. 16, BYU 6
January 1, 1991	Louisville 34, Alabama 7	December 21, 1973	Arizona St. 28, Pittsburgh 7
January 1, 1990	Florida St. 41, Nebraska 17	December 23, 1972	Arizona St. 49, Missouri 35
January 2, 1989	Notre Dame 34, West Virginia 21	December 27, 1971	Arizona St. 45, Florida St. 38

NCAA DIVISION I-AA CHAMPIONSHIPS

YEAR	WINNER	RUNNER-UP	SCORE	YEAR	WINNER	RUNNER-UP	SCORE
2004	James Madison	Montana	31–21	1990	Georgia Southern	Nevada-Reno	36–13
2003	Delaware	Colgate	40–0	1989	Georgia Southern	Stephen F. Austin	37–34
2002	Western Kentucky	McNeese St.	34–14	1988	Furman	Georgia Southern	17–12
2001	Montana	Furman	13–6	1987	Northeast Louisiana	Marshall	43–42
2000	Georgia Southern	Montana	27–25	1986	Georgia Southern	Arkansas St.	48–21
1999	Georgia Southern	Youngstown St.	59–24	1985	Georgia Southern	Furman	44–42
1998	Massachusetts	Georgia Southern	55–43	1984	Montana St.	Louisiana Tech	19–6
1997	Youngstown St.	McNeese St.	10–9	1983	Southern Illinois	Western Carolina	43–7
1996	Marshall	Montana	49–29	1982	Eastern Kentucky	Delaware	17–14
1995	Montana	Marshall	22–20	1981	Idaho St.	Eastern Kentucky	34–23
1994	Youngstown St.	Boise St.	28–14	1980	Boise St.	Eastern Kentucky	31–29
1993	Youngstown St.	Marshall	17–5	1979	Eastern Kentucky	Lehigh	30–7
1992	Marshall	Youngstown St.	31–28	1978	Florida A&M	Massachusetts	35–28
1991	Youngstown St.	Marshall	25–17				

HEISMAN MEMORIAL TROPHY

Awarded to the nation's best college player by the Downtown Athletic Club (DAC) of New York City. The trophy is named after John W. Heisman, who coached Georgia Tech to the national championship in 1917 and later served as DAC athletic director.

YEAR	WINNER, COLLEGE	RUNNER-UP, COLLEGE
2004	*† Matt Leinart, USC	Adrian Peterson, Oklahoma
2003	* Jason White, Oklahoma	Larry Fitzgerald, Pittsburgh
2002	Carson Palmer, USC	Brad Banks, Iowa
2001	Eric Crouch, Nebraska	Rex Grossman, Florida
2000	Chris Weinke, Florida St.	Josh Heupel, Oklahoma
1999	Ron Dayne, Wisconsin	Joe Hamilton, Georgia Tech
1998	Ricky Williams, Texas	Michael Bishop, Kansas St.

*Juniors (all others were seniors)
†Winners who played for national championship teams the same year

HEISMAN MEMORIAL TROPHY (cont.)

YEAR	WINNER, COLLEGE	RUNNER-UP, COLLEGE
1997	†Charles Woodson, Michigan	Peyton Manning, Tennessee
1996	†Danny Wuerffel, Florida	Troy Davis, Iowa St.
1995	Eddie George, Ohio St.	Tommie Frazier, Nebraska
1994	Rashaan Salaam, Colorado	Ki-Jana Carter, Penn St.
1993	†Charlie Ward, Florida St.	Heath Shuler, Tennessee
1992	Gino Torretta, Miami (Florida)	Marshall Faulk, San Diego St.
1991	* Desmond Howard, Michigan	Casey Weldon, Florida St.
1990	* Ty Detmer, BYU	Raghib Ismail, Notre Dame
1989	* Andre Ware, Houston	Anthony Thompson, Indiana
1988	* Barry Sanders, Oklahoma St.	Rodney Peete, USC
1987	Tim Brown, Notre Dame	Don McPherson, Syracuse
1986	Vinny Testaverde, Miami (Florida)	Paul Palmer, Temple
1985	Bo Jackson, Auburn	Chuck Long, Iowa
1984	Doug Flutie, Boston College	Keith Byars, Ohio St.
1983	Mike Rozier, Nebraska	Steve Young, BYU
1982	* Herschel Walker, Georgia	John Elway, Stanford
1981	Marcus Allen, USC	Herschel Walker, Georgia
1980	George Rogers, South Carolina	Hugh Green, Pittsburgh
1979	Charles White, USC	Billy Sims, Oklahoma
1978	* Billy Sims, Oklahoma	Chuck Fusina, Penn St.
1977	Earl Campbell, Texas	Terry Miller, Oklahoma St.
1976	†Tony Dorsett, Pittsburgh	Ricky Bell, USC
1975	Archie Griffin, Ohio St.	Chuck Muncie, California
1974	* Archie Griffin, Ohio St.	Anthony Davis, USC
1973	John Cappelletti, Penn St.	John Hicks, Ohio St.
1972	Johnny Rodgers, Nebraska	Greg Pruitt, Oklahoma
1971	Pat Sullivan, Auburn	Ed Marinaro, Cornell
1970	Jim Plunkett, Stanford	Joe Theismann, Notre Dame
1969	Steve Owens, Oklahoma	Mike Phipps, Purdue
1968	O.J. Simpson, USC	Leroy Keyes, Purdue
1967	Gary Beban, UCLA	O.J. Simpson, USC
1966	Steve Spurrier, Florida	Bob Griese, Purdue
1965	Mike Garrett, USC	Howard Twilley, Tulsa
1964	John Huarte, Notre Dame	Jerry Rhome, Tulsa
1963	* Roger Staubach, Navy	Billy Lothridge, Georgia Tech
1962	Terry Baker, Oregon St.	Jerry Stovall, LSU
1961	Ernie Davis, Syracuse	Bob Ferguson, Ohio St.
1960	Joe Bellino, Navy	Tom Brown, Minnesota
1959	Billy Cannon, LSU	Rich Lucas, Penn St.
1958	Pete Dawkins, Army	Randy Duncan, Iowa
1957	John David Crow, Texas A&M	Alex Karras, Iowa
1956	Paul Hornung, Notre Dame	Johnny Majors, Tennessee
1955	Howard Cassady, Ohio St.	Jim Swink, TCU
1954	Alan Ameche, Wisconsin	Kurt Burris, Oklahoma
1953	John Lattner, Notre Dame	Paul Giel, Minnesota
1952	Billy Vessels, Oklahoma	Jack Scarbath, Maryland
1951	Dick Kazmaier, Princeton	Hank Lauricella, Tennessee
1950	* Vic Janowicz, Ohio St.	Kyle Rote, SMU
1949	†Leon Hart, Notre Dame	Charlie Justice, North Carolina
1948	* Doak Walker, SMU	Charlie Justice, North Carolina
1947	†John Lujack, Notre Dame	Bob Chappius, Michigan
1946	Glenn Davis, Army	Charley Trippi, Georgia
1945	*†Doc Blanchard, Army	Glenn Davis, Army
1944	Les Horvath, Ohio St.	Glenn Davis, Army
1943	Angelo Bertelli, Notre Dame	Bob Odell, Pennsylvania
1942	Frank Sinkwich, Georgia	Paul Governali, Columbia
1941	†Bruce Smith, Minnesota	Angelo Bertelli, Notre Dame
1940	Tom Harmon, Michigan	John Kimbrough, Texas A&M
1939	Nile Kinnick, Iowa	Tom Harmon, Michigan
1938	†Davey O'Brien, TCU	Marshall Goldberg, Pittsburgh
1937	Clint Frank, Yale	Byron White, Colorado
1936	Larry Kelley, Yale	Sam Francis, Nebraska
1935	Jay Berwanger, Chicago	Monk Meyer, Army

*Juniors (all others were seniors)
†Winners who played for national championship teams the same year
Note: Former Heisman winners and members of the national media cast votes with ballots allowing for three names (3 points for
first, 2 points for second, and 1 point for third).

MAXWELL AWARD

Given to the nation's outstanding college football player by the Maxwell Football Club of Philadelphia.

YEAR	PLAYER, COLLEGE	YEAR	PLAYER, COLLEGE
2004	Jason White, Oklahoma	1970	Jim Plunkett, Stanford
2003	Eli Manning, Mississippi	1969	Mike Reid, Penn St.
2002	Larry Johnson, Penn St.	1968	O.J. Simpson, USC
2001	Ken Dorsey, Miami (Florida)	1967	Gary Beban, UCLA
2000	Drew Brees, Purdue	1966	Jim Lynch, Notre Dame
1999	Ron Dayne, Wisconsin	1965	Tommy Nobis, Texas
1998	Ricky Williams, Texas	1964	Glenn Ressler, Penn St.
1997	Peyton Manning, Tennessee	1963	Roger Staubach, Navy
1996	Danny Wuerffel, Florida	1962	Terry Baker, Oregon St.
1995	Eddie George, Ohio St.	1961	Bob Ferguson, Ohio St.
1994	Kerry Collins, Penn St.	1960	Joe Bellino, Navy
1993	Charlie Ward, Florida St.	1959	Rich Lucas, Penn St.
1992	Gino Torretta, Miami (Florida)	1958	Pete Dawkins, Army
1991	Desmond Howard, Michigan	1957	Bob Reifsnyder, Navy
1990	Ty Detmer, BYU	1956	Tommy McDonald, Oklahoma
1989	Anthony Thompson, Indiana	1955	Howard Cassady, Ohio St.
1988	Barry Sanders, Oklahoma St.	1954	Ron Beagle, Navy
1987	Don McPherson, Syracuse	1953	John Lattner, Notre Dame
1986	Vinny Testaverde, Miami (Florida)	1952	John Lattner, Notre Dame
1985	Chuck Long, Iowa	1951	Dick Kazmaier, Princeton
1984	Doug Flutie, Boston College	1950	Reds Bagnell, Pennsylvania
1983	Mike Rozier, Nebraska	1949	Leon Hart, Notre Dame
1982	Herschel Walker, Georgia	1948	Chuck Bednarik, Pennsylvania
1981	Marcus Allen, USC	1947	Doak Walker, SMU
1980	Hugh Green, Pittsburgh	1946	Charley Trippi, Georgia
1979	Charles White, USC	1945	Doc Blanchard, Army
1978	Chuck Fusina, Penn St.	1944	Glenn Davis, Army
1977	Ross Browner, Notre Dame	1943	Bob Odell, Pennsylvania
1976	Tony Dorsett, Pittsburgh	1942	Paul Governali, Columbia
1975	Archie Griffin, Ohio St.	1941	Bill Dudley, Virginia
1974	Steve Joachim, Temple	1940	Tom Harmon, Michigan
1973	John Cappelletti, Penn St.	1939	Nile Kinnick, Iowa
1972	Brad Van Pelt, Michigan St.	1938	Davey O'Brien, TCU
1971	Ed Marinaro, Cornell	1937	Clint Frank, Yale

Jason White led Oklahoma to a 12–1 record in 2004.

VINCE LOMBARDI/ROTARY AWARD

Given to the outstanding college lineman of the year. The award is sponsored by the Rotary Club of Houston, Texas.

YEAR	PLAYER, COLLEGE	YEAR	PLAYER, COLLEGE
2004	David Pollack, Georgia	1984	Tony Degrate, Texas
2003	Tommie Harris, Oklahoma	1983	Dean Steinkuhler, Nebraska
2002	Terrell Suggs, Arizona St.	1982	Dave Rimington, Nebraska
2001	Julius Peppers, North Carolina	1981	Kenneth Sims, Texas
2000	Jamal Reynolds, Florida St.	1980	Hugh Green, Pittsburgh
1999	Corey Moore, Virginia Tech	1979	Brad Budde, USC
1998	Dat Nguyen, Texas A&M	1978	Bruce Clark, Penn St.
1997	Grant Wistrom, Nebraska	1977	Ross Browner, Notre Dame
1996	Orlando Pace, Ohio St.	1976	Wilson Whitley, Houston
1995	Orlando Pace, Ohio St.	1975	Lee Roy Selmon, Oklahoma
1994	Warren Sapp, Miami (Florida)	1974	Randy White, Maryland
1993	Aaron Taylor, Notre Dame	1973	John Hicks, Ohio St.
1992	Marvin Jones, Florida St.	1972	Rich Glover, Nebraska
1991	Steve Emtman, Washington	1971	Walt Patulski, Notre Dame
1990	Chris Zorich, Notre Dame	1970	Jim Stillwagon, Ohio St.
1989	Percy Snow, Michigan St.		
1988	Tracy Rocker, Auburn		
1987	Chris Spielman, Ohio St.		
1986	Cornelius Bennett, Alabama		
1985	Tony Casillas, Oklahoma		

DID YOU KNOW?

Running back Adrian Peterson of Oklahoma came in second in the voting for the 2004 Heisman Trophy, the highest finish ever by a freshman.

DAVEY O'BRIEN NATIONAL QUARTERBACK AWARD

Given to the nation's top quarterback by the Davey O'Brien Educational and Charitable Trust of Fort Worth. Named for TCU Hall of Fame quarterback Davey O'Brien (1936-38).

YEAR	PLAYER, COLLEGE	YEAR	PLAYER, COLLEGE
2004	Jason White, Oklahoma	1992	Gino Torretta, Miami (Florida)
2003	Jason White, Oklahoma	1991	Ty Detmer, BYU
2002	Brad Banks, Iowa	1990	Ty Detmer, BYU
2001	Eric Crouch, Nebraska	1989	Andre Ware, Houston
2000	Chris Weinke, Florida St.	1988	Troy Aikman, UCLA
1999	Joe Hamilton, Georgia Tech	1987	Don McPherson, Syracuse
1998	Michael Bishop, Kansas St.	1986	Vinny Testaverde, Miami (Florida)
1997	Peyton Manning, Tennessee	1985	Chuck Long, Iowa
1996	Danny Wuerffel, Florida	1984	Doug Flutie, Boston College
1995	Danny Wuerffel, Florida	1983	Steve Young, BYU
1994	Kerry Collins, Penn St.	1982	Todd Blackledge, Penn St.
1993	Charlie Ward, Florida St.	1981	Jim McMahon, BYU

2004-05 TIME LINE

■ **September 10, 2004:** The Florida State Seminoles take on the Miami Hurricanes for the first time as conference rivals (Miami joined the Atlantic Coast Conference in 2004). Miami beats Florida State in overtime, 16–10. Hurricane running back Frank Gore finishes with 89 yards, including an 18-yard touchdown run in overtime to give Miami the victory.

■ **November 6, 2004:** Texas comes back from a 35–7 first-half deficit to defeat Oklahoma State, 56–35. It is the biggest comeback in the school's 111 years of playing football.

■ **November 20, 2004:** In one of college football's biggest rivalries, Michigan meets Ohio State for the 100th time. Ohio State easily defeats its Big Ten rival, 37–21.

■ **December 4, 2004:** Running back Adrian Peterson of Oklahoma sets an NCAA freshman record for most total 100-yard rushing games (11). He gains 172 yards in the Sooners' 42–3 win over Colorado in the Big 12 championship game.

■ **January 1, 2005:** Utah, the first team from a non-BCS conference to advance to a BCS bowl game, walks all over Big East champion Pittsburgh in the Fiesta Bowl, 35–7. The win gives the Utes their first unbeaten season (12–0) since 1930.

■ **January 3, 2005:** The Auburn Tigers (13–0) hold off Virginia Tech, 16–13, in the Sugar Bowl to complete an undefeated season. They finish Number 2 in the BCS rankings.

■ **January 4, 2005:** USC crushes Oklahoma, 55–19, in the Orange Bowl to win its second straight national championship. The Trojans were co-champions with the Louisiana State Tigers the year before.

■ **January 14, 2005:** Junior quarterback Matt Leinart of USC announces he will return to school for his senior season instead of opting to leave school early and enter the 2005 NFL Draft.

BASEBALL

Manny Ramirez batted .412 in the World Series and was named Most Valuable Player.

AL TIELEMANS/SPORTS ILLUSTRATED

Baseball hit a high note on October 27, 2004. Boston Red Sox fans watched with joy as their team finally ended The Curse of the Bambino and won its first World Series since 1918. But as the off-season unfolded, baseball sunk to a new low as a steroid scandal once again gripped the sport.

Dogged off the field by steroid accusations in 2004, Barry Bonds of the San Francisco Giants still managed to post a successful season. He batted .362 with 45 home runs and 101 RBIs, and easily won his record seventh MVP award.

Bonds wasn't the only one setting records. Ichiro Suzuki of the Seattle Mariners broke George Sisler's 84-year-old record for the most hits in a single season (262). Randy Johnson of the Arizona Diamondbacks became just the 17th pitcher in history to throw a perfect game, and 41-year-old Roger Clemens of the Houston Astros won his record seventh Cy Young Award.

In January 2005, Johnson was traded to the New York Yankees. The Yanks were desperate to revive a pitching staff that had come up short in the American League Championship Series against the Red Sox. Boston became the first team in baseball history to overcome a three-games-to-none deficit in the ALCS. The Sox then swept the St. Louis Cardinals in the World Series.

After the Series, Major League Baseball faced accusations of steroid use by players. In January 2005, baseball announced a tougher drug policy: a first-time steroid offense would result in a 10-day suspension; a second offense would bring a 30-day suspension; a third offense a 60-day suspension; and a fourth offense a full year's suspension.

On February 14, 2005, former American League MVP Jose Canseco released a book, *Juiced*, in which he admitted to using steroids during his career. He said that other former and active players, including Mark McGwire and Sammy Sosa, also used them.

The book's publication prompted Congress to investigate what baseball was doing about steroids. On March 17, 2005, Sosa, McGwire, Rafael Palmeiro, Curt Schilling, and Frank Thomas testified before Congress about steroid use in baseball. Members of the House of Representatives and the Senate criticized Major League Baseball and said it needed stiffer punishments for steroid use.

As the 2005 season began, it was unclear whether baseball's new policy or the congressional hearings would make a difference in removing steroids from the game.

2004 MAJOR LEAGUE BASEBALL FINAL STANDINGS

NATIONAL LEAGUE

EASTERN DIVISION

TEAM	WON	LOST	PCT	GB	HOME	AWAY
Braves	96	66	.593	—	49–32	47–34
Phillies	86	76	.531	10.0	42–39	44–37
Marlins	83	79	.512	13.0	42–38	41–41
Mets	71	91	.438	25.0	38–43	33–48
Expos	67	95	.414	29.0	35–45	32–50

CENTRAL DIVISION

TEAM	WON	LOST	PCT	GB	HOME	AWAY
Cardinals	105	57	.648	—	53–28	52–29
†Astros	92	70	.568	13.0	48–33	44–37
Cubs	89	73	.549	16.0	45–37	44–36
Reds	76	86	.469	29.0	40–41	36–45
Pirates	72	89	.447	32.5	39–41	33–48
Brewers	67	94	.416	37.5	36–45	31–49

WESTERN DIVISION

TEAM	WON	LOST	PCT	GB	HOME	AWAY
Dodgers	93	69	.574	—	49–32	44–37
Giants	91	71	.562	2.0	47–35	44–36
Padres	87	75	.537	6.0	42–39	45–36
Rockies	68	94	.420	25.0	38–43	30–51
Diamondbacks	51	111	.315	42.0	29–52	22–59

†Wild-card team

AMERICAN LEAGUE

EASTERN DIVISION

TEAM	WON	LOST	PCT	GB	HOME	AWAY
Yankees	101	61	.623	—	57–24	44–37
†Red Sox	98	64	.605	3.0	55–26	43–38
Orioles	78	84	.481	23.0	38–43	40–41
Devil Rays	70	91	.435	30.5	41–39	29–52
Blue Jays	67	94	.416	33.5	40–41	27–53

CENTRAL DIVISION

TEAM	WON	LOST	PCT	GB	HOME	AWAY
Twins	92	70	.568	—	49–32	43–38
White Sox	83	79	.512	9.0	46–35	37–44
Indians	80	82	.494	12.0	44–37	36–45
Tigers	72	90	.444	20.0	38–43	34–47
Royals	58	104	.358	34.0	33–47	25–57

WESTERN DIVISION

TEAM	WON	LOST	PCT	GB	HOME	AWAY
Angels	92	70	.568	—	45–36	47–34
A's	91	71	.562	1.0	52–29	39–42
Rangers	89	73	.549	3.0	51–30	38–43
Mariners	63	99	.389	29.0	38–44	25–55

†Wild-card team

Albert Pujols led the St. Louis Cardinals to their first World Series appearance since 1987.

Curt Schilling of the Red Sox pitched Game 6 of the ALCS against the New York Yankees despite an injured ankle (inset).

MAJOR LEAGUE TEAMS

NATIONAL LEAGUE
Arizona Diamondbacks
Atlanta Braves
Chicago Cubs
Cincinnati Reds
Colorado Rockies
Florida Marlins
Houston Astros
Los Angeles Dodgers
Milwaukee Brewers
*Montreal Expos
New York Mets
Philadelphia Phillies
Pittsburgh Pirates
San Diego Padres
San Francisco Giants
St. Louis Cardinals

* Became the Washington Nationals in 2005.

AMERICAN LEAGUE
**Anaheim Angels
Baltimore Orioles
Boston Red Sox
Chicago White Sox
Cleveland Indians
Detroit Tigers
Kansas City Royals
Minnesota Twins
New York Yankees
Oakland Athletics
Seattle Mariners
Tampa Bay Devil Rays
Texas Rangers
Toronto Blue Jays

** Became the Los Angeles Angels in 2005.

MLB 2004 PLAYOFFS – NATIONAL LEAGUE

NATIONAL LEAGUE DIVISION SERIES

October 5	Cardinals 8, Dodgers 3	October 9	Dodgers 4, Cardinals 0
October 7	Cardinals 8, Dodgers 3	October 10	Cardinals 6, Dodgers 2

(ST. LOUIS CARDINALS WON SERIES, 3–1)

October 6	Astros 9, Braves 3	October 10	Braves 6, Astros 5
October 7	Braves 4, Astros 2	October 11	Astros 12, Braves 3
October 9	Astros 8, Braves 5		

(HOUSTON ASTROS WON SERIES, 3–2)

NATIONAL LEAGUE CHAMPIONSHIP SERIES

October 13	Cardinals 10, Astros 7	October 18	Astros 3, Cardinals 0
October 14	Cardinals 6, Astros 4	October 20	Cardinals 6, Astros 4
October 16	Astros 5, Cardinals 2	October 21	Cardinals 5, Astros 2
October 17	Astros 6, Cardinals 5		

(ST. LOUIS CARDINALS WON SERIES, 4–3)

GAME 1

Astros	2	0	0	2	0	0	0	2	1		**7**
Cardinals	2	0	0	0	2	6	0	0	x		**10**

W—Williams. **L**—Qualls. **SV**—Isringhausen. **E**—Hou: Vizcaino. **LOB**—Hou: 4; StL: 6. **2B**—Hou: Palmeiro, Biggio; StL: Williams, Walker, Edmonds. **3B**—StL: Walker. **HR**—Hou: Beltran, Kent, Berkman, Lamb; StL: Pujols. **S**—StL: Matheny. **SB**—StL: Womack. **GIDP**—StL: Sanders. **HBP**—StL: Edmonds. **T**—3:15. **A**—52,323.

Recap: Ahead 4–3 in the fifth inning, the Astros fell behind 10–4 in the sixth when Cardinal hitters battered Astro relievers Chad Qualls and Chad Harville. Astro rightfielder Lance Berkman closed the gap in the eighth inning with a two-run home run. A solo homer in the ninth by pinch-hitter Mike Lamb brought the Astros even closer, but reliever Jason Isringhausen got the last out for the Cardinals.

GAME 2

Astros	1	0	0	1	1	0	1	0	0		**4**
Cardinals	0	0	0	0	4	0	0	2	x		**6**

W—Tavarez. **L**—Miceli. **SV**—Isringhausen. **E**—Hou: Munro. **LOB**—Hou: 11; StL: 4. **2B**—Hou: Kent, Berkman; StL: Edmonds. **HR**—Hou: Beltran, Ensberg; StL: Walker, Rolen, 2; Pujols. **S**—StL: Morris. **SB**—StL: Womack. **CS**—Hou: Bagwell, Ensberg. **WP**—StL: Morris, 2. **T**—3:02. **A**—52,347.

Recap: Astro pitcher Pete Munro held his own against Cardinal ace Matt Morris, pitching four shutout innings before giving up a two-run homer to rightfielder Larry Walker in the fifth. The Astros were able to keep the game close, but two home runs by the Cardinals in the eighth sealed the win. Houston suddenly found itself in a two-games-to-none hole.

GAME 3

Cardinals	1	1	0	0	0	0	0	0	0		**2**
Astros	3	0	0	0	0	0	2	x			**5**

W—Clemens. **L**—Suppan. **SV**—Lidge. **LOB**—StL: 7; Hou: 5. **2B**—Hou: Beltran. **HR**—StL: Walker, Edmonds; Hou: Kent, Beltran, Berkman. **WP**—Hou: Clemens. **GIDP**—Hou: Bagwell. **HBP**—StL: Anderson. **T**—2:57. **A**—42,896.

Recap: Roger Clemens grounded the Cardinals with a 5–2 victory in Game 3. "The Rocket" hit his stride as the game went on, striking out seven of the last 13 batters he faced. He left after seven innings and reliever Brad Lidge closed out the victory.

GAME 4

Cardinals	3	0	1	1	0	0	0	0	0		**5**
Astros	1	0	2	0	0	2	1	0	x		**6**

W—Wheeler. **L**—Tavarez. **SV**—Lidge. **LOB**—StL: 8; Hou: 6. **2B**—StL: Rolen; Hou: Bagwell, Berkman, Vizcaino. **HR**—StL: Pujols; Hou: Berkman, Beltran. **S**—StL: Taguchi. **SF**—StL: Edmonds. **WP**—StL: Tavarez. **GIDP**—Hou: Ensberg. **HBP**—Hou: Kent. **CS**—Hou: Biggio. **PB**—Hou: Chavez. **T**—3:01. **A**—42,760.

Recap: The Astros, powered by centerfielder Carlos Beltran's solo homer in the seventh inning, came from behind to beat the Cardinals, 6–5. After giving up the run, Cardinal pitcher Julian Tavarez lost his cool, hitting one batter with a pitch and later smashing the dugout phone.

GAME 5

Cardinals	0	0	0	0	0	0	0	0	0		**0**
Astros	0	0	0	0	0	0	0	3			**3**

W—Lidge. **L**—Isringhausen. **LOB**—StL: 3; Hou: 4. **HR**—Hou: Kent. **SB**—Hou: Beltran. **HBP**—Hou: Ensberg. **T**—2:33. **A**—43,045.

Recap: The Astros scored three runs, including a homer by second baseman Jeff Kent, to take a 3–2 lead in the series. Cardinal pitcher Woody Williams gave up just one hit in seven innings but Houston's bats came alive in the ninth inning with reliever Jason Isringhausen of the Cardinals on the mound. Astro pitcher Brandon Backe lasted eight innings and gave up just one hit. Reliever Brad Lidge took over in the ninth and earned the win.

KEY W=winning pitcher; L=losing pitcher; SV=save; E=errors; LOB=left on base; S=single; SF=sacrifice fly; 2B=double; 3B=triple; HR=home run; SB=stolen bases; CS=caught stealing; HBP=hit by pitch; GIDP=grounded into double plays; WP=wild pitch; PB=passed ball; T=time; A=attendance

NATIONAL LEAGUE CHAMPIONSHIP SERIES (cont.)

GAME 6

Astros	1	0	1	1	0	0	0	0	1	0	0	0	**4**
Cardinals	2	0	2	0	0	0	0	0	0	0	0	2	**6**

W—Tavarez. **L**—Miceli. **LOB**—Hou: 9; StL: 10. **2B**—Hou: Bagwell, Kent; StL: Pujols, Sanders, 2; Rolen. **HR**—Hou: Lamb; StL: Pujols, Edmonds. **S**—Hou: Bruntlett. **SF**—Hou: Berkman. **GIDP**—Hou: Lamb. **HBP**—Hou: Ensberg. **SB**—Hou: Beltran, 2; Bagwell. **CS**—Hou: Vizcaino. **T**—3:54. **A**—52,144.

Recap: Centerfielder Jim Edmonds launched the decisive homer in the 12th inning for the Redbirds and the Cardinals forced a Game 7 with a 6–4 win. Pitcher Dan Miceli was the fifth reliever to take the mound for the Astros and the first to give up a run.

GAME 7

Astros	1	0	1	0	0	0	0	0	0	**2**
Cardinals	0	0	1	0	0	3	0	1	x	**5**

E—StL: Edmonds. **W**—Suppan. **L**—Clemens. **SV**—Isringhausen. **LOB**—Hou: 5; StL: 2. **2B**—StL: Womack, Pujols, Anderson. **HR**—Hou: Biggio; StL: Rolen. **S**—StL: Suppan, Renteria, 2. **GIDP**—StL: Rolen. **SB**—Hou: Beltran. **T**—2:51. **A**—52,140.

Recap: It looked as though Roger Clemens would carry the Astros to the World Series. But he gave up three runs in the sixth inning, including a go-ahead two-run homer to Scott Rolen. An insurance run in the eighth gave the Cards a three-run victory and a trip to the World Series.

MLB 2004 PLAYOFFS – AMERICAN LEAGUE

AMERICAN LEAGUE DIVISION SERIES

October 5	Twins 2, Yankees 0	October 8	Yankees 8, Twins 4
October 6	Yankees 7, Twins 6	October 9	Yankees 6, Twins 5

(NEW YORK YANKEES WON SERIES, 3–1)

October 5	Red Sox 9, Angels 3	October 8	Red Sox 8, Angels 6
October 6	Red Sox 8, Angels 3		

(BOSTON RED SOX WON SERIES, 3–0)

AMERICAN LEAGUE CHAMPIONSHIP SERIES

October 12	Yankees 10, Red Sox 7	October 18	Red Sox 5, Yankees 4
October 13	Yankees 3, Red Sox 1	October 19	Red Sox 4, Yankees 2
October 16	Yankees 19, Red Sox 8	October 20	Red Sox 10, Yankees 3
October 17	Red Sox 6, Yankees 4		

(BOSTON RED SOX WON SERIES, 4–3)

GAME 1

Red Sox	0	0	0	0	0	0	5	2	0	**7**
Yankees	2	0	4	0	0	0	2	2	x	**10**

W—Mussina. **L**—Schilling. **SV**—Rivera. **LOB**—Bos: 2; NY: 8. **2B**—Bos: Bellhorn, Millar; NY: Sheffield, Matsui, 2; Williams. **3B**—Bos: Ortiz. **HR**—Bos: Varitek; NY: Lofton. **SF**—NY: Posada. **GIDP**—Bos: Mueller; NY: Rodriguez. **HBP**—NY: Posada. **PB**—NY: Posada. **T**—3:20. **A**—56,135.

Recap: Mike Mussina pitched 6 ⅔ innings of perfect baseball and the Yankees had an 8–0 lead going into the seventh inning. But the Red Sox rallied in the seventh and drew to within one run in the eighth, thanks to a two-run triple by designated hitter David Ortiz. Mariano Rivera earned the save for the Yanks by getting Red Sox third baseman Bill Mueller into a game-ending double play.

GAME 2

Red Sox	0	0	0	0	0	0	0	1	0	**1**
Yankees	1	0	0	0	0	2	0	0	x	**3**

W—Lieber. **L**—Martinez. **SV**—Rivera. **LOB**—Bos: 4; NY: 11. **2B**—Bos: Varitek, Ramirez. **HR**—NY: Olerud. **GIDP**—Bos: Millar. **SB**—NY: Jeter. **HBP**—NY: Rodriguez. **T**—3:15. **A**—56,136.

Recap: Yankee pitcher Jon Lieber went head-to-head with Red Sox ace Pedro Martinez and won the duel. Lieber lasted through the seventh inning, allowing just three hits and one earned run. Martinez allowed four hits and three runs in six innings. Slumping Red Sox centerfielder Johnny Damon went 0-for-4 for the second straight game.

GAME 3

Yankees	3	0	3	5	2	0	4	0	2	**19**
Red Sox	0	4	2	0	0	0	2	0	0	**8**

W—Vazquez. **L**—Mendoza. **E**—NY: Jeter. **LOB**—NY: 7; Bos: 9. **2B**—NY: Rodriguez, 2; Sierra, Matsui, 2; Sheffield, Williams, Posada; Bos: Mueller, Millar, Cabrera, 2; Nixon. **3B**—NY: Sierra. **HR**—NY: Matsui, 2; Rodriguez, Sheffield; Bos: Nixon, Varitek. **GIDP**—NY: Posada. **WP**—NY: Brown, Gordon. **HBP**—NY: Cairo. **T**—4:20. **A**—35,126.

Recap: The Yankees set several League Championship Series game records as they pounded the Red Sox. New York set marks for the most runs (19) and extra base hits (13), and tied the record for most hits (22), doubles (8), and home runs (4). The game was also the longest nine-inning contest in post-season history.

GAME 4

Yankees	0	0	2	0	0	2	0	0	0	0	0	0	**4**
Red Sox	0	0	0	3	0	0	0	1	0	0	2		**6**

W—Leskanic. **L**—Quantrill. **E**—NY: Clark. **LOB**—NY: 14; Bos: 10. **2B**—NY: Matsui. **3B**—NY: Matsui. **HR**—NY: Rodriguez; Bos: Ortiz. **S**—NY: Cairo, Jeter. Bos: Mientkiewicz. **GIDP**—Bos: Mueller. **SB**—Bos: Roberts, Damon. **WP**—Bos: Timlin. **T**—5:02. **A**—34,826.

Recap: The Yankees were three outs away from the World Series, but Mariano Rivera blew the save as pinch-runner Dave Roberts scored the tying run in the ninth. David Ortiz hit a two-run homer in the 12th to keep the Red Sox alive.

AMERICAN LEAGUE CHAMPIONSHIP SERIES (cont.)

GAME 5

Yankees	0	1	0	0	0	3	0	0	0	0	0	0	0	0	**4**
Red Sox	2	0	0	0	0	0	0	2	0	0	0	0	0	1	**5**

W—Wakefield. **L**—Loaiza. **E**—NY: Jeter; Bos: Ramirez. **LOB**—NY: 18; Bos: 12. **2B**—NY: Jeter, Cairo, Clark; Bos: Bellhorn, Mientkiewicz. **HR**—NY: Williams; Bos: Ortiz. **S**—NY: Jeter. **SF**—Bos: Varitek. **GIDP**—NY: Sheffield; Bos: Ramirez, Cabrera. **PB**—Bos: Varitek, 3. **HBP**—NY: Cairo, Rodriguez. **CS**—Bos: Damon, Ortiz. **T**—5:49. **A**—35,120.

Recap: For the second day in a row, Mariano Rivera couldn't hold a lead for the Yankees, while David Ortiz came through for the Red Sox again. Ortiz hit an RBI single off Esteban Loaiza in the 14th inning to give Boston a 5–4 victory.

GAME 6

Red Sox	0	0	0	4	0	0	0	0	0	**4**
Yankees	0	0	0	0	0	0	1	1	0	**2**

W—Schilling. **L**—Lieber. **SV**—Foulke. **LOB**— Bos: 7; NY: 6. **2B**—Bos: Millar; NY: Cairo, 2. **HR**—Bos: Bellhorn; NY: Williams. **GIDP**— Bos: Bellhorn, Mueller. **SB**—Bos: Cabrera. **WP**—NY: Lieber. **HBP**—Bos: Mueller. **T**—3:50. **A**—56,128.

Recap: Red Sox pitcher Curt Schilling overcame an injured ankle to lead Boston to a decisive Game 7. Schilling lasted seven innings, giving up four hits and one run. He struck out four batters. But the turning point for the Red Sox came in the fourth inning. A slumping Mark Bellhorn hit a shot to deep left field, which was ruled a two-run double. The call was overturned to a three-run homer because the ball had hit a fan before bouncing back into play.

GAME 7

Red Sox	2	4	0	2	0	0	0	1	1	**10**
Yankees	0	0	1	0	0	0	2	0	0	**3**

W—Lowe. **L**—Brown. **E**—NY: Loaiza. **LOB**— Bos: 9; NY: 5. **2B**—NY: Matsui, Williams. **HR**—Bos: Ortiz, Damon, 2; Bellhorn. **SF**—Bos: Cabrera. **GIDP**—Bos: Damon. **SB**—NY: Cairo. Bos: Damon. **HBP**—NY: Cairo. **T**—3:31. **A**—56,129.

Recap: No team had ever come back from a 3–0 deficit to win a major league playoff series. Until now. The Red Sox defeated the Yankees, gaining sweet revenge from 2003 when they lost to New York in Game 7. David Ortiz got the Sox started with a two-run homer in the first inning. He was named the ALCS MVP. Johnny Damon hit a grand slam and a two-run homer. Derek Lowe allowed just one hit in six innings.

2004 WORLD SERIES

October 23	Red Sox 11, Cardinals 9	October 26	Red Sox 4, Cardinals 1
October 24	Red Sox 6, Cardinals 2	October 27	Red Sox 3, Cardinals 0

(BOSTON RED SOX WON SERIES, 4–0)

GAME 1

Cardinals	0	1	1	3	0	2	0	2	0	**9**
Red Sox	4	0	3	0	0	0	2	2	x	**11**

W—Foulke. **L**—Tavarez. **E**—StL: Renteria; Bos: Millar, Arroyo, Ramirez, 2. **LOB**—StL: 9; Bos: 12. **2B**—StL: Walker, 2; Renteria, Anderson; Bos: Damon, Millar. **HR**—StL: Walker; Bos: Ortiz, Bellhorn. **S**—StL: Womack. **SF**—StL: Matheny, 2. **GIDP**—StL: Rolen. **PB**—Bos: Mirabelli. **HBP**—Bos: Cabrera; StL: Pujols. **T**—4:00. **A**—35,035.

Recap: The Cardinals rallied after falling behind, 7–2, but the Red Sox didn't let up. Boston's offense (13 hits) made up for its sloppy defense (4 errors, including 2 by leftfielder Manny Ramirez). Red Sox second baseman Mark Bellhorn hit a two-run homer to break an eighth-inning tie and give Boston the victory.

GAME 2

Cardinals	0	0	0	1	0	0	0	1	0	**2**
Red Sox	2	0	0	2	0	2	0	0	x	**6**

W—Schilling. **L**—Morris. **E**—Bos: Bellhorn, Mueller, 3. **LOB**—StL: 6; Bos: 9. **2B**—StL: Pujols, 2; Bos: Mueller, Bellhorn. **3B**—Bos: Varitek. **SF**—StL: Rolen. **GIDP**—StL: Renteria; Bos: Bellhorn. **HBP**—Bos: Millar, Varitek. **T**—3:20. **A**—35,001.

Recap: Boston's defense performed sloppily again, committing four errors for the second straight game. But the Cardinals were unable to use that to their advantage. The Red Sox got two runs in the first inning off St. Louis starter Matt Morris and the Sox never looked back.

GAME 3

Red Sox	1	0	0	1	2	0	0	0	0	**4**
Cardinals	0	0	0	0	0	0	0	0	1	**1**

W—Martinez. **L**—Suppan. **LOB**—Bos: 8; StL: 3. **2B**—Bos: Mueller, Damon, Cabrera; StL: Renteria. **HR**—Bos: Ramirez; StL: Walker. **HBP**—Bos: Bellhorn. **T**—2:58. **A**—52,015.

Recap: Red Sox ace Pedro Martinez shut down the Cardinals to put his team within one win of a championship. Martinez held St. Louis to just three hits in seven shutout innings. He retired the last 14 batters he faced.

GAME 4

Red Sox	1	0	2	0	0	0	0	0	0	**3**
Cardinals	0	0	0	0	0	0	0	0	0	**0**

W—Lowe. **L**—Marquis. **SV**—Foulke. **LOB**—Bos: 12; StL: 6. **2B**—Bos: Nixon, 3; Ortiz; StL: Renteria. **3B**—Bos: Damon. **HR**—Bos: Damon. **S**—Bos: Lowe; StL: Walker. **SB**—StL: Sanders. **WP**—Bos: Lowe. **T**—3:14. **A**—52,037.

Recap: The Boston Red Sox won their first World Series since 1918 and became the third straight wild-card team to win the championship. Derek Lowe pitched seven strong innings for the Sox, giving up three hits and one walk, while striking out four. Manny Ramirez earned MVP honors, batting .412 for the Series.

TODAY'S STARS

Former American League MVP Miguel Tejada joined the Baltimore Orioles in 2004 and led the majors in RBIs (150).

■ **Miguel Tejada, shortstop,** b. May 25, 1976, Bani, Dominican Republic. Tejada signed a six-year contract with the Baltimore Orioles before the 2004 season and established himself as baseball's best offensive shortstop. He led the major leagues with a career-best 150 RBIs and added career-highs in batting average (.311), slugging percentage (.534), and on-base percentage (.360). Tejada played in his second All-Star Game in 2004 and won the Home Run Derby. Prior to joining the O's, Tejada spent six seasons with the Oakland A's. He helped the team to four straight post-season appearances and was named the American League MVP in 2002.

■ **Vladimir Guerrero, rightfielder,** b. February 9, 1976, Nizao Bani, Dominican Republic. Guerrero had the biggest impact of any player on a new team during the 2004 regular season. He signed a five-year $70 million deal with the Anaheim (now Los Angeles) Angels, then led them to the American League West title. Guerrero finished in the Top 5 in the league in batting average (.337), home runs (39), RBIs (126), slugging percentage (.598), hits (206), and runs (124). Guerrero carried the Angels down the stretch and easily won the American League MVP award.

■ **Roger Clemens, pitcher,** b. August 4, 1962, Dayton, Ohio. Clemens has long been considered one of the best pitchers of his generation. In 2004, he strengthened his case as one of the best pitchers of *any* generation. At age 41, he joined the Houston Astros in a new league (National) and still dominated opposing batters. His sparkling 18–4 record, 2.98 ERA, and 218 strikeouts earned Clemens his major-league-record seventh Cy Young Award. He also started the All-Star Game for the third time and pitched the Astros to a wild-card playoff berth and the franchise's first post-season series victory. Clemens had previously won Cy Young Awards with the Boston Red Sox (three), Toronto Blue Jays (two), and New York Yankees (one). He is second all-time in strikeouts (4,317) and is the only pitcher with two 20-strikeout games.

SIMON BRUTY/SPORTS ILLUSTRATED

TRIVIA CHALLENGE

The last three World Series winners were wild-card teams. Which team was the first wild-card entrant to win the World Series?

The Florida Marlins in 1997

MLB 2004 PLAYOFFS COMPOSITE BOX SCORES

NATIONAL LEAGUE CHAMPIONSHIP SERIES

ST. LOUIS CARDINALS

BATTING	AB	R	H	HR	RBI	BA
Rolen	29	6	9	3	6	.310
Walker	29	6	7	2	5	.241
Pujols	28	10	14	4	9	.500
Womack	26	5	7	0	1	.269
Edmonds	24	2	7	2	7	.292
Renteria	24	1	4	0	2	.167
Sanders	21	1	4	0	0	.190
Matheny	19	0	2	0	0	.105
Cedeno	6	1	1	0	1	.167
Mabry	6	0	1	0	1	.167
Luna	4	0	0	0	0	.000
Molina	4	0	1	0	0	.250
Williams	4	1	1	0	0	.250
Anderson	3	1	1	0	0	.333
Marquis	2	0	1	0	0	.500
Morris	2	0	0	0	0	.000
Suppan	2	0	0	0	1	.000
Taguchi	2	0	0	0	0	.000

PITCHING	G	IP	H	BB	SO	ERA
Williams	2	13.0	5	3	9	2.77
Suppan	2	12.0	8	4	9	3.00
Morris	2	10.0	11	8	6	5.40
Isringhausen	6	7.2	4	4	3	4.70
Calero	5	7.0	8	1	7	3.86
Tavarez	5	6.0	3	2	3	3.00
Marquis	1	4.0	5	2	2	6.75
Haren	2	1.2	3	0	2	10.80
King	4	1.2	4	0	1	10.80
Eldred	1	0.1	0	1	0	0.00

HOUSTON ASTROS

BATTING	AB	R	H	HR	RBI	BA
Biggio	32	3	6	1	1	.188
Vizcaino	28	1	7	0	0	.250
Bagwell	27	1	7	0	3	.259
Kent	25	3	6	3	7	.240
Beltran	24	12	10	4	5	.417
Berkman	24	7	7	3	9	.292
Ensberg	22	2	3	1	2	.136
Ausmus	19	0	2	0	0	.105
Palmeiro	6	0	2	0	0	.333
Backe	5	0	0	0	0	.000
Lamb	5	2	2	2	2	.400
Chavez	4	0	1	1	1	.250
Clemens	4	0	0	0	0	.000
Bruntlett	2	0	0	0	0	.000
Munro	2	0	0	0	0	.000
Oswalt	2	0	0	0	0	.000
Everett	1	0	0	0	0	.000
Lane	1	0	0	0	0	.000

PITCHING	G	IP	H	BB	SO	ERA
Clemens	2	13.0	10	2	9	4.15
Backe	2	12.2	6	4	10	2.84
Lidge	4	8.0	1	2	14	0.00
Oswalt	2	8.0	11	4	2	6.75
Munro	2	7.0	14	1	5	9.00
Wheeler	4	7.0	4	0	9	0.00
Qualls	2	4.0	8	2	4	11.25
Harville	3	1.1	3	1	3	13.50
Miceli	2	1.1	3	1	0	27.00

AMERICAN LEAGUE CHAMPIONSHIP SERIES

BOSTON RED SOX

BATTING	AB	R	H	HR	RBI	BA
Damon	35	5	6	2	7	.171
Ortiz	31	6	12	3	11	.387
Mueller	30	4	8	0	1	.267
Ramirez	30	3	9	0	0	.300
Cabrera	29	5	11	0	5	.379
Nixon	29	4	6	1	3	.207
Varitek	28	5	9	2	7	.321
Bellhorn	26	3	5	2	4	.192
Millar	24	4	6	0	2	.250
Mientkiewicz	4	0	2	0	0	.500
Kapler	3	0	1	0	0	.333
Mirabelli	1	0	0	0	0	.000
Reese	1	0	0	0	0	.000
Roberts	0	2	0	0	0	.000

PITCHING	G	IP	H	BB	SO	ERA
Martinez	3	13.0	14	9	14	6.23
Lowe	2	11.1	7	1	6	3.18
Schilling	2	10.0	10	2	5	6.30
Wakefield	3	7.1	9	3	6	8.59
Foulke	5	6.0	1	6	6	0.00
Timlin	5	5.2	10	5	2	4.76
Embree	6	4.2	9	1	2	3.86
Arroyo	3	4.0	8	2	3	15.75
Leskanic	3	2.2	3	3	2	10.12
Myers	3	2.1	5	1	4	7.71
Mendoza	2	2.0	2	0	1	4.50

NEW YORK YANKEES

BATTING	AB	R	H	HR	RBI	BA
Williams	36	4	11	2	10	.306
Matsui	34	9	14	2	10	.412
Rodriguez	31	8	8	2	5	.258
Jeter	30	5	6	0	5	.200
Sheffield	30	7	10	1	5	.333
Posada	27	4	7	0	2	.259
Cairo	25	4	7	0	0	.280
Clark	21	0	3	0	1	.143
Sierra	21	1	7	0	3	.333
Olerud	12	1	2	1	2	.167
Lofton	10	1	3	1	2	.300
Crosby	0	1	0	0	0	.000

PITCHING	G	IP	H	BB	SO	ERA
Lieber	2	14.1	12	1	5	3.14
Mussina	2	12.2	10	2	15	4.26
Rivera	5	7.0	6	2	6	1.29
Gordon	6	6.2	10	2	3	8.10
Loaiza	2	6.1	5	3	5	1.42
Vazquez	2	6.1	9	7	6	9.95
Hernandez	1	5.0	3	5	6	5.40
Brown	2	3.1	9	4	2	21.60
Quantrill	4	3.1	8	0	2	5.40
Sturtze	4	3.1	2	2	2	2.70
Heredia	3	1.1	1	0	1	0.00

KEY AB=at-bats; R=runs; H=hits; HR=home runs; RBI=runs batted in; BA=batting average; G=games; IP=innings pitched; BB=bases on balls; SO=strikeouts; ERA=earned run average

2004 WORLD SERIES COMPOSITE BOX SCORES

BOSTON RED SOX

BATTING	AB	R	H	HR	RBI	BA
Damon	21	4	6	1	2	.286
Cabrera	17	3	4	0	3	.235
Ramirez	17	2	7	1	4	.412
Mueller	14	3	6	0	2	.429
Nixon	14	1	5	0	3	.357
Ortiz	13	3	4	1	4	.308
Varitek	13	2	2	0	2	.154
Bellhorn	10	3	3	1	4	.300
Millar	8	2	1	0	0	.125
Mirabelli	3	1	1	0	0	.333
Kapler	2	0	0	0	0	.000
Lowe	2	0	0	0	0	.000
Martinez	2	0	0	0	0	.000
Mientkiewicz	1	0	0	0	0	.000
Reese	1	0	0	0	0	.000
Arroyo	0	0	0	0	0	.000
Embree	0	0	0	0	0	.000
Foulke	0	0	0	0	0	.000
Timlin	0	0	0	0	0	.000

PITCHING	G	IP	H	BB	SO	ERA
Lowe	1	7.0	3	1	4	0.00
Martinez	1	7.0	3	2	6	0.00
Schilling	1	6.0	4	1	4	0.00
Foulke	4	5.0	4	1	8	1.80
Wakefield	1	3.2	3	5	2	12.27
Timlin	3	3.0	2	1	0	6.00
Arroyo	2	2.2	4	1	4	6.75
Embree	3	1.2	1	0	4	0.00

ST. LOUIS CARDINALS

BATTING	AB	R	H	HR	RBI	BA
Edmonds	15	2	1	0	0	.067
Pujols	15	1	5	0	0	.333
Renteria	15	2	5	0	1	.333
Rolen	15	0	0	0	1	.000
Walker	14	2	5	2	3	.357
Womack	11	1	2	0	0	.182
Sanders	9	1	0	0	0	.000
Matheny	8	0	2	0	2	.250
Anderson	6	0	1	0	0	.167
Cedeno	4	1	1	0	0	.250
Mabry	4	0	0	0	0	.000
Taguchi	4	1	1	0	1	.250
Molina	3	0	0	0	0	.000
Luna	1	0	0	0	0	.000
Marquis	1	1	0	0	0	.000
Suppan	1	0	1	0	0	1.000
Calero	0	0	0	0	0	.000
Haren	0	0	0	0	0	.000
Isringhausen	0	0	0	0	0	.000
King	0	0	0	0	0	.000
Reyes	0	0	0	0	0	.000
Tavarez	0	0	0	0	0	.000

PITCHING	G	IP	H	BB	SO	ERA
Marquis	2	7.0	6	7	4	3.86
Haren	2	4.2	4	3	2	0.00
Suppan	1	4.2	8	1	4	7.71
Morris	1	4.1	4	4	3	8.31
King	3	2.2	1	1	1	0.00
Williams	1	2.1	8	3	1	27.00
Isringhausen	1	2.0	1	1	2	0.00
Tavarez	2	2.0	1	0	1	4.50
Eldred	2	1.2	4	0	2	10.80
Calero	2	1.1	2	4	0	13.50
Reyes	2	1.1	0	0	0	0.00

DID YOU KNOW?

The American League team that has the longest World Series title drought is now the Chicago White Sox. They last won the Series in 1917. The Sox' local rivals, the Cubs, haven't won a Series since 1908, the longest drought in baseball.

BASEBALL

2004 MLB INDIVIDUAL LEADERS

NATIONAL LEAGUE BATTING

BATTING AVERAGE	
Barry Bonds, SF	.362
Todd Helton, Col	.347
Mark Loretta, SD	.335
Adrian Beltre, LA	.334
Albert Pujols, StL	.331
Juan Pierre, Fla	.326
Sean Casey, Cin	.324
Jason Kendall, Pitt	.319
Aramis Ramirez, Chi	.318
Lance Berkman, Hou	.316
Johnny Estrada, Atl	.314
Scott Rolen, StL	.314

HITS	
Juan Pierre, Fla	221
Mark Loretta, SD	208
Jack Wilson, Pitt	201
Adrian Beltre, LA	200
Albert Pujols, StL	196
Cesar Izturis, LA	193
Todd Helton, Col	190
Jimmy Rollins, Phil	190
Sean Casey, Cin	185
Jason Kendall, Pitt	183
Craig Biggio, Hou	178

DOUBLES	
Lyle Overbay, Mil	53
Albert Pujols, StL	51
Todd Helton, Col	49
Bobby Abreu, Phil	47
Craig Biggio, Hou	47
Mark Loretta, SD	47

TRIPLES	
Juan Pierre, Fla	12
Jimmy Rollins, Phil	12
Jack Wilson, Pitt	12
Cesar Izturis, LA	9
Four tied with 8.	

HOME RUNS	
Adrian Beltre, LA	48
Adam Dunn, Cin	46
Albert Pujols, StL	46
Barry Bonds, SF	45
Jim Edmonds, StL	42
Jim Thome, Phil	42
Moises Alou, Chi	39
Jeromy Burnitz, Col	37
Steve Finley, LA	36
Aramis Ramirez, Chi	36

RUNS SCORED	
Albert Pujols, Stl	133
Barry Bonds, SF	129
Jimmy Rollins, Phil	119
Bobby Abreu, Phil	118
J.D. Drew, Atl	118
Todd Helton, Col	115
Brad Wilkerson, Mon	112
Scott Rolen, StL	109
Mark Loretta, SD	108
Moises Alou, Chi	106

TOTAL BASES	
Albert Pujols, StL	389
Adrian Beltre, LA	376
Todd Helton, Col	339
Moises Alou, Chi	335
Adam Dunn, Cin	323

STOLEN BASES	
Scott Podsednik, Mil	70
Juan Pierre, Fla	45
Bobby Abreu, Phil	40
Ryan Freel, Cin	37
Dave Roberts, LA	33
Endy Chavez, Mon	32

RUNS BATTED IN	
Vinny Castilla, Col	131
Scott Rolen, StL	124
Albert Pujols, StL	123
Adrian Beltre, LA	121
Miguel Cabrera, Fla	112
Jim Edmonds, StL	111
Tony Batista, Mon	110
Jeromy Burnitz, Col	110
Jeff Kent, Hou	107
Moises Alou, Chi	106

SLUGGING PERCENTAGE	
Barry Bonds, SF	.812
Albert Pujols, StL	.657
Jim Edmonds, StL	.643
Adrian Beltre, LA	.629
Todd Helton, Col	.620

ON-BASE PERCENTAGE	
Barry Bonds, SF	.609
Todd Helton, Col	.469
Lance Berkman, Hou	.450
J.D. Drew, Atl	.436
Bobby Abreu, Phil	.428

BASES ON BALLS	
Barry Bonds, SF	232
Bobby Abreu, Phil	127
Lance Berkman, Hou	127
Todd Helton, Col	127
J.D. Drew, Atl	118

Albert Pujols

NATIONAL LEAGUE PITCHING

EARNED RUN AVERAGE	
Jake Peavy, SD	2.27
Randy Johnson, Ari	2.60
Ben Sheets, Mil	2.70
Carlos Zambrano, Chi	2.75
Roger Clemens, Hou	2.98
Oliver Perez, Pitt	2.98
Carl Pavano, Fla	3.00
Jason Schmidt, SF	3.20
Al Leiter, NY	3.21
Odalis Perez, LA	3.25

SAVES	
Armando Benitez, Fla	47
Jason Isringhausen, StL	47
Eric Gagne, LA	45
John Smoltz, Atl	44
Jose Mesa, Pitt	43
Danny Graves, Cin	41
Trevor Hoffman, SD	41
Dan Kolb, Mil	39
Shawn Chacon, Col	35
Brad Lidge, Hou	29
Braden Looper, NY	29

Note: Players listed under batting average must have had at least 3.1 plate appearances per game.

WINS	
Roy Oswalt, Hou	20
Roger Clemens, Hou	18
Carl Pavano, Fla	18
Jason Schmidt, SF	18
Randy Johnson, Ari	16
Greg Maddux, Chi	16
Jeff Suppan, StL	16
Carlos Zambrano, Chi	16
Eight tied with 15.	

GAMES PITCHED	
Jim Brower, SF	89
Ray King, StL	86
Rheal Cormier, Phil	84
Chris Reitsma, Atl	84
Salomon Torres, Pitt	84

INNINGS PITCHED	
Livan Hernandez, Mon	255.0
Randy Johnson, Ari	245.2
Roy Oswalt, Hou	237.0
Ben Sheets, Mil	237.0
Jason Schmidt, SF	225.0
Carl Pavano, Fla	222.1
Jeff Weaver, LA	220.0
Roger Clemens, Hou	214.1

STRIKEOUTS	
Randy Johnson, Ari	290
Ben Sheets, Mil	264
Jason Schmidt, SF	251
Oliver Perez, Pitt	239
Roger Clemens, Hou	218
Roy Oswalt, Hou	206
Matt Clement, Chi	190
Carlos Zambrano, Chi	188
Livan Hernandez, Mon	186
Jake Peavy, SD	173

COMPLETE GAMES	
Livan Hernandez, Mon	9
Cory Lidle, Phil	5
Ben Sheets, Mil	5
Randy Johnson, Ari	4
Jason Schmidt, SF	4

SHUTOUTS	
Cory Lidle, Phil	3
Jason Schmidt, SF	3
Six tied with 2.	

AMERICAN LEAGUE BATTING

BATTING AVERAGE

Ichiro Suzuki, Sea	.372
Melvin Mora, Bal	.340
Vladimir Guerrero, Ana	.337
Ivan Rodriguez, Det	.334
Erubiel Durzao, Oak	.321
Carlos Guillen, Det	.318
Javy Lopez, Bal	.316
Mark Kotsay, Oak	.314
Michael Young, Tex	.313
Travis Hafner, Cle	.311
Miguel Tejada, Bal	.311

HITS

Ichiro Suzuki, Sea	262
Michael Young, Tex	216
Vladimir Guerrero, Ana	206
Miguel Tejada, Bal	203
Mark Kotsay, Oak	190
Johnny Damon, Bos	189
Derek Jeter, NY	188
Melvin Mora, Bal	187
Carl Crawford, TB	185
Javy Lopez, Bal	183

DOUBLES

Brian Roberts, Bal	50
Ronnie Belliard, Cle	48
David Ortiz, Bos	47
Derek Jeter, NY	44
Manny Ramirez, Bos	44
Three tied with 41.	

TRIPLES

Carl Crawford, TB	19
Chone Figgins, Ana	17
Carlos Guillen, Det	10
Omar Infante, Det	9
Michael Young, Tex	9
Jose Cruz, TB	8
Five tied with 7.	

HOME RUNS

Manny Ramirez, Bos	43
Paul Konerko, Chi	41
David Ortiz, Bos	41
Vladimir Guerrero, Ana	39
Mark Teixeira, Tex	38
Alex Rodriguez, NY	36
Gary Sheffield, NY	36
Miguel Tejada, Bal	34
Hank Blalock, Tex	32
Carlos Delgado, Tor	32

RUNS SCORED

Vladimir Guerrero, Ana	124
Johnny Damon, Bos	123
Gary Sheffield, NY	117
Michael Young, Tex	114
Alex Rodriguez, NY	112
Derek Jeter, NY	111
Melvin Mora, Bal	111
Matt Lawton, Cle	109
Hideki Matsui, NY	109
Manny Ramirez, Bos	108
Three tied with 107.	

TOTAL BASES

Vladimir Guerrero, Ana	366
David Ortiz, Bos	351
Miguel Tejada, Bal	349
Manny Ramirez, Bos	348
Michael Young, Tex	333
Ichiro Suzuki, Sea	320

STOLEN BASES

Carl Crawford, TB	59
Ichiro Suzuki, Sea	36
Chone Figgins, Ana	34
Brian Roberts, Bal	29
Alex Rodriguez, NY	28

RUNS BATTED IN

Miguel Tejada, Bal	150
David Ortiz, Bos	139
Manny Ramirez, Bos	130
Vladimir Guerrero, Ana	126
Gary Sheffield, NY	121
Paul Konerko, Chi	117
Mark Teixeira, Tex	112
Hank Blalock, Tex	110
Travis Hafner, Cle	109

SLUGGING PERCENTAGE

Manny Ramirez, Bos	.613
David Ortiz, Bos	.603
Vladimir Guerrero, Ana	.598
Travis Hafner, Cle	.583
Melvin Mora, Bal	.562

ON-BASE PERCENTAGE

Melvin Mora, Bal	.419
Ichiro Suzuki, Sea	.414
Travis Hafner, Cle	.410
Jorge Posada, NY	.400
Eric Chavez, Oak	.397
Manny Ramirez, Bos	.397

BASES ON BALLS

Eric Chavez, Oak	95
Gary Sheffield, NY	92
Mark Bellhorn, Bos	88
Hideki Matsui, NY	88
Jorge Posada, NY	88

AMERICAN LEAGUE PITCHING

EARNED RUN AVERAGE

Johan Santana, Min	2.61
Curt Schilling, Bos	3.26
Jake Westbrook, Cle	3.38
Brad Radke, Min	3.48
Tim Hudson, Oak	3.53
Rodrigo Lopez, Bal	3.59
Freddy Garcia, Chi	3.81
Mark Buehrle, Chi	3.89
Pedro Martinez, Bos	3.90
Kelvim Escobar, Ana	3.93
Rich Harden, Oak	3.99

SAVES

Mariano Rivera, NY	53
Francisco Cordero, Tex	49
Joe Nathan, Min	44
Troy Percival, Ana	33
Keith Foulke, Bos	32
Danys Baez, TB	30
Octavio Dotel, Oak	22
Jorge Julio, Bal	22
Ugueth Urbina, Det	21
Shingo Takatsu, Chi	19

WINS

Curt Schilling, Bos	21
Johan Santana, Min	20
Bartolo Colon, Ana	18
Kenny Rogers, Tex	18
Mark Mulder, Oak	17
Mark Buehrle, Chi	16
Pedro Martinez, Bos	16
Nine tied with 14.	

GAMES PITCHED

Paul Quantrill, NY	86
Tom Gordon, NY	80
Juan Rincon, Min	77
B.J. Ryan, Bal	76
Mike Timlin, Bos	76
Mike Myers, Bos	75

INNINGS PITCHED

Mark Buehrle, Chi	245.1
Johan Santana, Min	228.0
Curt Schilling, Bos	226.2
Mark Mulder, Oak	225.2
Brad Radke, Min	219.2

STRIKEOUTS

Johan Santana, Min	265
Pedro Martinez, Bos	227
Curt Schilling, Bos	203
Kelvim Escobar, Ana	191
Freddy Garcia, Chi	184
Jeremy Bonderman, Det	168
Ted Lilly, Tor	168
Rich Harden, Oak	167
Mark Buehrle, Chi	165
Barry Zito, Oak	163

COMPLETE GAMES

Mark Mulder, Oak	5
Sidney Ponson, Bal	5
Jake Westbrook, Cle	5
Mark Buehrle, Chi	4
Three tied with 3.	

SHUTOUTS

Jeremy Bonderman, Det	2
Tim Hudson, Oak	2
Sidney Ponson, Bal	2
Twenty-seven tied with 1.	

Mariano Rivera

BASEBALL

2004 REGULAR SEASON TEAM STATS

NATIONAL LEAGUE

TEAM BATTING	G	AB	R	H	2B	3B	HR	RBI	TB	BB	SO	SB	OBP	SLG	BA
St. Louis	162	5,555	855	1,544	319	24	214	817	2,553	548	1,085	111	.344	.460	.278
Colorado	162	5,577	833	1,531	331	34	202	795	2,536	568	1,181	44	.345	.455	.275
San Diego	162	5,573	768	1,521	304	32	139	722	2,306	566	910	52	.342	.414	.273
Atlanta	162	5,570	803	1,503	304	37	178	767	2,415	587	1,158	86	.343	.434	.270
San Francisco	162	5,546	850	1,500	314	33	183	805	2,429	705	874	43	.357	.438	.270
Chicago	162	5,628	789	1,508	308	29	235	755	2,579	489	1,080	66	.328	.458	.268
Houston	162	5,468	803	1,458	294	36	187	756	2,385	590	999	89	.342	.436	.267
Philadelphia	162	5,643	840	1,505	303	23	215	802	2,499	645	1,133	100	.345	.443	.267
Florida	162	5,486	718	1,447	275	32	148	677	2,230	499	968	96	.329	.406	.264
Los Angeles	162	5,542	761	1,450	226	30	203	731	2,345	536	1,092	102	.332	.423	.262
Pittsburgh	161	5,483	680	1,428	267	39	142	648	2,199	415	1,066	63	.321	.401	.260
Arizona	162	5,544	615	1,401	295	38	135	582	2,177	441	1,022	53	.310	.393	.253
Cincinnati	162	5,518	750	1,380	287	28	194	713	2,305	599	1,335	77	.331	.418	.250
Montreal	162	5,474	635	1,361	276	27	151	605	2,144	496	925	109	.313	.392	.249
New York	162	5,532	684	1,376	289	20	185	658	2,260	512	1,159	107	.317	.409	.249
Milwaukee	161	5,483	634	1,358	295	32	135	601	2,122	540	1,312	138	.321	.387	.248

TEAM PITCHING	W	L	ERA	CG	SHO	SV	INN	H	R	ER	BB	SO
Atlanta	96	66	3.74	4	13	48	1,450.0	1,475	668	603	523	1,025
St. Louis	105	57	3.75	4	12	57	1,453.2	1,378	659	605	440	1,041
Chicago	89	73	3.81	3	6	42	1,465.1	1,363	665	621	545	1,346
Los Angeles	93	69	4.01	2	6	51	1,453.1	1,386	684	647	521	1,066
San Diego	87	75	4.03	3	8	44	1,441.0	1,460	705	645	422	1,079
Houston	92	70	4.05	2	13	47	1,443.0	1,416	698	650	525	1,282
New York	71	91	4.09	2	6	31	1,449.0	1,452	731	658	592	977
Florida	83	79	4.10	6	14	53	1,439.0	1,395	700	655	513	1,116
Milwaukee	67	94	4.24	6	10	42	1,442.0	1,440	757	679	476	1,098
Pittsburgh	72	89	4.29	3	8	46	1,428.0	1,451	744	680	576	1,079
San Francisco	91	71	4.29	8	8	46	1,457.0	1,481	770	695	548	1,020
Montreal	67	95	4.33	11	11	31	1,447.0	1,477	769	696	582	1,032
Philadelphia	86	76	4.45	4	5	43	1,462.2	1,488	781	724	502	1,070
Arizona	51	111	4.98	5	6	33	1,436.0	1,480	899	794	668	1,153
Cincinnati	76	86	5.19	5	8	47	1,443.2	1,595	907	832	572	992
Colorado	68	64	5.54	3	2	36	1,435.1	1,634	923	883	697	947

AMERICAN LEAGUE

TEAM BATTING	G	AB	R	H	2B	3B	HR	RBI	TB	BB	SO	SB	OBP	SLG	BA
Anaheim	162	5,675	836	1,603	272	37	162	783	2,435	450	942	143	.341	.429	.282
Boston	162	5,720	949	1,613	373	25	222	912	2,702	659	1,189	68	.360	.472	.282
Baltimore	162	5,376	842	1,614	319	18	169	803	2,476	528	949	101	.345	.432	.281
Cleveland	162	5,676	858	1,565	345	29	184	820	2,520	606	1,009	94	.351	.444	.276
Detroit	162	5,623	827	1,531	284	54	201	800	2,526	518	1,144	86	.337	.449	.272
Oakland	162	5,728	793	1,545	336	15	189	752	2,478	608	1,061	47	.343	.433	.270
Seattle	162	5,722	698	1,544	276	20	136	658	2,268	492	1,058	110	.331	.396	.270
Chicago	163	5,534	865	1,481	284	19	242	823	2,529	499	1,030	78	.333	.457	.268
New York	162	5,527	897	1,483	281	20	242	863	2,530	670	982	84	.353	.458	.268
Minnesota	162	5,623	780	1,494	310	24	191	735	2,425	513	982	116	.332	.431	.266
Texas	162	5,615	860	1,492	323	34	227	825	2,564	500	1,099	69	.329	.457	.266
Toronto	161	5,531	719	1,438	290	34	145	680	2,231	513	1,083	58	.328	.403	.260
Kansas City	162	5,538	720	1,432	261	29	150	675	2,201	461	1,057	67	.322	.397	.259
Tampa Bay	161	5,483	714	1,416	278	46	145	685	2,221	469	944	132	.320	.405	.258

TEAM PITCHING	W	L	ERA	CG	SHO	SV	INN	H	R	ER	BB	SO
Minnesota	92	70	4.03	4	9	48	1,476.0	1,523	715	661	431	1,123
Oakland	91	71	4.17	10	8	35	1,471.1	1,466	742	682	544	1,034
Boston	98	64	4.18	4	12	36	1,451.1	1,430	768	674	447	1,132
Anaheim	92	70	4.28	2	11	50	1,454.1	1,476	734	692	502	1,164
Texas	89	73	4.53	5	9	52	1,439.2	1,536	794	724	547	979
New York	101	61	4.69	1	5	59	1,443.2	1,532	808	752	445	1,058
Baltimore	78	84	4.70	8	10	27	1,455.1	1,488	830	760	687	1,090
Seattle	63	99	4.76	7	7	28	1,459.1	1,498	823	772	575	1,036
Cleveland	80	82	4.81	8	8	32	1,466.2	1,553	857	784	579	1,115
Tampa Bay	70	91	4.81	3	5	35	1,417.0	1,459	842	757	580	923
Chicago	83	79	4.91	8	8	34	1,432.1	1,505	831	782	527	1,013
Toronto	67	94	4.91	6	11	37	1,421.0	1,505	823	775	608	956
Detroit	72	90	4.93	7	9	35	1,439.2	1,542	844	788	530	995
Kansas City	58	104	5.15	6	3	25	1,420.1	1,638	905	813	518	887

KEY G=games; AB=at bat; R=run; H=hit; 2B=double; 3B=triple; HR=home run; RBI=run batted in; TB=total bases; BB=walk; SO=strikeout; SB=stolen base; OBP=on-base percentage; SLG=slugging percentage; BA=batting average; W=win; L=loss; ERA=earned run average; CG=complete games; SHO=shutouts; SV=saves; INN=innings; ER=earned runs

NATIONAL LEAGUE TEAM-BY-TEAM STATS

ARIZONA DIAMONDBACKS

BATTING

BATTING	G	AB	R	H	2B	3B	HR	RBI	TB	BB	SO	SB	OBP	SLG	BA
Shea Hillenbrand	148	562	68	174	36	3	15	80	261	24	49	2	.348	.464	.310
Roberto Alomar	38	110	14	34	5	2	3	16	52	12	18	0	.382	.473	.309
Quinton McCracken	55	156	20	45	11	1	2	13	64	13	23	2	.341	.410	.288
Danny Bautista	141	539	64	154	27	1	11	65	216	35	66	6	.332	.401	.286
Chad Tracy	143	481	45	137	29	3	8	53	196	45	60	2	.343	.407	.285
Alex Cintron	154	564	56	148	31	7	4	49	205	31	59	3	.301	.363	.262
Luis Gonzalez	105	379	69	98	28	5	17	48	187	68	58	2	.373	.493	.259
Scott Hairston	101	339	39	84	15	6	13	29	150	21	88	3	.293	.442	.248
Matt Kata	42	162	17	40	9	2	2	13	59	13	29	4	.301	.364	.247
Luis Terrero	62	229	21	56	14	0	4	14	82	20	70	10	.319	.358	.245
Robby Hammock	62	195	22	47	16	2	4	18	79	13	39	3	.287	.405	.241
Chris Snyder	29	96	10	23	6	0	5	15	44	13	25	0	.327	.458	.240
Carlos Baerga	79	85	6	20	2	0	2	11	28	6	12	0	.309	.329	.235
Richie Sexson	23	90	20	21	4	0	9	23	52	14	21	0	.337	.578	.233
Doug DeVore	50	107	5	24	3	2	3	13	40	7	31	1	.272	.374	.224
Andy Green	46	109	13	22	2	1	1	4	29	5	17	1	.241	.266	.202

PITCHING

PITCHING	W–L	ERA	G	GS	CG	SV	INN	H	R	ER	BB	SO
Randy Johnson	16–14	2.60	35	35	4	0	245.2	177	88	71	44	290
Greg Aquino	0–2	3.06	34	0	0	16	35.1	24	15	12	17	26
Brandon Webb	7–16	3.59	35	35	1	0	208.0	194	111	83	119	164
Mike Koplove	4–4	4.05	76	0	0	2	86.2	86	42	39	37	55
Brandon Villafuerte	0–3	4.05	20	0	0	0	20.0	25	9	9	14	12
Jose Valverde	1–2	4.25	29	0	0	8	29.2	23	17	14	17	38
Brian Bruney	3–4	4.31	30	0	0	0	31.1	20	16	15	27	31
Randy Choate	2–4	4.62	74	0	0	0	50.2	52	26	26	20	49
Andrew Good	1–2	5.31	17	2	0	0	40.2	43	25	24	13	26
Jeff Fassero	3–8	5.46	41	12	0	0	112.0	136	73	68	44	60
Stephen Randolph	2–5	5.51	45	6	0	0	81.2	73	56	50	76	62
Steve Sparks	3–7	6.04	29	18	0	0	120.2	139	89	81	45	57
Casey Fossum	4–15	6.65	27	27	0	0	142.0	171	111	105	63	117

ATLANTA BRAVES

BATTING

BATTING	G	AB	R	H	2B	3B	HR	RBI	TB	BB	SO	SB	OBP	SLG	BA
Eli Marrero	90	250	37	80	18	1	10	40	130	23	50	4	.374	.520	.320
Johnny Estrada	134	462	56	145	36	0	9	76	208	39	66	0	.378	.450	.314
Marcus Giles	102	379	61	118	22	2	8	48	168	36	70	17	.378	.443	.311
Julio Franco	125	320	37	99	18	3	6	57	141	36	68	4	.378	.441	.309
J.D. Drew	145	518	118	158	28	8	31	93	295	118	116	12	.436	.569	.305
Charles Thomas	83	236	35	68	8	4	7	31	105	21	45	3	.368	.445	.288
Rafael Furcal	143	563	103	157	24	5	14	59	233	58	71	29	.344	.414	.279
Adam LaRoche	110	324	45	90	27	1	13	45	158	27	78	0	.333	.488	.278
Nick Green	95	264	40	72	15	3	3	26	102	12	63	1	.312	.386	.273
Andruw Jones	154	570	85	149	34	4	29	91	278	71	147	6	.345	.488	.261
Jesse Garcia	50	115	14	29	4	1	1	10	38	1	16	1	.265	.330	.252
Chipper Jones	137	472	69	117	20	1	30	96	229	84	96	2	.362	.485	.248
Mark DeRosa	118	309	33	74	16	0	3	31	99	23	53	1	.293	.320	.239
Eddie Perez	74	170	14	39	12	0	3	13	60	11	29	0	.286	.353	.229
Dewayne Wise	77	162	24	37	9	4	6	17	72	9	28	6	.272	.444	.228

PITCHING

PITCHING	W–L	ERA	G	GS	CG	SV	INN	H	R	ER	BB	SO
Horacio Ramirez	2–4	2.39	10	9	1	0	60.1	51	24	16	30	31
Antonio Alfonseca	6–4	2.57	79	0	0	0	73.2	71	24	21	28	45
Juan Cruz	6–2	2.75	50	0	0	0	72.0	59	24	22	30	70
John Smoltz	0–1	2.76	73	0	0	44	81.2	75	25	25	13	85
Kevin Gryboski	3–2	2.84	69	0	0	2	50.2	54	22	16	23	24
Jaret Wright	15–8	3.28	32	32	0	0	186.1	168	79	68	70	159
John Thomson	14–8	3.72	33	33	0	0	198.1	210	93	82	52	133
Paul Byrd	8–7	3.94	19	19	0	0	114.1	123	57	50	19	79
Tom Martin	0–2	3.97	76	0	0	1	45.1	49	20	20	19	30
Chris Reitsma	6–4	4.07	84	0	0	2	79.2	89	38	36	20	60
Russ Ortiz	15–9	4.13	34	34	2	0	204.2	197	98	94	112	143
Mike Hampton	13–9	4.28	29	29	1	0	172.1	198	86	82	65	87
C.J. Nitkowski	1–0	4.50	22	0	0	0	20.0	22	11	10	10	16

CHICAGO CUBS

BATTING	G	AB	R	H	2B	3B	HR	RBI	TB	BB	SO	SB	OBP	SLG	BA
Todd Hollandsworth	57	148	28	47	6	2	8	22	81	17	26	1	.392	.547	.318
Aramis Ramirez	145	547	99	174	32	1	36	103	316	49	62	0	.373	.578	.318
Mark Grudzielanek	81	257	32	79	12	1	6	23	111	15	32	1	.347	.432	.307
Nomar Garciaparra	43	165	28	49	14	0	4	20	75	16	14	2	.364	.455	.297
Moises Alou	155	601	106	176	36	3	39	106	335	68	80	3	.361	.557	.293
Michael Barrett	134	456	55	131	32	6	16	65	223	33	64	1	.337	.489	.287
Derrek Lee	161	605	90	168	39	1	32	98	305	68	128	12	.356	.504	.278
Todd Walker	129	372	60	102	19	4	15	50	174	43	52	0	.352	.468	.274
Jose Macias	98	194	23	52	6	3	3	22	73	5	38	4	.292	.376	.268
Craig Patterson	157	631	91	168	33	6	24	72	285	45	168	32	.320	.452	.266
Ben Grieve	123	250	30	65	17	0	8	35	106	39	70	0	.361	.424	.260
Neifi Perez	126	381	40	97	17	1	4	39	128	24	41	1	.296	.336	.255
Sammy Sosa	126	478	69	121	21	0	35	80	247	56	133	0	.332	.517	.253
Paul Bako	49	138	13	28	8	0	1	10	39	15	29	1	.288	.283	.203
Tom Goodwin	77	105	11	21	8	0	0	3	29	8	22	5	.254	.276	.200

PITCHING	W–L	ERA	G	GS	CG	SV	INN	H	R	ER	BB	SO
Kent Mercker	3–1	2.55	71	0	0	0	53.0	39	15	15	27	51
LaTroy Hawkins	5–4	2.63	77	0	0	25	82.0	72	27	24	14	69
Carlos Zambrano	16–8	2.75	31	31	1	0	209.2	174	73	64	81	188
Mike Remlinger	1–2	3.44	48	0	0	2	36.2	33	16	14	16	35
Glendon Rusch	6–2	3.47	32	16	0	2	129.2	127	54	50	33	90
Matt Clement	9–13	3.68	30	30	0	0	181.0	155	79	74	77	190
Kerry Wood	8–9	3.72	22	22	0	0	140.1	127	62	58	51	144
Jon Leicester	5–1	3.89	32	0	0	0	41.2	40	20	18	15	35
Ryan Dempster	1–1	3.92	23	0	0	2	20.2	16	9	9	13	18
Greg Maddux	16–11	4.02	33	33	2	0	212.2	218	103	95	33	151
Mark Prior	6–4	4.02	21	21	0	0	118.2	112	53	53	48	139

CINCINNATI REDS

BATTING	G	AB	R	H	2B	3B	HR	RBI	TB	BB	SO	SB	OBP	SLG	BA
Sean Casey	146	571	101	185	44	2	24	99	305	46	36	2	.381	.534	.324
Barry Larkin	111	346	55	100	15	3	8	44	145	34	39	2	.352	.419	.289
Ryan Freel	143	505	74	140	21	8	3	28	186	67	88	37	.375	.368	.277
D'Angelo Jimenez	152	563	76	152	28	3	12	67	222	82	99	13	.364	.394	.270
Adam Dunn	161	568	105	151	34	0	46	102	323	108	195	6	.388	.569	.266
Wily Mo Pena	110	336	45	87	10	1	26	66	177	22	108	5	.316	.527	.259
Ken Griffey, Jr.	83	300	49	76	18	0	20	60	154	44	67	1	.351	.513	.253
Jason LaRue	114	390	46	98	24	2	14	55	168	26	108	0	.334	.431	.251
Juan Castro	111	299	36	73	21	2	5	26	113	14	51	1	.277	.378	.244
Felipe Lopez	79	264	35	64	18	2	7	31	107	25	81	1	.314	.405	.242
Javier Valentin	82	202	18	47	10	1	6	20	77	17	36	0	.293	.381	.233
Austin Kearns	64	217	28	50	10	2	9	32	91	28	71	2	.321	.419	.230
Jacob Cruz	96	147	22	33	8	0	3	28	50	16	43	0	.317	.340	.224
Tim Hummel	56	110	10	24	4	0	1	7	31	8	17	1	.281	.282	.218
Brandon Larson	40	118	13	25	6	0	3	14	40	14	35	1	.304	.339	.212
Darren Bragg	47	101	13	19	3	1	4	9	36	10	31	1	.261	.356	.188

PITCHING	W–L	ERA	G	GS	CG	SV	INN	H	R	ER	BB	SO
Luke Hudson	4–2	2.42	9	9	0	0	48.1	36	16	13	25	38
Danny Graves	1–6	3.95	68	0	0	41	68.1	77	39	30	13	40
Paul Wilson	11–6	4.36	29	29	1	0	183.2	192	93	89	63	117
Ryan Wagner	3–2	4.70	49	0	0	0	51.2	59	31	27	27	37
Aaron Harang	10–9	4.86	28	28	1	0	161.0	177	90	87	53	125
Phil Norton	2–5	5.07	69	0	0	0	65.2	71	41	37	38	48
Josh Hancock	5–2	5.09	16	11	0	0	63.2	73	43	36	28	36
John Riedling	5–3	5.10	70	0	0	0	77.2	90	54	44	40	46
Joe Valentine	2–3	5.22	24	1	0	4	29.1	23	18	17	25	29
Jose Acevedo	5–12	5.94	39	27	0	0	157.2	188	108	104	45	117
Todd Van Poppel	4–6	6.09	48	11	0	0	115.1	136	80	78	32	72
Brandon Claussen	2–8	6.14	14	14	0	0	66.0	80	50	45	35	45
Gabe White	1–2	6.23	40	0	0	1	39.0	39	27	27	5	33

COLORADO ROCKIES

BATTING	G	AB	R	H	2B	3B	HR	RBI	TB	BB	SO	SB	OBP	SLG	BA
Todd Helton	154	547	115	190	49	2	32	96	339	127	72	3	.469	.620	.347
J.D. Closser	36	113	5	36	6	0	1	10	45	6	22	0	.364	.398	.319
Jorge Piedra	38	91	15	27	8	0	3	10	44	5	19	0	.340	.484	.297
Aaron Miles	134	522	75	153	15	3	6	47	192	29	53	12	.329	.368	.293
Luis Gonzalez	102	322	42	94	17	2	12	40	151	15	67	1	.330	.469	.292
Matt Holliday	121	400	65	116	31	3	14	57	195	31	86	3	.349	.488	.290
Jeromy Burnitz	150	540	94	153	30	4	37	110	302	58	124	5	.356	.559	.283
Todd Greene	75	195	23	55	14	0	10	35	99	13	38	0	.325	.508	.282
Royce Clayton	146	574	95	160	36	4	8	54	228	48	125	10	.338	.397	.279
Vinny Castilla	148	583	93	158	43	3	35	131	312	51	113	0	.332	.535	.271
Mark Sweeney	122	177	25	47	12	2	9	40	90	32	51	1	.377	.508	.266
Brad Hawpe	42	105	12	26	3	2	3	9	42	11	34	1	.322	.400	.248
Preston Wilson	58	202	24	50	11	0	6	29	79	17	49	2	.315	.391	.248
Kit Pellow	59	121	15	29	5	1	2	10	42	8	43	1	.308	.347	.240
Charles Johnson	109	305	42	72	20	0	13	47	131	49	91	2	.350	.430	.236

PITCHING	W–L	ERA	G	GS	CG	SV	INN	H	R	ER	BB	SO
Joe Kennedy	9–7	3.66	27	27	1	0	162.1	163	68	66	67	117
Steve Reed	3–8	3.68	65	0	0	0	66.0	72	29	27	17	38
Chin-hui Tsao	0–0	3.86	10	0	0	1	9.1	7	4	4	1	11
Scott Dohmann	0–3	4.11	41	0	0	0	46.0	41	22	21	19	49
Jamey Wright	2–3	4.13	14	14	0	0	78.2	82	39	36	45	41
Aaron Cook	6–4	4.28	16	16	1	0	96.2	112	47	46	39	40
Tim Harikkala	6–6	4.74	55	0	0	0	62.2	55	34	33	23	30
Allan Simpson	2–1	5.08	32	0	0	0	39.0	44	26	22	20	46
Jason Jennings	11–12	5.51	33	33	0	0	201.0	241	125	123	101	133
Adam Bernero	1–1	5.57	16	2	0	0	32.1	36	20	20	17	21
Brian Fuentes	2–4	5.64	47	0	0	0	44.2	46	30	28	19	48
Shawn Estes	15–8	5.84	34	34	1	0	202.0	233	133	131	105	117
Shawn Chacon	1–9	7.11	66	0	0	35	63.1	71	52	50	52	52

FLORIDA MARLINS

BATTING	G	AB	R	H	2B	3B	HR	RBI	TB	BB	SO	SB	OBP	SLG	BA
Juan Pierre	162	678	100	221	22	12	3	49	276	45	35	45	.374	.407	.326
Miguel Cabrera	160	603	101	177	31	1	33	112	309	68	148	5	.366	.512	.294
Mike Lowell	158	598	87	175	44	1	27	85	302	64	77	5	.365	.505	.293
Luis Castillo	150	564	91	164	12	7	2	47	196	75	68	21	.373	.348	.291
Paul Lo Duca	143	535	68	153	29	2	13	80	225	36	49	4	.338	.421	.286
Jeff Conine	140	521	55	146	35	1	14	83	225	48	78	5	.340	.432	.280
Damion Easley	98	223	26	53	20	1	9	43	102	24	36	4	.331	.457	.238
Juan Encarnacion	135	484	63	114	30	2	16	62	196	38	86	5	.299	.405	.236
Alex Gonzalez	159	561	67	130	30	3	23	79	235	27	126	3	.270	.419	.232
Mike Mordecai	69	84	7	19	3	0	1	5	25	6	18	0	.278	.298	.226
Chris Aguila	29	45	10	10	2	1	3	5	23	2	12	0	.255	.511	.222
Lenny Harris	79	95	7	20	5	0	1	17	28	3	8	0	.232	.295	.211

PITCHING	W–L	ERA	G	GS	CG	SV	INN	H	R	ER	BB	SO
Armando Benitez	2–2	1.29	64	0	0	47	69.2	36	11	10	21	62
Rudy Seanez	3–1	2.74	23	0	0	0	23.0	18	7	7	8	25
Carl Pavano	18–8	3.00	31	31	2	0	222.1	212	80	74	49	139
Guillermo Mota	9–8	3.07	78	0	0	4	96.2	75	33	33	37	85
Billy Koch	1–2	3.51	23	0	0	0	25.2	21	10	10	20	25
A.J. Burnett	7–6	3.68	20	19	1	0	120.0	102	50	49	38	113
Josh Beckett	9–9	3.79	26	26	1	0	156.2	137	72	66	54	152
Dontrelle Willis	10–11	4.02	32	32	2	0	197.0	210	99	88	61	139
David Weathers	7–7	4.15	66	2	0	0	82.1	85	44	38	35	61
Matt Perisho	5–3	4.40	66	0	0	0	47.0	45	23	23	26	42
Nate Bump	2–4	5.01	50	2	0	1	73.2	86	46	41	32	44
Ismael Valdez	14–9	5.19	34	31	1	0	170.0	202	105	98	49	67

BASEBALL

HOUSTON ASTROS

BATTING

BATTING	G	AB	R	H	2B	3B	HR	RBI	TB	BB	SO	SB	OBP	SLG	BA
Lance Berkman	160	544	104	172	40	3	30	106	308	127	101	9	.450	.566	.316
Jeff Kent	145	540	96	156	34	8	27	107	287	49	96	7	.348	.531	.289
Mike Lamb	112	278	38	80	14	3	14	58	142	31	63	1	.356	.511	.288
Craig Biggio	156	633	100	178	47	0	24	63	297	40	94	7	.337	.469	.281
Morgan Ensberg	131	411	51	113	20	3	10	66	169	36	46	6	.330	.411	.275
Jose Vizcaino	138	358	34	98	21	3	3	33	134	20	39	1	.311	.374	.274
Adam Everett	104	384	66	105	15	2	8	31	148	17	56	13	.317	.385	.273
Jason Lane	107	136	21	37	10	2	4	19	63	16	33	1	.348	.463	.272
Jeff Bagwell	156	572	104	152	29	2	27	89	266	96	131	6	.377	.465	.266
Carlos Beltran	90	333	70	86	17	7	23	53	186	55	57	28	.368	.559	.258
Eric Bruntlett	45	52	14	13	2	0	4	8	27	7	13	4	.328	.519	.250
Brad Ausmus	129	403	38	100	14	1	5	31	131	33	56	2	.306	.325	.248
Orlando Palmeiro	102	133	19	32	5	0	3	12	46	18	19	2	.344	.346	.241
Raul Chavez	64	162	9	34	8	0	0	23	42	10	38	0	.256	.259	.210

PITCHING

PITCHING	W–L	ERA	G	GS	CG	SV	INN	H	R	ER	BB	SO
Brad Lidge	6–5	1.90	80	0	0	29	94.2	57	21	20	30	157
Roger Clemens	18–4	2.98	33	33	0	0	214.1	169	76	71	79	218
Octavio Dotel	0–4	3.12	32	0	0	14	34.2	27	15	12	15	50
Wade Miller	7–7	3.35	15	15	0	0	88.2	76	35	33	44	74
Roy Oswalt	20–10	3.49	36	35	2	0	237.0	233	100	92	62	206
Chad Qualls	4–0	3.55	25	0	0	1	33.0	34	13	13	8	24
Dan Miceli	6–6	3.59	74	0	0	2	77.2	74	34	31	27	83
Andy Pettitte	6–4	3.90	15	15	0	0	83.0	71	37	36	31	79
Dan Wheeler	3–1	4.29	46	1	0	0	65.0	76	33	31	20	55
Brandon Backe	5–3	4.30	33	9	0	0	67.0	75	33	32	27	54
Mike Gallo	2–0	4.74	69	0	0	0	49.1	55	27	26	20	34
Chad Harville	3–2	4.75	56	0	0	0	53.0	54	35	28	26	46
Pete Munro	4–7	5.15	21	19	0	0	99.2	120	59	57	26	63
Tim Redding	5–7	5.72	27	17	0	0	100.2	125	73	65	43	56

LOS ANGELES DODGERS

BATTING

BATTING	G	AB	R	H	2B	3B	HR	RBI	TB	BB	SO	SB	OBP	SLG	BA
Adrian Beltre	156	598	104	200	32	0	48	121	376	53	87	7	.388	.629	.334
Jose Hernandez	95	211	32	61	12	1	13	29	114	26	61	3	.370	.540	.289
Cesar Izturis	159	670	90	193	32	9	4	62	255	43	70	25	.330	.381	.288
Olmedo Saenz	77	111	17	31	1	0	8	22	56	12	33	0	.352	.505	.279
Steve Finley	162	628	92	170	28	1	36	94	308	61	82	9	.333	.490	.271
Milton Bradley	141	516	72	138	24	0	19	67	219	71	123	15	.362	.424	.267
Shawn Green	157	590	92	157	28	1	28	86	271	71	114	5	.352	.459	.266
Alex Cora	138	405	47	107	9	4	10	47	154	47	41	3	.364	.380	.264
Jayson Werth	89	290	56	76	11	3	16	47	141	30	85	4	.338	.486	.262
Dave Roberts	68	233	45	59	4	7	2	21	83	28	31	33	.340	.356	.253
Hee-Seop Choi	126	343	53	86	21	1	15	46	154	63	96	1	.370	.449	.251
Robin Ventura	102	152	19	37	3	0	5	28	55	22	31	0	.337	.362	.243
Brent Mayne	83	190	14	42	6	1	0	15	50	27	41	1	.314	.263	.221
Jason Grabowski	113	173	18	38	7	0	7	20	66	19	50	0	.297	.382	.220

PITCHING

PITCHING	W–L	ERA	G	GS	CG	SV	INN	H	R	ER	BB	SO
Giovanni Carrara	5–2	2.18	42	0	0	2	53.2	46	15	13	20	48
Eric Gagne	7–3	2.19	70	0	0	45	82.1	53	24	20	22	114
Yhency Brazoban	6–2	2.48	31	0	0	0	32.2	25	9	9	15	27
Brad Penny	9–10	3.15	24	24	0	0	143.0	130	55	50	45	111
Odalis Perez	7–6	3.25	31	31	0	0	196.1	180	76	71	44	128
Duaner Sanchez	3–1	3.38	67	0	0	0	80.0	81	34	30	27	44
Jeff Weaver	13–13	4.01	34	34	0	0	220.0	219	103	98	67	153
Wilson Alvarez	7–6	4.03	40	15	0	1	120.2	109	56	54	31	102
Jose Lima	13–5	4.07	36	24	0	0	170.1	178	81	77	34	93
Darren Dreifort	1–4	4.44	60	0	0	1	50.1	43	25	25	36	63
Elmer Dessens	2–6	4.46	50	10	0	2	105.0	123	61	52	31	73
Kazuhisa Ishii	13–8	4.71	31	31	2	0	172.0	155	97	90	98	99
Hideo Nomo	4–11	8.25	18	18	0	0	84.0	105	77	77	42	54

MILWAUKEE BREWERS

BATTING	G	AB	R	H	2B	3B	HR	RBI	TB	BB	SO	SB	OBP	SLG	BA
Lyle Overbay	159	579	83	174	53	1	16	87	277	81	128	2	.385	.478	.301
Brady Clark	138	353	41	99	18	1	7	46	140	53	48	15	.385	.397	.280
Junior Spivey	59	228	33	62	13	0	7	28	96	25	48	5	.359	.421	.272
Geoff Jenkins	157	617	88	163	36	6	27	93	292	46	152	3	.325	.473	.264
Wes Helms	92	274	24	72	13	1	4	28	99	24	60	0	.331	.361	.263
Keith Ginter	113	386	47	101	23	2	19	60	185	37	100	8	.333	.479	.262
Scott Podsednik	154	640	85	156	27	7	12	39	233	58	105	70	.313	.364	.244
Craig Counsell	140	473	59	114	19	5	2	23	149	59	88	17	.330	.315	.241
Bill Hall	126	390	43	93	20	3	9	53	146	20	119	12	.276	.374	.238
Chris Magruder	56	89	11	21	6	1	2	10	35	8	21	0	.310	.393	.236
Russell Branyan	51	158	21	37	11	1	11	27	83	20	68	1	.324	.525	.234
Trent Durrington	53	82	13	19	2	3	2	4	33	4	23	4	.267	.402	.232
Gary Bennett	75	219	18	49	14	0	3	20	72	22	32	1	.297	.329	.224
Chad Moeller	101	317	25	66	13	1	5	27	98	21	74	0	.265	.303	.208

PITCHING	W–L	ERA	G	GS	CG	SV	INN	H	R	ER	BB	SO
Ben Sheets	12–14	2.70	34	34	5	0	237.0	201	85	71	32	264
Dan Kolb	0–4	2.98	64	0	0	39	57.1	50	22	19	15	21
Doug Davis	12–12	3.39	34	34	0	0	207.1	192	84	78	79	166
Mike Adams	2–3	3.40	46	0	0	0	53.0	50	21	20	11	39
Luis Vizcaino	4–4	3.75	73	0	0	1	72.0	61	35	30	24	63
Brooks Kleschnick	1–1	3.77	32	0	0	0	43.0	44	19	18	13	39
Pedro Liriano	0–0	4.02	11	0	0	0	15.2	15	10	7	3	10
Matt Wise	1–2	4.44	30	3	0	0	52.2	51	27	26	15	30
Jeff Bennett	1–5	4.79	60	0	0	0	71.1	78	43	38	26	45
Victor Santos	11–12	4.97	31	29	0	0	154.0	109	93	85	57	115
Wes Obermueller	6–8	5.80	25	20	1	0	118.0	138	80	76	42	59

MONTREAL EXPOS

BATTING	G	AB	R	H	2B	3B	HR	RBI	TB	BB	SO	SB	OBP	SLG	BA
Juan Rivera	134	391	48	120	24	1	12	49	182	34	45	6	.364	.465	.307
Jose Vidro	110	412	51	121	24	0	14	60	187	49	43	3	.367	.454	.294
Jamey Carroll	102	218	36	63	14	3	0	16	81	22	21	5	.374	.372	.289
Endy Chavez	132	502	65	139	20	6	5	34	186	30	40	32	.318	.371	.277
Henry Mateo	40	44	3	12	2	0	0	0	14	1	9	2	.289	.318	.273
Terrmel Sledge	133	398	45	107	20	6	15	62	184	40	66	3	.336	.462	.269
Brian Schneider	135	436	40	112	20	3	12	49	174	42	63	0	.325	.399	.257
Brad Wilkerson	160	572	112	146	39	2	32	67	285	106	152	13	.374	.498	.255
Carl Everett	39	127	8	32	10	0	2	14	48	8	19	0	.319	.378	.252
Nick Johnson	73	251	35	63	16	0	7	33	100	40	58	6	.359	.398	.251
Livan Hernandez	34	81	2	20	7	0	1	10	30	1	8	0	.256	.370	.247
Orlando Cabrera	103	390	41	96	19	2	4	31	131	28	31	12	.298	.336	.246
Tony Batista	157	606	76	146	30	2	32	110	276	26	78	14	.272	.455	.241
Einar Diaz	55	139	9	31	6	1	1	11	42	11	10	2	.293	.302	.223
Maicer Izturis	32	107	10	22	5	2	1	4	34	10	20	4	.286	.318	.206

PITCHING	W–L	ERA	G	GS	CG	SV	INN	H	R	ER	BB	SO
Luis Ayala	6–12	2.69	81	0	0	2	90.1	92	30	27	15	63
Chad Cordero	7–3	2.94	69	0	0	14	82.2	68	28	27	43	83
Joe Horgan	4–1	3.15	47	0	0	2	40.0	35	18	14	22	30
Tomo Ohka	3–7	3.40	15	15	0	0	84.2	98	40	32	20	38
Livan Hernandez	11–15	3.60	35	35	9	0	255.0	234	105	102	83	186
T.J. Tucker	4–2	3.72	54	1	0	0	67.2	73	28	28	17	44
Gary Majewski	0–1	3.86	16	0	0	1	21.0	28	15	9	5	12
Zach Day	5–10	3.93	19	19	1	0	116.2	117	53	51	45	61
Joey Eischen	0–1	3.93	21	0	0	0	18.1	16	10	8	8	17
Sunny Kim	4–6	4.58	43	17	0	0	135.2	145	80	69	55	87
Tony Armas	2–4	4.88	16	16	0	0	72.0	66	41	39	45	54
John Patterson	4–7	5.03	19	19	0	0	98.1	100	58	55	46	99
Scott Downs	3–6	5.14	12	12	1	0	63.0	79	47	36	23	38
Claudio Vargas	5–5	5.25	45	14	0	0	118.1	120	75	69	64	89

BASEBALL

NEW YORK METS

BATTING	G	AB	R	H	2B	3B	HR	RBI	TB	BB	SO	SB	OBP	SLG	BA
David Wright	69	263	41	77	17	1	14	40	138	14	40	6	.332	.525	.293
Wilson Delgado	42	130	11	38	4	1	2	13	50	15	29	1	.366	.385	.292
Jeff Keppinger	33	116	9	33	2	0	3	9	44	6	7	2	.317	.379	.284
Shane Spencer	74	185	21	52	10	1	4	26	76	13	37	6	.332	.411	.281
Vance Wilson	79	157	18	43	10	1	4	21	67	11	24	1	.335	.427	.274
Kazuo Matsui	114	460	65	125	32	2	7	44	182	40	97	14	.331	.396	.272
Eric Valent	130	270	39	72	15	2	13	34	130	28	61	0	.337	.481	.267
Mike Piazza	129	455	47	121	21	0	20	54	202	68	78	0	.362	.444	.266
Cliff Floyd	113	396	55	103	26	0	18	63	183	47	103	11	.352	.462	.260
Jose Reyes	53	220	33	56	16	2	2	14	82	5	31	19	.271	.373	.255
Joe McEwing	75	138	17	35	3	1	1	16	43	9	32	4	.297	.312	.254
Richard Hidalgo	144	523	67	125	26	3	25	82	232	44	129	4	.301	.444	.239
Karim Garcia	62	192	24	45	7	2	7	22	77	10	35	3	.272	.401	.234
Gerald Williams	57	129	17	30	8	2	4	11	54	8	26	2	.277	.419	.233
Todd Zeile	137	348	30	81	16	0	9	35	124	44	83	0	.319	.356	.233
Danny Garcia	58	138	23	32	7	1	3	17	50	22	34	3	.371	.362	.232
Mike Cameron	140	493	76	114	30	1	30	76	236	57	143	22	.319	.479	.231
Jason Phillips	128	362	34	79	18	0	7	34	118	35	42	0	.298	.326	.218

PITCHING	W–L	ERA	G	GS	CG	SV	INN	H	R	ER	BB	SO
Mike DeJean	0–0	1.69	17	0	0	0	21.1	21	5	4	5	24
Braden Looper	2–5	2.70	71	0	0	29	83.1	86	28	25	16	60
Mike Stanton	2–6	3.16	83	0	0	0	77.0	70	32	27	33	58
Al Leiter	10–8	3.21	30	30	0	0	173.2	138	65	62	97	117
Heath Bell	0–2	3.33	17	0	0	0	24.1	22	9	9	6	27
Ricky Bottalico	3–2	3.38	60	0	0	0	69.1	54	30	26	34	61
Orber Moreno	3–1	3.38	33	0	0	1	34.2	29	17	13	11	29
Tom Glavine	11–14	3.60	33	33	1	0	212.1	204	94	85	70	109
Bartolome Fortunato	1–0	3.86	15	0	0	1	10.2	14	0	0	13	20
Steve Trachsel	12–13	4.00	33	33	0	0	202.2	203	104	90	83	117
Kris Benson	12–12	4.31	31	31	1	0	200.1	202	106	96	61	134
Jae Weong Seo	5–10	4.90	24	21	0	0	117.2	133	67	64	50	54
John Franco	2–7	5.28	52	0	0	0	46.0	46	28	27	24	36
Pedro Feliciano	1–1	5.40	22	0	0	0	18.1	14	12	11	12	14

PHILADELPHIA PHILLIES

BATTING	G	AB	R	H	2B	3B	HR	RBI	TB	BB	SO	SB	OBP	SLG	BA
Bobby Abreu	159	574	118	173	47	1	30	105	312	127	116	40	.428	.544	.301
Placido Polanco	126	503	74	150	21	0	17	55	222	27	39	7	.345	.441	.298
David Bell	143	533	67	155	33	1	18	77	244	57	75	1	.363	.458	.291
Jimmy Rollins	154	657	119	190	43	12	14	73	299	57	73	30	.348	.455	.289
Lou Collier	32	36	7	10	1	0	1	4	14	5	10	1	.381	.389	.278
Jason Michaels	115	299	44	82	12	0	10	40	124	42	80	2	.364	.415	.274
Jim Thome	143	508	97	139	28	1	42	105	295	104	144	0	.396	.581	.274
Mike Lieberthal	131	476	58	129	31	1	17	61	213	37	69	1	.335	.447	.271
Chase Utley	94	267	36	71	11	2	13	57	125	15	40	4	.308	.468	.266
Todd Pratt	45	128	16	33	5	0	3	16	47	18	38	0	.351	.367	.258
Pat Burrell	127	448	66	115	17	0	24	84	204	78	130	2	.365	.455	.257
Marlon Byrd	106	346	48	79	13	2	5	33	111	22	68	2	.287	.321	.228
Tomas Perez	86	176	22	38	13	2	6	21	73	9	44	0	.257	.415	.216
Doug Glanville	87	162	21	34	1	1	2	14	43	8	21	8	.244	.265	.210
Brett Myers	29	51	6	10	4	0	0	1	14	2	17	0	.226	.275	.196

PITCHING	W–L	ERA	G	GS	CG	SV	INN	H	R	ER	BB	SO
Ryan Madson	9–3	2.34	52	1	0	1	77.0	68	23	20	19	55
Billy Wagner	4–0	2.42	45	0	0	21	48.1	31	16	13	6	59
Felix Rodriguez	5–8	3.29	76	0	0	1	65.2	61	25	24	29	59
Gavin Floyd	2–0	3.49	6	4	0	0	28.1	25	11	11	16	24
Rheal Cormier	4–5	3.56	84	0	0	0	81.0	70	32	32	26	46
Tim Worrell	5–6	3.68	77	0	0	19	78.1	75	36	32	21	64
Todd Jones	11–5	4.15	78	0	0	2	82.1	84	39	38	33	59
Randy Wolf	5–8	4.28	23	23	1	0	136.2	145	73	65	36	89
Amaury Telemaco	0–2	4.31	42	0	0	0	54.1	51	27	26	19	32
Vicente Padilla	7–7	4.53	20	20	0	0	115.1	119	63	58	36	82
Eric Milton	14–6	4.75	34	34	0	0	201.0	196	110	106	75	161
Roberto Hernandez	3–5	4.76	63	0	0	0	56.2	66	39	30	29	44
Kevin Millwood	9–6	4.85	25	25	0	0	141.0	155	81	76	51	125
Cory Lidle	12–12	4.90	34	34	5	0	211.1	224	123	115	61	126

PITTSBURGH PIRATES

BATTING	G	AB	R	H	2B	3B	HR	RBI	TB	BB	SO	SB	OBP	SLG	BA
Jason Kendall	147	574	86	183	32	0	3	51	224	60	41	11	.399	.390	.319
Jack Wilson	157	652	82	201	41	12	11	59	299	26	71	8	.335	.459	.308
Raul Mondesi	26	99	8	28	8	0	2	14	42	11	27	0	.355	.424	.283
Jason Bay	120	411	61	116	24	4	26	82	226	41	129	4	.358	.550	.282
Tike Redman	155	546	65	153	19	4	8	51	204	23	52	18	.310	.374	.280
Bobby Hill	126	233	28	62	7	2	2	27	79	20	39	0	.353	.339	.266
Craig Wilson	155	561	97	148	35	5	29	82	280	50	169	2	.354	.499	.264
Ty Wigginton	144	494	63	129	30	2	17	66	214	45	82	7	.324	.433	.261
Jose Castillo	129	383	44	98	15	2	8	39	141	23	92	3	.298	.368	.256
Daryle Ward	79	293	39	73	17	2	15	57	139	22	45	0	.305	.474	.249
Rob Mackowiak	155	491	65	121	22	6	17	75	206	50	114	13	.319	.420	.246
Abraham Nunez	112	182	17	43	9	0	2	13	58	10	36	1	.275	.319	.236
Humberto Cota	36	66	10	15	1	1	5	8	33	3	20	0	.271	.500	.227
Chris Stynes	74	162	16	35	10	0	1	16	48	9	23	0	.266	.296	.216

PITCHING	W–L	ERA	G	GS	CG	SV	INN	H	R	ER	BB	SO
Mike Gonzalez	3–1	1.25	47	0	0	1	43.1	32	7	6	6	55
Salomon Torres	7–7	2.64	84	0	0	0	92.0	87	33	27	22	62
Oliver Perez	12–10	2.98	30	30	2	0	196.0	145	71	65	81	239
Jose Mesa	5–2	3.25	70	0	0	43	69.1	78	26	25	20	37
Brian Meadows	2–4	3.58	68	0	0	1	78.0	76	40	31	19	46
Mike Johnston	0–3	4.37	24	0	0	0	22.2	29	16	11	15	18
Dave Williams	2–3	4.42	10	6	0	0	38.2	31	21	19	13	33
Mark Corey	1–2	4.54	31	0	0	0	35.2	39	20	18	19	28
Kip Wells	5–7	4.55	24	24	0	0	138.1	145	71	70	66	116
Brian Boehringer	1–1	4.62	21	0	0	0	25.1	27	14	10	17	20
Josh Fogg	11–10	4.64	32	32	0	0	178.1	193	98	92	66	82
Ryan Vogelsong	6–13	6.50	31	26	0	0	133.0	148	97	96	67	92

ST. LOUIS CARDINALS

BATTING	G	AB	R	H	2B	3B	HR	RBI	TB	BB	SO	SB	OBP	SLG	BA
Albert Pujols	154	592	133	196	51	2	46	123	389	84	52	5	.415	.657	.331
Scott Rolen	142	500	109	157	32	4	34	124	299	72	92	4	.409	.598	.314
Tony Womack	145	553	91	170	22	3	5	38	213	36	60	26	.349	.385	.307
Jim Edmonds	153	498	102	150	38	3	42	111	320	101	100	0	.410	.643	.301
Larry Walker	82	258	51	77	16	4	17	47	152	49	57	6	.424	.589	.298
John Mabry	87	240	32	71	11	0	13	40	121	26	63	0	.363	.504	.296
Jason Marquis	34	72	6	21	6	0	0	9	27	1	17	1	.297	.375	.292
So Taguchi	109	179	26	52	10	2	3	25	75	12	23	6	.337	.419	.291
Edgar Renteria	149	586	84	168	37	0	10	72	235	39	78	17	.327	.401	.287
Yadier Molina	51	135	12	36	6	0	2	15	48	13	20	0	.329	.356	.267
Roger Cedeno	95	200	22	53	9	2	3	23	75	19	41	5	.327	.375	.265
Reggie Sanders	135	446	64	116	27	3	22	67	215	33	118	21	.315	.482	.260
Ray Lankford	92	200	36	51	14	1	6	22	85	29	55	2	.349	.425	.255
Hector Luna	83	173	25	43	7	2	3	22	63	13	37	6	.304	.364	.249
Mike Matheny	122	385	28	95	22	1	5	50	134	23	83	0	.292	.348	.247
Marlon Anderson	113	253	31	60	12	0	8	28	96	12	38	6	.269	.379	.237

PITCHING	W–L	ERA	G	GS	CG	SV	INN	H	R	ER	BB	SO
Steve Kline	2–2	1.79	67	0	0	3	50.1	37	12	10	17	35
Julian Tavarez	7–4	2.38	77	0	0	4	64.1	57	21	17	19	48
Ray King	5–2	2.61	86	0	0	0	62.0	43	19	18	24	40
Kiko Calero	3–1	2.78	41	0	0	2	45.1	27	14	14	10	47
Jason Isringhausen	4–2	2.87	74	0	0	47	75.1	55	27	24	23	71
Chris Carpenter	15–5	3.46	28	28	1	0	182.0	169	75	70	38	152
Jason Marquis	15–7	3.71	32	32	0	0	201.1	215	90	83	70	138
Cal Eldred	4–2	3.76	52	0	0	1	67.0	71	31	28	17	54
Jeff Suppan	16–9	4.16	31	31	0	0	188.0	192	98	87	65	110
Woody Williams	11–8	4.18	31	31	0	0	189.2	193	93	88	58	131
Danny Haren	3–3	4.50	14	5	0	0	46.0	45	23	23	17	32
Matt Morris	15–10	4.72	32	32	3	0	202.0	205	116	106	56	131

SAN DIEGO PADRES

BATTING	G	AB	R	H	2B	3B	HR	RBI	TB	BB	SO	SB	OBP	SLG	BA
Mark Loretta	154	620	108	208	47	2	16	76	307	58	45	5	.391	.495	.335
Sean Burroughs	130	523	76	156	23	3	2	47	191	31	52	5	.348	.365	.298
Terrence Long	136	288	31	85	19	4	3	28	121	19	51	3	.335	.420	.295
Kerry Robinson	80	92	20	27	4	0	0	5	31	5	8	11	.330	.337	.293
Ryan Klesko	127	402	58	117	32	2	9	66	180	73	67	3	.399	.448	.291
Phil Nevin	147	547	78	158	31	1	26	105	269	66	121	0	.368	.492	.289
Brian Giles	159	609	97	173	33	7	23	94	289	89	80	10	.374	.475	.284
Ramon Hernandez	111	384	45	106	23	0	18	63	183	35	45	1	.341	.477	.276
Khalil Greene	139	484	67	132	31	4	15	65	216	53	94	4	.349	.446	.273
Jay Payton	143	458	57	119	17	4	8	55	168	43	56	2	.326	.367	.260
Miguel Ojeda	62	156	23	40	3	0	8	26	67	15	34	0	.322	.429	.256
Rich Aurilia	51	138	22	35	8	2	2	16	53	15	28	0	.331	.384	.254
Humberto Quintero	23	72	7	18	3	0	2	10	27	5	16	0	.295	.375	.250
Ramon Vazquez	52	115	12	27	3	2	1	13	37	11	24	1	.297	.322	.235
Alex Gonzalez	83	285	36	64	18	1	7	27	105	14	64	2	.263	.368	.225

PITCHING	W–L	ERA	G	GS	CG	SV	INN	H	R	ER	BB	SO
Akinori Otsuka	7–2	1.75	73	0	0	2	77.1	56	16	15	26	87
Scott Linebrink	7–3	2.14	73	0	0	0	84.0	61	22	20	26	83
Jake Peavy	15–6	2.27	27	27	0	0	166.1	146	49	42	53	173
Trevor Hoffman	3–3	2.30	55	0	0	41	54.2	42	14	14	8	53
Antonio Osuna	2–1	2.45	31	0	0	0	36.2	32	11	10	11	36
Jay Witasick	0–1	3.21	44	0	0	1	61.2	57	28	22	26	57
David Wells	12–8	3.73	31	31	0	0	195.2	203	85	81	20	101
Blaine Neal	1–1	4.07	40	0	0	0	42.0	49	19	19	11	36
Brian Lawrence	15–14	4.12	34	34	2	0	203.0	226	101	93	55	121
Adam Eaton	11–14	4.61	33	33	0	0	199.1	204	113	102	52	153
Rod Beck	0–2	6.38	26	0	0	0	24.0	27	18	17	9	15
Ricky Stone	2–2	6.45	43	0	0	0	51.2	66	39	37	16	38

SAN FRANCISCO GIANTS

BATTING	G	AB	R	H	2B	3B	HR	RBI	TB	BB	SO	SB	OBP	SLG	BA
Barry Bonds	147	373	129	135	27	3	45	101	303	232	41	6	.609	.812	.362
J.T. Snow	107	346	62	113	32	1	12	60	183	58	61	4	.429	.529	.327
Deivi Cruz	127	397	46	116	30	2	7	55	171	17	32	1	.322	.431	.292
Edgardo Alfonzo	139	519	46	150	26	1	11	77	211	46	40	1	.350	.407	.289
Ray Durham	120	471	95	133	28	8	17	65	228	57	60	10	.364	.484	.282
Brian Dallimore	20	43	8	12	2	0	1	7	17	4	7	0	.347	.395	.279
Marquis Grissom	145	562	78	157	26	2	22	90	253	37	83	3	.323	.450	.279
Pedro Feliz	144	503	72	139	33	3	22	84	244	23	85	5	.305	.485	.276
Dustan Mohr	117	263	52	72	20	1	7	28	115	46	64	0	.394	.437	.274
A.J. Pierzynski	131	471	45	128	28	2	11	77	193	19	27	0	.319	.410	.272
Michael Tucker	140	464	77	119	21	6	13	62	191	70	106	5	.353	.412	.256
Cody Ransom	78	68	13	17	6	0	1	11	26	6	20	2	.320	.382	.250
Damon Minor	24	58	8	14	2	0	0	6	16	12	18	0	.405	.276	.241
Ricky Ledee	104	176	25	41	9	0	7	30	71	27	47	3	.337	.403	.233
Yorvit Torrealba	64	172	19	39	7	3	6	23	70	17	31	2	.302	.407	.227
Jeffrey Hammonds	40	95	14	20	5	0	3	6	34	15	22	1	.336	.358	.211

PITCHING	W–L	ERA	G	GS	CG	SV	INN	H	R	ER	BB	SO
Jason Schmidt	18–7	3.20	32	32	4	0	225.0	165	84	80	77	251
Jim Brower	7–7	3.29	89	0	0	1	93.0	90	42	34	36	63
Noah Lowry	6–0	3.82	16	14	2	0	92.0	91	41	39	28	72
Brett Tomko	11–7	4.04	32	31	2	0	194.0	196	98	87	64	108
Scott Eyre	2–2	4.10	83	0	0	1	52.2	43	26	24	27	49
Dave Burba	4–1	4.21	51	0	0	2	77.0	70	40	36	26	50
Tyler Walker	5–1	4.24	52	0	0	1	63.2	69	31	30	24	48
Jerome Williams	10–7	4.24	22	22	0	0	129.1	123	69	61	44	80
Jason Christiansen	4–3	4.50	60	0	0	3	36.0	34	20	18	26	22
Dustin Hermanson	6–9	4.53	47	18	0	17	131.0	132	71	66	46	102
Kirk Reuter	9–12	4.73	33	33	0	0	190.1	225	108	100	66	56
Matt Herges	4–5	5.23	70	0	0	23	65.1	90	44	38	21	39
Wayne Franklin	2–1	6.39	43	2	0	0	50.2	55	37	36	22	40

AMERICAN LEAGUE TEAM-BY-TEAM STATS

ANAHEIM ANGELS

BATTING	G	AB	R	H	2B	3B	HR	RBI	TB	BB	SO	SB	OBP	SLG	BA
Robb Quinlan	56	160	23	55	14	0	5	23	84	14	26	3	.401	.525	.344
Vladimir Guerrero	156	612	124	206	39	2	39	126	366	52	74	15	.391	.598	.337
Garret Anderson	112	442	57	133	20	1	14	75	197	29	75	2	.343	.446	.301
Chone Figgins	148	577	83	171	22	17	5	60	242	49	94	34	.350	.419	.296
Darin Erstad	125	495	79	146	29	1	7	69	198	37	74	16	.346	.400	.295
Jose Guillen	148	565	88	166	28	3	27	104	281	37	92	5	.352	.497	.294
Adam Kennedy	144	468	70	130	20	5	10	48	190	41	92	15	.351	.406	.278
Joff DaVanon	108	285	41	79	11	4	7	34	119	46	54	18	.372	.418	.277
David Eckstein	142	566	92	156	24	1	2	35	188	42	49	16	.339	.332	.276
Bengie Molina	97	337	36	93	13	0	10	54	136	18	35	0	.313	.404	.276
Jose Molina	73	203	26	53	10	2	3	25	78	10	52	4	.296	.374	.261
Tim Salmon	60	186	15	47	7	0	2	23	60	14	41	1	.306	.323	.253
Troy Glaus	58	207	47	52	11	1	18	42	119	31	52	2	.355	.575	.251

PITCHING	W–L	ERA	G	GS	CG	SV	INN	H	R	ER	BB	SO
Francisco Rodriguez	4–1	1.82	69	0	0	12	84.0	51	21	17	33	123
Troy Percival	2–3	2.90	52	0	0	33	49.2	43	10	16	19	33
Brendan Donnelly	5–2	3.00	40	0	0	0	42.0	34	14	14	15	56
Scot Sheilds	8–2	3.33	60	0	0	4	105.1	97	42	39	40	109
Kelvim Escobar	11–12	3.93	33	33	0	0	208.1	192	91	91	76	191
Kevin Gregg	5–2	4.21	55	0	0	1	87.2	86	43	41	28	84
Ramon Ortiz	5–7	4.43	34	14	0	0	128.0	139	64	63	38	82
Jarrod Washburn	11–8	4.64	25	25	1	0	140.1	158	81	77	40	86
John Lackey	14–13	4.67	33	32	1	0	198.1	215	108	103	60	144
Matt Hensley	0–0	4.00	10	0	0	0	27.2	32	15	15	7	30
Bartolo Colon	18–12	5.01	34	34	0	0	208.1	215	122	116	71	158
Aaron Sele	9–4	5.05	28	24	0	0	132.0	163	84	74	51	51

BALTIMORE ORIOLES

BATTING	G	AB	R	H	2B	3B	HR	RBI	TB	BB	SO	SB	OBP	SLG	BA
Melvin Mora	140	550	111	187	41	0	27	104	309	66	95	11	.419	.562	.340
Javy Lopez	150	579	83	183	33	3	23	86	291	47	97	0	.370	.503	.316
David Newhan	95	373	66	116	15	7	8	54	169	27	72	11	.361	.453	.311
Miguel Tejada	162	653	107	203	40	2	34	150	349	48	73	4	.360	.534	.311
B.J. Surhoff	100	343	49	106	12	1	8	50	144	30	46	2	.365	.420	.309
Jerry Hairston	86	287	43	87	19	1	2	24	114	29	29	13	.378	.397	.303
Larry Bigbie	139	478	76	134	23	1	15	68	204	45	113	8	.341	.427	.280
Brian Roberts	159	641	107	175	50	2	4	53	241	71	95	29	.344	.376	.273
Rafael Palmeiro	154	550	68	142	29	0	23	88	240	86	61	2	.359	.436	.258
Tim Raines	48	94	14	24	6	0	0	5	30	4	16	7	.293	.319	.255
Jay Gibbons	97	346	36	85	14	1	10	47	131	29	64	1	.303	.379	.246
Luis Matos	89	330	36	74	18	0	6	28	110	19	60	12	.275	.333	.224
Karim Garcia	23	66	9	14	0	0	3	11	23	4	15	0	.247	.348	.212
Jose Leon	31	66	4	12	2	0	2	8	20	2	19	0	.203	.303	.182
Luis Lopez	56	88	7	16	5	0	1	8	24	3	20	0	.211	.273	.182

PITCHING	W–L	ERA	G	GS	CG	SV	INN	H	R	ER	BB	SO
B.J. Ryan	4–6	2.28	76	0	0	3	87.0	64	24	22	35	122
Todd Williams	2–0	2.87	29	0	0	0	31.1	26	10	10	9	13
Bruce Chen	2–1	3.02	8	7	1	0	47.2	39	19	16	16	32
John Parrish	6–3	3.46	56	1	0	1	78.0	68	39	30	55	71
Rodrigo Lopez	14–9	3.59	37	23	1	0	170.2	164	71	68	54	121
Jason Grimsley	5–7	3.86	73	0	0	0	63.0	61	36	27	35	39
Jorge Julio	2–5	4.57	65	0	0	22	69.0	59	35	35	39	70
Erik Bedard	6–10	4.59	27	26	0	0	137.1	149	83	70	71	121
Rick Bauer	2–1	4.70	23	2	0	0	53.2	49	31	28	20	37
Buddy Groom	4–1	4.78	60	0	0	0	52.2	67	30	28	16	32
Eddy Rodriguez	1–0	4.78	29	0	0	0	43.1	36	23	23	30	37
Daniel Cabrera	12–8	5.00	28	27	1	1	147.2	145	85	82	89	76
Dave Borkowski	3–4	5.14	17	8	0	0	56.0	65	37	32	15	45
Sidney Ponson	11–15	5.30	33	33	5	0	215.2	265	136	127	69	115

BOSTON RED SOX

BATTING	G	AB	R	H	2B	3B	HR	RBI	TB	BB	SO	SB	OBP	SLG	BA
Nomar Garciaparra	38	156	24	50	7	3	5	21	78	8	16	2	.367	.500	.321
Trot Nixon	48	149	24	47	9	1	6	23	76	15	24	0	.377	.510	.315
Manny Ramirez	152	568	108	175	44	0	43	130	348	82	124	2	.397	.613	.308
Johnny Damon	150	621	123	189	35	6	20	94	296	76	71	19	.380	.477	.304
David Ortiz	150	582	94	175	47	3	41	139	351	75	133	0	.380	.603	.301
Kevin Millar	150	508	74	151	36	0	18	74	241	57	91	1	.383	.474	.297
Jason Varitek	137	463	67	137	30	1	18	73	223	62	126	10	.390	.482	.296
Orlando Cabrera	58	228	33	67	19	1	6	31	106	11	23	4	.320	.465	.294
Bill Mueller	110	399	75	113	27	1	12	57	178	51	56	2	.365	.446	.283
Doug Mirabelli	59	160	27	45	12	0	9	32	84	19	46	0	.368	.525	.281
Gabe Kapler	136	290	51	79	14	1	6	33	113	15	49	5	.311	.390	.272
Mark Bellhorn	138	523	93	138	37	3	17	82	232	88	177	6	.373	.444	.264
Kevin Youkilis	72	208	38	54	11	0	7	35	86	33	45	0	.367	.413	.260
David McCarty	91	151	24	39	8	1	4	17	61	14	40	1	.327	.404	.258
Dave Roberts	45	86	19	22	10	0	2	14	38	10	17	5	.330	.442	.256
Doug Mientkiewicz	127	391	47	93	24	1	6	35	137	48	56	2	.326	.350	.238
Pokey Reese	96	244	32	54	7	2	3	29	74	17	60	6	.271	.303	.221

PITCHING	W–L	ERA	G	GS	CG	SV	INN	H	R	ER	BB	SO
Scott Williamson	0–1	1.26	28	0	0	1	28.2	11	6	4	18	28
Keith Foulke	5–3	2.17	72	0	0	32	83.0	63	22	20	15	79
Curt Schilling	21–6	3.26	32	32	3	0	226.2	206	84	82	35	203
Ramiro Mendoza	2–1	3.52	27	0	0	0	30.2	25	12	12	7	13
Pedro Martinez	16–9	3.90	33	33	1	0	217.0	193	99	94	61	227
Bronson Arroyo	10–9	4.03	32	29	0	0	178.2	171	99	80	47	142
Alan Embree	2–2	4.13	71	0	0	0	52.1	49	28	24	11	37
Mike Timlin	5–4	4.13	76	0	0	1	76.1	75	35	35	19	56
Mike Myers	5–1	4.64	75	0	0	0	42.2	45	22	22	23	32
Terry Adams	6–4	4.76	61	0	0	3	70.0	84	39	37	28	56
Tim Wakefield	12–10	4.87	32	30	0	0	188.1	197	121	102	63	116
Curtis Leskanic	3–5	5.19	51	0	0	4	43.1	47	27	25	30	37
Derek Lowe	14–12	5.42	33	33	0	0	182.2	224	138	110	71	105

CHICAGO WHITE SOX

BATTING	G	AB	R	H	2B	3B	HR	RBI	TB	BB	SO	SB	OBP	SLG	BA
Jamie Burke	57	120	22	40	9	0	0	15	49	10	13	0	.386	.408	.333
Ross Gload	110	234	28	75	16	0	7	44	112	20	37	0	.375	.479	.321
Aaron Rowand	140	487	94	151	38	2	24	69	265	30	91	17	.361	.544	.310
Carlos Lee	153	591	103	180	37	0	31	99	310	54	86	11	.366	.525	.305
Magglio Ordonez	52	202	32	59	8	2	9	37	98	16	22	0	.351	.485	.292
Juan Uribe	134	502	82	142	31	6	23	74	254	32	96	9	.327	.506	.283
Paul Konerko	155	563	84	156	22	0	41	117	301	69	107	1	.359	.535	.277
Frank Thomas	74	240	53	65	16	0	18	49	135	64	57	0	.434	.563	.271
Carl Everett	43	154	21	41	7	1	5	21	65	8	26	1	.320	.422	.266
Willie Harris	129	409	68	107	15	2	2	27	132	51	79	19	.343	.323	.262
Timo Perez	103	293	38	72	12	0	5	40	99	15	29	3	.285	.338	.246
Sandy Alomar, Jr.	50	146	16	35	4	0	2	14	45	11	13	0	.298	.308	.240
Joe Crede	144	490	67	117	25	0	21	69	205	34	81	1	.299	.418	.239
Jose Valentin	125	450	73	97	20	3	30	70	213	43	139	8	.287	.473	.216
Ben Davis	68	193	22	40	9	0	6	18	67	12	49	1	.256	.347	.207

PITCHING	W–L	ERA	G	GS	CG	SV	INN	H	R	ER	BB	SO
Shingo Takatsu	6–4	2.31	59	0	0	19	62.1	40	17	16	21	50
Damaso Marte	6–5	3.42	74	0	0	6	73.2	56	28	28	34	68
Freddy Garcia	13–11	3.81	31	31	1	0	210.0	192	92	89	64	184
Mark Buehrle	16–10	3.89	35	35	4	0	245.1	257	119	106	51	165
Cliff Politte	0–3	4.38	54	0	0	1	51.1	52	26	25	22	48
Jon Adkins	2–3	4.65	50	0	0	0	62.0	75	35	32	20	44
Jon Garland	12–11	4.89	34	33	1	0	217.0	223	125	118	76	113
Mike Jackson	2–0	5.01	45	0	0	0	46.2	55	27	26	15	26
Billy Koch	1–1	5.40	24	0	0	8	23.1	24	15	14	16	25
Jose Contreras	13–9	5.50	31	31	0	0	170.1	166	114	104	84	150
Scott Schoeneweis	6–9	5.59	20	19	0	0	112.2	129	74	70	49	69

CLEVELAND INDIANS

BATTING	G	AB	R	H	2B	3B	HR	RBI	TB	BB	SO	SB	OBP	SLG	BA
Travis Hafner	140	482	96	150	41	3	28	109	281	68	111	3	.410	.583	.311
Coco Crisp	139	491	78	146	24	2	15	71	219	36	69	20	.344	.446	.297
Omar Vizquel	148	567	82	165	28	3	7	59	220	57	62	19	.353	.388	.291
Lou Merloni	71	190	25	55	12	1	4	28	81	14	41	1	.343	.426	.289
Victor Martinez	141	520	77	147	38	1	23	108	256	60	69	0	.359	.492	.283
Ronnie Belliard	152	599	78	169	48	1	12	70	255	60	98	3	.348	.426	.282
Matt Lawton	150	591	109	164	25	0	20	70	249	74	84	23	.366	.421	.277
Ben Broussard	139	418	57	115	28	5	17	82	204	52	95	4	.370	.488	.275
Casey Blake	152	587	93	159	36	3	28	88	285	68	139	5	.354	.486	.271
Jody Gerut	134	481	72	121	31	5	11	51	195	54	59	13	.334	.405	.252
Josh Phelps	103	371	51	93	19	2	17	61	167	22	93	0	.304	.450	.251
Grady Sizemore	43	138	15	34	6	2	4	24	56	14	34	2	.333	.406	.246
Tim Laker	43	117	12	25	2	0	3	17	36	7	28	0	.262	.308	.214
Alex Escobar	46	152	20	32	8	2	1	12	47	23	42	1	.318	.309	.211
John McDonald	66	93	17	19	5	1	2	7	32	4	11	0	.237	.344	.204

PITCHING	W–L	ERA	G	GS	CG	SV	INN	H	R	ER	BB	SO
Bob Howry	4–2	2.74	37	0	0	0	42.2	37	14	13	12	39
Matt Miller	4–1	3.09	57	0	0	1	55.1	42	22	19	23	55
Jake Westbrook	14–9	3.38	33	30	5	0	215.2	208	95	81	61	116
David Riske	7–3	3.72	72	0	0	5	77.1	69	32	32	41	78
Rafael Betancourt	5–6	3.92	68	0	0	4	66.2	71	32	29	18	76
C.C. Sabathia	11–10	4.12	30	30	1	0	188.0	176	90	86	72	139
Bob Wickman	0–2	4.25	30	0	0	13	29.2	33	14	14	10	26
Scott Elarton	3–5	4.53	21	21	1	0	117.1	107	62	59	42	90
Cliff Bartosh	1–0	4.66	34	0	0	0	19.1	22	10	10	11	25
Rick White	5–5	5.29	59	0	0	1	78.1	99	52	46	20	44
Cliff Lee	14–8	5.43	33	33	0	0	179.0	188	113	108	81	161
Jason Davis	2–7	5.51	26	19	0	0	114.1	148	81	70	51	72

DETROIT TIGERS

BATTING	G	AB	R	H	2B	3B	HR	RBI	TB	BB	SO	SB	OBP	SLG	BA
Ivan Rodriguez	135	527	72	176	32	2	19	86	269	41	91	7	.383	.510	.334
Alex Sanchez	70	002	41	107	8	3	2	26	128	7	50	19	.335	.386	.322
Carlos Guillen	136	522	97	166	37	10	20	97	283	52	87	12	.379	.542	.318
Craig Monroe	128	447	65	131	27	3	18	72	218	29	79	3	.337	.488	.293
Brandon Inge	131	408	43	117	15	7	13	64	185	32	72	5	.340	.453	.287
Nook Logan	47	133	12	37	5	2	0	10	46	13	24	8	.340	.346	.278
Dmitri Young	104	389	72	106	23	2	18	60	187	33	71	0	.336	.481	.272
Rondell White	121	448	78	121	21	2	19	67	203	39	77	1	.337	.453	.270
Omar Infante	142	503	69	133	27	9	16	55	226	40	112	13	.317	.449	.264
Marcus Thames	61	165	24	42	12	0	10	33	84	16	42	0	.326	.509	.255
Bobby Higginson	131	448	63	110	24	2	12	64	174	70	84	5	.353	.388	.246
Carlos Pena	142	481	89	116	22	4	27	82	227	70	146	7	.338	.472	.241
Jason Smith	61	155	20	37	7	4	5	19	67	8	37	1	.280	.432	.239
Fernando Vina	29	115	21	26	5	0	0	7	31	9	9	2	.308	.270	.226
Eric Munson	109	321	36	68	14	2	19	49	143	29	90	1	.289	.445	.212

PITCHING	W–L	ERA	G	GS	CG	SV	INN	H	R	ER	BB	SO
Jamie Walker	3–4	3.20	70	0	0	1	64.2	69	28	23	12	53
Esteban Yan	3–6	3.83	69	0	0	7	87.0	92	43	37	32	69
Mike Maroth	11–13	4.31	33	33	2	0	217.0	244	112	104	59	108
Wilfredo Ledezma	4–3	4.39	15	8	0	0	53.1	55	28	26	18	29
Ugeth Urbina	4–6	4.50	54	0	0	21	54.0	38	28	27	32	56
Al Levine	3–4	4.58	65	0	0	0	70.2	83	37	36	24	32
Danny Patterson	0–4	4.75	37	0	0	2	41.2	44	24	22	16	24
Jeremy Bonderman	11–13	4.89	33	32	2	0	184.0	168	101	100	73	168
Nate Robertson	12–10	4.90	34	32	1	1	196.2	210	116	107	66	155
Jason Johnson	8–15	5.13	33	33	2	0	196.2	222	121	112	60	125
Gary Knotts	7–6	5.25	36	19	0	2	135.1	142	83	79	58	81
Roberto Novoa	1–1	5.57	16	0	0	0	21.0	25	15	13	6	15
Steve Colyer	1–0	6.47	41	0	0	0	32.0	33	24	23	24	31
Craig Dingman	2–2	6.75	24	0	0	0	29.1	33	22	22	22	16

KANSAS CITY ROYALS

BATTING	G	AB	R	H	2B	3B	HR	RBI	TB	BB	SO	SB	OBP	SLG	BA
David DeJesus	96	363	58	104	15	3	7	39	146	33	53	8	.360	.402	.287
Ken Harvey	120	456	47	131	20	1	13	55	192	28	89	1	.338	.421	.287
Joe Randa	128	485	65	139	31	2	8	56	198	40	77	0	.343	.408	.287
Mike Sweeney	106	411	56	118	23	0	22	79	207	33	44	3	.347	.504	.287
Carlos Beltran	69	266	51	74	19	2	15	51	142	37	44	14	.367	.534	.278
Juan Gonzalez	33	127	17	35	4	1	5	17	56	9	19	0	.326	.441	.276
Benito Santiago	49	175	15	48	10	0	6	23	76	8	32	1	.312	.434	.274
Ruben Gotay	44	152	17	41	7	3	1	16	57	9	36	0	.315	.375	.270
Matt Stairs	126	439	48	117	21	3	18	66	198	49	92	1	.345	.451	.267
Tony Graffanino	75	278	37	73	11	0	3	26	93	27	38	10	.332	.335	.263
Angel Berroa	134	512	72	134	27	6	8	43	197	23	87	14	.308	.385	.262
Dee Brown	59	195	19	49	7	0	4	24	68	11	50	2	.293	.349	.251
Calvin Pickering	35	122	21	30	8	1	7	26	61	18	42	0	.338	.500	.246
John Buck	71	238	36	56	9	0	12	30	101	15	79	1	.280	.424	.235
Abraham Nunez	59	221	31	50	9	0	5	29	74	25	48	0	.304	.335	.226
Desi Relaford	114	380	45	84	14	0	6	34	116	34	56	5	.296	.305	.221

PITCHING	W–L	ERA	G	GS	CG	SV	INN	H	R	ER	BB	SO
Jaime Cerda	1–4	3.15	53	0	0	2	45.2	41	21	16	30	33
Rudy Seanez	0–1	3.91	16	0	0	0	23.0	21	10	10	11	21
Shawn Camp	2–2	3.92	42	0	0	2	66.2	74	37	29	16	51
Zach Greinke	8–11	3.97	24	24	0	0	145.0	143	64	64	26	100
Nate Field	2–3	4.26	43	0	0	3	44.1	40	25	21	19	30
Dennys Reyes	4–8	4.75	40	12	0	0	108.0	114	64	57	50	91
Scott Sullivan	3–4	4.77	49	0	0	0	60.1	73	34	32	24	45
D.J. Carrasco	2–2	4.84	30	0	0	0	35.1	41	22	19	15	22
Jeremy Affeldt	3–4	4.95	38	8	0	13	76.1	91	49	42	32	49
Jimmy Gobble	9–8	5.35	25	24	1	0	148.0	157	94	88	43	49
Mike MacDougal	1–1	5.56	13	0	0	1	11.1	16	8	7	9	14
Darrell May	9–19	5.61	31	31	3	0	186.0	234	130	116	55	120
Brian Anderson	6–12	5.64	35	26	2	0	166.0	217	123	104	53	70
Mike Wood	3–8	5.94	17	17	0	0	100.0	112	67	66	28	54

MINNESOTA TWINS

BATTING	G	AB	R	H	2B	3B	HR	RBI	TB	BB	SO	SB	OBP	SLG	BA
Augie Ojeda	30	59	16	20	1	0	2	7	27	10	3	1	.429	.458	.339
Joe Mauer	35	107	18	33	8	1	6	17	61	11	14	1	.369	.570	.308
Shannon Stewart	92	378	46	115	17	2	11	47	169	47	44	6	.380	.447	.304
Jason Kubel	23	60	10	18	2	0	2	7	26	6	9	1	.358	.433	.300
Lew Ford	154	569	89	170	31	4	15	72	254	67	75	20	.381	.446	.299
Cristian Guzman	145	576	84	158	31	4	8	46	221	30	64	10	.309	.384	.274
Torii Hunter	138	520	79	141	37	0	23	81	247	40	101	21	.330	.475	.271
Justin Morneau	74	280	39	76	17	0	19	58	150	28	54	0	.340	.536	.271
Matthew LeCroy	88	264	25	71	14	0	9	39	112	16	60	0	.321	.424	.269
Michael Cuddyer	115	339	49	89	22	1	12	45	149	37	74	5	.339	.440	.263
Jose Offerman	77	172	22	44	14	2	2	22	68	29	31	1	.363	.395	.256
Luis Rivas	109	336	44	86	19	5	10	34	145	13	53	15	.283	.432	.256
Michael Restovich	29	47	9	12	3	0	2	6	21	4	10	0	.314	.447	.255
Jacque Jones	151	55	69	141	22	1	24	80	237	40	117	13	.315	.427	.254
Nick Punto	38	91	17	23	0	0	2	12	29	12	19	6	.340	.319	.253
Corey Koskie	118	422	68	106	24	2	25	71	209	49	103	9	.342	.495	.251
Henry Blanco	114	315	36	65	19	1	10	37	116	21	56	0	.260	.368	.206

PITCHING	W–L	ERA	G	GS	CG	SV	INN	H	R	ER	BB	SO
Joe Nathan	1–2	1.62	73	0	0	44	72.1	48	14	13	23	89
Jesse Crain	3–0	2.00	22	0	0	0	27.0	17	6	6	12	14
Johan Santana	20–6	2.61	34	34	1	0	228.0	156	70	66	54	265
Juan Rincon	11–6	2.63	77	0	0	2	82.0	52	27	24	32	106
Brad Radke	11–8	3.48	34	34	1	0	219.2	229	92	85	26	143
J.C. Romero	7–4	3.51	74	0	0	1	74.1	61	32	29	38	69
Carlos Silva	14–8	4.21	33	33	1	0	203.0	255	100	95	35	76
Grant Balfour	4–1	4.35	36	0	0	0	39.1	35	19	19	21	42
Joe Roa	2–3	4.50	48	0	0	0	70.0	84	38	35	24	47
Aaron Fultz	3–3	5.04	55	0	0	1	50.0	50	28	28	23	37
Terry Mulholland	5–9	5.18	39	15	0	0	123.1	163	76	71	33	60
Kyle Lohse	9–13	5.34	35	34	1	0	194.0	240	128	115	76	111

NEW YORK YANKEES

BATTING	G	AB	R	H	2B	3B	HR	RBI	TB	BB	SO	SB	OBP	SLG	BA
Hideki Matsui	162	584	109	174	34	2	31	108	305	88	103	3	.390	.522	.298
Miguel Cairo	122	360	48	105	17	5	6	42	150	18	49	11	.346	.417	.292
Derek Jeter	154	643	111	188	44	1	23	78	303	46	99	23	.352	.471	.292
Gary Sheffield	154	573	117	166	30	1	36	121	306	92	83	5	.393	.534	.290
Alex Rodriguez	155	601	112	172	24	2	36	106	308	80	131	28	.375	.512	.286
Kenny Lofton	83	276	51	76	10	7	3	18	109	31	27	7	.346	.395	.275
Jorge Posada	137	449	72	122	31	0	21	81	216	88	92	1	.400	.481	.272
Bernie Williams	148	561	105	147	29	1	22	70	244	85	96	1	.360	.435	.262
John Olerud	127	425	45	110	20	1	9	48	159	61	61	0	.359	.374	.259
John Flaherty	47	127	11	32	9	0	6	16	59	5	25	0	.286	.465	.252
Ruben Sierra	107	307	40	75	12	1	17	65	140	25	55	1	.296	.456	.244
Tony Clark	106	253	37	56	12	0	16	49	116	26	92	0	.297	.458	.221
Enrique Wilson	93	240	19	51	9	0	6	31	78	15	20	1	.254	.325	.213
Jason Giambi	80	264	33	55	9	0	12	40	100	47	62	0	.342	.379	.208
Bubba Crosby	55	53	8	8	2	0	2	7	16	2	13	2	.196	.302	.151

PITCHING	W–L	ERA	G	GS	CG	SV	INN	H	R	ER	BB	SO
Mariano Rivera	4–2	1.94	74	0	0	53	78.2	65	17	17	20	66
Tom Gordon	9–4	2.21	80	0	0	4	89.2	56	23	22	23	96
Orlando Hernandez	8–2	3.30	15	15	0	0	84.2	73	31	31	06	04
Kevin Brown	10–0	4.09	22	22	0	0	132.0	132	65	60	35	83
Jon Lieber	14–8	4.33	27	27	0	0	176.2	216	95	85	18	102
Mike Mussina	12–9	4.59	27	27	1	0	164.2	178	91	84	40	132
Paul Quantrill	7–3	4.72	86	0	0	1	95.1	124	54	50	20	37
Javier Vazquez	14–10	4.91	32	32	0	0	198.0	195	114	108	60	150
Bret Prinz	1–0	5.08	26	0	0	0	28.1	28	17	16	14	22
Scott Proctor	2–1	5.40	26	0	0	0	25.0	29	18	15	14	21
Tanyon Sturtze	6–2	5.47	28	3	0	1	77.1	75	40	47	33	56
Esteban Loaiza	10–7	5.70	31	27	2	0	183.0	217	124	116	71	117

OAKLAND ATHLETICS

BATTING	G	AB	R	H	2B	3B	HR	RBI	TB	BB	SO	SB	OBP	SLG	BA
Erubiel Durazo	142	511	80	164	35	1	22	88	267	56	104	3	.396	.523	.321
Mark Kotsay	148	606	78	190	37	3	15	63	278	55	70	8	.370	.459	.314
Scott Hatteberg	152	550	87	156	30	0	15	82	231	72	48	0	.367	.420	.284
Eric Byrnes	143	569	91	161	39	3	20	73	266	46	111	17	.347	.467	.283
Eric Chavez	125	475	87	131	20	0	29	77	238	95	99	6	.397	.501	.276
Marco Scutaro	137	455	50	124	32	1	7	43	179	16	58	0	.297	.393	.273
Damian Miller	110	397	39	108	25	0	9	58	160	39	87	0	.339	.403	.272
Jermaine Dye	137	532	87	141	29	4	23	80	247	49	128	4	.329	.464	.265
Adam Melhuse	69	214	23	55	11	0	11	31	99	16	47	0	.309	.463	.257
Esteban German	31	60	9	15	1	1	0	7	18	4	13	0	.297	.300	.250
Mark McLemore	77	250	29	62	14	0	2	21	82	41	33	0	.355	.328	.248
Bobby Crosby	151	545	70	130	34	1	22	64	232	58	141	7	.319	.426	.239
Bobby Kielty	83	238	29	51	14	1	7	31	88	35	47	1	.321	.370	.214
Eric Karros	40	103	8	20	6	0	2	11	32	7	16	1	.243	.311	.194
Billy McMillon	52	92	10	17	4	0	3	11	30	8	22	0	.255	.326	.185

PITCHING	W–L	ERA	G	GS	CG	SV	INN	H	R	ER	BB	SO
Chris Hammond	4–1	2.68	41	0	0	1	53.2	56	21	16	13	34
Justin Duchscherer	7–6	3.27	53	0	0	0	96.1	85	37	35	32	59
Tim Hudson	12–6	3.53	27	27	3	0	188.2	194	82	74	44	103
Jim Mecir	0–5	3.59	65	0	0	2	47.2	45	21	19	19	49
Ricardo Rincon	1–1	3.68	67	0	0	0	44.0	45	22	18	22	40
Rich Harden	11–7	3.99	31	31	0	0	189.2	171	90	84	81	167
Octavio Dotel	6–2	4.09	45	0	0	22	50.2	41	23	23	18	72
Chad Bradford	5–7	4.42	68	0	0	1	59.0	51	32	29	24	34
Mark Mulder	17–8	4.43	33	33	5	0	225.2	223	119	111	83	140
Barry Zito	11–11	4.48	34	34	0	0	213.0	216	116	106	81	163
Mark Redman	11–12	4.71	32	32	2	0	191.0	218	110	100	68	102
Arthur Rhodes	3–3	5.12	37	0	0	9	38.2	46	23	22	21	34
Justin Lehr	1–1	5.23	27	0	0	0	32.2	35	19	19	14	16

SEATTLE MARINERS

BATTING	G	AB	R	H	2B	3B	HR	RBI	TB	BB	SO	SB	OBP	SLG	BA
Ichiro Suzuki	161	704	101	262	24	5	8	60	320	49	63	36	.414	.455	.372
Raul Ibanez	123	481	67	146	31	1	16	62	227	36	72	1	.353	.472	.304
Randy Winn	157	626	84	179	34	6	14	81	267	53	98	21	.346	.427	.286
Dave Hansen	57	78	14	22	5	0	2	12	33	18	16	0	.412	.423	.282
Bucky Jacobsen	42	160	17	44	9	0	9	28	80	14	47	0	.335	.500	.275
Jolbert Cabrera	113	359	38	97	19	2	6	47	138	16	70	10	.312	.384	.270
Edgar Martinez	141	486	45	128	23	0	12	63	187	58	107	1	.342	.385	.263
Bret Boone	148	593	74	149	30	0	24	83	251	56	135	10	.317	.423	.251
Dan Wilson	103	319	23	80	13	0	2	33	99	26	57	0	.305	.310	.251
Willie Bloomquist	93	188	27	46	10	0	2	18	62	10	48	13	.283	.330	.245
Hiram Bocachica	50	90	9	22	5	0	3	6	36	12	27	5	.337	.400	.244
Rich Aurilia	73	261	27	63	13	0	4	28	88	22	43	1	.304	.337	.241
Miguel Olivo	96	301	46	70	15	4	13	40	132	20	84	7	.286	.439	.233
Jose Lopez	57	207	28	48	13	0	5	22	76	8	31	0	.263	.367	.232
Justin Leone	31	102	15	22	5	0	6	13	45	9	32	1	.298	.441	.216
Scott Spezio	112	367	38	79	12	3	10	41	127	36	60	4	.288	.346	.215

PITCHING	W–L	ERA	G	GS	CG	SV	INN	H	R	ER	BB	SO
Eddie Guardado	2–2	2.78	41	0	0	18	45.1	31	14	14	14	45
Bobby Madritsch	6–3	3.27	15	11	1	0	88.0	74	33	32	33	60
Scott Atchison	2–3	3.52	25	0	0	0	30.2	29	12	12	14	36
George Sherrill	2–1	3.80	21	0	0	0	23.2	24	12	10	9	16
Ron Villone	8–6	4.08	56	10	0	0	117.0	102	64	53	64	86
Matt Thornton	1–2	4.13	19	1	0	0	32.2	30	15	15	25	30
Joel Pineiro	6–11	4.67	21	21	1	0	140.2	144	77	73	43	111
Julio Mateo	1–2	4.68	45	0	0	1	57.2	56	30	30	16	43
J.J. Putz	0–3	4.71	54	0	0	9	63.0	66	35	33	24	47
Ryan Franklin	4–16	4.90	32	32	2	0	200.1	224	116	109	61	104
Gil Meche	7–7	5.01	23	23	1	0	127.2	139	73	71	47	99
Shigetoshi Hasegawa	4–6	5.16	68	0	0	0	68.0	67	42	39	31	46
Jamie Moyer	7–13	5.21	34	33	1	0	202.0	217	127	117	63	125

TAMPA BAY DEVIL RAYS

BATTING	G	AB	R	H	2B	3B	HR	RBI	TB	BB	SO	SB	OBP	SLG	BA
Jorge Cantu	50	173	25	52	20	1	2	17	80	9	44	0	.341	.462	.301
Aubrey Huff	157	600	92	178	27	2	29	104	296	56	74	5	.360	.493	.297
Carl Crawford	152	626	104	185	26	19	11	55	282	35	81	59	.331	.450	.296
Rocco Baldelli	136	518	79	145	27	3	16	74	226	30	88	17	.326	.436	.280
Midre Cummings	22	54	10	15	4	0	2	7	25	5	12	1	.361	.463	.278
Julio Lugo	157	581	83	160	41	4	7	75	230	54	106	21	.338	.396	.275
Tino Martinez	138	458	63	120	20	1	23	76	211	66	72	3	.362	.461	.262
B.J. Upton	45	159	19	41	8	2	4	12	65	15	46	4	.324	.409	.258
Toby Hall	119	404	35	103	21	0	8	60	148	24	41	0	.300	.366	.255
Rey Sanchez	91	285	23	70	14	3	2	26	96	12	28	0	.281	.337	.246
Jose Cruz	153	545	76	132	25	8	21	78	236	76	117	11	.333	.433	.242
Geoff Blum	112	339	38	73	21	0	8	35	118	24	58	2	.266	.348	.215
Brook Fordyce	54	151	14	31	6	0	2	9	43	9	34	0	.259	.285	.205
Robert Fick	76	214	12	43	5	2	6	26	70	20	32	0	.273	.327	.201

PITCHING	W–L	ERA	G	GS	CG	SV	INN	H	R	ER	BB	SO
Bobby Seay	0–0	2.38	21	0	0	0	22.2	21	6	6	5	17
Trever Miller	1–1	3.12	60	0	0	1	49.0	48	21	17	15	43
Jesus Colome	2–2	3.27	33	0	0	3	41.1	28	16	15	18	40
Lance Carter	3–3	3.47	56	0	0	0	80.1	77	32	31	23	36
Danys Baez	4–4	3.57	62	0	0	30	68.0	60	31	27	29	52
Travis Harper	6–2	3.89	52	0	0	0	78.2	69	37	34	23	59
Victor Zambrano	9–7	4.43	23	22	0	0	128.0	107	68	63	96	109
Rob Bell	8–8	4.46	24	19	1	0	123.0	121	71	61	41	57
John Halama	7–6	4.70	34	14	0	0	118.2	134	68	62	27	59
Dewon Brazelton	6–8	4.77	22	21	0	0	120.2	121	71	64	53	64
Mark Hendrickson	10–15	4.81	32	30	2	0	183.1	211	113	98	46	87
Chad Gaudin	1–2	4.85	26	4	0	0	42.2	59	27	23	16	30
Jorge Sosa	4–7	5.53	43	8	0	1	99.1	100	67	61	54	94
Doug Waechter	5–7	6.01	14	14	0	0	70.1	68	54	47	33	36

TEXAS RANGERS

BATTING

BATTING	G	AB	R	H	2B	3B	HR	RBI	TB	BB	SO	SB	OBP	SLG	BA
Michael Young	160	690	114	216	33	9	22	99	333	44	89	12	.353	.483	.313
Eric Young	104	344	55	99	25	2	1	27	131	43	28	14	.377	.381	.288
Mark Teixeira	145	545	101	153	34	2	38	112	305	68	117	4	.370	.560	.281
Alfonso Soriano	145	608	77	170	32	4	28	91	294	33	121	18	.324	.484	.280
Kevin Mench	125	438	69	122	30	3	26	71	236	33	63	0	.335	.539	.279
Hank Blalock	159	624	107	172	38	3	32	110	312	75	149	2	.355	.500	.276
Gary Matthews	87	280	37	77	17	1	11	36	129	33	64	5	.350	.461	.275
Rod Barajas	108	358	50	89	26	1	15	58	162	13	63	0	.276	.453	.249
Laynce Nix	115	371	58	92	20	4	14	46	162	23	113	1	.293	.437	.248
David Dellucci	107	331	59	80	13	1	17	61	146	47	88	9	.342	.441	.242
Chad Allen	20	58	4	14	4	1	0	6	20	2	13	0	.262	.345	.241
Manny Alexander	21	21	3	5	2	0	0	3	7	1	7	0	.273	.333	.238
Adrian Gonzalez	16	42	7	10	3	0	1	7	16	2	0	0	.273	.381	.238
Brad Fullmer	76	258	41	60	19	1	11	33	114	27	30	1	.310	.442	.233
Gerald Laird	49	147	20	33	6	0	1	16	42	12	35	0	.287	.286	.224
Herbert Perry	49	134	13	30	2	1	5	17	49	14	19	0	.307	.366	.224
Brian Jordan	61	212	27	47	13	1	5	23	77	16	35	2	.275	.363	.222

PITCHING

PITCHING	W–L	ERA	G	GS	CG	SV	INN	H	R	ER	BB	SO
Francisco Cordero	0–4	2.13	67	0	0	49	71.2	60	19	17	32	79
Brian Shouse	2–0	2.23	53	0	0	0	44.1	38	12	11	18	34
Ron Mahay	3–0	2.55	60	0	0	0	67.0	60	23	19	29	54
Frank Francisco	5–1	3.33	45	0	0	0	51.1	36	19	19	28	60
Jay Powell	1–1	3.38	23	0	0	0	24.0	24	11	9	11	17
Carlos Almanzar	7–3	3.72	67	0	0	0	72.2	66	33	30	19	44
Doug Brocail	4–1	4.13	43	0	0	1	52.1	54	29	24	20	43
Ryan Drese	14–10	4.20	34	33	2	0	207.2	233	104	97	58	98
Erasmo Ramirez	5–3	4.29	34	0	0	0	35.2	34	19	17	7	21
Kenny Rogers	18–9	4.76	35	35	2	0	211.2	248	117	112	66	126
Jeff Nelson	1–2	5.32	29	0	0	1	23.2	17	16	14	19	22
Chan Ho Park	4–7	5.46	16	16	0	0	95.2	105	63	58	33	63
R.A. Dickey	6–7	5.61	25	15	0	1	104.1	136	77	65	33	57
Joaquin Benoit	3–5	5.08	28	15	0	0	103.0	113	67	65	31	95

TORONTO BLUE JAYS

BATTING

BATTING	G	AB	R	H	2B	3B	HR	RBI	TB	BB	SO	SB	OBP	SLG	BA
Eric Hinske	155	570	66	140	23	3	15	69	214	54	109	12	.312	.375	.246
Reed Johnson	141	537	68	145	25	2	10	61	204	28	98	6	.320	.380	.270
Vernon Wells	134	536	82	146	34	2	23	67	253	51	83	9	.337	.472	.272
Orlando Hudson	135	489	73	132	32	7	12	58	214	51	98	7	.341	.438	.270
Carlos Delgado	128	458	74	123	26	0	32	99	245	69	115	0	.372	.535	.269
Alex Rios	111	426	55	122	24	7	1	28	163	31	84	15	.338	.383	.286
Chris Gomez	109	341	41	96	11	1	3	37	118	28	41	3	.337	.346	.282
Gregg Zaun	107	338	46	91	24	0	6	36	133	47	61	0	.367	.393	.269
Frank Menechino	84	269	40	74	13	4	9	26	122	37	52	0	.371	.454	.275
Frank Catalanotto	75	249	27	73	19	1	1	26	97	17	33	1	.344	.390	.293
Chris Woodward	69	213	21	50	13	4	1	24	74	14	46	1	.283	.347	.235
Kevin Cash	60	181	18	35	9	0	4	21	56	10	59	0	.249	.309	.193
Dave Berg	58	154	13	39	4	0	3	23	52	4	27	0	.278	.338	.253
Gabe Gross	44	129	18	27	4	0	3	16	40	19	31	2	.311	.310	.209
Howie Clark	40	115	17	25	6	0	3	12	40	13	15	0	.292	.348	.217

PITCHING

PITCHING	W–L	ERA	G	GS	CG	SV	INN	H	R	ER	BB	SO
Dave Bush	5–4	3.69	16	16	1	0	97.2	95	47	40	25	64
Justin Speier	3–8	3.91	62	0	0	7	69.0	61	32	30	25	52
Ted Lilly	12–10	4.06	32	32	2	0	197.1	171	92	89	89	168
Jason Frasor	4–6	4.08	63	0	0	17	68.1	64	31	31	36	54
Roy Halladay	8–8	4.20	21	21	1	0	133.0	140	66	62	39	95
Vinnie Chulk	1–3	4.66	47	0	0	2	56.0	59	30	29	27	44
Miguel Batista	10–13	4.80	38	31	2	5	198.2	206	115	106	96	104
Bob File	1–0	4.81	24	0	0	0	33.2	45	19	18	12	15
Josh Towers	9–9	5.11	21	21	0	0	116.1	148	70	66	26	51
Aquilino Lopez	1–1	6.00	18	0	0	0	21.0	21	15	14	13	13
Jason Kershner	0–1	6.04	24	2	0	0	22.1	30	16	15	8	15
Justin Miller	3–4	6.06	19	15	0	0	81.2	101	58	55	42	47

WORLD SERIES ALL-TIME RESULTS

2004	Boston (A) 4, St. Louis (N) 0	1953	New York (A) 4, Brooklyn (N) 2
2003	Florida (N) 4, New York (A) 2	1952	New York (A) 4, Brooklyn (N) 3
2002	Anaheim (A) 4, San Francisco (N) 3	1951	New York (A) 4, New York (N) 2
2001	Arizona (N) 4, New York (A) 3	1950	New York (A) 4, Philadelphia (N) 0
2000	New York (A) 4, New York (N) 1	1949	New York (A) 4, Brooklyn (N) 1
1999	New York (A) 4, Atlanta (N) 0	1948	Cleveland (A) 4, Boston (N) 2
1998	New York (A) 4, San Diego (N) 0	1947	New York (A) 4, Brooklyn (N) 3
1997	Florida (N) 4, Cleveland (A) 3	1946	St. Louis (N) 4, Boston (A) 3
1996	New York (A) 4, Atlanta (N) 2	1945	Detroit (A) 4, Chicago (N) 3
1995	Atlanta (N) 4, Cleveland (A) 2	1944	St. Louis (N) 4, St. Louis (A) 2
1994	Series canceled due to labor dispute.	1943	New York (A) 4, St. Louis (N) 1
1993	Toronto (A) 4, Philadelphia (N) 2	1942	St. Louis (N) 4, New York (A) 1
1992	Toronto (A) 4, Atlanta (N) 2	1941	New York (A) 4, Brooklyn (N) 1
1991	Minnesota (A) 4, Atlanta (N) 3	1940	Cincinnati (N) 4, Detroit (A) 3
1990	Cincinnati (N) 4, Oakland (A) 0	1939	New York (A) 4, Cincinnati (N) 0
1989	Oakland (A) 4, San Francisco (N) 0	1938	New York (A) 4, Chicago (N) 0
1988	Los Angeles (N) 4, Oakland (A) 1	1937	New York (A) 4, New York (N) 1
1987	Minnesota (A) 4, St. Louis (N) 3	1936	New York (A) 4, New York (N) 2
1986	New York (N) 4, Boston (A) 3	1935	Detroit (A) 4, Chicago (N) 2
1985	Kansas City (A) 4, St. Louis (N) 3	1934	St. Louis (N) 4, Detroit (A) 3
1984	Detroit (A) 4, San Diego (N) 1	1933	New York (N) 4, Washington (A) 1
1983	Baltimore (A) 4, Philadelphia (N) 1	1932	New York (A) 4, Chicago (N) 0
1982	St. Louis (N) 4, Milwaukee (A) 3	1931	St. Louis (N) 4, Philadelphia (A) 3
1981	Los Angeles (N) 4, New York (A) 2	1930	Philadelphia (A) 4, St. Louis (N) 2
1980	Philadelphia (N) 4, Kansas City (A) 2	1929	Philadelphia (A) 4, Chicago (N) 1
1979	Pittsburgh (N) 4, Baltimore (A) 3	1928	New York (A) 4, St. Louis (N) 0
1978	New York (A) 4, Los Angeles (N) 2	1927	New York (A) 4, Pittsburgh (N) 0
1977	New York (A) 4, Los Angeles (N) 2	1926	St. Louis (N) 4, New York (A) 3
1976	Cincinnati (N) 4, New York (A) 0	1925	Pittsburgh (N) 4, Washington (A) 3
1975	Cincinnati (N) 4, Boston (A) 3	1924	Washington (A) 4, New York (N) 3
1974	Oakland (A) 4, Los Angeles (N) 1	1923	New York (A) 4, New York (N) 2
1973	Oakland (A) 4, New York (N) 3	1922	New York (N) 4, New York (A) 0; 1 tie
1972	Oakland (A) 4, Cincinnati (N) 3	1921	New York (N) 5, New York (A) 3
1971	Pittsburgh (N) 4, Baltimore (A) 3	1920	Cleveland (A) 5, Brooklyn (N) 2
1970	Baltimore (A) 4, Cincinnati (N) 1	1919	Cincinnati (N) 5, Chicago (A) 3
1969	New York (N) 4, Baltimore (A) 1	1918	Boston (A) 4, Chicago (N) 2
1968	Detroit (A) 4, St. Louis (N) 3	1917	Chicago (A) 4, New York (N) 2
1967	St. Louis (N) 4, Boston (A) 3	1916	Boston (A) 4, Brooklyn (N) 1
1966	Baltimore (A) 4, Los Angeles (N) 0	1915	Boston (A) 4, Philadelphia (N) 1
1965	Los Angeles (N) 4, Minnesota (A) 3	1914	Boston (N) 4, Philadelphia (A) 0
1964	St. Louis (N) 4, New York (A) 3	1913	Philadelphia (A) 4, New York (N) 1
1963	Los Angeles (N) 4, New York (A) 0	1912	Boston (A) 4, New York (N) 3; 1 tie
1962	New York (A) 4, San Francisco (N) 3	1911	Philadelphia (A) 4, New York (N) 2
1961	New York (A) 4, Cincinnati (N) 1	1910	Philadelphia (A) 4, Chicago (N) 1
1960	Pittsburgh (N) 4, New York (A) 3	1909	Pittsburgh (N) 4, Detroit (A) 3
1959	Los Angeles (N) 4, Chicago (A) 2	1908	Chicago (N) 4, Detroit (A) 1
1958	New York (A) 4, Milwaukee (N) 3	1907	Chicago (N) 4, Detroit (A) 0; 1 tie
1957	Milwaukee (N) 4, New York (A) 3	1906	Chicago (A) 4, Chicago (N) 2
1956	New York (A) 4, Brooklyn (N) 3	1905	New York (N) 4, Philadelphia (A) 1
1955	Brooklyn (N) 4, New York (A) 3	1904	No series
1954	New York (N) 4, Cleveland (A) 0	1903	Boston (A) 5, Pittsburgh (N) 3

Note: A=American League; N=National League

WORLD SERIES MOST VALUABLE PLAYERS

2004	Manny Ramirez, Bos	1980	Mike Schmidt, Phil
2003	Josh Beckett, Fla	1979	Willie Stargell, Pitt
2002	Troy Glaus, Ana	1978	Bucky Dent, NY (A)
2001	Randy Johnson, Ari	1977	Reggie Jackson, NY (A)
	Curt Schilling, Ari	1976	Johnny Bench, Cin
2000	Derek Jeter, NY (A)	1975	Pete Rose, Cin
1999	Mariano Rivera, NY (A)	1974	Rollie Fingers, Oak
1998	Scott Brosius, NY (A)	1973	Reggie Jackson, Oak
1997	Livan Hernandez, Fla	1972	Gene Tenace, Oak
1996	John Wetteland, NY (A)	1971	Roberto Clemente, Pitt
1995	Tom Glavine, Atl	1970	Brooks Robinson, Bal
1994	Series canceled due to labor dispute.	1969	Donn Clendenon, NY (N)
1993	Paul Molitor, Tor	1968	Mickey Lolich, Det
1992	Pat Borders, Tor	1967	Bob Gibson, StL
1991	Jack Morris, Min	1966	Frank Robinson, Bal
1990	Jose Rijo, Cin	1965	Sandy Koufax, LA
1989	Dave Stewart, Oak	1964	Bob Gibson, StL
1988	Orel Hershiser, LA	1963	Sandy Koufax, LA
1987	Frank Viola, Min	1962	Ralph Terry, NY (A)
1986	Ray Knight, NY (N)	1961	Whitey Ford, NY (A)
1985	Bret Saberhagen, KC	1960	Bobby Richardson, NY (A)
1984	Alan Trammell, Det	1959	Larry Sherry, LA
1983	Rick Dempsey, Bal	1958	Bob Turley, NY (A)
1982	Darrell Porter, StL	1957	Lew Burdette, Mil
1981	Ron Cey, LA; Steve Yeager, LA;	1956	Don Larsen, NY (A)
	Pedro Guerrero, LA	1955	Johnny Podres, Bklyn

LEAGUE CHAMPIONSHIP SERIES

	NATIONAL LEAGUE		AMERICAN LEAGUE
2004	St. Louis (C) 4, Houston (WC) 3	2004	Boston (WC) 4, New York (E) 3
2003	Florida (WC) 4, Chicago (C) 3	2003	New York (E) 4, Boston (WC) 3
2002	San Francisco (WC) 4, St. Louis (C) 1	2002	Anaheim (WC) 4, Minnesota (C) 1
2001	Arizona (W) 4, Atlanta (E) 1	2001	New York (E) 4, Seattle (W) 1
2000	New York (WC) 4, St. Louis (C) 1	2000	New York (E) 4, Seattle (WC) 2
1999	Atlanta (E) 4, New York (WC) 2	1999	New York (E) 4, Boston (WC) 1
1998	San Diego (W) 4, Atlanta (E) 2	1998	New York (E) 4, Cleveland (C) 2
1997	Florida (WC) 4, Atlanta (E) 2	1997	Cleveland (C) 4, Baltimore (E) 2
1996	Atlanta (E) 4, St. Louis (C) 3	1996	New York (E) 4, Baltimore (WC) 1
1995	Atlanta (E) 4, Cincinnati (C) 0	1995	Cleveland (C) 4, Seattle (W) 2
1994	Playoffs canceled due to labor dispute.	1994	Playoffs canceled due to labor dispute.
1993	Philadelphia (E) 4, Atlanta (W) 2	1993	Toronto (E) 4, Chicago (W) 2
1992	Atlanta (W) 4, Pittsburgh (E) 3	1992	Toronto (E) 4, Oakland (W) 2
1991	Atlanta (W) 4, Pittsburgh (E) 3	1991	Minnesota (W) 4, Toronto (E) 1
1990	Cincinnati (W) 4, Pittsburgh (E) 2	1990	Oakland (W) 4, Boston (E) 0
1989	San Francisco (W) 4, Chicago (E) 1	1989	Oakland (W) 4, Toronto (E) 1
1988	Los Angeles (W) 4, New York (E) 3	1988	Oakland (W) 4, Boston (E) 0
1987	St. Louis (E) 4, San Francisco (W) 3	1987	Minnesota (W) 4, Detroit (E) 1
1986	New York (E) 4, Houston (W) 2	1986	Boston (E) 4, California (W) 3
1985	St. Louis (E) 4, Los Angeles (W) 2	1985	Kansas City (W) 4, Toronto (E) 3
1984	San Diego (W) 3, Chicago (E) 2	1984	Detroit (E) 3, Kansas City (W) 0
1983	Philadelphia (E) 3, Los Angeles (W) 1	1983	Baltimore (E) 3, Chicago (W) 1
1982	St. Louis (E) 3, Atlanta (W) 0	1982	Milwaukee (E) 3, California (W) 2
1981	Los Angeles (W) 3, Montreal (E) 2	1981	New York (E) 3, Oakland (W) 0
1980	Philadelphia (E) 3, Houston (W) 2	1980	Kansas City (W) 3, New York (E) 0
1979	Pittsburgh (E) 3, Cincinnati (W) 0	1979	Baltimore (E) 3, California (W) 1
1978	Los Angeles (W) 3, Philadelphia (E) 1	1978	New York (E) 3, Kansas City (W) 1
1977	Los Angeles (W) 3, Philadelphia (E) 1	1977	New York (E) 3, Kansas City (W) 2
1976	Cincinnati (W) 3, Philadelphia (E) 0	1976	New York (E) 3, Kansas City (W) 2
1975	Cincinnati (W) 3, Pittsburgh (E) 0	1975	Boston (E) 3, Oakland (W) 0
1974	Los Angeles (W) 3, Pittsburgh (E) 1	1974	Oakland (W) 3, Baltimore (E) 1
1973	New York (E) 3, Cincinnati (W) 2	1973	Oakland (W) 3, Baltimore (E) 2
1972	Cincinnati (W) 3, Pittsburgh (E) 2	1972	Oakland (W) 3, Detroit (E) 2
1971	Pittsburgh (E) 3, San Francisco (W) 1	1971	Baltimore (E) 3, Oakland (W) 0
1970	Cincinnati (W) 3, Pittsburgh (E) 0	1970	Baltimore (E) 3, Minnesota (W) 0
1969	New York (E) 3, Atlanta (W) 0	1969	Baltimore (E) 3, Minnesota (W) 0

Note: WC=wild-card team; W=Western Division; E=Eastern Division; C=Central Division

NLCS MOST VALUABLE PLAYER

2004	Albert Pujols, StL	1994	Playoffs canceled	1985	Ozzie Smith, StL
2003	Ivan Rodriguez, Fla	1993	Curt Schilling, Phil	1984	Steve Garvey, SD
2002	Benito Santiago, SF	1992	John Smoltz, Atl	1983	Gary Matthews, Phil
2001	Craig Counsell, Ari	1991	Steve Avery, Atl	1982	Darrell Porter, StL
2000	Mike Hampton, NY	1990	R. Myers/R. Dibble, Cin	1981	Burt Hooton, LA
1999	Eddie Perez, Atl	1989	Will Clark, SF	1980	Manny Trillo, Phil
1998	Sterling Hitchcock, SD	1988	Orel Hershiser, LA	1979	Willie Stargell, Pitt
1997	Livan Hernandez, Fla	1987	Jeffrey Leonard, SF	1978	Steve Garvey, LA
1996	Javier Lopez, Atl	1986	Mike Scott, Hou	1977	Dusty Baker, LA
1995	Mike Devereaux, Atl				

ALCS MOST VALUABLE PLAYER

2004	David Ortiz, Bos	1995	Orel Hershiser, Cle	1986	Marty Barrett, Bos
2003	Mariano Rivera, NY	1994	Playoffs canceled	1985	George Brett, KC
2002	Adam Kennedy, Ana	1993	Dave Stewart, Tor	1984	Kirk Gibson, Det
2001	Andy Pettitte, NY	1992	Roberto Alomar, Tor	1983	Mike Boddicker, Bal
2000	David Justice, NY	1991	Kirby Puckett, Min	1982	Fred Lynn, Cal
1999	Orlando Hernandez, NY	1990	Dave Stewart, Oak	1981	Graig Nettles, NY
1998	David Wells, NY	1989	Rickey Henderson, Oak	1980	Frank White, KC
1997	Marquis Grissom, Cle	1988	Dennis Eckersley, Oak		
1996	Bernie Williams, NY	1987	Gary Gaetti, Min		

ALL-STAR GAME

DATE	WINNER	SCORE	SITE	DATE	WINNER	SCORE	SITE
7-12-05	American	7–5	Comerica Park, Det	7-13-65	National	6–5	Metropolitan Stadium, Min
7-13-04	American	9–4	Minute Maid Park, Hou				
7-15-03	American	7–6	U.S. Cellular Field, Chi	7-7-64	National	7–4	Shea Stadium, NY
7-9-02	Tie (11 inn)	7–7	Miller Park, Mil	7-9-63	National	5–3	Municipal Stadium, Cle
7-10-01	American	4–1	Safeco Field, Sea	7-30-62	American	9–4	Wrigley Field, Chi
7-11-00	American	6–3	Turner Field, Atl	7-10-62	National	3–1	D.C. Stadium, Wash
7-13-99	American	4–1	Fenway Park, Bos	7-31-61	Tie*	1–1	Fenway Park, Bos
7-7-98	American	13–8	Coors Field, Col	7-11-61	National	5–4	Candlestick Park, SF
7-8-97	American	3–1	Jacobs Field, Cle	7-13-60	National	6–0	Yankee Stadium, NY
7-9-96	National	6–0	Veterans Stadium, Phil	7-11-60	National	5–3	Municipal Stadium, KC
7-11-95	National	3–2	The Ballpark in Arlington, Tex	8-3-59	American	5–3	Memorial Coliseum, LA
				7-7-59	National	5–4	Forbes Field, Pitt
7-12-94	National	8–7	Three Rivers Stadium, Pitt	7-8-58	American	4–3	Memorial Stadium, Bal
7-13-93	American	9–3	Camden Yards, Bal	7-9-57	American	6–5	Sportsman's Park, StL
7-14-92	American	13–6	Jack Murphy Stadium, SD	7-10-56	National	7–3	Griffith Stadium, Wash
7-9-91	American	4–2	SkyDome, Tor	7-12-55	National	6–5	County Stadium, Mil
7-10-90	American	2–0	Wrigley Field, Chi	7-13-54	American	11–9	Municipal Stadium, Cle
7-11-89	American	5–3	Anaheim Stadium, Cal	7-14-53	National	5–1	Crosley Field, Cin
7-12-88	American	2–1	Riverfront Stadium, Cin	7-8-52	National	3–2	Shibe Park, Phil
7-14-87	National	2–0	Oakland Coliseum, Oak	7-10-51	National	8–3	Briggs Stadium, Det
7-15-86	American	3–2	Astrodome, Hou	7-11-50	National	4–3	Comiskey Park, Chi
7-16-85	National	6–1	Metrodome, Min	7-12-49	American	11–7	Ebbets Field, Bklyn
7-10-84	National	3–1	Candlestick Park, SF	7-13-48	American	5–2	Sportsman's Park, StL
7-6-83	American	13–3	Comiskey Park, Chi	7-8-47	American	2–1	Wrigley Field, Chi
7-13-82	National	4–1	Olympic Stadium, Mon	7-9-46	American	12–0	Fenway Park, Bos
8-9-81	National	5–4	Municipal Stadium, Cle	1945	No game due to wartime travel restrictions.		
7-8-80	National	4–2	Dodger Stadium, LA	7-11-44	National	7–1	Forbes Field, Pitt
7-17-79	National	7–6	Kingdome, Sea	7-13-43	American	5–3	Shibe Park, Phil
7-11-78	National	7–3	Jack Murphy Stadium, SD	7-6-42	American	3–1	Polo Grounds, NY
7-19-77	National	7–5	Yankee Stadium, NY	7-8-41	American	7–5	Briggs Stadium, Det
7-13-76	National	7–1	Veterans Stadium, Phil	7-10-40	National	4–0	Sportsman's Park, StL
7-15-75	National	6–3	County Stadium, Mil	7-11-39	American	3–1	Yankee Stadium, NY
7-23-74	National	7–2	Three Rivers Stadium, Pitt	7-6-38	National	4–1	Crosley Field, Cin
7-24-73	National	7–1	Royals Stadium, KC	7-7-37	American	8–3	Griffith Stadium, Wash
7-25-72	National	4–3	Atlanta Stadium, Atl	7-7-36	National	4–3	Braves Field, Bos
7-13-71	American	6–4	Tiger Stadium, Det	7-8-35	American	4–1	Municipal Stadium, Cle
7-14-70	National	5–4	Riverfront Stadium, Cin	7-10-34	American	9–7	Polo Grounds, NY
7-23-69	National	9–3	R.F.K. Memorial Stadium, Wash	7-6-33	American	4–2	Comiskey Park, Chi
7-9-68	National	1–0	Astrodome, Hou				
7-11-67	National	2–1	Anaheim Stadium, Cal				
7-12-66	National	2–1	Busch Stadium, StL				

*Game called because of rain after nine innings.

ALL-STAR GAME – MOST VALUABLE PLAYERS

2005	Miguel Tejada, Bal	AL	1987	Tim Raines, Mon	NL	1971	Frank Robinson, Bal	AL
2004	Alfonso Soriano, Tex	AL	1986	Roger Clemens, Bos	AL	1970	Carl Yastrzemski, Bos	AL
2003	Garret Anderson, Ana	AL	1985	LaMarr Hoyt, SD	NL	1969	Willie McCovey, SF	NL
2002	None selected		1984	Gary Carter, Mon	NL	1968	Willie Mays, SF	NL
2001	Cal Ripken, Jr., Bal	AL	1983	Fred Lynn, Cal	AL	1967	Tony Perez, Cin	NL
2000	Derek Jeter, NY	AL	1982	Dave Concepcion, Cin	NL	1966	Brooks Robinson, Bal	AL
1999	Pedro Martinez, Bos	AL	1981	Gary Carter, Mon	NL	1965	Juan Marichal, SF	NL
1998	Roberto Alomar, Bal	AL	1980	Ken Griffey, Cin	NL	1964	Johnny Callison, Phil	NL
1997	Sandy Alomar, Cle	AL	1979	Dave Parker, Pitt	NL	1963	Willie Mays, SF	NL
1996	Mike Piazza, LA	NL	1978	Steve Garvey, LA	NL	1962	Maury Wills, LA	NL
1995	Jeff Conine, Fla	NL	1977	Don Sutton, LA	NL	1962	Leon Wagner, LA	AL
1994	Fred McGriff, Atl	NL	1976	George Foster, Cin	NL			
1993	Kirby Puckett, Min	AL	1975	Bill Madlock, Chi	NL			
1992	Ken Griffey, Jr., Sea	AL	1975	Jon Matlack, NY	NL			
1991	Cal Ripken, Jr., Bal	AL	1974	Steve Garvey, LA	NL			
1990	Julio Franco, Tex	AL	1973	Bobby Bonds, SF	NL			
1989	Bo Jackson, KC	AL	1972	Joe Morgan, Cin	NL	***Barry***	
1988	Terry Steinbach, Oak	AL					***Bonds***	

REGULAR SEASON – MOST VALUABLE PLAYERS

NATIONAL LEAGUE

YEAR	NAME AND TEAM	POSITION	YEAR	NAME AND TEAM	POSITION
2004	Barry Bonds, SF	Outfield	1961	Frank Robinson, Cin	Outfield
2003	Barry Bonds, SF	Outfield	1960	Dick Groat, Pitt	Shortstop
2002	Barry Bonds, SF	Outfield	1959	Ernie Banks, Chi	Shortstop
2001	Barry Bonds, SF	Outfield	1958	Ernie Banks, Chi	Shortstop
2000	Jeff Kent, SF	Second Base	1957	Hank Aaron, Mil	Outfield
1999	Chipper Jones, Atl	Third Base	1956	Don Newcombe, Bklyn	Pitcher
1998	Sammy Sosa, Chi	Outfield	1955	Roy Campanella, Bklyn	Catcher
1997	Larry Walker, Col	Outfield	1954	Willie Mays, NY	Outfield
1996	Ken Caminiti, SD	Third Base	1953	Roy Campanella, Bklyn	Catcher
1995	Barry Larkin, Cin	Shortstop	1952	Hank Sauer, Chi	Outfield
1994	Jeff Bagwell, Hou	First Base	1951	Roy Campanella, Bklyn	Catcher
1993	Barry Bonds, SF	Outfield	1950	Jim Konstanty, Phil	Pitcher
1992	Barry Bonds, Pitt	Outfield	1949	Jackie Robinson, Bklyn	Second Base
1991	Terry Pendleton, Atl	Third Base	1948	Stan Musial, StL	Outfield
1990	Barry Bonds, Pitt	Outfield	1947	Bob Elliott, Bos	Third Base
1989	Kevin Mitchell, SF	Outfield	1946	Stan Musial, StL	First Base, Outfield
1988	Kirk Gibson, LA	Outfield	1945	Phil Cavarretta, Chi	First Base
1987	Andre Dawson, Chi	Outfield	1944	Marty Marion, StL	Shortstop
1986	Mike Schmidt, Phil	Third Base	1943	Stan Musial, StL	Outfield
1985	Willie McGee, StL	Outfield	1942	Mort Cooper, StL	Pitcher
1984	Ryne Sandberg, Chi	Second Base	1941	Dolph Camilli, Bklyn	First Base
1983	Dale Murphy, Atl	Outfield	1940	Frank McCormick, Cin	First Base
1982	Dale Murphy, Atl	Outfield	1939	Bucky Walters, Cin	Pitcher
1981	Mike Schmidt, Phil	Third Base	1938	Ernie Lombardi, Cin	Catcher
1980	Mike Schmidt, Phil	Third Base	1937	Joe Medwick, StL	Outfield
1979	Keith Hernandez, StL	First Base	1936	Carl Hubbell, NY	Pitcher
	Willie Stargell, Pitt	First Base	1935	Gabby Hartnett, Chi	Catcher
1978	Dave Parker, Pitt	Outfield	1934	Dizzy Dean, StL	Pitcher
1977	George Foster, Cin	Outfield	1933	Carl Hubbell, NY	Pitcher
1976	Joe Morgan, Cin	Second Base	1932	Chuck Klein, Phil	Outfield
1975	Joe Morgan, Cin	Second Base	1931	Frankie Frisch, StL	Second Base
1974	Steve Garvey, LA	First Base	1930	No selection	
1973	Pete Rose, Cin	Outfield	1929	Rogers Hornsby, Chi	Second Base
1972	Johnny Bench, Cin	Catcher	1928	Jim Bottomley, StL	First Base
1971	Joe Torre, StL	Third Base	1927	Paul Waner, Pitt	Outfield
1970	Johnny Bench, Cin	Catcher	1926	Bob O'Farrell, StL	Catcher
1969	Willie McCovey, SF	First Base	1925	Rogers Hornsby, StL	Second Base, Manager
1968	Bob Gibson, StL	Pitcher			
1967	Orlando Cepeda, StL	First Base	1924	Dazzy Vance, Bklyn	Pitcher
1966	Roberto Clemente, Pitt	Outfield	1915-23	No selections	
1965	Willie Mays, SF	Outfield	1914	Johnny Evers, Bos	Second Base
1964	Ken Boyer, StL	Third Base	1913	Jake Daubert, Bklyn	First Base
1963	Sandy Koufax, LA	Pitcher	1912	Larry Doyle, NY	Second Base
1962	Maury Wills, LA	Shortstop	1911	Wildfire Schulte, Chi	Outfield

REGULAR SEASON – MOST VALUABLE PLAYERS (cont.)

AMERICAN LEAGUE

Vladimir Guerrero of the Anaheim Angels was the 2004 A.L. MVP.

PETER READ MILLER/SPORTS ILLUSTRATED

YEAR	NAME AND TEAM	POSITION
1964	Brooks Robinson, Bal	Third Base
1963	Elston Howard, NY	Catcher
1962	Mickey Mantle, NY	Outfield
1961	Roger Maris, NY	Outfield
1960	Roger Maris, NY	Outfield
1959	Nellie Fox, Chi	Second Base
1958	Jackie Jensen, Bos	Outfield
1957	Mickey Mantle, NY	Outfield
1956	Mickey Mantle, NY	Outfield
1955	Yogi Berra, NY	Catcher
1954	Yogi Berra, NY	Catcher
1953	Al Rosen, Cle	Third Base
1952	Bobby Shantz, Phil	Pitcher
1951	Yogi Berra, NY	Catcher
1950	Phil Rizzuto, NY	Shortstop
1949	Ted Williams, Bos	Outfield
1948	Lou Boudreau, Cle	Shortstop
1947	Joe DiMaggio, NY	Outfield
1946	Ted Williams, Bos	Outfield
1945	Hal Newhouser, Det	Pitcher
1944	Hal Newhouser, Det	Pitcher
1943	Spud Chandler, NY	Pitcher
1942	Joe Gordon, NY	Second Base
1941	Joe DiMaggio, NY	Outfield
1940	Hank Greenberg, Det	Outfield
1939	Joe DiMaggio, NY	Outfield
1938	Jimmie Foxx, Bos	First Base
1937	Charlie Gehringer, Det	Second Base
1936	Lou Gehrig, NY	First Base
1935	Hank Greenberg, Det	First Base
1934	Mickey Cochrane, Det	Catcher
1933	Jimmie Foxx, Phil	First Base
1932	Jimmie Foxx, Phil	First Base
1931	Lefty Grove, Phil	Pitcher
1930	No selection	
1929	No selection	
1928	Mickey Cochrane, Phil	Catcher
1927	Lou Gehrig, NY	First Base
1926	George Burns, Cle	First Base
1925	Roger Peckinpaugh, Wash	Shortstop
1924	Walter Johnson, Wash	Pitcher
1923	Babe Ruth, NY	Outfield
1922	George Sisler, StL	First Base
1915–21	No selections	
1914	Eddie Collins, Phil	Second Base
1913	Walter Johnson, Wash	Pitcher
1912	Tris Speaker, Bos	Outfield
1911	Ty Cobb, Det	Outfield

YEAR	NAME AND TEAM	POSITION
2004	Vladimir Guerrero, Ana	Outfield
2003	Alex Rodriguez, Tex	Shortstop
2002	Miguel Tejada, Oak	Shortstop
2001	Ichiro Suzuki, Sea	Outfield
2000	Jason Giambi, Oak	First Base
1999	Ivan Rodriguez, Tex	Catcher
1998	Juan Gonzalez, Tex	Outfield
1997	Ken Griffey, Jr., Sea	Outfield
1996	Juan Gonzalez, Tex	Outfield
1995	Mo Vaughn, Bos	First Base
1994	Frank Thomas, Chi	First Base
1993	Frank Thomas, Chi	First Base
1992	Dennis Eckersley, Oak	Pitcher
1991	Cal Ripken, Jr., Bal	Shortstop
1990	Rickey Henderson, Oak	Outfield
1989	Robin Yount, Mil	Outfield
1988	Jose Canseco, Oak	Outfield
1987	George Bell, Tor	Outfield
1986	Roger Clemens, Bos	Pitcher
1985	Don Mattingly, NY	First Base
1984	Willie Hernandez, Det	Pitcher
1983	Cal Ripken, Jr., Bal	Shortstop
1982	Robin Yount, Mil	Shortstop
1981	Rollie Fingers, Mil	Pitcher
1980	George Brett, KC	Third Base
1979	Don Baylor, Cal	Outfield, DH
1978	Jim Rice, Bos	Outfield, DH
1977	Rod Carew, Min	First Base
1976	Thurman Munson, NY	Catcher
1975	Fred Lynn, Bos	Outfield
1974	Jeff Burroughs, Tex	Outfield
1973	Reggie Jackson, Oak	Outfield
1972	Dick Allen, Chi	First Base
1971	Vida Blue, Oak	Pitcher
1970	Boog Powell, Bal	First Base
1969	Harmon Killebrew, Min	Third Base, First Base
1968	Denny McLain, Det	Pitcher
1967	Carl Yastrzemski, Bos	Outfield
1966	Frank Robinson, Bal	Outfield
1965	Zoilo Versalles, Min	Shortstop

TRIVIA CHALLENGE

On May 18, 2004, Randy Johnson became the 17th pitcher to throw a perfect game. Only one perfect game has ever come in the post-season. Name the pitcher who threw baseball's only perfecto in post-season play.

Don Larsen of the New York Yankees pitched a perfect game in Game 5 of the 1956 World Series, a 2–0 victory over the Brooklyn Dodgers.

REGULAR SEASON – ROOKIES OF THE YEAR

NATIONAL LEAGUE		AMERICAN LEAGUE	
2004	Jason Bay, Pitt (OF)	2004	Bobby Crosby, Oak (SS)
2003	Dontrelle Willis, Fla (P)	2003	Angel Berroa, KC (SS)
2002	Jason Jennings, Col (P)	2002	Eric Hinske, Tor (3B)
2001	Albert Pujols, StL (OF)	2001	Ichiro Suzuki, Sea (OF)
2000	Rafael Furcal, Atl (SS)	2000	Kazuhiro Sasaki, Sea (P)
1999	Scott Williamson, Cin (P)	1999	Carlos Beltran, KC (OF)
1998	Kerry Wood, Chi (P)	1998	Ben Grieve, Oak (OF)
1997	Scott Rolen, Phil (3B)	1997	Nomar Garciaparra, Bos (SS)
1996	Todd Hollandsworth, LA (OF)	1996	Derek Jeter, NY (SS)
1995	Hideo Nomo, LA (P)	1995	Marty Cordova, Min (OF)
1994	Raul Mondesi, LA (OF)	1994	Bob Hamelin, KC (DH)
1993	Mike Piazza, LA (C)	1993	Tim Salmon, Cal (OF)
1992	Eric Karros, LA (1B)	1992	Pat Listach, Mil (SS)
1991	Jeff Bagwell, Hou (3B)	1991	Chuck Knoblauch, Min (2B)
1990	David Justice, Atl (OF)	1990	Sandy Alomar, Jr., Cle (C)
1989	Jerome Walton, Chi (OF)	1989	Gregg Olson, Bal (P)
1988	Chris Sabo, Cin (3B)	1988	Walt Weiss, Oak (SS)
1987	Benito Santiago, SD (C)	1987	Mark McGwire, Oak (1B)
1986	Todd Worrell, StL (P)	1986	Jose Canseco, Oak (OF)
1985	Vince Coleman, StL (OF)	1985	Ozzie Guillen, Chi (SS)
1984	Dwight Gooden, NY (P)	1984	Alvin Davis, Sea (1B)
1983	Darryl Strawberry, NY (OF)	1983	Ron Kittle, Chi (OF)
1982	Steve Sax, LA (2B)	1982	Cal Ripken, Jr., Bal (SS)
1981	Fernando Valenzuela, LA (P)	1981	Dave Righetti, NY (P)
1980	Steve Howe, LA (P)	1980	Joe Charboneau, Cle (OF)
1979	Rick Sutcliffe, LA (P)	1979	Alfredo Griffin, Tor (SS)
			John Castino, Min (3B)
1978	Bob Horner, Atl (3B)	1978	Lou Whitaker, Det (2B)
1977	Andre Dawson, Mon (OF)	1977	Eddie Murray, Bal (DH)
1976	Pat Zachry, Cin (P)	1976	Mark Fidrych, Det (P)
	Butch Metzger, SD (P)		
1975	John Montefusco, SF (P)	1975	Fred Lynn, Bos (OF)
1974	Bake McBride, StL (OF)	1974	Mike Hargrove, Tex (1B)
1973	Gary Matthews, SF (OF)	1973	Al Bumbry, Bal (OF)
1972	Jon Matlack, NY (P)	1972	Carlton Fisk, Bos (C)
1971	Earl Williams, Atl (C)	1971	Chris Chambliss, Cle (1B)
1970	Carl Morton, Mon (P)	1970	Thurman Munson, NY (C)
1969	Ted Sizemore, LA (2B)	1969	Lou Piniella, KC (OF)
1968	Johnny Bench, Cin (C)	1968	Stan Bahnsen, NY (P)
1967	Tom Seaver, NY (P)	1967	Rod Carew, Min (2B)
1966	Tommy Helms, Cin (2B)	1966	Tommie Agee, Chi (OF)
1965	Jim Lefebvre, LA (2B)	1965	Curt Blefary, Bal (OF)
1964	Dick Allen, Phil (3B)	1964	Tony Oliva, Min (OF)
1963	Pete Rose, Cin (2B)	1963	Gary Peters, Chi (P)
1962	Ken Hubbs, Chi (2B)	1962	Tom Tresh, NY (SS)
1961	Billy Williams, Chi (OF)	1961	Don Schwall, Bos (P)
1960	Frank Howard, LA (OF)	1960	Ron Hansen, Bal (SS)
1959	Willie McCovey, SF (1B)	1959	Bob Allison, Wash (OF)
1958	Orlando Cepeda, SF (1B)	1958	Albie Pearson, Wash (OF)
1957	Jack Sanford, Phil (P)	1957	Tony Kubek, NY (OF, SS)
1956	Frank Robinson, Cin (OF)	1956	Luis Aparicio, Chi (SS)
1955	Bill Virdon, StL (OF)	1955	Herb Score, Cle (P)
1954	Wally Moon, StL (OF)	1954	Bob Grim, NY (P)
1953	Junior Gilliam, Bklyn (2B)	1953	Harvey Kuenn, Det (SS)
1952	Joe Black, Bklyn (P)	1952	Harry Byrd, Phil (P)
1951	Willie Mays, NY (OF)	1951	Gil McDougald, NY (3B)
1950	Sam Jethroe, Bos (OF)	1950	Walt Dropo, Bos (1B)
1949	Don Newcombe, Bklyn (P)	1949	Roy Sievers, StL (OF)
*1948	Alvin Dark, Bos (SS)		
*1947	Jackie Robinson, Bklyn (1B)		

*One selection for both leagues

Roger Clemens

Johan Santana went 20–6 in 2004 and won the A.L. Cy Young Award.

REGULAR SEASON –
CY YOUNG AWARD WINNERS

NATIONAL LEAGUE

YEAR	PITCHER	W–L	SV	ERA
2004	Roger Clemens, Hou	18–4	0	2.98
2003	Eric Gagne, LA	2–3	55	1.20
2002	Randy Johnson, Ari	24–5	0	2.32
2001	Randy Johnson, Ari	21–6	0	2.49
2000	Randy Johnson, Ari	19–7	0	2.64
1999	Randy Johnson, Ari	17–9	0	2.48
1998	Tom Glavine, Atl	20–6	0	2.47
1997	Pedro Martinez, Mon	17–8	0	1.90
1996	John Smoltz, Atl	24–8	0	2.94
1995	Greg Maddux, Atl	19–2	0	1.63
1994	Greg Maddux, Atl	16–6	0	1.56
1993	Greg Maddux, Atl	20–10	0	2.36
1992	Greg Maddux, Chi	20–11	0	2.18
1991	Tom Glavine, Atl	20–11	0	2.55
1990	Doug Drabek, Pitt	22–6	0	2.76
1989	Mark Davis, SD	4–3	44	1.85
1988	Orel Hershiser, LA	23–8	1	2.26
1987	Steve Bedrosian, Phil	5–3	40	2.83
1986	Mike Scott, Hou	18–10	0	2.22
1985	Dwight Gooden, NY	24–4	0	1.53
†1984	Rick Sutcliffe, Chi	16–1	0	2.69
1983	John Denny, Phil	19–6	0	2.37
1982	Steve Carlton, Phil	23–11	0	3.10
1981	Fernando Valenzuela, LA	13–7	0	2.48
1980	Steve Carlton, Phil	24–9	0	2.34
1979	Bruce Sutter, Chi	6–6	37	2.23
1978	Gaylord Perry, SD	21–6	0	2.72
1977	Steve Carlton, Phil	23–10	0	2.64
1976	Randy Jones, SD	22–14	0	2.74
1975	Tom Seaver, NY	22–9	0	2.38
1974	Mike Marshall, LA	15–12	21	2.42
1973	Tom Seaver, NY	19–10	0	2.08
1972	Steve Carlton, Phil	27–10	0	1.97
1971	Ferguson Jenkins, Chi	24–13	0	2.77
1970	Bob Gibson, StL	23–7	0	3.12
1969	Tom Seaver, NY	25–7	0	2.21
*1968	Bob Gibson, StL	22–9	0	1.12
1967	Mike McCormick, SF	22–10	0	2.85
1966	Sandy Koufax, LA (NL)	27–9	0	1.73
1965	Sandy Koufax, LA (NL)	26–8	2	2.04
1964	Dean Chance, LA (AL)	20–9	4	1.65
*1963	Sandy Koufax, LA (NL)	25–5	0	1.88
1962	Don Drysdale, LA (NL)	25–9	1	2.83
1961	Whitey Ford, NY (AL)	25–4	0	3.21
1960	Vernon Law, Pitt (NL)	20–9	0	3.08
1959	Early Wynn, Chi (AL)	22–10	0	3.17
1958	Bob Turley, NY (AL)	21–7	1	2.97
1957	Warren Spahn, Mil (NL)	21–11	3	2.69
*1956	Don Newcombe, Bklyn (NL)	27–7	0	3.06

* Won the MVP and Cy Young awards in the same season.
†NL games only. Sutcliffe pitched 15 games with Cleveland before being traded to the Cubs.
Note: One award was presented for both leagues from 1956-1966.

AMERICAN LEAGUE

YEAR	PITCHER	W–L	SV	ERA
2004	Johan Santana, Min	20–6	0	2.61
2003	Roy Halladay, Tor	22–7	0	3.25
2002	Barry Zito, Oak	23–5	0	2.75
2001	Roger Clemens, NY	20–3	0	3.51
2000	Pedro Martinez, Bos	18–6	0	1.74
1999	Pedro Martinez, Bos	23–4	0	1.55
1998	Roger Clemens, Tor	20–6	0	2.65
1997	Roger Clemens, Tor	21–7	0	2.05
1996	Pat Hentgen, Tor	20–10	0	3.22
1995	Randy Johnson, Sea	18–2	0	2.48
1994	David Cone, KC	16–4	0	2.94
1993	Jack McDowell, Chi	22–10	0	3.37
*1992	Dennis Eckersley, Oak	7–1	51	1.91
1991	Roger Clemens, Bos	18–10	0	2.62
1990	Bob Welch, Oak	27–6	0	2.95
1989	Bret Saberhagen, KC	23–6	0	2.16
1988	Frank Viola, Min	24–7	0	2.64
1987	Roger Clemens, Bos	20–9	0	2.97
*1986	Roger Clemens, Bos	24–4	0	2.48
1985	Bret Saberhagen, KC	20–6	0	2.87
*1984	Willie Hernandez, Det	9–3	32	1.92
1983	LaMarr Hoyt, Chi	24–10	0	3.66
1982	Pete Vuckovich, Mil	18–6	0	3.34
*1981	Rollie Fingers, Mil	6–3	28	1.04
1980	Steve Stone, Bal	25–7	0	3.23
1979	Mike Flanagan, Bal	23–9	0	3.08
1978	Ron Guidry, NY	25–3	0	1.74
1977	Sparky Lyle, NY	13–5	26	2.17
1976	Jim Palmer, Bal	22–13	0	2.51
1975	Jim Palmer, Bal	23–11	1	2.09
1974	Catfish Hunter, Oak	25–12	0	2.49
1973	Jim Palmer, Bal	22–9	1	2.40
1972	Gaylord Perry, Cle	24–16	1	1.92
*1971	Vida Blue, Oak	24–8	0	1.82
1970	Jim Perry, Min	24–12	0	3.03
1969	Denny McLain, Det	24–9	0	2.80
	(tie) Mike Cuellar, Bal	23–11	0	2.38
1968	*Denny McLain, Det	31–6	0	1.96
1967	Jim Lonborg, Bos	22–9	0	3.16

REGULAR SEASON – CAREER INDIVIDUAL BATTING

GAMES

Pete Rose	3,562
Carl Yastrzemski	3,308
Hank Aaron	3,298
Rickey Henderson	3,081
Ty Cobb	3,034
Stan Musial	3,026
Eddie Murray	3,026
Cal Ripken, Jr.	3,001
Willie Mays	2,992
Dave Winfield	2,973
Rusty Staub	2,951
Brooks Robinson	2,896
Robin Yount	2,856
Al Kaline	2,834
Harold Baines	2,830
Eddie Collins	2,826
Reggie Jackson	2,820
Frank Robinson	2,808
Honus Wagner	2,794
Tris Speaker	2,789

AT-BATS

Pete Rose	14,053
Hank Aaron	12,364
Carl Yastrzemski	11,988
Cal Ripken, Jr.	11,551
Ty Cobb	11,434
Eddie Murray	11,336
Robin Yount	11,008
Dave Winfield	11,003
Stan Musial	10,972
Rickey Henderson	10,961
Willie Mays	10,881
Paul Molitor	10,835
Brooks Robinson	10,654
Honus Wagner	10,439
George Brett	10,349
Lou Brock	10,332
Luis Aparicio	10,230
Tris Speaker	10,195
Al Kaline	10,116
Rabbit Maranville	10,078

HOME RUNS

Hank Aaron	755
Babe Ruth	714
*Barry Bonds	703
Willie Mays	660
Frank Robinson	586
Mark McGwire	583
*Sammy Sosa	574
Harmon Killebrew	573
Reggie Jackson	563
*Rafael Palmeiro	551
Mike Schmidt	548
Mickey Mantle	536
Jimmie Foxx	534
Ted Williams	521
Willie McCovey	521
Eddie Mathews	512
Ernie Banks	512
Mel Ott	511
Eddie Murray	504
*Ken Griffey, Jr.	501

* Active in 2004.
Note: Stats were compiled after the 2004 season.

HITS

Pete Rose	4,256
Ty Cobb	4,189
Hank Aaron	3,771
Stan Musial	3,630
Tris Speaker	3,515
Carl Yastrzemski	3,419
Honus Wagner	3,414
Paul Molitor	3,319
Eddie Collins	3,315
Willie Mays	3,283
Eddie Murray	3,255
Nap Lajoie	3,242
Cal Ripken, Jr.	3,184
George Brett	3,154
Paul Waner	3,152
Robin Yount	3,142
Tony Gwynn	3,141
Dave Winfield	3,110
Rod Carew	3,053
Rickey Henderson	3,055

BATTING AVERAGE (5,000 AB)

Ty Cobb	.366
Rogers Hornsby	.358
Ed Delahanty	.346
Tris Speaker	.345
Ted Williams	.344
Billy Hamilton	.344
Dan Brouthers	.342
Babe Ruth	.342
Harry Heilmann	.342
Willie Keeler	.341
Bill Terry	.341
George Sisler	.340
Lou Gehrig	.340
Jesse Burkett	.338
Tony Gwynn	.338
Nap Lajoie	.338
Al Simmons	.334
Paul Waner	.333
Eddie Collins	.333
Sam Thompson	.331

RUNS

Rickey Henderson	2,295
Ty Cobb	2,246
Babe Ruth	2,174
Hank Aaron	2,174
Pete Rose	2,165
*Barry Bonds	2,070
Willie Mays	2,062
Stan Musial	1,949
Lou Gehrig	1,888
Tris Speaker	1,882
Mel Ott	1,859
Frank Robinson	1,829
Eddie Collins	1,821
Carl Yastrzemski	1,816
Ted Williams	1,798
Paul Molitor	1,782
Charlie Gehringer	1,774
Jimmie Foxx	1,751
Honus Wagner	1,739
Cap Anson	1,722

DOUBLES

Tris Speaker	792
Pete Rose	746
Stan Musial	725
Ty Cobb	724
George Brett	665
Nap Lajoie	657
Carl Yastrzemski	646
Honus Wagner	643
Hank Aaron	624
Paul Molitor	605
Paul Waner	605
Cal Ripken, Jr.	603
Robin Yount	583
Wade Boggs	578
Charlie Gehringer	574
*Rafael Palmeiro	572
Eddie Murray	560
Tony Gwynn	543
Harry Heilmann	542
Rogers Hornsby	541

TRIPLES

Sam Crawford	309
Ty Cobb	295
Honus Wagner	252
Jake Beckley	244
Roger Connor	233
Tris Speaker	222
Fred Clarke	220
Dan Brouthers	205
Joe Kelley	194
Paul Waner	191
Bid McPhee	189
Eddie Collins	187
Ed Delahanty	186
Sam Rice	184
Jesse Burkett	182
Edd Roush	182
Ed Konetchy	182
Buck Ewing	178
Rabbit Maranville	177
Stan Musial	177

BASES ON BALLS

*Barry Bonds	2,302
Rickey Henderson	2,190
Babe Ruth	2,062
Ted Williams	2,019
Joe Morgan	1,865
Carl Yastrzemski	1,845
Mickey Mantle	1,733
Mel Ott	1,708
Eddie Yost	1,614
Darrell Evans	1,605
Stan Musial	1,599
Pete Rose	1,566
Harmon Killebrew	1,559
Lou Gehrig	1,508
Mike Schmidt	1,507
Eddie Collins	1,499
Willie Mays	1,464
Jimmie Foxx	1,452
Eddie Mathews	1,444
Frank Robinson	1,420

REGULAR SEASON – CAREER INDIVIDUAL BATTING (cont.)

RUNS BATTED IN

Hank Aaron	2,297
Babe Ruth	2,213
Lou Gehrig	1,995
Stan Musial	1,951
Ty Cobb	1,938
Jimmie Foxx	1,922
Eddie Murray	1,917
Willie Mays	1,903
Cap Anson	1,880
Mel Ott	1,860
Carl Yastrzemski	1,844
*Barry Bonds	1,843
Ted Williams	1,839
Dave Winfield	1,833
Al Simmons	1,827
Frank Robinson	1,812
*Rafael Palmeiro	1,775
Honus Wagner	1,732
Reggie Jackson	1,702
Cal Ripken, Jr.	1,695

SLUGGING PERCENTAGE (5,000 AB)

Babe Ruth	.690
Ted Williams	.634
Lou Gehrig	.632
*Barry Bonds	.611
Jimmie Foxx	.609
Hank Greenberg	.605
Mark McGwire	.588
Joe DiMaggio	.579
Rogers Hornsby	.577
*Larry Walker	.568
*Frank Thomas	.567
Albert Belle	.564
Johnny Mize	.562
*Mike Piazza	.562
*Juan Gonzalez	.561
*Ken Griffey, Jr.	.560
Stan Musial	.559
Willie Mays	.557
Mickey Mantle	.557
Hank Aaron	.555

STOLEN BASES

Rickey Henderson	1,406
Lou Brock	938
Billy Hamilton	914
Ty Cobb	892
Tim Raines	808
Vince Coleman	752
Arlie Latham	742
Eddie Collins	741
Max Carey	738
Honus Wagner	723
Joe Morgan	689
Willie Wilson	668
Tom Brown	657
Bert Campaneris	649
Otis Nixon	620
George Davis	619
Dummy Hoy	596
Maury Wills	586
George Van Haltren	583
Ozzie Smith	580

* Active in 2004.

Reggie Jackson is the career leader in strikeouts (2,597).

ON-BASE PERCENTAGE (5,000 AB)

Ted Williams	.482
Babe Ruth	.474
Billy Hamilton	.455
Lou Gehrig	.447
*Barry Bonds	.443
Rogers Hornsby	.434
Ty Cobb	.433
*Frank Thomas	.429
Jimmie Foxx	.428
Tris Speaker	.428
Eddie Collins	.424
Edgar Martinez	.423
Dan Brouthers	.423
Mickey Mantle	.421
Mickey Cochrane	.419
Stan Musial	.417
Cupid Childs	.416
Jesse Burkett	.415
Wade Boggs	.415
*Jeff Bagwell	.408

TOTAL BASES

Hank Aaron	6,856
Stan Musial	6,134
Willie Mays	6,066
Ty Cobb	5,854
Babe Ruth	5,793
Pete Rose	5,752
*Barry Bonds	5,556
Carl Yastrzemski	5,539
Eddie Murray	5,397
Frank Robinson	5,373
Dave Winfield	5,221
Cal Ripken, Jr.	5,168
Tris Speaker	5,101
Lou Gehrig	5,060
George Brett	5,044
Mel Ott	5,041
Jimmie Foxx	4,956
Ted Williams	4,884
Honus Wagner	4,870
Paul Molitor	4,854

STRIKEOUTS

Reggie Jackson	2,597
*Sammy Sosa	2,110
*Andres Galarraga	2,003
Jose Canseco	1,942
Willie Stargell	1,936
Mike Schmidt	1,883
*Fred McGriff	1,882
Tony Perez	1,867
Dave Kingman	1,816
Bobby Bonds	1,757
Dale Murphy	1,748
Lou Brock	1,730
Mickey Mantle	1,710
Harmon Killebrew	1,699
Chili Davis	1,698
Dwight Evans	1,697
Rickey Henderson	1,694
Dave Winfield	1,686
Gary Gaetti	1,602
Mark McGwire	1,596

REGULAR SEASON – CAREER INDIVIDUAL PITCHING

GAMES

Jesse Orosco	1,252
*John Franco	1,088
Dennis Eckersley	1,071
Hoyt Wilhelm	1,070
Dan Plesac	1,064
Kent Tekulve	1,050
Lee Smith	1,022
Goose Gossage	1,002
Lindy McDaniel	987
Mike Jackson	960
Rollie Fingers	944
Gene Garber	931
Cy Young	906
Sparky Lyle	899
Jim Kaat	898
Mike Stanton	885
Paul Assenmacher	884
Jeff Reardon	880
Don McMahon	874
Phil Niekro	864

INNINGS PITCHED

Cy Young	7,356.2
Pud Galvin	5,941.1
Walter Johnson	5,914.1
Phil Niekro	5,404.1
Nolan Ryan	5,386.0
Gaylord Perry	5,350.1
Don Sutton	5,282.1
Warren Spahn	5,243.2
Steve Carlton	5,217.1
Grover Alexander	5,190.0
Kid Nichols	5,056.1
Tim Keefe	5,049.1
Bert Blyleven	4,970.0
Mickey Welch	4,802.0
Tom Seaver	4,782.2
Christy Mathewson	4,780.2
Tommy John	4,710.1
Robin Roberts	4,688.2
Early Wynn	4,564.0
John Clarkson	4,536.1

WINS

Cy Young	511
Walter Johnson	417
Grover Alexander	373
Christy Mathewson	373
Warren Spahn	363
Pud Galvin	361
Kid Nichols	361
Tim Keefe	342
Steve Carlton	329
John Clarkson	328
*Roger Clemens	328
Eddie Plank	326
Nolan Ryan	324
Don Sutton	324
Phil Niekro	318
Gaylord Perry	314
Tom Seaver	311
Charley Radbourn	309
Mickey Welch	307
Lefty Grove	300
Early Wynn	300

*Active in 2004. **Minimum 100 victories.

LOSSES

Cy Young	316
Pud Galvin	308
Nolan Ryan	292
Walter Johnson	279
Phil Niekro	274
Gaylord Perry	265
Don Sutton	256
Jack Powell	254
Eppa Rixey	251
Bert Blyleven	250
Robin Roberts	245
Warren Spahn	245
Steve Carlton	244
Early Wynn	244
Jim Kaat	237
Frank Tanana	236
Gus Weyhing	232
Tommy John	231
Bob Friend	230
Ted Lyons	230

WINNING PERCENTAGE**

Al Spalding	.796
Spud Chandler	.717
*Pedro Martinez	.705
Whitey Ford	.690
Dave Foutz	.690
Bob Caruthers	.688
Don Gullett	.686
Lefty Grove	.680
Joe Wood	.671
Vic Raschi	.667
*Roger Clemens	.666
Larry Corcoran	.665
Christy Mathewson	.665
Sam Leever	.660
Sal Maglie	.658
*Randy Johnson	.657
Dick McBride	.656
Sandy Koufax	.655
Johnny Allen	.654
Ron Guidry	.651

SAVES

Lee Smith	478
*John Franco	424
*Trevor Hoffman	393
Dennis Eckersley	390
Jeff Reardon	367
Randy Myers	347
Rollie Fingers	341
*Mariano Rivera	336
John Wetteland	330
*Roberto Hernandez	320
Rick Aguilera	318
*Troy Percival	316
Robb Nen	314
Tom Henke	311
Goose Gossage	310
Jeff Montgomery	304
Doug Jones	303
Bruce Sutter	300
*Rod Beck	286
Todd Worrell	256

EARNED RUN AVERAGE

Ed Walsh	1.82
Al Spalding	2.04
Three Finger Brown	2.06
John Ward	2.10
Christy Mathewson	2.13
Tommy Bond	2.14
Rube Waddell	2.16
Walter Johnson	2.17
Ed Reulbach	2.28
Will White	2.28
Eddie Plank	2.35
Larry Corcoran	2.36
Eddie Cicotte	2.38
Candy Cummings	2.39
Doc White	2.39
Nap Rucker	2.42
George Bradley	2.43
Jim McCormick	2.43
Chief Bender	2.46

SHUTOUTS

Walter Johnson	110
Grover Alexander	90
Christy Mathewson	79
Cy Young	76
Eddie Plank	69
Warren Spahn	63
Nolan Ryan	61
Tom Seaver	61
Bert Blyleven	60
Don Sutton	58
Pud Galvin	57
Ed Walsh	57
Bob Gibson	56
Three Finger Brown	55
Steve Carlton	55
Jim Palmer	53
Gaylord Perry	53
Juan Marichal	52
Rube Waddell	50
Vic Willis	50

COMPLETE GAMES

Cy Young	749
Pud Galvin	639
Tim Keefe	554
Kid Nichols	532
Walter Johnson	531
Mickey Welch	525
Charley Radbourn	488
John Clarkson	485
Tony Mullane	468
Jim McCormick	466
Gus Weyhing	448
Grover Alexander	437
Christy Mathewson	435
Jack Powell	422
Eddie Plank	410
Will White	394
Amos Rusie	393
Vic Willis	388
Tommy Bond	386
Warren Spahn	382

BASEBALL

REGULAR SEASON – CAREER INDIVIDUAL PITCHING (cont.)

STRIKEOUTS		BASES ON BALLS	
Nolan Ryan	5,714	Nolan Ryan	2,795
*Roger Clemens	4,317	Steve Carlton	1,833
*Randy Johnson	4,161	Phil Niekro	1,809
Steve Carlton	4,136	Early Wynn	1,775
Bert Blyleven	3,701	Bob Feller	1,764
Tom Seaver	3,640	Bobo Newsom	1,732
Don Sutton	3,574	Amos Rusie	1,707
Gaylord Perry	3,534	Charlie Hough	1,665
Walter Johnson	3,509	Gus Weyhing	1,566
Phil Niekro	3,342	Red Ruffing	1,541
Ferguson Jenkins	3,192	Bump Hadley	1,442
Bob Gibson	3,117	Warren Spahn	1,434
*Greg Maddux	2,916	Earl Whitehill	1,431
Jim Bunning	2,855	Tony Mullane	1,408
Mickey Lolich	2,832	Sad Sam Jones	1,396
Cy Young	2,803	Jack Morris	1,390
Frank Tanana	2,773	Tom Seaver	1,390
David Cone	2,668	Gaylord Perry	1,379
Chuck Finley	2,610	Roger Clemens	1,379
Warren Spahn	2,583	Bobby Witt	1,375

Ichiro Suzuki

TOM DIPACE

REGULAR SEASON – INDIVIDUAL BATTING, SINGLE SEASON

HITS		TRIPLES		RUNS BATTED IN	
Ichiro Suzuki, 2004	262	Chief Wilson, 1912	36	Hack Wilson, 1930	190
George Sisler, 1920	257	Dave Orr, 1886	31	Lou Gehrig, 1931	184
Lefty O'Doul, 1929	254	Heinie Reitz, 1894	31	Hank Greenberg, 1937	183
Bill Terry, 1930	254	Perry Werden, 1893	29	Lou Gehrig, 1927	175
Al Simmons, 1925	253	Harry Davis, 1897	28	Jimmie Foxx, 1938	175
Rogers Hornsby, 1922	250	Sam Thompson, 1894	28	Lou Gehrig, 1930	174
Chuck Klein, 1930	250	George Davis, 1893	27	Babe Ruth, 1921	171
Ty Cobb, 1911	248	Sam Thompson, 1894	27	Chuck Klein, 1930	170
George Sisler, 1922	246	Jimmy Williams, 1899	27	Hank Greenberg, 1935	170
Ichiro Suzuki, 2001	242	John Reilly, 1890	26	Jimmie Foxx, 1932	169
Heinie Manush, 1928	241	George Treadway, 1894	26		
Babe Herman, 1930	241	Joe Jackson, 1912	26	STRIKEOUTS	
		Sam Crawford, 1914	26	Adam Dunn, 2004	195
BATTING AVERAGE		Kiki Cuyler, 1925	26	Bobby Bonds, 1970	189
Hugh Duffy, 1894	.440			Jose Hernandez, 2002	188
Tip O'Neill, 1887	.435	HOME RUNS		Bobby Bonds, 1969	187
Ross Barnes, 1876	.429	Barry Bonds, 2001	73	Preston Wilson, 2000	187
Nap Lajoie, 1901	.426	Mark McGwire, 1998	70	Rob Deer, 1987	186
Willie Keeler, 1897	.424	Sammy Sosa, 1998	66	Jose Hernandez, 2001	185
Rogers Hornsby, 1924	.424	Mark McGwire, 1999	65	Jim Thome, 2001	185
George Sisler, 1922	.420	Sammy Sosa, 2001	64	Pete Incaviglia, 1986	185
Ty Cobb, 1911	.420	Sammy Sosa, 1999	63	Cecil Fielder, 1990	182
Sam Thompson, 1894	.415	Roger Maris, 1961	61	Mo Vaughn, 2000	181
Fred Dunlap, 1884	.412	Babe Ruth, 1927	60		
		Babe Ruth, 1921	59	RUNS	
DOUBLES		Jimmie Foxx, 1932	58	Billy Hamilton, 1894	198
Earl Webb, 1931	67	Hank Greenberg, 1938	58	Tom Brown, 1891	177
George Burns, 1926	64	Mark McGwire, 1997	58	Babe Ruth, 1921	177
Joe Medwick, 1936	64			Tip O'Neill, 1887	167
Hank Greenberg, 1934	63	TOTAL BASES		Lou Gehrig, 1936	167
Paul Waner, 1932	62	Babe Ruth, 1921	457	Billy Hamilton, 1895	166
Charlie Gehringer, 1936	60	Rogers Hornsby, 1922	450	Willie Keeler, 1894	165
Tris Speaker, 1923	59	Lou Gehrig, 1927	447	Joe Kelley, 1894	165
Chuck Klein, 1930	59	Chuck Klein, 1930	445	Arlie Latham, 1887	163
Todd Helton, 2000	59	Jimmie Foxx, 1932	438	Babe Ruth, 1928	163
Billy Herman, 1936	57	Stan Musial, 1948	429	Lou Gehrig, 1931	163
Billy Herman, 1935	57	Sammy Sosa, 2001	425		
Carlos Delgado, 2000	57	Hack Wilson, 1930	423	
		Chuck Klein, 1932	420	
		Luis Gonzalez, 2001	419	
		Lou Gehrig, 1930	419	

■ **Fast Fact:** Barry Bonds received a major-league record 120 intentional walks in 2004. Had he not been walked any other time, he still would have finished fourth in the majors last year in bases on balls (three players tied with 127).

REGULAR SEASON – INDIVIDUAL BATTING, SINGLE SEASON (cont.)

STOLEN BASES		BASES ON BALLS		SLUGGING PERCENTAGE	
Hugh Nicol, 1887	138	Barry Bonds, 2004	232	Barry Bonds, 2001	.863
Rickey Henderson, 1982	130	Barry Bonds, 2002	198	Babe Ruth, 1920	.847
Arlie Latham, 1887	129	Barry Bonds, 2001	177	Babe Ruth, 1921	.846
Lou Brock, 1974	118	Babe Ruth, 1923	170	Barry Bonds, 2004	.812
Charlie Comiskey, 1887	117	Ted Williams, 1947	162	Barry Bonds, 2002	.799
John Ward, 1887	111	Ted Williams, 1949	162	Babe Ruth, 1927	.772
Billy Hamilton, 1889	111	Mark McGwire, 1998	162	Lou Gehrig, 1927	.765
Billy Hamilton, 1891	111	Ted Williams, 1946	156	Babe Ruth, 1923	.764
Vince Coleman, 1985	110	Eddie Yost, 1956	151	Rogers Hornsby, 1925	.756
Arlie Latham, 1888	109	Barry Bonds, 1996	151	Mark McGwire, 1998	.752
Vince Coleman, 1987	109	Babe Ruth, 1920	150	Jeff Bagwell, 1994	.750

REGULAR SEASON – INDIVIDUAL PITCHING, SINGLE SEASON

GAMES		LOSSES		SHUTOUTS	
Mike Marshall, 1974	106	John Coleman, 1883	48	George Bradley, 1876	16
Kent Tekulve, 1979	94	Will White, 1880	42	Grover Alexander, 1916	16
Mike Marshall, 1973	92	Larry McKeon, 1884	41	Jack Coombs, 1910	13
Kent Tekulve, 1978	91	George Bradley, 1879	40	Bob Gibson, 1968	13
Wayne Granger, 1969	90	Jim McCormick, 1879	40	Jim Galvin, 1884	12
Mike Marshall, 1970	90	Henry Porter, 1888	37	Ed Morris, 1886	12
Kent Tekulve, 1987	90	Kid Carsey, 1891	37	Grover Alexander, 1915	12
Steve Kline, 2001	89	George Cobb, 1892	37	Tommy Bond, 1879	11
Mark Eichhorn, 1987	89	Stump Weidman, 1886	36	Charley Radbourn, 1884	11
Paul Quantrill, 2003	89	Bill Hutchison, 1892	36	Dave Foutz, 1886	11
Julian Tavarez, 1997	89			Christy Mathewson, 1908	11
		WINNING PERCENTAGE		Ed Walsh, 1908	11
GAMES STARTED		Roy Face, 1959	.947	Walter Johnson, 1913	11
Will White, 1879	75	Johnny Allen, 1937	.938	Sandy Koufax, 1963	11
Jim Galvin, 1883	75	Greg Maddux, 1995	.905	Dean Chance, 1964	11
Jim McCormick, 1880	74	Randy Johnson, 1995	.900		
Charley Radbourn, 1884	73	Ron Guidry, 1978	.893	COMPLETE GAMES	
Guy Hecker, 1884	73	Freddie Fitzsimmons, 1940	.889	Will White, 1879	75
Jim Galvin, 1884	72	Lefty Grove, 1931	.886	Charley Radbourn, 1884	73
John Clarkson, 1889	72	Bob Stanley, 1978	.882	Jim McCormick, 1880	72
Bill Hutchison, 1892	71	Preacher Roe, 1951	.880	Jim Galvin, 1883	72
John Clarkson, 1885	70	Fred Goldsmith, 1880	.875	Guy Hecker, 1884	72
Matt Kilroy, 1887	69	Tom Seaver, 1981	.875	Jim Galvin, 1884	71
				Tim Keefe, 1883	68
INNINGS PITCHED		SAVES		John Clarkson, 1885	68
Will White, 1878	680.0	Bobby Thigpen, 1990	57	John Clarkson, 1889	68
Charley Radbourn, 1884	678.2	Eric Gagne, 2003	55	Bill Hutchison, 1892	67
Guy Hecker, 1884	670.2	John Smoltz, 2002	55		
Jim McCormick, 1880	657.2	Randy Myers, 1993	53	STRIKEOUTS	
Jim Galvin, 1883	656.1	Trevor Hoffman, 1998	53	Matt Kilroy, 1886	513
Jim Galvin, 1884	636.1	Mariano Rivera, 2004	53	Toad Ramsey, 1886	499
Charley Radbourn, 1883	632.1	Eric Gagne, 2002	52	Hugh Daily, 1884	483
Bill Hutchison, 1892	627.0	Dennis Eckersley, 1992	51	Dupee Shaw, 1884	451
John Clarkson, 1885	623.0	Rod Beck, 1998	51	Charley Radbourn, 1884	441
Jim Devlin, 1876	622.0	Mariano Rivera, 2001	50	Charlie Buffinton, 1884	417
Bill Hutchison, 1892	622.0	Francisco Cordero, 2004	49	Guy Hecker, 1884	385
		Dennis Eckersley, 1990	48	Nolan Ryan, 1973	383
WINS		Rod Beck, 1993	48	Sandy Koufax, 1965	382
Charley Radbourn, 1884	59	Jeff Shaw, 1998	48	Bill Sweeney, 1884	374
John Clarkson, 1885	53				
Guy Hecker, 1884	52	EARNED RUN AVERAGE		BASES ON BALLS	
John Clarkson, 1889	49	Tim Keefe, 1880	0.86	Amos Rusie, 1890	289
Charley Radbourn, 1883	48	Dutch Leonard, 1914	0.96	Mark Baldwin, 1889	274
Charlie Buffinton, 1884	48	Three Finger Brown, 1906	1.04	Amos Rusie, 1892	270
Al Spalding, 1876	47	Bob Gibson, 1968	1.12	Amos Rusie, 1891	262
John Ward, 1879	47	Christy Mathewson, 1909	1.14	Mark Baldwin, 1890	249
Jim Galvin, 1883	46	Walter Johnson, 1913	1.14	Jack Stivetts, 1891	232
Jim Galvin, 1884	46	Jack Pfiester, 1907	1.15	Mark Baldwin, 1891	227
Matt Kilroy, 1887	46	Addie Joss, 1908	1.16	Phil Knell, 1891	226
		Carl Lundgren, 1907	1.17	Bob Barr, 1890	219
		Denny Driscoll, 1882	1.21	Amos Rusie 1893	218

REGULAR SEASON – INDIVIDUAL BATTING, SINGLE GAME

MOST RUNS	
7	Guy Hecker, Lou	Aug. 15, 1886

MOST HITS	
7	Wilbert Robinson, Bal	June 10, 1892
	Rennie Stennett, Pitt	Sept. 16, 1975

MOST HOME RUNS	
4	Bobby Lowe, Bos (N)	May 30, 1894
	Ed Delahanty, Phil	July 13, 1896
	Lou Gehrig, NY (A)	June 3, 1932
	Gil Hodges, Bklyn	Aug. 31, 1950
	Joe Adcock, Mil (N)	July 31, 1954
	Rocky Colavito, Cle	June 10, 1959
	Willie Mays, SF	April 30, 1961
	Mike Schmidt, Phi	April 17, 1976
	Bob Horner, Atl	July 6, 1986
	Mark Whiten, StL	Sept. 7, 1993
	Mike Cameron, Sea	May 2, 2002
	Shawn Green, LA	May 23, 2002
	Carlos Delgado, Tor	Sept. 25, 2003

MOST GRAND SLAMS	
2	Tony Lazzeri, NY (A)	May 24, 1936
	Jim Tabor, Bos (A)	July 4, 1939
	Rudy York, Bos (A)	July 27, 1946
	Jim Gentile, Bal	May 9, 1961
	Tony Cloninger, Atl	July 3, 1966
	Jim Northrup, Det	June 24, 1968
	Frank Robinson, Bal	June 26, 1970
	Robin Ventura, Chi (A)	Sept. 4, 1995
	Chris Hoiles, Bal	Aug. 14, 1998
	Fernando Tatis, StL	April 23, 1999
	Nomar Garciaparra, Bos	May 10, 1999
	Bill Mueller, Bos	July 29, 2003

MOST RBIS	
12	Jim Bottomley, StL	Sept. 16, 1924
	Mark Whiten, StL	Sept. 7, 1993

REGULAR SEASON – INDIVIDUAL PITCHING, SINGLE GAME

MOST INNINGS PITCHED	
26	Leon Cadore, Bklyn	May 1, 1920, tie 1–1
	Joe Oeschger, Bos (N)	May 1, 1920, tie 1–1

MOST RUNS ALLOWED	
24	Al Travers, Det	May 18, 1912

MOST HITS ALLOWED	
36	Jack Wadsworth, Lou	Aug. 17, 1894

MOST STRIKEOUTS	
20	Roger Clemens, Bos	April 29, 1986
20	Roger Clemens, Bos	Sept. 18, 1996
20	Kerry Wood, Chi (N)	May 6, 1998
20	Randy Johnson, Ari	May 8, 2001

MOST WALKS ALLOWED	
16	Bill George, NY (N)	May 30, 1887
	George Van Haltren, Chi (N)	June 27, 1887
	Henry Gruber, Cle	April 19, 1890
	Bruno Haas, Phil (A)	June 2, 1915

MOST WILD PITCHES	
6	J.R. Richard, Hou	April 10, 1979
	Phil Niekro, Atl	Aug. 14, 1979
	Bill Gullickson, Mon	April 10, 1982

NOTABLE ACHIEVEMENTS
NO-HIT GAMES, NINE INNINGS OR MORE.

NATIONAL LEAGUE

DATE		PITCHER AND GAME	DATE		PITCHER AND GAME
1876	July 15	George Bradley, StL vs. Hart 2–0	1893	Aug. 16	Bill Hawke, Bal vs. Wash 5–0
1880	June 12	John Richmond, Wor vs. Cle 1–0	1897	Sept. 18	Cy Young, Cle vs. Cin 6–0
		(perfect game)	1898	April 22	Ted Breitenstein, Cin vs. Pitt 11–0
	June 17	Monte Ward, Prov vs. Buf 5–0		April 22	Jim Hughes, Bal vs. Bos 8–0
		(perfect game)		July 8	Frank Donahue, Phil vs. Bos 5–0
	Aug. 19	Larry Corcoran, Chi vs. Bos 6–0		Aug. 21	Walter Thornton, Chi vs. Bklyn 2–0
	Aug. 20	Pud Galvin, Buff vs. Wor 1–0	1899	May 25	Deacon Phillippe, Lou vs. NY 7–0
1882	Sept. 20	Larry Corcoran, Chi vs. Wor 5–0		Aug. 7	Vic Willis, Bos vs. Wash 7–1
	Sept. 22	Tim Lovett, Bklyn vs. NY 4–0	1900	July 12	Noodles Hahn, Cin vs. Phil 4–0
1883	July 25	Hoss Radbourn, Prov vs. Cle 8–0	1901	July 15	Christy Mathewson, NY vs. StL 5–0
	Sept. 13	Hugh Daily, Cle vs. Phil 1–0	1903	Sept. 18	Chick Fraser, Phil vs. Chi 10–0
1884	June 27	Larry Corcoran, Chi vs. Prov 6–0	1904	June 11	Bob Wicker, Chi vs. NY 1–0
	Aug. 4	Pud Galvin, Buf vs. Det 18–0			(hit in 10th; won in 12th)
1885	July 27	John Clarkson, Chi vs. Prov 4–0	1905	June 13	Christy Mathewson, NY vs. Chi 1–0
	Aug. 29	Charles Ferguson, Phil vs. Prov 1–0	1906	May 1	John Lush, Phil vs. Bklyn 6–0
1891	June 22	Tom Lovett, Bklyn vs. NY 4–0		July 20	Mal Eason, Bklyn vs. StL 2–0
	July 31	Amos Rusie, NY vs. Bklyn 6–0		Aug. 1	Harry McIntire, Bklyn vs. Pitt 0–1
1892	Aug. 6	Jack Stivetts, Bos vs. Bklyn 11–0			(hit in 11th; lost in 13th)
	Aug. 22	Alex Sanders, Lou vs. Bal 6–2	1907	May 8	Frank Pfeffer, Bos vs. Cin 6–0
	Oct. 15	Bumpus Jones, Cin vs. Pitt 7–1		Sept. 20	Nick Maddox, Pitt vs. Bklyn 2–1
		(first major league game)			

NOTABLE ACHIEVEMENTS
NO-HIT GAMES, NINE INNINGS OR MORE (cont.)

NATIONAL LEAGUE

DATE		PITCHER AND GAME	DATE		PITCHER AND GAME
1908	July 4	George Wiltse, NY vs. Phil 1–0	1969	April 17	Bill Stoneman, Mon vs. Phil 7–0
		(10 innings)		April 30	Jim Maloney, Cin vs. Hou 10–0
	Sept. 5	Nap Rucker, Bklyn vs. Bos 6–0		May 1	Don Wilson, Hou vs. Cin 4–0
1909	April 15	Leon Ames, NY vs. Bklyn 0–3		Aug. 19	Ken Holtzman, Chi vs. Atl 3–0
		(hit in 10th; lost in 13th)		Sept. 20	Bob Moose, Pitt vs. NY 4–0
1912	Sept. 6	Jeff Tesreau, NY vs. Phil 3–0	1970	June 12	Dock Ellis, Pitt vs. SD 2–0
1914	Sept. 9	George Davis, Bos vs. Phil 7–0		July 20	Bill Singer, LA vs. Phil 5–0
1915	April 15	Rube Marquard, NY vs. Bklyn 2–0	1971	June 3	Ken Holtzman, Chi vs. Cin 1–0
	Aug. 31	Jimmy Lavender, Chi vs. NY 2–0		June 23	Rick Wise, Phil vs. Cin 4–0
1916	June 16	Tom Hughes, Bos vs. Pitt 2–0		Aug. 14	Bob Gibson, StL vs. Pitt 11–0
1917	May 2	Jim Vaughn, Chi vs. Cin 0–1	1972	April 16	Burt Hooton, Chi vs. Phil 4–0
		(hit in 10th; lost in 10th)		Sept. 2	Milt Pappas, Chi vs. SD 8–0
	May 2	Fred Toney, Cin vs. Chi 1–0		Oct. 2	Bill Stoneman, Mon vs. NY 7–0
		(10 innings)	1973	Aug. 5	Phil Niekro, Atl vs. SD 9–0
1919	May 11	Hod Eller, Cin vs. StL 6–0	1975	Aug. 24	Ed Halicki, SF vs. NY 6–0
1922	May 7	Jesse Barnes, NY vs. Phil 6–0	1976	July 9	Larry Dierker, Hou vs. Mon 6–0
1924	July 17	Jesse Haines, StL vs. Bos 5–0		Aug. 9	John Candelaria, Pitt vs. LA 2–0
1925	Sept. 13	Dazzy Vance, Bklyn vs. Phil 10–1		Sept. 29	John Montefusco, SF vs. Atl 9–0
1929	May 8	Carl Hubbell, NY vs. Pitt 11–0	1978	April 16	Bob Forsch, StL vs. Phil 5–0
1934	Sept. 21	Paul Dean, StL vs. Bklyn 3–0		June 16	Tom Seaver, Cin vs. StL 4–0
1938	June 11	Johnny Vander Meer, Cin vs. Bos 3–0	1979	April 7	Ken Forsch, Hou vs. Atl 6–0
	June 15	Johnny Vander Meer, Cin vs. Bklyn 6–0	1980	June 27	Jerry Reuss, LA vs. SF 8–0
1940	April 30	Tex Carleton, Bklyn vs. Cin 3–0	1981	May 10	Charlie Lea, Mon vs. SF 4–0
1941	Aug. 30	Lon Warneke, StL vs. Cin 2–0		Sept. 26	Nolan Ryan, Hou vs. LA 5–0
1944	April 27	Jim Tobin, Bos vs. Bklyn 2–0	1983	Sept. 26	Bob Forsch, StL vs. Mon 3–0
	May 15	Clyde Shoun, Cin vs. Bos 1–0	1986	Sept. 25	Mike Scott, Hou vs. SF 2–0
1946	April 23	Ed Head, Bklyn vs. Bos 5–0	1988	Sept. 16	Tom Browning, Cin vs. LA 1–0
1947	June 18	Ewell Blackwell, Cin vs. Bos 6–0			(perfect game)
1948	Sept. 9	Rex Barney, Bklyn vs. NY 2–0	1990	June 29	Fernando Valenzuela, LA vs. StL 6–0
1950	Aug. 11	Vern Bickford, Bos vs. Bklyn 7–0		Aug. 15	Terry Mulholland, Phil vs. SF 6–0
1951	May 6	Cliff Chambers, Pitt vs. Bos 3–0	1991	May 23	Tommy Greene, Phil vs. Mon 2–0
1952	June 19	Carl Erskine, Bklyn vs. Chi 5–0		July 26	Mark Gardner, Mon vs. LA 0–1
1954	June 12	Jim Wilson, Mil vs. Phil 2–0			(hit in 10th, lost in 10th)
1955	May 12	Sam Jones, Chi vs. Pitt 4–0		July 28	Dennis Martinez, Mon vs. LA 2–0
1956	May 12	Carl Erskine, Bklyn vs. NY 3–0			(perfect game)
	Sept. 25	Sal Maglie, Bklyn vs. Phil 5–0		Sept. 11	Kent Mercker (6), Mark Wohlers (2),
1959	May 26	Harvey Haddix, Pitt vs. Mil 0–1			and Alejandro Pena (1), Atl vs. SD 1–0
		(hit in 13th; lost in 13th)	1992	Aug. 17	Kevin Gross, LA vs. SF 2–0
1960	May 15	Don Cardwell, Chi vs. StL 4–0	1993	Sept. 8	Darryl Kile, Hou vs. NY 7–1
	Aug. 18	Lew Burdette, Mil vs. Phil 1–0	1994	April 8	Kent Mercker, Atl vs. LA 6–0
	Sept. 16	Warren Spahn, Mil vs. Phil 4–0	1995	June 3	Pedro Martinez, Mon vs. SD 1–0
1961	April 28	Warren Spahn, Mil vs. SF 1–0			(perfect through nine, hit in 10th)
1962	June 30	Sandy Koufax, LA vs. NY 5–0		July 14	Ramon Martinez, LA vs. Fla 7–0
1963	May 11	Sandy Koufax, LA vs. SF 8–0	1996	May 11	Al Leiter, Fla vs. Col 11–0
	May 17	Don Nottebart, Hou vs. Phil 4–1		Sept. 17	Hideo Nomo, LA vs. Col 9–0
	June 15	Juan Marichal, SF vs. Hou 1–0	1997	June 10	Kevin Brown, Fla vs. SF 9–0
1964	April 23	Ken Johnson, Hou vs. Cin 0–1		July 12	Francisco Cordova (9) and
	June 4	Sandy Koufax, LA vs. Phil 3–0			Ricardo Rincon (1), Pitt vs. Col 3–0
	June 21	Jim Bunning, Phil vs. NY 6–0	1999	June 25	Jose Jimenez, StL vs. Ari 1–0
		(perfect game)	2001	May 12	A.J. Burnett, Fla vs. SD 3–0
1965	June 14	Jim Maloney, Cin vs. NY 0–1		Sept. 3	Bud Smith, StL vs. SD 4–0
		(hit in 11th; lost in 11th)	2003	April 27	Kevin Millwood, Phil vs. SF 1–0
	Aug. 19	Jim Maloney, Cin vs. Chi 1–0		June 11	Roy Oswalt (1), Pete Munro (2⅔),
		(10 innings)			Kirk Saarloos (1⅓), Brad Lidge (2),
	Sept. 9	Sandy Koufax, LA vs. Chi 1–0			Octavio Dotel (1), and Billy Wagner (1),
		(perfect game)			Hou vs. NY 8–0
1967	June 18	Don Wilson, Hou vs. Atl 2–0	2004	May 18	Randy Johnson, Ari vs. Atl 2–0
1968	July 29	George Culver, Cin vs. Phil 6–1			(perfect game)
	Sept. 17	Gaylord Perry, SF vs. StL 1–0			
	Sept. 18	Ray Washburn, StL vs. SF 2–0			

■ Fast Fact: In 2004, Cincinnati Reds outfielder Adam Dunn set a major-league record for strikeouts in a single season by whiffing 195 times, surpassing the old mark of 189, held by Bobby Bonds.

BASEBALL

NOTABLE ACHIEVEMENTS
NO-HIT GAMES, NINE INNINGS OR MORE (cont.)

AMERICAN LEAGUE

DATE		PITCHER AND GAME	DATE		PITCHER AND GAME
1901	May 9	Earl Moore, Cle vs. Chi 2–4 (hit in 10th; lost in 10th)	1956	July 14	Mel Parnell, Bos vs. Chi 4–0
1902	Sept. 20	Jimmy Callahan, Chi vs. Det 3–0		Oct. 8	Don Larsen, NY (A) vs. Bklyn (N) 2–0 (World Series, perfect game)
1904	May 5	Cy Young, Bos vs. Phil 3–0 (perfect game)	1957	Aug. 20	Bob Keegan, Chi vs. Wash 6–0
	Aug. 17	Jesse Tannehill, Bos vs. Chi 6–0	1958	July 20	Jim Bunning, Det vs. Bos 3–0
1905	July 22	Weldon Henley, Phil vs. StL 6–0		Sept. 20	Hoyt Wilhelm, Bal vs. NY 1–0
	Sept. 6	Frank Smith, Chi vs. Det 15–0	1962	May 5	Bo Belinsky, LA vs. Bal 2–0
	Sept. 27	Bill Dinneen, Bos vs. Chi 2–0		June 26	Earl Wilson, Bos vs. LA 2–0
1908	June 30	Cy Young, Bos vs. NY 8–0		Aug. 1	Bill Monbouquette, Bos vs. Chi 1–0
	Sept. 18	Bob Rhoades, Cle vs. Bos 2–1		Aug. 26	Jack Kralick, Min vs. KC 1–0
	Sept. 20	Frank Smith, Chi vs. Phil 1–0	1965	Sept. 16	Dave Morehead, Bos vs. Cle 2–0
	Oct. 2	Addie Joss, Cle vs. Chi 1–0 (perfect game)	1966	June 10	Sonny Siebert, Cle vs. Wash 2–0
1910	April 20	Addie Joss, Cle vs. Chi 1–0	1967	April 30	Steve Barber (8⅔) and Stu Miller (⅓), Bal vs. Det 1–2
	May 12	Chief Bender, Phil vs. Cle 4–0		Aug. 25	Dean Chance, Min vs. Cle 2–1
	Aug. 30	Tom Hughes, NY vs. Cle 0–5 (hit in 10th; lost in 11th)		Sept. 10	Joel Horlen, Chi vs. Det 6–0
1911	July 29	Joe Wood, Bos vs. StL 5–0	1968	April 27	Tom Phoebus, Bal vs. Bos 6–0
	Aug. 27	Ed Walsh, Chi vs. Bos 5–0		May 8	Catfish Hunter, Oak vs. Min 4–0 (perfect game)
1912	July 4	George Mullin, Det vs. StL 7–0	1969	Aug. 13	Jim Palmer, Bal vs. Oak 8–0
	Aug. 30	Earl Hamilton, StL vs. Det 5–1	1970	July 3	Clyde Wright, Cal vs. Oak 4–0
1914	May 14	Jim Scott, Chi vs. Wash 0–1 (hit in 10th; lost in 10th)		Sept. 21	Vida Blue, Oak vs. Min 6–0
	May 31	Joe Benz, Chi vs. Cle 6–1	1973	April 27	Steve Busby, KC vs. Det 3–0
1916	June 21	George Foster, Bos vs. NY 2–0		May 15	Nolan Ryan, Cal vs. KC 3–0
	Aug. 26	Joe Bush, Phil vs. Cle 5–0		July 15	Nolan Ryan, Cal vs. Det 6–0
	Aug. 30	Dutch Leonard, Bos vs. StL 4–0		July 30	Jim Bibby, Tex vs. Oak 6–0
1917	April 14	Ed Cicotte, Chi vs. StL 11–0	1974	June 19	Steve Busby, KC vs. Mil 2–0
	April 24	George Mogridge, NY vs. Bos 2–1		July 19	Dick Bosman, Cle vs. Oak 4–0
	May 5	Ernie Koob, StL vs. Chi 1–0		Sept. 28	Nolan Ryan, Cal vs. Min 4–0
	May 6	Bob Groom, StL vs. Chi 3–0	1975	June 1	Nolan Ryan, Cal vs. Bal 1–0
	June 23	Ernie Shore, Bos vs. Wash 4–0 (perfect game)		Sept. 28	Vida Blue (5), Glenn Abbott (1), Paul Lindblad (1), and Rollie Fingers (2), Oak vs. Cal 5–0
1918	June 3	Dutch Leonard, Bos vs. Det 5–0	1976	July 28	John Odom (5) and Francisco Barrios (4), Chi vs. Oak 2–1
1919	Sept. 10	Ray Caldwell, Cle vs. NY 3–0	1977	May 14	Jim Colborn, KC vs. Tex 6–0
1920	July 1	Walter Johnson, Wash vs. Bos 1–0		May 30	Dennis Eckersley, Cle vs. Cal 1–0
1922	April 30	Charlie Robertson, Chi vs. Det 2–0 (perfect game)		Sept. 22	Bert Blyleven, Tex vs. Cal 6–0
1923	Sept. 4	Sam Jones, NY vs. Phil 2–0	1981	May 15	Len Barker, Cle vs. Tor 3–0 (perfect game)
	Sept. 7	Howard Ehmke, Bos vs. Phil 4–0	1983	July 4	Dave Righetti, NY vs. Bos 4–0
1926	Aug. 21	Ted Lyons, Chi vs. Bos 6–0		Sept. 29	Mike Warren, Oak vs. Chi 3–0
1931	April 29	Wes Ferrell, Cle vs. StL 9–0	1984	April 7	Jack Morris, Det vs. Chi 4–0
	Aug. 8	Bob Burke, Wash vs. Bos 5–0		Sept. 30	Mike Witt, Cal vs. Tex 1–0 (perfect game)
1934	Sept. 18	Bobo Newsom, StL vs. Bos 1–2 (hit in 10th; lost in 10th)	1986	Sept. 19	Joe Cowley, Chi vs. Cal 7–1
1935	Aug. 31	Vern Kennedy, Chi vs. Cle 5–0	1987	April 15	Juan Nieves, Mil vs. Bal 7–0
1937	June 1	Bill Dietrich, Chi vs. StL 8–0	1990	April 11	Mark Langston (7) and Mike Witt (2), Cal vs. Sea 1–0
1938	Aug. 27	Monte Pearson, NY vs. Cle 13–0		June 2	Randy Johnson, Sea vs. Det 2–0
1940	April 16	Bob Feller, Cle vs. Chi 1–0 (Opening Day)		June 11	Nolan Ryan, Tex vs. Oak 5–0
1945	Sept. 9	Dick Fowler, Phil vs. StL 1–0		June 29	Dave Stewart, Oak vs. Tor 5–0
1946	April 30	Bob Feller, Cle vs. NY 1–0		July 1	Andy Hawkins, NY vs. Chi 0–4 (pitched eight innings of nine-inning game)
1947	July 10	Don Black, Cle vs. Phil 3–0		Sept. 2	Dave Stieb, Tor vs. Cle 3–0
	Sept. 3	Bill McCahan, Phil vs. Wash 3–0	1991	May 1	Nolan Ryan, Tex vs. Tor 3–0
1948	June 30	Bob Lemon, Cle vs. Det 2–0		July 13	Bob Milacki (6), Mike Flanagan (1), Mark Williamson (1), and Gregg Olson (1), Bal vs. Oak 2–0
1951	July 1	Bob Feller, Cle vs. Det 2–1		Aug. 11	Wilson Alvarez, Chi vs. Bal 7–0
	July 12	Allie Reynolds, NY vs. Cle 1–0		Aug. 26	Bret Saberhagen, KC vs. Chi 7–0
	Sept. 28	Allie Reynolds, NY vs. Bos 8–0	1993	April 22	Chris Bosio, Sea vs. Bos 7–0
1952	May 15	Virgil Trucks, Det vs. Wash 1–0		Sept. 4	Jim Abbott, NY vs. Cle 4–0
	Aug. 25	Virgil Trucks, Det vs. NY 1–0			
1953	May 6	Bobo Holloman, StL vs. Phil 6–0 (first major league start)			

NOTABLE ACHIEVEMENTS

NO-HIT GAMES, NINE INNINGS OR MORE (cont.)

AMERICAN LEAGUE

DATE		PITCHER AND GAME	DATE		PITCHER AND GAME
1994	April 27	Scott Erickson, Min vs. Mil 6–0	1999	July 18	David Cone, NY vs. Mon 6–0
	July 28	Kenny Rogers, Tex vs. Cal 4–0			(perfect game)
		(perfect game)		Sept. 11	Eric Milton, Min vs. Ana 7–0
1996	May 14	Dwight Gooden, NY vs. Sea 2–0	2001	April 4	Hideo Nomo, Bos vs. Bal 3–0
1998	May 17	David Wells, NY vs. Min 4–0	2002	April 27	Derek Lowe, Bos vs. TB 10–0
		(perfect game)			

LONGEST HITTING STREAKS

NATIONAL LEAGUE

PLAYER AND TEAM	YEAR	G
Willie Keeler, Bal	1897	44
Pete Rose, Cin	1978	44
Bill Dahlen, Chi	1894	42
Tommy Holmes, Bos	1945	37
Billy Hamilton, Phil	1894	36
Luis Castillo, Fla	2002	35
Fred Clarke, Lou	1895	35
Benito Santiago, SD	1987	34
George Davis, NY	1893	33
Rogers Hornsby, StL	1922	32

AMERICAN LEAGUE

PLAYER AND TEAM	YEAR	G
Joe DiMaggio, NY	1941	56
George Sisler, StL	1922	41
Ty Cobb, Det	1911	40
Paul Molitor, Mil	1987	39
Ty Cobb, Det	1917	35
Ty Cobb, Det	1912	34
George Sisler, StL	1925	34
John Stone, Det	1930	34
George McQuinn, StL	1938	34
Dom DiMaggio, Bos	1949	34

TRIPLE CROWN WINNERS*

NATIONAL LEAGUE

PLAYER AND TEAM	YEAR	HR	RBI	BA
Paul Hines, Prov	1878	4	50	.358
Hugh Duffy, Bos	1894	18	145	.438
**Heinie Zimmerman, Chi	1912	14	103	.372
Rogers Hornsby, StL	1922	42	152	.401
Rogers Hornsby, StL	1925	39	143	.403
Chuck Klein, Phil	1933	28	120	.368
Joe Medwick, StL	1937	31	154	.374

AMERICAN LEAGUE

PLAYER AND TEAM	YEAR	HR	RBI	BA
Nap Lajoie, Phil	1901	14	125	.422
Ty Cobb, Det	1909	9	115	.377
Jimmie Foxx, Phil	1933	48	163	.356
Lou Gehrig, NY	1934	49	165	.363
Ted Williams, Bos	1942	36	137	.356
Ted Williams, Bos	1947	32	114	.343
Mickey Mantle, NY	1956	52	130	.353
Frank Robinson, Bal	1966	49	122	.316
Carl Yastrzemski, Bos	1967	44	121	.326

* Player who leads in three categories: home runs, RBIs, and batting average.
** Zimmerman ranked first in RBIs as calculated by Ernie Lanigan, but only third as calculated by Information Concepts Inc.

TRIPLE CROWN PITCHERS***

NATIONAL LEAGUE

PLAYER AND TEAM	YEAR	W	L	SO	ERA	PLAYER AND TEAM	YEAR	W	L	SO	ERA
Tommy Bond, Bos	1877	40	17	170	2.11	Hippo Vaughn, Chi	1918	22	10	148	1.74
Hoss Radbourn, Prov	1884	60	12	441	1.38	Grover Alexander, Chi	1920	27	14	173	1.91
Tim Keefe, NY	1888	35	12	333	1.74	Dazzy Vance, Bklyn	1924	28	6	262	2.16
John Clarkson, Bos	1889	49	19	284	2.73	Bucky Walters, Cin	1939	27	11	137	2.29
Amos Rusie, NY	1894	36	13	195	2.78	Sandy Koufax, LA	1963	25	5	306	1.88
Christy Mathewson, NY	1905	31	8	206	1.27	Sandy Koufax, LA	1965	26	8	382	2.04
Christy Mathewson, NY	1908	37	11	259	1.43	Sandy Koufax, LA	1966	27	9	317	1.73
Grover Alexander, Phil	1915	31	10	241	1.22	Steve Carlton, Phil	1972	27	10	310	1.97
Grover Alexander, Phil	1916	33	12	167	1.55	Dwight Gooden, NY	1985	24	4	268	1.53
Grover Alexander, Phil	1917	30	13	201	1.86	Randy Johnson, Ari	2002	24	5	334	2.32

AMERICAN LEAGUE

PLAYER AND TEAM	YEAR	W	L	SO	ERA	PLAYER AND TEAM	YEAR	W	L	SO	ERA
Cy Young, Bos	1901	33	10	158	1.62	Lefty Gomez, NY	1934	26	5	158	2.33
Rube Waddell, Phil	1905	26	11	287	1.48	Lefty Gomez, NY	1937	21	11	194	2.33
Walter Johnson, Wash	1913	36	7	303	1.09	Hal Newhouser, Det	1945	25	9	212	1.81
Walter Johnson, Wash	1918	23	13	162	1.27	Roger Clemens, Tor	1997	21	7	292	2.05
Walter Johnson, Wash	1924	23	7	158	2.72	Roger Clemens, Tor	1998	20	6	271	2.64
Lefty Grove, Phil	1930	28	5	209	2.54	Pedro Martinez, Bos	1999	23	4	313	2.07
Lefty Grove, Phil	1931	31	4	175	2.06						

***Pitcher who leads in three categories: wins, strikeouts, and ERA.

NOTABLE ACHIEVEMENTS
CONSECUTIVE GAMES PLAYED, 500 OR MORE GAMES

Cal Ripken, Jr.	2,632	Frank McCormick	652
Lou Gehrig	2,130	Sandy Alomar, Sr.	648
Everett Scott	1,307	Eddie Brown	618
Steve Garvey	1,207	Roy McMillan	585
Billy Williams	1,117	George Pinckney	577
Joe Sewell	1,103	Steve Brodie	574
Stan Musial	895	Aaron Ward	565
Eddie Yost	829	Alex Rodriguez	546
Gus Suhr	822	Candy LaChance	540
Nellie Fox	798	Buck Freeman	535
Pete Rose	745	Fred Luderus	533
Dale Murphy	740	Clyde Milan	511
Richie Ashburn	730	Charlie Gehringer	511
Ernie Banks	717	Vada Pinson	508
Pete Rose	678	Tony Cuccinello	504
Earl Averill	673	Charlie Gehringer	504
		Omar Moreno	503

UNASSISTED TRIPLE PLAYS

PLAYER AND TEAM	DATE	POS	OPP	OPP BATTER
Neal Ball, Cle	7-19-09	SS	Bos	Amby McConnell
Bill Wambsganss, Cle	10-10-20	2B	Bklyn	Clarence Mitchell
George Burns, Bos	9-14-23	1B	Cle	Frank Brower
Ernie Padgett, Bos	10-6-23	SS	Phil	Walter Holke
Glenn Wright, Pitt	5-7-25	SS	StL	Jim Bottomley
Jimmy Cooney, Chi	5-30-27	SS	Pitt	Paul Waner
Johnny Neun, Det	5-31-27	1B	Cle	Homer Summa
Ron Hansen, Wash	7-30-68	SS	Cle	Joe Azcue
Mickey Morandini, Phil	9-20-92	2B	Pitt	Jeff King
John Valentin, Bos	7-15-94	SS	Min	Marc Newfield
Randy Velarde, Oak	5-29-00	2B	NYY	Shane Spencer
Rafael Furcal, Atl	5-10-03	SS	StL	Woody Williams

PENNANT WINNERS (PAST 50 YEARS)

NATIONAL LEAGUE

YEAR	TEAM	MANAGER	W	L	PCT	GA
††2004	St. Louis (C)	Tony LaRussa	105	57	.648	13
††2003	Florida (WC)	Jack McKeon	91	71	.562	-10
††2002	San Francisco (WC)	Dusty Baker	95	66	.590	-2.5
††2001	Arizona (W)	Bob Brenly	92	70	.568	2
††2000	New York (WC)	Bobby Valentine	94	68	.580	-6.5
††1999	Atlanta (E)	Bobby Cox	103	59	.636	6.5
††1998	San Diego (W)	Bruce Bochy	98	64	.605	9.5
††1997	Florida (WC)	Jim Leyland	92	70	.568	-9
††1996	Atlanta (E)	Bobby Cox	96	66	.593	8
††1995	Atlanta (E)	Bobby Cox	90	54	.625	21
1994	Season ended Aug. 11 due to labor dispute.					
††1993	Philadelphia (E)	Jim Fregosi	97	65	.599	3
††1992	Atlanta (W)	Bobby Cox	98	64	.605	8
††1991	Atlanta (W)	Bobby Cox	94	68	.580	1
††1990	Cincinnati (W)	Lou Piniella	91	71	.562	5
††1989	San Francisco (W)	Roger Craig	92	70	.568	3
††1988	Los Angeles (W)	Tommy Lasorda	94	67	.584	7
††1987	St. Louis (E)	Whitey Herzog	95	67	.586	3
††1986	New York (E)	Dave Johnson	108	54	.667	21.5
††1985	St. Louis (E)	Whitey Herzog	101	61	.623	3
††1984	San Diego (W)	Dick Williams	92	70	.568	12
††1983	Philadelphia (E)	Pat Corrales/Paul Owens	90	72	.556	6
††1982	St. Louis (E)	Whitey Herzog	92	70	.568	3
††1981	Los Angeles (W)	Tommy Lasorda	63	47	.573	**
††1980	Philadelphia (E)	Dallas Green	91	71	.562	1
††1979	Pittsburgh (E)	Chuck Tanner	98	64	.605	2
††1978	Los Angeles (W)	Tommy Lasorda	95	67	.586	2.5
††1977	Los Angeles (W)	Tommy Lasorda	98	64	.605	10
††1976	Cincinnati (W)	Sparky Anderson	102	60	.630	10
††1975	Cincinnati (W)	Sparky Anderson	108	54	.667	20

††Won championship series. **First half 36–21; second half 27–26, in season split by strike; defeated Houston in playoff for Western Division title.

LEGENDS

■ **Ted Williams, outfielder,** b. August 30, 1918, San Diego, California; d. July 5, 2002, Inverness, Florida. Despite missing three full seasons (1943-45) and most of two others (1952 and 1953) to serve in the United States military, Williams finished his career with 521 home runs and a .344 average. "The Splendid Splinter" batted .300 or better in 18 of his 19 seasons, all with the Boston Red Sox. Williams won two MVP Awards and two Triple Crowns, and he played in 17 All-Star Games. He was inducted into the Hall of Fame in 1966.

Ted Williams is the last major league player to bat more than .400 for a season (.406 in 1941).

■ **Nolan Ryan, pitcher,** b. January 31, 1947, Refugio, Texas. "The Ryan Express" was baseball's greatest strikeout artist. He pitched for the Mets, Angels, Astros, and Rangers from 1966-93. Armed with a 100 mph fastball and knee-buckling curve, Ryan established untouchable big-league marks for strikeouts (5,714) and career no-hitters (7). He led the league in strikeouts 11 times and is a member of baseball's 300-win club (324). Ryan was inducted into the Hall of Fame in 1999.

■ **Lou Gehrig, first baseman,** b. June 19, 1903, New York, New York; d. June 2, 1941, Riverdale, New York. Gehrig is considered to be the best first baseman in baseball history. He played an amazing 2,130 consecutive games from 1925-39. During that time, he won a Triple Crown and two MVP awards, hit a record 23 grand slams, and had 13 straight seasons of 100 runs scored and 100 RBIs. Gehrig was inducted into the Hall of Fame in 1939. He died two years later at age 38 of amyotrophic lateral sclerosis, a muscle disease that's now known as Lou Gehrig's Disease.

PENNANT WINNERS (PAST 50 YEARS cont.)

NATIONAL LEAGUE

YEAR	TEAM	MANAGER	W	L	PCT	GA
††1974	Los Angeles (W)	Walt Alston	102	60	.630	4
††1973	New York (E)	Yogi Berra	82	79	.509	1.5
††1972	Cincinnati (W)	Sparky Anderson	95	59	.617	10.5
††1971	Pittsburgh (E)	Danny Murtaugh	97	65	.599	7
††1970	Cincinnati (W)	Sparky Anderson	102	60	.630	14.5
††1969	New York (E)	Gil Hodges	100	62	.617	8
1968	St. Louis	Red Schoendienst	97	65	.599	9
1967	St. Louis	Red Schoendienst	101	60	.627	10.5
1966	Los Angeles	Walt Alston	95	67	.586	1.5
1965	Los Angeles	Walt Alston	97	65	.599	2
1964	St. Louis	Johnny Keane	93	69	.574	1
1963	Los Angeles	Walt Alston	99	63	.611	6
#1962	San Francisco	Al Dark	103	62	.624	1
1961	Cincinnati	Fred Hutchinson	93	61	.604	4
1960	Pittsburgh	Danny Murtaugh	95	59	.617	7
‡1959	Los Angeles	Walt Alston	88	68	.564	2
1958	Milwaukee	Fred Haney	92	62	.597	8
1957	Milwaukee	Fred Haney	95	59	.617	8
1956	Brooklyn	Walt Alston	93	61	.604	1
1955	Brooklyn	Walt Alston	98	55	.641	13.5
1954	New York	Leo Durocher	97	57	.630	5

††Won championship series. #Defeated Los Angeles, two games to one, in playoff for pennant. ‡Defeated Milwaukee, two games to none, in playoff for pennant.

PENNANT WINNERS (PAST 50 YEARS)

		AMERICAN LEAGUE				
YEAR	TEAM	MANAGER	W	L	PCT	GA
‡2004	Boston (WC)	Terry Francona	98	64	.605	-3
‡2003	New York (E)	Joe Torre	101	61	.623	6
‡2002	Anaheim (WC)	Mike Scioscia	99	63	.611	-4
‡2001	New York (E)	Joe Torre	95	65	.594	13.5
‡2000	New York (E)	Joe Torre	87	74	.540	2.5
‡1999	New York (E)	Joe Torre	98	64	.605	4
‡1998	New York (E)	Joe Torre	114	48	.704	22
‡1997	Cleveland (C)	Mike Hargrove	86	75	.534	6
‡1996	New York (E)	Joe Torre	92	70	.568	4
‡1995	Cleveland (C)	Mike Hargrove	100	44	.694	30
1994	Season ended Aug. 11 due to labor dispute.					
‡1993	Toronto (E)	Cito Gaston	95	67	.586	7
‡1992	Toronto (E)	Cito Gaston	96	66	.593	4
‡1991	Minnesota (W)	Tom Kelly	95	67	.586	8
‡1990	Oakland (W)	Tony La Russa	103	59	.636	9
‡1989	Oakland (W)	Tony La Russa	99	63	.611	7
‡1988	Oakland (W)	Tony La Russa	104	58	.642	13
‡1987	Minnesota (W)	Tom Kelly	85	77	.525	2
‡1986	Boston (E)	John McNamara	95	66	.590	5.5
‡1985	Kansas City (W)	Dick Howser	91	71	.562	1
‡1984	Detroit (E)	Sparky Anderson	104	58	.642	15
‡1983	Baltimore (E)	Joe Altobelli	98	64	.605	6
‡1982	Milwaukee (E)	Buck Rodgers, Harvey Kuenn	95	67	.586	1
‡1981	New York (E)	Gene Michael, Bob Lemon	59	48	.551	#
‡1980	Kansas City (W)	Jim Frey	97	65	.599	14
‡1979	Baltimore (E)	Earl Weaver	102	57	.642	8
†‡1978	New York (E)	Billy Martin, Bob Lemon	100	63	.613	1
‡1977	New York (E)	Billy Martin	100	62	.617	2.5
‡1976	New York (E)	Billy Martin	97	62	.610	10.5
‡1975	Boston (E)	Darrell Johnson	95	65	.594	4.5
‡1974	Oakland (W)	Al Dark	90	72	.556	5
‡1973	Oakland (W)	Dick Williams	94	68	.580	6
‡1972	Oakland (W)	Dick Williams	93	62	.600	5.5
‡1971	Baltimore (E)	Earl Weaver	101	57	.639	12
‡1970	Baltimore (E)	Earl Weaver	108	54	.667	15
‡1969	Baltimore (E)	Earl Weaver	109	53	.673	19
1968	Detroit	Mayo Smith	103	59	.636	12
1967	Boston	Dick Williams	92	70	.568	1
1966	Baltimore	Hank Bauer	97	63	.606	9
1965	Minnesota	Sam Mele	102	60	.630	7
1964	New York	Yogi Berra	99	63	.611	1
1963	New York	Ralph Houk	104	57	.646	10.5
1962	New York	Ralph Houk	96	66	.593	5
1961	New York	Ralph Houk	109	53	.673	8
1960	New York	Casey Stengel	97	57	.630	8
1959	Chicago	Al Lopez	94	60	.610	5
1958	New York	Casey Stengel	92	62	.597	10
1957	New York	Casey Stengel	98	56	.636	8
1956	New York	Casey Stengel	97	57	.630	9
1955	New York	Casey Stengel	96	58	.623	3
1954	Cleveland	Al Lopez	111	43	.721	8

‡Won championship series.
†Defeated Boston in a one-game playoff.
#First half 34–22; second half 25–26, in season split by strike; defeated Milwaukee in playoff for Eastern Division title.

2004 OFF-SEASON TRANSACTIONS

The following is a list of big-time players who switched teams for the 2005 season.

FAY STUEBLEBINE/FEUTERS

■ **Randy Johnson, pitcher, New York Yankees** After years of trying to land the Big Unit, Yankee owner George Steinbrenner finally got his man in a January trade with the Arizona Diamondbacks. In exchange for three players and cash, Johnson came to the Yankees after a dominant 2004 season that included a perfect game and a 16–14 record with a 2.60 ERA and 290 strikeouts for a team that won just 51 games. Despite his age (41), the Yanks hope Johnson will produce like the five-time Cy Young Award winner he is.

TOM DIPACE

■ **Carlos Beltran, centerfielder, New York Mets** If getting Martinez was a surprise, landing Beltran, baseball's most coveted free agent, was a stunner for the Mets. For $119 million over seven years, the Mets got a five-tool player who had 38 home runs and 42 stolen bases in 2004 for the Kansas City Royals and Houston Astros. Beltran is the first player in baseball history to put up four straight seasons of 20 home runs, 30 steals, 100 RBIs, and a .500 slugging percentage

JOHN IACONO/SPORTS ILLUSTRATED

■ **Pedro Martinez, pitcher, New York Mets** Martinez, who was with the Red Sox for seven seasons, bolted Boston for a new start in New York less than two months after he helped the Sox win their first World Series title since 1918. The Mets signed the right-hander to a four-year, $53-million contract to be the ace of their staff. Martinez slipped to a 16–9 record with a 3.90 ERA in 2004, but he is a three-time Cy Young Award winner. Pedro still possesses pinpoint control and an above-average fastball.

■ **Carlos Delgado, first baseman, Florida Marlins** Delgado, who left the Toronto Blue Jays to sign with Florida for four years and $52 million, adds punch to an already dangerous lineup. Delgado has driven in at least 90 runs in each of his nine full seasons (1996-2004), and his streak of eight straight years with at least 30 home runs is the fourth-longest in baseball.

TOM DIPACE

2005 YOUNG STARS TO WATCH

■ **Bobby Crosby, shortstop, Oakland A's**
Crosby had big cleats to fill in 2004 — those of former A.L. MVP Miguel Tejada. But his impressive rookie season earned him the 2004 American League Rookie of the Year Award. Though Crosby batted just .239, he showed plenty of pop, with 22 home runs (tops among A.L. rookies) and 64 RBIs. His stellar glove-work already has the 25-year-old listed among the best defensive shortstops in baseball.

BRAD MANGIN

■ **Oliver Perez, pitcher, Pittsburgh Pirates**
Though few people noticed, Perez had one of the best seasons by a pitcher in the history of the franchise. The 23-year-old went 12–10, but he finished among the National League leaders with a 2.98 ERA and 239 strikeouts. His 11.0 strikeouts per nine innings led the majors.

JASON COHN/ICON SMI

■ **Miguel Cabrera, outfielder, Florida Marlins** Cabrera first grabbed center stage as a rookie by being a major contributor to the Marlins' World Series title run in 2003. In his first full season in 2004, he blossomed even more. Cabrera batted .294 with 33 home runs and 112 RBIs and played in the All-Star Game just three months after his 21st birthday.

ALLEN KEE/WIREIMAGE.COM

■ **Victor Martinez, catcher, Cleveland Indians** A member of one of baseball's best young teams, Martinez revealed offensive ability to go with his sound defensive skills in 2004. After hitting just 2 home runs and driving in 21 runs in limited duty his first two seasons, Martinez, age 26, hit .283 with 23 home runs and 108 RBIs in 2004. He was one of four Indians named to the American League All-Star team.

RON SCHWANE/ICON SMI

DID YOU KNOW?

Minor league pitcher Mike Schultz of the Lancaster JetHawks tied a pro baseball record with five strikeouts in one inning on July 15, 2004. Two batters reached base on wild pitches. The major league record is four strikeouts in one inning, held by several pitchers.

2004-05 TIME LINE

■ **June 20, 2004:** Cincinnati Reds outfielder Ken Griffey, Jr., becomes the 20th player to reach 500 career home runs. His dad, former big league outfielder Ken Griffey, is in attendance on Father's Day as the Reds beat the Cardinals, 6–0.

■ **July 13, 2004:** In the All-Star Game in Houston, Texas, hometown hero Roger Clemens of the Astros is roughed up for six first-inning runs. The American League cruises to a 9–4 win.

■ **July 25, 2004:** Dennis Eckersley, one of the greatest closers in baseball history, and Paul Molitor, a member of the 3,000-hit club, are inducted into the National Baseball Hall of Fame in Cooperstown, New York.

■ **August 7, 2004:** Greg Maddux of the Chicago Cubs becomes the 22nd pitcher to win 300 games, with an 8–4 win over the Giants in San Francisco.

■ **September 18, 2004:** Barry Bonds becomes just the third player in baseball history to reach 700 career home runs. The Giants outfielder connects off San Diego Padres starter Jake Peavy during San Francisco's 4–1 win.

■ **September 29, 2004:** The Expos play their last game in Montreal, a 9–1 loss to the Florida Marlins. After 36 seasons in Canada, the team moves to Washington, D.C., for the 2005 season and becomes the Washington Nationals.

■ **October 1, 2004:** Seattle Mariners rightfielder Ichiro Suzuki breaks George Sisler's 84-year-old record for most hits in a single season (257) with a third-inning single. He finishes the season with 262 hits.

■ **October 2, 2004:** Centerfielder Steve Finley of the Dodgers hits a walk-off grand slam on the next-to-last day of the regular season to clinch Los Angeles's first National League West title since 1995. The Dodgers beat their archrivals, the San Francisco Giants, 7–3.

■ **October 11, 2004:** The Houston Astros win a post-season series for the first time in their 43-year history, defeating the Atlanta Braves 12–3 at Turner Field in Game 5 of the National League Division Series.

■ **October 20, 2004:** The Boston Red Sox complete the greatest comeback in baseball history by crushing the New York Yankees, 10–3, in Game 7 of the American League Championship Series. The Red Sox are the first team in baseball to rally from a three-games-to-none deficit to win a playoff series.

■ **October 27, 2004:** After 86 years, the Boston Red Sox are World Series champions again. Derek Lowe pitches seven shutout innings, and the Red Sox beat the St. Louis Cardinals, 3–0, in Game 4 to win their first Series since 1918.

■ **November 10, 2004:** Roger Clemens wins his major-league-record seventh Cy Young Award, and his first in the National League. Clemens went 18–4 with a 2.98 ERA for the Houston Astros in 2004.

■ **November 15, 2004:** Barry Bonds wins his fourth straight National League MVP Award. It's the seventh of his career, a big-league record.

■ **April 3, 2005:** In a rematch of the 2004 ALCS championship, Boston meets New York for the opening game of the 2005 season. The Yanks beat the Red Sox, 9–2.

BASKETBALL MEN'S

The 2004-05 NBA season will be remembered for being good, bad, and ugly.

The biggest story of the season was bad *and* ugly: On November 19, 2004, the Indiana Pacers led the Detroit Pistons, 97–82, with 45.9 seconds left in the fourth quarter. A scuffle broke out between Piston center Ben Wallace and Pacer forward Ron Artest. A fan threw a drink that hit Artest.

Artest stormed into the stands to fight the fan. A brawl erupted between players and fans. Artest was suspended for the rest of the season. Eight other players were given shorter suspensions. Several fans were arrested. The incident gave the league a black eye and was talked about for months.

But even with that unfortunate event, there were many positives during the season. The Phoenix Suns thrilled fans with an uptempo, high-scoring offense led by point guard Steve Nash. Nash, the league's MVP, dished out an NBA-leading 11.5 assists per game. The Suns raced to the NBA's best record, 62–20, 33 more wins than in 2003-04.

Tim Duncan led the San Antonio Spurs to their third NBA championship in seven seasons in 2004-05.

MANNY MILLAN/SPORTS ILLUSTRATED

NBA TEAMS

EASTERN CONFERENCE
Atlanta Hawks
Boston Celtics
Charlotte Bobcats
Chicago Bulls
Cleveland Cavaliers
Detroit Pistons
Indiana Pacers
Miami Heat
Milwaukee Bucks
New Jersey Nets
New York Knicks
Orlando Magic
Philadelphia 76ers
Toronto Raptors
Washington Wizards

WESTERN CONFERENCE
Dallas Mavericks
Denver Nuggets
Golden State Warriors
Houston Rockets
Los Angeles Clippers
Los Angeles Lakers
Memphis Grizzlies
Minnesota Timberwolves
New Orleans Hornets
Phoenix Suns
Portland Trail Blazers
Sacramento Kings
San Antonio Spurs
Seattle SuperSonics
Utah Jazz

The Seattle Super-Sonics (52–30) improved their record by 15 games from 2003-04. The Washington Wizards (45–37) won a playoff series for the first time since 1981-82.

LeBron James of the Cleveland Cavaliers, the 2003-04 Rookie of the Year, raised his game to another level. He averaged 27.2 points, 7.4 rebounds, and 7.2 assists per game. The rookie class of 2004-05 was impressive as well. Emeka Okafor of the Charlotte Bobcats was named Rookie of the Year and Ben Gordon of the Chicago Bulls won the Sixth Man Award.

Shaquille O'Neal, who was traded from the Lakers to the Miami Heat in July 2004, ruled the Eastern Conference (22.9 points and 10.4 rebounds per game). O'Neal proved to have great chemistry with guard Dwyane Wade (24.1 points and 6.8 assists). The dynamic duo led the Heat to the best regular-season record in the East (59–23), but lost to the Pistons in the Conference Finals.

The San Antonio Spurs quietly excelled during the regular season (59–23). They defeated the Pistons in seven games to win their third NBA title in seven seasons. Tim Duncan was named the MVP of the Finals for the third time.

Ben Wallace and the Detroit Pistons pushed the NBA Finals to seven games for the first time since 1993-94.

JOHN W. McDONOUGH/SPORTS ILLUSTRATED

2004-05 NBA FINAL STANDINGS

Eastern Conference

ATLANTIC	W	L	PCT	GB
a-Celtics (3)	45	37	.549	—
x-76ers (7)	43	39	.524	2.0
x-Nets (8)	42	40	.512	3.0
Raptors	33	49	.402	12.0
Knicks	33	49	.402	12.0

CENTRAL	W	L	PCT	GB
c-Pistons (2)	54	28	.659	—
x-Bulls (4)	47	35	.573	7.0
x-Pacers (6)	44	38	.537	10.0
Cavaliers	42	40	.512	12.0
Bucks	30	52	.366	24.0

SOUTHEAST	W	L	PCT	GB
e, se-Heat (1)	59	23	.720	—
x-Wizards (5)	45	37	.549	14.0
Magic	36	46	.439	23.0
Bobcats	18	64	.220	41.0
Hawks	13	69	.159	46.0

Western Conference

NORTHWEST	W	L	PCT	GB
nw-Sonics (3)	52	30	.634	—
x-Nuggets (7)	49	33	.598	3.0
Timberwolves	44	38	.537	8.0
Trail Blazers	27	55	.329	25.0
Jazz	26	56	.317	26.0

PACIFIC	W	L	PCT	GB
w, p-Suns (1)	62	20	.756	—
x-Kings (6)	50	32	.610	12.0
Clippers	37	45	.451	25.0
Lakers	34	48	.415	28.0
Warriors	34	48	.415	28.0

SOUTHWEST	W	L	PCT	GB
sw-Spurs (2)	59	23	.720	—
x-Mavericks (4)	58	24	.707	1.0
x-Rockets (5)	51	31	.622	8.0
x-Grizzlies (8)	45	37	.549	14.0
Hornets	18	64	.220	41.0

Note: Numbers in parentheses are seedings for the playoffs.

KEY x=clinched playoff berth; e=clinched Eastern Conference; a=clinched Atlantic Division; c=clinched Central Division; se=clinched Southeast Division; w=clinched Western Conference; sw=clinched Southwest Division; nw=clinched Northwest Division; p=clinched Pacific Division; W=wins; L=losses; PCT=winning percentage; GB=games back

2005 NBA PLAYOFFS

| EASTERN CONFERENCE | | | | WESTERN CONFERENCE |

Miami Heat (4–0)
Miami Heat (4–0)
New Jersey Nets
Miami Heat
Chicago Bulls
Washington Wizards
Washington Wizards (4–2)

DETROIT PISTONS vs. SAN ANTONIO SPURS
SAN ANTONIO SPURS WIN SERIES, 4 GAMES TO 3

Boston Celtics
Indiana Pacers
Indiana Pacers (4–3)
Detroit Pistons (4–3)
Detroit Pistons (4–1)
Detroit Pistons (4–2)
Philadelphia 76ers
San Antonio Spurs (4–1)

Phoenix Suns (4–2)
Phoenix Suns
Dallas Mavericks
Phoenix Suns (4–0)
Memphis Grizzlies
Dallas Mavericks (4–3)
Houston Rockets

Seattle SuperSonics
San Antonio Spurs (4–2)
Seattle SuperSonics (4–1)
Sacramento Kings
San Antonio Spurs (4–1)
Denver Nuggets

FIRST ROUND | CONF. SEMIFINALS | CONF. FINALS | NBA FINALS | CONF. FINALS | CONF. SEMIFINALS | FIRST ROUND

NBA PLAYOFF RESULTS

FIRST ROUND

Eastern Conference

MIAMI HEAT VS. NEW JERSEY NETS
GAME 1 April 23, 2005: Miami 116, New Jersey 98
GAME 2 April 26, 2005: Miami 104, New Jersey 87
GAME 3 April 28, 2005: Miami 108, New Jersey 105 (2 OT)
GAME 4 May 1, 2005: Miami 110, New Jersey 97
MIAMI HEAT WINS SERIES, 4–0

CHICAGO BULLS VS. WASHINGTON WIZARDS
GAME 1 April 24, 2005: Chicago 103, Washington 94
GAME 2 April 27, 2005: Chicago 113, Washington 103
GAME 3 April 30, 2005: Washington 117, Chicago 99
GAME 4 May 2, 2005: Washington 106, Chicago 99
GAME 5 May 4, 2005: Washington 112, Chicago 110
GAME 6 May 6, 2005: Washington 94, Chicago 91
WASHINGTON WIZARDS WIN SERIES, 4–2

BOSTON CELTICS VS. INDIANA PACERS
GAME 1 April 23, 2005: Boston 102, Indiana 82
GAME 2 April 25, 2005: Indiana 82, Boston 79
GAME 3 April 28, 2005: Indiana 99, Boston 74
GAME 4 April 30, 2005: Boston 110, Indiana 79
GAME 5 May 3, 2005: Indiana 90, Boston 85
GAME 6 May 5, 2005: Boston 92, Indiana 89
GAME 7 May 7, 2005: Indiana 97, Boston 70
INDIANA PACERS WIN SERIES, 4–3

DETROIT PISTONS VS. PHILADELPHIA 76ERS
GAME 1 April 23, 2005: Detroit 106, Philadelphia 85
GAME 2 April 26, 2005: Detroit 99, Philadelphia 84
GAME 3 April 29, 2005: Philadelphia 115, Detroit 104
GAME 4 May 1, 2005: Detroit 97, Philadelphia 92
GAME 5 May 3, 2005: Detroit 88, Philadelphia 76
DETROIT PISTONS WIN SERIES, 4–1

Western Conference

PHOENIX SUNS VS. MEMPHIS GRIZZLIES
GAME 1 April 24, 2005: Phoenix 114, Memphis 103
GAME 2 April 27, 2005: Phoenix 108, Memphis 103
GAME 3 April 29, 2005: Phoenix 110, Memphis 90
GAME 4 May 1, 2005: Phoenix 123, Memphis 115
PHOENIX SUNS WIN SERIES, 4–0

DALLAS MAVERICKS VS. HOUSTON ROCKETS
GAME 1 April 23, 2005: Houston 98, Dallas 86
GAME 2 April 25, 2005: Houston 113, Dallas 111
GAME 3 April 28, 2005: Dallas 106, Houston 102
GAME 4 April 30, 2005: Dallas 97, Houston 93
GAME 5 May 2, 2005: Dallas 103, Houston 100
GAME 6 May 5, 2005: Houston 101, Dallas 83
GAME 7 May 7, 2005: Dallas 116, Houston 76
DALLAS MAVERICKS WIN SERIES, 4–3

SEATTLE SUPERSONICS VS. SACRAMENTO KINGS
GAME 1 April 23, 2005: Seattle 87, Sacramento 82
GAME 2 April 26, 2005: Seattle 105, Sacramento 93
GAME 3 April 29, 2005: Sacramento 116, Seattle 104
GAME 4 May 1, 2005: Seattle 115, Sacramento 102
GAME 5 May 3, 2005: Seattle 122, Sacramento 118
SEATTLE SUPERSONICS WIN SERIES, 4–1

SAN ANTONIO SPURS VS. DENVER NUGGETS
GAME 1 April 24, 2005: Denver 93, San Antonio 87
GAME 2 April 27, 2005: San Antonio 104, Denver 76
GAME 3 April 30, 2005: San Antonio 86, Denver 78
GAME 4 May 2, 2005: San Antonio 126, Denver 115
GAME 5 May 4, 2005: San Antonio 99, Denver 89
SAN ANTONIO SPURS WIN SERIES, 4–1

CONFERENCE SEMIFINALS

Eastern Conference

MIAMI HEAT VS. WASHINGTON WIZARDS
GAME 1 May 8, 2005: Miami 105, Washington 86
GAME 2 May 10, 2005: Miami 108, Washington 102
GAME 3 May 12, 2005: Miami 102, Washington 95
GAME 4 May 14, 2005: Miami 99, Washington 95
MIAMI HEAT WINS SERIES, 4–0

DETROIT PISTONS VS. INDIANA PACERS
GAME 1 May 9, 2005: Detroit 96, Indiana 81
GAME 2 May 11, 2005: Indiana 92, Detroit 83
GAME 3 May 13, 2005: Indiana 79, Detroit 74
GAME 4 May 15, 2005: Detroit 89, Indiana 76
GAME 5 May 17, 2005: Detroit 86, Indiana 67
GAME 6 May 19, 2005: Detroit 88, Indiana 79
DETROIT PISTONS WIN SERIES, 4–2

NBA PLAYOFF RESULTS (cont.)

CONFERENCE SEMIFINALS (cont.)
Western Conference

PHOENIX SUNS VS. DALLAS MAVERICKS
GAME 1 May 9, 2005: Phoenix 127, Dallas 102
GAME 2 May 11, 2005: Dallas 108, Phoenix 106
GAME 3 May 13, 2005: Phoenix 119, Dallas 102
GAME 4 May 15, 2005: Dallas 119, Phoenix 109
GAME 5 May 18, 2005: Phoenix 114, Dallas 108
GAME 6 May 20, 2005: Phoenix 130, Dallas 126 (OT)
PHOENIX SUNS WIN SERIES, 4–2

SAN ANTONIO SPURS VS. SEATTLE SUPERSONICS
GAME 1 May 8, 2005: San Antonio 103, Seattle 81
GAME 2 May 10, 2005: San Antonio 108, Seattle 91
GAME 3 May 12, 2005: Seattle 92, San Antonio 91
GAME 4 May 14, 2005: Seattle 101, San Antonio 89
GAME 5 May 17, 2005: San Antonio 103, Seattle 90
GAME 6 May 19, 2005: San Antonio 98, Seattle 96
SAN ANTONIO SPURS WIN SERIES, 4–2

CONFERENCE FINALS
Eastern Conference

MIAMI HEAT VS. DETROIT PISTONS
GAME 1 May 23, 2005: Detroit 90, Miami 81
GAME 2 May 25, 2005: Miami 92, Detroit 86
GAME 3 May 29, 2005: Miami 113, Detroit 104
GAME 4 May 31, 2005: Detroit 106, Miami 96
GAME 5 June 2, 2005: Miami 88, Detroit 76
GAME 6 June 4, 2005: Detroit 91, Miami 66
GAME 7 June 6, 2005: Detroit 88, Miami 82
DETROIT PISTONS WIN SERIES, 4–3

Western Conference

PHOENIX SUNS VS. SAN ANTONIO SPURS
GAME 1 May 22, 2005: San Antonio 121, Phoenix 114
GAME 2 May 24, 2005: San Antonio 111, Phoenix 108
GAME 3 May 28, 2005: San Antonio 102, Phoenix 92
GAME 4 May 30, 2005: Phoenix 111, San Antonio 106
GAME 5 June 1, 2005: San Antonio 101, Phoenix 95
SAN ANTONIO SPURS WIN SERIES, 4–1

FINALS

DETROIT PISTONS VS. SAN ANTONIO SPURS
GAME 1 June 9, 2005: San Antonio 84, Detroit 69
GAME 2 June 12, 2005: San Antonio 97, Detroit 76
GAME 3 June 14, 2005: Detroit 96, San Antonio 79
GAME 4 June 16, 2005: Detroit 102, San Antonio 71
GAME 5 June 19, 2005: San Antonio 96, Detroit 95 (OT)
GAME 6 June 21, 2005: Detroit 95, San Antonio 86
GAME 7 June 23, 2005: San Antonio 81, Detroit 74
SAN ANTONIO SPURS WIN SERIES, 4–3

NBA FINALS COMPOSITE BOX SCORE

SAN ANTONIO SPURS

PLAYER	GP	Field Goals		3-PT FG		Free Throws		Rebounds		A	STL	TO	BLK	AVG
		FGM	PCT	FGM	PCT	FTM	PCT	OFF	TOTAL					
Duncan	7	54	41.9	0	00.0	36	66.7	33	99	15	3	17	15	20.6
Ginobili	7	42	49.4	12	38.7	35	85.4	8	41	28	9	23	1	18.7
Parker	7	44	45.8	2	14.3	7	43.8	2	17	24	2	22	1	13.9
Horry	7	24	44.4	15	48.4	11	73.3	13	34	15	7	8	5	10.6
Bowen	7	19	38.0	13	44.8	4	66.7	1	19	14	4	11	5	7.9
Mohammed	7	13	43.3	0	00.0	8	72.7	20	42	0	2	5	6	4.9
Barry	7	11	40.7	6	37.5	4	80.0	3	15	11	4	8	2	4.6
Udrih	5	4	36.4	2	50.0	2	100.0	2	5	4	1	8	0	2.4
Brown	6	3	27.3	1	50.0	4	57.1	1	6	3	0	1	0	1.8
Robinson	3	1	20.0	0	00.0	0	00.0	0	3	0	0	1	3	.7
Nesterovic	4	1	50.0	0	00.0	0	00.0	3	8	1	0	1	1	.5
Massenburg	3	0	00.0	0	00.0	0	00.0	0	3	0	0	0	0	.0
TOTALS	**7**	**216**	**42.9**	**51**	**39.8**	**111**	**69.8**	**86**	**292**	**115**	**32**	**110**	**39**	**84.9**

DETROIT PISTONS

PLAYER	GP	Field Goals		3-PT FG		Free Throws		Rebounds		A	STL	TO	BLK	AVG
		FGM	PCT	FGM	PCT	FTM	PCT	OFF	TOTAL					
Billups	7	46	43.4	11	29.7	40	90.9	9	35	44	7	9	1	20.4
Hamilton	7	49	38.6	1	16.7	18	75.0	9	37	18	4	14	1	16.7
R. Wallace	7	35	43.8	5	29.4	1	25.0	13	39	13	14	7	17	10.9
B. Wallace	7	33	56.9	0	00.0	9	42.9	27	72	7	12	7	21	10.7
McDyess	7	33	50.8	0	00.0	5	55.6	18	51	7	6	10	8	10.1
Prince	7	29	38.2	1	11.1	12	85.7	12	34	18	10	8	4	10.1
Hunter	7	16	38.1	0	00.0	7	87.5	5	13	19	9	4	1	5.6
Arroyo	5	5	50.0	0	00.0	1	50.0	0	1	3	1	2	0	2.2
Milicic	3	1	33.3	0	00.0	0	00.0	3	3	0	0	0	0	.7
Ham	5	1	50.0	0	00.0	0	00.0	0	2	0	0	0	0	.4
Dupree	5	0	00.0	0	00.0	0	00.0	0	0	0	0	0	0	.0
Campbell	1	0	00.0	0	00.0	0	00.0	0	1	0	0	0	0	.0
TOTALS	**7**	**248**	**43.4**	**18**	**24.0**	**93**	**73.8**	**96**	**287**	**130**	**63**	**69**	**53**	**86.7**

KEY GP=games played; FGM=field goals made; PCT=percentage; FTM=free throws made; OFF=offensive; A=assists; STL=steals; TO=turnovers; BLK=blocks; AVG=average

NBA FINALS BOX SCORES

GAME 1

SAN ANTONIO SPURS 84

	MIN	FG M-A	FT M-A	REB O-T	A	PF	STL	TO	PTS
Parker	41	7-17	1-2	1-4	3	1	0	4	15
Ginobili	39	10-16	4-4	3-9	2	3	1	4	26
Duncan	41	10-22	4-5	6-17	2	2	0	3	24
Bowen	35	0-6	0-0	0-2	2	4	0	1	0
Mohammed	26	4-8	2-2	4-7	0	1	1	0	10
Horry	28	2-6	1-2	0-3	3	2	1	0	7
Barry	10	0-1	0-0	0-1	0	4	0	1	0
Udrih	7	0-0	0-0	1-1	0	0	0	1	0
Brown	6	0-1	0-0	0-2	0	0	0	1	0
Robinson	6	1-2	0-0	0-3	0	0	0	0	2
Nesterovic	1	0-0	0-0	0-0	0	0	0	0	0
Massenburg									DNP
TOTALS	**240**	**34-79**	**12-15**	**15-49**	**12**	**17**	**3**	**15**	**84**

Percentages: Field goals—43%, Free throws—80%, 3-point field goals—4-13, 30.8% (Parker 0-1, Ginobili 2-4, Bowen 0-3, Horry 2-4, Barry 0-1). Team rebounds: 9. Blocked shots: 8 (Duncan 2, Bowen 1, Mohammed 2, Robinson 3).

DETROIT PISTONS 69

	MIN	FG M-A	FT M-A	REB O-T	A	PF	STL	TO	PTS
Billups	43	9-16	6-6	0-4	6	1	4	1	25
Hamilton	39	7-21	0-1	1-1	1	2	0	2	14
R. Wallace	33	3-6	0-0	4-8	1	4	2	1	6
Prince	32	4-12	3-4	2-5	4	2	1	3	11
B. Wallace	39	2-5	1-2	1-7	1	3	2	1	5
McDyess	23	1-8	0-1	1-7	0	2	1	1	2
Hunter	16	1-5	0-0	2-3	1	3	1	2	2
Arroyo	13	1-3	0-0	0-0	1	2	1	1	2
Ham	1	1-1	0-0	0-0	0	0	0	0	2
Dupree	1	0-0	0-0	0-0	0	0	0	0	0
Milicic									DNP
Campbell									DNP
TOTALS	**240**	**29-77**	**10-14**	**11-35**	**15**	**19**	**12**	**12**	**69**

Percentages: Field goals—37.7%, Free throws—71.4%, 3-point field goals—1-6, 16.7% (Billups 1-4, Hamilton 0-1, Hunter 0-1). Team rebounds: 7. Blocked shots: 10 (Billups 1, R. Wallace 6, B. Wallace 3).

GAME 2

SAN ANTONIO SPURS 97

	MIN	FG M-A	FT M-A	REB O-T	A	PF	STL	TO	PTS
Ginobili	32	6-8	11-13	1-3	7	3	3	3	27
Parker	28	6-9	0-1	0-1	2	5	0	0	12
Duncan	37	5-10	8-9	3-11	1	2	0	2	18
Bowen	36	5-13	1-2	0-3	1	3	1	1	15
Mohammed	25	1-2	4-5	3-5	0	2	0	2	6
Horry	28	4-10	2-2	1-6	5	2	4	2	12
Barry	26	0-3	0-0	0-1	5	1	2	2	0
Udrih	18	2-4	2-2	0-2	2	0	1	2	7
Robinson	3	0-1	0-0	0-0	0	0	0	1	0
Nesterovic	3	0-0	0-0	1-3	0	0	0	0	0
Brown	2	0-0	0-0	0-0	0	1	0	0	0
Massenburg	2	0-2	0-0	0-1	0	0	0	0	0
TOTALS	**240**	**29-62**	**28-34**	**9-36**	**23**	**19**	**11**	**15**	**97**

Percentages: Field goals—46.8%, Free throws—82.4%, 3-point field goals—11-24, 45.8% (Ginobili 4-5, Parker 0-1, Bowen 4-8, Horry 2-6, Barry 0-3, Udrih 1-1). Team rebounds: 5. Blocked shots: 7 (Duncan 4, Mohammed 2, Horry 1).

DETROIT PISTONS 76

	MIN	FG M-A	FT M-A	REB O-T	A	PF	STL	TO	PTS
Billups	40	6-14	1-1	1-5	3	3	0	4	13
Hamilton	35	5-15	4-5	2-7	3	4	1	0	14
Prince	33	1-7	1-1	1-3	0	4	0	1	3
R. Wallace	33	5-12	1-2	3-8	4	5	2	1	11
B. Wallace	33	4-6	1-3	4-8	2	3	0	3	9
Hunter	24	3-7	1-2	2-4	3	1	1	1	7
McDyess	24	7-14	1-2	3-7	2	4	1	2	15
Arroyo	8	2-3	0-0	0-1	0	1	0	1	4
Ham	4	0-1	0-0	2-2	0	0	0	0	0
Milicic	3	0-1	0-0	0-0	0	0	0	0	0
Dupree	3	0-2	0-0	0-0	0	0	0	0	0
Campbell									DNP
TOTALS	**240**	**33-82**	**10-16**	**18-45**	**17**	**25**	**5**	**13**	**76**

Percentages: Field goals—40.2%, Free throws—62.5%, 3-point field goals—0-6, 0% (Billups 0-3, R. Wallace 0-2, Hunter 0-1). Team rebounds: 8. Blocked shots: 2 (Prince 1, B. Wallace 1).

GAME 3

DETROIT PISTONS 96

	MIN	FG M-A	FT M-A	REB O-T	A	PF	STL	TO	PTS
Hamilton	43	11-23	2-3	1-3	4	5	2	3	24
Billups	37	6-12	5-7	2-6	7	5	1	2	20
Prince	40	4-10	4-4	0-6	5	0	1	2	12
R. Wallace	37	4-13	0-0	3-7	1	3	1	3	8
B. Wallace	39	7-10	1-2	6-11	1	2	3	1	15
Hunter	21	1-6	1-1	0-1	4	2	2	0	3
McDyess	19	6-9	0-0	4-9	0	1	3	1	12
Ham	1	0-0	0-0	1-1	0	0	0	0	0
Arroyo	1	1-1	0-0	0-0	0	0	0	0	2
Milicic	1	0-1	0-0	0-0	0	0	0	0	0
Dupree	1	0-0	0-0	0-0	0	0	0	0	0
Campbell									DNP
TOTALS	**240**	**40-85**	**13-17**	**17-44**	**22**	**18**	**12**	**11**	**96**

Percentages: Field goals—47.1%, Free throws—76.5%, 3-point field goals—3-14, 21.4% (Hamilton 0-1, Billups 3-7, R. Wallace 0-4, Hunter 0-2). Team rebounds: 5. Blocked shots: 10 (Prince 1, R. Wallace 1, B. Wallace 5, Hunter 1, McDyess 2).

SAN ANTONIO SPURS 79

	MIN	FG M-A	FT M-A	REB O-T	A	PF	STL	TO	PTS
Parker	40	8-16	5-8	0-2	4	4	2	4	21
Ginobili	29	2-6	2-2	0-4	0	4	0	6	7
Bowen	42	4-8	1-2	0-0	2	4	2	1	13
Duncan	38	5-15	4-4	3-10	4	3	3	2	14
Mohammed	18	2-4	0-2	3-7	0	3	0	1	4
Horry	30	2-7	1-2	1-5	2	0	0	0	6
Barry	21	4-5	0-0	0-4	1	1	0	1	10
Nesterovic	8	1-2	0-0	2-3	1	1	0	0	2
Udrih	7	0-0	0-0	1-2	2	1	0	3	0
Robinson	5	0-2	0-0	0-0	0	0	0	0	2
Brown	2	1-2	0-0	0-0	0	0	0	0	2
Massenburg									DNP
TOTALS	**240**	**29-67**	**13-20**	**10-37**	**16**	**21**	**7**	**18**	**79**

Percentages: Field goals—43.3%, Free throws—65%, 3-point field goals—8-17, 47.1% (Parker 0-2, Ginobili 1-3, Bowen 4-6, Horry 1-3, Barry 2-2, Robinson 0-1). Team rebounds: 8. Blocked shots: 3 (Bowen 1, Duncan 1, Horry 1).

KEY MIN=minutes played; FG M-A=field goals made-attempted; FT M-A=free throws made-attempted; REB O-T=rebounds offensive-total; A=assists; PF=personal fouls; STL=steals; TO=turnovers; PTS=points; DNP=did not play

GAME 4

DETROIT PISTONS 102

	MIN	FG M-A	FT M-A	REB O-T	A	PF	STL	TO	PTS
Billups	38	5-14	7-7	0-5	7	1	2	1	17
Hamilton	38	4-16	4-4	2-9	4	4	1	1	12
Prince	36	6-14	1-1	2-2	1	2	2	0	13
R. Wallace	33	6-10	0-1	2-8	2	3	2	0	14
B. Wallace	39	5-11	1-4	5-13	1	3	3	0	11
Hunter	22	7-10	3-3	0-1	5	4	2	0	17
McDyess	19	6-11	1-1	2-7	1	4	1	1	13
Arroyo	7	1-3	1-2	0-0	2	0	0	0	3
Ham	4	0-0	0-0	0-0	0	1	0	0	0
Milicic	2	1-1	0-0	0-2	0	0	0	0	2
Dupree	2	0-0	0-0	0-0	0	0	0	0	0
Campbell									DNP
TOTALS	**240**	**41-90**	**18-23**	**13-47**	**23**	**22**	**13**	**3**	**102**

Percentages: Field goals—45.6%, Free throws—78.3%, 3-point field goals—2-9, 22.2% (Billups 0-4, Hamilton 0-1, Prince 0-2, R. Wallace 2-2). Team rebounds: 7. Blocked shots: 6 (R. Wallace 2, B. Wallace 3, McDyess 1).

SAN ANTONIO SPURS 71

	MIN	FG M-A	FT M-A	REB O-T	A	PF	STL	TO	PTS
Parker	37	6-13	0-2	0-4	4	2	0	3	12
Ginobili	32	4-9	3-4	0-4	3	3	1	2	12
Duncan	39	5-17	6-9	3-16	2	0	0	3	16
Bowen	33	2-3	2-2	1-3	4	4	0	3	6
Mohammed	17	2-6	0-0	3-5	0	2	0	1	4
Brown	20	2-8	3-5	1-3	2	1	0	0	8
Horry	20	2-6	0-0	3-4	0	1	0	1	5
Nesterovic	14	0-0	0-2	0-2	0	1	0	1	0
Udrih	11	2-5	0-0	0-0	0	2	0	2	5
Barry	11	1-2	0-0	1-1	0	2	0	1	3
Massenburg	6	0-1	0-0	0-2	0	1	0	0	0
Robinson									DNP
TOTALS	**240**	**26-70**	**14-24**	**12-44**	**15**	**21**	**1**	**17**	**71**

Percentages: Field goals—37.1%, Free throws—58.3%, 3-point field goals—5-15, 33.3% (Parker 0-1, Ginobili 1-5, Brown 1-2, Horry 1-3, Udrih 1-2, Barry 1-2). Team rebounds: 10. Blocked shots: 9 (Parker 1, Ginobili 1, Duncan 3, Bowen 2, Horry 1, Nesterovic 1).

GAME 5

SAN ANTONIO SPURS 96 (OT)

	MIN	FG M-A	FT M-A	REB O-T	A	PF	STL	TO	PTS
Parker	45	7-16	0-0	1-2	3	4	0	6	14
Ginobili	44	5-10	5-5	3-6	9	4	1	2	15
Duncan	48	11-24	4-11	8-19	2	3	0	2	26
Bowen	44	4-8	0-0	0-5	3	4	1	3	10
Mohammed	26	3-4	0-0	1-3	0	3	1	0	6
Horry	32	7-12	2-3	5-7	2	5	0	3	21
Barry	22	1-3	0-0	1-2	0	2	0	0	0
Brown	4	0-0	1-2	0-1	1	0	0	0	1
Udrih									DNP
Robinson									DNP
Massenburg									DNP
Nesterovic									DNP
TOTALS	**265**	**38-82**	**12-21**	**19-45**	**20**	**26**	**3**	**16**	**96**

Percentages: Field goals—46.3%, Free throws—57.1%, 3-point field goals—8-20, 40% (Parker 0-3, Ginobili 0-4, Bowen 2-5, Horry 5-6, Barry 1-2). Team rebounds: 7. Blocked shots: 3 (Duncan 2, Barry 1).

DETROIT PISTONS 95

	MIN	FG M-A	FT M-A	REB O-T	A	PF	STL	TO	PTS
Hamilton	49	7-15	1-2	1-4	2	5	0	5	15
Billups	44	11-26	10-11	3-5	7	2	0	1	34
Prince	48	5-10	0-0	3-9	3	3	3	1	10
R. Wallace	41	6-15	0-0	1-5	1	5	3	0	12
B. Wallace	48	4-9	5-6	5-12	1	1	0	2	13
Hunter	18	0-3	2-2	0-1	2	1	1	1	2
McDyess	17	4-6	1-2	3-6	1	3	0	1	9
Ham									DNP
Arroyo									DNP
Milicic									DNP
Dupree									DNP
Campbell									DNP
TOTALS	**265**	**37-84**	**19-23**	**16-42**	**17**	**20**	**7**	**11**	**95**

Percentages: Field goals—44%, Free throws—82.6%, 3-point field goals—2-9, 22.2% (Billups 2-7, Prince 0-1, Hunter 0-1). Team rebounds: 10. Blocked shots: 11 (Prince 1, R. Wallace 4, B. Wallace 4, McDyess 2).

GAME 6

DETROIT PISTONS 95

	MIN	FG M-A	FT M-A	REB O-T	A	PF	STL	TO	PTS
Hamilton	44	9-19	4-5	1-5	3	0	0	2	23
Billups	39	6-16	4-4	2-6	6	4	0	0	21
Prince	44	5-10	3-4	3-7	4	3	1	0	13
R. Wallace	24	7-15	0-1	1-3	3	5	2	1	16
B. Wallace	44	4-6	0-2	3-9	0	2	2	0	8
McDyess	28	4-10	2-3	2-8	1	4	0	2	10
Hunter	16	2-3	0-0	1-2	2	3	1	0	4
Arroyo	1	0-0	0-0	0-0	0	0	0	0	0
Ham									DNP
Milicic									DNP
Dupree									DNP
Campbell									DNP
TOTALS	**240**	**37-79**	**13-19**	**13-40**	**19**	**21**	**6**	**5**	**95**

Percentages: Field goals—46.8%, Free throws—68.4%, 3-point field goals—8-17, 47.1% (Hamilton 1-1, Billups 5-9, Prince 0-2, R. Wallace 2-5). Team rebounds: 6. Blocked shots: 8 (Prince 1, R. Wallace 3, B. Wallace 3, McDyess 1).

SAN ANTONIO SPURS 86

	MIN	FG M-A	FT M-A	REB O-T	A	PF	STL	TO	PTS
Ginobili	41	7-17	5-8	1-10	3	3	2	3	21
Parker	38	7-15	0-1	0-2	5	4	0	4	15
Bowen	41	2-8	0-0	0-2	1	2	0	1	6
Duncan	40	8-14	5-10	5-15	1	2	0	0	21
Mohammed	24	1-3	2-2	5-8	0	1	0	1	4
Horry	30	3-6	0-0	1-4	2	4	1	1	8
Barry	25	3-10	4-5	1-2	3	2	0	1	11
Udrih	1	0-2	0-0	0-0	0	0	0	0	0
Brown									DNP
Robinson									DNP
Massenburg									DNP
Nesterovic									DNP
TOTALS	**240**	**31-75**	**16-26**	**13-43**	**15**	**18**	**3**	**11**	**86**

Percentages: Field goals—41.3%, Free throws—61.5%, 3-point field goals—8-28, 28.6% (Ginobili 2-8, Parker 1-3, Bowen 2-6, Horry 2-5, Barry 1-5, Udrih 0-1). Team rebounds: 13. Blocked shots: 2 (Duncan 1, Horry 1).

NBA FINALS BOX SCORES (cont.)

GAME 7

SAN ANTONIO SPURS 81

	MIN	FG M-A	FT M-A	REB O-T	A	PF	STL	TO	PTS
Parker	38	3-11	1-2	0-2	3	4	0	1	8
Ginobili	35	8-13	5-5	0-5	4	3	1	3	23
Duncan	42	10-27	5-6	5-11	3	2	0	5	25
Bowen	41	2-4	0-0	0-4	1	5	0	1	5
Mohammed	22	0-3	0-0	1-7	0	3	0	0	0
Horry	32	4-7	5-6	2-5	1	1	1	1	15
Barry	29	2-3	0-0	0-4	2	2	2	2	5
Brown	1	0-0	0-0	0-0	0	0	0	0	0
Udrih									DNP
Robinson									DNP
Massenburg									DNP
Nesterovic									DNP
TOTALS	240	29-68	16-19	8-38	14	20	4	13	81

Percentages: Field goals—42.6%, Free throws—84.2%, 3-point field goals—7-11, 63.6% (Parker 1-3, Ginobili 2-2, Bowen 1-1, Horry 2-4, Barry 1-1). Team rebounds: 8. Blocked shots: 7 (Duncan 2, Bowen 1, Mohammed 2, Horry 1, Barry 1).

DETROIT PISTONS 74

	MIN	FG M-A	FT M-A	REB O-T	A	PF	STL	TO	PTS
Hamilton	46	6-18	3-4	1-8	1	3	0	1	15
Billups	40	3-8	7-8	1-4	8	4	1	1	13
Prince	41	4-13	0-0	1-2	1	1	2	1	9
R. Wallace	28	5-10	0-0	0-1	1	5	2	1	11
B. Wallace	38	6-10	0-2	2-11	1	5	2	0	12
McDyess	23	5-7	0-0	3-7	2	4	0	2	10
Hunter	21	2-8	0-0	0-1	2	2	1	0	4
Ham	1	0-0	0-0	0-0	0	0	0	0	0
Dupree	1	0-0	0-0	0-0	0	0	0	0	0
Campbell	1	0-0	0-0	0-0	1	0	0	0	0
Arroyo									DNP
Milicic									DNP
TOTALS	240	31-74	10-14	8-34	17	24	8	6	74

Percentages: Field goals—41.9%, Free throws—71.4%, 3-point field goals—2-14, 14.3% (Hamilton 0-2, Billups 0-3, Prince 1-4, R. Wallace 1-4, Hunter 0-1). Team rebounds: 9. Blocked shots: 6 (Hamilton 1, R. Wallace 1, B. Wallace 2, McDyess 2).

LEGENDS

■ **Michael Jordan, guard,** b. February 17, 1963, Brooklyn, New York. Jordan is considered by many as the greatest player of all time. The five-time MVP led the Chicago Bulls to six NBA championships (1991-93 and 1996-98). Jordan was also a 14-time All-Star, and a record 10-time NBA scoring champion. The 6' 6" shooting guard retired from the NBA in 1993 and 1999, but returned to the league both times. Jordan became part-owner of the Washington Wizards in 2000 and played for the team in 2001-02 and 2002-03. He then retired for the third and final time with a 30.1 points-per-game average, the highest in NBA history.

Michael Jordan scored 32,292 career points, third on the all-time list.

■ **Willis Reed, center,** b. June 25, 1942, Hico, Louisiana. Reed, who played his entire career with the New York Knicks, will always be remembered for hobbling onto the floor with an injured leg in Game 7 of the 1970 NBA Finals. He made his first two shots and inspired the Knicks to win their first championship. Reed also led the Knicks to the NBA championship in 1973. He averaged 18.7 points and 12.9 rebounds per game in 10 seasons. In 1969-70, he was the MVP of the league, the All-Star game, and the NBA Finals, the first player to win all three awards in the same season. Reed was the first Knick to have his number retired. He was elected into the Basketball Hall of Fame in 1982.

■ **Wilt Chamberlain, center,** b. August 21, 1936, Philadelphia, Pennsylvania; d. October 12, 1999, Los Angeles, California. At 7' 1", "The Big Dipper" was the most dominant big man of the 1960's. He played for the Philadelphia/San Francisco Warriors, the Philadelphia 76ers, and the Los Angeles Lakers. Chamberlain led the NBA in scoring seven straight seasons (1960-66) and was tops in rebounding 11 times (1960-63, 1966-69, and 1971-73). He was a four-time league MVP and a member of two NBA championship teams, the 1966-67 Sixers and the 1971-72 Lakers. But he is best known for his individual stats. On March 2, 1962, he set an NBA record by scoring 100 points in a game against the New York Knicks. Chamberlain holds many other records, including most rebounds in a game (55), most games scoring 50 or more points (118), and most career rebounds (23,924). He retired in 1973 and was elected to the Basketball Hall of Fame in 1978.

2004-05 NBA INDIVIDUAL LEADERS

Allen Iverson,
Philadelphia 76ers

SCORING

	GP	PTS	AVG
Allen Iverson, Philadelphia 76ers	75	2,302	30.7
Kobe Bryant, Los Angeles Lakers	66	1,819	27.6
LeBron James, Cleveland Cavaliers	80	2,175	27.2
Dirk Nowitzki, Dallas Mavericks	78	2,032	26.1
Amare Stoudemire, Phoenix Suns	80	2,080	26.0

REBOUNDING

	GP	REB	AVG
Kevin Garnett, Minnesota Timberwolves	82	1,108	13.5
Ben Wallace, Detroit Pistons	74	902	12.2
Emeka Okafor, Charlotte Bobcats	81	915	11.3
Troy Murphy, Golden State Warriors	73	795	10.9
Shaquille O'Neal, Miami Heat	70	756	10.8
Kurt Thomas, New York Knicks	73	760	10.4
	80	831	10.4

ASSISTS

	GP	A	AVG
Steve Nash, Phoenix Suns	75	861	11.5
Brevin Knight, Charlotte Bobcats	66	591	9.0
Jason Kidd, New Jersey Nets	66	545	8.3
Stephon Marbury, New York Knicks	82	668	8.1
Allen Iverson, Philadelphia 76ers	75	596	7.9

FIELD GOAL PERCENTAGE

	FGA	FGM	PCT
Shaquille O'Neal, Miami Heat	1,095	658	60.1
Amare Stoudemire, Phoenix Suns	1,336	747	55.9
Yao Ming, Houston Rockets	975	538	55.2
Udonis Haslem, Miami Heat	641	346	54.0
Eddy Curry, Chicago Bulls	730	393	53.8

FREE THROW PERCENTAGE

	FTA	FTM	PCT
Reggie Miller, Indiana Pacers	268	250	93.3
Earl Boykins, Denver Nuggets	303	279	92.1
Peja Stojakovic, Sacramento Kings	275	253	92.0
Damon Stoudamire, Portland Trail Blazers	199	182	91.5
Chauncey Billups, Detroit Pistons	382	343	89.8

3-POINT FIELD GOAL PERCENTAGE

	FGA	FGM	PCT
Fred Hoiberg, Minnesota Timberwolves	145	70	48.3
Joe Johnson, Phoenix Suns	370	177	47.8
Cuttino Mobley, Sacramento Kings	342	150	43.9
Mike Miller, Memphis Grizzlies	323	140	43.3
Damon Jones, Miami Heat	521	225	43.2

STEALS

	GP	STL	AVG
Larry Hughes, Washington Wizards	61	176	2.89
Allen Iverson, Philadelphia 76ers	75	180	2.40
LeBron James, Cleveland Cavaliers	80	177	2.21
Shawn Marion, Phoenix Suns	81	163	2.01
Brevin Knight, Charlotte Bobcats	66	131	1.98

Larry Hughes,
Washington
Wizards

BLOCKS

	GP	BLK	AVG
Andrei Kirilenko, Utah Jazz	41	136	3.32
Marcus Camby, Denver Nuggets	66	199	3.02
Tim Duncan, San Antonio Spurs	66	174	2.64
Theo Ratliff, Portland Trail Blazers	63	158	2.51
Ben Wallace, Detroit Pistons	74	176	2.38

KEY GP=games played; PTS=points; AVG=average; REB=rebounds; A=assists; FGA=field goals attempted; FGM=field goals made; PCT=percentage; FTA=free throw attempts; FTM=free throws made; STL=steals; BLK=blocks

MANNY MILLAN/SPORTS ILLUSTRATED

JESSE D. GARRABRANT/NBAE/GETTY IMAGES

TEAM-BY-TEAM STATS

ATLANTA HAWKS

PLAYER	GP	MIN	Field Goals		3-PT FG	Free Throws		Rebounds		A	STL	TO	BLK	AVG
			FGM	PCT	FGA-FGM	FTM	PCT	OFF	TOTAL					
Al Harrington	66	2,550	453	45.9	74-16	236	67.2	145	461	208	85	204	16	17.5
Tyronn Lue	70	2,007	295	45.1	155-55	142	86.1	14	149	322	33	105	0	11.2
Tony Delk	56	1,340	246	41.6	202-72	103	75.7	28	130	104	47	54	3	11.9
Josh Childress	80	2,376	302	47.0	56-13	190	82.3	195	482	151	74	106	35	10.1
Josh Smith	74	2,050	274	45.5	23-4	163	68.8	147	457	127	59	135	144	9.7
Predrag Drobnjak	71	1,435	238	43.8	71-25	96	80.0	73	238	49	42	78	24	8.4
Jason Collier	70	942	174	46.3	14-6	48	67.6	84	184	18	15	63	13	5.7
Obinna Ekezie	42	732	79	43.4	1-0	72	77.4	69	179	11	22	45	12	5.5
Tom Gugliotta	47	966	99	41.1	26-8	33	76.7	56	191	68	41	57	17	5.1
Boris Diaw	66	1,201	124	42.2	50-9	57	74.0	54	170	149	37	87	18	4.8
Royal Ivey	62	809	85	42.9	9-3	47	70.1	19	84	103	39	58	7	3.5
Donta Smith	38	433	44	38.9	22-6	33	68.8	19	52	39	23	25	5	3.3
Kevin Willis	29	344	35	38.9	2-0	17	73.9	29	76	9	8	15	7	3.0
James Thomas	11	117	12	60.0	0-0	2	33.3	17	37	4	4	7	4	2.4
Michael Stewart	12	145	11	52.4	0-0	3	42.9	21	40	5	6	6	5	2.1
Anthony Miller	2	9	2	66.7	0-0	0	0.00	0	1	1	1	1	0	2.0
Jelani McCoy	10	88	7	53.8	0-0	1	20.0	7	21	0	3	6	8	1.5
TEAM TOTALS	82	19,855	2,942	44.1	973-304	1,417	71.1	1,100	3,435	1,614	629	1,319	344	92.7
OPPONENTS	82	–	3,044	47.6	1,232-467	1,846	77.0	902	3,385	1,803	716	1,210	484	102.5

KEY GP=games played; MIN=minutes played; FGM=field goals made; PCT=percentage; FGA=field goals attempted; FTM=free throws made; OFF=offensive; A=assists; STL=steals; TO=turnovers; BLK=blocks; AVG=average

BOSTON CELTICS

PLAYER	GP	MIN	Field Goals		3-PT FG	Free Throws		Rebounds		A	STL	TO	BLK	AVG
			FGM	PCT	FGA-FGM	FTM	PCT	OFF	TOTAL					
Paul Pierce	82	2,960	556	45.5	292-108	549	82.2	78	539	348	133	230	39	21.6
Antoine Walker	77	2,955	581	42.2	341-110	201	53.9	182	695	265	89	253	58	19.1
Ricky Davis	82	2,696	481	46.2	180-61	286	81.5	66	249	246	89	205	27	16.0
Gary Payton	77	2,541	339	46.8	129-42	153	76.1	48	236	469	88	148	12	11.3
Raef LaFrentz	80	2,196	341	49.6	225-82	120	81.1	154	553	98	42	70	99	11.1
Mark Blount	82	2,130	327	52.9	1-0	117	71.3	143	397	129	33	158	64	9.4
Al Jefferson	71	1,051	195	52.8	3-0	85	63.0	119	312	24	22	66	55	6.7
Tony Allen	77	1,262	184	47.5	31-12	112	73.7	85	221	64	76	77	24	6.4
Marcus Banks	81	1,145	115	40.2	59-21	121	74.2	29	126	155	63	79	13	4.6
Delonte West	39	507	66	42.6	67-24	19	70.4	14	65	53	21	24	8	4.5
Kendrick Perkins	60	548	56	47.1	0-0	37	63.8	53	176	21	9	43	37	2.5
Justin Reed	23	121	15	51.7	3-0	11	73.3	8	16	10	3	5	1	1.8
TEAM TOTALS	82	19,880	3,046	46.8	1,252-437	1,775	76.4	909	3,347	1,810	667	1,297	423	101.3
OPPONENTS	82	–	2,960	44.4	1,370-488	1,825	75.3	1,039	3,466	1,859	714	1,277	402	100.4

CHARLOTTE BOBCATS

PLAYER	GP	MIN	Field Goals		3-PT FG	Free Throws		Rebounds		A	STL	TO	BLK	AVG
			FGM	PCT	FGA-FGM	FTM	PCT	OFF	TOTAL					
Emeka Okafor	73	2,600	448	44.7	1-0	209	60.9	275	795	64	62	125	125	15.1
Primoz Brezec	72	2,276	387	51.2	0-0	164	74.5	226	531	86	33	106	55	13.0
Gerald Wallace	70	2,147	286	44.9	62-17	191	66.1	118	386	137	117	159	91	11.1
Brevin Knight	66	1,944	248	42.2	20-3	167	85.2	21	170	591	131	147	5	10.1
Keith Bogans	74	1,791	262	38.1	173-57	133	72.7	76	226	135	68	122	8	9.6
Jason Hart	74	1,887	257	44.9	95-35	157	78.5	18	203	367	99	102	14	9.5
Matt Carroll	25	430	70	38.9	39-13	71	85.5	13	60	17	17	25	2	9.0
Jason Kapono	81	1,491	269	40.1	194-80	70	82.4	32	164	61	40	46	6	8.5
Kareem Rush	48	968	157	38.7	137-51	37	77.1	20	89	68	20	47	7	8.4
Melvin Ely	79	1,649	227	43.2	0-0	122	57.5	142	326	76	32	115	69	7.3
Malik Allen	36	519	84	47.5	0-0	26	92.9	40	99	18	9	18	22	5.4
Tamar Slay	8	78	13	33.3	12-2	0	00.0	6	14	3	5	8	0	3.5
Jamal Sampson	23	329	28	45.2	0-0	23	59.0	36	122	8	4	17	17	3.4
Theron Smith	33	510	44	32.4	12-3	14	87.5	39	116	28	6	27	4	3.2
Cory Alexander	16	201	16	32.7	19-8	9	75.0	8	29	37	9	19	1	3.1
Bernard Robinson	31	328	36	44.4	8-3	18	69.2	14	48	30	11	20	4	3.0
Jahidi White	17	135	14	45.2	0-0	14	35.0	11	34	1	2	11	12	2.5
TEAM TOTALS	82	19,880	2,961	43.2	881-320	1,487	70.9	1,083	3,418	1,794	695	1,192	440	94.3
OPPONENTS	82	–	3,015	46.3	1,224-442	1,748	76.7	959	3,545	1,768	624	1,297	446	100.2

DID YOU KNOW?

The first NBA game was played on November 1, 1946 at Maple Leaf Gardens in Toronto, Ontario, Canada. The New York Knickerbockers beat the Toronto Huskies, 68–66.

CHICAGO BULLS

PLAYER	GP	MIN	Field Goals		3-PT FG	Free Throws		Rebounds		A	STL	TO	BLK	AVG
			FGM	PCT	FGA-FGM	FTM	PCT	OFF	TOTAL					
Eddy Curry	63	1,808	393	53.8	0-0	226	72.0	116	338	37	21	163	58	16.1
Kirk Hinrich	77	2,800	445	39.7	408-145	171	79.2	32	304	494	122	176	21	15.7
Ben Gordon	82	2,002	434	41.1	331-134	233	86.3	55	215	164	53	186	10	15.1
Luol Deng	61	1,663	280	43.4	117-31	120	74.1	92	322	135	48	118	27	11.7
Andres Nocioni	81	1,892	241	40.1	97-25	170	76.6	69	386	122	37	135	34	8.4
Tyson Chandler	80	2,189	207	49.4	2-0	226	67.3	261	775	65	69	118	141	8.0
Othella Harrington	70	1,271	217	51.2	0-0	127	71.8	106	292	56	24	84	18	8.0
Antonio Davis	72	1,843	193	46.1	0-0	115	75.7	152	428	80	27	96	41	7.0
Jannero Pargo	32	453	82	38.5	66-23	17	73.9	12	47	76	16	45	1	6.4
Chris Duhon	82	2,117	172	35.2	265-94	49	73.1	23	213	398	82	119	3	5.9
Eric Piatkowski	68	841	111	43.0	134-57	45	80.4	15	79	51	29	37	1	4.8
Lawrence Funderburke	2	21	3	50.0	0-0	3	60.0	1	3	0	0	0	0	4.5
Adrian Griffin	69	667	58	36.0	9-2	33	75.0	52	146	53	43	30	4	2.2
Jared Reiner	19	132	10	33.3	0-0	1	25.0	13	38	1	3	9	7	1.1
Frank Williams	9	71	3	15.0	4-0	0	00.0	2	6	11	2	3	3	.7
TEAM TOTALS	82	19,830	2,849	43.2	1,133-511	1,530	75.0	1,001	3,592	1,743	576	1,371	369	94.5
OPPONENTS	82	–	2,763	42.2	1,245-416	1,716	74.4	979	3,503	1,715	685	1,272	434	93.4

CLEVELAND CAVALIERS

PLAYER	GP	MIN	Field Goals		3-PT FG	Free Throws		Rebounds		A	STL	TO	BLK	AVG
			FGM	PCT	FGA-FGM	FTM	PCT	OFF	TOTAL					
LeBron James	80	3,388	795	47.2	308-108	477	75.0	111	588	577	177	262	52	27.2
Zydrunas Ilgauskas	78	2,615	458	46.8	7-2	402	79.9	299	672	100	53	191	165	16.9
Drew Gordon	82	2,523	464	49.2	28-5	251	81.0	207	753	130	77	133	76	14.4
Jeff McInnis	76	2,651	377	41.2	264-91	130	81.3	32	157	391	56	117	1	12.8
Jiri Welsch	71	1,317	149	40.2	110-34	129	76.3	26	167	103	44	73	5	6.5
Ira Newble	71	1,002	182	42.9	53-10	66	70.7	78	220	91	50	61	18	5.9
Robert Traylor	74	1,327	177	44.4	8-0	55	53.9	136	332	61	54	73	50	5.5
Anderson Varejao	54	863	99	51.3	2-0	68	53.5	109	257	27	41	26	38	4.9
Aleksander Pavlovic	65	862	120	43.5	78-30	44	68.8	15	71	49	29	47	4	4.8
Lucious Harris	73	1,128	118	39.5	65-21	56	81.2	39	121	49	27	29	6	4.3
Eric Snow	81	1,844	125	38.2	45-13	59	73.8	37	155	317	67	89	16	4.0
Dajuan Wagner	11	102	18	32.7	26-5	3	75.0	0	2	13	5	9	0	4.0
Luke Jackson	10	43	10	37.0	6-4	5	83.3	2	6	3	0	2	0	2.9
Scott Williams	19	152	12	29.3	1-0	9	81.8	15	30	8	4	5	6	1.7
Jerome Moiso	20	120	9	50.0	1-0	10	76.9	10	37	1	3	7	6	1.4
DeSagana Diop	39	306	20	29.0	2-0	0	00.0	30	70	15	8	12	27	1.0
TEAM TOTALS	82	19,855	2,990	44.7	904-300	1,634	75.2	1,117	3,469	1,851	654	1,141	461	96.5
OPPONENTS	82	–	2,913	45.2	1,122-422	1,601	75.0	938	3,262	1,737	549	1,213	419	95.7

DALLAS MAVERICKS

| PLAYER | GP | MIN | Field Goals | | 3-PT FG | Free Throws | | Rebounds | | | | | | |
			FGM	PCT	FGA-FGM	FTM	PCT	OFF	TOTAL	A	STL	TO	BLK	AVG
Dirk Nowitzki	78	3,020	663	45.9	228-91	615	86.9	96	757	240	97	176	119	26.1
Michael Finley	64	2,358	387	42.7	285-116	113	83.1	45	262	169	48	60	18	15.7
Jerry Stackhouse	56	1,617	274	41.4	120-32	253	84.9	38	183	127	53	106	10	14.9
Josh Howard	76	2,446	377	47.5	115-34	170	73.3	169	484	109	116	122	49	12.6
Jason Terry	80	2,401	372	50.1	245-103	146	84.4	38	188	429	109	147	15	12.4
Keith Van Horn	62	1,502	257	45.6	142-54	128	81.5	89	294	75	36	81	21	11.2
Erick Dampier	59	1,609	202	55.0	3-0	138	60.5	183	501	51	15	102	80	9.2
Marquis Daniels	60	1,412	220	43.7	35-7	98	73.7	87	216	128	83	86	14	9.1
Devin Harris	76	1,173	157	42.9	131-44	78	75.7	28	102	169	77	82	19	5.7
Darrell Armstrong	66	988	89	32.1	111-28	58	85.3	35	115	178	45	67	8	4.0
Alan Henderson	78	1,203	116	52.7	0-2	41	53.9	164	348	21	29	49	37	3.5
Shawn Bradley	77	885	84	45.2	0-0	43	68.3	70	214	15	25	33	63	2.7
Didier Ilunga-Mbenga	15	58	6	42.9	0-0	3	75.0	3	8	0	0	5	5	1.0
Pavel Podkolzin	5	10	0	00.0	0-0	1	50.0	0	2	0	0	2	0	.2
TEAM TOTALS	82	19,730	3,058	45.7	1,273-463	1,826	78.9	990	3,520	1,610	708	1,102	461	102.5
OPPONENTS	82	–	2,941	43.8	1,366-451	1,601	75.4	1,072	3,539	1,714	584	1,278	399	96.8

DENVER NUGGETS

| PLAYER | GP | MIN | Field Goals | | 3-PT FG | Free Throws | | Rebounds | | | | | | |
			FGM	PCT	FGA-FGM	FTM	PCT	OFF	TOTAL	A	STL	TO	BLK	AVG
Carmelo Anthony	75	2,608	530	43.1	158-42	456	79.6	141	426	194	68	224	30	20.8
Kenyon Martin	70	2,272	444	49.0	12-0	199	64.6	146	511	170	100	149	78	15.5
Andre Miller	82	2,852	427	47.7	39-6	253	83.8	100	338	569	121	220	8	13.6
Earl Boykins	82	2,162	340	41.3	166-56	279	92.1	37	143	372	78	121	12	12.4
Marcus Camby	66	2,015	279	46.5	4-0	125	72.3	131	661	152	61	103	199	10.3
Voshon Lenard	3	54	10	38.5	12-4	5	62.5	0	6	6	1	2	0	9.7
Nene	55	1,317	194	50.3	2-0	140	66.0	104	325	84	50	94	48	9.6
DerMarr Johnson	71	1,232	185	49.9	148-53	80	79.2	43	151	75	43	65	18	7.1
Wesley Person	41	667	107	47.3	89-41	9	69.2	3	83	39	19	17	4	6.4
Greg Buckner	70	1,522	160	52.8	121-49	63	77.8	66	208	133	75	49	6	6.2
Eduardo Najera	68	1,185	145	45.0	21-6	58	63.7	102	243	65	41	61	24	5.2
Bryon Russell	70	1,026	95	37.7	149-56	61	79.2	50	172	72	44	35	11	4.4
Francisco Elson	67	939	101	46.8	3-1	45	57.0	61	201	34	34	40	41	3.7
Luis Flores	16	77	14	48.3	10-5	2	100.0	1	3	11	2	11	0	2.2
Mark Pope	9	27	2	33.3	0-0	0	00.0	5	8	1	1	1	2	.4
TEAM TOTALS	82	19,755	3,038	45.9	940-320	1,765	76.3	967	3,440	1,958	750	1,224	489	99.5
OPPONENTS	82	–	2,950	44.7	1,342-463	1,632	74.6	975	3,416	1,778	636	1,342	458	97.5

DETROIT PISTONS

PLAYER	GP	MIN	Field Goals		3-PT FG	Free Throws		Rebounds		A	STL	TO	BLK	AVG
			FGM	PCT	FGA-FGM	FTM	PCT	OFF	TOTAL					
Richard Hamilton	76	2,926	510	44.0	118-36	368	85.8	74	295	372	77	217	13	18.7
Chauncey Billups	80	2,866	404	44.2	387-165	343	89.8	48	271	464	81	180	9	16.5
Tayshaun Prince	82	3,039	469	48.7	138-47	221	80.7	133	435	247	56	135	71	14.7
Rasheed Wallace	79	2,687	467	44.0	236-75	136	69.7	174	644	142	65	127	115	14.5
Ben Wallace	74	2,671	295	45.3	9-1	130	42.8	292	902	123	106	82	176	9.7
Antonio McDyess	77	1,797	307	51.3	1-0	126	65.6	177	482	71	46	93	52	9.6
Carlos Arroyo	70	1,448	167	38.9	30-8	119	79.9	26	104	280	44	107	4	6.6
Carlos Delfino	30	459	42	35.9	35-9	23	57.5	13	55	38	22	23	6	3.9
Lindsey Hunter	76	1,144	108	35.8	84-23	46	79.3	38	123	130	68	68	13	3.8
Ronald Dupree	47	472	61	48.0	2-1	29	61.7	34	95	24	7	22	10	3.2
Elden Campbell	40	390	39	31.7	2-0	42	76.4	28	93	19	8	29	7	3.0
Horace Jenkins	15	104	15	33.3	9-0	12	92.3	3	9	9	5	7	1	2.6
Darko Milicic	37	254	25	32.9	0-0	17	70.8	3	43	7	2	16	17	1.8
Derrick Coleman	5	50	3	21.4	2-0	3	100.0	3	15	0	0	2	0	1.8
Darvin Ham	47	275	17	45.9	0-0	12	38.7	19	35	5	6	0	7	1.0
TEAM TOTALS	82	19,955	2,851	44.4	1,053-363	1,500	73.9	1,054	3,561	1,787	576	1,133	497	93.3
OPPONENTS	82	–	2,791	43.0	1,213-410	1,344	75.1	928	3,249	1,618	610	1,135	367	89.5

GOLDEN STATE WARRIORS

PLAYER	GP	MIN	Field Goals		3-PT FG	Free Throws		Rebounds		A	STL	TO	BLK	AVG
			FGM	PCT	FGA-FGM	FTM	PCT	OFF	TOTAL					
Jason Richardson	72	2,724	610	44.6	370-125	214	69.3	125	424	281	105	169	32	21.7
Baron Davis	46	1,581	291	38.7	354-118	185	76.1	32	175	362	81	131	14	19.2
Troy Murphy	70	2,375	392	41.4	148-59	233	73.0	251	756	97	53	108	33	15.4
Mike Dunleavy	79	2,570	408	45.1	276-107	134	77.9	97	435	203	79	132	26	13.4
Derek Fisher	74	2,222	297	39.3	291-108	175	86.2	38	218	301	76	129	4	11.9
Mickael Pietrus	67	1,340	214	42.7	195-67	141	69.8	65	189	82	46	92	18	9.5
Zarko Cabarkapa	40	475	86	48.6	36-13	53	81.5	35	102	25	10	30	5	6.0
Rodney White	58	677	121	41.9	60-24	27	61.4	24	89	44	32	37	11	5.1
Adonal Foyle	78	1,700	156	50.2	0-0	40	55.6	165	429	56	26	58	159	4.5
Calbert Cheaney	55	951	113	42.6	3-0	24	64.9	32	124	64	17	35	15	4.5
Andris Biedrins	30	384	45	57.7	1-0	19	47.5	47	118	12	12	12	24	3.6
Ansu Sesay	16	128	17	40.5	8-2	13	54.2	18	38	12	2	8	3	3.1
Nikoloz Tskitishvili	35	220	22	29.7	17-2	4	57.1	12	41	10	8	19	11	1.4
TEAM TOTALS	82	19,905	3,029	43.0	1,774-624	1,412	72.2	1,069	3,505	1,811	642	1,112	420	98.7
OPPONENTS	82	–	3,133	45.8	1,239-450	1,555	74.5	1,057	3,828	1,858	570	1,257	417	100.9

HOUSTON ROCKETS

PLAYER	GP	MIN	Field Goals FGM	PCT	3-PT FG FGA-FGM	Free Throws FTM	PCT	Rebounds OFF	TOTAL	A	STL	TO	BLK	AVG
Tracy McGrady	78	3,182	715	43.1	435-142	431	77.4	71	484	448	135	201	52	25.7
Yao Ming	80	2,447	538	55.2	0-0	389	78.3	208	669	61	34	196	160	18.3
David Wesley	80	2,774	334	39.8	315-118	162	85.7	38	228	265	96	113	9	11.9
Mike James	74	1,859	331	44.1	259-100	109	75.2	35	208	263	65	106	6	11.8
Bob Sura	61	1,922	215	42.7	155-55	141	75.0	79	337	317	65	147	7	10.3
Juwan Howard	61	1,624	244	45.1	1-0	97	84.3	126	346	94	32	79	5	9.6
Jon Barry	69	1,505	161	43.8	165-71	62	87.3	26	159	167	60	67	9	6.6
Charlie Ward	14	360	24	31.2	51-16	11	84.6	6	39	43	15	18	0	5.4
Scott Padgett	66	942	98	42.1	126-50	29	72.5	47	185	55	33	30	10	4.2
Dikembe Mutombo	80	1,212	108	49.8	0-0	106	74.1	150	426	10	16	51	101	4.0
Clarence Weatherspoon	40	525	47	41.2	0-0	29	82.9	35	122	17	9	15	6	3.1
Moochie Norris	38	360	35	32.1	12-0	20	83.3	10	46	39	18	27	2	2.4
Rod Strickland	16	196	9	20.9	2-1	9	90.0	3	27	39	3	16	2	1.8
Ryan Bowen	66	604	47	42.3	6-3	14	66.7	21	76	18	23	7	5	1.7
Vin Baker	27	204	13	31.0	1-0	9	52.9	17	39	10	2	17	4	1.3
Torraye Braggs	7	24	3	42.9	0-0	0	00.0	7	12	0	0	2	0	.9
Brandin Knight	1	3	0	00.0	0-0	0	00.0	0	0	1	0	0	0	.0
TEAM TOTALS	82	19,855	2,846	44.3	1,521-553	1,551	78.1	874	3,475	1,733	563	1,135	378	95.1
OPPONENTS	82	–	2,720	42.3	1,343-454	1,571	74.2	892	3,336	1,696	607	1,087	335	91.0

INDIANA PACERS

PLAYER	GP	MIN	Field Goals FGM	PCT	3-PT FG FGA-FGM	Free Throws FTM	PCT	Rebounds OFF	TOTAL	A	STL	TO	BLK	AVG
Ron Artest	7	291	59	49.6	17-7	47	92.2	8	45	22	12	17	6	24.6
Jermaine O'Neal	44	1,530	386	45.2	6-1	295	75.4	85	388	82	25	131	88	24.3
Stephen Jackson	51	1,806	330	40.3	286-103	190	83.0	44	250	119	64	123	14	18.7
Jamaal Tinsley	40	1,301	218	41.8	156-58	122	74.4	26	160	257	81	134	12	15.4
Reggie Miller	66	2,105	314	43.7	298-96	250	93.3	18	156	146	50	77	5	14.8
Fred Jones	77	2,268	275	42.5	229-87	176	85.0	34	242	196	61	114	31	10.6
Austin Croshere	73	1,827	188	37.8	174-45	226	88.3	103	375	98	48	104	17	8.9
Anthony Johnson	63	1,747	203	44.5	108-41	85	75.2	32	179	302	59	96	15	8.4
Jeff Foster	61	1,594	168	51.9	5-0	90	63.4	205	550	43	46	55	12	7.0
David Harrison	43	760	106	57.6	0-0	52	57.1	48	135	13	16	53	55	6.1
Jonathan Bender	7	93	16	40.0	5-1	3	50.0	5	14	4	1	10	2	5.1
James Jones	75	1,330	126	39.6	166-66	53	85.5	39	174	57	31	43	28	4.9
Dale Davis	61	1,307	112	47.9	0-0	60	60.6	152	375	47	32	43	65	4.7
Scot Pollard	49	865	79	47.3	0-0	33	67.3	85	205	18	30	31	24	3.9
Eddie Gill	73	1,021	81	33.5	117-36	71	87.7	16	112	83	59	60	5	3.7
Marcus Haislip	9	106	13	34.2	1-0	6	54.5	5	15	3	2	6	2	3.6
Tremaine Fowlkes	8	56	9	52.9	3-1	0	00.0	3	8	0	2	5	0	2.4
Britton Johnsen	6	87	6	27.3	4-0	0	00.0	5	10	4	1	3	0	2.0
Michael Curry	18	249	13	44.8	0-0	4	50.0	8	27	15	5	5	4	1.7
John Edwards	25	139	11	36.7	0-0	7	50.0	8	19	3	3	8	4	1.2
TEAM TOTALS	82	19,905	2,668	43.2	1,575-542	1,748	79.2	868	3,286	1,489	615	1,173	357	93.0
OPPONENTS	82	–	2,768	44.0	1,071-391	1,637	74.3	972	3,388	1,540	549	1,142	398	92.2

LOS ANGELES CLIPPERS

PLAYER	GP	MIN	Field Goals		3-PT FG	Free Throws		Rebounds		A	STL	TO	BLK	AVG
			FGM	PCT	FGA-FGM	FTM	PCT	OFF	TOTAL	A	STL	TO	BLK	AVG
Corey Maggette	66	2,436	425	43.1	168-51	563	85.7	70	394	225	70	195	8	22.2
Elton Brand	81	3,001	629	50.3	3-0	364	75.2	296	770	208	62	183	169	20.0
Bobby Simmons	75	2,799	474	46.6	115-50	231	84.6	128	446	205	106	135	16	16.4
Marko Jaric	50	1,656	189	41.4	151-56	59	72.0	20	161	303	84	98	17	9.9
Chris Kaman	63	1,632	246	49.7	1-0	80	66.1	135	423	73	26	115	68	9.1
Chris Wilcox	54	1,005	169	51.4	0-0	88	61.1	63	228	38	26	77	24	7.9
Shaun Livingston	30	814	89	41.4	2-0	44	74.6	22	89	151	32	75	11	7.4
Kerry Kittles	11	243	28	38.4	21-7	6	60.0	1	32	20	8	7	3	6.3
Zeljko Rebraca	58	928	133	56.8	0-0	73	85.9	49	184	26	13	49	40	5.8
Rick Brunson	80	1,945	166	37.6	130-48	57	77.0	23	187	410	82	125	7	5.5
Mikki Moore	74	1,178	144	50.2	5-1	107	78.7	97	246	47	19	63	32	5.4
Quinton Ross	78	1,659	161	43.2	4-1	74	67.3	59	210	109	51	54	22	5.1
Kenny Anderson	43	744	85	42.3	13-0	27	73.0	24	88	103	33	49	0	4.7
Darrick Martin	11	190	16	32.0	18-5	5	62.5	3	10	28	6	6	0	3.8
Lionel Chalmers	36	433	42	33.6	49-12	15	62.5	4	31	51	13	24	0	3.1
Mamadou N'diaye	11	72	8	40.0	1-0	4	57.1	9	18	1	1	0	5	1.8
Kirk Penney	4	12	1	33.3	1-0	0	00.0	0	1	1	0	2	0	.5
TEAM TOTALS	82	20,030	2,924	45.9	669-231	1,770	77.8	980	3,435	1,901	599	1,290	422	95.7
OPPONENTS	82	–	2,936	44.4	1,317-485	1,555	76.2	986	3,241	1,732	638	1,122	393	96.5

LOS ANGELES LAKERS

PLAYER	GP	MIN	Field Goals		3-PT FG	Free Throws		Rebounds		A	STL	TO	BLK	AVG
			FGM	PCT	FGA-FGM	FTM	PCT	OFF	TOTAL	A	STL	TO	BLK	AVG
Kobe Bryant	66	2,689	573	43.3	387-131	542	81.6	95	392	398	86	270	53	27.6
Caron Butler	77	2,746	441	44.5	125-38	275	86.2	146	450	146	110	125	23	15.5
Lamar Odom	64	2,320	366	47.3	117-36	207	69.5	134	653	238	42	161	65	15.2
Chucky Atkins	82	2,000	308	42.6	455-176	163	80.3	31	197	358	73	151	2	13.6
Chris Mihm	75	1,870	280	50.7	2-0	175	67.8	197	502	50	14	110	108	9.8
Jumaine Jones	76	1,830	210	43.2	261-102	55	73.3	107	398	65	44	49	24	7.6
Devean George	15	306	37	35.6	58-21	15	75.0	13	53	14	8	12	2	7.3
Brian Cook	72	1,087	176	41.7	199-78	28	75.7	63	216	35	23	29	26	6.4
Tierre Brown	76	1,066	124	35.6	72-26	59	78.7	21	93	155	32	74	1	4.4
Brian Grant	69	1,136	103	49.3	0-0	57	72.2	101	257	34	23	43	23	3.8
Slava Medvedenko	43	423	71	45.5	1-0	23	82.1	31	79	13	9	13	2	3.8
Luke Walton	61	768	74	41.1	61-16	34	70.8	55	142	93	26	58	11	3.2
Sasha Vujacic	35	403	33	28.2	63-17	18	94.7	13	62	51	12	15	2	2.9
Tony Bobbit	2	12	2	40.0	2-1	0	00.0	0	3	0	0	0	0	2.5
Vlade Divac	15	130	13	41.9	0-0	8	66.7	18	32	19	4	14	1	2.3
TEAM TOTALS	82	19,780	2,895	43.7	1,813-644	1,661	77.7	1,028	3,539	1,672	508	1,176	344	98.7
OPPONENTS	82	–	3,141	45.3	1,522-549	1,507	78.0	1,023	3,476	2,001	627	965	420	101.7

MEMPHIS GRIZZLIES

PLAYER	GP	MIN	Field Goals		3-PT FG	Free Throws		Rebounds		A	STL	TO	BLK	AVG
			FGM	PCT	FGA-FGM	FTM	PCT	OFF	TOTAL					
Pau Gasol	56	1,790	357	51.4	6-1	282	76.8	130	410	135	37	137	93	17.8
Mike Miller	76	2,278	387	50.5	323-140	108	72.0	36	300	220	54	127	23	13.4
Bonzi Wells	69	1,489	272	44.1	104-36	141	75.0	49	229	80	85	90	27	10.4
Stromile Swift	60	1,279	219	44.9	4-0	166	75.8	92	273	43	41	90	92	10.1
Jason Williams	71	1,952	266	41.3	330-107	80	79.2	19	122	399	75	130	5	10.1
Shane Battier	80	2,516	271	44.2	177-70	180	78.9	158	413	126	91	75	77	9.9
Lorenzen Wright	80	2,287	320	46.9	3-0	131	66.2	177	613	87	58	100	69	9.6
Brian Cardinal	58	1,433	160	37.0	125-44	158	87.3	63	225	114	88	83	19	9.0
James Posey	50	1,382	127	35.7	178-55	96	86.5	45	219	88	48	69	23	8.1
Earl Watson	80	1,808	236	42.6	163-52	91	65.9	35	164	359	83	167	19	7.7
Dahntay Jones	52	649	83	43.7	60-23	44	68.8	11	69	21	13	29	11	4.5
Antonio Burks	24	219	28	46.7	11-3	14	73.7	1	12	28	13	12	1	3.0
Ryan Humphrey	35	317	42	40.8	2-0	18	48.6	50	87	6	10	23	1	2.9
Jake Tsakalidis	31	278	32	50.0	0-0	14	77.8	21	56	10	3	12	16	2.5
Andre Emmett	8	28	2	33.3	0-0	3	60.0	0	2	0	0	1	0	.9
TEAM TOTALS	82	19,705	2,802	44.7	1,486-531	1,526	75.4	887	3,194	1,716	699	1,197	476	93.4
OPPONENTS	82	–	2,684	43.2	1,215-426	1,679	77.1	993	3,380	1,633	612	1,303	476	91.1

MIAMI HEAT

PLAYER	GP	MIN	Field Goals		3-PT FG	Free Throws		Rebounds		A	STL	TO	BLK	AVG
			FGM	PCT	FGA-FGM	FTM	PCT	OFF	TOTAL					
Dwyane Wade	77	2,974	630	47.8	45-13	581	76.2	110	397	520	121	321	82	24.1
Shaquille O'Neal	73	2,492	658	60.1	0-0	353	46.1	253	760	200	36	203	171	22.9
Eddie Jones	80	2,839	351	42.8	382-142	174	80.6	38	405	212	86	99	38	12.7
Damon Jones	82	2,576	331	45.6	521-225	68	79.1	14	231	350	44	98	5	11.6
Udonis Haslem	80	2,675	346	54.0	4-0	178	79.1	239	726	108	63	113	41	10.9
Alonzo Mourning	37	702	100	47.2	0-0	82	58.2	53	198	18	8	57	74	7.6
Rasual Butler	65	1,203	163	39.9	153-57	37	77.1	15	151	62	18	37	29	6.5
Steve Smith	50	750	102	41.1	105-41	69	86.3	15	65	71	14	27	7	6.3
Christian Laettner	49	739	107	58.2	7-1	45	76.3	36	131	41	32	29	15	5.3
Keyon Dooling	74	1,184	139	40.3	75-19	85	78.0	11	90	132	39	65	11	5.2
Michael Doleac	80	1,175	148	44.7	2-0	25	61.0	74	259	47	23	36	22	4.0
Shandon Anderson	66	1,171	98	45.2	29-5	54	81.8	41	191	70	40	50	14	3.9
Qyntel Woods	3	40	5	41.7	0-0	0	00.0	2	6	0	4	2	0	3.3
Dorell Wright	3	27	3	27.3	4-0	1	100.0	0	1	3	4	3	0	2.3
Wang Zhizhi	20	92	17	47.2	3-2	7	58.3	6	18	5	3	5	2	2.2
TEAM TOTALS	82	19,980	3,097	48.6	1,260-475	1,658	67.2	887	3,526	1,790	528	1,127	474	101.5
OPPONENTS	82	–	2,865	42.7	1,269-441	1,621	76.0	922	3,319	1,620	611	1,085	264	95.0

MILWAUKEE BUCKS

PLAYER	GP	MIN	Field Goals		3-PT FG	Free Throws		Rebounds		A	STL	TO	BLK	AVG
			FGM	PCT	FGA-FGM	FTM	PCT	OFF	TOTAL					
Michael Redd	75	2,848	625	44.1	293-104	369	85.4	72	312	172	63	133	8	23.0
Desmond Mason	80	2,893	478	44.3	8-1	420	80.2	85	312	217	58	164	27	17.2
Joe Smith	74	2,265	319	51.4	1-0	175	76.8	179	541	67	43	79	38	11.0
Maurice Williams	80	2,254	323	43.8	99-32	136	85.0	50	244	484	74	196	11	10.2
Dan Gadzuric	81	1,783	243	53.9	0-0	107	53.8	261	674	30	47	81	106	7.3
Marcus Fizer	54	903	133	45.5	6-0	70	68.0	29	175	64	25	63	13	6.2
Zaza Pachulia	74	1,397	160	45.2	1-0	138	74.6	131	370	60	44	70	34	6.2
Kendall Gill	14	284	32	40.0	9-3	18	90.0	11	37	27	14	9	4	6.1
Toni Kukoc	53	1,099	105	41.0	116-42	44	72.1	31	160	160	39	64	13	5.6
Anthony Goldwire	33	537	57	41.9	80-32	26	83.9	10	59	78	15	15	0	5.2
Erick Strickland	62	1,014	114	37.5	83-21	52	81.3	11	103	115	30	64	1	4.9
Calvin Booth	51	451	49	45.4	1-0	20	81.3	29	107	0	15	16	28	2.4
Daniel Santiago	11	105	7	33.3	0-0	8	72.7	6	19	1	3	4	4	2.0
Reece Gaines	21	187	17	34.0	14-4	3	75.0	1	14	7	5	7	1	2.0
TEAM TOTALS	82	19,780	2,964	45.0	925-325	1,720	77.2	985	3,390	1,720	529	1,133	290	97.0
OPPONENTS	82	–	3,098	46.4	1,349-463	1,559	77.1	935	3,348	1,953	611	1,067	370	100.2

MINNESOTA TIMBERWOLVES

PLAYER	GP	MIN	Field Goals		3-PT FG	Free Throws		Rebounds		A	STL	TO	BLK	AVG
			FGM	PCT	FGA-FGM	FTM	PCT	OFF	TOTAL					
Kevin Garnett	82	3,121	683	50.2	25-6	445	81.1	247	1,108	466	121	222	112	22.2
Wally Szczerbiak	81	2,558	485	50.6	169-63	260	85.5	82	303	191	40	132	16	15.5
Ndudi Ebi	2	54	11	52.4	1-0	5	55.6	6	16	1	1	3	1	13.5
Sam Cassell	59	1,522	319	46.4	103-27	134	86.5	25	157	301	36	109	14	13.5
Latrell Sprewell	80	2,450	398	41.4	211-69	156	83.0	65	254	179	53	127	21	12.8
Troy Hudson	79	1,729	266	40.1	258-89	70	77.8	19	105	283	27	113	6	8.7
Eddie Griffin	70	1,492	202	38.7	204-67	56	71.8	128	453	53	23	55	118	7.5
Trenton Hassell	82	2,068	225	47.4	11-1	90	78.9	80	219	128	30	64	30	6.6
Michael Olowokandi	62	1,215	161	45.6	0-0	46	66.7	106	324	29	15	68	56	5.9
Fred Hoiberg	76	1,272	139	48.9	145-70	89	87.3	32	181	85	50	20	15	5.8
Anthony Carter	66	742	72	40.7	17-2	35	68.6	12	69	161	35	62	18	2.7
John Thomas	44	521	42	48.8	0-0	27	58.7	39	97	17	15	18	13	2.5
Mark Madsen	41	601	34	51.5	0-0	20	50.0	63	128	18	7	24	14	2.1
Ervin Johnson	46	410	28	51.9	1-1	16	64.0	43	113	6	7	18	13	1.6
TEAM TOTALS	82	19,755	3,045	45.9	1,145-395	1,449	79.6	947	3,527	1,918	460	1,079	447	96.8
OPPONENTS	82	–	2,967	43.8	1,291-468	1,413	75.2	1,032	3,391	1,783	540	963	323	95.3

sikids.com
Visit our website
for the latest stats
and sports info.

NEW JERSEY NETS

PLAYER	GP	MIN	Field Goals		3-PT FG	Free Throws		Rebounds		A	STL	TO	BLK	AVG
			FGM	PCT	FGA-FGM	FTM	PCT	OFF	TOTAL					
Vince Carter	77	2,828	696	45.2	313-127	367	79.8	106	401	327	109	168	48	24.5
Richard Jefferson	33	1,355	238	42.2	89-30	227	84.4	49	240	133	33	132	17	22.2
Jason Kidd	66	2,435	340	39.8	358-129	142	74.0	94	488	545	123	167	9	14.4
Nenad Krstic	75	1,965	281	49.3	2-0	185	72.5	161	401	77	32	112	63	10.0
Ron Mercer	18	390	65	41.1	3-0	7	70.0	9	40	20	16	14	2	7.6
Clifford Robinson	71	1,689	202	38.6	193-67	62	63.9	54	209	104	62	66	53	7.5
Rodney Buford	64	1,313	187	38.2	108-34	37	82.2	33	189	63	40	35	4	7.0
Travis Best	76	1,461	190	42.0	85-26	108	88.5	19	107	143	66	67	9	6.8
Jason Collins	80	2,542	186	41.2	6-2	137	65.6	153	488	105	71	91	71	6.4
Brian Scalabrine	54	1,167	132	39.8	68-22	53	76.8	83	244	88	34	66	18	6.3
Jacque Vaughn	71	1,410	146	44.9	15-5	76	83.5	17	107	135	41	62	1	5.3
Zoran Planinic	43	515	78	44.8	40-15	46	69.7	19	69	44	25	41	0	5.0
Jabari Smith	45	648	62	41.9	2-1	41	74.5	29	111	38	25	39	14	3.7
Billy Thomas	25	356	34	36.2	56-17	7	77.8	7	36	17	14	9	1	3.7
Donnell Harvey	3	16	2	100.0	0-0	4	100.0	2	7	1	1	1	1	2.7
Kaniel Dickens	11	61	4	28.6	9-3	2	100.0	3	9	1	2	2	1	1.2
Awvee Storey	9	32	3	30.0	2-1	1	50.0	4	5	1	0	0	0	.9
TEAM TOTALS	82	19,905	2,753	42.9	1,203-435	1,555	76.3	855	3,242	1,772	650	1,164	308	91.4
OPPONENTS	82	–	2,710	43.9	1,319-485	1,714	74.4	874	3,377	1,666	601	1,283	402	92.9

NEW ORLEANS HORNETS

PLAYER	GP	MIN	Field Goals		3-PT FG	Free Throws		Rebounds		A	STL	TO	BLK	AVG
			FGM	PCT	FGA-FGM	FTM	PCT	OFF	TOTAL					
Lee Nailon	68	2,017	415	47.8	2-0	133	80.6	128	298	109	36	110	16	14.2
Dan Dickau	71	2,090	306	40.5	245-85	190	83.3	34	180	347	76	145	4	12.5
Jamaal Magloire	23	703	98	43.2	0-0	74	60.2	79	205	29	8	59	23	11.7
Speedy Claxton	62	1,866	257	42.1	61-11	187	73.6	37	184	374	109	119	8	11.5
P.J. Brown	82	2,817	338	44.6	0-0	210	86.4	266	737	178	74	101	50	10.8
J.R. Smith	76	1,859	295	39.4	281-81	111	68.9	39	152	142	55	109	11	10.3
Chris Andersen	67	1,430	191	53.4	3-0	131	68.9	137	410	71	14	64	100	7.7
Bostjan Nachbar	71	1,341	161	39.2	196-75	97	82.9	24	182	74	29	73	16	7.0
Casey Jacobsen	84	1,798	165	40.4	177-66	151	78.6	35	167	113	33	71	8	6.5
David West	30	552	75	43.6	5-2	34	68.0	40	129	23	12	37	16	6.2
Junior Harrington	29	550	64	36.0	19-6	29	82.9	13	63	62	25	41	5	5.6
Alex Garcia	8	146	18	34.6	18-5	3	75.0	7	15	18	4	8	1	5.5
Jackson Vroman	46	705	82	41.2	3-0	48	64.0	64	175	40	25	64	19	4.6
Matt Freije	23	441	37	29.1	54-14	5	62.5	16	61	20	13	17	2	4.0
George Lynch	44	933	68	36.0	37-11	17	73.9	55	174	88	32	57	12	3.7
Maciej Lampe	37	380	49	37.1	4-2	15	68.2	24	89	11	5	17	7	3.1
Corsley Edwards	10	110	10	32.3	0-0	7	58.3	12	25	3	3	2	4	2.7
Lonny Baxter	4	36	3	27.3	0-0	0	00.0	4	8	0	0	4	0	1.5
TEAM TOTALS	82	19,930	2,718	41.5	1,316-415	1,401	76.6	1,019	3,300	1,724	550	1,217	310	88.4
OPPONENTS	82	–	2,847	45.2	1,346-494	1,644	77.5	947	3,432	1,742	634	1,168	452	95.5

NEW YORK KNICKS

PLAYER	GP	MIN	Field Goals		3-PT FG	Free Throws		Rebounds						
			FGM	PCT	FGA-FGM	FTM	PCT	OFF	TOTAL	A	STL	TO	BLK	AVG
Stephon Marbury	82	3,281	604	46.2	325-115	458	83.4	50	248	668	122	233	6	21.7
Jamal Crawford	70	2,688	437	39.8	512-185	182	84.3	33	203	302	92	148	19	17.7
Tim Thomas	71	1,940	315	43.9	208-85	136	78.6	45	237	110	41	113	17	12.0
Allan Houston	20	532	85	41.5	80-31	36	83.7	4	23	42	8	21	2	11.9
Kurt Thomas	80	2,855	424	47.1	4-2	66	78.6	170	831	160	70	99	79	11.5
Michael Sweetney	77	1,509	237	53.1	1-0	176	74.9	169	418	44	27	108	28	8.4
Anfernee Hardaway	37	894	110	42.3	50-15	34	73.9	19	89	74	20	50	3	7.3
Maurice Taylor	65	1,336	203	45.5	9-3	63	61.2	67	257	67	27	94	20	7.3
Malik Rose	76	1,475	198	44.9	10-1	137	73.7	129	341	59	46	102	16	7.0
Trevor Ariza	80	1,382	172	44.2	13-3	121	69.5	89	242	85	70	73	18	5.9
Jerome Williams	79	1,211	122	50.2	5-0	115	66.9	115	283	41	55	65	10	4.5
Jackie Butler	3	5	4	100.0	0-0	2	100.0	0	0	0	1	1	0	3.3
Jermaine Jackson	21	230	17	51.5	2-0	8	61.5	3	23	24	7	10	1	2.0
Jamison Brewer	18	185	11	29.7	15-3	6	46.2	6	22	12	8	13	1	1.7
Bruno Sundov	21	73	11	29.7	3-1	2	100.0	6	13	2	2	6	2	1.2
TEAM TOTALS	82	19,880	2,978	45.1	1,240-441	1,580	76.7	965	3,358	1,665	629	1,204	260	97.3
OPPONENTS	82	–	3,001	40.5	1,276-464	1,711	75.6	969	3,417	1,697	602	1,195	309	99.7

ORLANDO MAGIC

PLAYER	GP	MIN	Field Goals		3-PT FG	Free Throws		Rebounds						
			FGM	PCT	FGA-FGM	FTM	PCT	OFF	TOTAL	A	STL	TO	BLK	AVG
Steve Francis	78	2,978	563	42.3	127-38	499	82.3	126	450	547	112	317	28	21.3
Grant Hill	67	2,038	517	50.9	13-3	280	82.1	77	318	220	97	161	28	19.7
Hedo Turkoglu	67	1,757	328	41.9	245-93	188	83.6	62	233	153	41	119	18	14.0
Dwight Howard	82	2,670	352	52.0	2-0	277	67.1	287	823	75	77	165	136	12.0
Jameer Nelson	79	1,612	286	45.5	141-44	73	68.2	52	193	237	78	117	3	8.7
DeShawn Stevenson	55	1,089	174	40.8	67-25	56	55.4	38	102	69	16	57	9	7.8
Kelvin Cato	62	1,525	160	53.9	0-0	112	78.3	102	416	40	55	64	82	7.0
Doug Christie	52	1,525	130	39.2	62-15	70	89.7	38	177	199	80	104	18	6.6
Tony Battie	81	1,894	163	46.0	6-0	68	72.3	109	452	42	30	81	81	4.9
Pat Garrity	71	955	123	40.2	147-49	29	87.9	21	124	30	19	30	9	4.6
Stacey Augmon	55	663	68	40.7	0-0	57	74.0	45	99	36	23	31	8	3.5
Brandon Hunter	31	224	37	50.7	0-0	21	53.8	25	69	3	4	22	7	3.1
Andre Barrett	38	483	45	36.3	52-14	14	73.7	11	40	69	19	27	1	3.1
Mario Kasun	45	356	47	48.0	1-0	24	55.8	52	128	8	8	26	13	2.6
Mark Jones	10	116	9	29.0	4-0	5	50.0	6	13	6	5	3	2	2.3
Andrew DeClercq	8	49	4	44.4	0-0	1	33.3	7	10	0	2	1	0	1.1
TEAM TOTALS	82	19,705	3,034	45.4	916-320	1,772	75.9	1,038	3,582	1,583	633	1,322	441	99.5
OPPONENTS	82	–	3,081	45.1	1,291-443	1,739	75.4	1,024	3,452	1,747	698	1,190	354	101.8

PHILADELPHIA 76ers

PLAYER	GP	MIN	Field Goals		3-PT FG	Free Throws		Rebounds		A	STL	TO	BLK	AVG
			FGM	PCT	FGA-FGM	FTM	PCT	OFF	TOTAL					
Allen Iverson	75	3,174	771	42.4	338-104	656	83.5	51	299	596	180	344	9	30.7
Chris Webber	67	2,370	555	43.3	44-15	181	79.4	130	612	318	94	182	53	19.5
Marc Jackson	81	1,976	340	46.5	2-0	289	82.6	184	406	81	32	131	18	12.0
Kyle Korver	82	2,667	317	41.8	558-226	82	85.4	40	379	182	103	106	33	11.5
Andre Iguodala	82	2,686	269	49.3	142-47	156	74.3	89	464	246	138	139	48	9.0
Samuel Dalembert	72	1,785	250	52.4	0-0	89	60.1	187	542	35	46	114	121	8.2
Willie Green	57	1,066	155	36.6	105-30	97	77.6	22	133	100	34	75	6	7.7
Rodney Rogers	58	1,367	172	38.2	168-48	52	74.3	61	246	86	41	86	20	7.7
John Salmons	58	993	85	40.5	91-31	35	72.9	12	121	114	40	51	13	4.1
Josh Davis	42	328	42	37.8	53-19	14	82.4	29	79	12	8	15	4	2.8
Aaron McKie	68	1,118	61	43.0	62-20	10	62.5	20	172	103	48	31	17	2.2
Kedrick Brown	8	55	2	33.3	3-0	8	80.0	1	11	4	3	5	1	1.5
Michael Bradley	18	119	15	62.5	1-0	3	37.5	8	28	5	1	5	2	1.8
Kevin Ollie	26	158	11	35.5	0-0	6	66.7	3	19	19	5	6	0	1.1
TEAM TOTALS	82	19,855	2,946	43.7	1,453-505	1,731	78.9	909	3,445	1,710	756	1,274	321	99.1
OPPONENTS	82	–	2,930	44.3	1,560-565	1,764	76.7	962	3,615	1,878	681	1,394	383	99.9

PHOENIX SUNS

PLAYER	GP	MIN	Field Goals		3-PT FG	Free Throws		Rebounds		A	STL	TO	BLK	AVG
			FGM	PCT	FGA-FGM	FTM	PCT	OFF	TOTAL					
Amare Stoudemire	80	2,889	747	55.9	16-3	583	73.3	219	713	131	77	189	130	26.0
Shawn Marion	81	3,146	613	47.6	341-114	229	83.3	235	915	154	163	125	119	19.4
Joe Johnson	82	3,240	544	46.1	370-177	135	75.0	120	422	291	79	148	24	17.1
Steve Nash	75	2,573	430	50.2	218-94	211	88.7	57	249	861	74	245	6	15.5
Quentin Richardson	79	2,839	407	38.9	631-226	136	73.9	91	479	158	96	102	27	14.9
Jim Jackson	64	1,987	248	42.6	295-122	54	93.1	33	269	183	35	115	5	10.5
Leandro Barbosa	63	1,087	168	47.5	139-51	55	79.7	32	130	126	30	87	7	7.0
Steven Hunter	76	1,046	135	61.4	1-0	78	47.9	98	227	13	4	44	102	4.6
Walter McCarty	72	906	95	40.4	155-55	15	51.7	29	138	37	25	36	15	3.6
Smush Parker	16	144	18	41.9	13-3	9	69.2	4	12	15	5	19	0	3.0
Jake Voskuhl	38	360	27	45.8	0-0	26	68.4	30	92	17	4	20	11	2.1
Yuta Tabuse	4	17	1	16.7	1-1	4	100.0	2	4	3	0	1	0	1.8
Paul Shirley	9	30	5	45.5	0-0	2	50.0	1	2	3	0	1	0	1.3
Bo Outlaw	39	214	12	35.3	0-0	5	55.6	16	53	13	6	8	12	.7
TEAM TOTALS	82	19,780	3,351	47.7	2,026-796	1,556	74.8	967	3,619	1,927	572	1,125	453	110.4
OPPONENTS	82	–	3,328	44.5	1,476-494	1,320	74.4	1,233	3,783	1,741	627	1,131	342	103.3

■ Fast Fact: The Phoenix Suns finished the 2004-05 season averaging 110.4 points per game. It was the highest average for a team since 1994-95.

PORTLAND TRAIL BLAZERS

| PLAYER | GP | MIN | Field Goals | | 3-PT FG | Free Throws | | Rebounds | | A | STL | TO | BLK | AVG |
			FGM	PCT	FGA-FGM	FTM	PCT	OFF	TOTAL					
Zach Randolph	46	1,603	332	44.8	6-0	207	81.5	142	442	86	34	112	17	18.9
Shareef Abdur-Rahim	54	1,867	337	50.3	39-15	220	86.6	123	392	111	49	117	26	16.8
Damon Stoudamire	81	2,762	457	39.2	490-181	182	91.5	56	310	458	86	164	2	15.8
Darius Miles	63	1,699	336	48.2	23-8	129	60.0	71	299	129	75	157	78	12.8
Ruben Patterson	70	1,957	319	53.1	25-2	169	59.9	126	273	138	106	143	21	11.6
Nick Van Exel	53	1,619	214	38.1	257-100	58	78.4	20	161	227	44	92	0	11.1
Derek Anderson	47	1,239	152	38.9	151-58	70	80.5	25	128	143	36	70	4	9.2
Sebastian Telfair	68	1,330	169	39.3	69-17	105	78.9	10	104	224	35	125	4	6.8
Joel Przybilla	76	1,858	199	59.8	0-0	90	51.7	178	588	74	24	98	163	6.4
Travis Outlaw	59	793	133	49.8	10-4	49	65.3	40	121	35	30	39	40	5.4
Theo Ratliff	63	1,731	115	44.7	0-0	74	69.2	111	331	34	23	56	158	4.8
Viktor Khryapa	32	523	54	43.5	11-4	23	54.8	28	108	25	20	33	18	4.2
Richie Frahm	43	499	56	40.0	80-31	21	84.0	17	61	30	15	14	4	3.8
Ha Seung-Jin	19	104	10	43.5	0-0	6	54.5	6	18	2	1	12	5	1.4
Geno Carlisle	6	16	2	66.7	0-0	4	66.7	1	1	1	0	1	0	1.3
Maurice Baker	5	19	0	00.0	0-0	0	00.0	1	2	1	1	1	0	.0
TEAM TOTALS	82	19,730	2,896	45.1	1,161-420	1,409	72.5	970	3,374	1,722	583	1,308	544	92.9
OPPONENTS	82	–	3,056	44.7	1,283-440	1,397	75.5	1,149	3,461	1,923	700	1,102	414	96.9

SACRAMENTO KINGS

| PLAYER | GP | MIN | Field Goals | | 3-PT FG | Free Throws | | Rebounds | | A | STL | TO | BLK | AVG |
			FGM	PCT	FGA-FGM	FTM	PCT	OFF	TOTAL					
Peja Stojakovic	66	2,534	451	44.4	433-174	253	92.0	62	285	138	79	102	12	20.1
Mike Bibby	80	3,084	560	44.3	364-131	320	77.5	77	332	541	124	203	30	19.6
Cuttino Mobley	66	2,388	408	43.8	342-150	168	82.0	45	229	188	74	133	30	17.2
Brad Miller	56	2,089	319	52.4	19-5	233	81.2	139	521	220	69	82	68	15.6
Kenny Thomas	73	2,167	367	47.0	5-1	173	76.2	184	535	152	67	131	17	12.4
Bobby Jackson	25	536	109	42.7	96-33	50	86.2	23	85	59	14	28	2	12.0
Corliss Williamson	72	1,527	273	46.7	2-0	195	79.9	104	259	78	38	86	15	10.3
Darius Songaila	81	1,668	257	52.7	3-0	94	84.7	125	344	114	51	70	18	7.5
Maurice Evans	65	1,233	165	44.2	82-27	59	75.6	88	201	45	37	34	8	6.4
Eddie House	68	891	165	45.1	97-44	23	85.2	16	83	96	44	35	6	5.8
Brian Skinner	49	941	104	50.7	1-0	25	35.7	107	280	43	31	40	49	4.8
Kevin Martin	45	455	45	38.5	25-5	36	65.5	29	58	22	16	24	3	2.9
Greg Ostertag	56	556	37	44.0	2-0	13	34.2	55	167	37	7	24	40	1.6
Erik Daniels	21	72	6	33.3	2-1	0	00.0	7	18	4	2	6	0	.6
TEAM TOTALS	82	19,855	3,203	45.9	1,396-522	1,577	78.7	1,023	3,478	2,005	674	1,073	316	103.7
OPPONENTS	82	–	3,186	45.9	1,318-471	1,485	73.8	1,102	3,634	1,766	622	1,204	365	101.6

SAN ANTONIO SPURS

PLAYER	GP	MIN	Field Goals FGM	PCT	3-PT FG FGA-FGM	Free Throws FTM	PCT	Rebounds OFF	TOTAL	A	STL	TO	BLK	AVG
Tim Duncan	66	2,203	517	49.6	9-3	305	67.0	202	732	179	45	127	174	20.3
Tony Parker	80	2,735	539	48.2	156-43	210	65.0	47	298	491	98	215	4	16.6
Manu Ginobili	74	2,193	367	47.1	258-97	355	80.3	75	329	288	119	172	27	16.0
Glenn Robinson	9	157	34	44.2	6-2	20	87.0	4	24	8	4	7	3	10.0
Nazr Mohammed	77	1,933	289	48.0	1-0	153	67.4	247	586	34	58	108	86	9.5
Bruce Bowen	82	2,627	251	42.0	253-102	71	63.4	50	285	126	56	57	39	8.2
Brent Barry	81	1,742	194	42.3	280-100	113	83.7	29	190	178	39	64	20	7.4
Devin Brown	67	1,238	173	42.3	121-45	103	79.2	37	176	92	39	53	12	7.4
Robert Horry	75	1,396	157	41.9	138-51	86	78.9	91	268	80	67	69	60	6.0
Beno Udirh	80	1,149	173	44.4	142-58	67	75.3	16	83	150	41	77	10	5.9
Rasho Nesterovic	70	1,785	198	46.0	0-0	14	46.7	184	459	71	31	73	117	5.9
Dion Glover	7	68	8	36.4	8-1	8	80.0	3	11	4	3	2	3	3.6
Sean Marks	23	244	27	33.8	3-0	22	78.6	18	56	8	3	14	11	3.3
Tony Massenburg	61	699	74	40.7	0-0	48	76.2	54	163	14	18	40	20	3.2
Mike Wilks	48	278	32	41.6	16-5	12	75.0	4	25	33	14	14	1	1.7
Linton Johnson III	2	15	0	00.0	1-0	0	00.0	0	3	0	1	1	0	.0
TEAM TOTALS	82	19,805	2,923	45.3	1,395-507	1,535	72.4	987	3,476	1,771	613	1,126	543	96.2
OPPONENTS	82	–	2,712	42.6	881-321	1,501	76.8	893	3,296	1,385	594	1,240	421	88.4

SEATTLE SUPERSONICS

PLAYER	GP	MIN	Field Goals FGM	PCT	3-PT FG FGA-FGM	Free Throws FTM	PCT	Rebounds OFF	TOTAL	A	STL	TO	BLK	AVG
Ray Allen	78	3,064	640	42.8	556-209	378	88.3	79	347	289	84	171	5	23.9
Rashard Lewis	71	2,697	532	46.2	432-173	220	77.7	110	388	94	75	123	62	20.5
Vladimir Radmanovic	63	1,856	266	40.9	329-128	81	78.6	52	289	86	57	80	31	11.8
Antonio Daniels	75	2,026	273	43.8	165-49	248	81.6	20	169	309	51	78	3	11.2
Luke Ridnour	82	2,571	299	40.5	178-67	159	88.3	55	204	483	94	149	23	10.0
Danny Fortson	62	1,047	118	52.2	0-0	227	88.0	157	348	8	15	91	7	7.5
Ronald Murray	49	883	131	36.1	95-24	59	73.8	15	96	65	30	57	11	7.0
Damien Wilkins	29	520	73	43.5	59-16	21	61.8	29	66	26	22	16	10	6.3
Nick Collison	82	1,396	190	53.7	3-0	83	70.3	156	376	32	34	62	50	5.6
Reggie Evans	79	1,881	131	47.6	2-0	125	53.4	254	736	58	58	104	15	4.9
Jerome James	80	1,330	174	50.9	2-0	47	72.3	81	241	19	23	88	111	4.9
Vitaly Potapenko	33	335	45	51.7	1-0	27	87.1	30	78	9	7	12	3	3.5
Robert Swift	16	72	5	45.5	0-0	5	55.6	1	5	2	1	4	7	.9
Mateen Cleaves	14	65	5	35.7	2-0	3	75.0	2	6	7	2	2	0	.9
Ibrahim Kutluay	5	12	0	00.0	0-0	0	00.0	0	1	0	0	2	0	.0
TEAM TOTALS	82	19,755	2,882	44.4	1,824-666	1,683	79.0	1,041	3,352	1,487	553	1,113	338	98.9
OPPONENTS	82	–	2,932	45.9	1,317-470	1,591	74.9	930	3,104	1,698	508	1,085	390	96.6

TORONTO RAPTORS

PLAYER	GP	MIN	Field Goals		3-PT FG	Free Throws		Rebounds						
			FGM	PCT	FGA-FGM	FTM	PCT	OFF	TOTAL	A	STL	TO	BLK	AVG
Jalen Rose	81	2,710	527	45.5	274-108	333	85.4	44	276	209	63	180	10	18.5
Chris Bosh	81	3,017	473	47.1	10-3	412	76.0	194	718	153	76	187	113	16.8
Rafer Alston	80	2,717	403	41.4	389-139	191	74.0	42	279	514	118	170	7	14.2
Morris Peterson	82	2,510	356	42.0	335-129	188	83.2	71	340	169	91	93	18	12.5
Donyell Marshall	65	1,645	262	44.3	363-151	72	79.1	95	428	81	57	42	46	11.5
Matt Bonner	82	1,553	247	53.3	92-39	56	78.9	108	285	48	39	40	19	7.2
Lamond Murray	62	918	132	42.6	105-46	61	76.3	44	164	47	32	54	16	6.0
Milt Palacio	80	1,533	175	44.6	12-2	115	74.2	26	134	279	48	104	13	5.8
Eric Williams	55	1,322	142	43.0	73-28	112	69.6	44	172	92	38	60	4	7.7
Omar Cook	5	74	10	41.7	4-0	3	50.0	2	7	22	6	6	1	4.6
Loren Woods	45	712	71	43.3	1-0	34	57.6	81	220	17	8	37	39	3.9
Rafael Araujo	59	736	76	43.4	3-1	43	78.2	59	185	16	21	52	8	3.3
Pape Sow	27	255	23	39.7	0-0	16	59.3	18	57	2	12	10	4	2.3
Aaron Williams	42	315	29	46.0	0-0	15	88.2	17	60	8	5	17	8	1.7
TEAM TOTALS	82	19,805	2,952	44.4	1,681-648	1,626	77.4	844	3,288	1,670	621	1,087	317	99.7
OPPONENTS	82	–	3,133	46.7	1,222-435	1,610	74.4	991	3,711	1,814	507	1,182	360	101.4

UTAH JAZZ

PLAYER	GP	MIN	Field Goals		3-PT FG	Free Throws		Rebounds						
			FGM	PCT	FGA-FGM	FTM	PCT	OFF	TOTAL	A	STL	TO	BLK	AVG
Carlos Boozer	51	1,772	361	52.1	1-0	187	69.8	141	457	144	41	137	24	17.8
Andrei Kirilenko	41	1,349	207	49.3	77-23	203	78.4	89	255	132	67	90	136	15.6
Matt Harpring	78	2,584	418	48.9	43-9	245	77.8	196	480	142	70	133	16	14.0
Mehmet Okur	82	2,304	354	46.8	63-17	329	85.0	194	616	166	32	141	60	12.9
Raja Bell	63	1,790	303	45.4	134-54	112	74.7	48	201	91	44	79	8	12.3
Gordon Giricek	81	1,660	283	44.8	105-38	111	81.0	25	182	137	46	90	11	8.8
Keith McLeod	53	1,382	143	35.0	72-18	112	76.7	20	113	236	63	99	12	7.8
Howard Eisley	74	1,428	161	39.8	103-27	66	79.5	15	90	250	45	111	9	5.6
Raul Lopez	31	518	57	42.2	45-20	27	81.8	7	39	123	22	47	3	5.2
Kirk Snyder	68	906	122	37.2	85-30	64	66.7	50	121	36	26	58	19	5.0
Ben Handlogten	21	297	43	51.8	1-0	9	52.9	23	65	13	7	18	5	4.5
Jarron Collins	50	961	65	41.4	1-0	83	69.7	57	164	61	11	34	6	4.3
Kris Humphries	67	873	116	40.4	6-2	44	43.6	73	197	43	25	52	18	4.1
Randy Livingston	17	227	22	42.3	8-5	15	88.2	3	12	45	12	14	2	3.8
Curtis Borchardt	67	859	74	43.0	0-0	52	73.2	86	224	49	10	52	32	3.0
Aleksandar Radojevic	12	128	6	31.6	0-0	7	70.0	9	28	6	0	15	2	1.6
TEAM TOTALS	82	19,780	2,828	44.9	762-250	1,719	75.7	1,047	3,290	1,826	541	1,292	374	93.0
OPPONENTS	82	–	2,731	45.8	1,297-486	2,027	76.4	859	3,089	1,592	646	1,182	474	97.3

TRIVIA CHALLENGE

Who led all NBA players in scoring during the regular season (30.7 points) *and* the playoffs (31.2) in 2004-05?

Allen Iverson of the Philadelphia 76ers

WASHINGTON WIZARDS

PLAYER	GP	MIN	Field Goals		3-PT FG	Free Throws		Rebounds		A	STL	TO	BLK	AVG
			FGM	PCT	FGA-FGM	FTM	PCT	OFF	TOTAL					
Gilbert Arenas	80	3,274	656	43.1	562-205	521	81.4	83	378	411	139	242	23	25.5
Larry Hughes	61	2,358	467	43.0	209-59	352	77.7	74	382	285	176	153	18	22.0
Antawn Jamison	68	2,605	519	43.7	208-71	225	76.0	160	519	154	55	118	16	19.6
Jarvis Hayes	54	1,560	206	38.9	123-42	99	83.9	41	227	90	49	62	9	10.2
Brendan Haywood	68	1,865	239	56.0	0-0	159	60.9	202	464	57	52	96	114	9.4
Juan Dixon	63	1,054	186	41.6	147-48	87	89.7	32	119	111	43	68	4	8.0
Etan Thomas	47	976	128	50.2	0-0	76	52.8	85	244	20	17	50	51	7.1
Kwame Brown	42	908	109	46.0	0-0	74	57.4	72	206	39	25	67	15	7.0
Jared Jeffries	77	2,007	203	46.8	51-16	101	58.4	152	374	151	66	114	35	6.8
Steve Blake	44	648	61	32.8	93-36	33	80.5	18	71	69	13	39	0	4.3
Damone Brown	14	152	23	37.1	11-4	4	44.4	10	28	14	1	15	6	3.9
Anthony Peeler	40	529	56	37.3	65-25	16	88.9	14	65	57	18	28	2	3.8
Laron Profit	42	428	56	43.8	28-8	16	64.0	24	76	37	16	27	5	3.2
Peter Ramos	6	20	5	50.0	0-0	1	50.0	1	4	0	0	3	1	1.8
Samaki Walker	14	134	11	35.5	0-0	2	66.7	8	18	4	3	8	7	1.7
Michael Ruffin	79	1,262	41	41.4	1-0	29	43.3	157	332	64	43	44	41	1.4
TEAM TOTALS	82	19,780	2,966	43.7	1,498-514	1,795	72.5	1,133	3,507	1,563	716	1,172	347	100.5
OPPONENTS	82	–	3,099	45.9	1,432-521	1,549	76.2	1,017	3,527	1,885	586	1,306	412	100.8

TODAY'S STARS

Dwyane Wade fired up the Heat in 2004-05.

HEINZ KLUETMEIER/SPORTS ILLUSTRATED

■ **Dwyane Wade, guard,** b. January 17, 1982, Chicago, Illinois. Wade has established himself as one of the NBA's top players. "The Flash" earned his nickname for his speedy and aggressive play for the Miami Heat. In 2004-05, the 6' 4" guard ranked in the Top 10 in points per game (24.1) and assists (6.8), and was voted an NBA All-Star. Wade upped his scoring stats in the playoffs (27.4 points per game) as he and Shaquille O'Neal led the Miami Heat to the Eastern Conference Finals for the first time since 1996-97.

■ **Michael Redd, guard,** b. August 24, 1979, Columbus, Ohio. Redd is becoming one of the most exciting players in the NBA. He is a great outside shooter with explosive moves to the hoop. Redd's stats have improved steadily since he joined the Milwaukee Bucks in 2000-01. He led the Bucks in scoring in 2003-04 and 2004-05. He averaged 23 points per game, 11th in the league, in 2004-05. Redd holds the NBA record for most 3-pointers in one quarter. He hit eight 3-pointers in the fourth quarter against the Houston Rockets on February 20, 2002.

■ **Amare Stoudemire, center,** b. November 16, 1982, Lake Wales, Florida. At age 22, Stoudemire was fifth in the NBA in scoring (26 points per game) and second in field goal percentage (55.9 percent) in 2004-05. Stoudemire teamed with point guard Steve Nash to lead the Phoenix Suns to an NBA-best record of 62–20 and the Western Conference finals. He averaged 26 points and 8.9 rebounds per game during the regular season and 29.9 points and 10.7 rebounds per game in the playoffs. Stoudemire, the NBA Rookie of the Year in 2002-03, was selected to his first All-Star Game in 2005.

NBA CHAMPIONS

SEASON	CHAMPION	SERIES	RUNNER-UP	WINNING COACH	FINALS MVP
2004-05	San Antonio	4–3	Detroit Pistons	Gregg Popovich	Tim Duncan, SA
2003-04	Detroit	4–1	L.A. Lakers	Larry Brown	Chauncey Billups, Det
2002-03	San Antonio	4–2	New Jersey	Gregg Popovich	Tim Duncan, SA
2001-02	L.A. Lakers	4–0	New Jersey	Phil Jackson	Shaquille O'Neal, L.A.
2000-01	L.A. Lakers	4–1	Philadelphia	Phil Jackson	Shaquille O'Neal, L.A.
1999-00	L.A. Lakers	4–2	Indiana	Phil Jackson	Shaquille O'Neal, L.A.
1998-99	San Antonio	4–1	New York	Gregg Popovich	Tim Duncan, SA
1997-98	Chicago	4–2	Utah	Phil Jackson	Michael Jordan, Chi
1996-97	Chicago	4–2	Utah	Phil Jackson	Michael Jordan, Chi
1995-96	Chicago	4–2	Seattle	Phil Jackson	Michael Jordan, Chi
1994-95	Houston	4–0	Orlando	Rudy Tomjanovich	Hakeem Olajuwon, Hou
1993-94	Houston	4–3	New York	Rudy Tomjanovich	Hakeem Olajuwon, Hou
1992-93	Chicago	4–2	Phoenix	Phil Jackson	Michael Jordan, Chi
1991-92	Chicago	4–2	Portland	Phil Jackson	Michael Jordan, Chi
1990-91	Chicago	4–1	L.A. Lakers	Phil Jackson	Michael Jordan, Chi
1989-90	Detroit	4–1	Portland	Chuck Daly	Isiah Thomas, Det
1988-89	Detroit	4–0	L.A. Lakers	Chuck Daly	Joe Dumars, Det
1987-88	L.A. Lakers	4–3	Detroit	Pat Riley	James Worthy, L.A.
1986-87	L.A. Lakers	4–2	Boston	Pat Riley	Magic Johnson, L.A.
1985-86	Boston	4–2	Houston	K.C. Jones	Larry Bird, Bos
1984-85	L.A. Lakers	4–2	Boston	Pat Riley	Kareem Abdul-Jabbar, L.A.
1983-84	Boston	4–3	L.A. Lakers	K.C. Jones	Larry Bird, Bos
1982-83	Philadelphia	4–0	L.A. Lakers	Billy Cunningham	Moses Malone, Phil
1981-82	L.A. Lakers	4–2	Philadelphia	Pat Riley	Magic Johnson, L.A.
1980-81	Boston	4–2	Houston	Bill Fitch	Cedric Maxwell, Bos
1979-80	L.A. Lakers	4–2	Philadelphia	Paul Westhead	Magic Johnson, L.A.
1978-79	Seattle	4–1	Washington	Lenny Wilkens	Dennis Johnson, Sea
1977-78	Washington	4–3	Seattle	Dick Motta	Wes Unseld, Wash
1976-77	Portland	4–2	Philadelphia	Jack Ramsay	Bill Walton, Port
1975-76	Boston	4–2	Phoenix	Tom Heinsohn	Jo Jo White, Bos
1974-75	Golden State	4–0	Washington	Al Attles	Rick Barry, GS
1973-74	Boston	4–3	Milwaukee	Tom Heinsohn	John Havlicek, Bos
1972-73	New York	4–1	L.A. Lakers	Red Holzman	Willis Reed, N.Y.
1971-72	L.A. Lakers	4–1	New York	Bill Sharman	Wilt Chamberlain, L.A.
1970-71	Milwaukee	4–0	Baltimore	Larry Costello	Kareem Abdul-Jabbar, Mil
1969-70	New York	4–3	L.A. Lakers	Red Holzman	Willis Reed, N.Y.
1968-69	Boston	4–3	L.A. Lakers	Bill Russell	Jerry West, L.A.
1967-68	Boston	4–2	L.A. Lakers	Bill Russell	–
1966-67	Philadelphia	4–2	San Francisco	Alex Hannum	–
1965-66	Boston	4–3	L.A. Lakers	Red Auerbach	–
1964-65	Boston	4–1	L.A. Lakers	Red Auerbach	–
1963-64	Boston	4–1	San Francisco	Red Auerbach	–
1962-63	Boston	4–2	L.A. Lakers	Red Auerbach	–
1961-62	Boston	4–3	L.A. Lakers	Red Auerbach	–
1960-61	Boston	4–1	St. Louis	Red Auerbach	–
1959-60	Boston	4–3	St. Louis	Red Auerbach	–
1958-59	Boston	4–0	Minneapolis	Red Auerbach	–
1957-58	St. Louis	4–2	Boston	Alex Hannum	–
1956-57	Boston	4–3	St. Louis	Red Auerbach	–
1955-56	Philadelphia	4–1	Ft. Wayne	George Senesky	–
1954-55	Syracuse	4–3	Ft. Wayne	Al Cervi	–
1953-54	Minneapolis	4–3	Syracuse	John Kundla	–
1952-53	Minneapolis	4–1	New York	John Kundla	–
1951-52	Minneapolis	4–3	New York	John Kundla	–
1950-51	Rochester	4–3	New York	Les Harrison	–
1949-50	Minneapolis	4–2	Syracuse	John Kundla	–
1948-49	Minneapolis	4–2	Washington	John Kundla	–
1947-48	Baltimore	4–2	Philadelphia	Buddy Jeannette	–
1946-47	Philadelphia	4–1	Chicago	Ed Gottlieb	–

Note: The NBA did not name a Finals MVP from 1946-47 to 1967-68.

ALL-TIME INDIVIDUAL LEADERS

SCORING

MOST POINTS, CAREER	PTS	AVG
Kareem Abdul-Jabbar	38,387	24.6
Karl Malone	36,928	25.0
Michael Jordan	32,292	30.1
Wilt Chamberlain	31,419	30.1
Moses Malone	27,409	20.6
Elvin Hayes	27,313	21.0
Hakeem Olajuwon	26,946	21.8
Oscar Robertson	26,710	25.7
Dominique Wilkins	26,668	24.8
John Havlicek	26,395	20.8

Karl Malone retired in 2005, second on the all-time scoring list.

JOHN W. McDONOUGH/SPORTS ILLUSTRATED

HIGHEST SCORING AVERAGE, CAREER

Michael Jordan	30.1	1,072 games
Wilt Chamberlain	30.1	1,045 games
Allen Iverson	27.4	610 games
Elgin Baylor	27.4	846 games
Jerry West	27.0	932 games
Shaquille O'Neal	26.7	882 games
Bob Pettit	26.4	792 games
George Gervin	26.2	791 games
Oscar Robertson	25.7	1,040 games
Karl Malone	25.0	1,476 games

Note: Minimum 400 games or 10,000 points.

MOST POINTS, GAME		OPPONENT	DATE
100	Wilt Chamberlain, Phil	N.Y.	3/2/62
78	Wilt Chamberlain, Phil	L.A.	12/8/61
73	Wilt Chamberlain, Phil	Chi	1/13/62
73	Wilt Chamberlain, SF	N.Y.	11/16/62
73	David Thompson, Den	Det	4/9/78
72	Wilt Chamberlain, SF	L.A.	11/3/62
71	Elgin Baylor, L.A.	N.Y.	11/15/60
71	David Robinson, SA	LAC	4/24/94
70	Wilt Chamberlain, SF	Syr	3/10/63
69	Michael Jordan, Chi	Clev	3/28/90

HIGHEST FIELD-GOAL PERCENTAGE, CAREER
.599 Artis Gilmore

Note: Minimum 2,000 field goals made.

HIGHEST FREE-THROW PERCENTAGE, CAREER
.904 Mark Price

Note: Minimum 1,200 free throws made.

3-POINT FIELD GOALS
Most 3-point Field Goals, Career:
 2,560 Reggie Miller, Indiana
Highest 3-point Field-goal Percentage, Career:
 .454 Steve Kerr, San Antonio
Most 3-point Field Goals, Game:
 12 Kobe Bryant, L.A. Lakers vs. Seattle, 1/7/03
Note: First year of shot: 1979-80.

STEALS*

Most Steals, Career: 3,265 John Stockton, Utah
Most Steals, Game: 11 Kendall Gill, New Jersey vs. Miami, 4/3/99; Larry Kenon, San Antonio vs. Kansas City, 12/26/76

REBOUNDS

MOST REBOUNDS, CAREER

PLAYER	REBOUNDS	YRS	AVG
Wilt Chamberlain	23,924	14	22.9
Bill Russell	21,620	13	22.5
Kareem Abdul-Jabbar	17,440	20	11.2
Elvin Hayes	16,279	16	12.5
Moses Malone	16,212	19	12.2
Karl Malone	14,968	19	10.1
Robert Parish	14,715	21	9.1
Nate Thurmond	14,464	14	15.0
Walt Bellamy	14,241	14	13.7
Wes Unseld	13,769	13	14.0

MOST REBOUNDS, GAME

NO.	PLAYER, TEAM	OPPONENT	DATE
55	Wilt Chamberlain, Phil	Bos	11/24/60
51	Bill Russell, Bos	Syr	2/5/60
49	Bill Russell, Bos	Phil	11/16/57
49	Bill Russell, Bos	Det	3/11/65
45	Wilt Chamberlain, Phil	Syr	2/6/60
45	Wilt Chamberlain, Phil	L.A.	1/21/61

*Steals have only been an official stat since the 1973-74 season.

ASSISTS

MOST ASSISTS, CAREER

John Stockton	15,806
Mark Jackson	10,334
Magic Johnson	10,141
Oscar Robertson	9,887
Isiah Thomas	9,061

MOST ASSISTS, GAME

30 Scott Skiles, Orlando vs. Denver, 12/30/90

Hakeem Olajuwon is the NBA's all-time leader in blocks.

JOHN W. McDONOUGH/SPORTS ILLUSTRATED (2)

BLOCKS*

MOST BLOCKS, CAREER

Hakeem Olajuwon	3,830
Kareem Abdul-Jabbar	3,189
Dikembe Mutombo	3,097
Mark Eaton	3,064
David Robinson	2,954

MOST BLOCKS, GAME

17 Elmore Smith, L.A. Lakers vs. Portland, 10/28/73

*Blocks have only been an official stat since the 1973-74 season.

> **DID YOU KNOW?**
>
> Forward Larry Nance of the Phoenix Suns was the winner of the first NBA Slam Dunk contest in 1984. Forward Julius "Dr. J" Erving of the Philadelphia 76ers was the runner-up.

MOST VALUABLE PLAYER: MAURICE PODOLOFF TROPHY

SEASON	PLAYER, TEAM
2004–05	Steve Nash, Phoenix
2003–04	Kevin Garnett, Minnesota
2002–03	Tim Duncan, San Antonio
2001–02	Tim Duncan, San Antonio
2000–01	Allen Iverson, Philadelphia
1999–00	Shaquille O'Neal, L.A. Lakers
1998–99	Karl Malone, Utah
1997–98	Michael Jordan, Chicago
1996–97	Karl Malone, Utah
1995–96	Michael Jordan, Chicago
1994–95	David Robinson, San Antonio
1993–94	Hakeem Olajuwon, Houston
1992–93	Charles Barkley, Phoenix
1991–92	Michael Jordan, Chicago
1990–91	Michael Jordan, Chicago
1989–90	Magic Johnson, L.A. Lakers
1988–89	Magic Johnson, L.A. Lakers
1987–88	Michael Jordan, Chicago
1986–87	Magic Johnson, L.A. Lakers
1985–86	Larry Bird, Boston
1984–85	Larry Bird, Boston
1983–84	Larry Bird, Boston
1982–83	Moses Malone, Philadelphia
1981–82	Moses Malone, Houston
1980–81	Julius Erving, Philadelphia

Steve Nash, Phoenix Suns

SEASON	PLAYER, TEAM
1979–80	Kareem Abdul-Jabbar, L.A. Lakers
1978–79	Moses Malone, Houston
1977–78	Bill Walton, Portland
1976–77	Kareem Abdul-Jabbar, L.A. Lakers
1975–76	Kareem Abdul-Jabbar, L.A. Lakers
1974–75	Bob McAdoo, Buffalo
1973–74	Kareem Abdul-Jabbar, Milwaukee
1972–73	Dave Cowens, Boston
1971–72	Kareem Abdul-Jabbar, Milwaukee
1970–71	Kareem Abdul-Jabbar, Milwaukee
1969–70	Willis Reed, New York
1968–69	Wes Unseld, Baltimore
1967–68	Wilt Chamberlain, Philadelphia
1966–67	Wilt Chamberlain, Philadelphia
1965–66	Wilt Chamberlain, Philadelphia
1964–65	Bill Russell, Boston
1963–64	Oscar Robertson, Cincinnati
1962–63	Bill Russell, Boston
1961–62	Bill Russell, Boston
1960–61	Bill Russell, Boston
1959–60	Wilt Chamberlain, Philadelphia
1958–59	Bob Pettit, St. Louis
1957–58	Bill Russell, Boston
1956–57	Bob Cousy, Boston
1955–56	Bob Pettit, St. Louis

ROOKIE OF THE YEAR: EDDIE GOTTLIEB TROPHY

SEASON	PLAYER, TEAM
2004–05	Emeka Okafor, Charlotte
2003–04	LeBron James, Cleveland
2002–03	Amare Stoudemire, Phoenix
2001–02	Pau Gasol, Memphis
2000–01	Mike Miller, Orlando
1999–00	Steve Francis, Houston
	Elton Brand, Chicago
1998–99	Vince Carter, Toronto
1997–98	Tim Duncan, San Antonio
1996–97	Allen Iverson, Philadelphia
1995–96	Damon Stoudamire, Toronto
1994–95	Jason Kidd, Dallas
	Grant Hill, Detroit
1993–94	Chris Webber, Golden State
1992–93	Shaquille O'Neal, Orlando
1991–92	Larry Johnson, Charlotte
1990–91	Derrick Coleman, New Jersey
1989–90	David Robinson, San Antonio
1988–89	Mitch Richmond, Golden State
1987–88	Mark Jackson, New York
1986–87	Chuck Person, Indiana
1985–86	Patrick Ewing, New York
1984–85	Michael Jordan, Chicago
1983–84	Ralph Sampson, Houston
1982–83	Terry Cummings, San Diego
1981–82	Buck Williams, New Jersey
1980–81	Darrell Griffith, Utah
1979–80	Larry Bird, Boston
1978–79	Phil Ford, Kansas City
1977–78	Walter Davis, Phoenix
1976–77	Adrian Dantley, Buffalo
1975–76	Alvan Adams, Phoenix
1974–75	Keith Wilkes, Golden State
1973–74	Ernie DiGregorio, Buffalo
1972–73	Bob McAdoo, Buffalo
1971–72	Sidney Wicks, Portland
1970–71	Dave Cowens, Boston
	Geoff Petrie, Portland
1969–70	Kareem Abdul-Jabbar, Milwaukee
1968–69	Wes Unseld, Baltimore
1967–68	Earl Monroe, Baltimore
1966–67	Dave Bing, Detroit
1965–66	Rick Barry, San Francisco
1964–65	Willis Reed, New York
1963–64	Jerry Lucas, Cincinnati
1962–63	Terry Dischinger, Chicago
1961–62	Walt Bellamy, Chicago
1960–61	Oscar Robertson, Cincinnati
1959–60	Wilt Chamberlain, Philadelphia
1958–59	Elgin Baylor, Minneapolis
1957–58	Woody Sauldsberry, Philadelphia
1956–57	Tom Heinsohn, Boston
1955–56	Maurice Stokes, Rochester
1954–55	Bob Pettit, Milwaukee
1953–54	Ray Felix, Baltimore
1952–53	Don Meineke, Ft. Wayne

Emeka Okafor, Charlotte Bobcats

ROCKY WIDNER/NABE/GETTY IMAGES

Note: There were co-winners in 1999–00, 1994–95, and 1970–71

DEFENSIVE PLAYER OF THE YEAR

SEASON	PLAYER, TEAM
2004–05	Ben Wallace, Detroit
2003–04	Ron Artest, Indiana
2002–03	Ben Wallace, Detroit
2001–02	Ben Wallace, Detroit
2000–01	Dikembe Mutombo, Philadelphia/Atlanta
1999–00	Alonzo Mourning, Miami
1998–99	Alonzo Mourning, Miami
1997–98	Dikembe Mutombo, Atlanta
1996–97	Dikembe Mutombo, Atlanta
1995–96	Gary Payton, Seattle
1994–95	Dikembe Mutombo, Denver
1993–94	Hakeem Olajuwon, Houston
1992–93	Hakeem Olajuwon, Houston
1991–92	David Robinson, San Antonio
1990–91	Dennis Rodman, Detroit
1989–90	Dennis Rodman, Detroit
1988–89	Mark Eaton, Utah
1987–88	Michael Jordan, Chicago
1986–87	Michael Cooper, L.A. Lakers
1985–86	Alvin Robertson, San Antonio
1984–85	Mark Eaton, Utah
1983–84	Sidney Moncrief, Milwaukee
1982–83	Sidney Moncrief, Milwaukee

SIXTH MAN AWARD

SEASON	PLAYER, TEAM
2004–05	Ben Gordon, Chicago
2003–04	Antawn Jamison, Dallas
2002–03	Bobby Jackson, Sacramento
2001–02	Corliss Williamson, Detroit
2000–01	Aaron McKie, Philadelphia
1999–00	Rodney Rogers, Phoenix
1998–99	Darrell Armstrong, Orlando
1997–98	Danny Manning, Phoenix
1996–97	John Starks, New York
1995–96	Toni Kukoc, Chicago
1994–95	Anthony Mason, New York
1993–94	Dell Curry, Charlotte
1992–93	Clifford Robinson, Portland
1991–92	Detlef Schrempf, Indiana
1990–91	Detlef Schrempf, Indiana
1989–90	Ricky Pierce, Milwaukee
1988–89	Eddie Johnson, Phoenix
1987–88	Roy Tarpley, Dallas
1986–87	Ricky Pierce, Milwaukee
1985–86	Bill Walton, Boston
1984–85	Kevin McHale, Boston
1983–84	Kevin McHale, Boston
1982–83	Bobby Jones, Philadelphia

*Ben Gordon,
Chicago Bulls*

GREG NELSON

MOST IMPROVED PLAYER

SEASON	PLAYER, TEAM	SEASON	PLAYER, TEAM
2004–05	Bobby Simmons, L.A. Clippers	1994–95	Dana Barros, Philadelphia
2003–04	Zach Randolph, Portland	1993–94	Don MacLean, Washington
2002–03	Gilbert Arenas, Golden State	1992–93	Mahmoud Abdul-Rauf, Denver
2001–02	Jermaine O'Neal, Indiana	1991–92	Pervis Ellison, Washington
2000–01	Tracy McGrady, Orlando	1990–91	Scott Skiles, Orlando
1999–00	Jalen Rose, Indiana	1989–90	Rony Seikaly, Miami
1998–99	Darrell Armstrong, Orlando	1988–89	Kevin Johnson, Phoenix
1997–98	Alan Henderson, Atlanta	1987–88	Kevin Duckworth, Portland
1996–97	Isaac Austin, Miami	1986–87	Dale Ellis, Seattle
1995–96	Gheorghe Muresan, Washington	1985–86	Alvin Robertson, San Antonio

2005 NBA DRAFT — FIRST ROUND

**June 28, 2005,
New York, NY**

1. Andrew Bogut, Milwaukee
2. Marvin Williams, Atlanta
3. Deron Williams, Utah
   (from Portland)
4. Chris Paul, New Orleans
5. Raymond Felton, Charlotte
6. Martell Webster, Portland
   (from Utah)
7. Charlie Villanueva, Toronto
8. Channing Frye, New York
9. Ike Diogu, Golden State
10. Andrew Bynum, L.A. Lakers

11. Fran Vazquez, Orlando
12. Yaroslav Korolev, L.A. Clippers
13. Sean May, Charlotte
    (from Cleveland via Phoenix)
14. Rashad McCants, Minnesota
15. Antoine Wright, New Jersey
16. Joey Graham, Toronto
    (from Philadelphia via
    New Jersey)
17. Danny Granger, Indiana
18. Gerald Green, Boston
19. Hakim Warrick, Memphis
20. Julius Hodge, Denver
    (from Washington via Orlando)

21. Nate Robinson, Phoenix (from
    Chicago; traded to New York)
22. Jarrett Jack, Denver (traded to
    Portland)
23. Francisco Garcia, Sacramento
24. Luther Head, Houston
25. Johan Petro, Seattle
26. Jason Maxiell, Detroit
27. Linus Kleiza, Portland
    (from Utah via Dallas)
28. Ian Mahinmi, San Antonio
29. Wayne Simien, Miami
30. David Lee, New York
    (from Phoenix via San Antonio)

ALL-STAR GAME RESULTS

YEAR	RESULT	SITE	WINNING COACH	MOST VALUABLE PLAYER
2005	East 125, West 115	Denver, CO	Stan Van Gundy	Allen Iverson, Philadelphia
2004	West 136, East 132	Los Angeles, CA	Flip Saunders	Shaquille O'Neal, L.A. Lakers
2003	West 155, East 145 (2 OT)	Atlanta, GA	Rick Adelman	Kevin Garnett, Minnesota
2002	West 135, East 120	Philadelphia, PA	Don Nelson	Kobe Bryant, L.A. Lakers
2001	East 111, West 110	Washington, DC	Larry Brown	Allen Iverson, Philadelphia
2000	West 137, East 126	Oakland, CA	Phil Jackson	Shaquille O'Neal, L.A. Lakers/ Tim Duncan, San Antonio
1999	Canceled due to lockout			
1998	East 135, West 114	New York, NY	Larry Bird	Michael Jordan, Chicago
1997	East 132, West 120	Cleveland, OH	Doug Collins	Glen Rice, Charlotte
1996	East 129, West 118	San Antonio, TX	Phil Jackson	Michael Jordan, Chicago
1995	West 139, East 112	Phoenix, AZ	Paul Westphal	Mitch Richmond, Sacramento
1994	East 127, West 118	Minneapolis, MN	Lenny Wilkens	Scottie Pippen, Chicago
1993	West 135, East 132	Salt Lake City, UT	Paul Westphal	Karl Malone/John Stockton,Utah
1992	West 153, East 113	Orlando, FL	Don Nelson	Magic Johnson, L.A. Lakers
1991	East 116, West 114	Charlotte, NC	Chris Ford	Charles Barkley, Philadelphia
1990	East 130, West 113	Miami, FL	Chuck Daly	Magic Johnson, L.A. Lakers
1989	West 143, East 134	Houston, TX	Pat Riley	Karl Malone, Utah
1988	East 138, West 133	Chicago, IL	Mike Fratello	Michael Jordan, Chicago
1987	West 154, East 149 (OT)	Seattle, WA	Pat Riley	Tom Chambers, Seattle
1986	East 139, West 132	Dallas, TX	K.C. Jones	Isiah Thomas, Detroit
1985	West 140, East 129	Indianapolis, IN	Pat Riley	Ralph Sampson, Houston
1984	East 154, West 145 (OT)	Denver, CO	K.C. Jones	Isiah Thomas, Detroit
1983	East 132, West 123	Los Angeles, CA	Billy Cunningham	Julius Erving, Philadelphia
1982	East 120, West 118	East Rutherford, NJ	Bill Fitch	Larry Bird, Boston
1981	East 123, West 120	Cleveland, OH	Billy Cunningham	Nate Archibald, Boston
1980	East 144, West 135 (OT)	Washington, DC	Billy Cunningham	George Gervin, San Antonio
1979	West 134, East 129	Detroit, MI	Lenny Wilkens	David Thompson, Denver
1978	East 133, West 125	Atlanta, GA	Billy Cunningham	Randy Smith, Buffalo
1977	West 125, East 124	Milwaukee, WI	Larry Brown	Julius Erving, Philadelphia
1976	East 123, West 109	Philadelphia, PA	Tom Heinsohn	Dave Bing, Washington
1975	East 108, West 102	Phoenix, AZ	K.C. Jones	Walt Frazier, New York
1974	West 134, East 123	Seattle, WA	Larry Costello	Bob Lanier, Detroit
1973	East 104, West 84	Chicago, IL	Tom Heinsohn	Dave Cowens, Boston
1972	West 112, East 110	Los Angeles, CA	Bill Sharman	Jerry West, L.A. Lakers
1971	West 108, East 107	San Diego, CA	Larry Costello	Lenny Wilkens, Seattle
1970	East 142, West 135	Philadelphia, PA	Red Holzman	Willis Reed, New York
1969	East 123, West 112	Baltimore, MD	Gene Shue	Oscar Robertson, Cincinnati
1968	East 144, West 124	New York, NY	Alex Hannum	Hal Greer, Philadelphia
1967	West 135, East 120	San Francisco, CA	Fred Schaus	Rick Barry, San Francisco
1966	East 137, West 94	Cincinnati, OH	Red Auerbach	Adrian Smith, Cincinnati
1965	East 124, West 123	St. Louis, MO	Red Auerbach	Jerry Lucas, Cincinnati
1964	East 111, West 107	Boston, MA	Red Auerbach	Oscar Robertson, Cincinnati
1963	East 115, West 108	Los Angeles, CA	Red Auerbach	Bill Russell, Boston
1962	West 150, East 130	St. Louis, MO	Fred Schaus	Bob Pettit, St. Louis
1961	West 153, East 131	Syracuse, NY	Paul Seymour	Oscar Robertson, Cincinnati
1960	East 125, West 115	Philadelphia, PA	Red Auerbach	Wilt Chamberlain, Philadelphia
1959	West 124, East 108	Detroit, MI	Ed Macauley	Bob Pettit, St. Louis/ Elgin Baylor, Minnesota
1958	East 130, West 118	St. Louis, MO	Red Auerbach	Bob Pettit, St. Louis
1957	East 109, West 97	Boston, MA	Red Auerbach	Bob Cousy, Boston
1956	West 108, East 94	Rochester, NY	Charley Eckman	Bob Pettit, St. Louis
1955	East 100, West 91	New York, NY	Al Cervi	Bill Sharman, Boston
1954	East 98, West 93 (OT)	New York, NY	Joe Lapchick	Bob Cousy, Boston
1953	West 79, East 75	Ft. Wayne, IN	John Kundla	George Mikan, Minnesota
1952	East 108, West 91	Boston, MA	Al Cervi	Paul Arizin, Philadelphia
1951	East 111, West 94	Boston, MA	Joe Lapchick	Ed Macauley, Boston

■ **Fast Fact:** In 2004-05, LeBron James became the fifth player in history to average 27 points, 7 assists, and 7 rebounds in a season. The other players to achieve this feat are Michael Jordan, Larry Bird, Oscar Robertson, and John Havlicek.

TRIVIA CHALLENGE

Which player won the most regular-season MVP awards (6): Michael Jordan, Wilt Chamberlain, or Kareem Abdul-Jabbar?

Kareem Abdul-Jabbar (1970-71, 1971-72, 1973-74, 1975-76, 1976-77, and 1979-80)

2004-05 TIME LINE

■ **August 28, 2004:** The U.S. men's basketball team defeats Lithuania, 104–96, to win the bronze medal at the 2004 Summer Olympics. It is the first time since 1992 that the United States does not win the gold medal. (1992 was the first year NBA players were allowed to play in the Olympics.) Guard Allen Iverson leads the U.S. in scoring (13.8 points per game) during the eight-game tournament.

■ **November 19, 2004:** A brawl erupts between the Indiana Pacers and the Detroit Pistons with 45.9 seconds left in the fourth quarter at the Palace of Auburn Hills. Pacer forward Ron Artest storms the stands after a fan throws a drink at him. He is suspended for 73 games, the most severe non-drug-related punishment in NBA history. Eight other players are given less-severe suspensions.

■ **December 2, 2004:** Houston Rocket guard Tracy McGrady (48 points) and Dallas Maverick forward Dirk Nowitzki (53 points) score a combined 101 points as the Mavs beat the Rockets, 113–106, in overtime.

■ **February 12, 2005:** Allen Iverson of the Philadelphia 76ers scores an NBA-season high 60 points in a 112–99 Sixers win over the Orlando Magic.

■ **February 13, 2005:** Karl Malone announces his retirement. He played 18 seasons with the Utah Jazz and one with the Los Angeles Lakers. Malone finishes his career second on the NBA's all-time scoring list (36,928 points).

■ **February 20, 2005:** The Eastern Conference defeats the Western Conference, 125–115, in the NBA All-Star Game in Denver, Colorado. Allen Iverson (15 points, 9 assists, 4 rebounds, and 5 steals) is named MVP of the game.

■ **May 19, 2005:** Indiana Pacer guard Reggie Miller plays his final NBA game, a loss to the Detroit Pistons in Game 6 of the Eastern Conference semifinals. Miller finishes his 18-year career as the NBA's all-time leader in 3-pointers made (2,560).

■ **June 23, 2005:** The San Antonio Spurs defeat the Detroit Pistons, 81–74, to win their third NBA title in seven seasons.

■ **June 28, 2005:** The Milwaukee Bucks choose Andrew Bogut of Utah with the Number 1 overall pick in the NBA Draft.

WORLD CHAMPIONSHIP OF BASKETBALL

YEAR	WINNER	RUNNER-UP	SCORE	SITE
2002	Yugoslavia	Argentina	84–77 (OT)	Indianapolis, Indiana
1998	Yugoslavia	Russia	64–62	Athens, Greece
1994*	United States	Russia	137–91	Toronto, Ontario, Canada
1990	Yugoslavia	Soviet Union	92–75	Buenos Aires, Argentina
1986	United States	Soviet Union	87–85	Madrid, Spain
1982	Soviet Union	United States	95–94	Cali, Colombia
1978	Yugoslavia	Soviet Union	82–81 (OT)	Manila, Philippines
1974	Soviet Union	Yugoslavia	†	San Juan, Puerto Rico
1970	Yugoslavia	Brazil	†	Ljubljana, Yugoslavia
1967	Soviet Union	Yugoslavia	†	Montevideo, Uruguay
1963	Brazil	Yugoslavia	†	Rio de Janeiro, Brazil
1959	Brazil	United States	†	Santiago, Chile
1954	United States	Brazil	†	Rio de Janeiro, Brazil
1950	Argentina	United States	†	Rio de Janeiro, Brazil

* U.S. professionals began competing in 1994. In 1998, an NBA labor dispute resulted in a boycott of the World Championship by NBA stars. Players from the Continental Basketball Association, European professional leagues, and U.S. colleges were used to fill the U.S. team's roster.
† Result determined by overall record in final round of competition.

BASKETBALL WOMEN'S

The 2004 WNBA season went from May to October, a month longer than in past years. The league shut down for most of August because its stars, including center Lisa Leslie of the Los Angeles Sparks, forward Tamika Catchings of the Indiana Fever, and guard Sue Bird of the Seattle Storm, played in the Summer Olympics in Athens, Greece.

Once action resumed in September, there was plenty of gold medal-worthy play. Leslie was named the regular-season MVP and Defensive Player of the Year after leading the league in rebounding (9.9 per game) and blocked shots (2.88). She also finished third in scoring (17.6 points per game). The 6' 5" center played her best ball following the Olympic break, averaging 22.8 points and 9.5 boards. Guard Diana Taurasi of the Phoenix Mercury was named Rookie of the Year after leading all first-year players in scoring (17 points per game) and 3-pointers (62).

The WNBA Finals featured two teams that had never played for the championship before: the Connecticut Sun and Seattle Storm. The Sun won Game 1 at home, 68–64, but the Storm took the next two games on its home court to win the title.

Betty Lennox of the Seattle Storm was named MVP of the 2004 WNBA championship series.

NATHANIEL S. BUTLER/WNBAE VIA GETTY IMAGES

The Storm reached the Finals behind the stellar play of its stars, Bird and forward/center Lauren Jackson, the WNBA's leading scorer (20.5 points per game). But it was their teammate, Betty Lennox, who was named MVP of the championship round. The 5' 8" guard averaged 22.3 points during the Finals, 11.1 more points than her regular-season average. The Storm's victory was all about teamwork. Four players scored eight or more points and three players grabbed five or more rebounds in the deciding Game 3.

■ *Fast Fact:* Anne Donovan is the first female coach to win a WNBA championship. She led the Seattle Storm to the title in 2004.

WNBA TEAMS

EASTERN CONFERENCE

Charlotte Sting
Connecticut Sun
Detroit Shock
Indiana Fever
New York Liberty
Washington Mystics

WESTERN CONFERENCE

Houston Comets
Los Angeles Sparks
Minnesota Lynx
Phoenix Mercury
Sacramento Monarchs
San Antonio Silver Stars
Seattle Storm

A new, unnamed franchise based in
Chicago will begin play in 2006.

Lisa Leslie of the Los Angeles Sparks was the WNBA's MVP and Defensive Player of the Year in 2004.

BOB ROSATO/SPORTS ILLUSTRATED

2004 WNBA FINAL STANDINGS

EASTERN CONFERENCE					WESTERN CONFERENCE				
TEAM	W	L	PCT	GB	TEAM	W	L	PCT	GB
Sun	18	16	.529	—	Sparks	25	9	.735	—
Liberty	18	16	.529	—	Storm	20	14	.588	5.0
Shock	17	17	.500	1.0	Lynx	18	16	.529	7.0
Mystics	17	17	.500	1.0	Monarchs	18	16	.529	7.0
Sting	16	18	.471	2.0	Mercury	17	17	.500	8.0
Fever	15	19	.441	3.0	Comets	13	21	.382	12.0
					Silver Stars	9	25	.265	16.0

2004 WNBA Playoffs

EASTERN CONFERENCE

Connecticut Sun (2–1)
Connecticut Sun (2–0)
Washington Mystics

Detroit Shock
New York Liberty
New York Liberty (2–1)

Connecticut Sun

SEATTLE STORM (2–1)

Seattle Storm (2–1)

WESTERN CONFERENCE

Sacramento Monarchs
Sacramento Monarchs (2–1)
Los Angeles Sparks

Seattle Storm (2–0)
Minnesota Lynx

CONF. SEMIFINALS   CONF. FINALS   FINALS   CONF. FINALS   CONF. SEMIFINALS

2004 WNBA PLAYOFF RESULTS

EASTERN CONFERENCE SEMIFINALS

September 25: Mystics 67, Sun 59
September 28: Sun 80, Mystics 70
September 29: Sun 76, Mystics 56
Connecticut Sun won series, 2–1

September 24: Liberty 75, Shock 62
September 26: Shock 76, Liberty 66
September 28: Liberty 66, Shock 64
New York Liberty won series, 2–1

WESTERN CONFERENCE SEMIFINALS

September 24: Monarchs 72, Sparks 52
September 26: Sparks 71, Monarchs 57
September 28: Monarchs 73, Sparks 53
Sacramento Monarchs won series, 2–1

September 25: Storm 70, Lynx 58
September 27: Storm 64, Lynx 54
Seattle Storm won series, 2–0

EASTERN CONFERENCE FINALS

October 1: Sun 61, Liberty 51
October 3: Sun 60, Liberty 57
Connecticut Sun won series, 2–0

WESTERN CONFERENCE FINALS

October 1: Monarchs 74, Storm 72 (OT)
October 3: Storm 66, Monarchs 54
October 5: Storm 82, Monarchs 62
Seattle Storm won series, 2–1

WNBA FINALS

October 8: Sun 68, Storm 64
October 10: Storm 67, Sun 65
October 12: Storm 74, Sun 60
Seattle Storm won series, 2–1

WNBA FINALS COMPOSITE BOX SCORE

SEATTLE STORM

PLAYER	GP	MPG	FG%	3P%	FT%	REBOUNDS OFF	DEF	TOTAL	APG	SPG	BPG	TO	PF	PPG
Betty Lennox	3	34.3	50.0	60.0	87.5	.7	3.7	4.3	2.0	1.33	.00	2.67	3.30	22.3
Lauren Jackson	3	37.0	35.6	60.0	81.8	2.3	5.7	8.0	2.0	1.33	1.33	2.00	2.00	14.7
Sue Bird	3	31.3	39.1	12.5	84.6	1.0	3.7	4.7	3.7	1.33	.00	3.33	2.30	10.0
Kamila Vodichkova	3	21.3	38.1	00.0	55.6	1.7	3.3	5.0	.7	.33	.67	2.33	2.00	7.0
Sheri Sam	3	27.3	26.3	00.0	66.7	1.7	2.3	4.0	2.3	1.33	.00	1.67	2.30	4.0
Alicia Thompson	3	12.7	36.4	33.3	00.0	1.3	1.3	2.7	1.0	.33	.00	1.33	1.00	3.3
Simone Edwards	3	10.0	57.1	00.0	00.0	2.0	2.0	4.0	.3	.00	.33	.67	1.00	2.7
Tully Bevilaqua	3	12.3	42.9	100.0	00.0	.3	1.0	1.3	.3	.67	.00	1.00	2.30	2.3
Janell Burse	3	11.0	25.0	00.0	00.0	.7	1.7	2.3	.0	.67	1.00	.33	.70	2.0
Adia Barnes	2	3.5	00.0	00.0	00.0	.5	.0	.5	.0	.00	.00	.00	1.00	.0
Michelle Greco	1	1.0	00.0	00.0	00.0	.0	.0	.0	.0	.00	.00	.00	.00	.0
TEAM AVERAGES	3	200.0	39.1	37.0	78.8	12.0	24.7	36.7	12.3	7.3	3.3	15.7	17.7	68.3

CONNECTICUT SUN

PLAYER	GP	MPG	FG%	3P%	FT%	REBOUNDS OFF	DEF	TOTAL	APG	SPG	BPG	TO	PF	PPG
Nykesha Sales	3	33.3	53.7	63.6	85.7	2.0	4.7	6.7	.7	3.33	1.33	2.67	3.00	19.0
Katie Douglas	3	34.0	34.4	31.3	84.6	1.0	3.3	4.3	1.3	2.33	.00	2.00	2.00	12.7
Lindsay Whalen	3	32.3	37.0	16.7	60.0	.0	1.7	1.7	6.0	1.33	.67	2.00	3.00	10.0
Taj McWilliams-Franklin	3	32.7	31.3	00.0	50.0	2.3	4.0	6.3	2.0	1.67	1.00	1.67	2.70	7.3
Asjha Jones	3	19.7	52.9	00.0	25.0	1.0	1.0	2.0	1.0	.67	.00	3.00	1.30	6.3
Wendy Palmer	3	17.7	41.2	16.7	50.0	1.0	2.3	3.3	.0	.33	.67	1.00	1.70	5.3
Le'coe Willingham	3	8.7	33.3	00.0	100.0	1.3	2.0	3.3	.0	.00	.00	.33	.00	2.3
Candace Futrell	1	2.0	00.0	00.0	00.0	.0	.0	.0	.0	.00	.00	.00	.00	2.0
Debbie Black	3	9.0	20.0	00.0	00.0	.0	1.3	1.3	.3	.67	.00	1.00	2.00	.7
Jessica Brungo	3	12.0	00.0	00.0	00.0	.3	1.0	1.3	.7	.00	.00	.33	1.00	1.0
TEAM AVERAGES	3	200.0	39.8	33.3	67.4	9.0	21.3	30.3	12.0	10.3	3.7	14.0	16.7	64.3

KEY GP=games played; MPG=minutes per game; FG%=field-goal percentage; 3P%=3-point percentage; FT%=free-throw percentage; OFF=offensive; DEF=defensive; APG=assists per game; SPG=steals per game; BPG=blocks per game; TO=turnovers; PF=personal fouls; PPG=points per game

WNBA FINALS GAME 1 SUN 68, STORM 64 Time of Game: 1:59 Attendance: 9,341

10/8/2004 Mohegan Sun Arena, Uncasville, CT Officials: June Courteau, Lisa Mattingly, Michael Price

SEATTLE STORM

PLAYER	POS	MIN	FGM-A	3GM-A	FTM-A	REBOUNDS OFF	DEF	TOT	A	STL	BLK	TO	PF	PTS
Betty Lennox	G	38	7-17	3-4	0-0	2	6	8	3	1	0	1	3	17
Sue Bird	G	32	4-11	1-4	3-4	3	3	6	4	0	0	6	5	12
Lauren Jackson	F	40	6-19	2-4	2-2	5	1	6	1	2	1	3	1	16
Sherie Sam	F	24	2-7	0-1	1-1	2	1	3	2	2	0	2	2	5
Kamila Vodichkova	C	21	1-4	0-0	0-0	0	6	6	0	1	0	3	0	2
Alicia Thompson		16	1-7	0-3	0-0	3	0	3	2	0	0	2	1	2
Janell Burse		11	2-5	0-0	0-0	0	2	2	0	0	2	0	2	4
Tully Bevilaqua		10	2-2	0-0	0-0	0	0	0	0	0	0	0	3	4
Simone Edwards		8	1-2	0-0	0-0	5	3	8	1	0	0	0	0	2
Adia Barnes														DNP
Michelle Greco														DNP
TOTAL		**200**	**26-74** (35.1%)	**6-16** (37.5%)	**6-7** (85.7%)	**20**	**22**	**42**	**13**	**6**	**3**	**17**	**17**	**64**

CONNECTICUT SUN

PLAYER	POS	MIN	FGM-A	3GM-A	FTM-A	REBOUNDS OFF	DEF	TOT	A	STL	BLK	TO	PF	PTS
Lindsay Whalen	G	32	4-9	1-2	2-4	0	3	3	9	2	2	2	2	11
Katie Douglas	G	31	0-11	3-8	3-4	0	2	2	2	2	0	4	1	10
Nykesha Sales	F	32	3-7	0-0	1-2	4	5	9	2	4	1	4	1	7
Wendy Palmer	F	30	7-13	1-3	1-2	3	4	7	0	1	1	1	2	16
Taj McWilliams-Franklin	C	33	5-12	0-0	0-1	1	6	7	3	4	2	0	3	10
Jessica Brungo		17	0-4	0-2	0-0	1	2	3	2	0	0	0	1	0
Asjha Jones		13	3-4	0-0	0-1	0	1	1	0	0	0	3	1	6
Debbie Black		8	0-1	0-0	0-0	0	0	0	1	2	0	1	3	0
Le'coe Willingham		4	0-0	0-0	0-0	0	1	1	0	0	0	0	0	0
Candace Futrell														DNP
Jennifer Derevjanik														DNP
TOTAL		**200**	**28-61** (45.9%)	**5-13** (38.5%)	**7-14** (50%)	**9**	**24**	**33**	**19**	**15**	**6**	**15**	**14**	**68**

WNBA FINALS GAME 2 STORM 67, SUN 65 Time of Game: 2:09 Attendance: 17,072

10/10/2004 KeyArena, Seattle, WA Officials: Bob Trammell, Sally Bell, Tina Napier

CONNECTICUT SUN

PLAYER	POS	MIN	FGM-A	3GM-A	FTM-A	REBOUNDS OFF	DEF	TOT	A	STL	BLK	TO	PF	PTS
Katie Douglas	G	37	5-10	2-4	2-3	2	3	5	0	3	0	2	1	14
Lindsay Whalen	G	30	3-9	0-2	3-4	0	1	1	7	1	0	2	4	9
Nykesha Sales	F	35	14-22	4-6	0-0	0	5	5	0	4	2	2	3	32
Wendy Palmer	F	14	0-2	0-1	0-0	0	2	2	0	0	1	2	1	0
Taj McWilliams-Franklin	C	32	1-11	0-0	0-0	4	3	7	1	0	1	3	2	2
Asjha Jones		21	0-2	0-0	1-2	1	1	2	2	1	0	3	1	1
Debbie Black		12	1-3	0-0	0-0	0	3	3	0	0	0	2	2	2
Le'coe Willingham		12	2-5	0-0	1-1	1	3	4	0	0	0	0	0	5
Jessica Brungo		7	0-0	0-0	0-0	0	0	0	0	0	0	0	1	0
Candace Futrell														DNP
Jennifer Derevjanik														DNP
TOTAL		**200**	**26-64** (40.6%)	**6-13** (46.2%)	**7-10** (70.0%)	**8**	**21**	**29**	**10**	**9**	**4**	**16**	**15**	**65**

SEATTLE STORM

PLAYER	POS	MIN	FGM-A	3GM-A	FTM-A	REBOUNDS OFF	DEF	TOT	A	STL	BLK	TO	PF	PTS
Sue Bird	G	31	2-6	0-3	6-7	0	3	3	1	3	0	2	0	10
Betty Lennox	G	31	11-16	0-0	5-5	0	2	2	1	1	0	4	3	27
Lauren Jackson	F	37	5-15	1-1	4-4	2	9	11	2	1	1	2	1	15
Sheri Sam	F	29	1-6	0-0	0-0	1	3	4	3	2	0	2	4	2
Kamila Vodichkova	C	22	2-9	0-0	1-2	4	1	5	2	0	2	2	2	5
Tully Bevilaqua		14	0-2	0-0	0-0	0	1	1	1	0	0	1	2	0
Alicia Thompson		13	3-3	2-2	0-0	1	2	3	0	1	0	2	2	8
Janell Burse		12	0-4	0-0	0-0	1	2	3	0	2	1	1	0	0
Simone Edwards		8	0-0	0-0	0-0	0	0	0	0	0	0	0	2	0
Adia Barnes		3	0-1	0-0	0-0	0	0	0	0	0	0	0	0	0
Michelle Greco														DNP
TOTAL		**200**	**24-62** (38.7%)	**3-6** (50.0%)	**16-18** (88.9%)	**9**	**23**	**32**	**10**	**10**	**4**	**16**	**16**	**67**

KEY POS=position; MIN=minutes; FGM-A=field goals made-attempts; 3GM-A=3-point field goals made-attempts; FTM-A=free throws made-attempts; TOT=total; A=assists; STL=steals; BLK=blocks; PTS=points

WNBA FINALS GAME 3 STORM 74, SUN 60 Time of Game: 2:06 Attendance: 17,072
10/12/2004 KeyArena, Seattle, WA   Officials: June Courteau, Lisa Mattingly, Roy Gulbeyan

CONNECTICUT SUN

PLAYER	POS	MIN	FGM-A	3GM-A	FTM-A	OFF	DEF	TOT	A	STL	BLK	TO	PF	PTS
Lindsay Whalen	G	35	3-9	0-2	4-7	0	1	1	2	1	0	2	3	10
Katie Douglas	G	34	0-11	0-6	6-6	1	5	6	2	2	0	0	4	6
Nykesha Sales	F	33	5-12	3-5	5-5	2	4	6	0	2	1	2	5	18
Wendy Palmer	F	9	0-2	0-2	0-0	0	1	1	0	0	0	0	2	0
Taj McWilliams-Franklin	C	33	4-9	0-0	2-3	2	3	5	2	1	0	2	3	10
Asjha Jones		25	6-11	0-0	0-1	2	1	3	1	1	0	3	2	12
Jessica Brungo		12	0-1	0-1	0-0	0	1	1	0	0	0	1	1	0
Le'coe Willingham		10	1-4	0-0	0-0	3	2	5	0	0	0	1	0	2
Debbie Black		7	0-1	0-0	0-0	0	1	1	0	0	0	0	1	0
Candace Futrell		2	1-1	0-0	0-0	0	0	0	0	0	0	0	0	2
Jennifer Derevjanik														DNP
TOTAL		**200**	**20-61**	**3-16**	**17-22**	**10**	**19**	**29**	**7**	**7**	**1**	**11**	**21**	**60**
			(32.8%)	(18.8%)	(77.3%)									

SEATTLE STORM

PLAYER	POS	MIN	FGM-A	3GM-A	FTM-A	OFF	DEF	TOT	A	STL	BLK	TO	PF	PTS
Betty Lennox	G	34	7-17	0-1	9-11	0	3	3	2	2	0	3	4	23
Sue Bird	G	31	3-6	0-1	2-2	0	5	5	6	1	0	2	2	8
Lauren Jackson	F	34	5-11	0-0	3-5	0	7	7	3	1	2	1	4	13
Sheri Sam	F	29	2-6	0-1	1-2	0	3	5	2	0	0	1	1	5
Kamila Vodichkova	C	21	5-8	0-0	4-7	1	3	4	0	0	0	2	4	14
Simone Edwards		14	3-5	0-0	0-0	1	3	4	0	0	1	2	1	6
Tully Bevilaqua		13	1-3	1-1	0-0	1	2	3	0	2	0	2	2	3
Janell Burse		10	1-3	0-0	0-0	1	1	2	0	0	0	0	0	2
Alicia Thompson		9	0-1	0-1	0-0	0	2	2	1	0	0	0	0	0
Adia Barnes		4	0-1	0-0	0-0	1	0	1	0	0	0	0	2	0
Michelle Greco		1	0-0	0-0	0-0	0	0	0	0	0	0	0	0	0
TOTAL		**200**	**27-61**	**1-5**	**19-27**	**7**	**29**	**36**	**14**	**6**	**3**	**13**	**20**	**74**
			(44.3%)	(20.0%)	(70.4%)									

AWARD WINNERS

YEAR	MVP	ROOKIE	DEFENSIVE	IMPROVED	SPORTSMANSHIP	COACH
2004	Lisa Leslie	Diana Taurasi	Lisa Leslie	Kelly Miller/ Wendy Palmer	Teresa Edwards	Susie McConnell Serio
2003	Lauren Jackson	Cheryl Ford	Sheryl Swoopes	Michelle Snow	Edna Campbell	Bill Laimbeer
2002	Sheryl Swoopes	Tamika Catchings	Sheryl Swoopes	Coco Miller	Jennifer Gillom	Marianne Stanley
2001	Lisa Leslie	Jackie Stiles	Debbie Black	Janeth Arcain	Sue Wicks	Dan Hughes
2000	Sheryl Swoopes	Betty Lennox	Sheryl Swoopes	Tari Phillips	Susie McConnell Serio	Michael Cooper
1999	Yolanda Griffith	Chamique Holdsclaw	Yolanda Griffith	N/A	Dawn Staley	Van Chancellor
1998	Cynthia Cooper	Tracy Reid	Teresa Weatherspoon	N/A	Susie McConnell Serio	Van Chancellor
1997	Cynthia Cooper	N/A	Teresa Weatherspoon	N/A	Haixia Zheng	Van Chancellor

NEWCOMER*
1998   Susie McConnell Serio

1999   Yolanda Griffith

*No longer awarded

■ *Fast Fact:* Forward DeLisha Milton-Jones of the Los Angeles Sparks was an interim head coach for the Los Angeles Stars of the American Basketball Association in 2004-05. She is only the third woman in history to coach a men's professional basketball team.

WNBA CHAMPIONS

YEAR	CHAMPION	RUNNER-UP	MVP
2004	Seattle Storm	Connecticut Sun	Betty Lennox
2003	Detroit Shock	Los Angeles Sparks	Ruth Riley
2002	Los Angeles Sparks	New York Liberty	Lisa Leslie
2001	Los Angeles Sparks	Charlotte Sting	Lisa Leslie
2000	Houston Comets	New York Liberty	Cynthia Cooper
1999	Houston Comets	New York Liberty	Cynthia Cooper
1998	Houston Comets	Phoenix Mercury	Cynthia Cooper
1997	Houston Comets	New York Liberty	Cynthia Cooper

TEAM-BY-TEAM STATS

CHARLOTTE STING

PLAYER	GP	MIN	FGM	PCT	FGA	FGM	FTM	PCT	OFF	TOTAL	A	STL	TO	BLK	AVG
			FIELD GOALS		3-PT FG		FREE THROWS		REBOUNDS						
Allison Feaster	33	1,052	132	39.8	143	45	79	86.6	22	84	60	27	68	6	11.8
Tammy Sutton-Brown	34	970	106	47.3	0	0	113	69.8	63	211	15	31	71	71	9.6
Dawn Staley	34	1,143	106	43.1	59	24	66	75.9	12	58	171	43	74	2	8.9
Charlotte Smith-Taylor	34	977	99	48.1	58	29	53	72.6	50	139	40	18	55	13	8.2
Tynesha Lewis	34	617	91	43.3	60	20	44	75.9	23	57	44	27	44	7	7.2
Andrea Stinson	34	777	79	41.4	37	11	34	77.3	25	119	49	27	41	7	6.0
Nicole Powell	31	384	50	41.3	58	24	8	80.0	10	71	16	15	22	4	4.3
Ieana Miller	9	77	14	51.9	0	0	7	50.0	9	18	0	2	5	6	3.9
Kelly Mazzante	34	339	31	33.7	52	13	4	66.7	9	33	9	7	20	2	2.3
Olympia Scott-Richardson	34	398	27	40.3	1	0	19	59.4	28	65	10	9	36	13	2.1
Mery Andrade	12	65	3	42.9	1	0	3	100.0	1	4	7	0	3	1	.8
Jia Perkins	4	17	0	0	0	0	3	75.0	1	3	1	3	1	0	.8
Tera Bjorklund	4	13	1	33.3	0	0	0	00.0	0	0	0	0	1	0	.5
STING	34	6,900	745	42.7	459	166	436	73.9	256	872	426	210	479	134	61.5
OPPONENTS	34	–	800	41.4	349	130	438	74.6	368	996	516	243	437	114	63.8

> **KEY** FGM=field goals made; PCT=percentage; FGA=field-goal attempts; FTM=free throws made; A=assists; STL=steals; BLK=blocks; AVG=average

CONNECTICUT SUN

| PLAYER | GP | MIN | FIELD GOALS | | 3-PT FG | | FREE THROWS | | REBOUNDS | | A | STL | TO | BLK | AVG |
			FGM	PCT	FGA	FGM	FTM	PCT	OFF	TOTAL					
Nykesha Sales	34	1,096	210	43.2	129	41	56	72.7	33	135	97	75	76	8	15.2
Taj McWilliams-Franklin	34	1,133	168	47.7	12	0	77	60.2	83	244	63	48	73	45	12.1
Katie Douglas	34	1,120	125	38.9	153	53	61	79.2	33	132	90	50	52	13	10.7
Wendy Palmer	33	786	108	42.7	41	13	68	80.0	47	182	30	23	40	5	9.0
Lindsay Whalen	31	946	83	45.4	57	20	89	73.0	21	90	148	39	94	0	8.9
Asjha Jones	34	699	96	40.2	6	2	41	85.4	51	118	39	20	53	18	6.9
Le'coe Willingham	23	175	24	63.2	1	0	20	76.9	22	43	7	8	12	2	3.0
Candace Futrell	20	144	11	28.9	17	7	13	81.3	7	19	10	5	7	1	2.1
Debbie Black	31	347	26	46.4	1	0	3	75.0	13	36	47	19	15	0	1.8
Jessica Brungo	33	314	18	30.5	38	10	4	80.0	10	37	27	4	12	4	1.5
Jen Derevjanik	23	140	7	26.9	12	3	2	100.0	1	9	14	8	10	0	.8
SUN	**34**	**6,900**	**876**	**42.7**	**467**	**149**	**434**	**73.6**	**321**	**1,045**	**572**	**299**	**462**	**96**	**68.7**
OPPONENTS	**34**	**–**	**858**	**43.0**	**384**	**145**	**443**	**74.0**	**306**	**1,063**	**565**	**239**	**492**	**113**	**67.8**

DETROIT SHOCK

| PLAYER | GP | MIN | FIELD GOALS | | 3-PT FG | | FREE THROWS | | REBOUNDS | | A | STL | TO | BLK | AVG |
			FGM	PCT	FGA	FGM	FTM	PCT	OFF	TOTAL					
Swin Cash	32	1,105	180	46.9	23	8	158	72.1	78	208	135	44	81	29	16.4
Deanna Nolan	34	1,138	166	38.2	114	33	99	79.8	29	134	112	66	90	12	13.6
Ruth Riley	34	1,037	153	44.6	2	1	71	81.6	68	199	50	31	82	53	11.1
Cheryl Ford	31	912	118	41.1	0	0	93	58.9	104	297	34	41	54	25	10.6
Merlakia Jones	33	517	76	37.1	15	4	24	75.0	23	69	21	19	26	2	5.5
Barbara Farris	26	422	41	51.3	0	0	36	66.7	28	61	7	8	26	2	4.5
Elaine Powell	30	760	52	37.7	0	0	29	58.0	31	84	134	36	61	8	4.4
Chandi Jones	31	397	37	35.9	32	8	25	80.6	8	34	45	18	40	5	3.5
Iciss Tillis	31	287	35	47.3	18	6	7	58.3	13	39	13	9	23	8	2.7
Isabel Sanchez	10	62	6	42.9	5	2	8	72.7	3	5	3	2	11	0	2.2
Ayana Walker	18	148	8	28.6	0	0	2	33.3	10	26	6	1	5	4	1.0
Stacy Stephens	7	36	2	33.3	0	0	0	00.0	2	9	3	0	2	0	.6
Amisha Carter	2	13	0	0.0	0	0	1	50.0	0	4	0	2	3	0	.5
Stacey Thomas	1	1	0	0.0	0	0	0	70.2	0	0	0	0	0	0	.0
SHOCK	**34**	**6,850**	**874**	**41.7**	**209**	**62**	**556**	**70.2**	**397**	**1,170**	**564**	**277**	**513**	**148**	**69.6**
OPPONENTS	**34**	**–**	**860**	**41.0**	**533**	**191**	**470**	**77.2**	**325**	**1,055**	**515**	**289**	**496**	**131**	**70.0**

HOUSTON COMETS

| PLAYER | GP | MIN | FIELD GOALS | | 3-PT FG | | FREE THROWS | | REBOUNDS | | A | STL | TO | BLK | AVG |
			FGM	PCT	FGA	FGM	FTM	PCT	OFF	TOTAL					
Tina Thompson	26	943	180	40.2	108	44	116	78.9	44	157	48	22	70	23	20.0
Sheryl Swoopes	31	1,070	181	42.2	65	20	77	85.6	38	153	91	47	59	16	14.8
Michelle Snow	31	893	104	45.4	0	0	68	60.2	62	239	31	28	71	35	8.9
Kedra Holland-Corn	27	703	59	37.1	97	31	28	68.3	19	66	53	40	47	3	6.6
Sheila Lambert	34	788	75	42.4	27	7	40	78.4	19	68	88	26	82	4	5.8
Dominique Canty	32	770	63	42.0	2	0	51	70.8	40	84	64	32	45	1	5.5
Tiffani Johnson	33	660	59	50.0	0	0	24	75.0	30	122	27	9	31	17	4.3
Felicia Ragland	34	517	44	36.7	49	19	11	84.6	19	67	38	25	32	3	3.5
Octavia Blue	13	155	16	38.1	4	0	12	92.3	12	21	5	1	7	0	3.4
Lucienne Berthieu	16	134	12	35.3	0	0	13	72.2	12	27	4	6	9	2	2.3
Pollyanna Johns Kimbrough	19	157	3	17.6	0	0	16	76.2	16	24	1	4	0	0	1.2
LaTonya Johnson	6	36	2	28.6	6	2	0	00.0	0	1	1	2	2	0	1.0
Gordana Grubin	5	24	0	00.0	0	0	2	100.0	0	1	0	0	3	0	.4
COMETS	34	6,850	798	41.3	358	123	458	74.5	311	1,035	451	242	484	107	64.0
OPPONENTS	34	–	834	41.5	434	152	391	73.6	335	1,055	539	258	471	129	65.0

INDIANA FEVER

| PLAYER | GP | MIN | FIELD GOALS | | 3-PT FG | | FREE THROWS | | REBOUNDS | | A | STL | TO | BLK | AVG |
			FGM	PCT	FGA	FGM	FTM	PCT	OFF	TOTAL					
Tamika Catchings	34	1,149	180	38.5	167	56	152	86.4	79	249	115	67	77	38	16.7
Natalie Williams	34	956	133	45.4	4	0	83	69.7	93	235	62	40	65	23	10.3
Kelly Miller	34	1,096	126	38.7	112	46	50	87.7	28	108	106	37	74	5	10.2
Kelly Schumacher	32	601	92	46.9	13	5	35	77.8	36	104	25	10	52	31	7.0
Deanna Jackson	34	804	92	36.7	12	0	52	71.2	57	113	53	29	52	6	6.9
Kristen Rasmussen	33	692	56	41.5	27	10	30	78.9	41	113	47	21	35	14	4.6
Stephanie White	22	450	27	37.5	39	13	24	70.6	8	28	52	24	30	5	4.1
Coretta Brown	26	398	37	34.3	56	20	10	62.5	10	34	41	7	31	1	4.0
Niele Ivey	15	179	11	29.7	24	8	4	66.7	2	10	18	4	6	3	2.3
Ebony Hoffman	30	334	26	31.3	17	5	3	75.0	34	87	21	15	27	5	2.0
Kate Starbird	12	117	6	26.1	10	3	5	83.3	6	9	11	6	9	0	1.7
Astou Ndiaye-Diatta	10	74	5	26.3	0	0	2	50.0	2	11	4	1	8	3	1.2
FEVER	34	6,850	791	39.3	481	166	450	77.6	396	1,101	555	261	486	134	64.6
OPPONENTS	34	–	804	43.1	352	121	516	74.2	281	969	514	268	466	162	66.0

LOS ANGELES SPARKS

PLAYER	GP	MIN	FIELD GOALS		3-PT FG		FREE THROWS		REBOUNDS		A	STL	TO	BLK	AVG
			FGM	PCT	FGA	FGM	FTM	PCT	OFF	TOTAL					
Lisa Leslie	34	1,150	223	49.4	22	6	146	71.2	60	336	88	50	110	98	17.6
Mwadi Mabika	31	965	159	41.5	94	38	89	82.4	39	122	75	36	48	3	14.4
Nikki Teasley	34	1,105	108	38.8	165	68	52	76.5	29	116	207	43	103	7	9.9
DeLisha Milton-Jones	19	604	65	40.4	37	11	45	72.6	35	90	31	23	48	10	9.8
Tamecka Dixon	32	913	119	44.2	11	5	68	78.2	32	110	112	36	71	1	9.7
Tamika Whitmore	34	595	77	44.5	16	7	49	68.1	38	106	17	12	34	5	6.2
Laura Macchi	25	410	52	49.1	26	7	41	74.5	23	61	14	21	29	6	6.1
Christi Thomas	31	547	66	46.2	11	5	28	68.3	43	120	23	18	27	14	5.3
Doneeka Hodges	24	245	16	30.8	17	4	7	70.0	3	22	16	10	17	2	1.8
Raffaela Masciadri	17	116	10	40.0	11	4	4	40.0	1	5	8	1	5	0	1.6
Monique Coker	3	14	1	100.0	1	1	0	00.0	1	1	3	0	3	1	1.0
Teresa Weatherspoon	34	292	8	32.0	3	1	0	00.0	6	29	32	12	26	1	.5
Mfon Udoka	3	19	0	00.0	0	0	1	25.0	2	3	0	0	1	0	.3
SPARKS	34	6,975	904	43.7	414	157	530	73.4	312	1,121	626	262	529	148	73.4
OPPONENTS	34	–	815	38.9	511	174	557	73.2	339	1,066	532	288	523	114	69.4

MINNESOTA LYNX

PLAYER	GP	MIN	FIELD GOALS		3-PT FG		FREE THROWS		REBOUNDS		A	STL	TO	BLK	AVG
			FGM	PCT	FGA	FGM	FTM	PCT	OFF	TOTAL					
Katie Smith	23	800	137	43.1	139	60	98	89.9	17	84	52	23	51	6	18.8
Nicole Ohlde	34	1,018	136	44.2	2	0	125	70.6	83	194	60	16	74	45	11.7
Tamika Williams	34	978	102	54.0	4	1	49	56.3	82	205	38	39	66	5	7.5
Svetlana Abrosimova	22	462	49	35.3	53	20	28	60.9	17	74	45	30	43	2	6.6
Teresa Edwards	34	697	74	37.0	85	25	21	70.0	29	90	79	47	93	8	5.7
Vanessa Hayden	29	350	66	41.5	0	0	21	55.3	23	84	7	7	34	29	5.3
Helen Darling	33	707	43	33.1	55	12	42	66.7	11	67	115	30	74	4	4.2
Amanda Lassiter	33	563	47	34.8	89	27	6	66.7	15	80	37	21	40	22	3.8
Stacey Lovelace-Tolbert	34	388	49	40.2	17	3	20	83.3	25	66	20	18	45	9	3.6
Amber Jacobs	32	391	31	31.0	60	19	20	90.9	3	36	47	13	45	0	3.2
Michele Van Gorp	8	66	9	47.4	1	0	4	50.0	6	13	1	0	7	1	2.8
Tasha Butts	30	423	24	30.0	37	10	18	72.0	21	62	25	13	23	7	2.5
Gwen Slaughter	3	7	0	00.0	0	0	2	100.0	0	1	0	0	0	1	.7
LYNX	34	6,850	767	40.4	542	177	454	70.9	332	1,056	526	257	613	139	63.7
OPPONENTS	34	–	804	40.8	330	92	490	73.2	323	1,036	508	333	502	133	64.4

NEW YORK LIBERTY

| PLAYER | GP | MIN | FIELD GOALS | | 3-PT FG | | FREE THROWS | | REBOUNDS | | A | STL | TO | BLK | AVG |
			FGM	PCT	FGA	FGM	FTM	PCT	OFF	TOTAL					
Becky Hammon	34	1,130	153	43.2	170	57	97	83.6	17	118	150	58	118	2	13.5
Crystal Robinson	28	890	122	43.7	144	55	40	93.0	19	83	58	24	33	8	12.1
Elena Baranova	34	1,048	146	46.3	115	53	49	92.5	33	246	67	37	80	58	11.6
Vickie Johnson	34	1,119	121	41.3	60	17	62	88.6	37	121	124	25	71	4	9.4
Tari Phillips	13	311	33	34.7	0	0	21	45.7	28	70	16	14	33	10	6.7
Ann Wauters	13	271	29	43.9	3	1	23	79.3	10	40	21	4	21	8	6.3
Shameka Christon	33	560	67	35.4	82	24	33	64.7	19	68	23	9	32	9	5.8
Bethany Donaphin	26	479	49	46.2	0	0	33	54.1	30	71	16	11	21	8	5.0
La'Keshia Frett	26	347	47	48.0	0	0	23	62.2	17	50	18	10	24	7	4.5
DeTrina White	31	420	37	54.4	0	0	8	47.1	51	118	9	8	36	10	2.6
Erin Thorn	17	150	12	26.7	31	9	1	50.0	0	8	8	4	9	1	2.0
K.B. Sharp	30	240	9	24.3	12	0	11	01.7	5	21	33	6	20	1	1.0
LIBERTY	**34**	**6,900**	**819**	**42.4**	**617**	**216**	**398**	**75.0**	**263**	**1,004**	**539**	**209**	**506**	**124**	**66.2**
OPPONENTS	**34**	**–**	**867**	**41.4**	**416**	**132**	**431**	**74.4**	**371**	**1,101**	**517**	**288**	**430**	**123**	**67.6**

PHOENIX MERCURY

| PLAYER | GP | MIN | FIELD GOALS | | 3-PT FG | | FREE THROWS | | REBOUNDS | | A | STL | TO | BLK | AVG |
			FGM	PCT	FGA	FGM	FTM	PCT	OFF	TOTAL					
Diana Taurasi	34	1,130	200	41.0	188	62	48	76.0	28	140	132	43	90	25	17.0
Anna DeForge	34	1,152	165	41.7	181	70	88	86.3	23	123	107	51	68	8	14.4
Penny Taylor	33	1,076	150	48.4	96	41	93	86.1	51	160	82	52	81	14	13.2
Plenette Pierson	31	803	112	44.3	3	0	66	60.6	46	131	26	26	49	17	9.4
Gwen Jackson	33	426	46	49.5	6	1	24	75.0	31	81	15	6	15	4	3.5
Slobodanka Tuvic	33	691	37	37.4	1	0	17	70.8	25	123	32	25	41	37	2.8
Nikki McCray	27	371	30	44.8	11	5	4	57.1	10	29	13	7	18	0	2.6
Tamara Moore	32	387	27	44.3	10	3	25	86.2	7	28	53	26	34	9	2.6
Shereka Wright	24	243	13	31.0	13	6	25	78.1	17	27	8	3	15	1	2.4
Kayte Christensen	32	407	19	38.8	0	0	12	63.2	27	69	23	21	26	7	1.6
Jae Cross	18	143	6	33.3	7	3	8	72.7	5	14	13	5	9	2	1.3
Ashley Robinson	19	130	7	50.0	1	0	3	42.9	4	13	2	8	4	10	.9
Lindsay Taylor	5	26	1	20.0	3	1	0	00.0	0	3	2	1	1	1	.6
MERCURY	**34**	**6,825**	**826**	**43.0**	**519**	**192**	**456**	**76.3**	**264**	**916**	**501**	**282**	**464**	**137**	**67.6**
OPPONENTS	**34**	**–**	**784**	**42.5**	**348**	**133**	**534**	**73.8**	**309**	**1,020**	**456**	**226**	**536**	**137**	**65.7**

SACRAMENTO MONARCHS

PLAYER	GP	MIN	FIELD GOALS		3-PT FG		FREE THROWS		REBOUNDS		A	STL	TO	BLK	AVG
			FGM	PCT	FGA	FGM	FTM	PCT	OFF	TOTAL					
Yolanda Griffith	34	1,031	177	51.9	1	0	140	75.3	122	246	42	75	59	41	14.5
Tangela Smith	34	908	165	41.1	29	5	45	80.4	46	138	50	38	53	25	11.2
Kara Lawson	34	827	103	42.0	134	51	37	84.1	12	77	68	21	53	8	8.6
DeMya Walker	34	884	111	41.6	10	0	62	60.2	72	143	86	26	86	13	8.4
Ticha Penicheiro	33	970	63	35.4	68	23	50	71.4	14	102	163	64	72	2	6.0
Ruthie Bolton	34	469	57	37.0	79	32	14	73.7	17	49	31	23	15	0	4.7
Rebekkah Brunson	34	494	59	42.1	0	0	33	71.7	42	122	19	23	29	13	4.4
Hamchetou Maiga	34	480	62	47.0	0	0	16	55.2	35	71	25	29	49	6	4.1
Edna Campbell	22	332	29	38.2	39	16	0	00.0	3	19	16	5	15	2	3.4
Chantelle Anderson	30	231	25	39.1	0	0	27	73.0	14	34	5	3	25	6	2.6
Lady Grooms	28	235	19	28.8	0	0	11	91.7	10	18	11	7	2	2	1.8
Giuliana Mendiola	6	39	4	50.0	5	2	0	00.0	2	5	3	0	3	0	1.7
MONARCHS	34	6,900	874	42.2	365	129	435	72.0	389	1,024	519	314	485	118	68.0
OPPONENTS	34	–	803	42.9	458	161	474	75.1	310	986	513	241	593	117	65.9

SAN ANTONIO SILVER STARS

PLAYER	GP	MIN	FIELD GOALS		3-PT FG		FREE THROWS		REBOUNDS		A	STL	TO	BLK	AVG
			FGM	PCT	FGA	FGM	FTM	PCT	OFF	TOTAL					
LaToya Thomas	31	964	171	48.9	8	3	95	84.1	48	138	42	25	56	11	14.2
Marie Ferdinand	17	509	67	41.4	27	10	55	85.9	18	54	29	32	35	2	11.7
Adrienne Goodson	34	1,068	142	44.8	16	4	84	82.4	89	235	60	28	67	2	10.9
Shannon Johnson	31	954	89	38.0	76	27	82	76.6	14	82	136	48	99	4	9.3
Agnieszka Bibrzycka	24	465	55	36.4	84	26	23	88.5	5	28	40	21	32	7	6.6
Margo Dydek	34	682	90	43.3	2	1	44	75.9	30	168	60	20	64	48	6.6
Jessie Hicks	27	371	52	46.8	0	0	23	60.5	23	57	18	17	34	13	4.7
Semeka Randall	29	462	53	37.1	5	0	30	62.5	26	60	20	22	28	4	4.7
Adrian Williams	23	294	42	40.0	0	0	13	61.9	16	49	13	19	27	6	4.2
Jocelyn Penn	1	3	2	100.0	0	0	0	00.0	0	1	0	0	0	0	4.0
Nevriye Yilmaz	7	77	6	25.0	7	1	6	100.0	3	10	2	3	4	1	2.7
Toccara Williams	26	417	16	34.8	2	1	22	75.9	7	39	43	35	31	5	2.1
Tai Dillard	23	205	16	29.6	18	5	0	00.0	2	14	19	4	14	1	1.6
Mandisa Stevenson	29	259	15	33.3	1	1	7	87.5	11	35	5	6	11	4	1.3
SILVER STARS	34	6,875	812	41.9	247	79	488	77.7	302	1,003	493	272	513	106	64.4
OPPONENTS	34	–	888	44.3	469	172	416	73.8	324	1,034	575	280	492	129	69.5

SEATTLE STORM

| PLAYER | GP | MIN | FIELD GOALS | | 3-PT FG | | FREE THROWS | | REBOUNDS | | A | STL | TO | BLK | AVG |
			FGM	PCT	FGA	FGM	FTM	PCT	OFF	TOTAL					
Lauren Jackson	31	1,070	220	47.8	115	52	142	81.1	64	207	51	31	67	62	20.5
Sue Bird	34	1,136	151	46.3	146	64	73	85.9	22	106	184	51	87	5	12.9
Betty Lennox	32	920	139	42.1	83	22	58	85.3	28	159	79	34	77	3	11.2
Sheri Sam	34	1,018	117	41.2	42	11	65	85.5	42	139	82	53	63	6	9.1
Kamila Vodichkova	34	873	94	39.0	2	1	84	77.8	65	168	55	32	73	12	8.0
Janell Burse	29	514	51	42.9	0	0	39	58.2	51	96	19	23	41	36	4.9
Tully Bevilaqua	34	358	24	40.0	26	11	20	69.0	6	26	38	26	2	2.3
Alicia Thompson	23	182	24	44.4	16	3	1	50.0	8	24	9	6	7	0	2.3
Michelle Greco	13	73	10	55.6	2	0	9	69.2	3	10	8	3	8	0	2.2
Simone Edwards	23	257	20	36.4	0	0	8	42.1	25	56	5	8	13	3	2.1
Adia Barnes	34	402	21	30.4	6	3	22	71.0	33	63	31	23	24	2	2.0
Trina Frierson	5	22	2	22.2	1	0	3	100.0	3	5	0	0	1	0	1.4
STORM	34	6,825	873	43.1	439	167	524	77.5	350	1,059	552	302	499	131	71.7
OPPONENTS	34	–	851	42.8	391	139	423	71.5	303	982	507	252	527	127	66.6

WASHINGTON MYSTICS

| PLAYER | GP | MIN | FIELD GOALS | | 3-PT FG | | FREE THROWS | | REBOUNDS | | A | STL | TO | BLK | AVG |
			FGM	PCT	FGA	FGM	FTM	PCT	OFF	TOTAL					
Chamique Holdsclaw	23	801	162	40.2	17	7	106	80.3	51	191	58	39	57	18	19.0
Alana Beard	34	1,025	159	41.8	56	21	107	71.8	28	143	91	69	80	34	13.1
Chastity Melvin	34	825	104	40.6	0	0	85	76.6	63	131	37	15	52	18	8.6
Stacey Dales-Schuman	31	782	87	38.2	119	40	40	72.7	17	64	78	20	37	3	8.2
Murriel Page	33	809	81	46.3	3	0	22	55.0	40	140	36	25	30	16	5.6
Nakia Sanford	31	653	63	50.0	0	0	43	57.3	53	154	18	18	37	16	5.5
Tamicha Jackson	25	405	57	42.2	25	10	11	68.8	7	37	45	20	28	1	5.4
Coco Miller	33	637	72	43.1	19	5	11	78.6	35	63	43	18	27	3	4.8
Kiesha Brown	26	371	35	39.8	28	13	21	87.5	9	50	42	13	33	2	4.0
Aiysha Smith	29	403	42	40.8	16	9	22	64.7	26	69	15	17	21	12	4.0
Kaayla Chones	13	115	11	40.7	0	0	6	54.5	8	17	4	1	11	4	2.2
Shaunzinski Gortman	4	24	0	00.0	0	0	0	00.0	0	4	2	0	2	1	0.0
MYSTICS	34	6,850	873	41.8	283	105	474	71.7	337	1,063	467	255	424	128	68.4
OPPONENTS	34	–	864	42.9	425	146	510	74.3	336	1,106	534	237	492	111	70.1

TRIVIA CHALLENGE

Which of these teams has never played in the WNBA Finals: the Charlotte Sting, Phoenix Mercury, or Sacramento Monarchs?

The Sacramento Monarchs have never played for a WNBA championship. The Mercury reached the Finals in 1998 but lost to the Houston Comets. The Sting played in the Finals in 2001 but lost to the Los Angeles Sparks.

Yolanda Griffith of the Sacramento Monarchs tied for the league lead in steals per game (2.21).

2004 WNBA INDIVIDUAL LEADERS

POINTS	GP	PTS	AVG
Lauren Jackson, Seattle Storm	31	634	20.5
Tina Thompson, Houston Comets	26	520	20.0
Lisa Leslie, Los Angeles Sparks	34	598	17.6
Diana Taurasi, Phoenix Mercury	34	578	17.0
Tamika Catchings, Indiana Fever	34	568	16.7

REBOUNDS	GP	REB	AVG
Lisa Leslie, Los Angeles Sparks	34	336	9.9
Cheryl Ford, Detroit Shock	31	297	9.6
Michelle Snow, Houston Comets	31	239	7.7
Tamika Catchings, Indiana Fever	34	249	7.3

Three tied with 7.2.

ASSISTS	GP	A	AVG
Nikki Teasley, Los Angeles Sparks	34	207	6.1
Sue Bird, Seattle Storm	34	184	5.4
Dawn Staley, Charlotte Sting	34	171	5.0
Ticha Penicheiro, Sacramento Monarchs	33	163	4.9
Lindsay Whalen, Connecticut Sun	31	148	4.8

FIELD-GOAL PERCENTAGE	FGA	FGM	PCT
Tamika Williams, Minnesota Lynx	189	102	54.0
Yolanda Griffith, Sacramento Monarchs	341	177	51.9
Lisa Leslie, Los Angeles Sparks	451	223	49.4
LaToya Thomas, San Antonio Silver Stars	350	171	48.9
Penny Taylor, Phoenix Mercury	310	150	48.4

FREE-THROW PERCENTAGE	FTA	FTM	PCT
Katie Smith, Minnesota Lynx	109	98	89.9
Vickie Johnson, New York Liberty	70	62	88.6
Kelly Miller, Indiana Fever	57	50	87.7
Allison Feaster, Charlotte Sting	91	79	86.8
Anna DeForge, Phoenix Mercury	102	88	86.3

3-POINT FIELD-GOAL PERCENTAGE	FGA	FGM	PCT
Charlotte Smith-Taylor, Charlotte Sting	58	29	50.0
Elena Baranova, New York Liberty	115	53	46.1
Lauren Jackson, Seattle Storm	115	52	45.2
Sue Bird, Seattle Storm	146	64	43.8
Katie Smith, Minnesota Lynx	139	60	43.2

STEALS	GP	STL	AVG
Yolanda Griffith, Sacramento Monarchs	34	75	2.21
Nykesha Sales, Connecticut Sun	34	75	2.21
Alana Beard, Washington Mystics	34	69	2.03
Tamika Catchings, Indiana Fever	34	67	1.97
Deanna Nolan, Detroit Shock	34	66	1.94
Ticha Penicheiro, Sacramento Monarchs	33	64	1.94

BLOCKS	GP	BLK	AVG
Lisa Leslie, Los Angeles Sparks	34	98	2.88
Tammy Sutton-Brown, Charlotte Sting	34	71	2.09
Lauren Jackson, Seattle Storm	31	62	2.00
Elena Baranova, New York Liberty	34	58	1.71
Ruth Riley, Detroit Shock	34	53	1.56

TODAY'S STARS

Diana Taurasi led the Mercury in scoring and assists in 2004.

■ **Diana Taurasi, guard,** b. June 11, 1982, Glendale, California. Taurasi was the Number 1 pick in the 2004 WNBA Draft. She ranked 4th in the league in scoring (17 points per game) and 10th in assists (3.9). Most impressively, the 2004 Rookie of the Year led the Phoenix Mercury to a 17–17 record and a fifth-place finish in the Western Conference. In 2003, the Mercury finished 8–26, last in the league. Taurasi was a two-time Naismith Player of the Year at Connecticut (2003 and 2004) and led the Huskies to three NCAA national titles (2002, 2003, and 2004). Taurasi also won a gold medal at the 2004 Summer Olympics. She averaged 8.5 points in 8 games.

■ **Nikki Teasley, guard,** b. March 22, 1979, Washington, D.C. In 2004, Teasley led the WNBA in assists (6.1 per game), was seventh in 3-point field goal percentage (41.2), and averaged 9.9 points per game for the Los Angeles Sparks. The Portland Fire selected her as the fifth pick overall in the 2002 draft, but she was traded on the same day to the Sparks. In Game 2 of the 2002 WNBA Finals, Teasley hit a game-winning 3-pointer to give Los Angeles its second straight WNBA championship.

■ **Swin Cash, forward,** b. September 22, 1979, McKeesport, Pennsylvania. Cash is a proven winner. She won two NCAA championships with Connecticut (2000 and 2002), helped lead the Detroit Shock to its first WNBA title (2003), and won an Olympic gold medal as a member of the U.S. Women's National Team (2004). The two-time WNBA All-Star finished sixth in the league in scoring (16.4 points per game) and ninth in assists (4.2) in 2004.

> **DID YOU KNOW?**
> In 2004, the WNBA had 24 international players from 17 countries on its rosters. Australia had the most players, with four.

WNBA ALL-STAR GAME RESULTS

YEAR	RESULT	SITE	WINNING COACH	MVP
2004	U.S. National Team 74, WNBA All-Stars 58	New York, NY	Van Chancellor	Yolanda Griffith, Sacramento Monarchs
2003	West 84, East 75	New York, NY	Michael Cooper	Nikki Teasley, Los Angeles Sparks
2002	West 81, East 76	Washington, D.C.	Michael Cooper	Lisa Leslie, Los Angeles Sparks
2001	West 80, East 72	Orlando, FL	Van Chancellor	Lisa Leslie, Los Angeles Sparks
2000	West 73, East 61	Phoenix, AZ	Van Chancellor	Tina Thompson, Houston Comets
1999	West 79, East 61	New York, NY	Van Chancellor	Lisa Leslie, Los Angeles Sparks

2005 WNBA DRAFT

APRIL 16, 2005, SECAUCUS, NJ

FIRST ROUND PICK	TEAM	NAME/POSITION	SCHOOL		FIRST ROUND PICK	TEAM	NAME/POSITION	SCHOOL
1.	Charlotte	Janel McCarville, C	Minnesota		8.	Connecticut	Katie Feenstra, C	Liberty (rights
2.	Indiana	Tan White, G	Mississippi State				traded to San Antonio for Margo Dydek)
3.	Phoenix	Sandora Irvin, F	Texas Christian		9.	Sacramento	Kristin Haynie, G	Michigan State
4.	San Antonio	Kendra Wecker, F	Kansas State		10.	New York	Loree Moore, G	Tennessee
5.	Houston	Sancho Lyttle, C	Houston		11.	Minnesota	Kristen Mann, F	California-Santa
6.	Washington	Temeka Johnson, G	LSU					Barbara
7.	Detroit	Kara Braxton, F	Georgia		12.	Seattle	Tanisha Wright, G	Penn State
					13.	Detroit	Dionnah Jackson, F	Oklahoma

KEY G=guard; F=forward; C=center

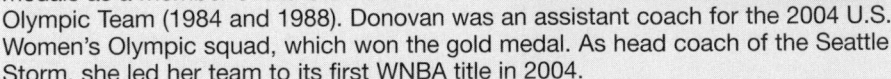

LEGENDS

Heading into 2005, Dawn Staley had dished out 1,055 assists, third-most in WNBA history.

JESSE D. GARRABRANT/WNBAE VIA GETTY IMAGES

■ **Dawn Staley, guard,** b. May 4, 1970, Philadelphia, Pennsylvania. Staley is a three-time WNBA All-Star and a three-time Olympic gold medalist (1996, 2000, and 2004). As the point guard for the Charlotte Sting, she ranked first in the league in assists-to-turnover ratio (2.31) and third in assists per game (5) in 2004. Staley is also the head coach of Temple University's women's basketball team. She led the Owls to the A-10 tournament title in 2004 and 2005.

■ **Anne Donovan, center,** b. November 1, 1961, Ridgewood, New Jersey. As a three-time All-America at Old Dominion, Donovan scored the most points (2,719), grabbed the most rebounds (1,976), and blocked the most shots (801) in school history. After college, the 6' 8" center won two gold medals as a member of the U.S. Women's Olympic Team (1984 and 1988). Donovan was an assistant coach for the 2004 U.S. Women's Olympic squad, which won the gold medal. As head coach of the Seattle Storm, she led her team to its first WNBA title in 2004.

■ **Lynette Woodard, guard/forward,** b. August 12, 1959, Wichita, Kansas. A four-time All-America at Kansas (1978-81), Woodard is the all-time career scoring leader (3,649 points) in women's college basketball. She was co-captain of the U.S. Women's Olympic Team that won the gold medal in 1984. In 1985, Woodard became the first woman to play for the Harlem Globetrotters. She played with the team for two years, then played overseas before she retired in 1992. Woodard came out of retirement in 1997 to play two seasons in the WNBA with the Cleveland Rockers and the Detroit Shock. She was inducted into the Naismith Memorial Basketball Hall of Fame in September 2004.

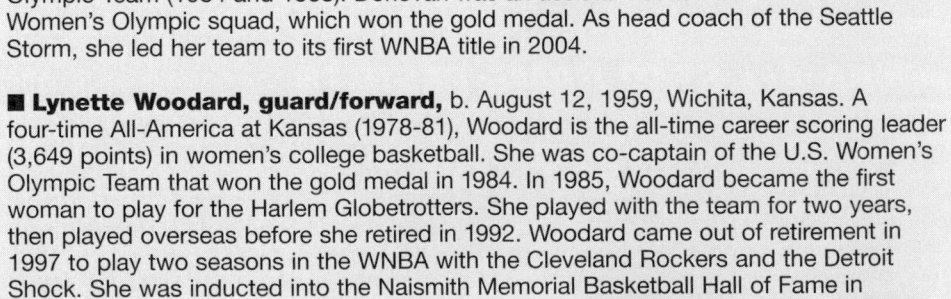

DID YOU KNOW?

After eight WNBA seasons, there are only 12 active players who have been in the league since it started in 1997.

2004-05 TIME LINE

■ **May 20, 2004:** Forward/center Lauren Jackson of the Seattle Storm scores 31 points in an 88–85 win over the Minnesota Lynx. It's the second-most points scored on a WNBA opening night.

■ **May 28, 2004:** Guard Diana Taurasi of the Phoenix Mercury scores 22 points. She becomes the first player to begin her WNBA career by scoring more than 20 points in three consecutive games.

■ **August 5, 2004:** A week before the 2004 Summer Olympics, the WNBA All-Stars take on the U.S. National Team at Radio City Music Hall in New York City. The U.S. wins easily, 74–58, behind center Lisa Leslie's 15 points.

■ **August 28, 2004:** The U.S women's basketball team beats Australia, 74–63, to win the Olympic gold medal in Athens, Greece. The U.S. roster features 12 WNBA players. Australia is led by forward/center Lauren Jackson of the Seattle Storm.

■ **October 12, 2004:** The Seattle Storm wins its first championship by beating the Connecticut Sun, 74–60, in Game 3 of the WNBA Finals. Storm guard Betty Lennox scores 23 points and is named Finals MVP.

■ **April 16, 2005:** The Charlotte Sting choose center Janel McCarville of Minnesota as the Number 1 pick in the WNBA Draft.

■ **May 21, 2005:** The WNBA tips off its ninth regular season.

TRIVIA CHALLENGE

True or False: A foreign player has never been the Number 1 pick in the WNBA Draft.

False: Three international players have been drafted first: Lauren Jackson of Australia (2001), Ann Wauters of Belgium (2000), and Margo Dydek of Poland (1998).

ALL-TIME WORLD CHAMPIONSHIP RESULTS

YEAR	WINNER	RUNNER-UP	SCORE	SITE
2002	United States	Russia	79–74	China
1998	United States	Russia	71–65	Germany
1994	Brazil	China	96–87	Australia
1990	United States	Yugoslavia	88–78	Malaysia
1986	United States	Soviet Union	108–88	Soviet Union
1983	Soviet Union	United States	84–82	Brazil
1979	United States	Canada	77–61	South Korea
1975	Soviet Union	Japan	106–75	Colombia
1971	Soviet Union	Czechoslovakia	88–69	Brazil
1967	Soviet Union	South Korea	83–50	Czechoslovakia
1964	Soviet Union	Czechoslovakia	70–35	Peru
1959*	Soviet Union	Bulgaria	51–38	Soviet Union
1957	United States	Soviet Union	51–48	Brazil
1953	United States	Chile	49–36	Chile

*The U.S. did not compete in 1959 because the worlds were held in Moscow, Soviet Union.

The North Carolina Tar Heels made a remarkable turnaround in just three seasons. In 2002-03, the team went 8–20. The next season, former Kansas head coach Roy Williams returned to UNC to take the top job. (He had been an assistant coach from 1978-88.) In 2003-04, the team improved to 19–11, but still struggled to combine its individual talents into one powerful force.

Fast forward one season. In 2004-05, Williams watched his collection of All-Americas and future NBA draft picks roll to a 33–4 record. The Tar Heels won the school's fourth NCAA championship with a 75–70 victory over Illinois in the championship game.

Ironically, the Fighting Illini had been the model for teamwork all season long. Each of the team's three starting guards — Dee Brown, Deron Williams, and Luther Head — averaged double figures in scoring.

Without question, Illinois entered the NCAA tournament as the favorite. The Illini held the Number 1 ranking all season. Only a last-second, one-point loss at Ohio State in the regular-season finale kept Illinois from entering the NCAA tournament undefeated.

As other national championship hopefuls were picked off in the tournament (Wake Forest: not enough defense; Kentucky: not enough offense; Duke: not enough depth; Kansas: not enough toughness),

Junior center Sean May led North Carolina to its fourth NCAA championship in 2005.

DAVID E. KLUTHO/SPORTS ILLUSTRATED

the nation's two best teams were on a collision course for a national title matchup. On April 4, 2005, Illinois (ranked Number 1) and North Carolina (Number 2) met in St. Louis, Missouri, the site of the Final Four. It was the first time since 1975 that the nation's top two teams would play for the national championship.

Using a perfect blend of ability and teamwork, North Carolina prevailed. The Tar Heels held Illinois to 30 percent shooting from 3-point range. North Carolina junior center Sean May was named Most

Outstanding Player after scoring 26 points and grabbing 10 rebounds.

One week later, junior Rashad McCants announced that he would declare for the 2005 NBA Draft. Two weeks later, May, junior Raymond Felton, and freshman Marvin Williams announced that they would do the same. In the blink of an eye, the foundation of UNC's title team had collapsed, leaving behind the most inexperienced squad in school history. The question now is how quickly Williams can rebuild the Tar Heels into a contender.

NCAA MEN'S DIVISION I CHAMPIONSHIP BOX SCORE

NORTH CAROLINA TAR HEELS: 75

PLAYER	POS	MIN	FG M-A	3-PT M-A	FT M-A	PF	PTS
Jawad Williams	F	22	3-6	3-4	0-0	1	9
Rashad McCants	F	31	6-15	2-5	0-0	0	14
Sean May	C	34	10-11	0-0	6-8	1	26
Raymond Felton	G	35	4-9	4-5	5-6	4	17
Jackie Manuel	G	18	0-1	0-0	0-2	4	0
Melvin Scott		13	0-2	0-1	0-0	0	0
Reyshawn Terry		2	0-0	0-0	0-0	0	0
Quentin Thomas		1	0-0	0-0	0-0	1	0
Marvin Williams		24	4-8	0-1	0-1	2	8
David Noel		20	0-0	0-0	1-2	0	1
TOTALS			**27-52**	**9-16**	**12-19**	**13**	**75**
			(51.9%)	(56.2%)	(63.2%)		

ILLINOIS FIGHTING ILLINI: 70

PLAYER	POS	MIN	FG M-A	3-PT M-A	FT M-A	PF	PTS
James Augustine	F	9	0-3	0-0	0-0	5	0
Roger Powell, Jr.	F	38	4-10	1-2	0-0	2	9
Luther Head	G	37	8-21	5-16	0-0	1	21
Deron Williams	G	40	7-16	3-10	0-2	4	17
Dee Brown	G	38	4-10	2-8	2-2	1	12
Rich McBride		2	0-0	0-0	0-0	0	0
Warren Carter		5	0-1	0-1	0-0	1	0
Nick Smith		1	0-0	0-0	0-0	0	0
Jack Ingram		30	4-9	1-3	2-2	4	11
TOTALS			**27-70**	**12-40**	**4-6**	**18**	**70**
			(38.6%)	(30%)	(66.7%)		

KEY POS=position; MIN=minutes played; FG M-A=field goals made-attempted; 3-PT M-A=3-point field goals made-attempted; FT M-A=free throws made-attempted; PF=personal fouls; PTS=points; F=forward; G=guard; C=center

TRIVIA CHALLENGE

Illinois was ranked Number 1 for 14 of 17 weeks in the AP college basketball poll. Which two other schools earned a Number 1 ranking during the 2004-05 regular season?

The Clash. San Jose changed its name to the Earthquakes before the start of the 2000 season.

Luther Head led Illinois in scoring with 15.9 points per game in 2004-05.

JOHN BIEVER/SPORTS ILLUSTRATED

USA TODAY/ESPN Coaches Top 25 Final Poll

RANK	SCHOOL	FINAL RECORD	POINTS
1	North Carolina	33-4	775
2	Illinois	36-1	744
3	Louisville	33-4	704
4	Michigan State	26-6	676
5	Kentucky	28-6	637
6	Arizona	30-7	612
7	Duke	27-6	560
8	Oklahoma State	26-7	515
9	Washington	29-6	511
10	Wisconsin	25-9	489
11	Wake Forest	27-6	399
12	West Virginia	24-11	384
13	Villanova	24-8	355
14	Utah	29-6	333
15	Kansas	23-7	253
16	Texas Tech	22-11	251
17	Connecticut	23-8	249
18	Gonzaga	26-5	239
19	Boston College	25-5	234
20	Oklahoma	25-8	218
21	Syracuse	27-7	179
22	North Carolina State	21-14	137
23	Wisconsin-Milwaukee	26-6	123
24	Florida	24-8	118
25	Cincinnati	25-8	96

NCAA MEN'S DIVISION I INDIVIDUAL LEADERS

SCORING

PLAYER	CLASS	GP	FG	3FG	FT	PTS	AVG
Keydren Clark, St. Peter's	Jr.	28	230	109	152	721	25.8
Taylor Coppenrath, Vermont	Sr.	31	271	9	226	777	25.1
Ronnie Price, Utah Valley State	Sr.	28	229	80	142	680	24.3
Juan Mendez, Niagara	Sr.	30	221	39	224	705	23.5
Rob Monroe, Quinnipiac	Sr.	26	173	72	171	589	22.7
Bo McCaleb, New Orleans	So.	30	261	25	132	679	22.6
Ike Diogu, Arizona State	Jr.	32	229	18	248	724	22.6
Tim Smith, East Tennessee State	Jr.	29	245	59	96	645	22.2
Jose Juan Barea, Northeastern	Jr.	30	233	68	131	665	22.2
J.J. Redick, Duke	Jr.	33	202	121	196	721	21.8

KEY GP=games played; FG=field goals; 3FG=3-point field goals; FT=free throws; PTS=points; AVG=average; So.=sophomore; Jr.=junior; Sr.=senior

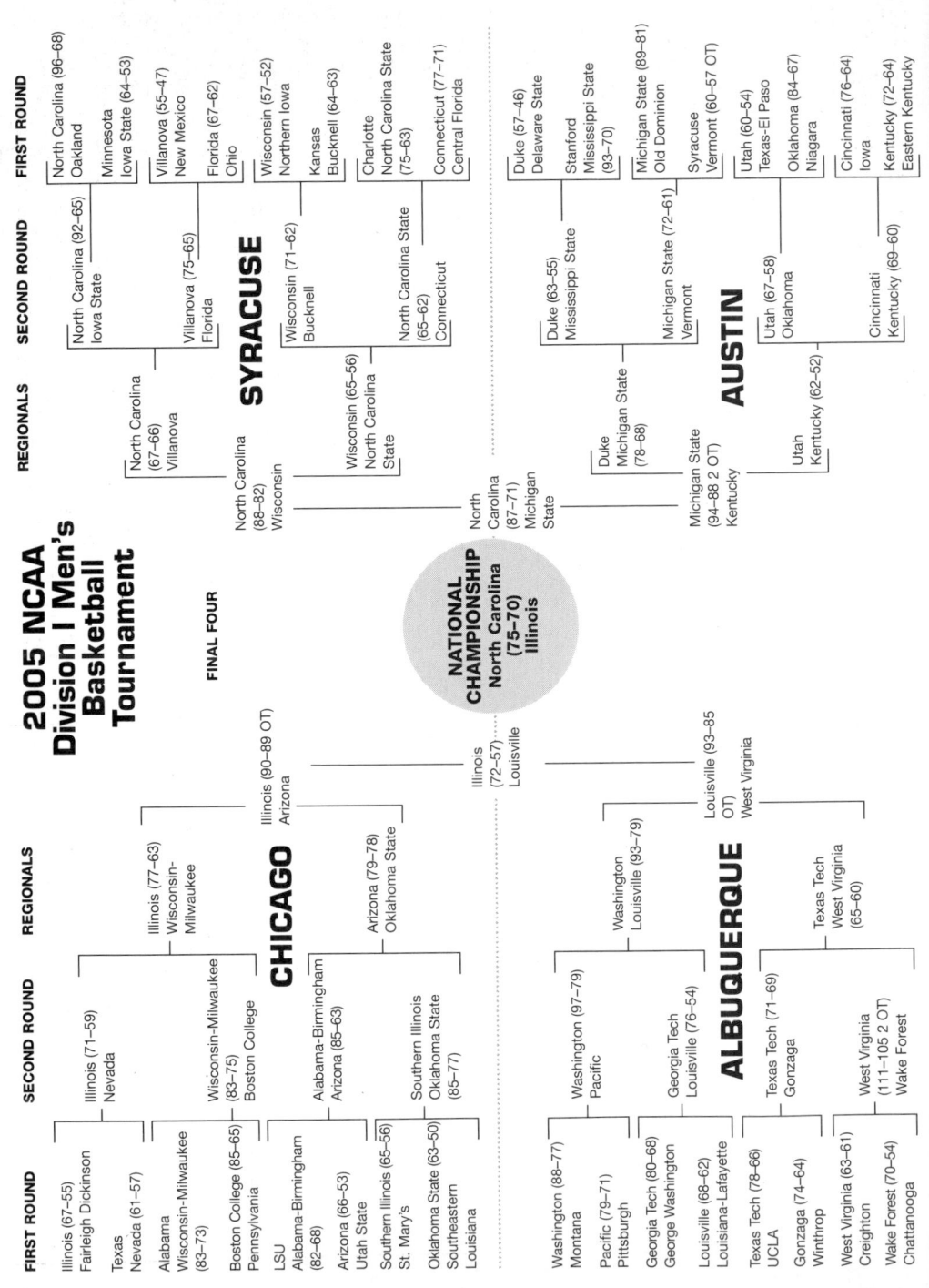

2005 NCAA Division I Men's Basketball Tournament

SYRACUSE

AUSTIN

CHICAGO

ALBUQUERQUE

FINAL FOUR

NATIONAL CHAMPIONSHIP
North Carolina (75–70)
Illinois

FIRST ROUND / SECOND ROUND / REGIONALS (Syracuse)

North Carolina (96–68)
Oakland
Minnesota
Iowa State (64–53)

North Carolina (92–65)
Iowa State

Villanova (55–47)
New Mexico
Florida (67–62)
Ohio

Villanova (75–65)
Florida

North Carolina (67–66)
Villanova

Wisconsin (57–52)
Northern Iowa
Kansas
Bucknell (64–63)

Wisconsin (71–62)
Bucknell

Charlotte
North Carolina State (75–63)
Connecticut (77–71)
Central Florida

North Carolina State (65–62)
Connecticut

Wisconsin (65–56)
North Carolina State

North Carolina (88–82)
Wisconsin

FIRST ROUND / SECOND ROUND / REGIONALS (Austin)

Duke (57–46)
Delaware State
Stanford
Mississippi State (93–70)

Duke (63–55)
Mississippi State

Michigan State (89–81)
Old Dominion
Syracuse
Vermont (60–57 OT)

Michigan State (72–61)
Vermont

Duke
Michigan State (78–68)

Utah (60–54)
Texas-El Paso
Oklahoma (84–67)
Niagara

Utah (67–58)
Oklahoma

Cincinnati (76–64)
Iowa
Kentucky (72–64)
Eastern Kentucky

Cincinnati
Kentucky (69–60)

Utah
Kentucky (62–52)

Michigan State (94–88 2 OT)
Kentucky

North Carolina (87–71)
Michigan State

FIRST ROUND / SECOND ROUND / REGIONALS (Chicago)

Illinois (67–55)
Fairleigh Dickinson
Texas
Nevada (61–57)

Illinois (71–59)
Nevada

Alabama
Wisconsin-Milwaukee (83–73)
Boston College (85–65)
Pennsylvania

Wisconsin-Milwaukee (83–75)
Boston College

Illinois (77–63)
Wisconsin-Milwaukee

LSU
Alabama-Birmingham (82–68)
Arizona (66–53)
Utah State

Alabama-Birmingham
Arizona (85–63)

Southern Illinois (65–56)
St. Mary's
Oklahoma State (63–50)
Southeastern Louisiana

Southern Illinois
Oklahoma State (85–77)

Arizona (79–78)
Oklahoma State

Illinois (90–89 OT)
Arizona

FIRST ROUND / SECOND ROUND / REGIONALS (Albuquerque)

Washington (88–77)
Montana
Pacific (79–71)
Pittsburgh

Washington (97–79)
Pacific

Georgia Tech (80–68)
George Washington
Louisville (68–62)
Louisiana-Lafayette

Georgia Tech
Louisville (76–54)

Washington
Louisville (93–79)

Texas Tech (78–66)
UCLA
Gonzaga (74–64)
Winthrop

Texas Tech (71–69)
Gonzaga

West Virginia (63–61)
Creighton
Wake Forest (70–54)
Chattanooga

West Virginia (111–105 2 OT)
Wake Forest

Texas Tech
West Virginia (65–60)

Louisville (93–85 OT)
West Virginia

Illinois (72–57)
Louisville

RISING SUN

No one expected the Phoenix Suns to be among the NBA's elite teams at the start of 2004-05. But behind the ferocious play of center Amare Stoudemire, the Suns scorched the competition, posting a 41–13 record before the All-Star break. The 6' 10" dunk artist was averaging 26.2 points and 8.7 rebounds per game.

HALL'S HAUL

Freestyle skier Tanner Hall of Kalispell, Montana, nearly made history at the 2005 Winter X Games. He placed second in the Slopestyle event, in which skiers go through a course of jumps and rails. Hall had won the event three years in a row and was going for a record fourth straight gold medal.

FAST FORWARD

On April 17, 2004, forward Freddy Adu of the D.C. United became the youngest player to score a goal in Major League Soccer. That was no surprise, considering the then 14-year-old was the youngest player ever drafted into the league. Adu played in all 30 matches for the United in 2004, starting 14 of them. He finished the season with 5 goals and 3 assists, good enough for fourth on the team in points (13). Adu also saw action in the MLS Championship Game, in which the United defeated the Kansas City Wizards, 3–2.

CHART TOPPER

Vijay Singh won nine PGA Tour events in 2004, including the PGA Championship. He took over the Number 1 ranking in the world from Tiger Woods and won his first money title, collecting a record $10,905,166. Singh piled up 18 Top 10 finishes on his way to being named the PGA Tour Player of the Year.

BOOMING SOONER

Adrian Peterson of Oklahoma broke records as easily as he did tackles in 2004. The running back set NCAA freshman marks for most rushing yards in a season (1,925) and most 100-yard games (11). Peterson finished second in voting for the Heisman Trophy and helped lead the Sooners to the Number 2 ranking and a second straight berth in the Bowl Championship Series (BCS) national championship game.

TALENTED TIGER

Seimone Augustus of Louisiana State earned her reputation as the country's best women's college player in 2004-05. The junior guard scored 33 points and grabbed 14 rebounds in her third game of the season, a 71–70 victory over eighth-ranked Baylor. Augustus led LSU to a 23–1 start and a Number 1 national ranking. She was the leading vote-getter for the 2004-05 pre-season All-America team and the favorite to win the Naismith Player of the Year award.

WORLD ON ICE

With the National Hockey League on thin ice due to a lockout by the owners, the 2004 World Cup of Hockey gave fans reason to cheer. Jaromir Jagr, a forward on the NHL's New York Rangers, played through injury to help lead the Czech Republic to the semifinals, where it lost 4–3 in overtime to eventual champion Canada. Jagr scored 1 goal and had 1 assist for the tournament.

SWISS CLIMBER

Roger Federer of Switzerland became the first male tennis player in 14 years to win three Grand Slam titles in a season (U.S. Open, Australian Open, and Wimbledon). He won eight other ATP tournaments and finished the season ranked Number 1 in the world.

RECORD BREAKER

Quarterback Peyton Manning of the Indianapolis Colts threw 49 touchdown passes in 2004, breaking the 20-year-old NFL regular-season record held by Miami Dolphins quarterback Dan Marino. Manning led the Colts to their second straight AFC South title and was named the league's MVP for the second year in a row.

COMEBACK KID

In a dramatic come-from-behind victory at the 2004 Summer Olympics, gymnast Paul Hamm propelled himself from 12th place to 1st and won the United States' first men's all-around gold medal. (He also won two silver medals.) But South Korea insisted a judging error was made and that Tae Young Yang, who was awarded the bronze medal, deserved the gold. In October 2004, the Court of Arbitration for Sport ruled that the all-around title belonged to Hamm.

HOT SPARK

Lisa Leslie of the Los Angeles Sparks earned her second WNBA Most Valuable Player award in 2004. She led the Sparks to a league-best 25–9 record and finished the season ranked first in rebounds (9.9 per game), second in minutes played (1,150), and third in points (17.6). The 6' 5" center also led the U.S. Women's Team to the gold medal — her third — at the Summer Olympics, in Athens, Greece.

SAND MASTERS

The Summer Olympics' biggest party broke out at the Beach Volleyball Centre, where top-seeded Misty May (left) and Kerri Walsh of the United States did not lose a single set. In the gold-medal match, they needed just 43 minutes to defeat Shelda Bede and Adriana Behar of Brazil, 21–17, 21–11. Success is nothing new to May and Walsh: They had an 89-match, 15-tournament winning streak that lasted from July 2003 to June 2004.

DEMON DEACON

Sophomore point guard Chris Paul of Wake Forest lived up to the hype. The 2003-04 Atlantic Coast Conference Rookie of the Year led his team to the Number 1 pre-season ranking and a 22–3 record to start the 2004-05 season. Paul was averaging 14.6 points and 6.8 assists per game, through 25 games. In one of his biggest games, he had 26 points, 6 rebounds, 8 assists, and 5 steals in a 95–82 victory over third-ranked North Carolina, on January 15, 2005.

SUPER SCORER

In 2004, forward Abby Wambach of the U.S. Women's National Team scored a team-leading 31 goals and had 13 assists in 33 matches, including the game-winning header in overtime of the Olympic gold-medal soccer match. The 24-year-old earned her second straight Chevy Female Athlete of the Year award from U.S. Soccer.

DRIVEN TO WIN

NASCAR's championship series changed its name from the Winston Cup to the Nextel Cup in 2004. That wasn't the only change. To keep the excitement high as the season wore on, drivers ranked in the Top 10 competed in a 10-race "Chase for the Championship." Kurt Busch, who had the fewest Top 5 finishes of any champion in NASCAR history, secured the title with a fifth-place finish in the season's final race, the Ford 400.

SMOOTH SKATING

Short-track speed skater Apolo Ohno of the U.S. won his third World Cup overall championship in 2004-05. He also won individual titles in the 1,000-meter and 1,500-meter events. The 22-year-old, who won one gold medal and one silver medal at the 2002 Winter Olympics, hopes to win more gold at the 2006 Winter Games, in Turin, Italy.

CURSE REVERSED

The Boston Red Sox finally ended "The Curse of the Bambino" in 2004. The long-suffering franchise was baseball's big winner, capturing the World Series championship for the first time since 1918. Pitcher Curt Schilling, MVP outfielder Manny Ramirez, designated hitter David Ortiz, and the rest of the self-proclaimed "Idiots" first beat the New York Yankees in an epic seven-game American League Championship Series. The Sox then swept the St. Louis Cardinals, 4–0, to win the World Series.

FIELD GOAL PERCENTAGE

PLAYER	CLASS	GP	FGM	FGA	PCT
Bruce Brown, Hampton	Jr.	30	178	269	66.2
Nate Harris, Utah State	Jr.	32	172	264	65.2
Eric Williams, Wake Forest	Jr.	33	201	319	63.0
Chad McKnight, Morehead State	Sr.	27	155	246	63.0
Aaron Andrews, Morgan State	Sr.	28	140	224	62.5
Michael Haney, Eastern Kentucky	Sr.	31	174	279	62.4
Kyle Hines, North Carolina-Greensboro	Fr.	30	175	282	62.1
Andrew Bogut, Utah	So.	35	281	453	62.0
Carl Landry, Purdue	Jr.	25	160	259	61.8
Quincy Davis, Tulane	Jr.	28	153	250	61.2

Note: Minimum five field goals made per game.

FREE THROW PERCENTAGE

PLAYER	CLASS	GP	FTM	FTA	PCT
Blake Ahearn, Southwest Missouri State	So.	32	90	95	94.7
J.J. Redick, Duke	Jr.	33	196	209	93.8
Vince Green, Illinois State	Sr.	30	81	88	92.0
Salim Stoudamire, Arizona	Sr.	36	122	134	91.0
Jamaal Hilliard, Lafayette	So.	28	91	100	91.0
Chris McCray, Maryland	Jr.	31	102	113	90.3
Derek Raivio, Gonzaga	So.	31	102	113	90.3
Anthony Roberson, Florida	Jr.	32	81	90	90.0
David Doubley, Pacific	Sr.	31	94	105	89.5
Jerry Johnson, Rider	Sr.	30	107	120	89.2

Note: Minimum 2.5 free throws made per game.

REBOUNDING

PLAYER	CLASS	GP	REB	AVG
Paul Millsap, Louisiana Tech	So.	29	360	12.4
Andrew Bogut, Utah	So.	35	427	12.2
Lance Allred, Weber State	Sr.	29	348	12.0
Michael Harris, Rice	Sr.	31	363	11.7
Dwayne Jones, St. Joseph's	Jr.	36	418	11.6
Shelden Williams, Duke	Jr.	33	369	11.2
Wayne Simien, Kansas	Sr.	26	287	11.0
Lawrence Roberts, Mississippi State	Sr.	32	351	11.0
Sean May, North Carolina	Jr.	37	397	10.7
Juan Mendez, Niagara	Sr.	30	319	10.6

Paul Millsap, Louisiana Tech

ASSISTS

PLAYER	CLASS	GP	A	APG
Damitrius Coleman, Mercer	Jr.	28	224	8.0
Will Funn, Portland State	Sr.	28	224	8.0
Marcus Williams, Connecticut	So.	31	243	7.8
Walker Russell, Jacksonville State	Jr.	29	211	7.3
Jose Juan Barea, Northeastern	Jr.	30	218	7.3
Aaron Miles, Kansas	Sr.	30	216	7.2
Filiberto Rivera, Texas-El Paso	Sr.	32	229	7.2

3-POINT FIELD GOAL PERCENTAGE

PLAYER	CLASS	GP	3FGM	3FGA	PCT
Matt McCraw, Air Force	So.	30	55	108	50.9
Jarrett Howell, Texas-Arlington	Jr.	28	43	85	50.6
Salim Stoudamire, Arizona	Sr.	36	120	238	50.4
Jeremiah Boswell, Columbia	Sr.	27	44	88	50.0
Will Whittington, Marist	So.	28	97	197	49.2

Note: Minimum 2.5 three-point field goals made per game.

KEY GP=games played; FGM=field goals made; FGA=field goals attempted; PCT=percentage; FTM=free throws made; FTA=free throws attempted; REB=rebounds; AVG=average; A=assists; APG=assists per game; 3FGM=3-point field goals made; 3FGA=3-point field goals attempted

JOHN RED/US PRESSWIRE

NCAA MEN'S DIVISION I INDIVIDUAL LEADERS (cont.)

STEALS

PLAYER	CLASS	GP	STL	SPG
Obie Trotter, Alabama A&M	Jr.	32	125	3.9
Chakowby Hicks, Norfolk State	Sr.	27	91	3.4
Keydren Clark, St. Peter's	Jr.	28	93	3.3
Hosea Butler, Mississippi Valley	Sr.	28	91	3.3
Eddie Basden, North Carolina-Charlotte	Sr.	29	93	3.2

Deng Gai, Fairfield

BLOCKS

PLAYER	CLASS	GP	BLK	BPG
Deng Gai, Fairfield	Sr.	30	165	5.5
Shawn James, Northeastern	Fr.	25	136	5.4
Shelden Williams, Duke	Jr.	33	122	3.7
Kyle Hines, North Carolina-Greensboro	Fr.	30	106	3.5

LOU CAPOZZOLA

KEY GP=games played; STL=steals; SPG=steals per game; BLK=blocks; BPG=blocks per game

DID YOU KNOW?

Illinois tied the NCAA single-season record with 37 wins in 2004-05, joining Duke (1985-86 and 1998-99) and UNLV (1986-87). All four of those teams reached the Final Four, but none won the national championship.

2004-05 TIME LINE

■ **December 1, 2004:** Number 3 Illinois routs Number 1 Wake Forest, 91–73, in the first big matchup of the season. The Fighting Illini take over the Number 1 spot in the polls and hold on to it for the rest of the season.

■ **December 11, 2004:** Arizona coach Lute Olson wins his 1,000th career game, including high school, junior college, and college, as the Wildcats defeat Utah, 67–62.

■ **February 14, 2005:** Savannah State becomes just the second Division I program in 50 years to have a winless season when the Tigers lose to Florida A&M, 49–44. The Tigers finish 0–28 and enter 2005-06 with a 55-game losing streak.

■ **March 18, 2005:** The two biggest upsets of the NCAA tournament's first round come on the same night. Bucknell, a 14th seed, stuns Number 3-seeded Kansas, 64–63, in the Syracuse Region, and Number 13 Vermont shocks Number 4 Syracuse, 60–57, in overtime in the Austin Region.

■ **March 26, 2005:** Louisville rallies from 20 points down in the first half to beat West Virginia, 93–85, in overtime in the Albuquerque Regional final. Illinois erases a 15-point Arizona lead with less than four minutes remaining in regulation to beat the Wildcats, 90–89, in overtime to reach the Final Four. North Carolina and Michigan State join the Cardinals and Fighting Illini the next day.

■ **March 31, 2005:** South Carolina's Tarence Kinsey hits a 3-pointer with 0.9 seconds remaining to give the Gamecocks a 60–57 victory over St. Joseph's in the NIT championship game.

■ **April 2, 2005:** Illinois and North Carolina win their Final Four games to set up a highly anticipated national championship matchup. The Fighting Illini top Louisville, 72–57, and the Tar Heels beat Michigan State, 87–71.

■ **April 4, 2005:** North Carolina wins its fourth NCAA championship with a 75–70 victory over Illinois. Sean May, the Tar Heels' junior center, is named Most Outstanding Player.

NCAA MEN'S DIVISION I CHAMPIONSHIP RESULTS

YEAR	WINNER	SCORE	RUNNER-UP	THIRD PLACE	FOURTH PLACE	WINNING COACH
2005	North Carolina	75–70	Illinois	* Michigan State	* Louisville	Roy Williams
2004	UConn	82–73	Georgia Tech	* Duke	* Oklahoma State	Jim Calhoun
2003	Syracuse	81–78	Kansas	* Texas	* Marquette	Jim Boeheim
2002	Maryland	64–52	Indiana	* Kansas	* Oklahoma	Gary Williams
2001	Duke	82–72	Arizona	* Maryland	* Michigan St.	Mike Krzyzewski
2000	Michigan St.	89–76	Florida	* Wisconsin	* North Carolina	Tom Izzo
1999	UConn	77–74	Duke	* Michigan St.	* Ohio St.	Jim Calhoun
1998	Kentucky	78–69	Utah	* Stanford	* North Carolina	Tubby Smith
1997	Arizona	84–79 (OT)	Kentucky	* Minnesota	* North Carolina	Lute Olson
1996	Kentucky	76–67	Syracuse	‡ Vacated	* Mississippi St.	Rick Pitino
1995	UCLA	89–78	Arkansas	* North Carolina	* Oklahoma St.	Jim Harrick
1994	Arkansas	76–72	Duke	* Arizona	* Florida	Nolan Richardson
1993	North Carolina	77–71	‡Vacated	* Kansas	* Kentucky	Dean Smith
1992	Duke	71–51	‡Vacated	* Cincinnati	* Indiana	Mike Krzyzewski
1991	Duke	72–65	Kansas	* UNLV	* North Carolina	Mike Krzyzewski
1990	UNLV	103–73	Duke	* Arkansas	* Georgia Tech	Jerry Tarkanian
1989	Michigan	80–79 (OT)	Seton Hall	* Duke	* Illinois	Steve Fisher
1988	Kansas	83–79	Oklahoma	* Arizona	* Duke	Larry Brown
1987	Indiana	74–73	Syracuse	* UNLV	* Providence	Bobby Knight
1986	Louisville	72–69	Duke	* Kansas	* Louisiana St	Denny Crum
1985	Villanova	66–64	Georgetown	St. John's (N.Y.)	‡ Vacated	Rollie Massimino
1984	Georgetown	84–75	Houston	* Kentucky	* Virginia	John Thompson
1983	North Carolina St.	54–52	Houston	* Georgia	* Louisville	Jim Valvano
1982	North Carolina	63–62	Georgetown	* Houston	* Louisville	Dean Smith
1981	Indiana	63–50	North Carolina	Virginia	Louisiana St.	Bobby Knight
1980	Louisville	59–54	‡Vacated	Purdue	Iowa	Denny Crum
1979	Michigan St	75–64	Indiana St	DePaul	Penn	Jud Heathcote
1978	Kentucky	94–88	Duke	Arkansas	Notre Dame	Joe Hall
1977	Marquette	67–59	North Carolina	UNLV	NC Charlotte	Al McGuire
1976	Indiana	86–68	Michigan	UCLA	Rutgers	Bobby Knight
1975	UCLA	92–85	Kentucky	Louisville	Syracuse	John Wooden
1974	North Carolina St.	76–64	Marquette	UCLA	Kansas	Norm Sloan
1973	UCLA	87–66	Memphis St.	Indiana	Providence	John Wooden
1972	UCLA	81–76	Florida St.	North Carolina	Louisville	John Wooden
1971	UCLA	68–62	‡Vacated	‡Vacated	Kansas	John Wooden
1970	UCLA	80–69	Jacksonville	New Mexico St.	St. Bonaventure	John Wooden
1969	UCLA	92–72	Purdue	Drake	North Carolina	John Wooden
1968	UCLA	78–55	North Carolina	Ohio St.	Houston	John Wooden
1967	UCLA	79–64	Dayton	Houston	North Carolina	John Wooden
1966	Texas Western	72–65	Kentucky	Duke	Utah	Don Haskins
1965	UCLA	91–80	Michigan	Princeton	Wichita St.	John Wooden
1964	UCLA	98–83	Duke	Michigan	Kansas St.	John Wooden
1963	Loyola (Illinois)	60–58 (OT)	Cincinnati	Duke	Oregon St.	George Ireland
1962	Cincinnati	71–59	Ohio St.	Wake Forest	UCLA	Edwin Jucker
1961	Cincinnati	70–65 (OT)	Ohio St.	‡Vacated	Utah	Edwin Jucker
1960	Ohio St.	75–55	California	Cincinnati	NYU	Fred Taylor
1959	California	71–70	West Virginia	Cincinnati	Louisville	Pete Newell
1958	Kentucky	84–72	Seattle	Temple	Kansas St.	Adolph Rupp
1957	North Carolina	54–53 (3 OT)	Kansas	San Francisco	Michigan St.	Frank McGuire
1956	San Francisco	83–71	Iowa	Temple	SMU	Phil Woolpert
1955	San Francisco	77–63	La Salle	Colorado	Iowa	Phil Woolpert
1954	La Salle	92–76	Bradley	Penn St.	USC	Kenneth Loeffler
1953	Indiana	69–68	Kansas	Washington	Louisiana St.	Branch McCracken
1952	Kansas	80–63	St. John's (N.Y.)	Illinois	Santa Clara	Forrest Allen
1951	Kentucky	68–58	Kansas St.	Illinois	Oklahoma St.	Adolph Rupp
1950	CCNY	71–68	Bradley	North Carolina St.	Baylor	Nat Holman
1949	Kentucky	46–36	Oklahoma St.	Illinois	Oregon St.	Adolph Rupp
1948	Kentucky	58–42	Baylor	Holy Cross	Kansas St.	Adolph Rupp
1947	Holy Cross	58–47	Oklahoma	Texas	CCNY	Alvin Julian
1946	Oklahoma A&M	43–40	North Carolina	Ohio St.	California	Hank Iba
1945	Oklahoma A&M	49–45	NYU	* Arkansas	* Ohio St.	Hank Iba
1944	Utah	42–40 (OT)	Dartmouth	* Iowa St.	* Ohio St.	Vadal Peterson
1943	Wyoming	46–34	Georgetown	* Texas	* DePaul	Everett Shelton
1942	Stanford	53–38	Dartmouth	* Colorado	* Kentucky	Everett Dean
1941	Wisconsin	39–34	Washington St.	* Pittsburgh	* Arkansas	Harold Foster
1940	Indiana	60–42	Kansas	* Duquesne	* USC	Branch McCracken
1939	Oregon	46–33	Ohio St.	* Oklahoma	* Villanova	Howard Hobson

* Tied for third place. ‡Student-athletes representing St. Joseph's (Pa.) in 1961, Villanova in 1971, Western Kentucky in 1971, UCLA in 1980, Memphis State in 1985, Michigan in 1992 and 1993, and Massachusetts in 1996 were declared ineligible subsequent to the tournament. Under NCAA rules, the teams' and ineligible student-athletes' records were deleted, and the teams' places in the standings were vacated.

TODAY'S STARS

■ **Dee Brown, guard,** b. August 17, 1984, Jackson, Mississippi. Nicknamed the "One Man Fast Break," Brown was college basketball's speediest player and one of its best all-around talents in 2004-05. He averaged 13.3 points, 4.5 assists, and 1.8 steals per game for Illinois in 2004-05 and led the team to its best season in school history (37–2 and national championship runner-up). Brown earned consensus first-team All-America honors in 2004-05 and was named the Big Ten's Player of the Year and Defensive Player of the Year.

Dee Brown led Illinois to a 37–2 record in 2004-05, the best season in school history.

JOHN BIEVER/SPORTS ILLUSTRATED

■ **Daniel Gibson, guard,** b. February 27, 1986, Houston, Texas. Gibson is likely to challenge former Texas point guard T.J. Ford as the best player in school history. He has the same speed and eye-catching moves. In 2004-05, Gibson was named Big 12 Freshman of the Year and a first-team Freshman All-America. He led the team in minutes (32.8 per game), points (14.2), steals (1.77), and assists (3.9). Gibson was the only Longhorn to start all 31 games. He led Texas to a 20–11 record and an NCAA tournament appearance.

■ **Rudy Gay, forward,** b. August 17, 1986, Baltimore, Maryland. One of college basketball's most athletic players, Gay will be at the head of the Huskies' pack as Connecticut looks to regain its championship form in 2005-06. As a freshman in 2004-05, the former high school All-America was named co-Big East Rookie of the Year and earned national Freshman of the Year honors from *The Sporting News*. He averaged 11.8 points and 5.4 rebounds per game while shooting 46.7 percent from 3-point range.

NCAA FINAL FOUR MOST OUTSTANDING PLAYERS

YEAR	WINNER, SCHOOL	YEAR	WINNER, SCHOOL	YEAR	WINNER, SCHOOL
2005	Sean May, North Carolina	1981	Isiah Thomas, Indiana	1958	* Elgin Baylor, Seattle
2004	Emeka Okafor, UConn	1980	Darrell Griffith, Louisville	1957	* Wilt Chamberlain, Kansas
2003	Carmelo Anthony, Syracuse	1979	Earvin Johnson, Michigan St.	1956	* Hal Lear, Temple
2002	Juan Dixon, Maryland	1978	Jack Givens, Kentucky	1955	Bill Russell, San Francisco
2001	Shane Battier, Duke	1977	Butch Lee, Marquette	1954	Tom Gola, La Salle
2000	Mateen Cleaves, Michigan St.	1976	Kent Benson, Indiana	1953	* B.H. Born, Kansas
1999	Richard Hamilton, UConn	1975	Richard Washington, UCLA	1952	Clyde Lovellette, Kansas
1998	Jeff Sheppard, Kentucky	1974	David Thompson, North Carolina St.	1951	Bill Spivey, Kentucky
1997	Miles Simon, Arizona	1973	Bill Walton, UCLA	1950	Irwin Dambrot, CCNY
1996	Tony Delk, Kentucky	1972	Bill Walton, UCLA	1949	Alex Groza, Kentucky
1995	Ed O'Bannon, UCLA	1971	*† Howard Porter, Villanova	1948	Alex Groza, Kentucky
1994	Corliss Williamson, Arkansas	1970	Sidney Wicks, UCLA	1947	George Kaftan, Holy Cross
1993	Donald Williams, North Carolina	1969	** Lew Alcindor, UCLA	1946	Bob Kurland, Oklahoma A&M
1992	Bobby Hurley, Duke	1968	** Lew Alcindor, UCLA	1945	Bob Kurland, Oklahoma A&M
1991	Christian Laettner, Duke	1967	** Lew Alcindor, UCLA	1944	Arnie Ferrin, Utah
1990	Anderson Hunt, UNLV	1966	* Jerry Chambers, Utah	1943	Ken Sailors, Wyoming
1989	Glen Rice, Michigan	1965	* Bill Bradley, Princeton	1942	Howard Dallmar, Stanford
1988	Danny Manning, Kansas	1964	Walt Hazzard, UCLA	1941	John Kotz, Wisconsin
1987	Keith Smart, Indiana	1963	Art Heyman, Duke	1940	Marv Huffman, Indiana
1986	Pervis Ellison, Louisville	1962	Paul Hogue, Cincinnati	1939	* Jimmy Hull, Ohio St.
1985	Ed Pinckney, Villanova	1961	* Jerry Lucas, Ohio St.		
1984	Patrick Ewing, Georgetown	1960	Jerry Lucas, Ohio St.		
1983	* Akeem Olajuwon, Houston	1959	* Jerry West, West Virginia		
1982	James Worthy, North Carolina				

* Not a member of the championship-winning team.
† Record later vacated.
** Now known as Kareem Abdul-Jabbar.

■ ***Fast Fact:*** For the first time in NCAA tournament history, three of the four regional final games went into overtime.

NATIONAL INVITATION TOURNAMENT (NIT) CHAMPIONSHIP RESULTS

YEAR	WINNER	SCORE	RUNNER-UP	YEAR	WINNER	SCORE	RUNNER-UP
2005	South Carolina	60–57	St. Joseph's	1971	North Carolina	84–66	Georgia Tech
2004	Michigan	62–55	Rutgers	1970	Marquette	65–53	St. John's (N.Y.)
2003	St. John's (N.Y.)	70–67	Georgetown	1969	Temple	89–76	Boston College
2002	Memphis	72–62	South Carolina	1968	Dayton	61–48	Kansas
2001	Tulsa	79–60	Alabama	1967	Southern Illinois	71–56	Marquette
2000	Wake Forest	71–61	Notre Dame	1966	BYU	97–84	NYU
1999	California	61–60	Clemson	1965	St. John's (N.Y.)	55–51	Villanova
1998	Minnesota	79–72	Penn St.	1964	Bradley	86–54	New Mexico
1997	Michigan	82–73	Florida St.	1963	Providence	81–66	Canisius
1996	Nebraska	60–56	St. Joseph's	1962	Dayton	73–67	St. John's (N.Y.)
1995	Virginia Tech	65–64 (OT)	Marquette	1961	Providence	62–59	St. Louis
1994	Villanova	80–73	Vanderbilt	1960	Bradley	88–72	Providence
1993	Minnesota	62–61	Georgetown	1959	St. John's (N.Y.)	76–71 (OT)	Bradley
1992	Virginia	81–76	Notre Dame	1958	Xavier	78–74 (OT)	Dayton
1991	Stanford	78–72	Oklahoma	1957	Bradley	84–83	Memphis St.
1990	Vanderbilt	74–72	St. Louis	1956	Louisville	93–80	Dayton
1989	St. John's (N.Y.)	73–65	St. Louis	1955	Duquesne	70–58	Dayton
1988	Connecticut	72–67	Ohio St.	1954	Holy Cross	71–62	Duquesne
1987	Southern Miss.	84–80	La Salle	1953	Seton Hall	58–46	St. John's (N.Y.)
1986	Ohio St.	73–63	Wyoming	1952	La Salle	75–64	Dayton
1985	UCLA	65–62	Indiana	1951	BYU	62–43	Dayton
1984	Michigan	83–63	Notre Dame	1950	CCNY	69–61	Bradley
1983	Fresno State	69–60	DePaul	1949	San Francisco	48–47	Loyola (Illinois)
1982	Bradley	67–58	Purdue	1948	St. Louis	65–52	NYU
1981	Tulsa	86–84 (OT)	Syracuse	1947	Utah	49–45	Kentucky
1980	Virginia	58–55	Minnesota	1946	Kentucky	46–45	Rhode Island
1979	Indiana	53–52	Purdue	1945	DePaul	71–54	Bowling Green
1978	Texas	101–93	North Carolina St.	1944	St. John's (N.Y.)	47–39	DePaul
1977	St. Bonaventure	94–91	Houston	1943	St. John's (N.Y.)	48–27	Toledo
1976	Kentucky	71–67	North Carolina-Charlotte	1942	West Virginia	47–45	Western Kentucky
1975	Princeton	80–69	Providence	1941	Long Island Univ.	56–42	Ohio University
1974	Purdue	87–81	Utah	1940	Colorado	51–40	Duquesne
1973	Virginia Tech	92–91 (OT)	Notre Dame	1939	Long Island Univ.	44–32	Loyola (Illinois)
1972	Maryland	100–69	Niagara	1938	Temple	60–36	Colorado

DID YOU KNOW?

North Carolina is the only school to reach a Final Four in each of the past seven decades and the only school to win a national championship in each of the last three decades.

NCAA MEN'S DIVISION I SINGLE-SEASON LEADERS

POINTS

PLAYER	YEAR	GP	FG	3FG	FT	PTS
Pete Maravich, LSU	1970	31	522	—	337	1,381
Elvin Hayes, Houston	1968	33	519	—	176	1,214
Frank Selvy, Furman	1954	29	427	—	355	1,209
Pete Maravich, LSU	1969	26	433	—	282	1,148
Pete Maravich, LSU	1968	26	432	—	274	1,138
Bo Kimble, Loyola Marymount	1990	32	404	92	231	1,131
Hersey Hawkins, Bradley	1988	31	377	87	284	1,125
Austin Carr, Notre Dame	1970	29	444	—	218	1,106
Austin Carr, Notre Dame	1971	29	430	—	241	1,101
Otis Birdsong, Houston	1977	36	452	—	186	1,090

Austin Carr, Notre Dame

SCORING AVERAGE

PLAYER	YEAR	GP	FG	FT	PTS	AVG
Pete Maravich, LSU	1970	31	522	337	1,381	44.5
Pete Maravich, LSU	1969	26	433	282	1,148	44.2
Pete Maravich, LSU	1968	26	432	274	1,138	43.8
Frank Selvy, Furman	1954	29	427	355	1,209	41.7
Johnny Neumann, Mississippi	1971	23	366	191	923	40.1

KEY GP=games played; FG=field goals; 3FG=3-point field goals; FT=free throws; PTS=points; AVG=average

HEINZ KLUETMEIER/SPORTS ILLUSTRATED

NCAA MEN'S DIVISION I SINGLE-SEASON LEADERS (cont.)

SCORING AVERAGE (CONT.)

PLAYER	YEAR	GP	FG	FT	PTS	AVG
Freeman Williams, Portland State	1977	26	417	176	1,010	38.8
Billy McGill, Utah	1962	26	394	221	1,009	38.8
Calvin Murphy, Niagara	1968	24	337	242	916	38.2
Austin Carr, Notre Dame	1970	29	444	218	1,106	38.1
Austin Carr, Notre Dame	1971	29	430	241	1,101	38.0

REBOUND AVERAGE (BEFORE 1973)

PLAYER	YEAR	GP	REB	AVG
Charlie Slack, Marshall	1955	21	538	25.6
Leroy Wright, Pacific	1959	26	652	25.1
Art Quimby, UConn	1955	25	611	24.4
Charlie Slack, Marshall	1956	22	520	23.6
Ed Conlin, Fordham	1953	26	612	23.5

REBOUND AVERAGE (SINCE 1973*)

PLAYER	YEAR	GP	REB	AVG
Kermit Washington, American	1973	25	511	20.4
Marvin Barnes, Providence	1973	30	571	19.0
Marvin Barnes, Providence	1974	32	597	18.7
Pete Padgett, Nevada	1973	26	462	17.8
Jim Bradley, Northern Illinois	1973	24	426	17.8

*Freshmen became eligible for varsity play before the 1972-73 season.

ASSISTS

PLAYER	YEAR	GP	A
Mark Wade, UNLV	1987	38	406
Avery Johnson, Southern University	1988	30	399
Anthony Manuel, Bradley	1988	31	373
Avery Johnson, Southern University	1987	31	333
Mark Jackson, St. John's (N.Y.)	1986	32	328

FIELD GOAL PERCENTAGE

PLAYER	YEAR	FGM	FGA	PCT
Steve Johnson, Oregon State	1981	235	315	74.6
Dwayne Davis, Florida	1989	179	248	72.2
Keith Walker, Utica	1985	154	216	71.3
Steve Johnson, Oregon State	1980	211	297	71.0
Adam Mark, Belmont	2002	150	212	70.8

J.J. Redick, Duke

FREE THROW PERCENTAGE

PLAYER	YEAR	FTM	FTA	PCT
Blake Ahearn, Southwest Missouri State	2004	117	120	97.5
Craig Collins, Penn State	1985	94	98	95.9
J.J. Redick, Duke	2004	143	150	95.3
Steve Drabyn, Belmont	2003	78	82	95.1
Rod Foster, UCLA	1982	95	100	95.0

3-POINT FIELD GOAL PERCENTAGE

PLAYER	YEAR	3FGM	3FGA	PCT
Glenn Tropf, Holy Cross	1988	52	82	63.4
Sean Wightman, Western Michigan	1992	48	76	63.2
Keith Jennings, East Tennessee State	1991	84	142	59.2
Dave Calloway, Monmouth	1989	48	82	58.5
Steve Kerr, Arizona	1988	114	199	57.3

BOB ROSATO/SPORTS ILLUSTRATED

KEY GP=games played; FG=field goals; FT=free throws; PTS=points; AVG=average; REB=rebounds; A=assists; FGM=field goals made; FGA=field goals attempted; PCT=percentage; FTM=free throws made; FTA=free throws attempted; 3FGM=3-point field goals made; 3FGA=3-point field goals attempted

■ **Fast Fact:** Andrew Bogut, Utah's sophomore center, became the first Australian to win the National Player of the Year Award.

STEALS

PLAYER	YEAR	GP	STL
Desmond Cambridge, Alabama A&M	2002	29	160
Mookie Blaylock, Oklahoma	1988	39	150
Aldwin Ware, Florida A&M	1988	29	142
Darron Brittman, Chicago State	1986	28	139
John Linehan, Providence	2002	31	139

John Linehan, Providence

BLOCKS

PLAYER	YEAR	GP	BLK
David Robinson, Navy	1986	35	207
Adonal Foyle, Colgate	1997	28	180
Keith Closs, Central Connecticut State	1996	28	178
Shawn Bradley, BYU	1991	34	177
Wojciech Myrda, LA–Monroe	2002	32	172

BOB BREIDENBACH/PROVIDENCE JOURNAL/AP

TRIVIA CHALLENGE

How many different schools has Louisville head coach Rick Pitino directed to the Final Four?

An NCAA-record three (Providence in 1987, Kentucky in 1993, 1996, and 1997, and Louisville in 2005).

KEY GP=games played; STL=steals, BLK=blocks

LEGENDS

David Robinson set two NCAA records at Navy.

MANNY MILLAN/SPORTS ILLUSTRATED

■ **David Robinson, center,** b. August 6, 1965, Key West, Florida. Robinson, nicknamed "The Admiral," was a two-time All-America at Navy. He was the first player in Division I history to score 2,500 points, grab 1,300 rebounds, and shoot 60 percent from the field. Robinson set NCAA records for most blocked shots in a game (14) and a season (207). In 1987, he became the first Midshipman to be the Number 1 pick in the NBA Draft. Robinson was a 10-time NBA All-Star with the San Antonio Spurs and the 1994-95 NBA MVP.

■ **Magic Johnson, guard,** b. August 14, 1959, Lansing, Michigan. Earvin "Magic" Johnson was a two-time first-team All-Big Ten selection and a two-time All-America at Michigan State (1978 and 1979). A 6' 9" point guard, Johnson did everything for the Spartans — scoring, rebounding, and passing. He capped his career by winning the Most Outstanding Player Award at the 1979 Final Four. He scored 24 points in the championship game to lead Michigan State to its first national title, 75–64, over Larry Bird and Indiana State. Johnson later won three NBA MVP Awards and led the Los Angeles Lakers to five NBA titles.

■ **James Worthy, forward,** b. February 27, 1961, Gastonia, North Carolina. "Big Game James" earned the nickname for his outstanding play with the North Carolina Tar Heels. Worthy led UNC to the national title in 1982, scoring 28 points in the Tar Heels' 63–62 win over Georgetown in the championship game. Worthy also earned MVP honors that season at the ACC Tournament and the NCAA East Regional. He was named Most Outstanding Player at the Final Four. He averaged 14.5 points and 7.4 rebounds in his career at Carolina, which ended after his junior season, when the Los Angeles Lakers chose him as the Number 1 pick in the 1982 NBA Draft. In 1996, Worthy was named one of the 50 Greatest Players in NBA history.

BASKETBALL WOMEN'S COLLEGE

The Baylor Lady Bears provided a breath of fresh air to women's college basketball in 2004-05. They proved that a team other than Tennessee or Connecticut could win a national championship.

But the boost the Lady Bears gave *their* school was even more important. Just two years after a scandal rocked the men's basketball program (a player was charged with shooting and killing a teammate, and the coach resigned), Baylor women's head coach Kim Mulkey-Robertson and her team gave the university something to be proud of.

During their march to their first-ever women's championship, the Lady Bears beat three Number 1 seeds. Baylor defeated North Carolina, the top seed in the Tempe Region; ousted the tournament's Number 1 overall seed, Louisiana State, in the national semifinal; and then toppled Michigan State, the Number 1 seed in the Kansas City Region, for the national championship.

Baylor became just the third team other than Connecticut or Tennessee to win the national championship since 1995. The UConn Huskies, who had won three straight titles, saw their 20-game NCAA tournament winning streak come to an end with a 76–59 loss to Stanford in the Sweet 16. Stanford had ended the season ranked

Number 1 in the country but was bounced from the NCAAs by Michigan State in the regional finals.

Stanford wasn't the only team to be upset by Michigan State. Tennessee had had a memorable season. Head coach Pat Summitt surpassed Dean Smith (North Carolina men's coach, 1961-97) with her 880th career win, a new all-time record. The milestone win came in the second round of the NCAA tournament, a 75–54 victory over Purdue.

The Lady Vols then advanced to their 16th — and fourth straight — Final Four. But in the national semifinals, Tennessee fell to Michigan State, 68–64. The Spartans rallied from a 16-point second-half deficit, which tied the largest comeback in Final Four history.

In the championship game, the Spartans ran into a team that was also familiar with comebacks. The Lady Bears had bounced back from a 15-point deficit to defeat LSU in their own Final Four victory. They

Junior Sophia Young led Baylor to its first NCAA title in 2005.

BILL FRAKES/SPORTS ILLUSTRATED

completed their school's remarkable turnaround with one final win. Tournament MVP Sophia Young had 26 points, 9 rebounds, and 4 assists in the title game, as Baylor cruised to an 84–62 triumph.

TRIVIA CHALLENGE

Since The Associated Press started naming women's All-America teams in 1994-95, Connecticut has had at least one All-America player every season but one. Which season was it?

2004-05

DID YOU KNOW?

Both of 2005's national championship game participants were recently among the worst teams in college basketball. Baylor went 7–20 in 1999-2000, and Michigan State was 10–18 in 2000-01.

NCAA WOMEN'S DIVISION I CHAMPIONSHIP BOX SCORE

BAYLOR BEARS: 84

PLAYER	MIN	FGM-A	FTM-A	REB OFF	REB TOT	A	PF	PTS
Sophia Young	36	10-10	6-0	4	0	4	1	20
Abiola Wabara	10	0-1	0-0	0	2	1	1	0
Steffanie Blackmon	35	8-19	6-8	2	7	1	2	22
Chelsea Whitaker	32	0-2	0-1	3	5	6	1	0
Chameka Scott	18	3-3	0-0	1	4	3	0	7
Monique Jones	1	0-0	0-0	0	0	0	0	0
Chisa Ononiwu	1	0-0	0-0	0	0	0	0	0
Chanelle Fox	2	0-0	0-0	0	2	0	0	0
Latoya Wyatt	20	3-5	2-4	1	6	0	4	8
Victoria Jones	1	0-0	0-0	0	0	0	0	0
Angela Tisdale	8	0-2	2-2	0	0	1	2	2
Jordan Davis	1	0-0	0-0	0	0	0	0	0
Melanie Hamerly	2	0-0	0-0	0	0	0	0	0
Emily Niemann	33	6-10	2-2	1	3	1	1	19
TOTALS		**30-61**	**18-26**	**12**	**38**	**17**	**12**	**84**
		(49.2%)	**(69.2%)**					

MICHIGAN STATE SPARTANS: 62

PLAYER	MIN	FGM-A	FTM-A	REB OFF	REB TOT	A	PF	PTS
Liz Shimek	37	3-6	0-0	0	5	2	3	7
Kelli Roehrig	30	3-8	2-2	0	5	0	3	8
Kristin Haynie	37	7-14	3-5	0	1	5	4	17
Lindsay Bowen	37	5-14	8-10	1	3	1	0	20
Victoria Lucas-Perry	25	3-6	0-0	0	2	0	3	7
Rene Haynes	19	0-3	1-2	0	2	1	2	1
Maggie Dwyer	1	0-0	0-0	1	1	0	0	0
Melanie Small	1	0-0	0-0	0	0	0	0	0
Katrina Grantham	3	0-0	0-0	0	0	0	2	0
Myisha Bannister	1	0-0	0-0	0	0	0	0	0
Laura Hall	9	1-2	0-0	0	1	0	2	2
TOTALS		**22-53**	**14-19**	**2**	**20**	**9**	**19**	**62**
		(41.5%)	**(73.7%)**					

KEY — MIN=minutes played; FGM-A=field goals made-attempted; FTM-A=free throws made-attempted; REB=rebounds; OFF=offensive; TOT=total; A=assists; PF=personal fouls; PTS=points

BILL FRAKES/SPORTS ILLUSTRATED

Michigan State's Lindsay Bowen scored a team-high 20 points in the title game.

USA TODAY/ESPN TOP 25 FINAL POLL

RANK	TEAM	RECORD	POINTS
1.	Baylor	28–3	1,000
2.	Michigan State	29–3	950
3.	LSU	28–2	913
4.	Tennessee	27–4	891
5.	Stanford	29–2	813
6.	North Carolina	28–3	756
7.	Rutgers	26–6	747
8.	Duke	29–4	724
9.	Ohio State	29–4	656
10.	Connecticut	24–7	610
11.	Minnesota	25–7	589
12.	Texas Tech	23–7	527
13.	Georgia	23–9	444
14.	Vanderbilt	23–7	433
15.	Notre Dame	27–5	393
16.	Arizona State	23–8	391
17.	Texas	22–8	379
18.	Temple	28–3	352
19.	Kansas State	24–7	312
20.	DePaul	26–4	242
21.	Liberty	25–6	214
22.	USC	20–10	91
23.	Boston College	20–9	84
24.	Maryland	22–9	82
25.	Iowa State	23–7	79

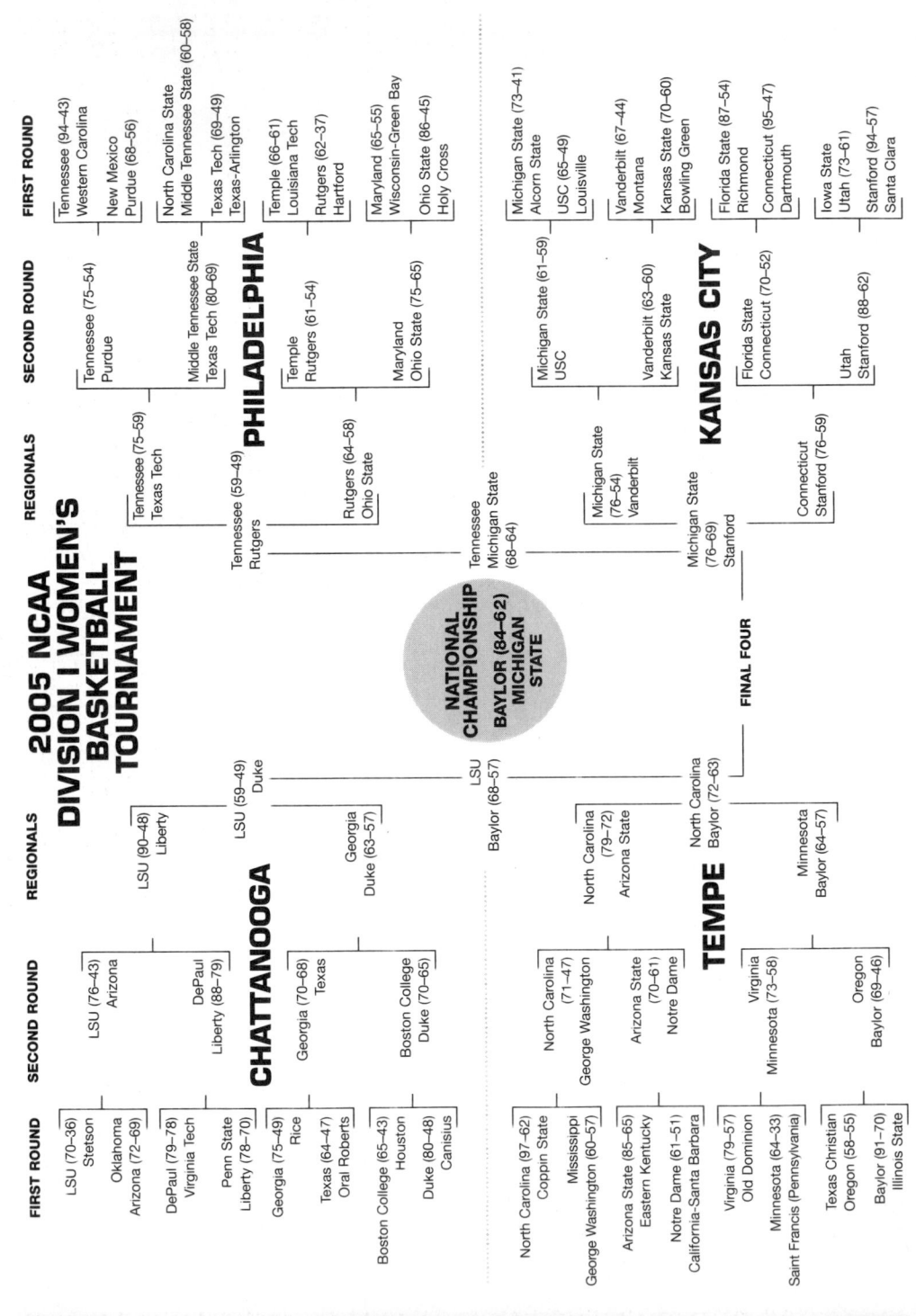

2005 NCAA DIVISION I WOMEN'S BASKETBALL TOURNAMENT

NATIONAL CHAMPIONSHIP
BAYLOR (84–62) MICHIGAN STATE

FIRST ROUND

Tennessee (94–43)
Western Carolina
New Mexico
Purdue (68–56)
North Carolina State
Middle Tennessee State (60–58)
Texas Tech (69–49)
Texas-Arlington
Temple (66–61)
Louisiana Tech
Rutgers (62–37)
Hartford
Maryland (65–55)
Wisconsin–Green Bay
Ohio State (86–45)
Holy Cross

Michigan State (73–41)
Alcorn State
USC (65–49)
Louisville
Vanderbilt (67–44)
Montana
Kansas State (70–60)
Bowling Green
Florida State (87–54)
Richmond
Connecticut (95–47)
Dartmouth
Iowa State
Utah (73–61)
Stanford (94–57)
Santa Clara

SECOND ROUND

Tennessee (75–54)
Purdue
Middle Tennessee State
Texas Tech (80–69)
Temple
Rutgers (61–54)
Maryland
Ohio State (75–65)

Michigan State (61–59)
USC
Vanderbilt (63–60)
Kansas State
Florida State
Connecticut (70–52)
Utah
Stanford (88–62)

REGIONALS — **PHILADELPHIA**

Tennessee (75–59)
Texas Tech
Rutgers (64–58)
Ohio State
Tennessee (59–49)
Rutgers

REGIONALS — **KANSAS CITY**

Michigan State (76–54)
Vanderbilt
Connecticut
Stanford (76–59)
Michigan State (76–69)
Stanford

Tennessee
Michigan State (68–64)

FINAL FOUR

LSU
Baylor (68–57)

REGIONALS — **CHATTANOOGA**

LSU (90–48)
Liberty
DePaul
Liberty (88–79)
Georgia (70–68)
Texas
Boston College
Duke (70–65)
LSU (59–49)
Duke
Georgia
Duke (63–57)

REGIONALS — **TEMPE**

North Carolina (79–72)
Arizona State
Virginia
Minnesota (64–67)
North Carolina
Baylor (72–63)
Minnesota
Baylor (64–67)

SECOND ROUND

LSU (76–43)
Arizona
DePaul (79–78)
Virginia Tech
Georgia (75–49)
Rice
Texas (64–47)
Oral Roberts
Boston College (65–43)
Houston
Duke (80–48)
Canisius

North Carolina (71–47)
George Washington
Arizona State (70–61)
Notre Dame
Virginia (79–57)
Old Dominion
Minnesota (73–58)
Saint Francis (Pennsylvania)
Texas Christian
Oregon (58–55)
Baylor (91–70)
Illinois State

FIRST ROUND

LSU (70–36)
Stetson
Oklahoma
Arizona (72–69)
DePaul (79–78)
Virginia Tech
Penn State
Liberty (78–70)
Georgia (75–49)
Rice
Texas (64–47)
Oral Roberts
Boston College (65–43)
Houston
Duke (80–48)
Canisius

North Carolina (97–62)
Coppin State
Mississippi
George Washington (60–57)
Arizona State (85–65)
Eastern Kentucky
Notre Dame (61–51)
California–Santa Barbara
Virginia (79–57)
Old Dominion
Minnesota (64–33)
Saint Francis (Pennsylvania)
Texas Christian
Oregon (58–55)
Baylor (91–70)
Illinois State

NCAA WOMEN'S DIVISION I INDIVIDUAL LEADERS

SCORING

PLAYER	CLASS	GP	FG	3FG	FT	PTS	AVG
Tan White, Mississippi State	Sr.	29	241	61	138	681	23.5
Emily Faurholt, Idaho	Jr.	30	241	46	169	697	23.2
Tori Talbert, Texas State	Sr.	25	208	0	144	560	22.4
Tamara James, Miami (Florida)	Jr.	29	242	39	124	647	22.3
Beth Swink, St. Francis (Pennsylvania)	Sr.	31	255	1	177	688	22.2
Rolanda Monroe, Southern	Jr.	30	219	67	135	640	21.3
Kendra Wecker, Kansas State	Sr.	29	240	40	89	609	21.0
Reka Cserny, Harvard	Sr.	27	192	26	154	564	20.9
Tara Boothe, Xavier	Jr.	32	254	30	121	659	20.6
Seimone Augustus, LSU	Jr.	36	303	5	113	724	20.1
Sugiery Monsac, Robert Morris	Jr.	30	218	15	151	602	20.1

KEY GP—games played; FG=field goals; 3FG=3-point field goals; FT=free throws; PTS=points; AVG=average

LEGENDS

Cindy Blodgett led Maine to the NCAA tournament four times from 1994 to 1998.

■ **Cindy Blodgett, guard,** b. December 23, 1975, Clinton, Maine. Blodgett averaged 25.5 points per game during her four seasons at Maine (1994-98), set 20 school records, and twice led the country in scoring. She led Maine to the America East Conference title four times and to the NCAA tournament four times, the first NCAA appearances in school history. She was named All-America and Conference Player of the Year as a senior in 1997-98 and had her number retired after graduation. Blodgett played four seasons in the WNBA with the Cleveland Rockers and Sacramento Monarchs.

■ **Jennifer Rizzotti, guard,** b. May 15, 1974, New Fairfield, Connecticut. Rizzotti was the floor general who ignited Connecticut's dynasty. She was named an All-America as a junior in 1994-95 after leading the Huskies to an undefeated season and the national championship. She was named The Associated Press National Player of the Year in 1995-96 and left UConn as the school's all-time leader in assists (637) and steals (349). Rizzotti played five seasons in the WNBA for the Cleveland Rockers and Houston Comets. In 1999, she became the youngest Division I head coach in the country (age 25) when she took over the women's program at the University of Hartford.

■ **Semeka Randall, guard,** b. February 7, 1979, Cleveland, Ohio. Part of the "Meek" trio, along with Tennessee teammates Chamique Holdsclaw and Tamika Catchings, Randall helped lead the Lady Vols to the 1997-98 national championship and a perfect 39–0 record. A two-time first-team All-Southeastern Conference selection, she also earned first-team All-America honors in 1999 and 2000 and was a member of the All-SEC Academic team. Randall played for four seasons in the WNBA. She retired in 2004 and is now an assistant coach for the Michigan State women's team.

NCAA WOMEN'S DIVISION I INDIVIDUAL LEADERS (cont.)

R. DAVID DUNCAN III/THE NEWS & ADVANCE/AP

FIELD GOAL PERCENTAGE

PLAYER	CLASS	GP	FGM	FGA	PCT
Katie Feenstra, Liberty	Sr.	32	230	343	67.1
Amber Jackson, San Jose State	Fr.	30	205	311	65.9
Ashley Earley, Vanderbilt	Sr.	32	240	375	64.0
LaToya Davis, Texas Tech	Jr.	31	157	256	61.3
Becky O'Neil, Weber State	So.	29	145	237	61.2
Crystal Kelly, Western Kentucky	Fr.	30	214	350	61.1
Brooke Smith, Stanford	So.	35	199	326	61.0
Tiffany Mor, Wisconsin-Green Bay	Sr.	31	203	333	61.0
Erlana Larkins, North Carolina	Fr.	34	181	297	60.9
Khara Smith, DePaul	Jr.	31	232	386	60.1

Note: Minimum 5 field goals made per game.

Katie Feenstra, Liberty

FREE THROW PERCENTAGE

PLAYER	CLASS	GP	FTM	FTA	PCT
Kristin Iwanaga, California	Sr.	29	85	91	93.4
Nefertiti Walker, Stetson	Jr.	31	80	87	92.0
Melissa Yeagley, Iowa	Jr.	26	83	92	90.2
Megan Duffy, Notre Dame	Jr.	33	137	153	89.5
Tynisha Alexander, Tennessee Tech	Sr.	29	109	122	89.3
Katie Gearlds, Purdue	So.	30	81	91	89.0
Kate Endress, Ball State	Sr.	29	86	97	88.7
Nicole Louden, Auburn	Sr.	29	85	97	87.6
Leilani Mitchell, Idaho	So.	30	168	192	87.5
Jess Strom, Penn State	Sr.	29	129	148	87.2

Note: Minimum 2.5 free throws made per game.

REBOUNDING

PLAYER	CLASS	GP	REB	AVG
Sancho Lyttle, Houston	Sr.	30	362	12.1
Sandora Irvin, Texas Christian	Sr.	33	390	11.8
Nakeya Downing, Southeastern Louisiana	Sr.	27	318	11.8
Khara Smith, DePaul	Jr.	31	364	11.7
Sugiery Monsac, Robert Morris	Jr.	30	348	11.6
Kemie Nkele, California-Riverside	Fr.	28	321	11.5
Evena Morency, South Carolina State	Sr.	29	321	11.1
Kristy Brown, Stetson	Sr.	31	334	10.8
Jen Perugini, Youngstown State	Sr.	27	288	10.7

ASSISTS

PLAYER	CLASS	GP	A	APG
Yolanda Paige, West Virginia	Sr.	34	297	8.7
Temeka Johnson, LSU	Sr.	36	278	7.7
Erin Grant, Texas Tech	Jr.	31	218	7.0
Corrie Mizusawa, Oregon	Sr.	30	209	7.0
Anesia Smith, Maryland	Sr.	32	214	6.7
Shona Thorburn, Utah	Sr.	34	221	6.5
Carolyn Kieger, Marquette	Jr.	30	185	6.2
Erica McGlaston, San Jose State	Sr.	30	185	6.2
Shannon Matthews, Gonzaga	Sr.	32	197	6.2
Anedra Gilmore, South Florida	Sr.	31	190	6.1

KEY GP=games played; FGM=field goals made; FGA=field goals attempted; PCT=percentage; FTM=free throws made; FTA=free throws attempted; REB=rebounds; AVG=average; A=assists; APG=assists per game

DID YOU KNOW?

Baylor coach Kim Mulkey-Robertson is the first woman to play for and coach a national champion. She was the starting point guard on Louisiana Tech's 1982 title team and coached the Lady Bears to the 2005 championship.

3-POINT FIELD GOAL PERCENTAGE

PLAYER	CLASS	GP	3FGM	3FGA	PCT
K.C. Cowgill, Southwest Missouri State	Sr.	33	74	139	53.2
Ashley Cazee, Eastern Kentucky	Fr.	28	56	113	49.6
Matea Pender, Maryland-Baltimore County	Jr.	28	62	127	48.8
Jill Marano, LaSalle	Sr.	28	57	123	46.3
Kate Endress, Ball State	Sr.	29	70	152	46.1
Allie Quigley, DePaul	Fr.	31	79	173	45.7
Meg Bulger, West Virginia	So.	34	88	197	44.7
Caity Matter, Ohio State	Sr.	35	73	164	44.5
Lisa Verhoff, Indiana State	Jr.	32	68	155	43.9
Jayme Wilson, Oakland	Jr.	29	62	142	43.7

Note: Minimum 2 3-point field goals made per game

STEALS

PLAYER	CLASS	GP	STL	SPG
Kristen Boone, North Carolina-Greensboro	Fr.	28	121	4.3
Leilani Mitchell, Idaho	So.	30	118	3.9
Melanie Boeglin, Indiana State	Jr.	32	123	3.8
Stephanie Raymond, Northern Illinois	So.	28	107	3.8
Kyle DeHaven, William & Mary	So.	27	100	3.7
Lisa Willis, UCLA	Jr.	28	102	3.6
Nina Randle, Louisiana-Monroe	Sr.	30	107	3.6

BLOCKS

PLAYER	CLASS	GP	BLK	BPG
Marita Payne, Auburn	Jr.	28	111	5.0
Ashley Sparkman, Northwestern State	Sr.	27	132	4.9
Sandora Irvin, Texas Christian	Sr.	33	150	4.5
Cassie Hager, Northern Iowa	Jr.	31	135	4.4
Brooke McAfee, IUPUI	Jr.	28	105	3.8
Alison Bales, Duke	So.	36	134	3.7
Zane Teilane, Western Illinois	Jr.	20	90	3.4
Jessica Davenport, Ohio State	So.	35	116	3.3
Kemie Nkele, California-Riverside	Fr.	28	92	3.3
Cisti Greenwalt, Texas Tech	Sr.	32	105	3.3

Kristen Boone, North Carolina-Greensboro

JOHN MILLER/AP

KEY GP=games played; 3FGM=3-point field goals made; 3FGA=3-point field goals attempted; PCT=percentage; STL=steals; SPG=steals per game; BLK=blocks; BPG=blocks per game

NCAA WOMEN'S DIVISION I CHAMPIONSHIP RESULTS

YEAR	WINNER	SCORE	RUNNER-UP	WINNING COACH
2005	Baylor	84–62	Michigan State	Kim Mulkey-Robertson
2004	UConn	70–61	Tennessee	Geno Auriemma
2003	UConn	73–68	Tennessee	Geno Auriemma
2002	UConn	82–70	Oklahoma	Geno Auriemma
2001	Notre Dame	68–66	Purdue	Muffet McGraw
2000	UConn	71–52	Tennessee	Geno Auriemma
1999	Purdue	62–45	Duke	Carolyn Peck
1998	Tennessee	93–75	Louisiana Tech	Pat Summitt
1997	Tennessee	68–59	Old Dominion	Pat Summitt
1996	Tennessee	83–65	Georgia	Pat Summitt
1995	UConn	70–64	Tennessee	Geno Auriemma
1994	North Carolina	60–59	Louisiana Tech	Sylvia Hatchell
1993	Texas Tech	84–82	Ohio State	Marsha Sharp
1992	Stanford	78–62	Western Kentucky	Tara VanDerveer
1991	Tennessee	70–67 (OT)	Virginia	Pat Summitt
1990	Stanford	88–81	Auburn	Tara VanDerveer
1989	Tennessee	76–60	Auburn	Pat Summitt
1988	Louisiana Tech	56–54	Auburn	Leon Barmore
1987	Tennessee	67–44	Louisiana Tech	Pat Summitt
1986	Texas	97–81	USC	Jody Conradt
1985	Old Dominion	70–65	Georgia	Marianne Stanley
1984	USC	72–61	Tennessee	Linda Sharp
1983	USC	69–67	Louisiana Tech	Linda Sharp
1982	Louisiana Tech	76–62	Cheyney	Sonja Hogg

2004-05 TIME LINE

■ **December 4, 2004:** Illinois hands Louisiana Tech its first home loss to an unranked team since 1992. The Lady Techsters, whose head coach, Kurt Budke, resigns at season's end, drop out of The Associated Press Top 25 for the first time since 1981.

■ **December 8, 2004:** Rutgers coach C. Vivian Stringer becomes the fourth women's basketball coach to win 700 games when the Scarlet Knights defeat Princeton, 68–46.

■ **January 16, 2005:** Texas Christian senior Sandora Irvin sets a Division I record with 16 blocked shots, part of a triple double (20 points, 18 rebounds) in the Horned Frogs' 75–34 win over Alabama-Birmingham.

■ **January 30, 2005:** Three-time defending NCAA champion UConn loses to Notre Dame, 65–59. It is the Huskies' first Big East loss at home since 1993, ending a 112-game home winning streak in conference play.

■ **February 10, 2005:** All-America guard Seimone Augustus scores 25 points as Number 1 LSU defeats Tennessee, 68–58. The loss ends the Lady Vols' 42-game Southeastern Conference regular-season winning streak.

■ **March 22, 2005:** Tennessee head coach Pat Summitt sets the all-time Division I record for coaching victories when her Lady Vols beat Purdue, 75–54, in the second round of the NCAA tournament. She passes Dean Smith, who won 879 games as the men's coach at North Carolina from 1961-97.

■ **March 29, 2005:** Michigan State advances to the Final Four for the first time in school history with a 76–69 win over Number 2-seed Stanford in the Kansas City Regional final. The Spartans join Tennessee, LSU, and Baylor in Indianapolis, Indiana, to battle for the championship.

■ **April 5, 2005:** Baylor wins its first national championship in women's basketball with an 84–62 dismantling of Michigan State. The Lady Bears jump out to a 19-point first-half lead and are never seriously threatened as they win their 20th straight game.

TRIVIA CHALLENGE

This four-time All-America and two-time Naismith Player of the Year led Tennessee to three national championships. In 1998, she was the first women's college basketball player to win the Sullivan Award as the nation's best amateur athlete. She now plays for the Los Angeles Sparks of the WNBA. Who is she?

Chamique Holdsclaw

Fast Fact: Texas finished the regular season ranked Number 1 in 1984, 1985, 1986, and 1987, a record for consecutive season-ending Number 1 finishes. But the Longhorns won just one national championship (1986) in those years.

sikids.com
Visit our website for the latest stats and sports info.

NCAA WOMEN'S DIVISION I SINGLE-SEASON LEADERS

POINTS

PLAYER	YEAR	GP	PTS
Jackie Stiles, Southwest Missouri State	2001	35	1,062
Cindy Brown, Long Beach State	1987	35	974
Genia Miller, California State-Fullerton	1991	33	969
Sheryl Swoopes, Texas Tech	1993	34	955
Andrea Congreaves, Mercer	1992	28	925
Wanda Ford, Drake	1986	30	919
Chamique Holdsclaw, Tennessee	1998	39	915
Barbara Kennedy, Clemson	1982	31	908
Patricia Hoskins, Mississippi Valley State	1989	27	908
LaTaunya Pollard, Long Beach State	1983	31	907

SCORING AVERAGE

PLAYER	YEAR	GP	FG	3FG	FT	PTS	AVG
Patricia Hoskins, Mississippi Valley State	1989	27	345	13	205	908	33.6
Andrea Congreaves, Mercer	1992	28	353	77	142	926	33.0
Deborah Temple, Delta State	1984	28	373	—	127	873	31.2
Andrea Congreaves, Mercer	1993	26	302	51	150	805	31.0
Wanda Ford, Drake	1986	30	390	—	139	919	30.6
Anucha Brown, Northwestern	1985	28	341	—	173	855	30.5
LeChandra LeDay, Grambling	1988	28	334	36	146	860	30.4
Jackie Stiles, Southwest Missouri State	2001	35	365	65	207	1,002	30.3
Kim Perrot, Louisiana Lafayette	1990	28	309	95	128	841	30.0

TODAY'S STARS

Sophia Young led Baylor to a season-end Number 1 ranking in 2004-05.

BILL FRAKES/SPORTS ILLUSTRATED

■ **Sophia Young, forward,** b. December 15, 1983, St. Vincent, West Indies. Young didn't start playing basketball until she came to the United States as a high school sophomore. She blossomed into an All-America as a junior for the Baylor Lady Bears in 2004-05. Young averaged 18.4 points and 9.3 rebounds per game and was even better in the NCAA tournament. She was the Final Four's Most Outstanding Player and averaged 23 points and 8.5 rebounds per game during the tournament.

■ **Candice Wiggins, guard,** b. February 14, 1987, Baltimore, Maryland. Wiggins made quite an impression as a Stanford freshman in 2004-05. She led the team in scoring (17.5 points per game), steals (2.4), and tied for second in rebounds (5.4). Wiggins was named a Kodak All-America, the seventh Stanford player and just the ninth freshman to earn the honor. She led Stanford to a 32–3 record, the Pacific-10 championship, and an NCAA tournament appearance. The Cardinal made it to the Elite Eight before losing to eventual national champion runner-up Michigan State.

■ **Monique Currie, guard/forward,** b. February 25, 1983, Washington, D.C. Currie averaged 17.5 points, 7.1 rebounds, 3.4 assists, and 2.14 steals for Duke in 2004-05. She was named a first-team All-America and the Atlantic Coast Conference Player of the Year. She scored in double figures 35 times in 36 games as the Blue Devils went 31–5 and advanced to the Elite Eight. Currie finished in the Top 15 in the ACC in scoring (4th), rebounding (9th), assists (13th), and steals (8th).

HOCKEY

Vincent Lecavalier led Canada to the 2004 World Cup of Hockey championship.

JEFF VINNICK/AP

The sun was shining on the world of hockey in the summer of 2004. First, the Tampa Bay Lightning defeated the Calgary Flames in one of the most exciting Stanley Cup Finals in years. Two months later, the world's best players took to the ice from August 30 to September 14, 2004, to represent their countries in the World Cup of Hockey. Eight nations participated. The European pool included Finland, Sweden, Germany, and the Czech Republic. The North American pool included Canada, Russia, Slovakia, and the United States.

On September 14, Canada and Finland met in the championship game at the Air Canada Centre in Toronto. Just 52 seconds into the game, captain Mario Lemieux set up Joe Sakic to give Canada an early 1–0 lead. The teams exchanged goals until Shane Doan scored on a pass from Joe Thornton to put Canada ahead for good, 3–2. Vincent Lecavalier, a member of Tampa Bay's Stanley Cup champs, was named tournament MVP

after tallying seven points in six games. Goaltender Martin Brodeur posted a stingy 1.00 goals-against average and a perfect 5–0 record.

But that warm, sunny feeling was short-lived. The day after the championship game, the labor agreement between National Hockey League team owners and the players' union expired. The owners said they were losing too much money and wanted to limit player salaries with a salary cap. The players refused to agree to a cap. The owners locked the players out of the arenas, putting the 2004-05 season on hold.

In December, the players offered to take a 24 percent pay cut and make other concessions. However, the owners turned down

2004 WORLD CUP OF HOCKEY POOLS

EUROPE
Czech Republic
Finland
Germany
Sweden

NORTH AMERICA
Canada
Russia
Slovakia
United States

Goalie Mikka Kiprusoff and Team Finland fell to Canada, 3–2, in the final game.

Canada's netminder, Martin Brodeur, was a perfect 5–0 in the World Cup tournament.

tho offor. Two montho later, the players finally agreed to a salary cap, but the two sides were unable to decide on an amount. On February 16, 2005, Commissioner Gary Bottman announced that the 2004-05 season was canceled.

On March 24, 2005, the league canceled the NHL Entry Draft, which was scheduled to take place the weekend of June 25-26 in Ottawa, Ontario, Canada.

Many players spent the winter skating overseas for European hockey clubs. Finally, on July 22, a new agreement was approved, ending the 311-day lockout.

2004 WORLD CUP OF HOCKEY FINAL STANDINGS

OVERALL STANDINGS

EUROPE	W	L	T	OTL	GF	GA	PTS
Finland	2	0	1	0	11	4	5
Sweden	2	0	1	0	13	9	5
Czech Republic	1	2	0	0	10	10	2
Germany	0	3	0	0	4	15	0

NORTH AMERICA	W	L	T	OTL	GF	GA	PTS
Canada	3	0	0	0	10	3	6
Russia	2	1	0	0	9	6	4
United States	1	2	0	0	5	6	2
Slovakia	0	3	0	0	4	13	0

2004 WORLD CUP OF HOCKEY BRACKET

United States (5-3)						Canada (5-0)	
	United States		CANADA		Canada (4-3, OT)		
Russia		Finland	3 – 2	Canada		Slovakia	
Finland (2-1)						Czech Republic (6-1)	
	Finland (2-1)				Czech Republic		
Germany						Sweden	

QUARTERFINALS	SEMIFINALS	WORLD CUP	SEMIFINALS	QUARTERFINALS

KEY W=win; L=loss; T=tie; OTL=overtime loss; GF=goals for; GA=goals against; PTS=points

WORLD CUP OF HOCKEY RESULTS

SCOREBOARD

MONDAY, AUGUST 30, 2004
FINLAND VS. CZECH REPUBLIC

TEAM	1	2	3	T
Czech Republic	0	0	0	0
Finland	1	0	3	4

FINLAND WINS, 4–0

TUESDAY, AUGUST 31, 2004
SWEDEN VS. GERMANY

TEAM	1	2	3	T
Germany	1	1	0	2
Sweden	1	4	0	5

SWEDEN WINS, 5–2

CANADA VS. UNITED STATES

TEAM	1	2	3	T
United States	0	1	0	1
Canada	1	1	0	2

CANADA WINS, 2–1

WEDNESDAY, SEPTEMBER 1, 2004
SWEDEN VS. CZECH REPUBLIC

TEAM	1	2	3	T
Czech Republic	0	0	3	3
Sweden	1	3	0	4

SWEDEN WINS, 4–3

CANADA VS. SLOVAKIA

TEAM	1	2	3	T
Canada	2	1	2	5
Slovakia	0	0	1	1

CANADA WINS, 5–1

THURSDAY, SEPTEMBER 2, 2004
FINLAND VS. GERMANY

TEAM	1	2	3	T
Finland	1	1	1	3
Germany	0	0	0	0

FINLAND WINS, 3–0

RUSSIA VS. UNITED STATES

TEAM	1	2	3	T
Russia	0	1	2	3
United States	0	1	0	1

RUSSIA WINS, 3–1

FRIDAY, SEPTEMBER 3, 2004
CZECH REPUBLIC VS. GERMANY

TEAM	1	2	3	T
Germany	0	0	2	2
Czech Republic	0	5	2	7

CZECH REPUBLIC WINS, 7–2

UNITED STATES VS. SLOVAKIA

TEAM	1	2	3	T
Slovakia	1	0	0	1
United States	2	0	1	3

UNITED STATES WINS, 3–1

SATURDAY, SEPTEMBER 4, 2004
RUSSIA VS. CANADA

TEAM	1	2	3	T
Russia	0	0	1	1
Canada	0	2	1	3

CANADA WINS, 3–1

SWEDEN VS. FINLAND

TEAM	1	2	3	OT	T
Sweden	3	0	1	0	4
Finland	3	1	0	0	4

SWEDEN AND FINLAND TIE, 4–4

SUNDAY, SEPTEMBER 5, 2004
SLOVAKIA VS. RUSSIA

TEAM	1	2	3	T
Slovakia	1	0	1	2
Russia	1	2	2	5

RUSSIA WINS, 5–2

MONDAY, SEPTEMBER 6, 2004
GERMANY VS. FINLAND

TEAM	1	2	3	T
Germany	0	0	1	1
Finland	0	1	1	2

FINLAND WINS, 2–1

TUESDAY, SEPTEMBER 7, 2004
CZECH REPUBLIC VS. SWEDEN

TEAM	1	2	3	T
Czech Republic	2	1	3	6
Sweden	0	0	1	1

CZECH REPUBLIC WINS, 6–1

UNITED STATES VS. RUSSIA

TEAM	1	2	3	T
United States	1	1	3	5
Russia	0	1	2	3

UNITED STATES WINS, 5–3

WORLD CUP OF HOCKEY RESULTS (cont.)

CANADA VS. SLOVAKIA

TEAM	1	2	3	T
Slovakia	0	0	0	0
Canada	0	4	1	5

CANADA WINS, 5–0

UNITED STATES VS. FINLAND

TEAM	1	2	3	T
United States	0	1	0	1
Finland	0	0	2	2

FINLAND WINS, 2–1

CANADA VS. CZECH REPUBLIC

TEAM	1	2	3	OT	T
Czech Republic	0	1	2	0	3
Canada	0	2	1	1	4

CANADA WINS, 4–3

CANADA VS. FINLAND

TEAM	1	2	3	T
Finland	1	1	0	2
Canada	1	1	1	3

CANADA WINS, 3–2

WORLD CUP OF HOCKEY BOX SCORES

SEMIFINALS

SEPTEMBER 10, 2004

FINLAND 2, UNITED STATES 1

TEAM	1	2	3	T
UNITED STATES	0	1	0	1
FINLAND	0	0	2	2

FIRST-PERIOD SCORING: None
SECOND-PERIOD SCORING: Doug Weight, United States, power play (12:57) Assists: Scott Gomez, Paul Martin
THIRD-PERIOD SCORING: Olli Jokinen, Finland (5:04) Assist: Teppo Numminen
Saku Koivu, Finland (16:06) Assists: Ossi Vaananen, Teemu Selanne

SEPTEMBER 11, 2004

CANADA 4, CZECH REPUBLIC 3

TEAM	1	2	3	OT	T
CZECH REPUBLIC	0	1	2	0	3
CANADA	0	2	1	1	4

FIRST-PERIOD SCORING: None
SECOND-PERIOD SCORING: Eric Brewer, Canada (11:15) Assists: Kris Draper, Joe Thornton
Mario Lemieux, Canada, power play (14:25) Assists: Vincent Lecavalier, Brad Richards
Petr Cajanek, Czech Republic (15:07) Assists: Milan Hejduk, Martin Rucinsky
THIRD-PERIOD SCORING: Martin Havlat, Czech Republic, power play (7:21) Assists: Tomas Kaberle, Milan Hejduk
Kris Draper, Canada (13:47) Assist: Joe Thornton
Patrik Elias, Czech Republic (13:53) Assist: Martin Havlat
OVERTIME SCORING: Vincent Lecavalier, Canada (3:45) Assist: Ryan Smyth

FINAL

SEPTEMBER 14, 2004

CANADA 3, FINLAND 2

TEAM	1	2	3	T
FINLAND	1	1	0	2
CANADA	1	1	1	3

FIRST-PERIOD SCORING: Joe Sakic, Canada (0:52) Assists: Mario Lemieux, Eric Brewer
Riku Hahl, Finland (6:34) Assists: Toni Lydman, Aki Berg
SECOND-PERIOD SCORING: Scott Niedermayer, Canada (3:15) Assists: Kris Draper, Joe Thornton
Tuomo Ruutu, Finland (19:00) Assist: Toni Lydman
THIRD-PERIOD SCORING: Shane Doan, Canada (0:34) Assists: Joe Thornton, Adam Foote

> ■ **Fast Fact:** In 1990-91, Brett Hull won the Hart Trophy as NHL MVP. His father, Bobby, won the award in 1964-65 and 1965-66. The Hulls are the only father-son duo in NHL history to receive the league's top honor.

HOCKEY

WORLD CUP OF HOCKEY TEAM-BY-TEAM STATS

CANADA

PLAYER	GP	G	A	PTS	+/-	PIM
Vincent Lecavalier	6	2	5	7	1	8
Joe Sakic	6	4	2	6	4	2
Joe Thornton	6	1	5	6	4	0
Mario Lemieux	6	1	4	5	4	2
Kris Draper	5	2	2	4	5	2
Ryan Smyth	6	3	1	4	0	2
Eric Brewer	6	1	3	4	6	4
Martin St. Louis	6	2	2	4	1	0
Brad Richards	6	1	3	4	2	0
Adam Foote	6	0	3	3	7	0
Jarome Iginla	6	2	1	3	5	2
Scott Niedermayer	6	1	1	2	1	9
Shane Doan	6	1	1	2	4	2
Simon Gagne	6	1	1	2	2	0
Dany Heatley	6	0	2	2	0	2
Wade Redden	2	0	1	1	0	0
Scott Hannan	5	0	1	1	3	4
Ed Jovanovski	1	0	0	0	0	0
Brenden Morrow	1	0	0	0	0	4
Robyn Regehr	6	0	0	0	2	6
Jay Bouwmeester	4	0	0	0	3	0

GOALTENDER	GP	GA	SA	GAA	SV	SV%	SO
Martin Brodeur	5	5	129	1.00	124	.961	1
Roberto Luongo	1	3	40	2.82	37	.925	0

CZECH REPUBLIC

PLAYER	GP	G	A	PTS	+/-	PIM
Martin Havlat	5	3	3	6	6	2
Patrik Elias	5	3	2	5	3	10
Milan Hejduk	4	3	2	5	1	2
Vaclav Prospal	4	1	3	4	1	0
Marek Zidlicky	5	3	1	4	3	2
Martin Straka	5	1	2	3	1	0
Petr Cajanek	4	1	2	3	3	0
Jaromir Jagr	5	1	1	2	1	2
Martin Rucinsky	4	1	1	2	2	10
Roman Hamrlik	4	0	2	2	4	0
Tomas Kaberle	4	0	1	1	3	0
Jiri Slegr	3	1	0	1	1	2
Jiri Dopita	5	0	1	1	1	0
Tomas Vlasak	2	0	1	1	2	0
Petr Sykora	3	0	1	1	-1	2
Radek Dvorak	4	1	0	1	0	0
Robert Reichel	4	0	0	0	-4	2
David Vyborny	5	0	0	0	5	2
Marek Malik	4	0	0	0	0	4
Martin Skoula	2	0	0	0	-2	2
Jiri Fischer	4	0	0	0	5	2
Josef Vasicek	1	0	0	0	-1	0
Jaroslav Spacek	4	0	0	0	0	0

GOALTENDER	GP	GA	SA	GAA	SV	SV%	SO
Tomas Vokoun	5	15	126	2.98	111	.881	0

FINLAND

PLAYER	GP	G	A	PTS	+/-	PIM
Kimmo Timonen	6	1	5	6	3	2
Teemu Selanne	6	1	3	4	1	4
Jere Lehtinen	6	1	3	4	1	2
Saku Koivu	6	3	1	4	2	2
Ville Peltonen	6	1	2	3	3	2
Toni Lydman	6	0	3	3	3	6
Olli Jokinen	6	2	1	3	4	6
Ossi Vaananen	4	1	2	3	3	0
Niko Kapanen	6	1	2	3	0	0
Tuomo Ruutu	6	1	2	3	4	4
Teppo Numminen	6	0	2	2	3	0
Mikko Eloranta	6	2	0	2	2	2
Jukka Hentunen	6	1	1	2	1	2
Aki Berg	5	0	1	1	1	2
Sami Salo	6	0	1	1	0	2
Niklas Hagman	5	1	0	1	1	2
Riku Hahl	2	1	0	1	0	0
Mikko Koivu	4	0	1	1	1	2
Janne Niinimaa	3	0	0	0	0	0
Ville Nieminen	2	0	0	0	1	0
Antti Laaksonen	1	0	0	0	0	0
Jarkko Ruutu	4	0	0	0	1	6

GOALTENDER	GP	GA	SA	GAA	SV	SV%	SO
Miikka Kiprusoff	6	9	149	1.48	140	.940	2

GERMANY

PLAYER	GP	G	A	PTS	+/-	PIM
Marco Sturm	4	2	0	2	-2	0
Lino Boos	4	1	1	2	0	2
Daniel Kreutzer	4	1	1	2	1	4
Rob Leask	4	0	1	1	1	6
Jochen Hecht	4	1	0	1	-2	2
Marcel Goc	3	0	1	1	-1	2
Eduard Lewandowski	4	0	1	1	2	4
Martin Reichel	2	0	0	0	-1	0
Stefan Ustorf	4	0	0	0	-2	0
Sascha Goc	3	0	0	0	0	2
Christian Ehrhoff	4	0	0	0	-2	2
Christoph Schubert	2	0	0	0	-1	6
Dennis Seidenberg	4	0	0	0	-3	0
Lasse Kopitz	3	0	0	0	-1	4
Mirko Ludemann	4	0	0	0	-3	0
Andreas Renz	3	0	0	0	-1	2
Tobias Abstreiter	4	0	0	0	-2	2
Klaus Kathan	3	0	0	0	-1	2
Tomas Martinec	3	0	0	0	-2	2
Stephan Retzer	2	0	0	0	-1	0
Petr Fical	4	0	0	0	-2	2

GOALTENDER	GP	GA	SA	GAA	SV	SV%	SO
Olaf Kolzig	3	10	105	3.34	95	.905	0
Robert Muller	1	3	26	5.94	23	.885	0
Oliver Jonas	1	4	30	8.08	26	.867	0

HOCKEY

RUSSIA

PLAYER	GP	G	A	PTS	+/-	PIM
Alex Kovalev	4	2	1	3	-2	4
Alexei Yashin	4	1	2	3	3	4
Sergei Gonchar	4	1	2	3	-1	6
Dainius Zubrus	4	2	1	3	2	4
Sergei Samsonov	4	1	2	3	1	0
Alexander Frolov	4	0	2	2	0	2
Dimitri Afanasenkov	2	1	1	2	2	0
Darius Kasparaitis	4	0	1	1	0	8
Viktor Kozlov	4	1	0	1	-1	0
Oleg Kvasha	2	0	1	1	0	0
Maxim Afinogenov	4	0	1	1	-2	2
Artem Chubarov	4	0	1	1	1	0
Andrei Markov	2	0	1	1	-1	2
Pavel Datsyuk	4	1	0	1	0	0
Alexander Khavanov	4	0	1	1	-2	4
Ilya Kovalchuk	4	1	0	1	-4	4
Alexander Ovechkin	2	1	0	1	2	0
Andrei Kovalenko	2	0	0	0	-1	6
Oleg Tverdovsky	3	0	0	0	1	0
Vitaly Vishnevski	3	0	0	0	5	0
Dmitri Kalinin	3	0	0	0	1	0
Anton Volchenkov	1	0	0	0	0	0

GOALTENDER	GP	GA	SA	GAA	SV	SV%	SO
Ilja Bryzgalov	3	7	68	2.34	61	.897	0
Maxim Sokolov	1	3	28	3.01	25	.893	0

SLOVAKIA

PLAYER	GP	G	A	PTS	+/-	PIM
Pavol Demira	4	0	2	2	-2	2
Zdeno Chara	4	0	2	2	-5	8
Marian Hossa	4	1	0	1	-2	2
Ladislav Nagy	4	1	0	1	-4	0
Lubos Bartecko	4	0	1	1	1	2
Martin Cibak	4	1	0	1	0	0
Branko Radivojevic	4	0	1	1	-4	2
Marian Gaborik	4	1	0	1	-2	2
Jozef Stumpel	4	0	0	0	-4	2
Miroslav Satan	4	0	0	0	-7	4
Martin Strbak	4	0	0	0	-1	4
Richard Zednik	3	0	0	0	-2	0
Radovan Somik	1	0	0	0	-2	0
Vladimir Orszach	4	0	0	0	-5	6
Jaroslav Obsut	3	0	0	0	-4	0
Richard Lintner	3	0	0	0	-5	2
Radoslav Suchy	3	0	0	0	-4	0
Rastislav Pavlikovsky	2	0	0	0	-4	2
Branislav Mezei	2	0	0	0	-3	0
Lubomir Visnovsky	4	0	0	0	-5	6
Miroslav Hlinka	2	0	0	0	-3	2
Ladislav Cierny	1	0	0	0	1	0

GOALTENDER	GP	GA	SA	GAA	SV	SV%	SO
Rastislav Stana	2	6	43	4.08	37	.860	0
Jan Lasak	3	12	72	4.75	60	.833	0

SWEDEN

PLAYER	GP	G	A	PTS	+/-	PIM
Fredrik Modin	4	4	4	8	1	2
Daniel Alfredsson	4	0	6	6	1	2
Mats Sundin	4	1	4	5	1	0
Tomas Holmstrom	4	3	2	5	-3	8
Kim Johnsson	4	1	3	4	-1	0
Peter Forsberg	4	1	2	3	-6	0
Markus Naslund	4	0	3	3	-5	0
Henrik Zetterberg	4	1	1	2	-7	4
Nicklas Lidstrom	4	1	0	1	0	2
Mattias Ohlund	4	1	0	1	-3	0
Marcus Nilson	4	1	0	1	1	4
Andreas Johansson	4	0	0	0	-2	4
Mattias Norstrom	4	0	0	0	-6	0
Marcus Ragnarsson	3	0	0	0	-4	0
Jorgen Jonsson	4	0	0	0	-2	0
Dick Tarnstrom	2	0	0	0	-4	0
Daniel Tjarnqvist	3	0	0	0	0	2
Per Johan Axelsson	4	0	0	0	-2	2
Samuel Pahlsson	4	0	0	0	-5	6

GOALTENDER	GP	GA	SA	GAA	EV	SV%	SO
Tommy Salo	1	2	19	2.00	17	.895	0
Mikael Tellqvist	3	12	96	4.03	84	.875	0

UNITED STATES

PLAYER	GP	G	A	PTS	+/-	PIM
Mike Modano	5	0	6	6	4	0
Keith Tkachuk	5	5	1	6	5	20
Bill Guerin	5	2	2	4	6	8
Scott Gomez	5	1	3	4	2	0
Brian Rafalski	4	0	3	3	3	6
Chris Chelios	5	0	1	1	0	6
Brian Leetch	5	0	1	1	-1	6
Tony Amonte	5	0	1	1	-5	0
Bryan Smolinski	3	1	0	1	-2	0
Doug Weight	5	1	0	1	-4	4
Jason Blake	4	1	0	1	-1	2
Paul Martin	3	0	1	1	3	0
Brett Hull	2	0	0	0	0	2
Eric Weinrich	2	0	0	0	-1	0
Craig Conroy	2	0	0	0	0	0
Ken Klee	4	0	0	0	2	0
Aaron Miller	5	0	0	0	-1	4
Brian Rolston	2	0	0	0	1	0
Steve Konowalchuk	5	0	0	0	-1	4
Jamie Langenbrunner	3	0	0	0	-1	4
Chris Drury	5	0	0	0	0	0
Jeff Halpern	4	0	0	0	-1	7
John-Michael Liles	2	0	0	0	-3	0

GOALTENDER	GP	GA	SA	GAA	SV	SV%	SO
Robert Esche	4	10	110	2.53	100	.909	0
Rick DiPietro	1	1	17	1.00	16	.941	0

2004 WORLD CUP OF HOCKEY INDIVIDUAL LEADERS

SCORING

POINTS	GP	PTS
Fredrik Modin, Sweden	4	8
Vincent Lecavalier, Canada	6	7
Keith Tkachuk, United States	5	6
Joe Sakic, Canada	6	6
Martin Havlat, Czech Republic	5	6
Kimmo Timonen, Finland	6	6
Joe Thornton, Canada	6	6
Mike Modano, United States	5	6
Daniel Alfredsson, Sweden	4	6
Patrik Elias, Czech Republic	5	5
Milan Hejduk, Czech Republic	4	5
Tomas Holmstrom, Sweden	4	5
Mario Lemieux, Canada	6	5
Mats Sundin, Sweden	4	5

ASSISTS	GP	A
Mike Modano, United States	5	6
Daniel Alfredsson, Sweden	4	6
Vincent Lecavalier, Canada	6	5
Kimmo Timonen, Finland	6	5
Joe Thornton, Canada	6	5
Fredrik Modin, Sweden	4	4
Mario Lemieux, Canada	6	4
Mats Sundin, Sweden	4	4
Martin Havlat, Czech Republic	5	3
Teemu Selanne, Finland	6	3
Jere Lehtinen, Finland	6	3
Vaclav Prospal, Czech Republic	4	3
Kim Johnsson, Sweden	4	3
Eric Brewer, Canada	6	3
Scott Gomez, United States	5	3
Brad Richards, Canada	6	3
Adam Foote, Canada	6	3
Markus Naslund, Sweden	4	3
Toni Lydman, Finland	6	3
Brian Rafalski, United States	4	3

**Keith Tkachuk,
United States**

GOALS	GP	G
Keith Tkachuk, United States	5	5
Fredrik Modin, Sweden	4	4
Joe Sakic, Canada	6	4
Martin Havlat, Czech Republic	5	3
Patrik Elias, Czech Republic	5	3
Milan Hejduk, Czech Republic	4	3
Tomas Holmstrom, Sweden	4	3
Saku Koivu, Finland	6	3
Ryan Smyth, Canada	6	3
Marek Zidlicky, Czech Republic	5	3
Vincent Lecavalier, Canada	6	2
Kris Draper, Canada	5	2
Bill Guerin, United States	5	2
Martin St. Louis, Canada	6	2
Alex Kovalev, Russia	4	2
Jarome Iginla, Canada	6	2
Dainius Zubrus, Russia	4	2
Olli Jokinen, Finland	6	2
Marco Sturm, Germany	4	2
Mikko Eloranta, Finland	6	2

PLUS/MINUS	GP	+/-
Adam Foote, Canada	6	7
Martin Havlat, Czech Republic	5	6
Bill Guerin, United States	5	6
Eric Brewer, Canada	6	6
Keith Tkachuk, United States	5	5
Kris Draper, Canada	5	5
Jarome Iginla, Canada	6	5
David Vyborny, Czech Republic	5	5
Jiri Fischer, Czech Republic	4	5
Vitaly Vishnevski, Russia	3	5
Mike Modano, United States	5	4
Joe Sakic, Canada	6	4
Joe Thornton, Canada	6	4
Mario Lemieux, Canada	6	4
Olli Jokinen, Finland	6	4
Tuomo Ruutu, Finland	6	4
Roman Hamrlik, Czech Republic	4	4
Shane Doan, Canada	6	4

Note: +/-=plus/minus rating (A player is awarded a plus [+1] each time he is on the ice when his team scores an even-strength or shorthanded goal. He receives a minus [-1] each time he is on the ice when the opposing team scores an even-strength or shorthanded goal. Power-play goals are not included in the rating.)

KEY GP=games played; PTS=points; G=goals; A=assists; +/-=plus/minus

TRIVIA CHALLENGE

The 2004-05 season was the second in history that the Stanley Cup was not awarded. When was the first?

1918-19. The league's championship series between the Montreal Canadiens and the Seattle Metropolitans was never completed because of a flu epidemic.

GOALTENDING

GOALS-AGAINST	GP	GA	GAA
Martin Brodeur, Canada	5	5	1.00
Rick DiPietro, United States	1	1	1.00
Miikka Kiprusoff, Finland	6	9	1.48
Tommy Salo, Sweden	1	2	2.00
Ilja Bryzgalov, Russia	3	7	2.34
Robert Esche, United States	4	10	2.53
Roberto Luongo, Canada	1	3	2.82
Tomas Vokoun, Czech Republic	5	15	2.98
Maxim Sokolov, Russia	1	3	3.01
Olaf Kolzig, Germany	3	10	3.34
Mikael Tellqvist, Sweden	3	12	4.03
Ratislav Stana, Slovakia	2	6	4.08
Jan Lasak, Slovakia	3	12	4.75
Robert Muller, Germany	1	3	5.94
Oliver Jonas, Germany	1	4	8.08

Olaf Kolzig, Germany

DAVE SANDFORD/GETTY IMAGES

SHUTOUTS	GP	SO
Miikka Kiprusoff, Finland	6	2
Martin Brodeur, Canada	5	1
Olaf Kolzig, Germany	3	0
Tommy Salo, Sweden	1	0
Tomas Vokoun, Czech Republic	5	0
Robert Esche, United States	4	0
Roberto Luongo, Canada	1	0
Rastislav Stana, Slovakia	2	0
Jan Lasak, Slovakia	3	0
Rick DiPietro, United States	1	0
Ilja Bryzgalov, Russia	3	0
Mikael Tellqvist, Sweden	3	0
Robert Muller, Germany	1	0
Oliver Jonas, Germany	1	0
Maxim Sokolov, Russia	1	0

SAVE PERCENTAGE	GP	GA	SA	SAVE PCT
Martin Brodeur, Canada	5	5	129	.961
Rick DiPietro, United States	1	1	17	.941
Miikka Kiprusoff, Finland	6	9	149	.940
Roberto Luongo, Canada	1	3	40	.925
Robert Esche, United States	4	10	110	.000
Olaf Kolzig, Germany	3	10	105	.905
Ilja Bryzgalov, Russia	3	7	68	.897
Tommy Salo, Sweden	1	2	19	.895
Maxim Sokolov, Russia	1	3	28	.893
Robert Muller, Germany	1	3	26	.885
Tomas Vokoun, Czech Republic	5	15	120	.881
Mikael Tellqvist, Sweden	3	12	96	.875
Oliver Jonas, Germany	1	4	30	.867
Rastislav Stana, Slovakia	2	6	43	.860
Jan Lasak, Slovakia	3	12	72	.833

SAVES	GP	SV
Miikka Kiprusoff, Finland	6	140
Martin Brodeur, Canada	5	124
Tomas Vokoun, Czech Republic	5	111
Robert Esche, United States	4	100
Olaf Kolzig, Germany	3	95
Mikael Tellqvist, Sweden	3	84
Ilja Bryzgalov, Russia	3	61
Jan Lasak, Slovakia	3	60
Roberto Luongo, Canada	1	37
Rastislav Stana, Slovakia	2	37
Oliver Jonas, Germany	1	26
Maxim Sokolov, Russia	1	25
Robert Muller, Germany	1	23
Tommy Salo, Sweden	1	17
Rick DiPietro, United States	1	16

DID YOU KNOW?

In August 2003, the Stanley Cup was temporarily lost by baggage handlers who had forgotten to load it on a plane leaving Toronto, Ontario, Canada, for Kosice, Slovakia. It was recovered and returned the next day.

KEY GP=games played; GA=goals allowed; GAA=goals-against average; SO=shutout; SA=shots allowed; SAVE PCT=save percentage; SV=saves

THE STANLEY CUP

Awarded annually to the team that wins the NHL's best-of-seven final-round playoffs. The Stanley Cup is the oldest trophy for which professional athletes in North America compete. It was donated in 1893 by Frederick Arthur, Lord Stanley of Preston.

SEASON	CHAMPION	FINALIST	GAMES PLAYED IN FINAL
2003–04	Tampa Bay Lightning	Calgary Flames	7
2002–03	New Jersey Devils	Anaheim Mighty Ducks	7
2001–02	Detroit Red Wings	Carolina Hurricanes	5
2000–01	Colorado Avalanche	New Jersey Devils	7
1999–00	New Jersey Devils	Dallas Stars	6
1998–99	Dallas Stars	Buffalo Sabres	6
1997–98	Detroit Red Wings	Washington Capitals	4
1996–97	Detroit Red Wings	Philadelphia Flyers	4
1995–96	Colorado Avalanche	Florida Panthers	4
1994–95	New Jersey Devils	Detroit Red Wings	4
1993–94	New York Rangers	Vancouver Canucks	7
1992–93	Montreal Canadiens	Los Angeles Kings	5
1991–92	Pittsburgh Penguins	Chicago Blackhawks	4
1990–91	Pittsburgh Penguins	Minnesota North Stars	6
1989–90	Edmonton Oilers	Boston Bruins	5
1988–89	Calgary Flames	Montreal Canadiens	6
1987–88	Edmonton Oilers	Boston Bruins	4
1986–87	Edmonton Oilers	Philadelphia Flyers	7
1985–86	Montreal Canadiens	Calgary Flames	5
1984–85	Edmonton Oilers	Philadelphia Flyers	5
1983–84	Edmonton Oilers	New York Islanders	5
1982–83	New York Islanders	Edmonton Oilers	4
1981–82	New York Islanders	Vancouver Canucks	4
1980–81	New York Islanders	Minnesota North Stars	5
1979–80	New York Islanders	Philadelphia Flyers	6
1978–79	Montreal Canadiens	New York Rangers	5
1977–78	Montreal Canadiens	Boston Bruins	6
1976–77	Montreal Canadiens	Boston Bruins	4
1975–76	Montreal Canadiens	Philadelphia Flyers	4
1974–75	Philadelphia Flyers	Buffalo Sabres	6
1973–74	Philadelphia Flyers	Boston Bruins	6
1972–73	Montreal Canadiens	Chicago Blackhawks	6
1971–72	Boston Bruins	New York Rangers	6
1970–71	Montreal Canadiens	Chicago Blackhawks	7
1969–70	Boston Bruins	St. Louis Blues	4
1968–69	Montreal Canadiens	St. Louis Blues	4
1967–68	Montreal Canadiens	St. Louis Blues	4
1966–67	Toronto Maple Leafs	Montreal Canadiens	6
1965–66	Montreal Canadiens	Detroit Red Wings	6
1964–65	Montreal Canadiens	Chicago Blackhawks	7
1963–64	Toronto Maple Leafs	Detroit Red Wings	7
1962–63	Toronto Maple Leafs	Detroit Red Wings	5
1961–62	Toronto Maple Leafs	Chicago Blackhawks	6
1960–61	Chicago Blackhawks	Detroit Red Wings	6
1959–60	Montreal Canadiens	Toronto Maple Leafs	4
1958–59	Montreal Canadiens	Toronto Maple Leafs	5
1957–58	Montreal Canadiens	Boston Bruins	6
1956–57	Montreal Canadiens	Boston Bruins	5
1955–56	Montreal Canadiens	Detroit Red Wings	5
1954–55	Detroit Red Wings	Montreal Canadiens	7
1953–54	Detroit Red Wings	Montreal Canadiens	7
1952–53	Montreal Canadiens	Boston Bruins	5

LEGENDS

Mario Lemieux has won the NHL scoring title six times in his 16-year career.

PAUL BERESWILL

■ **Mario Lemieux, center,** b. October 5, 1965, Montreal, Quebec, Canada. Lemieux wasted no time making his mark on the NHL after he was drafted by the Pittsburgh Penguins with the first pick in the 1984 draft. He scored in his first game with his first shot. Lemieux earned the nickname "The Magnificent One," a play on Wayne Gretzky's "The Great One." His jersey number, 66, is Gretzky's number 99 flipped upside down. Lemieux helped the Penguins win Stanley Cup titles in 1990-91 and 1991-92. He won the league's scoring title six times and was named MVP three times before retiring because of back problems in 1997. Lemieux and a group of investors bought the Penguins in 1999, making him the first former player to own a professional sports team in the modern era. He returned to the ice in 2000 and led the Penguins to the Eastern Conference finals. He also helped Canada win the gold medal at the 2002 Winter Olympics and captained the Canadian team that won the 2004 World Cup of Hockey.

■ **Ray Bourque, defenseman,** b. December 28, 1960, Montreal, Quebec, Canada. Bourque is the highest-scoring defenseman in NHL history. He played 22 seasons, all but one with the Boston Bruins, and totaled 410 goals and 1,169 assists. Those are astounding numbers for a defenseman. Bourque tallied at least 90 points in a season four times and won the Norris Trophy as the league's top defenseman five times. In 2000, Bourque was traded to the Colorado Avalanche so that he might win a Stanley Cup championship. He and the Avs won the Cup in 2000-01. Bourque retired 17 days later.

■ **Patrick Roy, goaltender,** b. October 5, 1965, Quebec City, Quebec, Canada. Roy revolutionized the goaltender position with his ferocious play, gritty determination, and use of the butterfly style. In the butterfly, he would spread his arms and legs wide across the goal. Roy began his career with the Montreal Canadiens, where he won the Stanley Cup and the Conn Smythe Trophy as the playoff MVP in 1985-86, his first full season in the league. He also led the Canadiens to the Cup in 1992-93 by winning a playoff-record 10 straight overtime games. He found even more success when he was traded to the Colorado Avalanche in 1995-96. In eight seasons with the Avalanche, Roy won 262 games, giving him 551 career victories, the most in NHL history. He never had a losing season, and in 2001-02 he had nine shutouts and posted a league-best 1.94 goals-against average. Roy won two Stanley Cups with Colorado (1995-96 and 2000-01). Over the course of a career that's sure to put him in the Hall of Fame, Roy won the Vezina Trophy as the NHL's best goalie three times. He retired after the 2002-03 season.

THE STANLEY CUP (cont.)

SEASON	CHAMPION	FINALIST	GAMES PLAYED IN FINAL
1951–52	Detroit Red Wings	Montreal Canadiens	4
1950–51	Toronto Maple Leafs	Montreal Canadiens	5
1949–50	Detroit Red Wings	New York Rangers	7
1948–49	Toronto Maple Leafs	Detroit Red Wings	4
1947–48	Toronto Maple Leafs	Detroit Red Wings	4
1946–47	Toronto Maple Leafs	Montreal Canadiens	6
1945–46	Montreal Canadiens	Boston Bruins	5
1944–45	Toronto Maple Leafs	Detroit Red Wings	7
1943–44	Montreal Canadiens	Chicago Blackhawks	4
1942–43	Detroit Red Wings	Boston Bruins	4
1941–42	Toronto Maple Leafs	Detroit Red Wings	7
1940–41	Boston Bruins	Detroit Red Wings	4
1939–40	New York Rangers	Toronto Maple Leafs	6
1938–39	Boston Bruins	Toronto Maple Leafs	5
1937–38	Chicago Blackhawks	Toronto Maple Leafs	4
1936–37	Detroit Red Wings	New York Rangers	5
1935–36	Detroit Red Wings	Toronto Maple Leafs	4
1934–35	Montreal Maroons	Toronto Maple Leafs	3
1933–34	Chicago Blackhawks	Detroit Red Wings	4
1932–33	New York Rangers	Toronto Maple Leafs	4
1931–32	Toronto Maple Leafs	New York Rangers	3
1930–31	Montreal Canadiens	Chicago Blackhawks	5
1929–30	Montreal Canadiens	Boston Bruins	2
1928–29	Boston Bruins	New York Rangers	2
1927–28	New York Rangers	Montreal Maroons	5
1926–27	Ottawa Senators	Boston Bruins	4
1925–26	Montreal Maroons	Victoria Cougars	4
1924–25	Victoria Cougars	Montreal Canadiens	4
1923–24	Montreal Canadiens	Vancouver Maroons, Calgary Tigers	2, 2*
1922–23	Ottawa Senators	Edmonton Eskimos, Vancouver Maroons	2, 4*
1921–22	Toronto St. Pats	Vancouver Millionaires	5
1920–21	Ottawa Senators	Vancouver Millionaires	5
1919–20	Ottawa Senators	Seattle Metropolitans	5
1918–19	No decision*	No decision*	5
1917–18	Toronto Arenas	Vancouver Millionaires	5
1916–17	Seattle Metropolitans	—	—
1915–16	Montreal Canadiens	—	—
1914–15	Vancouver Millionaires	—	—
1913–14	Toronto Blueshirts	—	—
1912–13	Quebec Bulldogs	—	—
1911–12	Quebec Bulldogs	—	—
1910–11	Ottawa Senators	—	—
1909–10	Montreal Wanderers	—	—
1908–09	Ottawa Senators	—	—
1907–08	Montreal Wanderers	—	—
1906–07	Montreal Wanderers (Mar.)	—	—
1906–07	Kenora Thistles (Jan.)	—	—
1905–06	Montreal Wanderers (Mar.)	—	—
1905–06	Ottawa Silver Seven (Feb.)	—	—
1904–05	Ottawa Silver Seven	—	—
1903–04	Ottawa Silver Seven	—	—
1902–03	Ottawa Silver Seven (Mar.)	—	—
1902–03	Montreal A.A.A. (Feb.)	—	—
1901–02	Montreal A.A.A. (Mar.)	—	—

*In 1923-24, the Montreal Canadiens beat the Vancouver Maroons in two games and the Calgary Tigers in two games. In 1922-23, the Ottawa Senators beat the Edmonton Eskimos in two games and the Vancouver Maroons in four games. In 1918-19, the Montreal Canadiens traveled to meet the Seattle Metropolitans. After five games had been played — the teams were tied at two wins apiece and one tie — the series was called off by the local Department of Health because of an influenza epidemic and the death of Canadien defenseman Joe Hall from influenza.

SEASON	CHAMPION	FINALIST	GAMES PLAYED IN FINAL
1901–02	Winnipeg Victorias (Jan.)	—	—
1900–01	Winnipeg Victorias	—	—
1899–00	Montreal Shamrocks	—	—
1898–99	Montreal Shamrocks (Mar.)	—	—
1898–99	Montreal Victorias (Feb.)	—	—
1897–98	Montreal Victorias	—	—
1896–97	Montreal Victorias	—	—
1895–96	Montreal Victorias (Dec.)	—	—
1895–96	Winnipeg Victorias (Feb.)	—	—
1894–95	Montreal Victorias	—	—
1893–94	Montreal A.A.A.	—	—
1892–93	Montreal A.A.A.	—	—

2004-05 TIME LINE

■ **September 14, 2004:** Team Canada defeats Finland, 3–2, in the championship game of the 2004 World Cup of Hockey. Canada is led by goaltender Martin Brodeur of the New Jersey Devils, captain Mario Lemieux of the Pittsburgh Penguins, and tournament MVP Vincent Lecavalier of the Tampa Bay Lightning. The team wins all six of its games.

■ **September 15, 2004:** The labor agreement between the NHL's owners and players officially expires. Since a new agreement is not in place, the owners vote to lock out the players. It is the first work stoppage in the NHL since 1994-95.

■ **October 13, 2004:** Opening night in the NHL comes and goes without a new labor agreement. Team owners and players have not met since September 9.

■ **November 3, 2004:** With talks still stalled, the league announces the cancellation of the 2005 All-Star Game, scheduled for February 13, 2005, in Atlanta, Georgia.

■ **February 15, 2005:** The league makes its final offer to the players' union. It includes a $42.5 million salary cap, which is $2.5 million higher than its offer from the previous day. The players are given a deadline of 11 a.m. the following day to accept the proposal. The offer is rejected.

■ **February 16, 2005:** With the lockout three months old, NHL Commissioner Gary Bettman holds a news conference to announce the formal cancellation of the 2004-05 season. It marks the first time in the history of North American professional sports that an entire season is lost because of a labor dispute.

■ **February 19, 2005:** In an effort to help save the sport, Wayne Gretzky and Mario Lemieux join last-ditch negotiations in New York. After initial rumors that an agreement has been reached, talks break down for good.

■ **May 15, 2005:** The Czech Republic defeats Canada, 3–0, in the final game of the 2005 IIHF World Championships in Vienna, Austria. Tomas Vokoun of the Czech Republic was named the tournament's best goalie. He had 29 saves in earning the shutout.

CONN SMYTHE TROPHY (PAST 20 SEASONS)

Awarded to the Most Valuable Player of the Stanley Cup playoffs, as selected by the Professional Hockey Writers Association. The trophy was named for the former coach, general manager, president, and owner of the Toronto Maple Leafs.

SEASON	PLAYER	SEASON	PLAYER
2003-04	Brad Richards, Tampa Bay Lightning	1993-94	Brian Leetch, New York Rangers
2002-03	Jean-Sebastien Giguere, Anaheim Mighty Ducks	1992-93	Patrick Roy, Montreal Canadiens
		1991-92	Mario Lemieux, Pittsburgh Penguins
2001-02	Nicklas Lidstrom, Detroit Red Wings	1990-91	Mario Lemieux, Pittsburgh Penguins
2000-01	Patrick Roy, Colorado Avalanche	1989-90	Bill Ranford, Edmonton Oilers
1999-00	Scott Stevens, New Jersey Devils	1988-89	Al MacInnis, Calgary Flames
1998-99	Joe Nieuwendyk, Dallas Stars	1987-88	Wayne Gretzky, Edmonton Oilers
1997-98	Steve Yzerman, Detroit Red Wings	1986-87	Ron Hextall, Philadelphia Flyers
1996-97	Mike Vernon, Detroit Red Wings	1985-86	Patrick Roy, Montreal Canadiens
1995-96	Joe Sakic, Colorado Avalanche	1984-85	Wayne Gretzky, Edmonton Oilers
1994-95	Claude Lemieux, New Jersey Devils		

HART MEMORIAL TROPHY (PAST 20 SEASONS)

Awarded annually "to the player adjudged to be the most valuable to his team." The original trophy was donated by Dr. David A. Hart, father of Cecil Hart, former manager-coach of the Montreal Canadiens.

SEASON	WINNER	SEASON	WINNER
2003-04	Martin St. Louis, Tampa Bay Lightning	1993-94	Sergei Fedorov, Detroit Red Wings
2002-03	Peter Forsberg, Colorado Avalanche	1992-93	Mario Lemieux, Pittsburgh Penguins
2001-02	Jose Theodore, Montreal Canadiens	1991-92	Mark Messier, New York Rangers
2000-01	Joe Sakic, Colorado Avalanche	1990-91	Brett Hull, St. Louis Blues
1999-00	Chris Pronger, St. Louis Blues	1989-90	Mark Messier, Edmonton Oilers
1998-99	Jaromir Jagr, Pittsburgh Penguins	1988-89	Wayne Gretzky, Los Angeles Kings
1997-98	Dominik Hasek, Buffalo Sabres	1987-88	Mario Lemieux, Pittsburgh Penguins
1996-97	Dominik Hasek, Buffalo Sabres	1986-87	Wayne Gretzky, Edmonton Oilers
1995-96	Mario Lemieux, Pittsburgh Penguins	1985-86	Wayne Gretzky, Edmonton Oilers
1994-95	Eric Lindros, Philadelphia Flyers	1984-85	Wayne Gretzky, Edmonton Oilers

ART ROSS TROPHY (PAST 20 SEASONS)

Awarded annually "to the player who leads the league in scoring points at the end of the regular season." The trophy was presented to the NHL in 1947 by Arthur Howie Ross, former manager-coach of the Boston Bruins. If two or more players are tied, the tie-breakers, in order, are: (1) player with most goals, (2) player with fewer games played, (3) player who scored the first goal of the season.

SEASON	WINNER	POINTS	SEASON	WINNER	POINTS
2003-04	Martin St. Louis, Tampa Bay Lightning	94	1993-94	Wayne Gretzky, Los Angeles Kings	130
2002-03	Peter Forsberg, Colorado Avalanche	106	1992-93	Mario Lemieux, Pittsburgh Penguins	160
2001-02	Jarome Iginla, Calgary Flames	96	1991-92	Mario Lemieux, Pittsburgh Penguins	131
2000-01	Jaromir Jagr, Pittsburgh Penguins	121	1990-91	Wayne Gretzky, Los Angeles Kings	163
1999-00	Jaromir Jagr, Pittsburgh Penguins	96	1989-90	Wayne Gretzky, Los Angeles Kings	142
1998-99	Jaromir Jagr, Pittsburgh Penguins	127	1988-89	Mario Lemieux, Pittsburgh Penguins	199
1997-98	Jaromir Jagr, Pittsburgh Penguins	102	1987-88	Mario Lemieux, Pittsburgh Penguins	168
1996-97	Mario Lemieux, Pittsburgh Penguins	122	1986-87	Wayne Gretzky, Edmonton Oilers	183
1995-96	Mario Lemieux, Pittsburgh Penguins	161	1985-86	Wayne Gretzky, Edmonton Oilers	215
1994-95	Jaromir Jagr, Pittsburgh Penguins	70	1984-85	Wayne Gretzky, Edmonton Oilers	208

LADY BYNG MEMORIAL TROPHY (PAST 20 SEASONS)

Awarded annually "to the player adjudged to have exhibited the best type of sportsmanship and gentlemanly conduct combined with a high standard of playing ability." Lady Byng, who first presented the trophy in 1925, was the wife of Canada's Governor-General. She donated a second trophy in 1936 because the first one was given permanently to Frank Boucher of the New York Rangers, who had won it seven times in eight seasons.

SEASON	WINNER	SEASON	WINNER
2003-04	Brad Richards, Tampa Bay Lightning	1993-94	Wayne Gretzky, Los Angeles Kings
2002-03	Alexander Mogilny, Toronto Maple Leafs	1992-93	Pierre Turgeon, New York Islanders
2001-02	Ron Francis, Carolina Hurricanes	1991-92	Wayne Gretzky, Los Angeles Kings
2000 01	Joe Sakic, Colorado Avalanche	1990-91	Wayne Gretzky, Los Angeles Kings
1999-00	Pavol Demitra, St. Louis Blues	1989-90	Brett Hull, St. Louis Blues
1998-99	Wayne Gretzky, New York Rangers	1988-89	Joe Mullen, Calgary Flames
1997-98	Ron Francis, Pittsburgh Penguins	1987-88	Mats Naslund, Montreal Canadiens
1996-97	Paul Kariya, Anaheim Mighty Ducks	1986-87	Joe Mullen, Calgary Flames
1995-96	Paul Kariya, Anaheim Mighty Ducks	1985-86	Mike Bossy, New York Islanders
1994-95	Ron Francis, Pittsburgh Penguins	1984-85	Jari Kurri, Edmonton Oilers

JAMES NORRIS MEMORIAL TROPHY (PAST 20 SEASONS)

Awarded annually "to the defense player who demonstrates throughout the season the greatest all-around ability in the position." James Norris was the former owner-president of the Detroit Red Wings.

SEASON	WINNER	SEASON	WINNER
2003-04	Scott Niedermayer, New Jersey Devils	1993-94	Ray Bourque, Boston Bruins
2002-03	Nicklas Lidstrom, Detroit Red Wings	1992-93	Chris Chelios, Chicago Blackhawks
2001-02	Nicklas Lidstrom, Detroit Red Wings	1991-92	Brian Leetch, New York Rangers
2000-01	Nicklas Lidstrom, Detroit Red Wings	1990-91	Ray Bourque, Boston Bruins
1999-00	Chris Pronger, St. Louis Blues	1989-90	Ray Bourque, Boston Bruins
1998-99	Al MacInnis, St. Louis Blues	1988-89	Chris Chelios, Montreal Canadiens
1997-98	Rob Blake, Los Angeles Kings	1987-88	Ray Bourque, Boston Bruins
1996-97	Brian Leetch, New York Rangers	1986-87	Ray Bourque, Boston Bruins
1995-96	Chris Chelios, Chicago Blackhawks	1985-86	Paul Coffey, Edmonton Oilers
1994-95	Paul Coffey, Detroit Red Wings	1984-85	Paul Coffey, Edmonton Oilers

CALDER MEMORIAL TROPHY (PAST 20 SEASONS)

Awarded annually "to the player selected as the most proficient in his first year of competition in the National Hockey League." Frank Calder was a former NHL president. Sergei Makarov, who won the award in 1989-90, was the oldest recipient of the trophy, at 31. If a player is 26 or older as of September 15 of a season, he is not eligible to win the award.

SEASON	WINNER	SEASON	WINNER
2003-04	Andrew Raycroft, Boston Bruins	1993-94	Martin Brodeur, New Jersey Devils
2002-03	Barret Jackman, St. Louis Blues	1992-93	Teemu Selanne, Winnipeg Jets
2001-02	Dany Heatley, Atlanta Thrashers	1991-92	Pavel Bure, Vancouver Canucks
2000-01	Evgeni Nabokov, San Jose Sharks	1990-91	Ed Belfour, Chicago Blackhawks
1999-00	Scott Gomez, New Jersey Devils	1989-90	Sergei Makarov, Calgary Flames
1998-99	Chris Drury, Colorado Avalanche	1988-89	Brian Leetch, New York Rangers
1997-98	Sergei Samsonov, Boston Bruins	1987-88	Joe Nieuwendyk, Calgary Flames
1996-97	Bryan Berard, New York Islanders	1986-87	Luc Robitaille, Los Angeles Kings
1995-96	Daniel Alfredsson, Ottawa Senators	1985-86	Gary Suter, Calgary Flames
1994-95	Peter Forsberg, Quebec Nordiques	1984-85	Mario Lemieux, Pittsburgh Penguins

VEZINA TROPHY (PAST 20 SEASONS)

Awarded annually "to the goalkeeper adjudged to be the best at his position." The trophy was named for Georges Vezina, an outstanding goalie for the Montreal Canadiens who collapsed during a game on November 28, 1925, and died four months later of tuberculosis. The general managers of the NHL teams vote on the award.

SEASON	WINNER	SEASON	WINNER
2003-04	Martin Brodeur, New Jersey Devils	1993-94	Dominik Hasek, Buffalo Sabres
2002-03	Martin Brodeur, New Jersey Devils	1992-93	Ed Belfour, Chicago Blackhawks
2001-02	Jose Theodore, Montreal Canadiens	1991-92	Patrick Roy, Montreal Canadiens
2000-01	Dominik Hasek, Buffalo Sabres	1990-91	Ed Belfour, Chicago Blackhawks
1999-00	Olaf Kolzig, Washington Capitals	1989-90	Patrick Roy, Montreal Canadiens
1998-99	Dominik Hasek, Buffalo Sabres	1988-89	Patrick Roy, Montreal Canadiens
1997-98	Dominik Hasek, Buffalo Sabres	1987-88	Grant Fuhr, Edmonton Oilers
1996-97	Dominik Hasek, Buffalo Sabres	1986-87	Ron Hextall, Philadelphia Flyers
1995-96	Jim Carey, Washington Capitals	1985-86	John Vanbiesbrouck, New York Rangers
1994-95	Dominik Hasek, Buffalo Sabres	1984-85	Pelle Lindbergh, Philadelphia Flyers

SELKE TROPHY (PAST 20 SEASONS)

Awarded annually "to the forward who best excels in the defensive aspects of the game." The trophy was named for Frank J. Selke, the architect of the Montreal Canadiens dynasty that won the Stanley Cup five consecutive times in the late 1950's. The winner is selected by a vote of the Professional Hockey Writers Association.

SEASON	WINNER	SEASON	WINNER
2003-04	Kris Draper, Detroit Red Wings	1993-94	Sergei Fedorov, Detroit Red Wings
2002-03	Jere Lehtinen, Dallas Stars	1992-93	Doug Gilmour, Toronto Maple Leafs
2001-02	Michael Peca, New York Islanders	1991-92	Guy Carbonneau, Montreal Canadiens
2000-01	John Madden, New Jersey Devils	1990-91	Dirk Graham, Chicago Blackhawks
1999-00	Steve Yzerman, Detroit Red Wings	1989-90	Rick Meagher, St. Louis Blues
1998-99	Jere Lehtinen, Dallas Stars	1988-89	Guy Carbonneau, Montreal Canadiens
1997-98	Jere Lehtinen, Dallas Stars	1987-88	Guy Carbonneau, Montreal Canadiens
1996-97	Michael Peca, Buffalo Sabres	1986-87	Dave Poulin, Philadelphia Flyers
1995-96	Sergei Fedorov, Detroit Red Wings	1985-86	Troy Murray, Chicago Blackhawks
1994-95	Ron Francis, Pittsburgh Penguins	1984-85	Craig Ramsay, Buffalo Sabres

CAREER RECORDS

All-time Points Leaders

PLAYER	YRS	GP	G	A	PTS	PTS/GAME
Wayne Gretzky, Edm, LA, StL, NYR	20	1,487	894	1,963	2,857	1.921
Mark Messier, Edm, Van, NYR	25	1,756	694	1,193	1,887	1.075
Gordie Howe, Det, Hart	26	1,767	801	1,049	1,850	1.047
Ron Francis, Hart, Pitt, Car, Tor	23	1,731	549	1,249	1,798	1.039
Marcel Dionne, Det, LA, NYR	18	1,348	731	1,040	1,771	1.314

All-time Goal-Scoring Leaders

PLAYER	YRS	GP	G	G/GAME
Wayne Gretzky, Edm, LA, StL, NYR	20	1,487	894	.601
Gordie Howe, Det, Hart	26	1,767	801	.453
Brett Hull, Cal, StL, Dal, Det	19	1,264	741	.586
Marcel Dionne, Det, LA, NYR	18	1,348	731	.542
Phil Esposito, Chi, Bos, NYR	18	1,282	717	.559

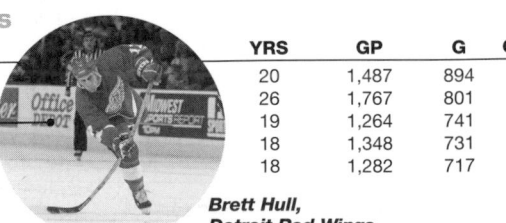

Brett Hull, Detroit Red Wings

KEY YRS=years; GP=games played; G=goals; A=assists; PTS=points; PTS/GAME=points per game; G/Game=goals per game

CAREER RECORDS (cont.)

All-time Assists Leaders

PLAYER	YRS	GP	A	A/GAME
Wayne Gretzky, Edm, LA, StL, NYR	20	1,487	1,963	1.320
Ron Francis, Hart, Pitt, Car, Tor	23	1,731	1,249	.721
Mark Messier, Edm, NYR, Van	25	1,756	1,193	.679
Ray Bourque, Bos, Col	22	1,612	1,169	.725
Paul Coffey, Edm, Pitt, LA, Det, Hart, Phi, Chi, Car, Bos	21	1,409	1,135	.806

GOALTENDING

All-time Win Leaders

GOALTENDER	W	L	T
Patrick Roy, Mtl, Col	551	315	131
Terry Sawchuk, Det, Bos, Tor, LA, NYR	447	330	172
Jacques Plante, Mtl, NYR, StL, Tor, Bos	435	247	145
Tony Esposito, Mtl, Chi	423	306	151
Glenn Hall, Det, Chi, StL	407	326	163

Patrick Roy,
Colorado Avalanche

LOU CAPOZZO

All-time Shutout Leaders

GOALTENDER	TEAM	YRS	GP	SO
Terry Sawchuk	Det, Bos, Tor, LA, NYR	21	971	103
George Hainsworth	Mtl, Tor	11	465	94
Glenn Hall	Det, Chi, StL	18	906	84
Jacques Plante	Mtl, NYR, StL, Tor, Bos	18	837	82
Tiny Thompson	Bos, Det	12	553	81
Alex Connell	Ott, Det, NYA, Mtl M	12	417	81

All-time Goals-Against Average Leaders (Pre-1950)

GOALTENDER	TEAM	YRS	GP	GA	GAA
George Hainsworth	Mtl, Tor	11	465	937	1.91
Alex Connell	Ott, Det, NYA, Mtl M	12	417	830	1.91
Chuck Gardiner	Chi	7	316	664	2.02
Lorne Chabot	NYR, Tor, Mtl, Chi, Mtl M, NYA	11	411	861	2.04
Tiny Thompson	Bos, Det	12	553	1,183	2.08

All-time Goals-Against Average Leaders (Post-1950)

GOALTENDER	TEAM	YRS	GP	GA	GAA
Martin Brodeur	NJ	12	740	1,573	2.17
Dominik Hasek	Chi, Buf, Det	13	595	1,284	2.23
Ken Dryden	Mtl	8	397	870	2.24
Jacques Plante	Mtl, NYR, StL, Tor, Bos	18	837	1,965	2.38
Ed Belfour	Chi, SJ, Dal, Tor	15	856	2,006	2.43

Note: Minimum 350 games played. Goals-against average equals goals against per 60 minutes played.

 KEY YRS=years; GP=games played; A/GAME=assists per game; W=win; L=loss; T=tie; SO=shutout; GA=goals allowed; GAA=goals-against average

■ **Fast Fact:** Since the NHL expanded in 1967, the Stanley Cup Finals have gone to a seventh game only six times. During that same span, the World Series has gone seven games 15 times.

TRIVIA CHALLENGE

During his playing career, Wayne Gretzky skated for the Edmonton Oilers, Los Angeles Kings, St. Louis Blues, and the New York Rangers. What team is he now part of?

The Phoenix Coyotes. "The Great One" is the managing partner of the team.

NHL ALL-STAR GAME

First played in 1947, this game was scheduled before the start of the regular season and used to match the defending Stanley Cup champions against a squad of NHL All-Stars from other teams. In 1966, the game was moved to mid-season, although there was no game that year. The format was changed to a conference-versus-conference showdown in 1969.

YEAR	SITE	SCORE	MVP	ATTENDANCE
2004	St. Paul, MN	East 6, West 4	Joe Sakic, Col (West)	19,434
2003	Sunrise, FL	West 6, East 5	Dany Heatley, Atl (East)	19,250
2002	Los Angeles, CA	World 8, N America 5	Eric Daze, Chi (N America)	18,118
2001	Denver, CO	N America 14, World 12	Bill Guerin, Bos (N America)	18,646
2000	Toronto, ONT	World 9, N America 4	Pavel Bure, Fla (World)	19,300
1999	Tampa Bay, FL	N America 8, World 6	Wayne Gretzky, NYR (N America)	19,758
1998	Vancouver, BC	N America 8, World 7	Teemu Selanne, Ana (World)	18,422
1997	San Jose, CA	East 11, West 7	Mark Recchi, Mtl	17,422
1996	Boston, MA	East 5, West 4	Ray Bourque, Bos	17,565
1994	New York, NY	East 9, West 8	Mike Richter, NYR	18,200
1993	Montreal, QUE	Wales 16, Campbell 6	Mike Gartner, NYR	17,137
1992	Philadelphia, PA	Campbell 10, Wales 6	Brett Hull, StL	17,380
1991	Chicago, IL	Campbell 11, Wales 5	Vince Damphousse, Tor	18,472
1990	Pittsburgh, PA	Wales 12, Campbell 7	Mario Lemieux, Pitt	16,236
1989	Edmonton, ALB	Campbell 9, Wales 5	Wayne Gretzky, LA	17,503
1988	St. Louis, MO	Wales 6, Campbell 5 (OT)	Mario Lemieux, Pitt	17,878
1986	Hartford, CT	Wales 4, Campbell 3 (OT)	Grant Fuhr, Edm	15,100
1985	Calgary, ALB	Wales 6, Campbell 4	Mario Lemieux, Pitt	16,825
1984	East Rutherford, NJ	Wales 7, Campbell 6	Don Maloney, NYR	18,939
1983	Uniondale, NY	Campbell 9, Wales 3	Wayne Gretzky, Edm	15,230
1982	Washington, DC	Wales 4, Campbell 2	Mike Bossy, NYI	18,130
1981	Los Angeles, CA	Campbell 4, Wales 1	Mike Liut, StL	15,761
1980	Detroit, MI	Wales 6, Campbell 3	Reg Leach, Phi	21,002
1978	Buffalo, NY	Wales 3, Campbell 2 (OT)	Billy Smith, NYI	16,433
1977	Vancouver, BC	Wales 4, Campbell 3	Rick Martin, Buf	15,607
1976	Philadelphia, PA	Wales 7, Campbell 5	Pete Mahovlich, Mtl	16,436
1975	Montreal, QUE	Wales 7, Campbell 1	Syl Apps Jr., Pitt	16,080
1974	Chicago, IL	West 6, East 4	Garry Unger, StL	16,426
1973	New York, NY	East 5, West 4	Greg Polis, Pitt	16,986
1972	Minneapolis, MN	East 3, West 2	Bobby Orr, Bos	15,423
1971	Boston, MA	West 2, East 1	Bobby Hull, Chi	14,790
1970	St. Louis, MO	East 4, West 1	Bobby Hull, Chi	16,587
1969	Montreal, QUE	East 3, West 3	Frank Mahovlich, Det	16,260
1968	Toronto, ONT	Toronto 4, All-Stars 3	Bruce Gamble, Tor	15,753
1967	Montreal, QUE	Montreal 3, All-Stars 0	Henri Richard, Mtl	14,284
1965	Montreal, QUE	All-Stars 5, Montreal 2	Gordie Howe, Det	13,529
1964	Toronto, ONT	All-Stars 3, Toronto 2	Jean Beliveau, Mtl	14,232
1963	Toronto, ONT	All-Stars 3, Toronto 3	Frank Mahovlich, Tor	14,034
1962	Toronto, ONT	Toronto 4, All-Stars 1	Eddie Shack, Tor	14,236
1961	Chicago, IL	All-Stars 3, Chicago 1	None named	14,534
1960	Montreal, QUE	All-Stars 2, Montreal 1	None named	13,949
1959	Montreal, QUE	Montreal 6, All-Stars 1	None named	13,818
1958	Montreal, QUE	Montreal 6, All-Stars 3	None named	13,989
1957	Montreal, QUE	All-Stars 5, Montreal 3	None named	13,003
1956	Montreal, QUE	All-Stars 1, Montreal 1	None named	13,095
1955	Detroit, MI	Detroit 3, All-Stars 1	None named	10,111
1954	Detroit, MI	All-Stars 2, Detroit 2	None named	10,689
1953	Montreal, QUE	All-Stars 3, Montreal 1	None named	14,153
1952	Detroit, MI	1st team 1, 2nd team 1	None named	10,680
1951	Toronto, ONT	1st team 2, 2nd team 2	None named	11,469
1950	Detroit, MI	Detroit 7, All-Stars 1	None named	9,166
1949	Toronto, ONT	All-Stars 3, Toronto 1	None named	13,541
1948	Chicago, IL	All-Stars 3, Toronto 1	None named	12,794
1947	Toronto, ONT	All-Stars 4, Toronto 3	None named	14,169

Note: The Challenge Cup, a series between the NHL All-Stars and the Soviet Union, was played instead of the All-Star Game in 1979. Eight years later, Rendez-Vous '87, a two-game series matching the Soviet Union and the NHL All-Stars, replaced the All-Star Game. The 1995 NHL All-Star Game was canceled because of a labor dispute. The 1998 NHL All-Star Game, billed as a preview to the 1998 Winter Olympics, in Nagano, Japan, matched North American–born All-Stars and All-Stars born elsewhere. NHL All-Star Games from 1999 through 2002 also followed this format.

TODAY'S STARS

■ **Martin St. Louis, right wing,** b. June 18, 1975, Laval, Quebec, Canada. St. Louis's journey to NHL stardom was not easy. He was a finalist for the Hobey Baker Award as college hockey's best player for three seasons (1994-95, 1995-96, and 1996-97) while at the University of Vermont. Yet St. Louis went undrafted by NHL teams because at 5' 9", teams felt he wasn't big enough to succeed in the league. He signed as a free agent with the Calgary Flames in 1998, but was used mostly as a checking forward during the next two seasons before being released in 2000. That summer, he signed with Tampa Bay. Over the next four seasons, St. Louis rose from part-time player to full-time star. In 2003-04, he played in all 82 games,

Martin St. Louis led the Tampa Bay Lightning to its first Stanley Cup Championship in 2003-04.

scored 38 goals, and led the league in assists (56) and points (94) to win the Art Ross Trophy as the scoring leader. St. Louis also won the Hart Trophy as the NHL's Most Valuable Player and led Tampa Bay to its first Stanley Cup championship. The Lightning defeated St. Louis's former team in seven games.

■ **Miikka Kiprusoff, goaltender,** b. October 26, 1976, Turku, Finland. Kiprusoff spent his first three NHL seasons as a backup goalie for the San Jose Sharks. The Calgary Flames, desperate for a goaltender after their top two netminders were injured, traded a draft pick for Kiprusoff on November 16, 2003. Kiprusoff then carried the Flames to the playoffs for the first time in eight seasons. He went 24-10-4 with four shutouts and broke the modern era record for lowest goals-against average (1.69). Kiprusoff continued his brilliant goaltending in the playoffs — he finished with a 15-11 record, including five shutouts. He became the first Calgary goalie to record back-to-back playoff shutouts and came within one win of leading the Flames to their first Stanley Cup since 1989.

■ **Kris Draper, center,** b. May 24, 1971, Toronto, Ontario, Canada. Draper's play was instrumental in the Detroit Red Wings' three Stanley Cup titles (1996-97, 1997-98, and 2001-02). In his 11 seasons with the Wings, Draper scored 105 goals and 128 assists. But his real contributions were as a defensive forward and a penalty-killer. Draper was awarded the Frank Selke Trophy as the NHL's best defensive forward for the 2003-04 season.

Visit our website for the latest stats and sports info.

DID YOU KNOW?

Brothers Brian, Darryl, Duane, Brent, Rich, and Ron Sutter all played in the NHL at the same time. Darryl is the only Sutter still in the NHL. He is the head coach and general manager of the Calgary Flames, who reached the 2004 Stanley Cup Finals.

Major League Soccer fans will remember 2004 as the "Year of Adu" — Freddy Adu, that is. When the 14-year-old made his debut with D.C. United on April 3, he became the youngest player to appear on a top-level U.S. pro team since 1887. Adu scored 5 goals and added 3 assists for the season. But his power reached far beyond the pitch. Wherever D.C. United played, fans turned out in droves to see him in action. Adu and company averaged 23,686 fans on the road — 6,000 more per game than the next-closest team.

In November, United's season turned even more glorious when it won the MLS Cup by beating the Kansas City Wizards, 3–2. Second-year forward Alecko Eskandarian of United scored two goals in the match and was named MVP.

Elsewhere in MLS, the lowly Dallas Burn fizzled and missed the playoffs for the second straight season. But the emergence of striker Eddie Johnson was a positive note. The lightning-fast 20-year-old tied for the league lead in goals (12). Johnson also made his mark with the U.S. National Team on October 13, scoring a hat trick in a 6–0 win over Panama.

MLS said good-bye to one of its brightest stars on December 31, 2004. Midfielder Landon Donovan left the San Jose Earthquakes after four seasons to join Bayer Leverkusen in the Bundesliga, Germany's

Alecko Eskandarian led D.C. United to the 2004 MLS Cup championship.

ROBERT BECK/SPORTS ILLUSTRATED

MLS TEAMS

EASTERN CONFERENCE
Chicago Fire
Columbus Crew
D.C. United
Kansas City Wizards
MetroStars
New England Revolution

WESTERN CONFERENCE
Club Deportivo Chivas USA
Colorado Rapids
FC Dallas
Los Angeles Galaxy
Real Salt Lake
San Jose Earthquakes

most competitive league. Five months earlier, another MLS star, midfielder DaMarcus Beasley of the Chicago Fire, had signed with PSV Eindhoven in Holland.

Finally, two new teams joined MLS for 2005. Real Salt Lake began play in Salt Lake City, Utah. And in Los Angeles, California, Club Deportivo Chivas USA kicked off its inaugural season. Chivas USA is owned by Chivas Rayadas de Guadalajara, the most popular club in Mexico's pro league. The team will share The Home Depot Center with the Los Angeles Galaxy.

■ **Fast Fact:** D.C. United forward Alecko Eskandarian, MVP of the 2004 MLS Cup, is the second member of his family to win a major U.S. soccer championship. His father, Andranik, won two titles (1980 and 1982) in the North American Soccer League as a defender with the New York Cosmos.

Teenage phenom Freddy Adu of D.C. United revved up MLS attendance in 2004.

Goalie Tony Meola of the Kansas City Wizards earned a shutout against the Chicago Fire in the 2004 U.S. Open Cup.

2004 MLS FINAL STANDINGS

EASTERN CONFERENCE

TEAM	GP	W	L	T	PTS	GF	GA
y-Crew	30	12	5	13	49	40	32
x-United	30	11	10	9	42	43	42
x-MetroStars	30	11	12	7	40	47	49
x-Revolution	30	8	13	9	33	42	43
Fire	30	8	13	9	33	36	44

WESTERN CONFERENCE

TEAM	GP	W	L	T	PTS	GF	GA
y-Wizards	30	14	9	7	49	38	30
x-Galaxy	30	11	9	10	43	42	40
x-Rapids	30	10	9	11	41	29	32
x-Earthquakes	30	9	10	11	38	41	35
Burn	30	10	14	6	36	34	45

Note: Three points for a win. One point for a tie.
x=clinched playoffs; y=conference champion

KEY GP=games played; W=win; L=loss; T=tie; PTS=points; GF=goals for; GA=goals against

MLS CUP 2004

The Home Depot Center, Carson, California
November 14, 2004
Attendance: 25,797

	1st Half	2nd Half	Final
D.C. United	3	0	3
Kansas City Wizards	1	1	2

Scoring Summary:
KC: Burciaga, Jr. (unassisted) 6
D.C.: Eskandarian (Carroll) 19
D.C.: Eskandarian (unassisted) 23
D.C.: own goal (Zotinca) 26
KC: Wolff (penalty kick) 58

United: Nick Rimando, Bryan Namoff, Ryan Nelsen, Mike Petke, Earnie Stewart (Brandon Prideaux 82), Brian Carroll, Christian Gomez (Joshua Gros 59), Ben Olsen, Dema Kovalenko, Jaime Moreno, Alecko Eskandarian (Freddy Adu 65)

Wizards: Bo Oshoniyi, Alex Zotinca (Diego Walsh 82), Jimmy Conrad, Nick Garcia, Jose Burciaga, Jr., Khari Stephenson (Igor Simutenkov 46), Diego Gutierrez, Kerry Zavagnin, Jack Jewsbury (Matt Taylor 66), Josh Wolff, Davy Arnaud

Note: Numbers next to player names indicate time of game.

2004 MLS PLAYOFFS

Crew
Revolution
Revolution
United
United
MetroStars

UNITED
3 – 2
United
(3–3; United advances on
penalty kicks, 4–3)

Wizards
(2–0)

Wizards
Galaxy

Wizards
Earthquakes
Galaxy
Rapids

PLAYOFF LEADERS

SCORING	GP	G	A	PTS
Alecko Eskandarian, United	4	4	1	9
Davy Arnaud, Wizards	4	2	1	5
Jaime Moreno, United	4	2	1	5
Steve Ralston, Revolution	3	1	2	4
Earnie Stewart, United	4	1	2	4
Taylor Twellman, Revolution	3	2	0	4
Jose Burciaga, Jr., Wizards	4	1	1	3
Jack Jewsbury, Wizards	4	1	1	3
Josh Wolff, Wizards	4	1	1	3
Edson Buddle, Crew	2	1	0	2

GOALS	GP	G
Alecko Eskandarian, United	4	4
Davy Arnaud, Wizards	4	2
Jaime Moreno, United	4	2
Taylor Twellman, Revolution	3	2

16 tied with 1

ASSISTS	GP	A
Steve Ralston, Revolution	3	2
Earnie Stewart, United	4	2

23 tied with 1

GOALS-AGAINST AVERAGE	GP	GAA
Jon Busch, Crew	2	1.00
Joe Cannon, Rapids	2	1.00
Kevin Hartman, Galaxy	3	1.00
Nick Rimando, United	4	1.15
Matt Reis, Revolution	3	1.20
Bo Oshoniyi, Wizards	4	1.25
Pat Onstad, Earthquakes	2	1.50

KEY GP=games played; G=goals; A=assists;
PTS=points; GAA=goals-against average

TRIVIA CHALLENGE

What was the original team nickname of the San Jose Earthquakes?

The Clash. San Jose changed its name to the Earthquakes before the start of the 2000 season.

TEAM-BY-TEAM STATS

CHICAGO FIRE

PLAYER	GP	MIN	G	A	PTS	SHOTS	SOG
Damani Ralph	26	2,250	11	3	25	89	36
Andy Williams	25	2,023	4	9	17	48	20
Nate Jaqua	26	1,836	4	4	12	45	19
Justin Mapp	24	1,627	3	4	10	23	8
Ante Razov	13	996	4	2	10	52	25
Chris Armas	21	1,821	1	7	9	18	5
Andy Herron	4	310	4	0	8	8	4
Dipsy Selolwane	19	627	2	0	4	14	5
*DaMarcus Beasley	15	1,290	0	3	3	23	6
Scott Buete	13	702	0	2	2	2	0
Craig Capano	13	440	1	0	2	5	2
Kelly Gray	25	2,112	1	0	2	20	6
Logan Pause	21	1,482	0	2	2	2	1
C.J. Brown	24	2,130	0	1	1	5	2
Jim Curtin	30	2,700	0	1	1	12	7
Orlando Perez	17	1,075	0	1	1	7	2
Evan Whitfield	23	1,665	0	1	1	1	0
Alexandre Boucicot	5	164	0	0	0	4	1
Chris Carrieri	1	34	0	0	0	1	0
Denny Clanton	10	500	0	0	0	0	0
Leonard Griffin	9	330	0	0	0	2	1
Sumed Ibrahim	3	82	0	0	0	0	0
Jesse Marsch	10	681	0	0	0	0	0
FIRE			**36**	**40**	**112**	**381**	**150**
OPPONENTS			**44**	**50**	**138**	**393**	**179**

INDIVIDUAL GOALKEEPING

GOALKEEPER	GP	MIN	SHO	SVS	C/P	GA	GAA
Henry Ring	28	2,520	7	128	95	40	1.43
D.J. Countess	2	180	0	4	12	4	2.00
TOTALS	**30**	**2,700**	**7**	**132**	**107**	**44**	**1.47**

COLORADO RAPIDS

PLAYER	GP	MIN	G	A	PTS	SHOTS	SOG
Jean Phillippe Peguero	18	1,389	7	4	10	42	22
Chris Henderson	29	2,562	3	5	11	59	28
Mark Chung	22	1,914	3	4	10	49	20
Jordan Cila	21	1,310	4	2	10	24	16
John Spencer	22	1,752	4	1	9	52	21
Matt Crawford	30	2,534	1	4	6	20	9
Nat Borchers	29	2,610	2	1	5	11	5
Antonio de la Torre	28	2,409	0	5	5	29	7
Alberto Delgado	13	742	1	3	5	15	6
Kyle Beckerman	29	2,241	1	2	4	29	13
Seth Trembly	24	761	1	1	3	13	8
Zizi Roberts	5	363	1	0	2	10	1
Joey DiGiamarino	8	413	0	1	1	2	0
Ritchie Kotschau	28	2,351	0	1	1	7	0
Rey Angel Martinez	7	314	0	1	1	9	2
Ricky Lewis	5	289	0	0	0	1	0
Pablo Mastoeni	17	1,467	0	0	0	4	2
Daryl Powell	13	1,013	0	0	0	8	1
Gary Sullivan	16	339	0	0	0	8	3
*Adrian Cann	2	11	0	0	0	0	0
*David Castellanos	3	132	0	0	0	3	1
*Zach Kingsley	2	78	0	0	0	1	0
RAPIDS			**29**	**35**	**93**	**396**	**165**
OPPONENTS			**32**	**32**	**96**	**431**	**187**

INDIVIDUAL GOALKEEPING

GOALKEEPER	GP	MIN	SHO	SVS	C/P	GA	GAA
Joe Cannon	30	2,700	10	150	126	32	1.07
TOTALS	**30**	**2,700**	**10**	**150**	**126**	**32**	**1.07**

*Player no longer with team

KEY GP=games played; MIN=minutes played; G=goals; A=assists; PTS=points; SOG=shots on goal; SHO=shutouts; SVS=saves; C/P=catches/punches; GA=goals allowed; GAA=goals-against average

COLUMBUS CREW

PLAYER	GP	MIN	G	A	PTS	SHOTS	SOG
Edson Buddle	24	1,721	11	2	24	65	31
Jeff Cunningham	30	1,856	9	4	22	63	26
Ross Paule	25	2,059	7	2	16	23	13
Kyle Martino	29	2,301	5	2	12	31	17
Simon Elliot	27	2,353	0	10	10	18	4
Duncan Oughton	28	2,020	2	1	5	20	8
Tony Sanneh	6	513	2	1	5	5	2
Frankie Hejduk	20	1,644	2	0	4	28	14
Manny Lagos	18	766	1	2	4	10	3
Michael Ritch	12	397	1	1	3	9	4
Eric Denton	18	1,310	0	2	2	4	2
Chris Wingert	22	1,488	0	2	2	11	5
Chad Marshall	28	2,446	0	1	1	24	10
Danny Szetela	8	374	0	1	1	6	1
David Testo	16	443	0	1	1	7	4
Nelson Akwari	19	1,400	0	0	0	0	0
Devin Barclay	3	72	0	0	0	0	0
Robin Fraser	28	2,520	0	0	0	1	0
Stephen Herdsman	8	675	0	0	0	3	0
Brian Maisonneuve	9	427	0	0	0	6	2
Erick Scott	6	143	0	0	0	0	0
Jamal Sutton	1	5	0	0	0	0	0
Dante Washington	1	19	0	0	0	1	1
*Jake Traeger	1	3	0	0	0	0	0
CREW			**40**	**32**	**112**	**335**	**147**
OPPONENTS			**32**	**30**	**94**	**404**	**176**

INDIVIDUAL GOALKEEPING

GOALKEEPER	GP	MIN	SHO	SVS	C/P	GA	GAA
Jon Busch	29	2,610	10	132	124	31	1.07
Matt Jordan	1	90	0	5	9	1	1.00
TOTALS	**30**	**2,700**	**10**	**137**	**133**	**32**	**1.07**

DALLAS BURN

PLAYER	GP	MIN	G	A	PTS	SHOTS	SOG
Eddie Johnson	26	2,269	12	3	27	75	32
Toni Nhleko	23	1,186	6	2	14	49	23
Ronnie O'Brien	29	2,581	2	10	14	67	30
Jason Kreis	25	1,703	5	2	12	42	16
Oscar Pareja	24	1,096	1	6	8	12	3
Brad Davis	29	1,945	2	2	6	34	11
Bobby Rhine	19	693	2	2	6	21	9
Simo Valakari	26	2,297	1	4	6	11	5
Eric Quill	23	1,377	1	3	5	23	12
Matt Behncke	17	1,239	1	0	2	7	2
Steve Jolley	28	2,428	1	0	2	13	6
Chris Gbandi	23	1,771	0	1	1	5	0
Cory Gibbs	21	1,850	0	1	1	12	2
Carey Talley	23	1,688	0	1	1	11	7
Clarence Goodson	5	247	0	0	0	2	0
Ramon Nunez	8	107	0	0	0	7	0
Milton Reyes	12	828	0	0	0	9	1
Philip Salyer	17	1,407	0	0	0	6	1
Jordan Stone	5	145	0	0	0	1	0
BURN			**34**	**38**	**106**	**407**	**160**
OPPONENTS			**45**	**52**	**142**	**362**	**166**

INDIVIDUAL GOALKEEPING

GOALKEEPER	GP	MIN	SHO	SVS	C/P	GA	GAA
Jeff Cassar	19	1,632	4	65	105	27	1.49
Scott Garlick	12	1,068	4	52	34	18	1.52
TOTALS	**30**	**2,700**	**8**	**117**	**139**	**45**	**1.50**

*Player no longer with team

D.C. UNITED

PLAYER	GP	MIN	G	A	PTS	SHOTS	SOG
Jaime Moreno	27	2,279	7	14	28	39	25
Alecko Eskandarian	24	1,627	10	2	22	58	32
Dema Kovalenko	25	2,163	2	10	14	37	20
Freddy Adu	30	1,440	5	3	13	33	16
Ben Olsen	25	2,046	3	4	10	41	26
Earnie Stewart	26	2,093	3	4	10	33	16
Christian Gomez	9	582	4	0	8	12	7
Joshua Gros	29	2,087	1	4	6	30	17
*Ronald Cerritos	10	545	2	1	5	20	9
Ryan Nelson	17	1,417	2	0	4	7	4
Bobby Convey	10	823	0	3	3	16	4
Bryan Namoff	27	2,384	0	2	2	4	1
Mike Petke	26	2,027	1	0	2	7	3
Brian Carroll	30	2,438	0	1	1	12	3
Kevin Ara	6	114	0	0	0	0	0
Ezra Hendrickson	12	787	0	0	0	6	3
Nana Kuffour	5	90	0	0	0	1	0
Brandon Prideaux	23	1,458	0	0	0	1	0
Santino Quaranta	1	23	0	0	0	1	0
David Stokes	11	410	0	0	0	7	1
Jason Thompson	1	60	0	0	0	0	0
*G.R. Cannon	1	35	0	0	0	0	0
D.C. UNITED			**43**	**48**	**134**	**365**	**187**
OPPONENTS			**42**	**43**	**127**	**327**	**131**

INDIVIDUAL GOALKEEPING

GOALKEEPER	GP	MIN	SHO	SVS	C/P	GA	GAA
Troy Perkins	16	1,440	3	52	53	26	1.62
Nick Rimando	13	1,170	4	26	36	13	1.00
Doug Warren	1	90	0	6	0	3	3.00
TOTALS	**30**	**2,700**	**7**	**84**	**89**	**42**	**1.40**

KANSAS CITY WIZARDS

PLAYER	GP	MIN	G	A	PTS	SHOTS	SOG
Josh Wolff	26	2,252	10	7	27	59	33
Davy Arnaud	30	2,626	9	8	26	61	27
Chris Klein	19	1,694	4	8	16	47	23
Diego Gutierrez	28	2,520	3	4	10	28	8
Matt Taylor	17	524	3	1	7	11	6
Jack Jewsbury	22	1,408	2	2	6	23	12
Jose Burciaga, Jr.	24	1,876	1	1	3	15	6
Jimmy Conrad	29	2,610	1	0	2	12	6
Francisco Gomez	23	1,097	1	0	2	30	10
Taylor Graham	17	750	1	0	2	4	2
Igor Simutenkov	9	456	1	0	2	16	5
Shavar Thomas	25	1,880	1	0	2	7	3
Kerry Zavagnin	24	2,160	0	2	2	12	2
Nick Garcia	26	2,295	0	1	1	4	1
Justin Detter	6	162	0	0	0	3	2
Preki	2	90	0	0	0	2	0
Vuk Rasovic	1	45	0	0	0	0	0
Khari Stephenson	3	44	0	0	0	1	0
Diego Walsh	15	688	0	0	0	16	7
Alex Zotinca	25	1,779	0	0	0	17	9
WIZARDS			**38**	**34**	**110**	**368**	**162**
OPPONENTS			**30**	**31**	**91**	**397**	**158**

INDIVIDUAL GOALKEEPING

GOALKEEPER	GP	MIN	SHO	SVS	C/P	GA	GAA
Tony Meola	21	1,890	7	76	107	22	1.05
Bo Oshoniyi	9	810	5	42	31	8	0.89
TOTALS	**30**	**2,700**	**12**	**118**	**138**	**30**	**1.00**

*Player no longer with team

SOCCER MEN'S

LOS ANGELES GALAXY

PLAYER	GP	MIN	G	A	PTS	SHOTS	SOG
*Carlos Ruiz	20	1,587	11	2	24	63	36
Jovan Kirovski	24	1,984	8	2	18	59	25
Andreas Herzog	27	2,048	4	7	15	68	26
Alejandro Moreno	25	1,297	6	2	14	29	12
Joseph Ngwenya	22	880	4	2	10	17	8
Sasha Victorine	26	2,265	3	3	9	21	9
Chris Albright	24	2,111	1	6	8	15	6
Ned Grabavoy	15	928	1	3	5	7	7
Cobi Jones	23	1,751	0	5	5	19	6
Tyrone Marshall	18	1,449	2	1	5	3	3
Arturo Torres	18	599	1	2	4	13	6
*Ricky Lewis	13	855	0	2	2	0	0
Paul Broome	22	1,758	0	1	1	5	3
Marcelo Saragosa	26	2,123	0	1	1	9	1
Peter Vagenas	12	913	0	1	1	2	0
Chris Aloisi	4	281	0	0	0	1	0
Danny Califf	13	855	0	0	0	3	2
Josh Gardner	2	25	0	0	0	1	0
Guillermo Gonzalez	6	114	0	0	0	3	0
Alan Gordon	3	142	0	0	0	4	2
Hong Myung-Bo	13	858	0	0	0	1	1
Ryan Suarez	26	2,154	0	0	0	4	3
Scot Thompson	1	1	0	0	0	0	0
GALAXY			**42**	**40**	**124**	**347**	**156**
OPPONENTS			**40**	**36**	**116**	**382**	**167**

INDIVIDUAL GOALKEEPING

GOALKEEPER	GP	MIN	SHO	SVS	C/P	GA	GAA
Kevin Hartman	30	2,655	7	117	96	39	1.32
Dan Popik	1	45	0	2	1	1	2.00
TOTALS	**30**	**2,700**	**7**	**119**	**97**	**40**	**1.33**

METROSTARS

PLAYER	GP	MIN	G	A	PTS	SHOTS	SOG
Amado Guevara	24	2,110	10	10	30	65	30
John Wolyniec	30	2,051	10	3	23	56	27
Eddie Gaven	29	2,578	7	7	21	46	22
Cornell Glen	18	966	6	2	14	42	21
Fabian Taylor	21	883	5	1	11	45	18
Mike Magee	22	1,536	3	4	10	30	15
Sergio Galvan Rey	20	871	2	1	5	23	9
Mark Lisi	11	695	0	4	4	14	5
Ricardo Clark	26	1,769	1	1	3	25	7
Jeff Parke	28	2,409	1	1	3	23	10
Joselito Vaca	22	1,673	1	1	3	31	13
Kenny Arena	10	707	1	0	2	2	1
Chris Leitch	29	2,610	0	2	2	13	3
Craig Ziadie	15	1,289	0	2	2	4	0
Gilberto Flores	7	451	0	1	1	7	1
Tenywa Bonseu	14	1,164	0	0	0	4	1
Pablo Brenes	14	709	0	0	0	13	4
Eddie Pope	22	1,928	0	0	0	10	5
Tim Regan	12	578	0	0	0	3	1
Seth Stammler	1	1	0	0	0	0	0
METROSTARS			**47**	**40**	**134**	**456**	**193**
OPPONENTS			**49**	**47**	**145**	**376**	**156**

INDIVIDUAL GOALKEEPING

GOALKEEPER	GP	MIN	SHO	SVS	C/P	GA	GAA
Jonny Walker	28	2,520	5	99	86	45	1.61
Zach Wells	2	180	0	4	9	4	2.00
TOTALS	**30**	**2,700**	**5**	**103**	**95**	**49**	**1.63**

*Player no longer with team

NEW ENGLAND REVOLUTION

PLAYER	GP	MIN	G	A	PTS	SHOTS	SOG
Pat Noonan	29	2,545	11	8	30	75	37
Steve Ralston	30	2,700	7	8	22	25	11
Taylor Twellman	23	2,050	9	1	19	70	39
Jose Cancela	25	1,957	3	10	16	41	20
Clint Dempsey	24	2,024	7	1	15	47	25
Richie Baker	20	1,052	0	6	6	14	7
Andy Dorman	20	365	2	1	5	6	5
Felix Brillant	19	856	1	2	4	8	4
Jay Heaps	28	2,415	1	2	4	11	6
Shalrie Joseph	23	2,032	0	3	3	17	4
Joe Franchino	20	1,693	1	0	2	21	7
Brian Kamler	22	1,653	0	2	2	14	6
Joe-Max Moore	3	246	0	2	2	4	2
Marshall Leonard	25	1,992	0	1	1	5	2
Steve Howey	3	193	0	0	0	0	0
Avery John	21	1,808	0	0	0	4	2
Rusty Pierce	14	1,179	0	0	0	1	0
Luke Vercollone	2	2	0	0	0	0	0
*Daouda Kante	4	222	0	0	0	1	0
REVOLUTION			**42**	**47**	**131**	**364**	**177**
OPPONENTS			**43**	**38**	**124**	**388**	**185**

INDIVIDUAL GOALKEEPING

GOALKEEPER	GP	MIN	SHO	SVS	C/P	GA	GAA
Matt Reis	24	2,115	3	97	110	32	1.36
Adin Brown	7	585	1	39	26	11	1.69
TOTALS	**30**	**2,700**	**4**	**136**	**136**	**43**	**1.43**

SAN JOSE EARTHQUAKES

PLAYER	GP	MIN	G	A	PTS	SHOTS	SOG
Brian Ching	26	1,954	12	4	28	51	26
*Landon Donovan	23	2,018	6	10	22	51	22
Brian Mullan	28	2,408	3	8	14	41	20
Dwayne De Rosario	21	1,214	5	3	13	40	14
Ronnie Ekelund	26	2,018	4	3	11	32	12
Richard Mulrooney	30	2,700	1	8	10	28	13
Ramiro Corrales	29	2,475	3	1	7	42	12
*Jeff Agoos	24	2,152	1	4	6	15	7
Chris Brown	11	561	2	1	5	15	5
Craig Waibel	23	2,005	1	1	3	15	7
Arturo Alvarez	11	374	1	0	2	7	4
Troy Dayak	16	1,367	1	0	2	8	4
Ryan Cochrane	18	1,459	0	1	1	3	3
Ian Russell	22	1,091	0	1	1	13	6
Tighe Dombrowski	4	44	0	0	0	0	0
Todd Dunivant	16	1,212	0	0	0	7	3
Wes Hart	18	1,180	0	0	0	1	0
Eddie Robinson	8	458	0	0	0	0	0
Jamil Walker	10	237	0	0	0	4	0
EARTHQUAKES			**41**	**45**	**127**	**373**	**158**
OPPONENTS			**35**	**40**	**110**	**332**	**150**

INDIVIDUAL GOALKEEPING

GOALKEEPER	GP	MIN	SHO	SVS	C/P	GA	GAA
Pat Onstad	25	2,250	6	98	101	32	1.28
Jon Conway	5	450	2	15	24	3	0.60
TOTALS	**30**	**2,700**	**8**	**113**	**125**	**35**	**1.17**

*Player no longer with team

2004 MLS
Statistical Leaders

SCORING	GP	G	A	PTS
Amado Guevara, MetroStars	24	10	10	30
Pat Noonan, Revolution	29	11	8	30
Brian Ching, Earthquakes	25	12	4	28
Jaime Moreno, United	27	7	14	28
Eddie Johnson, Burn	26	12	3	27
Josh Wolff, Wizards	26	10	7	27
Davy Arnaud, Wizards	30	9	8	26
Damani Ralph, Fire	26	11	3	25
Edson Buddle, Crew	24	11	2	24
Carlos Ruiz, Galaxy	20	11	2	24
John Wolyniec, MetroStars	30	10	3	23

GOALS	GP	G
Brian Ching, Earthquakes	25	12
Eddie Johnson, Burn	26	12
Edson Buddle, Crew	24	11
Pat Noonan, Revolution	29	11
Damani Ralph, Fire	26	11
Carlos Ruiz, Galaxy	20	11
Alecko Eskandarian, United	24	10
Amado Guevara, MetroStars	24	10
Josh Wolff, Wizards	26	10
John Wolyniec, MetroStars	30	10

ASSISTS	GP	A
Jaime Moreno, United	27	14
Jose Cancela, Revolution	25	10
Landon Donovan, Earthquakes	23	10
Simon Elliott, Crew	27	10
Amado Guevara, MetroStars	24	10
Dema Kovalenko, United	25	10
Ronnie O'Brien, Burn	29	10

GOALS-AGAINST AVERAGE	GAA
Nick Rimando, United	1.00
Tony Meola, Wizards	1.05
Joe Cannon, Rapids	1.07
Jon Busch, Crew	1.07
Pat Onstad, Earthquakes	1.28
Kevin Hartman, Galaxy	1.32
Matt Reis, Revolution	1.36
Henry Ring, Fire	1.43
Jeff Cassar, Burn	1.49
Scott Garlick, Burn	1.52

KEY GP=games played; G=goals; A=assists; PTS=points; GAA=goals-against average; W=win; L=loss; T=tie

UNITED SOCCER LEAGUE RESULTS

2004 A-LEAGUE* FINAL STANDINGS

EASTERN CONFERENCE				
Team	GP	W	L	T
Montreal Impact	28	17	6	5
Richmond Kickers	28	17	8	3
Syracuse Salty Dogs	28	15	8	5
Rochester Raging Rhinos	28	15	10	3
Atlanta Silverbacks	28	14	11	3
Virginia Beach Mariners	28	11	14	3
Toronto Lynx	28	10	16	2
Charleston Battery	28	7	15	6
Puerto Rico Islanders	28	5	17	6

WESTERN CONFERENCE				
Team	GP	W	L	T
Portland Timbers	28	18	7	3
Vancouver Whitecaps	28	14	9	5
Minnesota Thunder	28	13	9	6
Seattle Sounders	28	13	11	4
Milwaukee Wave United	28	12	12	4
Calgary Mustangs	28	4	18	6
Edmonton FC	28	4	18	6

2004 A-LEAGUE* CHAMPIONSHIP

Claude Robillard Sports Complex, Montreal, Quebec
September 18, 2004

Montreal Impact 2, Seattle Sounders 0

*A-League is called United Soccer League First Division as of the 2005 season.

DID YOU KNOW?

The first pro soccer league in the United States was formed in 1894. The league lasted just one year. A second pro league was created in 1921 and lasted until the early 1930's. It was called the American Soccer League.

sikids.com

Visit our website
for the latest stats
and sports info.

2004 LAMAR HUNT U.S. OPEN CUP RESULTS

The annual Lamar Hunt U.S. Open Cup is open to all amateur and professional teams in the United States. The tournament is a single-elimination event running at the same time as the MLS season. The winner advances to the CONCACAF (Confederation of North, Central American, and Caribbean Association Football) Cup, a tournament of the top club teams from North and Central America and the Caribbean.

QUARTERFINALS
San Jose Earthquakes 2, Minnesota Thunder 2
(Earthquakes advance 5–4 on penalty kicks)
Kansas City Wizards 4, Dallas Burn 0
Chicago Fire 1, Richmond Kickers 0
Charleston Battery 1, Rochester Raging Rhinos 0

SEMIFINALS
Kansas City Wizards 1, San Jose Earthquakes 0
Chicago Fire 1, Charleston Battery 0 (OT)

**2004 LAMAR HUNT
U.S. OPEN CUP FINAL RESULTS**
September 22, 2004, Kansas City, Missouri
Kansas City Wizards 1, Chicago Fire 0 (OT)
Scoring summary: Kansas City — Igor Simutenkov (unassisted) 95

ALL-TIME MLS CUP RESULTS

YEAR	CHAMPION	SCORE	RUNNER-UP
2004	D.C. United	3–2	Kansas City Wizards
2003	San Jose Earthquakes	4–2	Chicago Fire
2002	Los Angeles Galaxy	1–0 (OT)	New England Revolution
2001	San Jose Earthquakes	2–1 (OT)	Los Angeles Galaxy
2000	Kansas City Wizards	1–0	Chicago Fire
1999	D.C. United	2–0	Los Angeles Galaxy
1998	Chicago Fire	2–0	D.C. United
1997	D.C. United	2–1	Colorado Rapids
1996	D.C. United	3–2 (OT)	Los Angeles Galaxy

■ **Fast Fact:** Defender Jeff Agoos, who joined the MetroStars for the 2005 season, has played in MLS since the league began in 1996 and has won five MLS Cups (1996, 1997, and 1999 with D.C. United; 2001 and 2003 with the San Jose Earthquakes).

MLS ALL-STAR GAME RESULTS

YEAR	RESULT	SITE	MVP
2004	East 3, West 2	Washington, D.C.	Amado Guevara, MetroStars
2003	MLS 3, Guadalajara Chivas 1	Carson, California	Carlos Ruiz, Los Angeles Galaxy
2002	MLS 3, USA 2	Washington, D.C.	Marco Etcheverry, D.C. United
2001	East 6, West 6	San Jose, California	Landon Donovan, San Jose Earthquakes
2000	East 9, West 4	Columbus, Ohio	Mamadou Diallo, Tampa Bay Mutiny
1999	West 6, East 4	San Diego, California	Preki, Kansas City Wizards
1998	MLS USA 6, World 1	Orlando, Florida	Brian McBride, Columbus Crew
1997	East 5, West 4	East Rutherford, New Jersey	Carlos Valderrama, Tampa Bay Mutiny
1996	East 3, West 2	East Rutherford, New Jersey	Carlos Valderrama, Tampa Bay Mutiny

MLS AWARD WINNERS

YEAR	MVP	SCORING CHAMPION	GOAL OF THE YEAR	COACH
2004	Amado Guevara, MetroStars	Amado Guevara, MetroStars	Dwayne De Rosario, Earthquakes	Greg Andrulis, Crew
2003	Preki, Wizards	Preki, Wizards	Damani Ralph, Fire	Dave Sarachan, Fire
2002	Carlos Ruiz, Galaxy	Taylor Twellman, Revolution	Carlos Ruiz, Galaxy	Steve Nicol, Revolution
2001	Alex Pineda Chacon, Fusion	Alex Pineda Chacon, Fusion	Clint Mathis, MetroStars	Frank Yallop, Earthquakes
2000	Tony Meola, Wizards	Mamadou Diallo, Mutiny	Marcelo Balboa, Rapids	Bob Gansler, Wizards
1999	Jason Kreis, Burn	Jason Kreis, Burn	Marco Etcheverry, United	Sigi Schmid, Galaxy
1998	Marco Etcheverry, United	Stern John, Crew	Brian McBride, Crew	Bob Bradley, Fire
1997	Preki, Wizards	Preki, Wizards	Marco Etcheverry, United	Bruce Arena, United
1996	Carlos Valderrama, Mutiny	Roy Lassiter, Mutiny	Eric Wynalda, Clash	Thomas Rongen, Mutiny

YEAR	GOALKEEPER	DEFENDER	ROOKIE	COMEBACK PLAYER
2004	Joe Cannon, Rapids	Robin Fraser, Crew	Clint Dempsey, Revolution	Brian Ching, Earthquakes
2003	Pat Onstad, Earthquakes	Carlos Bocanegra, Fire	Damani Ralph, Fire	Chris Armas, Fire
2002	Joe Cannon, Earthquakes	Carlos Bocanegra, Fire	Kyle Martino, Crew	Chris Klein, Wizards
2001	Tim Howard, MetroStars	Jeff Agoos, Earthquakes	Rodrigo Faria, MetroStars	Troy Dayak, Earthquakes
2000	Tony Meola, Wizards	Peter Vermes, Wizards	Carlos Bocanegra, Fire	Tony Meola, Wizards
1999	Kevin Hartman, Galaxy	Robin Fraser, Galaxy	Jay Heaps, Fusion	N/A
1998	Zach Thornton, Fire	Lubos Kubik, Fire	Ben Olsen, United	N/A
1997	Brad Friedel, Crew	Eddie Pope, United	Mike Duhaney, Mutiny	N/A
1996	Mark Dodd, Burn	John Doyle, Clash	Steve Ralston, Mutiny	N/A

UNITED SOCCER LEAGUE FIRST DIVISION * CHAMPIONS

YEAR	CHAMPION	SCORE	RUNNER-UP
2004	Montreal Impact	2–0	Seattle Sounders
2003	Charleston Battery	3–0	Minnesota Thunder
2002	Milwaukee Rampage	2–1 (2 OT)	Richmond Kickers
2001	Rochester Raging Rhinos	2–0	Hershey Wildcats
2000	Rochester Raging Rhinos	3–1	Minnesota Thunder
1999	Minnesota Thunder	2–1	Rochester Raging Rhinos
1998	Rochester Raging Rhinos	3–1	Minnesota Thunder
1997	Milwaukee Rampage	2–1 (SO)	Carolina Dynamo
1996	Seattle Sounders	2–0	Rochester Raging Rhinos
1995	Seattle Sounders	1–2 (SO), 3–0, 2–1 (SO)	Atlanta Ruckus
1994	Montreal Impact	1–0	Colorado Foxes
1993	Colorado Foxes	3–1 (OT)	Los Angeles Salsa
1992	Colorado Foxes	1–0	Tampa Bay Rowdies
1991	San Francisco Bay Blackhawks	1–3, 2–0 (1–0 on PKs)	Albany Capitals

*United Soccer League serves as a minor league system for Major League Soccer.

LAMAR HUNT U.S. OPEN CUP RESULTS

YEAR	CHAMPION	YEAR	CHAMPION
2004	Kansas City Wizards (MLS)	1958	Los Angeles Kickers (CA)
2003	Chicago Fire (MLS)	1957	Kutis SC (St. Louis, MO)
2002	Columbus Crew (MLS)	1956	Harmarville SC (PA)
2001	Los Angeles Galaxy (MLS)	1955	Eintracht Sport Club (New York City)
2000	Chicago Fire (MLS)	1954	New York Americans (New York City)
1999	Rochester Rhinos (A-League)	1953	Falcons SC (Chicago, IL)
1998	Chicago Fire (MLS)	1952	Harmarville SC (PA)
1997	Dallas Burn (MLS)	1951	German Hungarian SC (New York City)
1996	D.C. United (MLS)	1950	Simpkins-Ford SC (St. Louis, MO)
1995	Richmond Kickers (VA)	1949	Morgan SC (PA)
1994	Greek American AC (San Francisco, CA)	1948	Simpkins-Ford SC (St. Louis, MO)
1993	Club Deportivo Mexico (San Francisco, CA)	1947	Ponta Delgada SC (Fall River, MA)
1992	San Jose Oaks (CA)	1946	Chicago Viking FC (IL)
1991	Brooklyn Italians SC (East New York, NY)	1945	Brookhattan FC (New York City)
1990	AAC Eagles (Chicago, IL)	1944	Brooklyn Hispano SC (New York City)
1989	HRC Kickers (St. Petersburg, FL)	1943	Brooklyn Hispano SC (New York City)
1988	Busch SC (St. Louis, MO)	1942	Gallatin SC (PA)
1987	Club España (Washington, D.C.)	1941	Pawtucket FC (RI)
1986	Kutis SC (St. Louis, MO)	1940	No winner
1985	Greek American AC (San Francisco, CA)	1939	St. Mary's Celtic SC (Brooklyn, NY)
1984	AO Krete (New York City)	1938	Sparta A and BA (Chicago, IL)
1983	NY Pancyprian-Freedoms (New York City)	1937	New York American FC (New York City)
1982	NY Pancyprian-Freedoms (New York City)	1936	German-Americans (Philadelphia, PA)
1981	Maccabee SC (Los Angeles, CA)	1935	Central Breweries FC (Chicago, IL)
1980	NY Pancyprian-Freedoms (New York City)	1934	Stix, Baer and Fuller FC (St. Louis, MO)
1979	Brooklyn Dodgers SC (New York City)	1933	Stix, Baer and Fuller FC (St. Louis, MO)
1978	Maccabee SC (Los Angeles, CA)	1932	New Bedford FC (MA)
1977	Maccabee SC (Los Angeles, CA)	1931	Fall River FC (MA)
1976	San Francisco AC (CA)	1930	Fall River FC (MA)
1975	Maccabee SC (Los Angeles, CA)	1929	Hakoah All Stars SC (New York City)
1974	Greek American AA (New York City)	1928	New York National FC (New York City)
1973	Maccabee SC (Los Angeles, CA)	1927	Fall River FC (MA)
1972	Elizabeth SC (Union, NJ)	1926	Bethlehem Steel FC (PA)
1971	Hota SC (New York City)	1925	Shawsheen FC (Andover, MA)
1970	Elizabeth SC (Union, NJ)	1924	Fall River FC (MA)
1969	Greek American AA (New York City)	1923	Paterson FC (NJ)
1968	Greek American AA (New York City)	1922	Scullin Steel FC (St. Louis, MO)
1967	Greek American AA (New York City)	1921	Robbins Dry Dock FC (Brooklyn, NY)
1966	Ukrainian Nationals (Philadelphia, PA)	1920	Ben Miller FC (St. Louis, MO)
1965	New York Hungaria (New York City)	1919	Bethlehem Steel FC (PA)
1964	Los Angeles Kickers (CA)	1918	Bethlehem Steel FC (PA)
1963	Ukrainian Nationals (Philadelphia, PA)	1917	Fall River Rovers (MA)
1962	New York Hungaria (New York City)	1916	Bethlehem Steel FC (PA)
1961	Ukrainian Nationals (Philadelphia, PA)	1915	Bethlehem Steel FC (PA)
1960	Ukrainian Nationals (Philadelphia, PA)	1914	Brooklyn Field Club (New York City)
1959	McIlvaine Canvasbacks (Los Angeles, CA)		

LEGENDS

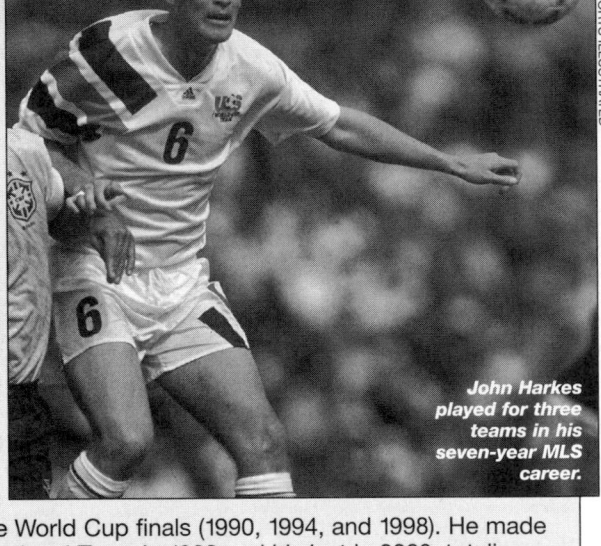

JOHN IACONO/SPORTS ILLUSTRATED

John Harkes played for three teams in his seven-year MLS career.

■ **John Harkes, midfielder,** b. March 8, 1967, Kearny, New Jersey. Harkes was a rock for the U.S. National Team for eight years. He played on the World Cup squads of 1990 and 1994 and served as team captain from March 1996 to March 1998. Harkes began his pro career in 1990 with Sheffield Wednesday in England's Premier League. He returned to the U.S. after six seasons and joined D.C. United for Major League Soccer's first season in 1996. As team captain, Harkes helped United win MLS Cup titles in 1996 and 1997. He retired after the 2002 season.

■ **Marcelo Balboa, defender,** b. August 8, 1967, Chicago, Illinois. Balboa is one of only three U.S. players to appear in three World Cup finals (1990, 1994, and 1998). He made his first appearance with the U.S. National Team in 1988 and his last in 2000, totaling 128 career caps or appearances, third among U.S. players. Balboa joined the Colorado Rapids in MLS's first season and scored the team's first goal on April 21, 1996. On May 30, 2001, he became the first defender in league history to score 20 goals and 20 assists in a career. He retired after the 2002 season.

■ **Paul Caligiuri, midfielder,** b. March 9, 1964, Walnut, California. In 1990, Caligiuri became the first American to play in the Bundesliga, Germany's top professional league. He joined MLS in 1996 with the Columbus Crew and later played with the Los Angeles Galaxy through the 2001 season. Caligiuri earned 110 career caps with the U.S. men's team. His game-winning goal against Trinidad and Tobago in a 1989 match sent the U.S. to its first World Cup finals (1990) in 40 years. Caligiuri retired after the 2001 season.

2004 EUROPEAN CHAMPIONSHIP PLAYOFF RESULTS

Portugal		Greece
	Portugal (2-2)*	Greece (1-0)
England		France
	Portugal (2-1) **GREECE 1 – 0** Greece (1-0)	
Sweden		Czech Republic
	Netherlands (0-0)*	Czech Republic (3-0)
Netherlands		Denmark

*Portugal and Netherlands advanced on penalty kicks, 6–5 and 5–4, respectively.

2004 EUROPEAN CHAMPIONSHIP GROUP STANDINGS

GROUP A	GP	W	L	T	GF	GA	PTS
Portugal	3	2	1	0	4	2	6
Greece	3	1	1	1	4	4	4
Spain	3	1	1	1	2	2	4
Russia	3	1	2	0	2	4	3

GROUP B	GP	W	L	T	GF	GA	PTS
France	3	2	0	1	7	4	7
England	3	2	1	0	8	4	6
Croatia	3	0	1	2	4	6	2
Switzerland	3	0	2	1	1	6	1

GROUP C	GP	W	L	T	GF	GA	PTS
Sweden	3	1	0	2	8	3	5
Denmark	3	1	0	2	4	2	5
Italy	3	1	0	2	3	2	5
Bulgaria	3	0	3	0	1	9	0

GROUP D	GP	W	L	T	GF	GA	PTS
Czech Republic	3	3	0	0	7	4	9
Netherlands	3	1	1	1	6	4	4
Germany	3	0	1	2	2	3	2
Latvia	3	0	2	1	1	5	1

2004 EUROPEAN CHAMPIONSHIP GAME RESULTS

GROUP A

Greece 2, Portugal 1
Spain 1, Russia 0
Greece 1, Spain 1
Portugal 2, Russia 0
Portugal 1, Spain 0
Russia 2, Greece 1

GROUP B

Switzerland 0, Croatia 0
France 2, England 1
England 3, Switzerland 0
France 2, Croatia 2
England 4, Croatia 2
France 3, Switzerland 1

GROUP C

Denmark 0, Italy 0
Sweden 5, Bulgaria 0
Denmark 2, Bulgaria 0
Italy 1, Sweden 1
Italy 2, Bulgaria 1
Sweden 2, Denmark 2

GROUP D

Germany 1, Netherlands 1
Czech Republic 2, Latvia 1
Latvia 0, Germany 0
Czech Republic 3, Netherlands 2
Netherlands 3, Latvia 0
Czech Republic 2, Germany 1

ALL-TIME WORLD CUP RESULTS

YEAR	CHAMPION	SCORE	RUNNER-UP	WINNING COACH
2002	Brazil	2–0	Germany	Luiz Felipe Scolari
1998	France	3–0	Brazil	Aime Jacquet
1994	Brazil	0–0 (3–2)	Italy	Carlos Alberto Parreira
1990	West Germany	1–0	Argentina	Franz Beckenbauer
1986	Argentina	3–2	West Germany	Carlos Bilardo
1982	Italy	3–1	West Germany	Enzo Bearzot
1978	Argentina	3–1	Netherlands	César Menotti
1974	West Germany	2–1	Netherlands	Helmut Schön
1970	Brazil	4–1	Italy	Mario Zagallo
1966	England	4–2	West Germany	Alf Ramsey
1962	Brazil	3–1	Czechoslovakia	Aymore Moreira
1958	Brazil	5–2	Sweden	Vicente Feola
1954	West Germany	3–2	Hungary	Sepp Herberger
1950	Uruguay	2–1	Brazil	Juan Lopez
1938	Italy	4–2	Hungary	Vittorio Pozzo
1934	Italy	2–1	Czechoslovakia	Vittorio Pozzo
1930	Uruguay	4–2	Argentina	Alberto Supicci

TODAY'S STARS

■ **Amado Guevara, midfielder,**
b. May 2, 1976, Tegucigalpa, Honduras.
The MetroStars' ace tied for the MLS
lead in points (30) in 2004 and was
named league MVP. Guevara is also
the captain of the Honduran national
team and has appeared in more
international games (77) than any
other player on the team. Nicknamed
El Lobo ("The Wolf"), he has also
played professionally in Mexico and
Spain.

■ **Joe Cannon, goalkeeper,**
b. January 1, 1975, Sun Valley, Idaho.
The netminder for the Colorado Rapids
won the MLS Goalkeeper of the Year
award in 2004. Cannon led the league
in saves (150) and tied for the lead in
shutouts (10). Cannon was also
named Goalkeeper of the Year in
2002 with the San Jose Earthquakes.

Amado Guevara led the MetroStars to the 2004 playoffs, where they lost to eventual champion D.C. United.

EVAN VUCCI/AP

■ **Damani Ralph, forward,**
b. November 6, 1980, Kingston, Jamaica. Ralph creates trouble near the opposition's
net. In 2004, the Chicago Fire forward led MLS in shots (89) and scored 11 goals, tied
for third in the league. He led all first-year players with 11 goals and won the Rookie of
the Year award in 2003. Ralph is also a starter on the Jamaican national team.

ALL-TIME WORLD CUP SCORING LEADERS

PLAYER, NATION	TOURNAMENTS	GOALS
Gerd Müller, West Germany	1970, 1974	14
Just Fontaine, France	1958	13
Pelé, Brazil	1958, 1962, 1966, 1970	12
Ronaldo, Brazil	1998, 2002	12
Sandor Kocsis, Hungary	1954	11
Teofilo Cubillas, Peru	1970, 1978	10
Gregorz Lato, Poland	1974, 1978, 1982	10
Helmut Rahn, West Germany	1954, 1958	10
Gary Lineker, England	1986, 1990	10
Ademir, Brazil	1950	9
Eusebio, Portugal	1966	9
Jairzinho, Brazil	1970, 1974	9
Paolo Rossi, Italy	1982, 1986	9
K.H. Rummenigge, West Germany	1978, 1982, 1986	9
Uwe Seeler, West Germany	1958, 1962, 1966, 1970	9
Vava, Brazil	1958, 1962	9

2004-05 TIME LINE

■ **April 3, 2004:** Teen phenom Freddy Adu of D.C. United makes his professional debut in a game against the San Jose Earthquakes. At age 14, the forward is the youngest player to appear in a game for a top-level U.S. pro team since 1887.

■ **April 17, 2004:** Adu scores his first professional goal during a 3–2 loss to the MetroStars.

■ **July 4, 2004:** In a stunning upset, Greece beats Portugal, 1–0, to win the 2004 European Championship.

■ **September 22, 2004:** The Kansas City Wizards defeat the Chicago Fire, 1–0, in overtime to win the Lamar Hunt U.S. Open Cup.

■ **October 9, 2004:** MLS announces that the expansion team that will play in Salt Lake City, Utah, beginning in 2005 will be named Real Salt Lake. Another expansion team, Club Deportivo Chivas USA, will play in Los Angeles, California.

■ **October 13, 2004:** The U.S. men's team defeats Panama, 6–0, to earn a spot in the final qualifying round of the CONCACAF region for the 2006 World Cup.

■ **November 11, 2004:** Midfielder Amado Guevara of the MetroStars is named MLS's MVP. He ties with forward Pat Noonan of the New England Revolution for most points (30).

■ **November 14, 2004:** D.C. United defeats the Kansas City Wizards, 3–2, to win its fourth MLS Cup. Forward Alecko Eskandarian of United scores two goals and is named the game's MVP.

■ **December 31, 2004:** Midfielder Landon Donovan of the San Jose Earthquakes leaves MLS and joins Bayer Leverkusen of Germany's Bundesliga. Donovan helped San Jose win two MLS Cup titles (2001 and 2003) and was MVP of both championship games.

■ **March 31, 2005:** Landon Donovan returns from Germany to play for MLS. He joins the Los Angeles Galaxy, who trade forward Carlos Ruiz to FC Dallas.

■ **April 2, 2005:** The 2005 MLS season kicks off with all 12 teams in action.

■ **August 6, 2005:** The Frisco Soccer & Entertainment Center opens in Dallas, Texas. It is the new home of FC Dallas, formerly known as the Dallas Burn, and the site of MLS Cup 2005.

TRIVIA CHALLENGE

Which current MLS coach was named MVP of the 1998 MLS Cup as a player with the Chicago Fire?

Peter Nowak of D.C. United

DID YOU KNOW?

Midfielder Landon Donovan is the only player to have won the Honda Player of the Year award three times (2002, 2003, and 2004). The award is given to the best player on the U.S. Men's National Team.

he Women's United Soccer Association (WUSA) folded in 2003, so soccer fans were happy that the Summer Olympics took place in 2004. But there was more than gold on the minds of the U.S. women's soccer team when it arrived in Athens, Greece. An era was about to end. The Games would be the last major international tournament for three U.S. stars — forward Mia Hamm, midfielder Julie Foudy, and defender Joy Fawcett. All three had announced that they would retire after the Olympics.

The trio went out on top. The U.S. beat Brazil, 2–1, in the gold medal match when forward Abby Wambach headed in the winning goal in overtime.

The retirement of Hamm, Foudy, and Fawcett marked the conclusion of a golden age for U.S. soccer. For 18 years, the three-some was the heart of a dazzling team that helped put women's soccer on the map. During that time, they won two World Cup titles (1991 and 1999) and two Olympic gold medals (1996 and 2004).

Foudy, age 33, became team captain in 1999. She was known for her superb vision on the field. Fawcett, age 36, earned a reputation as one of the toughest backliners in the world. But it was Hamm, age 32, who really propelled the women's game into the spotlight.

Hamm was aggressive and technically brilliant on the pitch. Her twisting, shifting moves and swerving free kicks forced opposing teams to concentrate on trying to shut her down. When that happened, Hamm simply set up her teammates with pinpoint passes. It's no surprise that

Three U.S. women's soccer legends said good-bye in 2004.

JOHN TODD/INTERNATIONAL SPORTS IMAGES

the "Golden Girl" of U.S. soccer became the idol of millions of young soccer-playing girls.

After the Olympics, the U.S. team enjoyed a "Fan Celebration Tour," playing 10 exhibition matches against international teams. The U.S. posted an 8–1–1 record. Hamm, Foudy, and Fawcett made their last appearance with the team in a 5–0 win over Mexico on December 8, 2004.

Despite the departure of three of its legendary talents, the future of the U.S. women's team is bright. Young players such as the 24-year-old Wambach (a team-leading 31 goals in 2004), 20-year-old forward Heather O'Reilly (1 goal in four games at the Summer Olympics), and 23-year-old defender Cat Reddick (2,527 minutes played in 2004, third-most on the team) have the potential to continue the winning tradition of Hamm, Foudy, and Fawcett.

In her last game, Hamm wore the name of her husband, Chicago Cub shortstop Nomar Garciaparra.

2004 WUSA FESTIVALS

Blaine, Minnesota   June 18, 2004

	1st Half	2nd Half	Final
New York Power	0	2	2
Atlanta Beat	0	2	2

Scoring Summary:
ATL: Dominguez (Hooper) 73
NY: Boxx (Clemens) 74
NY: Boxx (PK) 80
ATL: Hooper (PK) 90

Blaine, Minnesota   June 19, 2004

	1st Half	2nd Half	Final
Washington Freedom	3	0	3
Boston Breakers	1	2	3

Scoring Summary:
WAS: Hamm (Hucles) 3
WAS: Hamm (unassisted) 34
BOS: Pichon (Lilly) 44
WAS: Wambach (unassisted) 45
BOS: Popper (Splaine) 70
BOS: Smith (Splaine) 82

Carson, California   June 27, 2004

	1st Half	2nd Half	Final
San Diego Spirit	0	2	2
Carolina Courage	0	1	1

Scoring Summary:
SD: Hucles (Fleeting) 27
SD: Wambach (Connors) 61
CAR: Hooper (PK) 67

	1st Half	2nd Half	Final
Philadelphia Charge	1	1	2
San Jose CyberRays	0	0	0

Scoring Summary:
PHI: Pichon (Smith) 27
PHI: Lilly (Pichon) 52

Note: Hoping to revive interest, the defunct WUSA held two soccer festivals featuring the league's eight teams in 2004.

Numbers next to player names indicate time of game; PK=penalty kick.

DID YOU KNOW?

The final of the 1999 Women's World Cup drew 90,185 fans, the largest crowd to watch a women's sports event in history. The match was held at the Rose Bowl, in Pasadena, California.

2004 U.S. WOMEN'S NATIONAL TEAM STATS

FINAL INDIVIDUAL STATS

PLAYER	GP	MIN	G	A	PTS	CAREER CAPS/GOALS
Nicole Barnhart	1	4	0	0	0	1/0
Kylie Bivens	1	45	0	0	0	17/0
Shannon Boxx	32	2,714	8	5	21	41/12
Lori Chalupny	4	96	1	0	2	8/1
Brandi Chastain	20	1,148	0	2	2	192/30
Joy Fawcett	15	1,341	1	1	3	239/27
Julie Foudy	32	2,445	3	6	12	271/45
Mia Hamm	30	2,296	14	22	50	275/158
Angela Hucles	21	916	4	2	10	45/5
Amy LePeilbet	6	437	0	1	1	6/0
Kristine Lilly	28	2,457	8	8	24	291/101
Kristin Luckenbill	14	630	0	0	0	14
Shannon MacMillan	15	602	1	6	8	174/60
Kate Markgraf	33	2,812	0	3	3	137/0
Heather Mitts	28	1,905	2	0	4	33/2
Siri Mullinix	4	360	0	0	0	45
Heather O'Reilly	12	274	1	2	4	30/4
Leslie Osborne	9	493	0	0	0	9/0
Cindy Parlow	24	1,081	10	8	28	158/75
Christie Rampone	28	2,265	0	0	0	136/4
Cat Reddick	32	2,527	3	1	7	74/5
Tiffany Roberts	2	80	0	0	0	107/7
Briana Scurry	28	2,130	0	0	0	155
Lindsay Tarpley	25	1,222	8	3	19	33/8
Aly Wagner	27	1,586	6	6	18	80/18
Abby Wambach	33	2,319	31	13	75	55/45
Christie Welsh	2	56	1	1	3	23/13
TOTAL	**34**	**3,120**	**102**	**90**	**294**	
OPPONENTS	**34**	**3,120**	**23**	**16**	**62**	

FINAL GOALKEEPER STATS

GOALKEEPER	GP	MIN	W	L	T	SHO	GA	GAA
Kristin Luckenbill	14	630	4	0	2	2	5	0.72
Siri Mullinix	4	360	4	0	0	3	2	0.50
Briana Scurry	28	2,130	20	2	2	7	16	0.70
TOTAL	**34**	**3,120**	**28**	**2**	**4**	**12**	**23**	**0.66**
OPPONENTS	**34**	**3,120**	**2**	**28**	**4**	**1**	**104**	**3.00**

 KEY GP=games played; MIN=minutes played; G=goals; A=assists; PTS= points; W= win; L=loss; T=tie; SHO=shutouts; GA=goals allowed; GAA=goals-against average

■ **Fast Fact:** Joy Fawcett of the U.S. women's team retired in 2004 as the team's career leader in goals scored by a defender (27).

2004 U.S. WOMEN'S NATIONAL TEAM "FAN CELEBRATION TOUR" RESULTS

	DATE	RESULT	VENUE	CITY	ATTENDANCE
1.	September 25	USA 4, Iceland 3	Frontier Field	Rochester, New York	14,870 (sellout)
2.	September 29	USA 2, Iceland 0	Heinz Field	Pittsburgh, Pennsylvania	6,386
3.	October 3	USA 5, New Zealand 0	PGE Park	Portland, Oregon	16,554
4.	October 10	USA 6, New Zealand 0	Paul Brown Stadium	Cincinnati, Ohio	18,806
5.	October 16	USA 1, Mexico 0	Arrowhead Stadium	Kansas City, Missouri	20,435
6.	October 20	USA 5, Ireland 1	Soldier Field	Chicago, Illinois	12,856
7.	October 23	USA 5, Ireland 0	Reliant Stadium	Houston, Texas	16,991
8.	November 3	USA 1, Denmark 1	Giants Stadium	East Rutherford, New Jersey	18,885
9.	November 6	Denmark 3, USA 1	Lincoln Financial Field	Philadelphia, Pennsylvania	14,812
10.	December 8	USA 5, Mexico 0	Home Depot Center	Carson, California	15,549

OVERALL RECORD: USA, 8–1–1

ALL-TIME WUSA AWARD WINNERS

MVP

2003 Maren Meinert, Boston Breakers
2002 Marinette Pichon, Philadelphia Charge
2001 Tiffeny Milbrett, New York Power

GOALKEEPER OF THE YEAR

2003 Briana Scurry, Atlanta Beat
2002 Kristin Luckenbill, Carolina Courage
2001 LaKeysia Beene, San Jose CyberRays

OFFENSIVE PLAYER OF THE YEAR

2002 Marinette Pichon, Philadelphia Charge
2001 Tiffeny Milbrett, New York Power

ROOKIE OF THE YEAR

2003 Christine Latham, San Diego Spirit
2002 Abby Wambach, Washington Freedom

DEFENSIVE PLAYER OF THE YEAR

2003 Joy Fawcett, San Diego Spirit
2002 Danielle Slaton, Carolina Courage
2001 Doris Fitschen, Philadelphia Charge

GOAL OF THE YEAR

2003 Abby Wambach, Washington Freedom
2002 Katia, San Jose CyberRays

TODAY'S STARS

Heather O'Reilly came back from a broken leg to make the 2004 Olympic team.

■ **Heather O'Reilly, forward,** b. January 2, 1985, East Rutherford, New Jersey. O'Reilly is one of the fastest players on the U.S. Women's National Team. She joined the team at age 17 after scoring 143 goals in high school. In 2003, as a freshman at North Carolina, she helped lead the Tar Heels to the NCAA championship. She scored in all six of Carolina's playoff matches, including twice in the title game, and was named Offensive MVP of the Final Four.

■ **Kristine Lilly, midfielder,** b. July 22, 1971, New York, New York. Lilly debuted with the U.S. National Team in 1987 when she was 16. Tough and durable, she was the world's leader in international appearances (291) and the U.S. team's active career goal leader (101) at the end of the 2004 season. Lilly played in each of the WUSA's three seasons, all with the Boston Breakers (2001, 2002, and 2003). She was the only player to be named first-team All-WUSA in each season.

■ **Brandi Chastain, defender,** b. July 7, 1968, San Jose, California. Chastain scored perhaps the most famous goal in U.S. soccer history during the final of the 1999 Women's World Cup when she buried the deciding penalty kick against China in a shootout. The goal clinched the Cup title for the United States. Chastain began her national-team career in 1991 as a forward and switched to defender in 1996. The versatile, two-footed kicker shuts down attackers with strength and power. She played for the WUSA's San Jose CyberRays and helped the team win the league's first championship in 2001.

DID YOU KNOW?

The first college varsity women's soccer team in the United States was founded at Castleton State College in Vermont in the mid-1960's.

LEGENDS

JOHN CHAPMAN/NEWSPORT

Mia Hamm is the leading goal-scorer in international play.

■ **Mia Hamm, forward,** b. March 17, 1972, Selma, Alabama. Hamm is considered the greatest women's soccer player of all time. She joined the U.S. women's team in 1987 at age 15 and went on to win two Women's World Cup titles (1991 and 1999), two Olympic gold medals (1996 and 2004), and two FIFA Women's World Player of the Year awards (2001 and 2002). The talented striker attended North Carolina and won four NCAA titles (1989, 1990, 1992, and 1993). She played all three WUSA seasons with the Washington Freedom (2001, 2002, and 2003), and won a championship in 2003. Hamm is the world's all-time top international goal-scorer among women or men (158). She retired in 2004 at age 32.

■ **Julie Foudy, midfielder,** b. January 23, 1971, San Diego, California. Energetic, outgoing, and blessed with excellent field vision, "Loudy Foudy" joined the U.S. women's team in 1988 and was named captain in 1999. She helped the team win the Women's World Cup twice (1991 and 1999) and the Olympic gold medal twice (1996 and 2004). As a member of the San Diego Spirit, Foudy was named to the all-WUSA second team in each of the league's three seasons (2001, 2002, and 2003). She retired in 2004 at age 33.

■ **Birgit Prinz, forward,** b. October 25, 1977, Frankfurt, Germany. Prinz won her second straight FIFA Women's World Player of the Year award in 2004. She powered Germany to the 2003 World Cup title and led all scorers with 7 goals. Playing professionally with FFC Frankfurt (Germany), Prinz has led the team to four league titles. She played two seasons in the WUSA with the Carolina Courage (2002 and 2003), finishing second in the league in scoring in 2002 (12 goals, 8 assists).

ALL-TIME WUSA FOUNDER'S CUP RESULTS

YEAR	CHAMPION	SCORE	RUNNER-UP
2003	Washington Freedom	2–1 (OT)	Atlanta Beat
2002	Carolina Courage	3–2	Washington Freedom
2001	San Jose CyberRays	4–2 (on penalty kicks)	Atlanta Beat

sikids.com
Visit our website for the latest stats and sports info.

TRIVIA CHALLENGE

Notre Dame and North Carolina are the only schools to win the NCAA women's soccer championship more than once. Notre Dame won its second title in 2004. How many titles has North Carolina won?

17

YEAR	CHAMPION	SCORE	RUNNER-UP
2003	Germany	2–1	Sweden
1999	U.S.	5–4 (penalty kicks)	China
1995	Norway	2–0	Germany
1991	U.S.	2–1	Norway

ALL-TIME WORLD CUP SCORING

PLAYER	NATION	TOURNAMENTS	GOALS
Michelle Akers	U.S.	1991, 1995, 1999	12
Ann Kristin Aarones	Norway	1995, 1999	10
Heidi Mohr	Germany	1991, 1995	10
Sun Wen	China	1991, 1995, 1999	10

■ **Fast Fact:** The largest margin of victory in a Women's World Cup game is 8–0, and it happened twice: Sweden over Japan (1991) and Norway over Nigeria (1995).

TRIVIA CHALLENGE

FIFA released a list of the 100 greatest living soccer players — men and women — in 2004. Name the two Americans on the list.

Michelle Akers and Mia Hamm

2004-05 TIME LINE

■ **March 20, 2004:** The U.S. women's team wins the Algarve Cup championship for the third time by beating Norway, 4–1, in Fargo, Portugal. Forward Abby Wambach scores a hat trick and an assist in the title match, and finishes as the tournament's top scorer.

■ **May 5, 2004:** Michelle Akers, the former captain of the U.S. women's team (1985–2000), is elected to the Soccer Hall of Fame. The midfielder scored 105 goals in her career and was named FIFA Women's Player of the Century in 1999.

■ **June 18, 2004:** Hoping to revive interest, the defunct Women's United Soccer Association (WUSA) holds a "festival" in Blaine, Minnesota, with four of its former teams playing in a mini-tournament over two days. One week later, the league holds a second four-team festival in Carson, California.

■ **August 26, 2004:** Forward Abby Wambach sends a header into the back of the net in overtime to help the U.S. women's team defeat Brazil, 2–1, in the gold medal match at the Summer Olympics.

■ **November 27, 2004:** The U.S. Under-19 women's team beats Brazil, 3–0, for third place at the FIFA Under-19 Women's World Championship in Bangkok, Thailand.

■ **December 5, 2004:** After 90 minutes of regulation play, plus two overtimes and a shootout, Notre Dame and UCLA are still tied in the NCAA Division I women's soccer championship game. Notre Dame wins the title on sudden-death penalty kicks.

■ **December 8, 2004:** Legendary forward Mia Hamm of the U.S. women's team retires. The 32-year-old forward scored 158 goals in international play, the most in history by a woman or man. Hamm's longtime teammates, Julie Foudy and Joy Fawcett, also retire.

■ **December 20, 2004:** For the second year in a row, Germany's Birgit Prinz is named FIFA Women's World Player of the Year. The 27-year-old striker helped Germany finish as the world's top-rated women's national team in 2004.

■ **December 21, 2004:** The 2004 Chevrolet Female Athlete of the Year award goes to forward Abby Wambach. Her 31 goals and 13 assists were the second-highest single-year point total in U.S. women's soccer history. Wambach also won the award in 2003.

ACTION SPORTS

Shaun White won his sixth medal in snowboarding at the 2005 Winter X Games.

JAMIE SQUIRE/GETTY IMAGES

Snowboarder Shaun White was up to his old tricks — and some new ones — at the 2005 Winter X Games, held in Aspen, Colorado. After a knee injury cut short his 2003-04 season, White returned to the Winter X Games and won his third straight gold medal in Slopestyle. But White was unable to achieve his goal of winning gold medals in Slopestyle *and* Superpipe. Antti Autti of Finland won the Superpipe gold medal by pulling back-to-back 1080s.

Autti's airs were big, but freestyle motocross rider Brian Deegan's were even bigger in the Moto X Best Trick event. Deegan had broken both of his wrists and his left leg while attempting an off-axis 360 at the 2004 Winter X Games. He returned to the 2005 event, and landed a no-footed backflip one-hander to win Best Trick gold.

The Summer X Games, held in Los Angeles, California, celebrated its 10-year anniversary in 2004. Freestyle motocross rider Chuck Carothers unveiled the Carolla, a trick in which he lets go of his motorcycle in midair, spins his body 360 degrees, grabs the bike while he's still in the air, and then lands. The maneuver blew away the competition and earned Carothers the Moto X Best Trick gold medal.

In addition to new tricks, a new skateboarding event debuted at the Summer X Games. In Big Air, riders rocketed down a 50-foot-tall roll-in, soared off a jump across a 50-foot-wide gap, and landed right onto a 27-foot-tall quarterpipe. Danny Way, who pioneered this type of mega-ramp skating, easily won the inaugural gold medal, going bigger than any of his fellow competitors.

In the water, Andy Irons became the third male surfer to win three consecutive world championships. Sofia Mulanovich of Peru became the first South American, male or female, to win a world title.

Back on land, Chad Reed won his first 250cc Supercross title in 2004, ending Ricky Carmichael's three-year reign. But Carmichael was able to hold off Reed in the 250cc Motocross ranks, securing his fifth straight title. James "Bubba" Stewart won his second 125cc Motocross championship in three years.

WINTER X GAMES RESULTS

MOTO X

YEAR	EVENT	GOLD	SILVER	BRONZE
2005	Best Trick	Brian Deegan, U.S.	Jeff Kargola, U.S.	Dustin Miller, U.S.
2004	Best Trick	Caleb Wyatt, U.S.	Mike Metzger, U.S.	Nate Adams, U.S.
2003	Big Air	Mike Metzger, U.S.	Dane Kinnaird, Australia	Caleb Wyatt, U.S.
2002	Big Air	Brian Deegan, U.S.	Mike Jones, U.S.	Tommy Clowers, U.S.
2001	Big Air	Mike Jones, U.S.	Tommy Clowers, U.S.	Clifford Adoptante, U.S.

SKIING — MEN

YEAR	EVENT	GOLD	SILVER	BRONZE
2005	Skier X	Reggie Crist, U.S.	Zach Crist, U.S.	Enak Gavaggio, France
2004	Skier X	Casey Puckett, U.S.	Lars Lewen, Sweden	Reggie Crist, U.S.
2003	Skier X	Lars Lewen, Sweden	Reggie Crist, U.S.	Enak Gavaggio, France
2002	Skier X	Reggie Crist, U.S.	Peter Lind, Sweden	Enak Gavaggio, France
2001	Skier X	Zach Crist, U.S.	Tomas Andersson, Sweden	Enak Gavaggio, France
2000	Skier X	Shaun Palmer, U.S.	Bill Hudson, U.S.	Zach Crist, U.S.
1999	Skier X	Enak Gavaggio, France	Shane McConkey, U.S.	Jeremy Nobis, U.S.
1998	Skier X	Denis Rey, France	Kent Kreitler, U.S.	Chris Davenport, U.S.
2005	Slopestyle	Charles Gagnier, Canada	Tanner Hall, U.S	Jon Olsson, Sweden
2004	Slopestyle	Tanner Hall, U.S.	Peter Olenick, U.S.	Jon Olsson, Sweden
2003	Slopestyle	Tanner Hall, U.S.	Pep Fujas, U.S.	Jon Olsson, Sweden
2002	Slopestyle	Tanner Hall, U.S.	C.R. Johnson, U.S.	Jon Olsson, Sweden
2005	Superpipe	Simon Dumont, U.S.	Tanner Hall, U.S.	Jon Olsson, Sweden
2004	Superpipe	Simon Dumont, U.S.	Jon Olsson, Sweden	Peter Olenick, U.S.
2003	Superpipe	Candide Thovex, France	Tanner Hall, U.S.	Jon Olsson, Sweden
2002	Superpipe	Jon Olsson, Sweden	Philippe Larose, Canada	Philippe Poirier, Canada
2001	Big Air	Tanner Hall, U.S.	Evan Raps, U.S.	C.R. Johnson, U.S.
2000	Big Air	Candide Thovex, France	Skogen Sprang, U.S.	Evan Raps, U.S.
1999	Big Air	J.F. Cusson, Canada	Jonny Moseley, U.S.	Vincent Dorion, Canada

SKIING — WOMEN

YEAR	EVENT	GOLD	SILVER	BRONZE
2005	Skier X	Sanna Tidstrand, Sweden	Karin Huttary, Austria	Magdalena Jonsson, Sweden
2004	Skier X	Karin Huttary, Austria	Aleisha Cline, Canada	Sanna Tidstrand, Sweden
2003	Skier X	Aleisha Cline, Canada	Karin Huttary, Austria	Cecilie Larsen, Norway
2002	Skier X	Aleisha Cline, Canada	Magdalena Jonsson, Sweden	Patti Sherman-Kauf, U.S.
2001	Skier X	Aleisha Cline, Canada	Magdalena Jonsson, Sweden	Chiara Lawrence, U.S.
2000	Skier X	Anik Demers, Canada	Chiara Lawrence, U.S.	Patti Sherman-Kauf, U.S.
1999	Skier X	Aleisha Cline, Canada	Darian Boyle, U.S.	Patti Sherman-Kauf, U.S.
2005	Superpipe	Grete Eliassen, Norway	Sarah Burke, Canada	Kristi Leskinen, U.S.

SNOWBOARDING — MEN

YEAR	EVENT	GOLD	SILVER	BRONZE
2005	Slopestyle	Shaun White, U.S.	Danny Kass, U.S.	Travis Rice, U.S.
2004	Slopestyle	Shaun White, U.S.	Danny Kass, U.S.	Andreas Wiig, Norway
2003	Slopestyle	Shaun White, U.S.	Jussi Oksanen, Finland	Jimi Tomer, U.S.
2002	Slopestyle	Travis Rice, U.S.	Shaun White, U.S.	Todd Richards, U.S.
2001	Slopestyle	Kevin Jones, U.S.	Todd Richards, U.S.	Jussi Oksanen, Finland
2000	Slopestyle	Kevin Jones, U.S.	Todd Richards, U.S.	Peter Line, U.S.
1999	Slopestyle	Peter Line, U.S.	Kevin Jones, U.S.	Jimmy Halopoff, U.S.
1998	Slopestyle	Ross Powers, U.S.	Kevin Jones, U.S.	Rob Kingwill, U.S.
1997	Slopestyle	Daniel Franck, Norway	Jimmy Halopoff, U.S.	Bryan Iguchi, U.S.

WINTER X GAMES RESULTS (cont.)

SNOWBOARDING — MEN (cont.)

YEAR	EVENT	GOLD	SILVER	BRONZE
2005	Snowboarder X	Xavier de le Rue, France	Seth Wescott, U.S.	Marco Huser, Switzerland
2004	Snowboarder X	Ueli Kestenholz, Switzerland	Seth Wescott, U.S.	Xavier de le Rue, France
2003	Snowboarder X	Ueli Kestenholz, Switzerland	Xavier de le Rue, France	Michael Rosengren, U.S.
2002	Snowboarder X	Philippe Conte, Switzerland	Seth Wescott, U.S.	Berti Denervaud, Switzerland
2001	Snowboarder X	Scott Gaffney, Canada	Mark Schulz, U.S.	Seth Wescott, U.S.
2000	Snowboarder X	Drew Neilson, Canada	Scott Gaffney, Canada	Jason Ford, U.S.
1999	Snowboarder X	Shaun Palmer, U.S.	Drew Neilson, Canada	Scott Gaffney, Canada
1998	Snowboarder X	Shaun Palmer, U.S.	Jason Brown, U.S.	Seth Wescott, U.S.
1997	Snowboarder X	Shaun Palmer, U.S.	Berti Denervaud, Switzerland	Mike Basich, U.S.
2005	Superpipe	Antti Autti, Finland	Andy Finch, U.S.	Danny Kass, U.S.
2004	Superpipe	Steve Fisher, U.S.	Danny Kass, U.S.	Keir Dillon, U.S.
2003	Superpipe	Shaun White, U.S.	Danny Kass, U.S.	Markku Koski, Finland
2002	Superpipe	J.J. Thomas, U.S.	Shaun White, U.S.	Keir Dillon, U.S.
2001	Superpipe	Danny Kass, U.S.	Tommy Czeschin, U.S.	Ross Powers, U.S.
2000	Superpipe	Todd Richards, U.S.	Ross Powers, U.S.	Tommy Czeschin, U.S.
1999	Halfpipe	Jimi Scott, U.S.	Mike Michalchuk, Canada	Luke Wynen, U.S.
1998	Halfpipe	Ross Powers, U.S.	Guillaume Chastagnol, France	Todd Richards, U.S.
1997	Halfpipe	Todd Richards, U.S.	Daniel Franck, Norway	Fabien Rohrer, Switzerland
2001	Big Air	Jussi Oksanen, Finland	Todd Richards, U.S.	Josh Dirksen, U.S.
2000	Big Air	Peter Line, U.S.	Jason Borgstede, U.S.	Kevin Jones, U.S.
1999	Big Air	Kevin Sansalone, Canada	Peter Line, U.S.	Kevin Jones, U.S.
1998	Big Air	Jason Borgstede, U.S.	Ryan W. Williams, U.S.	Kevin Jones, U.S.
1997	Big Air	Jimmy Halopoff, U.S.	Steve Adkins, U.S.	Bjorn Leines, U.S.

■ **Fast Fact:** The only two people other than Dave Mirra who have won BMX Vert at the Summer X Games are Mat Hoffman (1995 and 1996) and Jamie Bestwick (2000 and 2003).

Lindsey Jacobellis (center) has won three straight Snowboarder X gold medals.

AGENCE ZOOM/GETTY IMAGES

SNOWBOARDING — WOMEN

YEAR	EVENT	GOLD	SILVER	BRONZE
2005	Slopestyle	Janna Meyen, U.S.	Silvia Mittermueller, Germany	Natasza Zurek, Canada
2004	Slopestyle	Janna Meyen, U.S.	Tara Dakides, U.S.	Jessica Dalpiaz, U.S.
2003	Slopestyle	Janna Meyen, U.S.	Hana Beaman, U.S.	Lindsey Jacobellis, U.S.
2002	Slopestyle	Tara Dakides, U.S.	Janna Meyen, U.S.	Barrett Christy, U.S.
2001	Slopestyle	Jaime MacLeod, U.S.	Shannon Dunn, U.S.	Marni Yamada, U.S.
2000	Slopestyle	Tara Dakides, U.S.	Jaime MacLeod, U.S.	Barrett Christy, U.S.
1999	Slopestyle	Tara Dakides, U.S.	Barrett Christy, U.S.	Jaime MacLeod, U.S.
1998	Slopestyle	Jennie Waara, Sweden	Barrett Christy, U.S.	Aurelie Sayres, U.S.
1997	Slopestyle	Barrett Christy, U.S.	Cara-Beth Burnside, U.S.	Jennie Waara, Sweden
2005	Snowboarder X	Lindsey Jacobellis, U.S.	Erin Simmons, Canada	Karine Ruby, France
2004	Snowboarder X	Lindsey Jacobellis, U.S.	Karine Ruby, France	Yvonne Mueller, Switzerland
2003	Snowboarder X	Lindsey Jacobellis, U.S.	Tanja Frieden, Switzerland	Yvonne Mueller, Switzerland
2002	Snowboarder X	Ine Poetzl, Austria	Erin Simmons, Canada	Tanja Frieden, Switzerland
2001	Snowboarder X	Line Oestvold, Norway	Erin Simmons, Canada	Amy Johnson, U.S.
2000	Snowboarder X	Leslee Olson, U.S.	Carlee Baker, Canada	Line Oestvold, Norway
1999	Snowboarder X	Maelle Ricker, Canada	Leslee Olson, U.S.	Candice Drouin, Canada
1998	Snowboarder X	Tina Dixon, U.S.	Corrie Rudishauser, U.S.	Katrina Warnick, U.S.
1997	Snowboarder X	Jennie Waara, Sweden	Hillary Maybery, U.S.	Aurelie Sayres, U.S.

SNOWBOARDING — WOMEN (cont.)

YEAR	EVENT	GOLD	SILVER	BRONZE
2005	Superpipe	Gretchen Bleiler, U.S.	Doriane Vidal, France	Hannah Teter, U.S.
2004	Superpipe	Hannah Teter, U.S.	Kelly Clark, U.S.	Doriane Vidal, France
2003	Superpipe	Gretchen Bleiler, U.S.	Kelly Clark, U.S.	Hannah Teter, U.S.
2002	Superpipe	Kelly Clark, U.S.	Stine Brun Kjeldaas, Norway	Natasza Zurek, Canada
2001	Superpipe	Shannon Dunn, U.S.	Natasza Zurek, Canada	Fabienne Reuteler, Switzerland
2000	Superpipe	Stine Brun Kjeldaas, Norway	Barrett Christy, U.S.	Natasza Zurek, Canada
1999	Halfpipe	Michelle Taggart, U.S.	Shannon Dunn, U.S.	Cara-Beth Burnside, U.S.
1998	Halfpipe	Cara-Beth Burnside, U.S.	Michelle Taggart, U.S.	Nicola Thost, Germany
1997	Halfpipe	Shannon Dunn, U.S.	Jennie Waara, Sweden	Nicole Angelrath, Switzerland
2001	Big Air	Tara Dakides, U.S.	Barrett Christy, U.S.	Jenna Murano, U.S.
2000	Big Air	Tara Dakides, U.S.	Leah Wagner, Canada	Jessica Dalpiaz, U.S.
1999	Big Air	Barrett Christy, U.S.	Tara Dakides, U.S.	Janet Matthews, Canada
1998	Big Air	Tina Basich, U.S.	Barrett Christy, U.S.	Tara Zwink, U.S.
1997	Big Air	Barrett Christy, U.S.	Tara Zwink, U.S.	Tina Basich, U.S.

SNOWMOBILING

YEAR	EVENT	GOLD	SILVER	BRONZE
2005	SnoCross	Blair Morgan, Canada	Tucker Hibbert, U.S.	Steve Martin, Canada
2004	SnoCross	Michael Island, Canada	Tucker Hibbert, U.S.	Blair Morgan, Canada
2003	SnoCross	Blair Morgan, Canada	D.J. Eckstrom, U.S.	Tucker Hibbert, U.S.
2002	SnoCross	Blair Morgan, Canada	Tucker Hibbert, U.S.	Tomi Ahmasalo, Finland
2001	SnoCross	Blair Morgan, Canada	Kent Ipsen, U.S.	D.J. Eckstrom, U.S.
2000	SnoCross	Tucker Hibbert, U.S.	Blair Morgan, Canada	T.J. Gulla, U.S.
1999	SnoCross	Chris Vincent, U.S.	Blair Morgan, Canada	Trevor John, U.S.
1998	SnoCross	Toni Haikonen, Finland	Dennis Burks, U.S.	Per Berggren, Sweden
2004	HillCross	Levi LaVallee, U.S.	Justin Tate, U.S.	Carl Kuster, Canada
2003	HillCross	T.J. Gulla, U.S.	Carl Kuster, Canada	Steve Martin, Canada
2002	HillCross	Carl Kuster, Canada	Steve Martin, Canada	Rick Ward, U.S.
2001	HillCross	Carl Kuster, Canada	Vinny Clark, Canada	Matt Luczynski, U.S.

ULTRACROSS *

YEAR	GOLD	SILVER	BRONZE
2005	Marco Huser, Switzerland	Xavier de le Rue, France	Nate Holland, U.S.
	Eric Andersson, Sweden	Davey Barr, Canada	Eric Archer, U.S.
2004	Nate Holland, U.S.	Lars Lewen, Sweden	Xavier Kuhn, France
	Reggie Crist, U.S.	Xavier de le Rue, France	Drew Neilson, Canada
2003	Xavier de le Rue, France	Seth Wescott, U.S.	Ben Jacobellis, U.S.
	Kaj Zackrisson, Sweden	Peter Lind, Sweden	Lars Lewen, Sweden
2002	Seth Wescott, U.S.	Scott Gaffney, Canada	Rob Fagan, Canada
	Peter Lind, Sweden	Eric Archer, U.S.	Enak Gavaggio, France
2001	Shaun Palmer, U.S.	Jason Evans, U.S.	Pontus Staahlkloo, Sweden
	Hiroomi Takizawa, Japan	Isidor Gruener, Austria	Matt Murphy, U.S.
2000	Travis McLain, U.S.	Scott Gaffney, Canada	Terry Plum, U.S.
	Peter Lind, Sweden	Sverre Liliequist, Sweden	Mike Dill, U.S.

*First athlete listed in each category is a snowboarder; the second athlete is a skier.

U.S. OPEN SNOWBOARDING CHAMPIONSHIPS RESULTS

HALFPIPE — MEN

YEAR	GOLD	SILVER	BRONZE
2005	Danny Kass, U.S.	Steve Fisher, U.S.	Antti Autti, Finland
2004	Danny Kass, U.S.	Steve Fisher, U.S.	Keir Dillon, U.S.
2003	Ross Powers, U.S.	Kazuhiro Kokubo, Japan	Daniel Franck, Norway

ACTION SPORTS

U.S. OPEN SNOWBOARDING CHAMPIONSHIPS RESULTS (cont.)

HALFPIPE — MEN (cont.)

YEAR	GOLD	SILVER	BRONZE
2002	Danny Kass, U.S.	Markku Koski, Finland	Keir Dillon, U.S.
2001	Danny Kass, U.S.	Abe Teter, U.S.	Daniel Franck, Norway
2000	Guillaume Morisset, Canada	Ross Powers, U.S.	Xavier Hoffman, Germany
1999	Ross Powers, U.S.	Xavier Hoffman, Germany	Tommy Czeschin, U.S.
1998	Rob Kingwill, U.S.	Terje Haakonsen, Norway	Todd Richards, U.S.
1997	Todd Richards, U.S.	Terje Haakonsen, Norway	Sebu Kuhlberg, Finland
1996	Jimi Scott, U.S.	Sami Hyry, Finland	Max Ploetzender, Austria
1995	Terje Haakonsen, Norway	Jason Evans, U.S.	J.J. Collier, U.S.
1994	Todd Richards, U.S.	Lael Gregory, U.S.	Jason Evans, U.S.
1993	Terje Haakonsen, Norway	Keith Wallace, U.S.	Sebu Kuhlberg, Finland
1992	Terje Haakonsen, Norway	Jeff Brushie, U.S.	Todd Richards, U.S.
1991	Jimi Scott, U.S.	Craig Kelly, U.S.	Shaun Palmer, U.S.
1990	Craig Kelly, U.S.	Shaun Palmer, U.S.	Jeff Brushie, U.S.
1989	Craig Kelly, U.S.	Bert Lamar, U.S.	Terry Kidwell, U.S.
1988	Terry Kidwell, U.S.	Bert Lamar, U.S.	Craig Kelly, U.S.

HALFPIPE — WOMEN

YEAR	GOLD	SILVER	BRONZE
2005	Gretchen Bleiler, U.S.	Torah Bright, Australia	Hannah Teter, U.S.
2004	Kelly Clark, U.S.	Tricia Byrnes, U.S.	Stine Brun Kjeldaas, Norway
2003	Gretchen Bleiler, U.S.	Natasza Zurek, Canada	Hannah Teter, U.S.
2002	Kelly Clark, U.S.	Tricia Byrnes, U.S.	Stine Brun Kjeldaas, Norway
2001	Natasza Zurek, Canada	Shannon Dunn, U.S.	Gretchen Bleiler, U.S.
2000	Natasza Zurek, Canada	Shannon Dunn, U.S.	Barrett Christy, U.S.
1999	Nicola Thost, Germany	Tricia Byrnes, U.S.	Shannon Dunn, U.S.
1998	Nicola Thost, Germany	Tricia Byrnes, U.S.	Tara Teigen, Canada
1997	Barrett Christy, U.S.	Tricia Byrnes, U.S.	Michelle Taggart, U.S.
1996	Satu Jarvela, Finland	Michelle Taggart, U.S.	Jennie Waara, Sweden
1995	Satu Jarvela, Finland	Nicole Angelrath, Switzerland	Jennie Waara, Sweden
1994	Shannon Dunn, U.S	Tina Basich, U.S.	Sandra Farmand, Germany
1993	Shannon Dunn, U.S.	Janna Meyen, U.S.	Tricia Byrnes, U.S.
1992	Tricia Byrnes, U.S.	Nicole Angelrath, Switzerland	Tina Basich, U.S.
1991	Janna Meyen, U.S.	Tina Basich, U.S.	Michelle Taggart, U.S.
1990	Tina Basich, U.S.	Lisa Vinciguerra, U.S.	Jean Higgins, U.S.
1989	Jean Higgins, U.S.	Tara Eberhard, U.S.	Ashild Lofthus, Norway
1988	Petra Mussig, Germany	Jean Higgins, U.S.	Gayle Guerin, U.S.

RAIL JAM — MEN

YEAR	GOLD	SILVER	BRONZE
2005	Eddie Wall, U.S.	Yale Cousino, U.S.	Jed Anderson, U.S.
2004	Rahm Klampert, U.S.	Travis Rice, U.S.	Chris Rotax, U.S.
2003	Travis Rice, U.S.	Shaun White, U.S.	Zach Leach, U.S.

RAIL JAM — WOMEN

YEAR	GOLD	SILVER	BRONZE
2005	Leanne Pelosi, Canada	Hana Beaman, U.S.	Spencer O'Brien, Canada
2004	Leanne Pelosi, Canada	Erin Comstock, U.S.	Natasza Zurek, Canada

SLOPESTYLE — MEN

YEAR	GOLD	SILVER	BRONZE
2005	Risto Mattila, Finland	Jussi Oksanen, Finland	Andreas Wiig, Norway
2004	Jake Blauvelt, U.S.	Travis Rice, U.S.	Christopher Schmidt, Germany
2003	Shaun White, U.S.	Travis Rice, U.S.	Nate Sheehan, U.S.
2002	Rahm Klampert, U.S.	Travis Rice, U.S.	Ryan Paris, U.S.

SLOPESTYLE — WOMEN

YEAR	GOLD	SILVER	BRONZE
2005	Janna Meyen, U.S.	Leanne Pelosi, Canada	Natasza Zurek, Canada
2004	Priscilla Levac, Canada	Kelly Clark, U.S.	Hana Beaman, U.S.
2003	Hana Beaman, U.S.	Priscilla Levac, Canada	Hannah Teter, U.S.
2002	Annie Boulanger, Canada	Hannah Teter, U.S.	Jaime MacLeod, U.S.

SUMMER X GAMES RESULTS

AGGRESSIVE IN-LINE — MEN

YEAR	EVENT	GOLD	SILVER	BRONZE
2003	Park	Bruno Lowe, Germany	Stephane Alfano, France	Sven Boekhorst, Netherlands
2002	Park	Jaren Grob, U.S.	Bruno Lowe, Germany	Blake Dennis, Australia
2001	Park	Jaren Grob, U.S.	Louie Zamora, U.S.	Franky Morales, U.S.
2000	Park	Sven Boekhorst, Netherlands	Jaren Grob, U.S.	Sam Fogarty, Australia
1999	Street	Nicky Adams, Canada	Blake Dennis, Australia	Aaron Feinberg, U.S.
1998	Street	Jonathan Bergeron, Canada	Marco Hintze, Mexico	Aaron Feinberg, U.S.
1997	Street	Aaron Feinberg, U.S.	Tim Ward, Australia	Chris Edwards, U.S.
1996	Street	Arlo Eisenberg, U.S.	Matt Mantz, U.S.	Chris Edwards, U.S.
1995	Street	Matt Salerno, Australia	Scott Bentley, New Zealand	Ryan Jacklone, U.S.

DID YOU KNOW?

Snowboarder Hannah Teter has two older brothers, Abe and Elijah, who are also pro snowboarders.

Takeshi Yasutoko won his sixth Summer X Games Vert medal in 2004.

YEAR	EVENT	GOLD	SILVER	BRONZE
2004	Vert	Takeshi Yasutoko, Japan	Marco De Santi, Brazil	Eito Yasutoko, Japan
2003	Vert	Eito Yasutoko, Japan	Takeshi Yasutoko, Japan	Nel Martin, Spain
2002	Vert	Takeshi Yasutoko, Japan	Eito Yasutoko, Japan	Marc Englehart, U.S.
2001	Vert	Taig Khris, France	Takeshi Yasutoko, Japan	Shane Yost, Australia
2000	Vert	Eito Yasutoko, Japan	Takeshi Yasutoko, Japan	Cesar Mora, Australia
1999	Vert	Eito Yasutoko, Japan	Cesar Mora, Australia	Matt Salerno, Australia
1998	Vert	Cesar Mora, Australia	Matt Salerno, Australia	Taig Khris, France
1997	Vert	Tim Ward, Australia	Taig Khris, France	Chris Edwards, U.S.
1996	Vert	Rene Hulgreen, Denmark	Tom Fry, Australia	Chris Edwards, U.S.
1995	Vert	Tom Fry, Australia	Cesar Mora, Australia	Manuel Billiris, Australia
1999	Vert Triples	Sven Boekhorst, Netherlands Javier Bujanda, Spain Taig Khris, France	Mike Budnik, U.S. Cesar Mora, Australia Matt Salerno, Australia	Maki Komori, Japan Eito Yasutoko, Japan Takeshi Yasutoko, Japan
1998	Vert Triples	Paul Malina, Australia Viorel Popa, U.S. Sam Fogarty, Australia	Mike Budnik, U.S. Cesar Mora, Australia Matt Salerno, Australia	Sven Boekhorst, Netherlands Javier Bujanda, Spain Taig Khris, France

SUMMER X GAMES RESULTS (cont.)

AGGRESSIVE IN-LINE — MEN (cont.)

YEAR	EVENT	GOLD	SILVER	BRONZE
1996	Best Trick	Dion Antony, Australia	Ryan Jacklone, U.S.	Eric Schrijn, U.S.
1995	Best Trick	B. Hardin, U.S.	Ryan Jacklone, U.S. Brooke Howard-Smith, New Zealand	
1995	High Air	Chris Edwards, U.S.	Manuel Billiris, Australia	Ichi Komori, Japan

AGGRESSIVE IN-LINE — WOMEN

YEAR	EVENT	GOLD	SILVER	BRONZE
2003	Park	Fabiola da Silva, Brazil	Jenny Logue, Great Britain	Martina Svobodova, Slovakia
2002	Park	Martina Svobodova, Slovakia	Jenna Downing, Great Britain	Fallon Heffernan, U.S.
2001	Park	Martina Svobodova, Slovakia	Fallon Heffernan, U.S.	Anneke Winter, Germany
2000	Park	Fabiola da Silva, Brazil	Martina Svobodova, Slovakia	Kelly Matthews, U.S.
1999	Street	Sayaka Yabe, Japan	Kelly Matthews, U.S.	Jenny Curry, U.S.
1998	Street	Jenny Curry, U.S.	Salima Sanga, Switzerland	Sayaka Yabe, Japan
1997	Street	Sayaka Yabe, Japan	Katie Brown, U.S.	True Otis, U.S.
2001	Vert	Fabiola da Silva, Brazil	Ayumi Kawasaki, Japan	N/A
2000	Vert	Fabiola da Silva, Brazil	Ayumi Kawasaki, Japan	Merce Borrull, Spain
1999	Vert	Ayumi Kawasaki, Japan	Fabiola da Silva, Brazil	Maki Komori, Japan
1998	Vert	Fabiola da Silva, Brazil	Ayumi Kawasaki, Japan	Maki Komori, Japan
1997	Vert	Fabiola da Silva, Brazil	Claudia Trachsel, Switzerland	Ayumi Kawasaki, Japan
1996	Vert	Fabiola da Silva, Brazil	Jodie Tyler, Australia	Tasha Hodgson, Australia
1995	Vert	Tasha Hodgson, Australia	Angie Walton, New Zealand	Laura Connery, U.S.

BAREFOOT JUMPING

YEAR	GOLD	SILVER	BRONZE
1998	Peter Fleck, U.S.	Ron Scarpa, U.S.	Massimiliano Colosio, Italy
1997	Peter Fleck, U.S.	Evan Berger, South Africa	Warren Fine, South Africa
1996	Ron Scarpa, U.S.	Jon Kretchman, U.S.	Rael Nurick, South Africa
1995	Justin Seers, Australia	Ron Scarpa, U.S.	Rael Nurick, South Africa

Corey Bohan won his first gold medal in Bike Stunt Dirt at the 2004 Summer X Games.

TRIVIA CHALLENGE

Which surfer has won the most world championships?

Kelly Slater of the U.S. has won six world titles (1992 and 1994-98).

BIKE STUNT

YEAR	EVENT	GOLD	SILVER	BRONZE
2004	Dirt	Corey Bohan, Australia	Chris Doyle, U.S.	T.J. Lavin, U.S.
2003	Dirt	Ryan Nyquist, U.S.	Corey Bohan, Australia	Chris Doyle, U.S.
2002	Dirt	Allan Cooke, U.S.	Ryan Nyquist, U.S.	Chris Doyle, U.S.
2001	Dirt	Stephen Murray, Great Britain	Ryan Nyquist, U.S.	T.J. Lavin, U.S.
2000	Dirt	Ryan Nyquist, U.S.	Cory Nastazio, U.S.	T.J. Lavin, U.S.
1999	Dirt	T.J. Lavin, U.S.	Brian Foster, U.S.	Ryan Nyquist, U.S.
1998	Dirt	Brian Foster, U.S.	Ryan Nyquist, U.S.	Joey Garcia, U.S.
1997	Dirt	T.J. Lavin, U.S.	Brian Foster, U.S.	Ryan Nyquist, U.S.

PETE DEMOS/SHAZAMM/ESPN

TODAY'S STARS

■ **Tanner Hall, skier,** b. October 26, 1983, Kalispell, Montana. Hall continued to heat up the snow in 2004-05. Although he was unable to win his fourth straight Winter X Games gold medal in Slopestyle in 2005, he did win silver in that event and in Superpipe. At the 2005 U.S. Freeskiing Open Championships, Hall won gold in Superpipe and finished second in Slopestyle.

■ **Luke Mitrani, snowboarder,** b. July 20, 1990, New York, New York. By age 12, Mitrani had made a name for himself in

Tanner Hall has won seven Winter X Games medals since 2001.

snowboarding. He was invited to the Arctic Challenge, snowboard legend Terje Haakonsen's exclusive contest. Mitrani was also the youngest person invited to join the U.S. Snowboard Team. Since then, he has finished first in Halfpipe and Slopestyle at the 2004 European Open Junior Jam. Mitrani hopes to compete in the 2006 Winter Olympics.

■ **Lyn-Z Adams Hawkins, skateboarder,** b. September 21, 1989, San Diego, California. Hawkins rips on both Vert and Street. She won the gold medal in Vert at the 2004 Summer X Games and the bronze medal in Street at the 2004 Summer Gravity Games. Hawkins's strong performances helped her become the first female skateboarder on the DC Shoes team, along with skating legends Danny Way and Rob Dyrdek.

SUMMER X GAMES RESULTS (cont.)

BIKE STUNT (cont.)

YEAR	EVENT	GOLD	SILVER	BRONZE
1996	Dirt	Joey Garcia, U.S.	T.J. Lavin, U.S.	Brian Foster, U.S.
1995	Dirt	Jay Miron, Canada	Taj Mihelich, U.S.	Joey Garcia, U.S.
2003	Flatland	Simon O'Brien, Australia	Nathan Penonzek, Canada	Trevor Meyer, U.S.
2002	Flatland	Martti Kuoppa, Finland	Michael Steingraeber, Germany	Phil Dolan, Great Britain
2001	Flatland	Martti Kuoppa, Finland	Phil Dolan, Great Britain	Matt Wilhelm, U.S.
2000	Flatland	Martti Kuoppa, Finland	Michael Steingraeber, Germany	Phil Dolan, Great Britain
1999	Flatland	Trevor Meyer, U.S.	Phil Dolan, Great Britain	Nathan Penonzek, Canada
1998	Flatland	Trevor Meyer, U.S.	Andrew Faris, Canada	Martti Kuoppa, Finland
1997	Flatland	Trevor Meyer, U.S.	Nate Hanson, U.S.	Andrew Faris, Canada
2004	Park	Dave Mirra, U.S.	Ryan Nyquist, U.S.	Ryan Guettler, Australia
2003	Park	Ryan Nyquist, U.S.	Gary Young, U.S.	Dave Mirra, U.S.
2002	Park	Ryan Nyquist, U.S.	Alistair Whitton, Great Britain	Chad Kagy, U.S.
2001	Park	Bruce Crisman, U.S.	Alistair Whitton, Great Britain	Jay Miron, Canada
2000	Park	Dave Mirra, U.S.	Markus Wilke, Germany	Ryan Nyquist, U.S.
1999	Street	Dave Mirra, U.S.	Jay Miron, Canada	Chad Kagy, U.S.
1998	Street	Dave Mirra, U.S.	Jay Miron, Canada	Dennis McCoy, U.S.
1997	Street	Dave Mirra, U.S.	Dennis McCoy, U.S.	Dave Voelker, U.S.
1996	Street	Dave Mirra, U.S.	Jay Miron, Canada	Rob Nolli, U.S.

SUMMER X GAMES RESULTS (cont.)

BIKE STUNT (cont.)

YEAR	EVENT	GOLD	SILVER	BRONZE
2004	Vert	Dave Mirra, U.S.	Simon Tabron, Great Britain	Kevin Robinson, U.S.
2003	Vert	Jamie Bestwick, Great Britain	Dave Mirra, U.S.	Kevin Robinson, U.S.
2002	Vert	Dave Mirra, U.S.	Mat Hoffman, U.S.	Simon Tabron, Great Britain
2001	Vert	Dave Mirra, U.S.	Jay Miron, Canada	Mat Hoffman, U.S.
2000	Vert	Jamie Bestwick, Great Britain	Dave Mirra, U.S.	Mat Hoffman, U.S.
1999	Vert	Dave Mirra, U.S.	Jay Miron, Canada	Simon Tabron, Great Britain
1998	Vert	Dave Mirra, U.S.	Dennis McCoy, U.S.	Simon Tabron, Great Britain
1997	Vert	Dave Mirra, U.S.	Dennis McCoy, U.S.	Mat Hoffman, U.S.
1996	Vert	Mat Hoffman, U.S.	Dave Mirra, U.S.	Jamie Bestwick, Great Britain
1995	Vert	Mat Hoffman, U.S.	Dave Mirra, U.S.	Jay Miron, Canada
1998	Vert Doubles	Dave Mirra, U.S. Dennis McCoy, U.S.	Jay Miron, Canada Dave Osato, Canada	Jason Davies, Great Britain John Parker, U.S.

BUNGY

YEAR	GOLD	SILVER	BRONZE
1996	Peter Bihun, Canada	Doug Anderson, Canada	Carolyn Anderson, Canada
1995	Doug Anderson, Canada	Mark Baldwin, U.S.	Todd Watkins, U.S.

DOWNHILL BMX

YEAR	GOLD	SILVER	BRONZE
2003	Brandon Meadows, U.S.	Kyle Bennett, U.S.	Michael Day, U.S.
2002	Robbie Miranda, U.S.	Kyle Bennett, U.S.	Robert de Wilde, Netherlands
2001	Brandon Meadows, U.S.	Brian Foster, U.S.	John Whipperman, U.S.

DOWNHILL IN-LINE — MEN

YEAR	EVENT	GOLD	SILVER	BRONZE
1998		Patrick Naylor, U.S.	Jeremy Anderson, U.S.	Dane Lewis, U.S.
1997		Derek Downing, U.S.	Keith Turner, U.S.	B.J. Steketee, U.S.
1996		Dante Muse, U.S.	Derek Parra, U.S.	Jim Wiederhold, U.S.
1995	Combined	Derek Downing, U.S.	Jim Wiederhold, U.S.	Jondon Trevena, U.S.

DOWNHILL IN-LINE — WOMEN

YEAR	GOLD	SILVER	BRONZE
1998	Julie Brandt, U.S.	Aimee Sanderson, U.S.	Theresa Cliff, U.S.
1997	Gypsy Tidwell, U.S.	Julie Brandt, U.S.	Jessica Apgar, U.S.
1996	Gypsy Tidwell, U.S.	Jennifer Jones, U.S.	Desly Hill, Australia

KITESKIING

YEAR	GOLD	SILVER	BRONZE
1995	Cory Roessler, U.S.	Clarin Mustad, Norway	Thomas Jeltsch, Germany

MOUNTAIN BIKING — MEN

YEAR	EVENT	GOLD	SILVER	BRONZE
1995	Dual Downhill	Robert Naughton, U.S.	Jurgen Beneke, Germany	Todd Tanner, U.S.
1995	Dual Slalom	Jimmy Knight, U.S.	Myles Rockwell, U.S.	Mike King, U.S.
1995	Observed Trials	Libor Karas, Czech Republic	Hans Rey, Germany	Marc Brooks, U.S.

SUMMER X GAMES RESULTS (cont.)

MOUNTAIN BIKING — WOMEN

YEAR	EVENT	GOLD	SILVER	BRONZE
1995	Dual Downhill	Cheri Elliott, U.S.	Kim Sonier, U.S.	Leigh Donovan, U.S.
1995	Dual Slalom	Leigh Donovan, U.S.	Cheri Elliott, U.S.	Giovanna Bonazzi, Italy

MOTO X

YEAR	EVENT	GOLD	SILVER	BRONZE
2003	Big Air	Brian Deegan, U.S.	Nate Adams, U.S.	Kenny Bartram, U.S.
2002	Big Air	Mike Metzger, U.S.	Carey Hart, U.S.	Brian Deegan, U.S.
2001	Big Air	Kenny Bartram, U.S.	Dustin Miller, U.S.	Brian Deegan, U.S.

SHAZAMM/ESPN

Nate Adams was the 2004 Summer X Games Freestyle champion.

2004	Freestyle	Nate Adams, U.S.	Travis Pastrana, U.S.	Adam Jones, U.S.
2003	Freestyle	Travis Pastrana, U.S.	Nate Adams, U.S.	Brian Deegan, U.S.
2002	Freestyle	Mike Metzger, U.S.	Kenny Bartram, U.S.	Drake McElroy, U.S.
2001	Freestyle	Travis Pastrana, U.S.	Clifford Adoptante, U.S.	Jake Windham, U.S.
2000	Freestyle	Travis Pastrana, U.S.	Tommy Clowers, U.S.	Brian Deegan, U.S.
1999	Freestyle	Travis Pastrana, U.S.	Mike Cinqmars, U.S.	Brian Deegan, U.S.
2004	Step Up	Jeremy McGrath, U.S.	Matt Buyten, U.S.	Tommy Clowers, U.S.
2003	Step Up	Matt Buyten, U.S.	Tommy Clowers, U.S.	Ronnie Renner, U.S.
2002	Step Up	Tommy Clowers, U.S.	Mike Metzger, U.S.	Brian Deegan, U.S.
2001	Step Up	Tommy Clowers, U.S.	Travis Pastrana, U.S.	Colin Morrison, U.S. (tie) Ronnie Renner, U.S. Kris Rourke, U.S. Jeremy Stenberg, U.S.
2000	Step Up	Tommy Clowers, U.S.	Kris Rourke, U.S.	Brian Deegan, U.S.
2004	Super Moto	Ben Bostrom, U.S.	Eddy Seel, Belgium	Jeremy McGrath, U.S.
2004	Best Trick	Chuck Carothers, U.S.	Nate Adams, U.S.	Travis Pastrana, U.S.

SUMMER X GAMES RESULTS (cont.)

SKATEBOARDING — MEN

YEAR	EVENT	GOLD	SILVER	BRONZE
2003	Park	Ryan Sheckler, U.S.	Rodil de Araujo, Jr., Brazil	Chad Bartie, Australia
2002	Park	Rodil de Araujo, Jr., Brazil	Wagner Ramos, Brazil	Eric Koston, U.S.
2001	Park	Rodil de Araujo, Jr., Brazil	Kerry Getz, U.S.	Caine Gayle, U.S.
2000	Park	Eric Koston, U.S.	Rodil de Araujo, Jr., Brazil	Kerry Getz, U.S.
2004	Street	Paul Rodriguez, U.S.	Andrew Reynolds, U.S.	Bastien Salabanzi, France
2003	Street	Eric Koston, U.S.	Rodil de Araujo, Jr., Brazil	Paul Rodriguez, U.S.
2002	Street	Rodil de Araujo, Jr., Brazil	Wagner Ramos, Brazil	Kyle Berard, U.S.
2001	Street	Kerry Getz, U.S.	Eric Koston, U.S.	Chris Senn, U.S.
1999	Street	Chris Senn, U.S.	Pat Channita, U.S.	Chad Fernandez, U.S.
1998	Street	Rodil de Araujo, Jr., Brazil	Andy Macdonald, U.S.	Chris Senn, U.S.
1997	Street	Chris Senn, U.S.	Andy Macdonald, U.S.	Brian Patch, U.S.
1996	Street	Rodil de Araujo, Jr., Brazil	Chris Senn, U.S.	Brian Patch, U.S.
1995	Street	Chris Senn, U.S.	Tony Hawk, U.S.	Willy Santos, U.S.
2003	Street Best Trick	Chad Muska, U.S.	Rodil de Araujo, Jr., Brazil	Wagner Ramos, Brazil
2002	Street Best Trick	Rodil de Araujo, Jr., Brazil	Wagner Ramos, Brazil	Dayne Brummet, U.S.
2001	Street Best Trick	Rick McCrank, Canada	Kerry Getz, U.S.	Eric Koston, U.S.
1996	Street Best Trick	Gershon Mosley, U.S.	Chris Senn, U.S.	Brian Patch, U.S.
1995	Street Best Trick	Jamie Thomas, U.S.	Gershon Mosley, U.S.	Kareem Campbell, U.S.
2004	Vert	Bucky Lasek, U.S.	Pierre-Luc Gagnon, Canada	Rune Glifberg, Denmark
2003	Vert	Bucky Lasek, U.S.	Andy Macdonald, U.S.	Rune Glifberg, Denmark
2002	Vert	Pierre-Luc Gagnon, Canada	Bob Burnquist, Brazil	Rune Glifberg, Denmark
2001	Vert	Bob Burnquist, Brazil	Bucky Lasek, U.S.	Tas Pappas, Australia
2000	Vert	Bucky Lasek, U.S.	Pierre-Luc Gagnon, Canada	Colin McKay, Canada
1999	Vert	Bucky Lasek, U.S.	Andy Macdonald, U.S.	Tony Hawk, U.S.
1998	Vert	Andy Macdonald, U.S.	Giorgio Zattoni, Italy	Tony Hawk, U.S.
1997	Vert	Tony Hawk, U.S.	Rune Glifberg, Denmark	Bob Burnquist, Brazil
1996	Vert	Andy Macdonald, U.S.	Tony Hawk, U.S.	Tas Pappas, Australia
1995	Vert	Tony Hawk, U.S.	Neal Hendrix, U.S.	Rune Glifberg, Denmark
2004	Vert Best Trick	Sandro Dias, Brazil	Pierre-Luc Gagnon, Canada	Danny Mayer, U.S.
2003	Vert Best Trick	Tony Hawk, U.S.	Sandro Dias, Brazil	Andy Macdonald, U.S.
2002	Vert Best Trick	Pierre-Luc Gagnon, Canada	Sandro Dias, Brazil	Tony Hawk, U.S.
2001	Vert Best Trick	Matt Dove, U.S.	Tony Hawk, U.S.	Bob Burnquist, Brazil
2000	Vert Best Trick	Bob Burnquist, Brazil	Colin McKay, Canada	Andy Macdonald, U.S.
1999	Vert Best Trick	Tony Hawk, U.S.	Colin McKay, Canada	Bob Burnquist, Brazil
2004	Big Air	Danny Way, U.S.	Pierre-Luc Gagnon, Canada	Andy Macdonald, U.S.
2003	Vert Doubles	Bucky Lasek, U.S. Bob Burnquist, Brazil	Rune Glifberg, Denmark Mike Crum, U.S.	Neal Hendrix, U.S. Buster Halterman, U.S.
2002	Vert Doubles	Tony Hawk, U.S. Andy Macdonald, U.S.	Bob Burnquist, Brazil Bucky Lasek, U.S.	Mike Crum, U.S. Rune Glifberg, Denmark
2001	Vert Doubles	Tony Hawk, U.S. Andy Macdonald, U.S.	Mike Crum, U.S. Chris Gentry, U.S.	Mike Frazier, U.S. Neal Hendrix, U.S.
2000	Vert Doubles	Tony Hawk, U.S. Andy Macdonald, U.S.	Pierre-Luc Gagnon, Canada Max Dufour, Canada	Sandro Dias, Brazil Cristiano Mateus, Brazil
1999	Vert Doubles	Tony Hawk, U.S. Andy Macdonald, U.S.	Bucky Lasek, U.S. Brian Patch, U.S.	Mike Crum, U.S. Rune Glifberg, Denmark
1998	Vert Doubles	Tony Hawk, U.S. Andy Macdonald, U.S.	Bucky Lasek, U.S. Brian Patch, U.S.	Bob Burnquist, Brazil Lincoln Ueda, Brazil
1997	Vert Doubles	Tony Hawk, U.S. Andy Macdonald, U.S.	Mike Frazier, U.S. Neal Hendrix, U.S.	Max Dufour, Canada Mathias Ringstrom, Sweden
1995	High Air	Danny Way, U.S.	Neal Hendrix, U.S.	Tas Pappas, Australia

DID YOU KNOW?

Skateboarder Danny Way holds the world record for highest air (23.5 feet).

Elissa Steamer won the first women's Street event at the 2004 Summer X Games.

SKATEBOARDING — WOMEN

YEAR	EVENT	GOLD	SILVER	BRONZE
2004	Street	Elissa Steamer, U.S.	Vanessa Torres, U.S.	Lauron Perkins, U.S.
2004	Vert	Lyn-Z Adams Hawkins, U.S.	Cara-Beth Burnside, U.S.	Mimi Knoop, U.S.

SNOWBOARDING — MEN

YEAR	EVENT	GOLD	SILVER	BRONZE
1999	Big Air	Peter Line, U.S.	Ben Hinkley, U.S.	Chris Engelsman, U.S.
1998	Big Air	Kevin Jones, U.S.	Ben Hinkley, U.S.	Jim Rippey, U.S.
1997	Big Air	Peter Line, U.S.	Kevin Jones, U.S.	Jason Borgstede, U.S.

SNOWBOARDING — WOMEN

YEAR	EVENT	GOLD	SILVER	BRONZE
1999	Big Air	Barrett Christy, U.S.	Tina Dixon, U.S.	Janet Matthews, Canada
1998	Big Air	Janet Matthews, Canada	Tina Basich, U.S.	Tina Dixon, U.S.
1997	Big Air	Tina Dixon, U.S.	Hillary Maybery, U.S.	Shelly Ueckert, U.S.

SPORT CLIMBING — MEN

YEAR	EVENT	GOLD	SILVER	BRONZE
2002	Speed	Maxim Stenkovoy, Ukraine	Alexandre Pechekhonov, Russia	Serguei Sinitsyn, Russia
2001	Speed	Maxim Stenkovoy, Ukraine	Vladimir Zakharov, Ukraine	Chris Bloch, U.S.
2000	Speed	Vladimir Zakharov, Ukraine	Chris Bloch, U.S.	Tomasz Oleksy, Poland
1999	Speed	Aaron Shamy, U.S.	Chris Bloch, U.S.	Vladimir Netsvetaev, Russia
1998	Speed	Vladimir Netsvetaev, Russia	Aaron Shamy, U.S.	Chris Bloch, U.S.
1997	Speed	Hans Florine, U.S.	Chris Bloch, U.S.	Jason Campbell, U.S.
1996	Speed	Hans Florine, U.S.	Chris Bloch, U.S.	Tim Fairfield, U.S.
1995	Speed	Hans Florine, U.S.	Salavat Rakhmetov, Russia	Yuji Hirayama, Japan
1999	Bouldering	Chris Sharma, U.S.	Francois Petit, France	Stephane Julien, France
1998	Difficulty	Christian Core, Italy	Francois Legrand, France	Vadim Vinokur, U.S.
1997	Difficulty	Francois Legrand, France	Yuji Hirayama, Japan	Chris Sharma, U.S.
1996	Difficulty	Arnaud Petit, France	Francois Lombard, France	Cristian Brenna, Italy
1995	Difficulty	Ian Vickers, Great Britain	Arnaud Petit, France	Francois Petit, France

2004-05 TIME LINE

■ **March 20, 2004:** Snowboarder Danny Kass becomes only the second rider to win three U.S. Open Halfpipe titles (2001, 2002, and 2004). He wins his fourth U.S. Open Halfpipe title in 2005.

■ **July 18, 2004:** Parks Bonifay captures his second consecutive Pro Wakeboard Tour Championship.

■ **July 25, 2004:** Warwick Stevenson of Australia wins the elite men's title at the BMX World Championships in Valkenswaard, Netherlands.

■ **August 5, 2004:** Freestyle motocross rider Chuck Carothers pulls the first Carolla, a move in which the rider does a midair 360 off the bike, at the Summer X Games. He wins the gold medal in Moto X Best Trick.

■ **August 6-7, 2004:** Dave Mirra wins gold medals in both BMX Vert and Park for the fourth time (1997-99 and 2004). Mirra, who has won more X Games medals than anyone, leaves with his 17th and 18th medals — 13 gold, 4 silver, and 1 bronze.

■ **August 8, 2004:** Skateboarding Big Air makes its debut at the Summer X Games. Danny Way easily wins the event and takes home the gold.

■ **August 29, 2004:** James "Bubba" Stewart wins his 26th 125cc race and passes Ricky Carmichael as the all-time 125cc wins leader in Motocross history. Stewart also captures his second 125cc title in three seasons.

■ **September 18, 2004:** Less than a month after winning the first women's Street competition at the Summer X Games, skateboarder Elissa Steamer wins the same event at the Gravity Games.

■ **November 8, 2004:** Surfer Andy Irons clinches his third straight World Championship Tour title.

■ **January 29, 2005:** Lindsey Jacobellis wins the Snowboarder X event at the Winter X Games for the third year in a row.

■ **January 30, 2005:** Brian Deegan wins Moto X Best Trick at the 2005 Winter X Games. At the 2004 Winter X Games, Deegan crashed and broke both his wrists and his left leg.

SUMMER X GAMES RESULTS (cont.)

SPORT CLIMBING — WOMEN

YEAR	EVENT	GOLD	SILVER	BRONZE
2002	Speed	Tori Allen, U.S.	Olga Zakharova, Ukraine	Etti Hendrawati, Indonesia
2001	Speed	Elena Repko, Ukraine	Olga Zakharova, Ukraine	Alena Ostapenko, Ukraine
2000	Speed	Etti Hendrawati, Indonesia	Elena Repko, Ukraine	Olga Zakharova, Ukraine
1999	Speed	Renata Piszczek, Poland	Olga Zakharova, Ukraine	Etti Hendrawati, Indonesia
1998	Speed	Elena Ovchinnikova, U.S.	Yuyun Yuniar, Indonesia	Venera Tchereshneva, Russia
1997	Speed	Elena Ovchinnikova, U.S.	Abby Watkins, Australia	Mi Sun Go, South Korea
1996	Speed	Cecile Le Flem, France	Elena Choumilova, Russia	Natalie Richer, France
1995	Speed	Elena Ovchinnikova, Russia	Diane Russell, U.S.	Georgia Phipps-Franklin, U.S.
1999	Bouldering	Stephanie Bodet, France	Liv Sansoz, France	Elena Choumilova, Russia
1998	Difficulty	Katie Brown, U.S.	Mi Sun Go, South Korea	Elena Choumilova, Russia

SUMMER X GAMES RESULTS (cont.)

SPORT CLIMBING — WOMEN (cont.)

YEAR	EVENT	GOLD	SILVER	BRONZE
1997	Difficulty	Katie Brown, U.S.	Liv Sansoz, France	Muriel Sarkany, Belgium
1996	Difficulty	Katie Brown, U.S.	Laurence Guyon, France	Liv Sansoz, France
1995	Difficulty	Robyn Erbesfield, U.S.	Elena Ovchinnikova, Russia	Mia Axon, U.S.

STREET LUGE

YEAR	EVENT	GOLD	SILVER	BRONZE
2001	Super Mass	Brent DeKeyser, U.S.	David Rogers, U.S.	Dave Auld, U.S.
2000	Super Mass	Bob Pereyra, U.S.	Lee Dansie, Great Britain	John Rogers, U.S.
1999	Super Mass	David Rogers, U.S.	Biker Sherlock, U.S.	Sean Slate, U.S.
1998	Super Mass	Rat Sult, U.S.	Bob Pereyra, U.S.	Todd Lehr, U.S.
1997	Super Mass	Chris Ponseti, U.S.	Biker Sherlock, U.S.	Rat Sult, U.S.
2000	Dual	Bob Ozman, U.S.	Wade Sokol, U.S.	Bob Pereyra, U.S.
1999	Dual	Dennis Derammelaere, U.S.	Lee Dansie, Great Britain	Biker Sherlock, U.S.
1998	Dual	Biker Sherlock, U.S.	Stefan Wagner, Germany	Dave Auld, U.S.
1997	Dual	Biker Sherlock, U.S.	Dennis Derammelaere, U.S.	Darren Lott, U.S.
1996	Dual	Shawn Goulart, U.S.	Stefan Wagner, Germany	Dennis Derammelaere, U.S.
1995	Dual	Bob Pereyra, U.S.	Stefan Wagner, Germany	Shawn Goulart, U.S.
1998	Mass	Rat Sult, U.S.	Sean Slate, U.S.	Steve Fernando, U.S.
1997	Mass	Biker Sherlock, U.S.	Dennis Derammelaere, U.S.	Lee Dansie, Great Britain
1996	Mass	Biker Sherlock, U.S.	Daryl Thompson, U.S.	Dennis Derammelaere, U.S.
1995	Mass	Shawn Goulart, U.S.	Lee Dansie, Great Britain	Stefan Wagner, Germany

SURFING — MEN

YEAR	GOLD	SILVER	BRONZE
2004	East Coast	West Coast	N/A
2003	East Coast	West Coast	N/A

WAKEBOARDING — MEN

YEAR	GOLD	SILVER	BRONZE
2004	Phillip Soven, U.S.	Chad Sharpe, Canada	Parks Bonifay, U.S.
2003	Danny Harf, U.S.	Parks Bonifay, U.S.	Daniel Watkins, U.S.
2002	Danny Harf, U.S.	Darin Shapiro, U.S.	Shaun Murray, U.S.
2001	Danny Harf, U.S.	Darin Shapiro, U.S.	Erik Ruck, U.S.
2000	Darin Shapiro, U.S.	Shaun Murray, U.S.	Shane Bonifay, U.S.
1999	Parks Bonifay, U.S.	Darin Shapiro, U.S.	Brannan Johnson, U.S.
1998	Darin Shapiro, U.S.	Shaun Murray, U.S.	Zane Schwenk, U.S.
1997	Jeremy Kovak, Canada	Darin Shapiro, U.S.	Parks Bonifay, U.S.
1996	Parks Bonifay, U.S.	Jeremy Kovak, Canada	Scott Byerly, U.S.

WAKEBOARDING — WOMEN

YEAR	GOLD	SILVER	BRONZE
2004	Dallas Friday, U.S.	Tara Hamilton, U.S.	Maeghan Major, U.S.
2003	Dallas Friday, U.S.	Melissa Marquardt, U.S.	Emily Copeland, U.S.
2002	Emily Copeland, U.S.	Dallas Friday, U.S.	Leslie Kent, U.S.
2001	Dallas Friday, U.S.	Emily Copeland, U.S.	Tara Hamilton, U.S.
2000	Tara Hamilton, U.S.	Dallas Friday, U.S.	Maeghan Major, U.S.
1999	Maeghan Major, U.S.	Emily Copeland, U.S.	Andrea Gaytan, Mexico
1998	Andrea Gaytan, Mexico	Dana Preble, U.S.	Tara Hamilton, U.S.
1997	Tara Hamilton, U.S.	Andrea Gaytan, Mexico	Jaime Necrason, U.S.

WINDSURFING — MEN

YEAR	GOLD	SILVER	BRONZE
1995	Bjorn Dunkerbeck, Spain	Micah Buzianis, U.S.	Al Aguera, U.S.

SUMMER X GAMES RESULTS (cont.)

WINDSURFING — WOMEN

YEAR	GOLD	SILVER	BRONZE
1995	Angela Cochran, U.S.	Jayne Fenner-Benedict, U.S.	Jutta Mueller, Germany

X VENTURE RACE

YEAR	GOLD	SILVER	BRONZE
1997	Team Presidio	Team Endeavour	Team Red Hot
	Ian Adamson, Australia	Louise Cooper-Lovelace, U.S.	Sharyn Davis, Australia
	John Howard, New Zealand	Neil Jones, New Zealand	John Jacoby, Australia
	Andrea Spitzer, Germany	Jeff Mitchell, New Zealand	Tim Smallwood, Australia
1996	Team Kobeer	Team Eco-Internet	Team Mirage
	Angelika Castaneda, U.S.	Ian Adamson, Australia	Kirk Boylston, U.S.
	John Howard, New Zealand	Robert Nagle, Ireland	Nancy Bristow, U.S.
	Keith Murray, New Zealand	Vivienne Prince, U.S.	Steve Gurney, New Zealand
1995	Team Thredbo	Twin Team	Team Eco-Internet
	Jane Hall, Australia	Angelika Castaneda, U.S.	Ian Adamson, Australia
	Andrew Hislop, Australia	Adrian Crane, U.S.	John Howard, New Zealand
	Rod Hislop, Australia	Tom Possert, U.S.	Keith Murray, New Zealand
	John Jacoby, Australia	Robert Rambach, U.S.	Robert Nagle, Ireland
	Novak Thompson, Australia	Marshall Ulrich, U.S.	Cathy Sassin-Smith, U.S.

WINTER GRAVITY GAMES RESULTS

SNOWBOARDING — MEN

YEAR	EVENT	GOLD	SILVER	BRONZE
2005	Snowboardcross	Xavier de le Rue, France	Jason Smith, U.S.	Mike Rosengren, U.S.
2005	Slopestyle	Chad Otterstrom, U.S.	Antti Autti, Finland	Wyatt Caldwell, U.S.
2005	Superpipe	Crispin Lipscomb, Canada	Danny Davis, U.S.	Risto Mattila, Finland
2005	Rail Jam	Chad Otterstrom, U.S.	N/A	N/A

SNOWBOARDING — WOMEN

YEAR	EVENT	GOLD	SILVER	BRONZE
2005	Snowboardcross	Leslee Olson, U.S.	Marni Yamada, U.S.	Jordan Karlinski, U.S.
2005	Slopestyle	Janna Meyen, U.S.	Silvia Mittermueller, Germany	Izumi Amaike, Japan
2005	Superpipe	Gretchen Bleiler, U.S.	Hannah Teter, U.S.	Elena Hight, U.S.
2005	Rail Jam	Leanne Pelosi, Canada	N/A	N/A

SKIING — MEN

YEAR	EVENT	GOLD	SILVER	BRONZE
2005	Skiercross	Casey Puckett, U.S.	Zach Crist, U.S.	Jakub Fiala, U.S.
2005	Slopestyle	T.J. Schiller, Canada	Simon Dumont, U.S.	Charles Gagnier, Canada
2005	Superpipe	Corey Vanular, U.S.	Andrew Woods, U.S.	Simon Dumont, U.S.
2005	Rail Jam	Tim Russell, U.S.	N/A	N/A

SKIING — WOMEN

YEAR	EVENT	GOLD	SILVER	BRONZE
2005	Skiercross	Brett Buckles, U.S.	Valentine Scuotto, France	Sara-Maude Boucher, Canada
2005	Superpipe	Kristi Leskinen, U.S.	Sarah Burke, Canada	Grete Eliassen, Norway
2005	Rail Jam	Grete Eliassen, Norway	N/A	N/A

LEGENDS

■ **Lisa Andersen, surfer,** b. March 8, 1969, Ormond Beach, Florida. Andersen learned to surf when she was 13. The next year, she moved to California to become a world champion. Andersen reached her goal after seven years on the pro surfing tour. She won consecutive titles on the women's World Championship Tour from 1994 through 1997. Only three other women have won as many surfing championships.

■ **Andy Macdonald, skateboarder,** b. July 31, 1973, Boston, Massachusetts. Macdonald has been a pro skateboarder since 1994. He has won 15 Summer X Games medals, including two golds in Vert (1996 and 1998) and six straight golds in Vert Doubles with partner Tony Hawk (1997-02). Andy Mac has also won five Summer Gravity Games medals.

■ **Tara Hamilton, wakeboarder,** b. January 16, 1982, Lantana, Florida. Hamilton won the first women's Wakeboarding gold medal awarded at the Summer X Games, in 1997. She was golden again in 2000 and took home the silver medal in 2004. Hamilton has also won three Pro Wakeboard Tour championships (1997, 1998, and 2000) and four world championships (1997-99 and 2002).

Lisa Andersen is one of four women to win three or more surfing world championships.

ALLSPORT

SUMMER GRAVITY GAMES RESULTS

BIKE

YEAR	EVENT	GOLD	SILVER	BRONZE
2004	Street	Morgan Wade, U.S.	Ryan Nyquist, U.S.	Steven McCann, Australia
2003	Street	Dave Mirra, U.S.	Ryan Nyquist, U.S.	Steven McCann, Australia
2002	Street	Dave Mirra, U.S.	Ryan Nyquist, U.S.	Tom Haugen, U.S.
2001	Street	Ryan Nyquist, U.S.	Dave Osato, Canada	Chad Kagy, U.S.
2000	Street	Dave Osato, Canada	Ryan Nyquist, U.S.	Mike Laird, U.S.
1999	Street	Dave Mirra, U.S.	Ryan Nyquist, U.S.	Jay Miron, Canada
2004	Dirt	Ryan Nyquist, U.S.	Steven McCann, Australia	Stephen Murray, Great Britain
2003	Dirt	Ryan Nyquist, U.S.	Chris Doyle, U.S.	Steven McCann, Australia
2002	Dirt	Stephen Murray, Great Britain	Allan Cooke, U.S.	Chris Doyle, U.S.
2001	Dirt	Stephen Murray, Great Britain	Todd Walkowiak, U.S.	Chris Doyle, U.S.
2000	Dirt	T.J. Lavin, U.S.	Chris Doyle, U.S.	Ryan Jordan, U.S.
1999	Dirt	Ryan Nyquist, U.S.	Todd Walkowiak, U.S.	T.J. Lavin, U.S.

Summer Gravity Games gold medalist Jamie Bestwick launches an Old School No-Hander.

2004	Vert	Jamie Bestwick, Great Britain	Chad Kagy, U.S.	Kevin Robinson, U.S.
2003	Vert	Dave Mirra, U.S.	Kevin Robinson, U.S.	Simon Tabron, Great Britain
2002	Vert	Simon Tabron, Great Britain	Dave Mirra, U.S.	Jay Miron, Canada
2001	Vert	Jamie Bestwick, Great Britain	Kevin Robinson, U.S.	Simon Tabron, Great Britain
2000	Vert	Dave Mirra, U.S.	Jamie Bestwick, Great Britain	Jay Miron, Canada
1999	Vert	Jamie Bestwick, Great Britain	Jay Miron, Canada	John Parker, U.S.

FREESTYLE MOTOCROSS

YEAR	GOLD	SILVER	BRONZE
2004	Nate Adams, U.S.	Jeremy Stenberg, U.S.	Ronnie Faisst, U.S.
2003	Nate Adams, U.S.	Travis Pastrana, U.S.	Ronnie Renner, U.S.
2002	Travis Pastrana, U.S.	Mike Metzger, U.S.	Kenny Bartram, U.S.
2001	Travis Pastrana, U.S.	Clifford Adoptante, U.S.	Tommy Clowers, U.S.
2000	Brian Deegan, U.S.	Mike Metzger, U.S.	Kenny Bartram, U.S.
1999	Travis Pastrana, U.S.	Brian Deegan, U.S.	Carey Hart, U.S.

Rune Glifberg won his second Gravity Games Vert gold medal in 2004.

MARKUS PAULSEN/SHAZAMM/ESPN

TRIVIA CHALLENGE

Who was the first freestyle motocross rider to successfully land a backflip in competition?

Mike Metzger landed a backflip at the 2002 Summer Gravity Games.

■ **Fast Fact:** Skateboarder Ryan Sheckler played Rod St. James in the 2003 movie *Grind*.

SKATEBOARDING — MEN

YEAR	EVENT	GOLD	SILVER	BRONZE
2004	Vert	Rune Glifberg, Denmark	Andy Macdonald, U.S.	Pierre-Luc Gagnon, Canada
2003	Vert	Bucky Lasek, U.S.	Andy Macdonald, U.S.	Rune Glifberg, Denmark
2002	Vert	Bucky Lasek, U.S.	Bob Burnquist, Brazil	Pierre-Luc Gagnon, Canada
2001	Vert	Rune Glifberg, Denmark	Bucky Lasek, U.S.	Andy Macdonald, U.S.
2000	Vert	Andy Macdonald, U.S.	Bob Burnquist, Brazil	Pierre-Luc Gagnon, Canada
1999	Vert	Bob Burnquist, Brazil	Bucky Lasek, U.S.	Andy Macdonald, U.S.
2004	Vert Best Trick	Sandro Diaz, Brazil	Danny Mayer, U.S.	Pierre-Luc Gagnon, Canada
2003	Vert Best Trick	Mathias Ringstrom, Sweden	Danny Mayer, U.S.	Sandro Diaz, Brazil
2002	Vert Best Trick	Pierre-Luc Gagnon, Canada	Bob Burnquist, Brazil	Sandro Diaz, Brazil
2004	Street	Rodil de Araujo, Jr., Brazil	Greg Lutzka, U.S.	Ryan Sheckler, U.S.
2003	Street	Ryan Sheckler, U.S.	Rick McCrank, Canada	Chris Senn, U.S.
2002	Street	Eric Koston, U.S.	Pat Channita, U.S.	Kerry Getz, U.S.
2001	Street	Eric Koston, U.S.	Rick McCrank, Canada	Kyle Berard, U.S.
2000	Street	Eric Koston, U.S.	Brian Anderson, U.S.	Kerry Getz, U.S.
1999	Street	Brian Anderson, U.S.	Rodil de Araujo, Jr., Brazil	Eric Koston, U.S.
2004	Street Best Trick	Paul Machnau, Canada	Nilton Neves, Brazil	Josh Evin, Canada
2003	Street Best Trick	Chris Haslam, Canada	Daniel Vieira, Brazil	Chad Bartie, Australia
2002	Downhill, 2-person	Mark Golter, U.S.	Dane Van Bommel, U.S.	Alex Wenk, Switzerland
2001	Downhill, 2-person	Dane Van Bommel, U.S.	Gary Hardwick, U.S.	Mark Golter, U.S.
2000	Downhill, 2-person	Dane Van Bommel, U.S.	John Gwiazdowski, U.S.	Alex Wenk, Switzerland
1999	Downhill, 2-person	Lee Dansie, Great Britain	Biker Sherlock, U.S.	Dane Van Bommel, U.S.
2002	Downhill, 4-person	Darryl Freeman, U.S.	Mark Golter, U.S.	Dane Van Bommel, U.S.
2001	Downhill, 4-person	Dane Van Bommel, U.S.	Alex Wenk, Switzerland	Lee Dansie, Great Britain
2000	Downhill, 4-person	Dane Van Bommel, U.S.	John Gwiazdowski, U.S.	Alex Wenk, Switzerland
1999	Downhill, 4-person	Biker Sherlock, U.S.	Dane Van Bommel, U.S.	Emanuel Antuna, France

SUMMER GRAVITY GAMES RESULTS (cont.)

SKATEBOARDING — WOMEN

YEAR	EVENT	GOLD	SILVER	BRONZE
2004	Street	Elissa Steamer, U.S.	Lauren Perkins, U.S.	Lyn-Z Adams Hawkins, U.S.

AGGRESSIVE IN-LINE — MEN

YEAR	EVENT	GOLD	SILVER	BRONZE
2001	Street	Blake Dennis, Australia	Louie Zamora, U.S.	Aaron Feinberg, U.S.
2000	Street	Sven Boekhorst, Netherlands	Blake Dennis, Australia	Wilfried Rossignol, France
1999	Street	Sven Boekhorst, Netherlands	Den Bosch, Netherlands	Louie Zamora, U.S.
2003	Street Best Trick	Richie Velasquez, U.S.	Stephane Alfano, France	Brian Aragon, U.S.
2003	Vert	Eito Yasutoko, Japan	Marco de Santi, Brazil	Marc Englehart, U.S.
2002	Vert	Marc Englehart, U.S.	Takeshi Yasutoko, Japan	Shane Yost, Tasmania
2001	Vert	Taig Khris, France	Takeshi Yasutoko, Japan	Matt Lindenmuth, U.S.
2000	Vert	Matt Salerno, Australia	Taig Khris, France	Eito Yasutoko, Japan
1999	Vert	Taig Khris, France	Shane Yost, Australia	Cesar Mora, Australia

AGGRESSIVE IN-LINE — WOMEN

YEAR	EVENT	GOLD	SILVER	BRONZE
2001	Street	Martina Svobodova, Slovakia	Fabiola da Silva, Brazil	Deborah West, U.S.
2000	Street	Martina Svobodova, Slovakia	Fabiola da Silva, Brazil	Kelly Matthews, U.S.
1999	Street	Fabiola da Silva, Brazil	Anneke Winter, Germany	Kelly Matthews, U.S.
2001	Vert	Ayumi Kawasaki, Japan	Fabiola da Silva, Brazil	N/A
2000	Vert	Fabiola da Silva, Brazil	Ayumi Kawasaki, Japan	Merce Borrull, Spain
1999	Vert	Fabiola da Silva, Brazil	Merce Borrull, Spain	Maki Komori, Japan

WAKEBOARDING — MEN

YEAR	GOLD	SILVER	BRONZE
2003	Parks Bonifay, U.S.	Shane Bonifay, U.S.	Brett Eisenhauer, Australia
2002	Mark Kenney, U.S.	Danny Harf, U.S.	Darin Shapiro, U.S.
2001	Darin Shapiro, U.S.	Parks Bonifay, U.S.	Daniel Watkins, Australia
2000	Parks Bonifay, U.S.	Darin Shapiro, U.S.	Ryan Wynne, U.S.
1999	Shaun Murray, U.S.	Parks Bonifay, U.S.	Rob Struharik, U.S.

WAKEBOARDING — WOMEN

YEAR	GOLD	SILVER	BRONZE
2003	Emily Copeland-Durham, U.S.	Tara Hamilton, U.S.	Leslie Kent, U.S.
2002	Emily Copeland, U.S.	Melissa Marquardt, U.S.	Dallas Friday, U.S.
2001	Dallas Friday, U.S.	Tara Hamilton, U.S.	Christy Smith, U.S.
2000	Maeghan Major, U.S.	Tara Hamilton, U.S.	Lauren Loe, U.S.
1999	Andrea Gaytan, Mexico	Tara Hamilton, U.S.	Christy Smith, U.S.

STREET LUGE

YEAR	EVENT	GOLD	SILVER	BRONZE
2002	4-person	Mike McIntyre, U.S.	John Rogers, U.S.	Dave Rogers, U.S.
2001	4-person	Rat Sult, U.S.	Biker Sherlock, U.S.	John Fryer, U.S.
1999	4-person	Sean Mallard, U.S.	Biker Sherlock, U.S.	George Orton, U.S.
2002	6-person	Dave Rogers, U.S.	Mike McIntyre, U.S.	John Rogers, U.S.
2001	6-person	Rat Sult, U.S.	Kurtis Head, U.S.	David Kelly, U.S.
1999	6-person	Biker Sherlock, U.S.	Sean Slate, U.S.	Wade Sokol, U.S.

SURFING — ALL-TIME RESULTS

ASSOCIATION OF SURFING PROFESSIONALS (ASP) WORLD CHAMPIONS

Andy Irons won his third straight world championship in 2004.

YEAR	MEN	YEAR	LONGBOARD
2004	Andy Irons, U.S.	2004	Joel Tudor, U.S.
2003	Andy Irons, U.S.	2003	Beau Young, Australia
2002	Andy Irons, U.S.	2002	Colin McPhillips, U.S.
2001	C.J. Hobgood, U.S.	2001	Colin McPhillips, U.S.
2000	Sunny Garcia, U.S.	2000	Beau Young, Australia
1999	Mark Occhilupo, Australia	1999	Colin McPhillips, U.S.
1998	Kelly Slater, U.S.	1998	Joel Tudor, U.S.
1997	Kelly Slater, U.S.	1997	Dino Miranda, U.S.
1996	Kelly Slater, U.S.	1996	Bonga Perkins, U.S.
1995	Kelly Slater, U.S.	1995	Rusty Keaulana, U.S.
1994	Kelly Slater, U.S.	1994	Rusty Keaulana, U.S.
1993	Derek Ho, U.S.	1993	Rusty Keaulana, U.S.
1992	Kelly Slater, U.S.	1992	Joey Hawkins, U.S.
1991	Damien Hardman, Australia	1991	Martin McMillan, Australia
1990	Tom Curren, U.S.	1990	Nat Young, Australia
1989	Martin Potter, Great Britain	1989	Nat Young, Australia
1988	Barton Lynch, Australia	1988	Nat Young, Australia
1987	Damien Hardman, Australia	1987	Stuart Entwistle, Australia
1986	Tom Curren, U.S.	1986	Nat Young, Australia
1985	Tom Curren, U.S.		
1984	Tom Carroll, Australia		
1983	Tom Carroll, Australia		
1982	Mark Richards, Australia		
1981	Mark Richards, Australia		
1980	Mark Richards, Australia		
1979	Mark Richards, Australia		
1978	Wayne Bartholomew, Australia		
1977	Shaun Tomson, South Africa		
1976	Peter Townend, Australia		

SURFING — ALL-TIME RESULTS (cont.)

ASSOCIATION OF SURFING PROFESSIONALS (ASP) WORLD CHAMPIONS (cont.)

Sofia Mulanovich was the women's pro surfing world champion in 2004.

YEAR	WOMEN	YEAR	WOMEN
2004	Sofia Mulanovich, Peru	1990	Pam Burridge, Australia
2003	Layne Beachley, Australia	1989	Wendy Botha, Australia
2002	Layne Beachley, Australia	1988	Freida Zamba, U.S.
2001	Layne Beachley, Australia	1987	Wendy Botha, South Africa
2000	Layne Beachley, Australia	1986	Freida Zamba, U.S.
1999	Layne Beachley, Australia	1985	Freida Zamba, U.S.
1998	Layne Beachley, Australia	1984	Freida Zamba, U.S.
1997	Lisa Andersen, U.S.	1983	Kim Mearig, U.S.
1996	Lisa Andersen, U.S.	1982	Debbie Beacham, U.S.
1995	Lisa Andersen, U.S.	1981	Margo Oberg, U.S.
1994	Lisa Andersen, U.S.	1980	Margo Oberg, U.S.
1993	Pauline Menczer, Australia	1979	Lynne Boyer, U.S.
1992	Wendy Botha, Australia	1978	Lynne Boyer, U.S.
1991	Wendy Botha, Australia	1977	Margo Oberg, U.S.

MOTOCROSS — ALL-TIME RESULTS

250CC SUPERCROSS

YEAR	CHAMPION	HOMETOWN	YEAR	CHAMPION	HOMETOWN
2004	Chad Reed	Kurri Kurri, Australia	1988	Rick Johnson	El Cajon, California
2003	Ricky Carmichael	Havana, Florida	1987	Jeff Ward	Mission Viejo, California
2002	Ricky Carmichael	Havana, Florida	1986	Rick Johnson	El Cajon, California
2001	Ricky Carmichael	Havana, Florida	1985	Jeff Ward	Mission Viejo, California
2000	Jeremy McGrath	Menifee, California	1984	Johnny O'Mara	Simi Valley, California
1999	Jeremy McGrath	Menifee, California	1983	David Bailey	Axton, Virginia
1998	Jeremy McGrath	Menifee, California	1982	Donnie Hansen	Canyon Country, California
1997	Jeff Emig	Riverside, California	1981	Mark Barnett	Bridgeview, Illinois
1996	Jeremy McGrath	Menifee, California	1980	Mike Bell	Lakewood, California
1995	Jeremy McGrath	Murrieta, California	1979	Bob Hannah	Carson, Nevada
1994	Jeremy McGrath	Murrieta, California	1978	Bob Hannah	Whittier, California
1993	Jeremy McGrath	Murrieta, California	1977	Bob Hannah	Whittier, California
1992	Jeff Stanton	Sherwood, Michigan	1976	Jim Weinert	Laguna Beach, California
1991	Jean-Michel Bayle	Manosque, France	1975	Jim Ellis	Cobalt, Connecticut
1990	Jeff Stanton	Sherwood, Michigan	1974	Pierre Karsmakers	Netherlands
1989	Jeff Stanton	Sherwood, Michigan			

250CC MOTOCROSS

YEAR	CHAMPION	HOMETOWN
2004	Ricky Carmichael	Havana, Florida
2003	Ricky Carmichael	Havana, Florida
2002	Ricky Carmichael	Havana, Florida
2001	Ricky Carmichael	Havana, Florida
2000	Ricky Carmichael	Havana, Florida
1999	Greg Albertyn	Johannesburg, South Africa
1998	Doug Henry	Oxford, Connecticut
1997	Jeff Emig	Riverside, California
1996	Jeff Emig	Riverside, California
1995	Jeremy McGrath	Murrieta, California
1994	Mike LaRocco	South Bend, Indiana
1993	Mike Kiedrowski	Acton, California

YEAR	CHAMPION	HOMETOWN
1992	Jeff Stanton	Sherwood, Michigan
1991	Jean-Michel Bayle	Manosque, France
1990	Jeff Stanton	Sherwood, Michigan
1989	Jeff Stanton	Sherwood, Michigan
1988	Jeff Ward	Mission Viejo, California
1987	Rick Johnson	El Cajon, California
1986	Rick Johnson	El Cajon, California
1985	Jeff Ward	Mission Viejo, California
1984	Rick Johnson	El Cajon, California
1983	David Bailey	Axton, Virginia
1982	Donnie Hansen	Canyon Country, California
1981	Kent Howerton	San Antonio, Texas
1980	Kent Howerton	San Antonio, Texas
1979	Bob Hannah	Carson City, Nevada
1978	Bob Hannah	Whittier, California
1977	Tony DiStefano	Morrisville, Pennsylvania
1976	Tony DiStefano	Morrisville, Pennsylvania
1975	Tony DiStefano	Morrisville, Pennsylvania
1974	Gary Jones	Hacienda Heights, California
1973	Gary Jones	Hacienda Heights, California
1972	Gary Jones	Hacienda Heights, California

James Stewart, Jr., won his second 125cc Motocross title in 2004.

125CC MOTOCROSS

YEAR	CHAMPION	HOMETOWN
2004	James Stewart, Jr.	Haines City, Florida
2003	Grant Langston	Durban, South Africa
2002	James Stewart, Jr.	Haines City, Florida
2001	Michael Brown	Piney Flats, Tennessee
2000	Travis Pastrana	Annapolis, Maryland
1999	Ricky Carmichael	Havana, Florida
1998	Ricky Carmichael	Havana, Florida
1997	Ricky Carmichael	Havana, Florida
1996	Steve Lamson	Pollock Pines, California
1995	Steve Lamson	Pollock Pines, California
1994	Doug Henry	Oxford, Connecticut
1993	Doug Henry	Oxford, Connecticut
1992	Jeff Emig	Highland, California
1991	Mike Kiedrowski	Canyon Country, California
1990	Guy Cooper	Stillwater, Oklahoma
1989	Mike Kiedrowski	Canyon Country, California

YEAR	CHAMPION	HOMETOWN
1988	George Holland	Kerman, California
1987	Micky Dymond	Yorba Linda, California
1986	Micky Dymond	Yorba Linda, California
1985	Ron Lechien	El Cajon, California
1984	Jeff Ward	Mission Viejo, California
1983	Johnny O'Mara	Simi Valley, California
1982	Mark Barnett	Bridgeview, Illinois
1981	Mark Barnett	Bridgeview, Illinois
1980	Mark Barnett	Bridgeview, Illinois
1979	Broc Glover	El Cajon, California
1978	Broc Glover	El Cajon, California
1977	Broc Glover	El Cajon, California
1976	Bob Hannah	Whittier, California
1975	Marty Smith	San Diego, California
1974	Marty Smith	San Diego, California

STEVE BRUHN/GETTY IMAGES

GOLF

Much of the attention during the 2004 PGA Tour was on Tiger Woods – not for what he accomplished, but for what he *didn't* accomplish. After defending his title at the WGC-Accenture Match Play Championship in February 2004, Woods failed to win another official event for the rest of the year. By the end of the year, he had come up empty in the last 10 majors after winning eight of the first 20 in his career.

Vijay Singh, on the other hand, was a multiple winner in 2004. He became only the sixth player in PGA Tour history to win nine tournaments in a season. Singh wrestled the Number 1 ranking in the world from Woods, who had held it for 264 consecutive weeks. Singh also won the PGA Championship, his third major, and earned the Player of the Year award.

Phil Mickelson, Retief Goosen, and Todd Hamilton also won major championships in 2004. Mickelson edged Ernie Els at The Masters to win his first major title in 47 attempts. Goosen then outdueled Mickelson down the stretch at the U.S. Open to win the second major of his career. At the British Open, Hamilton, a 38-year-old rookie, claimed his second Tour victory by winning a four-hole playoff with Els.

Mickelson, Woods, and Singh each won during the first two months of 2005, setting up an exciting Masters showdown in April. Woods had a rough start, shooting a 74 in the first round. But he propelled himself to the top of the leader board and defeated Chris DiMarco on the first hole of a playoff to win his fourth Masters and ninth major.

On the LPGA Tour, Annika Sorenstam continued to distance herself from the competition. She won eight LPGA tournaments in 2004, including the McDonald's LPGA Championship, her seventh major. Sorenstam also locked up the Player of the Year award for the seventh time, tying Kathy Whitworth for the most in LPGA history.

By June 2005, Sorenstam had already won six tournaments, including her eighth and ninth major championships, the Kraft Nabisco Championship and the LPGA Championship. High school phenom Michelle Wie continued to make news when she played in the PGA Tour's Sony Open for the second straight year. In April 2005, the 15-year-old attempted to qualify for the men's U.S. Open in June but missed the cut. But Wie managed her third Top 10 finish (second place) in an LPGA event, the LPGA Championship in June.

Vijay Singh won nine tournaments in 2004 and was ranked Number 1 in the world.

JOHN BIEVER

CHUCK SOLOMON/SPORTS ILLUSTRATED

Tiger Woods's streak of consecutive tournament cuts made ended at 142 in May 2005.

DARREN CARROLL

Grace Park won two tournaments in 2004, her fifth and sixth LPGA titles

ALL-TIME CHAMPIONS — MEN

THE MASTERS

YEAR	WINNER	YEAR	WINNER	YEAR	WINNER
2005	*Tiger Woods	1982	*Craig Stadler	1958	Arnold Palmer
2004	Phil Mickelson	1981	Tom Watson	1957	Doug Ford
2003	*Mike Weir	1980	Seve Ballesteros	1956	Jack Burke, Jr.
2002	Tiger Woods	1979†	*Fuzzy Zoeller	1955	Cary Middlecoff
2001	Tiger Woods	1978	Gary Player	1954	*Sam Snead
2000	Vijay Singh	1977	Tom Watson	1953	Ben Hogan
1999	Jose Maria Olazabal	1976	Ray Floyd	1952	Sam Snead
1998	Mark O'Meara	1975	Jack Nicklaus	1951	Ben Hogan
1997	Tiger Woods	1974	Gary Player	1950	Jimmy Demaret
1996	Nick Faldo	1973	Tommy Aaron	1949	Sam Snead
1995	Ben Crenshaw	1972	Jack Nicklaus	1948	Claude Harmon
1994	Jose Maria Olazabal	1971	Charles Coody	1947	Jimmy Demaret
1993	Bernhard Langer	1970	*Billy Casper	1946	Herman Keiser
1992	Fred Couples	1969	George Archer	1943-45	No tournament
1991	Ian Woosnam	1968	Bob Goalby	1942	*Byron Nelson
1990	*Nick Faldo	1967	Gay Brewer, Jr.	1941	Craig Wood
1989	*Nick Faldo	1966	*Jack Nicklaus	1940	Jimmy Demaret
1988	Sandy Lyle	1965	Jack Nicklaus	1939	Ralph Guldahl
1987	*Larry Mize	1964	Arnold Palmer	1938	Henry Picard
1986	Jack Nicklaus	1963	Jack Nicklaus	1937	Byron Nelson
1985	Bernhard Langer	1962	Arnold Palmer	1936	Horton Smith
1984	Ben Crenshaw	1961	Gary Player	1935	*Gene Sarazen
1983	Seve Ballesteros	1960	Arnold Palmer	1934	Horton Smith
		1959	Art Wall, Jr.		

* Winner in playoff.
† Playoff cut from 18 holes to sudden death.
Note: Played at Augusta National Golf Club, Augusta, Georgia.

ALL-TIME CHAMPIONS — MEN (cont.)

U.S. OPEN

YEAR	WINNER	YEAR	WINNER	YEAR	WINNER
2005	Michael Campbell	1970	Tony Jacklin	1931	*Billy Burke
2004	Retief Goosen	1969	Orville Moody	1930	Bobby Jones
2003	Jim Furyk	1968	Lee Trevino	1929	*Bobby Jones
2002	Tiger Woods	1967	Jack Nicklaus	1928	*Johnny Farrell
2001	*Retief Goosen	1966	*Billy Casper	1927	*Tommy Armour
2000	Tiger Woods	1965	*Gary Player	1926	Bobby Jones
1999	Payne Stewart	1964	Ken Venturi	1925	*Willie MacFarlane
1998	Lee Janzen	1963	*Julius Boros	1924	Cyril Walker
1997	Ernie Els	1962	*Jack Nicklaus	1923	*Bobby Jones
1996	Steve Jones	1961	Gene Littler	1922	Gene Sarazen
1995	Corey Pavin	1960	Arnold Palmer	1921	Jim Barnes
1994	*Ernie Els	1959	Billy Casper	1920	Edward Ray
1993	Lee Janzen	1958	Tommy Bolt	1919	*Walter Hagen
1992	Tom Kite	1957	*Dick Mayer	1917-18	No tournament
1991	*Payne Stewart	1956	Cary Middlecoff	1916	Chick Evans
1990	*Hale Irwin	1955	*Jack Fleck	1915	Jerry Travers
1989	Curtis Strange	1954	Ed Furgol	1914	Walter Hagen
1988	*Curtis Strange	1953	Ben Hogan	1913	*Francis Ouimet
1987	Scott Simpson	1952	Julius Boros	1912	John McDermott
1986	Ray Floyd	1951	Ben Hogan	1911	*John McDermott
1985	Andy North	1950	*Ben Hogan	1910	*Alex Smith
1984	*Fuzzy Zoeller	1949	Cary Middlecoff	1909	George Sargent
1983	Larry Nelson	1948	Ben Hogan	1908	*Fred McLeod
1982	Tom Watson	1947	*Lew Worsham	1907	Alex Ross
1981	David Graham	1946	*Lloyd Mangrum	1906	Alex Smith
1980	Jack Nicklaus	1942-45	No tournament	1905	Willie Anderson
1979	Hale Irwin	1941	Craig Wood	1904	Willie Anderson
1978	Andy North	1940	*Lawson Little	1903	*Willie Anderson
1977	Hubert Green	1939	*Byron Nelson	1902	Laurie Auchterlonie
1976	Jerry Pate	1938	Ralph Guldahl	1901	*Willie Anderson
1975	*Lou Graham	1937	Ralph Guldahl	1900	Harry Vardon
1974	Hale Irwin	1936	Tony Manero	1899	Willie Smith
1973	Johnny Miller	1935	Sam Parks, Jr.	1898	Fred Herd
1972	Jack Nicklaus	1934	Olin Dutra	1897†	Joe Lloyd
1971	*Lee Trevino	1933	Johnny Goodman	1896†	James Foulis
		1932	Gene Sarazen	1895†	Horace Rawlins

*Winner in playoff. The 1990 playoff went to one hole of sudden death after an 18-hole playoff. In the 1994 playoff, Montgomerie was eliminated after 18 playoff holes and Els beat Roberts on the 20th.
†Before 1898, 36 holes; from 1898 on, 72 holes.

BRITISH OPEN

YEAR	WINNER	YEAR	WINNER	YEAR	WINNER
2005	Tiger Woods	1985	Sandy Lyle	1964	Tony Lema
2004	*Todd Hamilton	1984	Seve Ballesteros	1963	*Bob Charles
2003	Ben Curtis	1983	Tom Watson	1962	Arnold Palmer
2002	*Ernie Els	1982	Tom Watson	1961	Arnold Palmer
2001	David Duval	1981	Bill Rogers	1960	Kel Nagle
2000	Tiger Woods	1980	Tom Watson	1959	Gary Player
1999	*Paul Lawrie	1979	Seve Ballesteros	1958	*Peter Thomson
1998	*Mark O'Meara	1978	Jack Nicklaus	1957	Bobby Locke
1997	Justin Leonard	1977	Tom Watson	1956	Peter Thomson
1996	Tom Lehman	1976	Johnny Miller	1955	Peter Thomson
1995	*John Daly	1975	*Tom Watson	1954	Peter Thomson
1994	Nick Price	1974	Gary Player	1953	Ben Hogan
1993	Greg Norman	1973	Tom Weiskopf	1952	Bobby Locke
1992	Nick Faldo	1972	Lee Trevino	1951	Max Faulkner
1991	Ian Baker-Finch	1971	Lee Trevino	1950	Bobby Locke
1990	Nick Faldo	1970	*Jack Nicklaus	1949	*Bobby Locke
1989††	*Mark Calcavecchia	1969	Tony Jacklin	1948	Henry Cotton
1988	Seve Ballesteros	1968	Gary Player	1947	Fred Daly
1987	Nick Faldo	1967	Robert DeVicenzo	1946	Sam Snead
1986	Greg Norman	1966	Jack Nicklaus	1940-45	No tournament
		1965	Peter Thomson	1939	Richard Burton

*Winner in playoff.
††Playoff cut from 18 holes to 4 holes.

BRITISH OPEN (cont.)

YEAR	WINNER	YEAR	WINNER	YEAR	WINNER
1938	Reginald A. Whitcombe	1920	George Duncan	1897	Harold Hilton
1937	Henry Cotton	1915-19	No tournament	1896	*Harry Vardon
1936	Alfred Padgham	1914	Harry Vardon	1895	John H. Taylor
1935	Alfred Perry	1913	John H. Taylor	1894	John H. Taylor
1934	Henry Cotton	1912	Ted Ray	1893	William Auchterlonie
1933	*Denny Shute	1911	Harry Vardon	1892**	Harold Hilton
1932	Gene Sarazen	1910	James Braid	1891	Hugh Kirkaldy
1931	Tommy Armour	1909	John H. Taylor	1890	John Ball
1930	Bobby Jones	1908	James Braid	1889	*Willie Park, Jr.
1929	Walter Hagen	1907	Arnaud Massy	1888	Jack Burns
1928	Walter Hagen	1906	James Braid	1887	Willie Park, Jr.
1927	Bobby Jones	1905	James Braid	1886	David Brown
1926	Bobby Jones	1904	Jack White	1885	Bob Martin
1925	Jim Barnes	1903	Harry Vardon	1884	Jack Simpson
1924	Walter Hagen	1902	Alexander Herd	1883	*Willie Fernie
1923	Arthur G. Havers	1901	James Braid	1882	Robert Ferguson
1922	Walter Hagen	1900	John H. Taylor		
1921	*Jock Hutchison	1899	Harry Vardon		
		1898	Harry Vardon		

*Winner in playoff.
**Championship extended from 36 to 72 holes.

TRIVIA CHALLENGE

Which PGA Tour event is nicknamed the season's "fifth major"?

The Players Championship. It has the largest purse on the tour ($9 million).

LEGENDS

■ **Tom Watson,** b. September 4, 1949, Kansas City, Missouri. Watson's first PGA victory came at the 1974 Western Open. During the next 24 years, he added 38 more official wins, including a victory at the Colonial in 1998 at the age of 49. Watson won eight major championships, including five victories at the British Open. His most dominant stretch was 1980-83, when he won 14 tournaments. During that span he won the Masters once, the U.S. Open once, and the British Open three times. Watson joined the Champions Tour, for players age 50 years or older, in 1999.

Tom Watson
won the
British Open
five times.

JOHN IACONO/SPORTS ILLUSTRATED

■ **Chi Chi Rodriguez,** b. October 23, 1935, Rio Piedras, Puerto Rico. Rodriguez joined the PGA Tour in 1960 and won eight times. But his popularity and victory total began to soar after he joined the Champions Tour in 1986. Rodriguez won 22 times in the next 17 years. He was known for his funny antics on the course. After sinking difficult putts, Rodriguez waved his putter like a sword before holstering it in his belt. He was honored with the Ambassador of Golf Award in 1981 for his work raising money to help underprivileged kids.

■ **Ben Crenshaw,** b. January 11, 1952, Austin, Texas. Crenshaw won his first official tournament as a fourth grader, and later won three straight NCAA championships while attending the University of Texas. He may have been the best pure putter the game has ever seen. Crenshaw's amazing touch on the greens helped him win 19 times on the PGA Tour. In addition to victories at important events such as the Byron Nelson Classic, Crenshaw won the Masters twice, in 1984 and 1995.

ALL-TIME CHAMPIONS — MEN (cont.)

BRITISH OPEN (cont.)

YEAR	WINNER	YEAR	WINNER	YEAR	WINNER
1881	Robert Ferguson	1873	Tom Kidd	1865	Andrew Strath
1880	Robert Ferguson	1872	Tom Morris, Jr.	1864	Tom Morris, Sr.
1879	Jamie Anderson	1871	No tournament	1863	Willie Park
1878	Jamie Anderson	1870	Tom Morris, Jr.	1862	Tom Morris, Sr.
1877	Jamie Anderson	1869	Tom Morris, Jr.	1861‡	Tom Morris, Sr.
1876	#Bob Martin	1868	Tom Morris, Jr.	1860†	Willie Park
1875	Willie Park	1867	Tom Morris, Sr.		
1874	Mungo Park	1866	Willie Park		

#Tied, but opponent refused playoff. ‡The second annual Open was open to amateurs and pros. †The first event was open only to pro golfers.

TODAY'S STARS

Retief Goosen won his second U.S. Open Championship in 2004, becoming the 21st player to win it more than once.

■ **Retief Goosen,** b. February 3, 1969, Pietersburg, South Africa. Goosen joined the PGA Tour after success on the European and South African tours. He beat Mark Brooks in a playoff to win the 2001 U.S. Open, his first PGA Tour win. Goosen followed that with wins at the BellSouth Classic in 2002 and the Chrysler Championship in 2003. At Shinnecock Hills in June 2004, he outplayed Phil Mickelson in a final-round duel to become the 21st player to win multiple U.S. Open titles. Later that year, he won the Tour Championship, shooting a 64 to beat Tiger Woods in the final round.

■ **Mike Weir,** b. May 12, 1970, Sarnia, Ontario, Canada. Weir has developed a reputation as a contender in big tournaments. In 1999, he beat a tough field at the Air Canada Championship for his first PGA Tour victory. His next two Tour victories came at invitation-only events, the American Express Championship and the Tour Championship. In 2003, Weir won three events, including the Masters, his first major. He became the first left-hander and first Canadian to win the tournament.

■ **Padraig Harrington,** b. August 31, 1971, Dublin, Ireland. Harrington has been among the world's Top 10 golfers since 2002, playing on the European and PGA Tours. He finally broke out on the PGA Tour in March 2004 with a win at the Honda Classic. In his 63rd career start, Harrington rallied from seven strokes down in the final round to shoot a 63, his best round on the PGA Tour. He beat Vijay Singh and Joe Ogilvie in a playoff. Later in the year, Harrington was a member of the winning European team in the Ryder Cup. He still splits his time between the PGA and European Tours and captured his ninth international title at the 2004 German Masters.

FRED VUICH

2004-05 MEN'S TIME LINE

■ **June 20, 2004:** Retief Goosen wins his second U.S. Open by firing a 1-over-par 71 in the final round. Goosen holds off Masters champion Phil Mickelson by two shots.

■ **July 18, 2004:** Rookie Todd Hamilton outplays veteran Ernie Els to win the British Open. Hamilton opens the tournament with a 71, and then fires rounds of 67, 67, and 69 to win the Claret Jug.

■ **August 15, 2004:** Vijay Singh wins the PGA Championship for the second time, beating Justin Leonard and Chris DiMarco in a playoff.

■ **September 6, 2004:** Singh goes head-to-head with Tiger Woods on the back nine at Boston's Deutsche Bank Championship to win his sixth tournament of the season. He replaces Woods as the world's top-ranked player.

■ **September 19, 2004:** The European team dominates the United States in the Ryder Cup, held at Oakland Hills Country Club in Michigan. The Europeans defeat the Americans 18.5 to 9.5, tying the largest margin of victory in Ryder Cup history.

■ **January 9, 2005:** The PGA Tour season opens in Kapalua, Hawaii, at the Mercedes Championships. Stuart Appleby shoots a final-round 67 to overcome a four-shot deficit and win the tournament for the second straight year.

■ **January 23, 2005:** Woods ends one of the longest droughts of his career by edging Charles Howell III and Luke Donald at the Buick Invitational. It is his first Tour victory in almost a year.

■ **April 10, 2005:** Woods and Chris DiMarco play 28 holes on Sunday at the Masters because of rain delays. DiMarco opens the day with a four-shot lead, but Woods erases it in less than half an hour. DiMarco then makes up a two-shot deficit on the final two holes to force a playoff, but Woods birdies the first extra hole to win his ninth major and fourth Masters.

■ **Fast Fact:** PGA Tour rules state that a golfer may only carry 14 clubs in his bag. Carrying more than 14 results in a two-stroke penalty on every hole played with the extra equipment.

ALL-TIME CHAMPIONS — MEN (cont.)

PGA CHAMPIONSHIP

YEAR	WINNER	YEAR	WINNER	YEAR	WINNER
2004	Vijay Singh	1988	Jeff Sluman	1971	Jack Nicklaus
2003	Shaun Micheel	1987	*Larry Nelson	1970	Dave Stockton
2002	Rich Beem	1986	Bob Tway	1969	Ray Floyd
2001	David Toms	1985	Hubert Green	1968	Julius Boros
2000	*Tiger Woods	1984	Lee Trevino	1967	*Don January
1999	Tiger Woods	1983	Hal Sutton	1966	Al Geiberger
1998	Vijay Singh	1982	Raymond Floyd	1965	Dave Marr
1997	Davis Love III	1981	Larry Nelson	1964	Bobby Nichols
1996	*Mark Brooks	1980	Jack Nicklaus	1963	Jack Nicklaus
1995	*Steve Elkington	1979	*David Graham	1962	Gary Player
1994	Nick Price	1978	*John Mahaffey	1961	*Jerry Barber
1993	*Paul Azinger	1977†	*Lanny Wadkins	1960	Jay Hebert
1992	Nick Price	1976	Dave Stockton	1959	Bob Rosburg
1991	John Daly	1975	Jack Nicklaus	1958	Dow Finsterwald
1990	Wayne Grady	1974	Lee Trevino	1957	Lionel Hebert
1989	Payne Stewart	1973	Jack Nicklaus	1956	Jack Burke
		1972	Gary Player	1955	Doug Ford

*Winner in playoff.
†Playoff changed from 18 holes to sudden death.

ALL-TIME CHAMPIONS — MEN (cont.)

PGA CHAMPIONSHIP (cont.)

YEAR	WINNER	YEAR	WINNER	YEAR	WINNER
1954	Chick Harbert	1942	Sam Snead	1929	Leo Diegel
1953	Walter Burkemo	1941	Vic Ghezzi	1928	Leo Diegel
1952	Jim Turnesa	1940	Byron Nelson	1927	Walter Hagen
1951	Sam Snead	1939	Henry Picard	1926	Walter Hagen
1950	Chandler Harper	1938	Paul Runyan	1925	Walter Hagen
1949	Sam Snead	1937	Denny Shute	1924	Walter Hagen
1948	Ben Hogan	1936	Denny Shute	1923	Gene Sarazen
1947	Jim Ferrier	1935	Johnny Revolta	1922	Gene Sarazen
1946	Ben Hogan	1934	Paul Runyan	1921	Walter Hagen
1945	Byron Nelson	1933	Gene Sarazen	1920	Jock Hutchison
1944	Bob Hamilton	1932	Olin Dutra	1919	Jim Barnes
1943	No tournament	1931	Tom Creavy	1917-18	No tournament
		1930	Tommy Armour	1916	Jim Barnes

ALL-TIME CHAMPIONS — WOMEN

LPGA CHAMPIONSHIP

YEAR	WINNER	YEAR	WINNER	YEAR	WINNER
2005	Annika Sorenstam	1988	Sherri Turner	1971	Kathy Whitworth
2004	Annika Sorenstam	1987	Jane Geddes	1970	*Shirley Englehorn
2003	Annika Sorenstam	1986	Pat Bradley	1969	Betsy Rawls
2002	Se Ri Pak	1985	Nancy Lopez	1968	*Sandra Post
2001	Karrie Webb	1984	Patty Sheehan	1967	Kathy Whitworth
2000	*Juli Inkster	1983	Patty Sheehan	1966	Gloria Ehret
1999	Juli Inkster	1982	Jan Stephenson	1965	Sandra Haynie
1998	Se Ri Pak	1981	Donna Caponi	1964	Mary Mills
1997	*Chris Johnson	1980	Sally Little	1963	Mickey Wright
1996	Laura Davies	1979	Donna Caponi	1962	Judy Kimball
1995	Kelly Robbins	1978	Nancy Lopez	1961	Mickey Wright
1994	Laura Davies	1977	Chako Higuchi	1960	Mickey Wright
1993	Patty Sheehan	1976	Betty Burfeindt	1959	Betsy Rawls
1992	Betsy King	1975	Kathy Whitworth	1958	Mickey Wright
1991	Meg Mallon	1974	Sandra Haynie	1957	Louise Suggs
1990	Beth Daniel	1973	Mary Mills	1956	*Marlene Hagge
1989	Nancy Lopez	1972	Kathy Ahern	1955	†Beverly Hanson

*Won in playoff. The 1956 and 1997 titles were decided in sudden death; 1968 and 1970 were 18-hole playoffs.
†Won match-play final.

U.S. WOMEN'S OPEN

YEAR	WINNER	YEAR	WINNER	YEAR	WINNER
2005	Birdie Kim	1985	Kathy Baker	1965	Carol Mann
2004	Meg Mallon	1984	Hollis Stacy	1964	*Mickey Wright
2003	*Hilary Lunke	1983	Jan Stephenson	1963	Mary Mills
2002	Juli Inkster	1982	Janet Anderson	1962	Murle Breer
2001	Karrie Webb	1981	Pat Bradley	1961	Mickey Wright
2000	Karrie Webb	1980	Amy Alcott	1960	Betsy Rawls
1999	Juli Inkster	1979	Jerilyn Britz	1959	Mickey Wright
1998	†Se Ri Pak	1978	Hollis Stacy	1958	Mickey Wright
1997	Alison Nicholas	1977	Hollis Stacy	1957	Betsy Rawls
1996	Annika Sorenstam	1976	*JoAnne Carner	1956	*Kathy Cornelius
1995	Annika Sorenstam	1975	Sandra Palmer	1955	Fay Crocker
1994	Patty Sheehan	1974	Sandra Haynie	1954	Babe Zaharias
1993	Lauri Merten	1973	Susie Berning	1953	*Betsy Rawls
1992	*Patty Sheehan	1972	Susie Berning	1952	Louise Suggs
1991	Meg Mallon	1971	JoAnne Carner	1951	Betsy Rawls
1990	Betsy King	1970	Donna Caponi	1950	Babe Zaharias
1989	Betsy King	1969	Donna Caponi	1949	Louise Suggs
1988	Liselotte Neumann	1968	Susie Berning	1948	Babe Zaharias
1987	*Laura Davies	1967	Catherine LaCoste	1947	Betty Jameson
1986	*Jane Geddes	1966	Sandra Spuzich	1946	Patty Berg

*Winner in playoff.
†Winner on second hole of sudden death after 18-hole playoff ended in a tie.

LEGENDS

■ **Pat Bradley,** b. March 24, 1951, Westford, Massachusetts. Bradley won 31 official LPGA events over a 29-year span and was honored with two Player of the Year awards. Her best season was in 1986, when she won the season's first two major championships – the Nabisco Dinah Shore and the LPGA Championship. After tying for fifth at the U.S. Women's Open, she defended her title at the du Maurier Classic, making her the only female player to win three of the four modern majors in a single season. Bradley's last Tour win was in 1995. Since then, she has played on the U.S. Solheim Team, the women's equivalent to the men's Ryder Cup, three times and captained the team once.

Pat Bradley is the only female player to win three of the four modern major tournaments in one year.

■ **Louise Suggs,** b. September 7, 1923, Atlanta, Georgia. Suggs was one of the 13 original founders of the LPGA Tour. She turned pro in 1948 and won eight tournaments   including five majors — before the LPGA officially formed. In 1957, Suggs won the LPGA Championship to become the first woman to complete the career Grand Slam. She won 58 times during her career, and in 1966 she was the first woman elected to the Georgia Athletic Hall of Fame. In 2000, the LPGA named the Tour's Rookie of the Year award after Suggs.

■ **Judy Rankin,** b. February 18, 1945, St. Louis, Missouri. In 1959, Rankin won the Missouri Amateur title, becoming the youngest player (14 years old) to win the event, a record that still stands. She won her first LPGA event in 1968 and won a total of 26 times between then and 1979, including at least one win in every season from 1970 through 1979. Rankin never won a major tournament, though she finished second three times. But she was named Player of the Year twice and was elected to the LPGA Hall of Fame in 2000. Rankin now does color commentary on the men's tour for ESPN and ABC.

DID YOU KNOW?

Annika is not the only Sorenstam on the LPGA Tour. Her younger sister, Charlotta, joined the Tour in 1997, after seven years as a member of the Swedish National team. Charlotta's only LPGA victory came in 2000, when she beat Karrie Webb and her sister at the Standard Register PING tournament.

TODAY'S STARS

■ **Lorena Ochoa,** b. November 15, 1981, Guadalajara, Mexico. Ochoa is no stranger to success. She won 12 NCAA events while at the University of Arizona, including a record eight in a row during the 2001-02 season. In 2003, her first year on the LPGA Tour, Ochoa finished in the Top 10 eight times and won the Rookie of the Year award. But 2004 was her breakout season. She made the cut in all 27 events she entered, finished in the Top 10 18 times, and won twice. Ochoa also set the LPGA single-season records for birdies (442), most rounds under par (75), and most rounds in the 60s (51).

In 2004, Lorena Ochoa became the first Mexican-born player to win on the LPGA Tour.

TODD BIGELOW/AURORA

■ **Annika Sorenstam,** b. October 9, 1970, Stockholm, Sweden. Since turning pro in 1994, Sorenstam has dominated women's golf — and she shows no signs of slowing down. In 2004, she finished in the Top 10 in 16 of her 18 appearances, winning eight times. She also won her seventh Player of the Year award, tying her with Kathy Whitworth for the most in LPGA history. Sorenstam won six of the first eight events she entered in 2005, including her eighth and ninth major championships. In 2003, Sorenstam became the first woman in 58 years to compete on the PGA Tour. She played in the Colonial but didn't make the cut.

■ **Meg Mallon,** b. April 14, 1963, Natick, Massachusetts. Mallon shot a brilliant 65 in the final round to win her second U.S. Women's Open in 2004. In doing so, she set the record for most time (13 years) between victories at the LPGA's most important event. She won the first of her 15 career victories in 1991, her fifth year on Tour, and then went on a tear. Mallon won four tournaments that year and was recognized with the Female Golfer of the Year award. She also became just the sixth female golfer to win both the U.S. Women's Open and the LPGA Championship in the same year.

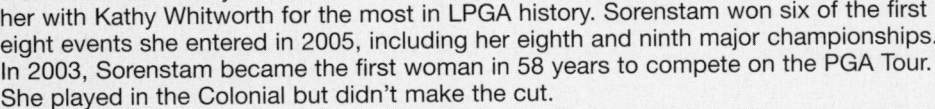

ALL-TIME CHAMPIONS — WOMEN (cont.)

NABISCO CHAMPIONSHIP

YEAR	WINNER	YEAR	WINNER	YEAR	WINNER
2005	Annika Sorenstam	1994	Donna Andrews	1982	Sally Little
2004	Grace Park	1993	Helen Alfredsson	1981	Nancy Lopez
2003	Patricia Meunier-Lebouc	1992	*Dottie Mochrie	1980	Donna Caponi
2002	Annika Sorenstam	1991	Amy Alcott	1979	Sandra Post
2001	Annika Sorenstam	1990	Betsy King	1978	*Sandra Post
2000	Karrie Webb	1989	Juli Inkster	1977	Kathy Whitworth
1999	Dottie Pepper	1988	Amy Alcott	1976	Judy Rankin
1998	Pat Hurst	1987	*Betsy King	1975	Sandra Palmer
1997	Betsy King	1986	Pat Bradley	1974	*Jo Ann Prentice
1996	Patti Sheehan	1985	Alice Miller	1973	Mickey Wright
1995	Nanci Bowen	1984	*Juli Inkster	1972	Jane Blalock
		1983	Amy Alcott		

*Winner in sudden-death playoff. *Note:* Designated fourth major in 1983; played at Mission Hills Country Club, Rancho Mirage, California.

DU MAURIER CLASSIC

YEAR	WINNER	YEAR	WINNER	YEAR	WINNER
2000	Meg Mallon	1991	Nancy Scranton	1981	Jan Stephenson
1999	Karrie Webb	1990	Cathy Johnston	1980	Pat Bradley
1998	Brandie Burton	1989	Tammie Green	1979	Amy Alcott
1997	Colleen Walker	1988	Sally Little	1978	JoAnne Carner
1996	Laura Davies	1987	Jody Rosenthal	1977	Judy Rankin
1995	Jenny Lidback	1986	*Pat Bradley	1976	*Donna Caponi
1994	Martha Nause	1985	Pat Bradley	1975	*JoAnne Carner
1993	Brandie Burton	1984	Juli Inkster	1974	Carole Jo Callison
1992	Sherri Steinhauer	1983	Hollis Stacy	1973	*Jocelyne Bourassa
		1982	Sandra Haynie		

*Winner in sudden-death playoff. Note: Designated third major in 1979; discontinued in 2001.

WOMEN'S BRITISH OPEN

YEAR	WINNER
2004	Karen Stupples
2003	Annika Sorenstam
2002	Karrie Webb
2001	Se Ri Pak

Note: Designated fourth major in 2001.

■ **Fast Fact:** Mickey Wright holds the women's record for most victories in a single season (13), set in 1963. She also occupies the second spot (11 in 1964) along with Annika Sorenstam (11 in 2002).

2004-05 WOMEN'S TIME LINE

■ **May 16, 2004:** Lorena Ochoa wins the Franklin American Mortgage Championship by one stroke to become the first Mexican-born player to win on the LPGA Tour. A little over three months later, she wins her second title of the season. She finishes the year ranked third on the money list.

■ **June 13, 2004:** Annika Sorenstam of Sweden beats Shi Hyun Ahn of Korea by three strokes to win the LPGA Championship for the second straight year. It is the seventh major championship of her career.

■ **July 4, 2004:** Meg Mallon of the United States shoots a final-round 65 for a come-from-behind victory at the U.S. Women's Open. It is her second Open title. She sets the LPGA record for the most years (13) between victories at the major championship. Sorenstam finishes second.

■ **November 21, 2004:** Sorenstam concludes a furious finish to the 2004 LPGA season by winning the ADT Championship in a playoff over Cristie Kerr of the United States. Sorenstam wins three tournaments in the final month of the season to run away with the money title and Player of the Year award.

■ **February 26, 2005:** Fifteen-year-old Michelle Wie of the U.S. finishes in a tie for second place with Cristie Kerr at the SBS Open. It is Wie's best result on the LPGA Tour. She shoots three straight rounds of 70 to finish at 6 under par, two strokes behind champion Jennifer Rosales of the Philippines.

■ **March 27, 2005:** Sorenstam wins the Kraft Nabisco Championship for her eighth major championship. After opening the tournament with a solid 70, she wins by eight strokes with rounds of 69, 66, and 68. The win is Sorenstam's fifth straight on the Tour.

TRIVIA CHALLENGE

In 2005, Annika Sorenstam tied the LPGA record for most consecutive victories, with five. Whose record did she match?

Nancy Lopez won five straight tournaments in 1978.

MOTOR SPORTS

Indy Car racing stole the motor sports headlines from NASCAR in the early part of 2005. Rookie driver Danica Patrick put the spotlight back on the Indianapolis 500, which had taken a backseat to the Daytona 500 as the biggest auto race in the United States.

Patrick, 23, became the first female driver to lead the Indy 500. She did so for 19 laps. Her fourth-place finish was the highest by a woman in Indy 500 history. Dan Wheldon of Great Britain won the race — his fourth win in the first five races of the year.

In NASCAR, Kurt Busch won the closest points race in the circuit's history when he edged Jimmie Johnson by eight points to win the 2004 Nextel Cup championship. It was Busch's first Nextel Cup title and the second straight for the Roush Racing team, which won the Cup with Matt Kenseth in 2003. Busch's title was also the first won under the Chase for the Championship format, which put the Top 10 points leaders (and any other driver within 400 points of the leader) after 26 races into a 10-race runoff to determine the champion.

Two veteran drivers, Mark Martin and Rusty Wallace, announced that they would retire from the NASCAR Nextel Cup series after the 2005 season. Between them, Martin and Wallace have 43 years of racing experience and 89 victories.

Meanwhile, three younger vets, Jeff Gordon, Greg Biffle, and Johnson, continued to burn up the track.

In February 2005, Gordon won the Daytona 500 for the third time in his career. He also won twice more in the season's first nine races. Gordon increased his career win total to 72, moving within

In 2004, Kurt Busch won the first Nextel Cup Championship.

four victories of tying the late Dale Earnhardt for sixth on the all-time wins list.

Before 2005, Biffle had only three career victories on NASCAR's top circuit. By the end of June 2005, he had won five of the season's first 15 races.

Johnson won twice in 12 races, including his third straight Coca-Cola 600. That victory gave him a slim lead over Biffle in the points standings as of June 2005.

Rookie Danica Patrick came in fourth in the 2005 Indianapolis 500.

For the second straight year, Jimmie Johnson finished second in the 2004 Nextel Cup standings.

INDY RACING LEAGUE (IRL)

ALL-TIME INDIANAPOLIS 500 WINNERS

Dan Wheldon

YEAR	DRIVER	MILES PER HOUR (M.P.H.)
2005	Dan Wheldon	157.603
2004	Buddy Rice (450*)	138.518
2003	Gil de Ferran	156.291
2002	Helio Castroneves	166.499
2001	Helio Castroneves	141.574
2000	Juan Montoya	167.607
1999	Kenny Brack	153.176
1998	Eddie Cheever, Jr.	145.155
1997	Arie Luyendyk	145.827
1996	Buddy Lazier	147.956
1995	Jacques Villeneuve	153.616
1994	Al Unser, Jr.	160.872
1993	Emerson Fittipaldi	157.207
1992	Al Unser, Jr.	134.477
1991	Rick Mears	176.457
1990	Arie Luyendyk	185.981
1989	Emerson Fittipaldi	167.581
1988	Rick Mears	144.809
1987	Al Unser	162.175
1986	Bobby Rahal	170.722
1985	Danny Sullivan	152.982
1984	Rick Mears	163.612
1983	Tom Sneva	162.117
1982	Gordon Johncock	162.029
1981	Bobby Unser	139.084
1980	Johnny Rutherford	142.862

YEAR	DRIVER	M.P.H.
1979	Rick Mears	158.899
1978	Al Unser	161.363
1977	A.J. Foyt, Jr.	161.331
1976	Johnny Rutherford (255*)	148.725
1975	Bobby Unser (435*)	149.213
1974	Johnny Rutherford	158.589
1973	Gordon Johncock (332.5*)	159.036
1972	Mark Donohue	162.962
1971	Al Unser	157.735
1970	Al Unser	155.749
1969	Mario Andretti	156.867
1968	Bobby Unser	152.882
1967	A.J. Foyt, Jr.	151.207
1966	Graham Hill	144.317
1965	Jim Clark	150.686
1964	A.J. Foyt, Jr.	147.350
1963	Parnelli Jones	143.137
1962	Rodger Ward	140.293
1961	A.J. Foyt, Jr.	139.130
1960	Jim Rathmann	138.767
1959	Rodger Ward	135.857
1958	Jimmy Bryan	133.791
1957	Sam Hanks	135.601
1956	Pat Flaherty	128.490
1955	Bob Sweikert	128.213
1954	Bill Vukovich	130.840
1953	Bill Vukovich	128.740
1952	Troy Ruttman	128.922
1951	Lee Wallard	126.244
1950	Johnnie Parsons (345*)	124.002
1949	Bill Holland	121.327
1948	Mauri Rose	119.814
1947	Mauri Rose	116.338
1946	George Robson	114.820
1942-45	No races held during World War II	
1941	Floyd Davis/Mauri Rose	115.117
1940	Wilbur Shaw	114.277

*Note: Miles per hour (M.P.H.) denotes average race speed. *Miles completed before race was called because of rain.*

INDY RACING LEAGUE (cont.)

ALL-TIME INDIANAPOLIS 500 WINNERS (cont.)

YEAR	DRIVER	MILES PER HOUR (M.P.H.)	YEAR	DRIVER	M.P.H.
1939	Wilbur Shaw	115.035	1925	Peter DePaolo	101.127
1938	Floyd Roberts	117.200	1924	L.L. Corum/Joe Boyer	98.234
1937	Wilbur Shaw	113.580	1923	Tommy Milton	90.954
1936	Louis Meyer	109.069	1922	Jimmy Murphy	94.484
1935	Kelly Petillo	106.240	1921	Tommy Milton	89.621
1934	Bill Cummings	104.863	1920	Gaston Chevrolet	88.618
1933	Louis Meyer	104.162	1919	Howdy Wilcox	88.050
1932	Fred Fame	104.144	1917-18	No races held during World War I	
1931	Louis Schneider	96.629	1916	Dario Resta (scheduled for 300 miles)	84.001
1930	Billy Arnold	100.448	1915	Ralph DePalma	89.840
1929	Ray Keech	97.585	1914	Rene Thomas	82.474
1928	Louis Meyer	99.482	1913	Jules Goux	75.933
1927	George Souders	97.545	1912	Joe Dawson	78.719
1926	Frank Lockhart (400*)	95.904	1911	Ray Harroun	74.602

*Miles completed before race was called because of rain.

ALL-TIME IRL CHAMPIONS

YEAR	DRIVER
2004	Tony Kanaan
2003	Scott Dixon
2002	Sam Hornish, Jr.
2001	Sam Hornish, Jr.
2000	Buddy Lazier
1999	Greg Ray
1998	Kenny Brack
1996-97*	Tony Stewart
1996 (Series' first year)	Buzz Calkins and Scott Sharp (co-champions)

Tony Kanaan was the 2004 IRL champion.

ALL-TIME IRL ROOKIES OF THE YEAR

YEAR	DRIVER
2004	Kosuke Matsuura
2003	Dan Wheldon
2002	Laurent Redon
2001	Felipe Giaffone
2000	Airton Dare
1999	Scott Harrington
1998	Robby Unser
1996-97*	Jim Guthrie
1996 (Series' first year)	No award

*This season started in 1996 and ended in 1997.

CHAMPIONSHIP AUTO RACING TEAMS (CART)

ALL-TIME CART CHAMPIONSHIP SERIES CHAMPIONS

YEAR	DRIVER	YEAR	DRIVER
2004	Sebastien Bourdais	1985	Al Unser
2003	Paul Tracy	1984	Mario Andretti
2002	Cristiano da Matta	1983	Al Unser
2001	Gil de Ferran	1982	Rick Mears
2000	Gil de Ferran	1981	Rick Mears
1999	Juan Montoya	1980	Johnny Rutherford
1998	Alex Zanardi	1979	Rick Mears
1997	Alex Zanardi		
1996	Jimmy Vasser		
1995	Jacques Villeneuve		
1994	Al Unser, Jr.		
1993	Nigel Mansell		
1992	Bobby Rahal		
1991	Michael Andretti		
1990	Al Unser, Jr.		
1989	Emerson Fittipaldi		
1988	Danny Sullivan		
1987	Bobby Rahal		
1986	Bobby Rahal		

DID YOU KNOW?

A car has to be at least 192 inches (16 feet) long to compete in the Indy Racing League.

Sebastien Bourdais was the 2004 CART champion.

JAMIE SQUIRE/GETTY IMAGES

JAIME PUEBLA/AP

TODAY'S STARS

■ **Dale Earnhardt, Jr.,** b. October 10, 1974, Concord, North Carolina. Earnhardt, Jr., is the most popular driver in NASCAR, just as his legendary father, the late Dale Earnhardt, was. But it took the elder Earnhardt 20 tries to win the Daytona 500, NASCAR's biggest race. Junior won Daytona on his fifth try, in 2004. He also finished in the Top 5 in the final points standings in 2003 and 2004. Since joining NASCAR's top circuit in 2000, "Little E" ranks third in victories (13), Top 5 finishes (52), and Top 10 finishes (78) through 2004.

■ **Tony Kanaan,** b. December 31, 1974, Salvador, Bahia, Brazil. In 2004, Kanaan was the Indy Racing League's IndyCar Series champion. During the season, he ran off a string of 15 straight Top 5 finishes, including three victories and six second-place finishes. Kanaan completed all 3,305 possible laps — the first IndyCar Series driver to accomplish that feat. He also set a Series record for laps led (889).

Dale Earnhardt, Jr., proves that driving talent runs in the family.

■ **Kurt Busch,** b. August 4, 1978, Las Vegas, Nevada. The hard-charging Busch won the NASCAR Nextel Cup championship in 2004. On his way to the title, Busch won three races, tied for fourth in Top 10 finishes (21), and was sixth in Top 5 finishes (10). He was runner-up for Rookie of the Year in 2001. Through 2004, Busch ranked fourth in victories (12) and seventh in Top 5s (38) and Top 10s (68).

■ *Fast Fact:* The most races won by a NASCAR Rookie of the Year is three, accomplished by Tony Stewart in 1999.

2004-05 TIME LINE

■ **August 30, 2004:** After 21 seasons, Rusty Wallace announces that the 2005 season will be his last in NASCAR's top series.

■ **October 3, 2004:** Tony Kanaan of Brazil wins his first career IRL championship with a second-place finish at the Toyota Indy 400.

■ **October 14, 2004:** Veteran driver Mark Martin announces that the 2005 season — his 22nd — will be his last in NASCAR racing.

■ **November 21, 2004:** Kurt Busch outlasts Jimmie Johnson and Jeff Gordon to win the Nextel Cup points championship with a fifth-place finish in the final race of the 2004 season, the Ford 400.

■ **November 23, 2004:** Kasey Kahne is named NASCAR's Rookie of the Year. He ends the season with 13 Top 5

finishes and 14 Top 10 finishes. Kahne, 24, is the youngest rookie winner since 1993, when Jeff Gordon won the award as a 22-year-old.

■ **February 20, 2005:** Gordon wins the Daytona 500 for the third time in his career. He is the fifth driver to win three or more Daytonas, joining Richard Petty (7), Cale Yarborough (4), Bobby Allison (3), and Dale Jarrett (3).

■ **May 29, 2005:** Danica Patrick, 23, of the United States, is the fourth woman to race in the Indianapolis 500. She finishes fourth at Indy, the best finish ever by a woman. Dan Wheldon of Great Britain wins the race, becoming the first British driver to win at Indy since 1966. In NASCAR, Jimmie Johnson wins his third straight Coca-Cola 600.

DID YOU KNOW?

The "silly season" is what NASCAR people call the period late in the racing season when some teams change drivers, crews, or sponsors.

NATIONAL ASSOCIATION FOR STOCK CAR AUTOMOBILE RACING (NASCAR)

ALL-TIME NASCAR CHAMPIONS

YEAR	DRIVER	YEAR	DRIVER	YEAR	DRIVER
2004	Kurt Busch	1985	Darrell Waltrip	1966	David Pearson
2003	Matt Kenseth	1984	Terry Labonte	1965	Ned Jarrett
2002	Tony Stewart	1983	Bobby Allison	1964	Richard Petty
2001	Jeff Gordon	1982	Darrell Waltrip	1963	Joe Weatherly
2000	Bobby Labonte	1981	Darrell Waltrip	1962	Joe Weatherly
1999	Dale Jarrett	1980	Dale Earnhardt	1961	Ned Jarrett
1998	Jeff Gordon	1979	Richard Petty	1960	Rex White
1997	Jeff Gordon	1978	Cale Yarborough	1959	Lee Petty
1996	Terry Labonte	1977	Cale Yarborough	1958	Lee Petty
1995	Jeff Gordon	1976	Cale Yarborough	1957	Buck Baker
1994	Dale Earnhardt	1975	Richard Petty	1956	Buck Baker
1993	Dale Earnhardt	1974	Richard Petty	1955	Tim Flock
1992	Alan Kulwicki	1973	Benny Parsons	1954	Lee Petty
1991	Dale Earnhardt	1972	Richard Petty	1953	Herb Thomas
1990	Dale Earnhardt	1971	Richard Petty	1952	Tim Flock
1989	Rusty Wallace	1970	Bobby Isaac	1951	Herb Thomas
1988	Bill Elliott	1969	David Pearson	1950	Bill Rexford
1987	Dale Earnhardt	1968	David Pearson	1949	Red Byron
1986	Dale Earnhardt	1967	Richard Petty		

NASCAR (cont.)

ALL-TIME NASCAR WINS LEADERS*

1. Richard Petty (200)
2. David Pearson (105)
3. (tie) Bobby Allison (84)
   Darrell Waltrip (84)
5. Cale Yarborough (83)
6. Dale Earnhardt (76)
7. Jeff Gordon (72)
8. (tie) Lee Petty (55)
   Rusty Wallace (55)
10. (tie) Ned Jarrett (50)
    Junior Johnson (50)
12. Herb Thomas (48)
13. Buck Baker (46)
14. Bill Elliott (44)
15. Tim Flock (40)
16. Bobby Isaac (37)
17. Mark Martin (34)
18. Fireball Roberts (32)
19. Dale Jarrett (31)
20. (tie) Rex White (28)
    Fred Lorenzen (28)

*Through June 2005

Kasey Kahne

ALL-TIME NASCAR ROOKIES OF THE YEAR

YEAR	DRIVER	YEAR	DRIVER
2004	Kasey Kahne	1980	Jody Ridley
2003	Jamie McMurray	1979	Dale Earnhardt
2002	Ryan Newman	1978	Ronnie Thomas
2001	Kevin Harvick	1977	Ricky Rudd
2000	Matt Kenseth	1976	Skip Manning
1999	Tony Stewart	1975	Bruce Hill
1998	Kenny Irwin	1974	Earl Ross
1997	Mike Skinner	1973	Lennie Pond
1996	Johnny Benson	1972	Larry Smith
1995	Ricky Craven	1971	Walter Ballard
1994	Jeff Burton	1970	Bill Dennis
1993	Jeff Gordon	1969	Dick Brooks
1992	Jimmy Hensley	1968	Pete Hamilton
1991	Bobby Hamilton	1967	Donnie Allison
1990	Rob Moroso	1966	James Hylton
1989	Dick Trickle	1965	Sam McQuagg
1988	Ken Bouchard	1964	Doug Cooper
1987	Davey Allison	1963	Billy Wade
1986	Alan Kulwicki	1962	Tom Cox
1985	Ken Schrader	1961	Woodie Wilson
1984	Rusty Wallace	1960	David Pearson
1983	Sterling Marlin	1959	Richard Petty
1982	Geoffrey Bodine	1958	Shorty Rollins
1981	Ron Bouchard		

ALL-TIME DAYTONA 500 WINNERS

YEAR	DRIVER	M.P.H.	YEAR	DRIVER	M.P.H.	YEAR	DRIVER	M.P.H.
2005	Jeff Gordon	135.173	1989	Darrell Waltrip	148.466	1973	Richard Petty	157.205
2004	Dale Earnhardt, Jr.	156.345	1988	Bobby Allison	137.531	1972	A.J. Foyt, Jr.	161.550
2003	Michael Waltrip	133.870	1987	Bill Elliott	170.200	1971	Richard Petty	144.462
2002	Ward Burton	142.971	1986	Geoffrey Bodine	148.124	1970	Pete Hamilton	149.601
2001	Michael Waltrip	161.783	1985	Bill Elliott	172.265	1969	Lee Roy Yarbrough	157.950
2000	Dale Jarrett	155.669	1984	Cale Yarborough	150.994	1968	Cale Yarborough	143.251
1999	Jeff Gordon	161.651	1983	Cale Yarborough	155.979	1967	Mario Andretti	146.926
1998	Dale Earnhardt	172.712	1982	Bobby Allison	153.991	1966	Richard Petty	160.627
1997	Jeff Gordon	148.295	1981	Richard Petty	169.651	1965	Fred Lorenzen	141.539
1996	Dale Jarrett	154.308	1980	Buddy Baker	177.602	1964	Richard Petty	154.334
1995	Sterling Marlin	141.710	1979	Richard Petty	143.977	1963	Tiny Lund	151.566
1994	Sterling Marlin	156.931	1978	Bobby Allison	159.730	1962	Fireball Roberts	152.529
1993	Dale Jarrett	154.972	1977	Cale Yarborough	153.218	1961	Marvin Panch	149.601
1992	Davey Allison	160.256	1976	David Pearson	152.181	1960	Junior Johnson	124.740
1991	Ernie Irvan	148.148	1975	Benny Parsons	153.649	1959	Lee Petty	135.521
1990	Derrike Cope	165.761	1974	Richard Petty	140.894			

ALL-TIME TALLADEGA 500* WINNERS

YEAR	DRIVER	M.P.H.	YEAR	DRIVER	M.P.H.	YEAR	DRIVER	M.P.H.
2005	Jeff Gordon	146.904	1992	Ernie Irvan	176.309	1979	Darrell Waltrip	161.229
2004	Jeff Gordon	129.396	1991	Dale Earnhardt	147.383	1978	Lennie Pond	174.700
2003	Dale Earnhardt, Jr.	144.625	1990	Dale Earnhardt	174.430	1977	Donnie Allison	162.524
2002	Dale Earnhardt, Jr.	159.022	1989	Terry Labonte	157.354	1976	Dave Marcis	157.547
2001	Bobby Hamilton	184.003	1988	Ken Schrader	154.505	1975	Buddy Baker	130.892
2000	Jeff Gordon	161.157	1987	Bill Elliott	171.293	1974	Richard Petty	148.637
1999	Dale Earnhardt	163.395	1986	Bobby Hillin	151.552	1973	Dick Brooks	145.454
1998	Bobby Labonte	163.439	1985	Cale Yarborough	148.772	1972	James Hylton	148.728
1997	Terry Labonte	156.601	1984	Dale Earnhardt	155.485	1971	Bobby Allison	145.945
1996	Jeff Gordon	133.387	1983	Dale Earnhardt	170.611	1970	Pete Hamilton	158.517
1995	Sterling Marlin	173.188	1982	Darrell Waltrip	168.157	1969	Richard Brickhouse	153.778
1994	Jimmy Spencer	163.217	1981	Ron Bouchard	156.737			
1993	Dale Earnhardt	153.858	1980	Neil Bonnett	166.894			

*From 1969 through 1988, the race was known as the Talladega 500. From 1989 through 2001, it was known as the Die Hard 500. In 2001, it was again called the Talladega 500. Since 2002, the race has been called the Aaron's 499.

NASCAR (cont.)

ALL-TIME COCA-COLA 600 WINNERS

YEAR	DRIVER	M.P.H.	YEAR	DRIVER	M.P.H.	YEAR	DRIVER	M.P.H.
2005	Jimmie Johnson	114.698	1989	Darrell Waltrip	144.077	1973	Buddy Baker	134.890
2004	Jimmie Johnson	142.763	1988	Darrell Waltrip	124.460	1972	Buddy Baker	142.255
2003	Jimmie Johnson	126.198	1987	Kyle Petty	131.483	1971	Bobby Allison	140.442
2002	Mark Martin	137.729	1986	Dale Earnhardt	140.406	1970	Donnie Allison	129.680
2001	Jeff Burton	138.107	1985	Darrell Waltrip	141.807	1969	Lee Roy Yarbrough	134.361
2000	Matt Kenseth	142.640	1984	Bobby Allison	129.233	1968	Buddy Baker	104.207
1999	Jeff Burton	151.367	1983	Neil Bonnett	140.707	1967	Jim Paschal	135.832
1998	Jeff Gordon	136.424	1982	Neil Bonnett	130.058	1966	Marvin Panch	135.042
1997	Jeff Gordon	136.745	1981	Bobby Allison	129.326	1965	Fred Lorenzen	121.772
1996	Dale Jarrett	147.581	1980	Benny Parsons	119.265	1964	Jim Paschal	125.772
1995	Bobby Labonte	151.952	1979	Darrell Waltrip	136.674	1963	Fred Lorenzen	132.418
1994	Jeff Gordon	139.445	1978	Darrell Waltrip	138.355	1962	Nelson Stacy	125.552
1993	Dale Earnhardt	145.504	1977	Richard Petty	137.676	1961	David Pearson	111.633
1992	Dale Earnhardt	132.980	1976	David Pearson	137.352	1960	Joe Lee Johnson	107.735
1991	Davey Allison	138.951	1975	Richard Petty	145.327			
1990	Rusty Wallace	137.650	1974	David Pearson	135.720			

ALL-TIME BRICKYARD 400 WINNERS

YEAR	DRIVER	M.P.H.	YEAR	DRIVER	M.P.H.
2004	Jeff Gordon	115.037	1998	Jeff Gordon	126.772
2003	Kevin Harvick	134.554	1997	Ricky Rudd	130.814
2002	Bill Elliott	125.033	1996	Dale Jarrett	139.508
2001	Jeff Gordon	130.790	1995	Dale Earnhardt	155.206
2000	Bobby Labonte	155.912	1994	Jeff Gordon	131.977
1999	Dale Jarrett	148.194			

■ **Fast Fact:** Sara Christian was the first woman to compete in a NASCAR race. She finished 14th in a race on a 3/4-mile dirt track in Charlotte, North Carolina, on June 19, 1949.

ALL-TIME SOUTHERN 500* WINNERS

YEAR	DRIVER	M.P.H.
2005	Greg Biffle	123.031
2004	Jimmie Johnson	125.044
2003	Terry Labonte	120.744
2002	Jeff Gordon	118.617
2001	Ward Burton	122.773
2000	Bobby Labonte	108.273
1999	Jeff Burton	107.816
1998	Jeff Gordon	139.031
1997	Jeff Gordon	121.149
1996	Jeff Gordon	135.757
1995	Jeff Gordon	121.231
1994	Bill Elliott	127.952
1993	Mark Martin	137.932
1992	Darrell Waltrip	129.114
1991	Harry Gant	133.508
1990	Dale Earnhardt	123.141
1989	Dale Earnhardt	135.462
1988	Bill Elliott	128.297
1987	Dale Earnhardt	115.520
1986	Tim Richmond	121.068
1985	Bill Elliott	121.254
1984	Harry Gant	128.270
1983	Bobby Allison	123.343
1982	Cale Yarborough	115.224
1981	Neil Bonnett	126.410
1980	Terry Labonte	115.210

*The race is now known as the Dodge Charger 500.

Jimmie Johnson makes a pit stop before winning the 2004 Southern 500.

ALL-TIME SOUTHERN 500 WINNERS (cont.)

YEAR	DRIVER	M.P.H.	YEAR	DRIVER	M.P.H.	YEAR	DRIVER	M.P.H.
1979	David Pearson	126.259	1969	Lee Roy Yarbrough	105.612	1959	Jim Reed	111.840
1978	Cale Yarborough	116.828	1968	Cale Yarborough	126.132	1958	Fireball Roberts	102.590
1977	David Pearson	106.797	1967	Richard Petty	130.423	1957	Speedy Thompson	100.094
1976	David Pearson	120.534	1966	Darel Dieringer	114.830	1956	Curtis Turner	95.067
1975	Bobby Allison	116.825	1965	Ned Jarrett	115.924	1955	Herb Thomas	93.281
1974	Cale Yarborough	111.075	1964	Buck Baker	117.757	1954	Herb Thomas	94.930
1973	Cale Yarborough	134.033	1963	Fireball Roberts	129.784	1953	Buck Baker	92.780
1972	Bobby Allison	128.124	1962	Larry Frank	117.965	1952	Fonty Flock	74.510
1971	Bobby Allison	131.398	1961	Nelson Stacy	117.787	1951	Herb Thomas	76.900
1970	Buddy Baker	128.817	1960	Buck Baker	105.901	1950	Johnny Mantz	76.260

LEGENDS

A.J. Foyt won the Indy 500 four times.

■ **A.J. Foyt,** b. January 16, 1935, Houston, Texas. Foyt was the first four-time winner of the Indianapolis 500. He is the only driver to win the Indy 500, the Daytona 500, and the 24 Hours of Le Mans in his career. Foyt holds Indy Car records for most victories (67), most championships (7), and most victories in one season (10). He was inducted into the International Motorsports Hall of Fame in 2000.

■ **Cale Yarborough,** b. March 27, 1940, Timmonsville, South Carolina. Yarborough is the only driver to win three straight NASCAR Cup championships (1976-78). His 83 career victories rank fifth all-time in NASCAR history. Yarborough won the Daytona 500 four times and the Southern 500 five times. He was inducted into the International Motorsports Hall of Fame in 1993.

■ **Rusty Wallace,** b. August 14, 1956, Fenton, Missouri. Wallace is second among active NASCAR drivers in victories (55) and is tied for eighth overall for career victories. In 1989, he won the NASCAR Winston (now Nextel) Cup championship after being named Rookie of the Year five years earlier. Wallace was honored as one of NASCAR's 50 Greatest Drivers in 1998.

TENNIS

Roger Federer of Switzerland had a year in 2004 that few players have matched. The Swiss star became the fourth male player, and the first since Mats Wilander in 1988, to capture three of the four Grand Slam tournaments in a single year. Not only that, but he did it without much trouble.

Federer started 2004 with a straight-set victory over Marat Safin of Russia in the Australian Open final. In July, he won his second straight Wimbledon title with a four-set victory over Andy Roddick of the United States. But Federer's most impressive win came at the U.S. Open in September, when he routed Australian Lleyton Hewitt, 6–0, 7–6, 6–0, in a match that took less than two hours.

The only one that got away from Federer was the French Open, where Gustavo Kuerten of Brazil upset him in straight sets in the third round. That opened the door for unseeded Gaston Gaudio of Argentina to win his first Grand Slam event.

On the women's side, the story was the rise of the Russians. With several top players, including Americans Serena and Venus Williams and Belgians Kim Clijsters and Justine Henin-Hardenne, struggling with injuries, players like Maria Sharapova, Elena Dementieva, Anastasia Myskina, and Svetlana Kuznetsova — all from Russia — filled their shoes.

None made a bigger impact than Sharapova. The 17-year-old pulled off one of the biggest upsets of the year by beating two-time defending champion Serena Williams in the Wimbledon final. It would be the start of the newest rivalry in tennis. Sharapova beat Williams again in the season-ending WTA Tour Championships.

Myskina defeated Dementieva to win her first French Open, a tournament that usually gives her trouble. Kuznetsova had a surprising win in the U.S. Open, beating Dementieva in the final.

At the start of 2005, three Russians were in the top 5 (Myskina at Number 3, Sharapova at Number 4, and Kuznetsova at Number 5).

SIMON BRUTY/SPORTS ILLUSTRATED

Roger Federer won 11 titles in 2004, including three Grand Slams.

GRAND SLAM TOURNAMENTS: ALL-TIME MEN'S CHAMPIONS

AUSTRALIAN CHAMPIONSHIPS

Year	Winner	Year	Winner	Year	Winner
2005	Marat Safin	1990	Ivan Lendl	1974	Jimmy Connors
2004	Roger Federer	1989	Ivan Lendl	1973	John Newcombe
2003	Andre Agassi	1988	Mats Wilander	1972	Ken Rosewall
2002	Thomas Johansson	1987	Stefan Edberg	1971	Ken Rosewall
2001	Andre Agassi	1986	no tournament	1970	Arthur Ashe
2000	Andre Agassi	1985	Stefan Edberg	*1969	Rod Laver
1999	Yevgeny Kafelnikov	1984	Mats Wilander	1968	Bill Bowrey
1998	Petr Korda	1983	Mats Wilander	1967	Roy Emerson
1997	Pete Sampras	1982	Johan Kriek	1966	Roy Emerson
1996	Boris Becker	1981	Johan Kriek	1965	Roy Emerson
1995	Andre Agassi	1980	Brian Teacher	1964	Roy Emerson
1994	Pete Sampras	1979	Guillermo Vilas	1963	Roy Emerson
1993	Jim Courier	1978	Guillermo Vilas	1962	Rod Laver
1992	Jim Courier	1977 (Dec.)	Vitas Gerulaitis	1961	Roy Emerson
1991	Boris Becker	1977 (Jan.)	Roscoe Tanner	1960	Rod Laver
		1976	Mark Edmondson	1959	Alex Olmedo
		1975	John Newcombe	1958	Ashley Cooper

* Became Open (amateur and professional) in 1969.
Note: Traditionally, the Australian Open was held in January. In 1977, it was moved to December, so there were two tournaments that year. It returned to January in 1987.

AUSTRALIAN CHAMPIONSHIPS (cont.)

Year	Winner
1957	Ashley Cooper
1956	Lew Hoad
1955	Ken Rosewall
1954	Mervyn Rose
1953	Ken Rosewall
1952	Ken McGregor
1951	Richard Savitt
1950	Frank Sedgman
1949	Frank Sedgman
1948	Adrian Quist
1947	Dinny Pails
1946	John Bromwich
1941-45	No tournament
1940	Adrian Quist
1939	John Bromwich
1938	Don Budge
1937	Vivian B. McGrath
1936	Adrian Quist
1935	Jack Crawford
1934	Fred Perry
1933	Jack Crawford
1932	Jack Crawford
1931	Jack Crawford
1930	Gar Moon
1929	John C. Gregory
1928	Jean Borotra
1927	Gerald Patterson
1926	John Hawkes
1925	James Anderson
1924	James Anderson
1923	Pat O'Hara Wood
1922	James Anderson
1921	Rhys H. Gemmell
1920	Pat O'Hara Wood
1919	A.R.F. Kingscote
1916-18	No tournament
1915	Francis G. Lowe
1914	Arthur Wood
1913	F. F. Parker
1912	J. Cecil Parke
1911	Norman Brookes
1910	Rodney Heath
1909	Tony Wilding
1908	Fred Alexander
1907	Horace M. Rice
1906	Tony Wilding
1905	Rodney Heath

FRENCH CHAMPIONSHIPS

Year	Winner
2005	Rafael Nadal
2004	Gaston Gaudio
2003	Juan Carlos Ferrero
2002	Albert Costa
2001	Gustavo Kuerten
2000	Gustavo Kuerten
1999	Andre Agassi

Year	Winner
1998	Carlos Moya
1997	Gustavo Kuerten
1996	Yevgeny Kafelnikov
1995	Thomas Muster
1994	Sergi Bruguera
1993	Sergi Bruguera
1992	Jim Courier
1991	Jim Courier
1990	Andres Gomez
1989	Michael Chang
1988	Mats Wilander
1987	Ivan Lendl
1986	Ivan Lendl
1985	Mats Wilander
1984	Ivan Lendl
1983	Yannick Noah
1982	Mats Wilander
1981	Bjorn Borg
1980	Bjorn Borg
1979	Bjorn Borg
1978	Bjorn Borg
1977	Guillermo Vilas
1976	Adriano Panatta
1975	Bjorn Borg
1974	Bjorn Borg
1973	Ilie Nastase
1972	Andres Gimeno
1971	Jan Kodes
1970	Jan Kodes
1969	Rod Laver
*1968	Ken Rosewall
1967	Roy Emerson
1966	Tony Roche
1965	Fred Stolle
1964	Manuel Santana
1963	Roy Emerson
1962	Rod Laver
1961	Manuel Santana
1960	Nicola Pietrangeli
1959	Nicola Pietrangeli
1958	Mervyn Rose
1957	Sven Davidson
1956	Lew Hoad
1955	Tony Trabert
1954	Tony Trabert
1953	Ken Rosewall
1952	Jaroslav Drobny
1951	Jaroslav Drobny
1950	Budge Patty
1949	Frank Parker
1948	Frank Parker
1947	Joseph Asboth
1946	Marcel Bernard
1940-45	No tournament
1939	Don McNeill
1938	Don Budge
1937	Henner Henkel
1936	Gottfried von Cramm
1935	Fred Perry
1934	Gottfried von Cramm

Year	Winner
1933	Jack Crawford
1932	Henri Cochet
1931	Jean Borotra
1930	Henri Cochet
1929	Rene Lacoste
1928	Henri Cochet
1927	Rene Lacoste
1926	Henri Cochet
†1925	Rene Lacoste

WIMBLEDON CHAMPIONSHIPS

Year	Winner
2005	Roger Federer
2004	Roger Federer
2003	Roger Federer
2002	Lleyton Hewitt
2001	Goran Ivanisevic
2000	Pete Sampras
1999	Pete Sampras
1998	Pete Sampras
1997	Pete Sampras
1996	Richard Krajicek
1995	Pete Sampras
1994	Pete Sampras
1993	Pete Sampras
1992	Andre Agassi
1991	Michael Stich
1990	Stefan Edberg
1989	Boris Becker
1988	Stefan Edberg
1987	Pat Cash
1986	Boris Becker
1985	Boris Becker
1984	John McEnroe
1983	John McEnroe
1982	Jimmy Connors
1981	John McEnroe
1980	Bjorn Borg
1979	Bjorn Borg
1978	Bjorn Borg
1977	Bjorn Borg
1976	Bjorn Borg
1975	Arthur Ashe
1974	Jimmy Connors
1973	Jan Kodes
1972	Stan Smith
1971	John Newcombe
1970	John Newcombe
1969	Rod Laver
*1968	Rod Laver
1967	John Newcombe
1966	Manuel Santana
1965	Roy Emerson
1964	Roy Emerson
1963	Chuck McKinley
1962	Rod Laver
1961	Rod Laver
1960	Neale Fraser
1959	Alex Olmedo
1958	Ashley Cooper
1957	Lew Hoad

* Became Open (amateur and professional) in 1968.
† 1925 was the first year in which players from all countries were allowed to compete.

TODAY'S STARS

■ **Andy Roddick,** b. August 30, 1982, Omaha, Nebraska. Roddick has taken his place as the next great American player. At the start of 2005, he had won 16 career singles titles, including the 2003 U.S. Open. He did not fare well in the Grand Slam tournaments in 2004. He advanced to only one Grand Slam final, a loss to Roger Federer at Wimbledon. However, Roddick won four singles titles in other tournaments during the year. He finished 2004 ranked Number 4 in the world. Roddick has the game's hardest serve, clocked at a record 155 miles per hour.

At the start of the 2005 season, Andy Roddick had won 16 tournaments.

■ **Tim Henman,** b. September 6, 1974, Oxford, England. Henman is the top British player on the tour. He always has the home crowd behind him at Wimbledon, where he has advanced to the semifinals four times. Henman is known for his consistency. He finished Number 6 in the final rankings in 2004, the fifth time in the past seven years that he has finished in the Top 10.

■ **Guillermo Coria,** b. January 13, 1982, Rufino, Argentina. Despite shoulder surgery in August 2004, Coria finished the season ranked in the Top 10 for the second straight year. He is one of the best clay-court players in the world, and he came within a point of winning the French Open in 2004. Coria led Gaston Gaudio, 6–0, 6–3, and had two match points even after he was slowed by leg cramps. Gaudio came back and won the third and fourth sets, and then took the fifth set, 8–6. Coria won two tournaments in 2004, both on clay — in Buenos Aires and Monte Carlo.

GRAND SLAM TOURNAMENTS: ALL-TIME MEN'S CHAMPIONS (cont.)

WIMBLEDON CHAMPIONSHIPS (cont.)

Year	Winner	Year	Winner	Year	Winner
1956	Lew Hoad	1931	Sidney B. Wood, Jr.	1906	H. Laurie Doherty
1955	Tony Trabert	1930	Bill Tilden	1905	H. Laurie Doherty
1954	Jaroslav Drobny	1929	Henri Cochet	1904	H. Laurie Doherty
1953	Vic Seixas	1928	Rene Lacoste	1903	H. Laurie Doherty
1952	Frank Sedgman	1927	Henri Cochet	1902	H. Laurie Doherty
1951	Dick Savitt	1926	Jean Borotra	1901	Arthur W. Gore
1950	Budge Patty	1925	Rene Lacoste	1900	Reggie F. Doherty
1949	Fred Schroeder, Jr.	1924	Jean Borotra	1899	Reggie F. Doherty
1948	Bob Falkenburg	1923	Bill Johnston	1898	Reggie F. Doherty
1947	Jack Kramer	1922	Gerald L. Patterson	1897	Reggie F. Doherty
1946	Yvon Petra	1921	Bill Tilden	1896	Harold S. Mahoney
1940-45	No tournament	1920	Bill Tilden	1895	Wilfred Baddeley
1939	Bobby Riggs	1919	Gerald L. Patterson	1894	Joshua Pim
1938	Don Budge	1915-18	No tournament	1893	Joshua Pim
1937	Don Budge	1914	Norman E. Brookes	1892	Wilfred Baddeley
1936	Fred Perry	1913	Anthony F. Wilding	1891	Wilfred Baddeley
1935	Fred Perry	1912	Anthony F. Wilding	1890	William J. Hamilton
1934	Fred Perry	1911	Anthony F. Wilding	1889	William Renshaw
1933	Jack Crawford	1910	Anthony F. Wilding	1888	Ernest Renshaw
1932	Ellsworth Vines	1909	Arthur W. Gore	1887	Herbert F. Lawford
		1908	Arthur W. Gore	1886	William Renshaw
		1907	Norman E. Brookes	1885	William Renshaw

WIMBLEDON CHAMPIONSHIPS (cont.)

Year	Winner
1884	William Renshaw
1883	William Renshaw
1882	William Renshaw
1881	William Renshaw
1880	John T. Harley
1879	John T. Harley
1878	P. Frank Hadow
1877	Spencer W. Gore

UNITED STATES CHAMPIONSHIPS

Year	Winner
2004	Roger Federer
2003	Andy Roddick
2002	Pete Sampras
2001	Lleyton Hewitt
2000	Marat Safin
1999	Andre Agassi
1998	Patrick Rafter
1997	Patrick Rafter

* Became Open (amateur and professional) in 1968.
** Separate amateur event held.

Year	Winner
1996	Pete Sampras
1995	Pete Sampras
1994	Andre Agassi
1993	Pete Sampras
1992	Stefan Edberg
1991	Stefan Edberg
1990	Pete Sampras
1989	Boris Becker
1988	Mats Wilander
1987	Ivan Lendl
1986	Ivan Lendl
1985	Ivan Lendl
1984	John McEnroe
1983	Jimmy Connors
1982	Jimmy Connors
1981	John McEnroe
1980	John McEnroe
1979	John McEnroe
1978	Jimmy Connors
1977	Guillermo Vilas
1976	Jimmy Connors
1975	Manuel Orantes
1974	Jimmy Connors
1973	John Newcombe
1972	Ilie Nastase

Year	Winner
1971	Stan Smith
1970	Ken Rosewall
**1969	Stan Smith
1969	Rod Laver
*1968	Arthur Ashe
**1968	Arthur Ashe
1967	John Newcombe
1966	Fred Stolle
1965	Manuel Santana
1964	Roy Emerson
1963	Rafael Osuna
1962	Rod Laver
1961	Roy Emerson
1960	Neale Fraser
1959	Neale Fraser
1958	Ashley Cooper
1957	Mal Anderson
1956	Ken Rosewall
1955	Tony Trabert
1954	Vic Seixas
1953	Tony Trabert
1952	Frank Sedgman
1951	Frank Sedgman
1950	Arthur Larsen
1949	Pancho Gonzales

2004-05 MEN'S TIME LINE

■ **February 1, 2004:** Roger Federer of Switzerland defeats Russian Marat Safin to win the Australian Open. Federer goes on to win 11 tournaments, including three Grand Slams, during the year.

■ **March 28, 2004:** Rising star Rafael Nadal of Spain, age 17, beats Federer in straight sets in the third round of the NASDAQ-100 Open. Nadal was named Newcomer of the Year in 2003.

■ **June 6, 2004:** Unseeded Gaston Gaudio of Argentina beats favored Guillermo Coria, also of Argentina, in the French Open final. Coria wins the first two sets easily, but Gaudio comes back after Coria suffers leg cramps in the fourth set.

■ **July 4, 2004:** After losing the first set, Federer comes back to beat Andy Roddick of the United States for his second straight Wimbledon title.

■ **August 22, 2004:** Nicolas Massu of Chile beats Mardy Fish of the United States in five sets to win the Olympic gold medal in men's singles. A day earlier, Massu and partner Fernando Gonzalez had won the gold medal in men's doubles. The gold medals are Chile's first in any Summer Olympic sport.

■ **September 12, 2004:** Roger Federer beats Australian Lleyton Hewitt to win the U.S. Open.

■ **September 24, 2004:** Andy Roddick breaks his serve record when he blasts a 155-mile-per-hour scorcher in his 6–1, 6–4, 6–4 win over Vladimir Voltchkov of Belarus in Davis Cup play.

■ **January 30, 2005:** Marat Safin defeats Lleyton Hewitt in four sets for his first Australian Open title.

DID YOU KNOW?

When he won the 2004 French Open, Gaston Gaudio of Argentina became the first player to win a Grand Slam title after losing the first set 6–0.

GRAND SLAM TOURNAMENTS: ALL-TIME MEN'S CHAMPIONS (cont.)

UNITED STATES CHAMPIONSHIPS (cont.)

Year	Winner	Year	Winner	Year	Winner
1948	Pancho Gonzales	1926	Rene Lacoste	1902	William A. Larned
1947	Jack Kramer	1925	Bill Tilden	1901	William A. Larned
1946	Jack Kramer	1924	Bill Tilden	1900	Malcolm D. Whitman
1945	Frank Parker	1923	Bill Tilden	1899	Malcolm D. Whitman
1944	Frank Parker	1922	Bill Tilden	1898	Malcolm D. Whitman
1943	Joseph R. Hunt	1921	Bill Tilden	1897	Robert D. Wrenn
1942	Fred R. Schroeder, Jr.	1920	Bill Tilden	1896	Robert D. Wrenn
1941	Bobby Riggs	1919	Bill Johnston	1895	Frederick H. Hovey
1940	Don McNeill	1918	R.L. Murray	1894	Robert D. Wrenn
1939	Bobby Riggs	1917	R.L. Murray	1893	Robert D. Wrenn
1938	Don Budge	1916	Richard N. Williams	1892	Oliver S. Campbell
1937	Don Budge	1915	Bill Johnston	1891	Oliver S. Campbell
1936	Fred Perry	1914	Richard N. Williams	1890	Oliver S. Campbell
1935	Wilmer L. Allison	1913	Maurice E. McLoughlin	1889	H. W. Slocum, Jr.
1934	Fred Perry	1912	Maurice E. McLoughlin	1888	H. W. Slocum, Jr.
1933	Fred Perry	1911	William A. Larned	1887	Richard D. Sears
1932	Ellsworth Vines	1910	William A. Larned	1886	Richard D. Sears
1931	Ellsworth Vines	1909	William A. Larned	1885	Richard D. Sears
1930	John H. Doeg	1908	William A. Larned	1884	Richard D. Sears
1929	Bill Tilden	1907	William A. Larned	1883	Richard D. Sears
1928	Henri Cochet	1906	William J. Clothier	1882	Richard D. Sears
1927	Rene Lacoste	1905	Beals C. Wright	1881	Richard D. Sears
		1904	Holcombe Ward		
		1903	H. Laurie Doherty		

LEGENDS

Boris Becker won 49 career titles, including six Grand Slams.

HEINZ KLUETMEIER/SPORTS ILLUSTRATED

■ **Boris Becker,** b. November 22, 1967, Leiman, Germany. Becker grabbed the attention of the tennis world by winning Wimbledon in 1985 when he was just 17 years and 7 months old. At the time, the victory made him the youngest male player to win a Grand Slam tournament. (In 1989, Michael Chang won the French Open at age 17 years and 3 months.) Becker went on to win five more Grand Slam events: Wimbledon and the Australian Open twice, and the U.S. Open once.

■ **Ilie Nastase,** b. July 19, 1946, Bucharest, Romania. Nastase's talent was often overshadowed by his bad temper and antics on the court, such as arguing with umpires and throwing his racket. He still had the talent to win seven Grand Slam singles titles and 17 doubles titles in his career. Nastase was the world's best player in 1973, when he won the French Open, Italian Open, and 13 other titles. He also helped to make Romania a respected competitor in the Davis Cup tournament. Romania reached the finals in 1969, 1971, and 1972, falling to the United States each time.

■ **Ivan Lendl,** b. March 7, 1960, Ostrava, Czechoslovakia. Lendl was the most dominant player of his era. From the early 1980's to the early 1990's, he won eight Grand Slam singles titles and was a finalist 11 other times. For 157 weeks, from 1985-88, Lendl was ranked Number 1 in the world, just three weeks short of Jimmy Connors' Open Era record. He finished four seasons ranked Number 1 (1985, 1986, 1987, and 1989). Lendl was also a powerhouse in Davis Cup play. He was 7-0 in singles and 3-0 in doubles competition, and led Czechoslovakia to its only Davis Cup title, in 1980.

GRAND SLAM TOURNAMENTS: ALL-TIME WOMEN'S CHAMPIONS

AUSTRALIAN CHAMPIONSHIPS

Year	Winner
2005	Serena Williams
2004	Justine Henin-Hardenne
2003	Serena Williams
2002	Jennifer Capriati
2001	Jennifer Capriati
2000	Lindsay Davenport
1999	Martina Hingis
1998	Martina Hingis
1997	Martina Hingis
1996	Monica Seles
1995	Mary Pierce
1994	Steffi Graf
1993	Monica Seles
1992	Monica Seles
1991	Monica Seles
1990	Steffi Graf
1989	Steffi Graf
1988	Steffi Graf
1987 (Jan.)	Hana Mandlikova
1985 (Dec.)	Martina Navratilova
1984	Chris Evert Lloyd
1983	Martina Navratilova
1982	Chris Evert Lloyd
1981	Martina Navratilova
1980	Hana Mandlikova
1979	Barbara Jordan
1978	Chris O'Neil
1977 (Dec.)	Evonne Goolagong Cawley
1977 (Jan.)	Kerry Melville Reid
1976	Evonne Goolagong Cawley
1975	Evonne Goolagong
1974	Evonne Goolagong
1973	Margaret Smith Court
1972	Virginia Wade
1971	Margaret Smith Court
1970	Margaret Smith Court
*1969	Margaret Smith Court
1968	Billie Jean King
1967	Nancy Richey
1966	Margaret Smith
1965	Margaret Smith
1964	Margaret Smith
1963	Margaret Smith
1962	Margaret Smith
1961	Margaret Smith
1960	Margaret Smith
1959	Mary Carter-Reitano
1958	Angela Mortimer
1957	Shirley Fry
1956	Mary Carter
1955	Beryl Penrose
1954	Thelma Long
1953	Maureen Connolly
1952	Thelma Long
1951	Nancye Wynne Bolton
1950	Louise Brough
1949	Doris Hart
1948	Nancye Wynne Bolton
1947	Nancye Wynne Bolton
1946	Nancye Wynne Bolton

Year	Winner
1941-45	No tournament
1940	Nancye Wynne Bolton
1939	Emily Westacott
1938	Dorothy Bundy
1937	Nancye Wynne Bolton
1936	Joan Hartigan
1935	Dorothy Round
1934	Joan Hartigan
1933	Joan Hartigan
1932	Coral Buttsworth
1931	Coral Buttsworth
1930	Daphne Akhurst
1929	Daphne Akhurst
1928	Daphne Akhurst
1927	Esna Boyd
1926	Daphne Akhurst
1925	Daphne Akhurst
1924	Sylvia Lance
1923	Margaret Molesworth
1922	Margaret Molesworth

FRENCH CHAMPIONSHIPS

Year	Winner
2005	Justine Henin-Hardenne
2004	Anastasia Myskina
2003	Justine Henin-Hardenne
2002	Serena Williams
2001	Jennifer Capriati
2000	Mary Pierce
1999	Steffi Graf
1998	Arantxa Sánchez-Vicario
1997	Iva Majoli
1996	Steffi Graf
1995	Steffi Graf
1994	Arantxa Sánchez-Vicario
1993	Steffi Graf
1992	Monica Seles
1991	Monica Seles
1990	Monica Seles
1989	Arantxa Sánchez-Vicario
1988	Steffi Graf
1987	Steffi Graf
1986	Chris Evert Lloyd
1985	Chris Evert Lloyd
1984	Martina Navratilova
1983	Chris Evert Lloyd
1982	Martina Navratilova
1981	Hana Mandlikova
1980	Chris Evert Lloyd
1979	Chris Evert Lloyd
1978	Virginia Ruzici
1977	Mima Jausovec
1976	Sue Barker
1975	Chris Evert
1974	Chris Evert
1973	Margaret Smith Court
1972	Billie Jean King
1971	Evonne Goolagong
1970	Margaret Smith Court
1969	Margaret Smith Court
**1968	Nancy Richey

Year	Winner
1967	Francoise Durr
1966	Ann Jones
1965	Lesley Turner
1964	Margaret Smith
1963	Lesley Turner
1962	Margaret Smith
1961	Ann Haydon
1960	Darlene Hard
1959	Christine Truman
1958	Zsuzsi Kormoczy
1957	Shirley Bloomer
1956	Althea Gibson
1955	Angela Mortimer
1954	Maureen Connolly
1953	Maureen Connolly
1952	Doris Hart
1951	Shirley Fry
1950	Doris Hart
1949	Margaret Osborne duPont
1948	Nelly Landry
1947	Patricia Todd
1946	Margaret Osborne
1940-45	No tournament
1939	Simone Mathieu
1938	Simone Mathieu
1937	Hilde Sperling
1936	Hilde Sperling
1935	Hilde Sperling
1934	Margaret Scriven
1933	Margaret Scriven
1932	Helen Wills Moody
1931	Cilly Aussem
1930	Helen Wills Moody
1929	Helen Wills
1928	Helen Wills
1927	Kea Bouman
1926	Suzanne Lenglen
†1925	Suzanne Lenglen

WIMBLEDON CHAMPIONSHIPS

Year	Winner
2005	Venus Williams
2004	Maria Sharapova
2003	Serena Williams
2002	Serena Williams
2001	Venus Williams
2000	Venus Williams
1999	Lindsay Davenport
1998	Jana Novotna
1997	Martina Hingis
1996	Steffi Graf
1995	Steffi Graf
1994	Conchita Martinez
1993	Steffi Graf
1992	Steffi Graf
1991	Steffi Graf
1990	Martina Navratilova
1989	Steffi Graf
1988	Steffi Graf
1987	Martina Navratilova
1986	Martina Navratilova
1985	Martina Navratilova
1984	Martina Navratilova
1983	Martina Navratilova
1982	Martina Navratilova

* Became Open (amateur and professional) in 1969.
** Became Open (amateur and professional) in 1968.
† 1925 was the first year in which players from all countries were allowed to compete.

TENNIS

TODAY'S STARS

Maria Sharapova won her first Grand Slam title, Wimbledon, in 2004.

■ **Maria Sharapova,** b. April 19, 1987, Nyagan, Russia. In 2004, Sharapova emerged as one of the best and most popular players in the world. She won Wimbledon even though she was playing in the famous tournament for just the second time. She was the lowest seed (13th) and second-youngest women's player (17 years old) to win Wimbledon. Sharapova won five singles titles during the year, including the season-ending WTA Championships. She finished the year ranked Number 4 in the world.

■ **Anastasia Myskina,** b. July 8, 1981, Moscow, Russia. After finishing 2003 ranked Number 7 in the world, Myskina had a breakout year in 2004. She became the first Russian woman to win a Grand Slam singles tournament when she beat Elena Dementieva, 6–1, 6–2, in the French Open. Overall, she won three singles titles and finished the season ranked Number 3. She also reached the semifinals of the singles tournament at the 2004 Summer Olympics.

■ **Elena Dementieva,** b. October 15, 1981, Moscow, Russia. Dementieva was the only women's player to reach the finals of two Grand Slam tournaments in 2004. She advanced to the finals of the French and U.S. Opens. Dementieva won more than twice as much prize money in 2004 ($1,825,688) as she did in her previous best season ($869,740, in 2003). She finished the year ranked Number 6 in the world, her highest ranking ever.

GRAND SLAM TOURNAMENTS: ALL-TIME WOMEN'S CHAMPIONS (cont.)

WIMBLEDON CHAMPIONSHIPS (cont.)

Year	Winner	Year	Winner	Year	Winner
1981	Chris Evert Lloyd	1959	Maria Bueno	1929	Helen Wills
1980	Evonne Goolagong Cawley	1958	Althea Gibson	1928	Helen Wills
		1957	Althea Gibson	1927	Helen Wills
1979	Martina Navratilova	1956	Shirley Fry	1926	Kathleen McKane Godfree
1978	Martina Navratilova	1955	Louise Brough		
1977	Virginia Wade	1954	Maureen Connolly	1925	Suzanne Lenglen
1976	Chris Evert	1953	Maureen Connolly	1924	Kathleen McKane
1975	Billie Jean King	1952	Maureen Connolly	1923	Suzanne Lenglen
1974	Chris Evert	1951	Doris Hart	1922	Suzanne Lenglen
1973	Billie Jean King	1950	Louise Brough	1921	Suzanne Lenglen
1972	Billie Jean King	1949	Louise Brough	1920	Suzanne Lenglen
1971	Evonne Goolagong	1948	Louise Brough	1919	Suzanne Lenglen
1970	Margaret Smith Court	1947	Margaret Osborne	1915-18	no tournament
1969	Ann Haydon Jones	1946	Pauline Betz	1914	Dorothea Lambert Chambers
**1968	Billie Jean King	1940-45	No tournament		
1967	Billie Jean King	1939	Alice Marble	1913	Dorothea Lambert Chambers
1966	Billie Jean King	1938	Helen Wills Moody		
1965	Margaret Smith	1937	Dorothy Round	1912	Ethel Larcombe
1964	Maria Bueno	1936	Helen Jacobs	1911	Dorothea Lambert Chambers
1963	Margaret Smith	1935	Helen Wills Moody		
1962	Karen Hantze Susman	1934	Dorothy Round	1910	Dorothea Lambert Chambers
1961	Angela Mortimer	1933	Helen Wills Moody		
1960	Maria Bueno	1932	Helen Wills Moody	1909	Dora Boothby
		1931	Cilly Aussem		
		1930	Helen Wills Moody		

**Became Open (amateur and professional) in 1968.

GRAND SLAM TOURNAMENTS: ALL-TIME WOMEN'S CHAMPIONS (cont.)

WIMBLEDON CHAMPIONSHIPS (cont.)

Year	Winner
1908	Charlotte Cooper Sterry
1907	May Sutton
1906	Dorothea Douglass
1905	May Sutton
1904	Dorothea Douglass
1903	Dorothea Douglass
1902	Muriel Robb
1901	Charlotte Cooper Sterry
1900	Blanche Bingley Hillyard
1899	Blanche Bingley Hillyard
1898	Charlotte Cooper
1897	Blanche Bingley Hillyard
1896	Charlotte Cooper
1895	Charlotte Cooper
1894	Blanche Bingley Hillyard
1893	Charlotte Dod
1892	Charlotte Dod
1891	Charlotte Dod
1890	Lena Rice
1889	Blanche Bingley Hillyard
1888	Charlotte Dod

Year	Winner
1887	Charlotte Dod
1886	Blanche Bingley
1885	Maud Watson
1884	Maud Watson

UNITED STATES CHAMPIONSHIPS

Year	Winner
2004	Svetlana Kuznetsova
2003	Justine Henin-Hardenne
2002	Serena Williams
2001	Venus Williams
2000	Venus Williams
1999	Serena Williams
1998	Lindsay Davenport
1997	Martina Hingis
1996	Steffi Graf
1995	Steffi Graf
1994	Arantxa Sánchez Vicario
1993	Steffi Graf
1992	Monica Seles
1991	Monica Seles
1990	Gabriela Sabatini
1989	Steffi Graf
1988	Steffi Graf
1987	Martina Navratilova
1986	Martina Navratilova
1985	Hana Mandlikova
1984	Martina Navratilova

Year	Winner
1983	Martina Navratilova
1982	Chris Evert Lloyd
1981	Tracy Austin
1980	Chris Evert Lloyd
1979	Tracy Austin
1978	Chris Evert
1977	Chris Evert
1976	Chris Evert
1975	Chris Evert
1974	Billie Jean King
1973	Margaret Smith Court
1972	Billie Jean King
1971	Billie Jean King
1970	Margaret Smith Court
1969	Margaret Smith Court
*1968	Virginia Wade
1967	Billie Jean King
1966	Maria Bueno
1965	Margaret Smith
1964	Maria Bueno
1963	Maria Bueno
1962	Margaret Smith
1961	Darlene Hard
1960	Darlene Hard
1959	Maria Bueno
1958	Althea Gibson
1957	Althea Gibson
1956	Shirley Fry
1955	Doris Hart
1954	Doris Hart
1953	Maureen Connolly

* Became Open (amateur and professional) in 1968.

2004-05 WOMEN'S TIME LINE

■ **January 31, 2004:** In an all-Belgian final, Justine Henin-Hardenne beats Kim Clijsters in three sets to win the Australian Open. Henin-Hardenne goes on to win her first 17 matches of the year.

■ **April 3, 2004:** After missing eight months because of knee surgery, Serena Williams of the United States returns and wins the NASDAQ-100 Open in Key Biscayne, Florida. She beats Elena Dementieva of Russia, 6–1, 6–1, in the final.

■ **June 5, 2004:** Anastasia Myskina becomes the first Russian woman to win a Grand Slam singles title. Myskina beats countrywoman Elena Dementieva in the French Open final.

■ **July 3, 2004:** Playing in just her second Wimbledon, 13th-seeded Maria Sharapova of Russia upsets two-time defending champion Serena Williams for the title.

■ **August 21, 2004:** Justine Henin-Hardenne defeats Amelie Mauresmo of France in straight sets to win her first Olympic gold medal in women's singles.

■ **September 11, 2004:** Svetlana Kuznetsova becomes the third Russian woman to win a Grand Slam singles final in 2004, beating Elena Dementieva to win the U.S. Open.

■ **January 29, 2005:** Serena Williams defeats Number 1-ranked Lindsay Davenport, 2–6, 6–3, 6–0, to win her second Australian Open and seventh Grand Slam title.

GRAND SLAM TOURNAMENTS: ALL-TIME WOMEN'S CHAMPIONS (cont.)

UNITED STATES CHAMPIONSHIPS (cont.)

Year	Winner	Year	Winner	Year	Winner
1952	Maureen Connolly	1931	Helen Wills Moody	1912	Mary K. Browne
1951	Maureen Connolly	1930	Betty Nuthall	1911	Hazel Hotchkiss
1950	Margaret Osborne duPont	1929	Helen Wills	1910	Hazel Hotchkiss
1949	Margaret Osborne duPont	1928	Helen Wills	1909	Hazel Hotchkiss
		1927	Helen Wills	1908	Maud Barger–Wallach
1948	Margaret Osborne duPont	1926	Molla Bjurstedt Mallory	1907	Evelyn Sears
		1925	Helen Wills	1906	Helen Homans
1947	Louise Brough	1924	Helen Wills	1905	Elisabeth Moore
1946	Pauline Betz	1923	Helen Wills	1904	May Sutton
1945	Sarah Palfrey Cooke	1922	Molla Bjurstedt Mallory	1903	Elisabeth Moore
1944	Pauline Betz	1921	Molla Bjurstedt Mallory	**1902	Marion Jones
1943	Pauline Betz	1920	Molla Bjurstedt Mallory	1901	Elisabeth Moore
1942	Pauline Betz	1919	Hazel Hotchkiss Wightman	1900	Myrtle McAteer
1941	Sarah Palfrey Cooke			1899	Marion Jones
1940	Alice Marble	1918	Molla Bjurstedt	1898	Juliette Atkinson
1939	Alice Marble	1917	Molla Bjurstedt	1897	Juliette Atkinson
1938	Alice Marble	1916	Molla Bjurstedt	1896	Elisabeth Moore
1937	Anita Lizane	1915	Molla Bjurstedt	1895	Juliette Atkinson
1936	Alice Marble	1914	Mary K. Browne	1894	Helen Hellwig
1935	Helen Jacobs	1913	Mary K. Browne	1893	Aline Terry
1934	Helen Jacobs			1892	Mabel Cahill
1933	Helen Jacobs			1891	Mabel Cahill
1932	Helen Jacobs			1890	Ellen C. Roosevelt
				1889	Bertha L. Townsend
				1888	Bertha L. Townsend
				1887	Ellen Hansell

** Five-set final abolished.

> ■ **Fast Fact:** Hall of Famer Jimmy Connors of the United States is the only player to have won the U.S. Open on three different surfaces — hardcourt, grass, and clay.

LEGENDS

Tracy Austin finished her career with 30 singles victories.

ADAM STOLTMAN/AP

■ **Tracy Austin,** b. December 12, 1962, Palos Verdes, California. Austin accomplished a lot in an injury-shortened career. At age 16 years and 9 months, she beat four-time champion Chris Evert to win the 1979 U.S. Open. She was the youngest champion in the tournament's history. Two years later, Austin won the U.S. Open again, defeating Martina Navratilova. Austin won her last tournament in 1982. Back injuries and a near-fatal car accident in 1989 forced her to retire from the game.

■ **Gabriela Sabatini,** b. May 16, 1970, Buenos Aires, Argentina. Sabatini won the 1990 U.S. Open, and is still the only Argentine to win that tournament. In 1985, at age 15 years and 3 weeks, she was the youngest player to advance to the French Open semifinals. She was named the WTA Tour's Most Impressive Newcomer that year. Sabatini retired in 1996 with 27 career singles titles and 12 doubles titles.

■ **Andrea Jaeger,** b. June 4, 1965, Chicago, Illinois. Jaeger turned pro at age 14, and 19 months later was ranked Number 2 in the world. At the 1980 Avon Futures of Las Vegas tournament, she won 13 consecutive matches to win the title, tying a women's pro record for most consecutive matches won in a single tournament. Jaeger reached the finals of Wimbledon in 1983. She won 10 singles titles in her seven-year career. She retired in 1987 because of a shoulder injury. In 1990, Jaeger founded the Silver Lining Foundation in Aspen, Colorado, which hosts camps for kids with cancer.

Pete Sampras retired in 2003 with 14 Grand Slam titles, the most in history.

SIMON BRUTY/SPORTS ILLUSTRATED

ALL-TIME GRAND SLAM SINGLES CHAMPIONS

MEN

PLAYER	AUS.	FR.	WIM.	U.S.	TOTAL
Pete Sampras	2	0	7	5	14
Roy Emerson	6	2	2	2	12
Bjorn Borg	0	6	5	0	11
Rod Laver	3	2	4	2	11
Bill Tilden	†	0	3	7	10
Jimmy Connors	1	0	2	5	8
Ivan Lendl	2	3	0	3	8
Fred Perry	1	1	3	3	8
Ken Rosewall	4	2	0	2	8
*Andre Agassi	4	1	1	2	8
Henri Cochet	†	4	2	1	7
Rene Lacoste	†	3	2	2	7
Bill Larned	†	†	0	7	7
John McEnroe	0	0	3	4	7
John Newcombe	2	0	3	2	7
Willie Renshaw	†	†	7	†	7
Dick Sears	†	†	0	7	7

*Active player. †Did not compete.

WOMEN

PLAYER	AUS.	FR.	WIM.	U.S.	TOTAL
Margaret Smith Court	11	5	3	5	24
Steffi Graf	4	6	7	5	22
Helen Wills Moody	†	4	8	7	19
Chris Evert	2	7	3	6	18
Martina Navratilova	3	2	9	4	18
Billie Jean King	1	1	6	4	12
Maureen Connolly	1	2	3	3	9
*Monica Seles	4	3	0	2	9
Suzanne Lenglen	†	#2	6	0	8
Molla Bjurstedt Mallory	†	†	0	8	8
Maria Bueno	0	0	3	4	7
Evonne Goolagong	4	1	2	0	7
Dorothea L. Chambers	†	†	7	0	7
*Serena Williams	2	1	2	2	7
Nancye Wynne Bolton	6	0	0	0	6
Louise Brough	1	0	4	1	6
Margaret Osborne duPont	†	2	1	3	6
Doris Hart	1	2	1	2	6
Blanche Bingley Hillyard	†	†	6	†	6

*Active player. †Did not compete.
#Suzanne Lenglen also won four singles titles at the French Championships before 1925, when the tournament was first opened to players from all nations.

SWIMMING

Michael Phelps of the United States began 2005 the same way he ended 2004: by proving himself to be the world's greatest all-around swimmer.

In April, Phelps won all five individual events he entered at the 2005 World Championship Trials. He announced that he would swim those five events, plus three relays, at the 2005 World Championships in July.

Phelps had already set and met huge goals at the 2004 Summer Olympics in Athens, Greece. The 19-year-old won eight medals — six of them gold — and set one world and two American records.

Phelps wasn't the only American smashing records. Brendan Hansen broke the 100-meter and 200-meter breaststroke world marks at the 2004 U.S. Olympic Trials. Ian Crocker broke the world record in the 100-meter butterfly at the same meet, and earlier in the year set the world mark in the 50-meter butterfly.

Backstroke specialist Aaron Peirsol set the world mark in the 200-meter event at the U.S. Olympic Trials, and then broke the world record in the 100-meter backstroke at the 2004 Summer Games. Eight months later, he lowered his own record in the 100-meter backstroke at the 2005 World Championship Trials.

Among the women, Amanda Beard broke the world record in the 200-meter breaststroke at the 2004 U.S. Olympic Trials just days after Australia's Leisel Jones had broken the previous mark. But no woman rewrote the record book more times than Australia's Jodie Henry.

Henry set three world records at the 2004 Summer Games. She won a gold medal and broke the world record in the 400-meter freestyle relay. She earned her second gold by breaking the world record in the 100-meter freestyle. Henry's third gold and world record came in the 400-meter medley relay.

A former world-record holder and legend retired in 2004. Jenny Thompson of the United States competed in her fourth and final Olympics. She won silver medals in the 400-meter freestyle relay and 400-meter medley relay. Thompson won a total of 12 Olympic medals in her career, the most by an American, man or woman.

While the U.S. team lost one star, another emerged. Katie Hoff, age 15, established herself as one of the U.S. team's strongest and most versatile performers. At the 2005 World Championship Trials, she lowered the American record in the 200-meter individual medley.

Michael Phelps won all five events he entered at the 2005 World Championship Trials.

SIMON BRUTY/SPORTS ILLUSTRATED

2004-05 MAJOR COMPETITIONS — MEN

U.S. NATIONAL CHAMPIONSHIPS (SUMMER) — Stanford, California, August 3–7, 2004

EVENT	SWIMMER, TEAM	TIME
50-meter freestyle	Randall Bal, Stanford Swimming	22.75
100-meter freestyle	Garrett Weber-Gale, Longhorn Aquatics	49.91
200-meter freestyle	Justin Mortimer, Mission Viejo	1:50.18
400-meter freestyle	Michael Klueh, Longhorn Aquatics	3:54.75
800-meter freestyle	Justin Mortimer, Mission Viejo	8:02.90
1,500-meter freestyle	Justin Mortimer, Mission Viejo	15:23.96
100-meter backstroke	Randall Bal, Stanford Swimming	54.67
200-meter backstroke	Trent Staley, Trojan SC	2:02.02
100-meter breaststroke	Kevin Swander, Indiana Swim Team	1:02.81
200-meter breaststroke	Julien Nicolardot, France	2:14.52
100-meter butterfly	Daniel Rohleder, Longhorn Aquatics	54.17
200-meter butterfly	William Stovall, Memphis Tiger SC	2:00.03
200-meter individual medley	Mark Stephens, Dynamo SC	2:04.34
400-meter individual medley	Justin Mortimer, Mission Viejo	4:21.15
400-meter medley relay	Longhorn Aquatics	3:46.02
400-meter freestyle relay	Longhorn Aquatics	3:25.59
800-meter freestyle relay	Mecklenburg Aquatic Club	7:35.84

WORLD CHAMPIONSHIP TRIALS — Indianapolis, Indiana, April 1–6, 2005

EVENT	SWIMMER, TEAM	TIME
50-meter freestyle	Jason Lezak, Irvine Novaquatics	22.29
100-meter freestyle	Michael Phelps, Club Wolverine/North Baltimore	49.00
200-meter freestyle	Michael Phelps, Club Wolverine/North Baltimore	1:46.44
400-meter freestyle	Michael Phelps, Club Wolverine/North Baltimore	3:47.79
800-meter freestyle	Larsen Jensen, University of Southern California	7:54.22
1,500-meter freestyle	Larsen Jensen, University of Southern California	15:04.06
100-meter backstroke	Aaron Peirsol, Longhorn Aquatics	53.17 (WR)
200-meter backstroke	Aaron Peirsol, Longhorn Aquatics	1:55.13
100-meter breaststroke	Brendan Hansen, Longhorn Aquatics	1:00.13
200-meter breaststroke	Brendan Hansen, Longhorn Aquatics	2:10.20
100-meter butterfly	Michael Phelps, Club Wolverine/North Baltimore	51.34
200-meter butterfly	David Tarwater, University of Michigan	1:58.71
200-meter individual medley	Michael Phelps, Club Wolverine/North Baltimore	1:57.44
400-meter individual medley	Ryan Lochte, University of Florida	4:16.83

2004-05 MAJOR COMPETITIONS — WOMEN

U.S. NATIONAL CHAMPIONSHIPS (SUMMER) — Stanford, California, August 3–7, 2004

EVENT	SWIMMER, TEAM	TIME
50-meter freestyle	Brooke Bishop, Palo Alto Stanford Aquatics	26.10
100-meter freestyle	Tanica Jamison, Longhorn Aquatics	55.96
200-meter freestyle	Lauren Medina, California Aquatics	2:01.89
400-meter freestyle	Kate Ziegler, The Fish-PV	4:12.06
800-meter freestyle	Alyssa Kiel, Lake Erie Silver Dolphins	8:33.08
1,500-meter freestyle	Kate Ziegler, The Fish-PV	16:22.03
100-meter backstroke	Hayley McGregory, Longhorn Aquatics	1:02.55
200-meter backstroke	Hayley McGregory, Longhorn Aquatics	2:13.59
100-meter breaststroke	Jessica Hardy, Irvine Novaquatics	1:08.33
200-meter breaststroke	Lindsey Ertter, Athens Bulldog SC	2:30.64
100-meter butterfly	Tanica Jamison, Longhorn Aquatics	59.23
200-meter butterfly	Kimberly Vandenberg, UCLA	2:11.08
200-meter individual medley	Danielle Townsend, Aggie SC	2:15.75
400-meter individual medley	Ariana Kukors, King Aquatic Club	4:45.41
400-meter medley relay	Longhorn Aquatics	4:10.34
400-meter freestyle relay	Longhorn Aquatics	3:48.76
800-meter freestyle relay	Longhorn Aquatics	8:18.05

KEY (WR)=World Record

2004-05 MAJOR COMPETITIONS — WOMEN (cont.)

WORLD CHAMPIONSHIP TRIALS
Indianapolis, Indiana, April 1–6, 2005

EVENT	SWIMMER, TEAM	TIME
50-meter freestyle	Kara Lynn Joyce, Athens Bulldog SC	25.17
100-meter freestyle	Natalie Coughlin, California Aquatics	54.76
200-meter freestyle	Katie Hoff, North Baltimore	1:59.56
400-meter freestyle	Carly Piper, University of Wisconsin	4:11.05
800-meter freestyle	Kate Ziegler, The Fish-PV	8:34.83
1,500-meter freestyle	Kate Ziegler, The Fish-PV	16:26.59
100-meter backstroke	Natalie Coughlin, California Aquatics	1:01.08
200-meter backstroke	Margaret Hoelzer, Auburn Aquatics	2:10.42
100-meter breaststroke	Tara Kirk, Palo Alto Stanford Aquatics	1:07.11
200-meter breaststroke	Tara Kirk, Palo Alto Stanford Aquatics	2:26.64
100-meter butterfly	Rachel Komisarz, Lakeside Swim Team	58.56
200-meter butterfly	Mary DeScenza, Athens Bulldog SC	2:09.00
200-meter individual medley	Katie Hoff, North Baltimore	2:11.24 (A)
400-meter individual medley	Katie Hoff, North Baltimore	4:39.25

KEY (A)=American Record

2004-05 TIME LINE

■ **April 13, 2004:** Michael Phelps of the United States receives the 2003 Sullivan Award, given to the nation's best amateur athlete. It is the 10th time a swimmer has won the award.

■ **July 7-14, 2004:** Brendan Hansen (100-meter and 200-meter breaststroke), Phelps (400-meter individual medley), Amanda Beard (200-meter breaststroke), Aaron Peirsol (200-meter backstroke), and Ian Crocker (100-meter butterfly) all break world records at the U.S. Olympic Trials.

■ **August 14, 2004:** Yana Klochkova of Ukraine wins gold in the 400-meter individual medley at the Summer Olympics in Athens, Greece. She becomes the first female swimmer to defend Olympic gold in the 200 and 400 individual medley. Michael Phelps wins gold and breaks his own world record in the men's 400-meter individual medley.

■ **August 16, 2004:** Ian Thorpe of Australia beats Pieter van den Hoogenband of Holland and Phelps to win the Olympic gold medal in the 200-meter freestyle. Two days earlier, Thorpe won the 400-meter freestyle.

■ **August 18, 2004:** Japan's Kosuke Kitajima wins the 200-meter breaststroke, making him the second swimmer to win Olympic gold in the 100 and 200 breaststroke.

■ **August 19, 2004:** Australia's Jodie Henry wins Olympic gold by breaking the world record in the 100-meter freestyle.

■ **February 2, 2005:** Phelps is voted the 2004 United States Olympic Committee Sportsman of the Year. He is the first swimmer to receive the award since Pablo Morales in 1992.

■ **April 2, 2005:** Aaron Peirsol lowers his own world record in the 100-meter backstroke with a time of 53.17 seconds at the World Championship Trials.

■ **April 4, 2005:** Phelps beats American-record-holder Jason Lezak to win the 100-meter freestyle at the World Championship Trials. He later wins the 200-meter individual medley to finish with five wins in five events. Phelps also wins the 100-meter butterfly and the 200-meter and 400-meter freestyle events.

WORLD AND AMERICAN RECORDS — MEN

FREESTYLE

EVENT	TIME	RECORD HOLDER	DATE	SITE
50 meters	21.64	Alexander Popov, Russia (WR)	6-16-00	Moscow, Russia
	21.76	Gary Hall, Jr. (A)	8-15-00	Indianapolis, Indiana
100 meters	47.84	Pieter van den Hoogenband, Netherlands (WR)	9-19-00	Sydney, Australia
	48.17	Jason Lezak (A)	7-10-04	Long Beach, California
200 meters	1:44.06	Ian Thorpe, Australia (WR)	7-25-01	Fukuoka, Japan
	1:45.20	Michael Phelps (A)	7-26-05	Montreal, Canada
400 meters	3:40.08	Ian Thorpe, Australia (WR)	7-30-02	Manchester, England
	3:44.11	Klete Keller (A)	8-14-04	Athens, Greece
800 meters	7:38.65	Grant Hackett, Australia (WR)	7-27-05	Montreal, Canada
	7:45.63	Larsen Jensen (A)	7-27-05	Montreal, Canada
1,500 meters	14:34.56	Grant Hackett, Australia (WR)	7-29-01	Fukuoka, Japan
	14:45.29	Larsen Jensen (A)	8-21-04	Athens, Greece

Ian Thorpe, Australia

THOMAS KIENZLE/AP

BACKSTROKE

EVENT	TIME	RECORD HOLDER	DATE	SITE
50 meters	24.80	Thomas Rupprath, Germany (WR)	7-27-03	Barcelona, Spain
	24.99	Lenny Krayzelburg (A)	8-28-99	Sydney, Australia
100 meters	53.17	Aaron Peirsol (WR, A)	4-2-05	Indianapolis, Indiana
200 meters	1:54.66	Aaron Peirsol (WR, A)	7-29-05	Montreal, Canada

BREASTSTROKE

EVENT	TIME	RECORD HOLDER	DATE	SITE
50 meters	27.18	Oleg Lisogor, Ukraine (WR)	8-2-02	Berlin, Germany
	27.39	Ed Moses (A)	3-31-01	Austin, Texas
100 meters	59.30	Brendan Hansen (WR, A)	7-8-04	Long Beach, California
200 meters	2:09.04	Brendan Hansen (WR, A)	7-11-04	Long Beach, California

BUTTERFLY

EVENT	TIME	RECORD HOLDER	DATE	SITE
50 meters	22.96	Roland Schoeman, South Africa (WR)	7-26-05	Montreal, Canada
	23.12	Ian Crocker (A)	7-25-05	Montreal, Canada
100 meters	50.40	Ian Crocker (WR, A)	7-30-05	Montreal, Canada
200 meters	1:53.93	Michael Phelps (WR, A)	7-22-03	Barcelona, Spain

INDIVIDUAL MEDLEY

EVENT	TIME	RECORD HOLDER	DATE	SITE
200 meters	1:55.94	Michael Phelps (WR, A)	8-9-03	College Park, Maryland
400 meters	4:08.26	Michael Phelps (WR, A)	8-14-04	Athens, Greece

RELAYS

EVENT	TIME	RECORD HOLDER	DATE	SITE
400-meter medley	3:30.68	United States (WR, A) (Aaron Peirsol, Brendan Hansen, Ian Crocker, Jason Lezak)	8-21-04	Athens, Greece
400-meter freestyle	3:13.17	South Africa (WR) (Lyndon Ferns, Ryk Neethling, Roland Schoeman, Darian Townsend)	8-14-04	Athens, Greece
	3:13.77	United States (A) (Michael Phelps, Neil Walker, Nate Dusing, Jason Lezak)	7-24-05	Montreal, Canada
800-meter freestyle	7:04.66	Australia (WR) (Grant Hackett, Michael Klim, Bill Kirby, Ian Thorpe)	7-27-01	Fukuoka, Japan
	7:06.56	United States (A) (Michael Phelps, Ryan Lochte, Peter Vanderkaay, Klete Keller)	7-29-05	Montreal, Canada

KEY (A)=American Record; (WR)=World Record

DID YOU KNOW?

Janet Evans of the United States holds the three longest-standing world records in swimming. She set the 400-meter freestyle and 1,500-meter freestyle records in 1988 and established the 800-meter freestyle record in 1989.

SWIMMING

WORLD AND AMERICAN RECORDS — WOMEN

FREESTYLE

EVENT	TIME	RECORD HOLDER	DATE	SITE
50 meters	24.13	Inge de Bruijn, Netherlands (WR)	9-22-00	Sydney, Australia
	24.63	Dara Torres (A)	9-23-00	Sydney, Australia
100 meters	53.52	Jodie Henry, Australia (WR)	8-18-04	Athens, Greece
	53.99	Natalie Coughlin (A)	8-29-02	Yokohama, Japan
200 meters	1:56.64	Franziska van Almsick, Germany (WR)	8-3-02	Berlin, Germany
	1:57.41	Lindsay Benko (A)	7-24-03	Barcelona, Spain
400 meters	4:03.85	Janet Evans (WR, A)	9-22-88	Seoul, South Korea
800 meters	8:16.22	Janet Evans (WR, A)	8-20-89	Tokyo, Japan
1,500 meters	15:52.10	Janet Evans (WR, A)	3-26-88	Orlando, Florida

BACKSTROKE

EVENT	TIME	RECORD HOLDER	DATE	SITE
50 meters	28.25	Sandra Volker, Germany (WR)	6-17-00	Berlin, Germany
	28.49	Natalie Coughlin (A)	7-23-01	Fukuoka, Japan
100 meters	59.58	Natalie Coughlin (WR, A)	8-13-02	Fort Lauderdale, Florida
200 meters	2:06.62	Krisztina Egerszegi, Hungary (WR)	8-25-91	Athens, Greece
	2:08.53	Natalie Coughlin (A)	8-16-02	Fort Lauderdale, Florida

BREASTSTROKE

EVENT	TIME	RECORD HOLDER	DATE	SITE
50 meters	30.57	Zoe Baker, Great Britain (WR)	7-30-02	Manchester, England
	30.85	Jessica Hardy (A)	7-31-05	Montreal, Canada
100 meters	1:06.20	Jessica Hardy (WR, A)	7-25-05	Montreal, Canada
200 meters	2:21.72	Leisel Jones, Australia (WR)	7-29-05	Montreal, Canada
	2:22.44	Amanda Beard (A)	7-12-04	Long Beach, California

**Amanda Beard,
United States**

ADAM PRETTY/GETTY IMAGES

BUTTERFLY

EVENT	TIME	RECORD HOLDER	DATE	SITE
50 meters	25.57	Anna-Karin Kammerling, Sweden (WR)	7-30-02	Berlin, Germany
	26.00	Jenny Thompson (A)	7-26-03	Barcelona, Spain
100 meters	56.61	Inge de Bruijn, Netherlands (WR)	9-17-00	Sydney, Australia
	57.58	Dara Torres (A)	8-9-00	Indianapolis, Indiana
200 meters	2:05.78	Otylia Jedrejczak, Poland (WR)	8-4-02	Berlin, Germany
	2:05.88	Misty Hyman (A)	9-20-00	Sydney, Australia

INDIVIDUAL MEDLEY

EVENT	TIME	RECORD HOLDER	DATE	SITE
200 meters	2:09.72	Yanyan Wu, China (WR)	10-17-97	Shanghai, China
	2:11.24	Katie Hoff (A)	4-1-05	Indianapolis, Indiana
400 meters	4:33.59	Yana Klochkova, Ukraine (WR)	9-16-00	Sydney, Australia
	4:34.95	Kaitlin Sandeno (A)	8-14-04	Athens, Greece

RELAYS

EVENT	TIME	RECORD HOLDER	DATE	SITE
400-meter medley	3:57.32	Australia (WR) (Giaan Rooney, Leisel Jones, Petria Thomas, Jodie Henry)	8-21-04	Athens, Greece
	3:58.30	United States (A) (B.J. Bedford, Megan Quann, Jenny Thompson, Dara Torres)	9-23-00	Sydney, Australia
400-meter freestyle	3:35.94	Australia (WR) (Jodie Henry, Lisbeth Lenton, Alice Mills, Petria Thomas)	8-14-04	Athens, Greece
	3:36.39	United States (A) (Natalie Coughlin, Kara Lynn Joyce, Jenny Thompson, Amanda Weir)	8-14-04	Athens, Greece
800-meter freestyle	7:53.42	United States (WR, A) (Natalie Coughlin, Carly Piper, Dana Vollmer, Kaitlin Sandeno)	8-18-04	Athens, Greece

LEGENDS

Jenny Thompson won a total of 12 medals at four Olympics (1992, 1996, 2000, and 2004).

AL BELLO/GETTY IMAGES

■ **Jenny Thompson,** b. February 26, 1973, Dover, New Hampshire. Thompson is one of just three female swimmers to compete in four Olympic Games (1992, 1996, 2000, and 2004). She won two silver medals at her final Olympics in 2004: in the 400-meter freestyle relay and 400-meter medley relay. Those gave her a total of 12 Olympic medals for her career, more than any U.S. Olympian. Thompson also has the most medals of any swimmer in international competitions (85).

■ **Tom Dolan,** b. September 15, 1975, Arlington, Virginia. Dolan overcame a severe case of asthma to become one of the greatest swimmers in the history of the sport. He won Olympic gold in the 400-meter individual medley at the 1996 and 2000 Summer Olympics and set a world record in the event at the 2000 Games. Dolan also won gold in the 400-meter individual medley at the 1994 and 1998 World Championships. He became the first man since Mark Spitz to win four events at a national tournament when he won four races at the 1994 Spring Nationals. He did it again at the 1998 Spring Nationals.

■ **Kieran Perkins,** b. August 14, 1973, Brisbane, Australia. Perkins is considered one of the greatest athletes in the history of Australia. He won the 1,500-meter freestyle at the 1992 and 1996 Summer Olympics. Perkins also won silver in the event at the 2000 Summer Games, making him the first swimmer to win three straight Olympic medals in the 1,500 freestyle. He is also the youngest swimmer to break the 15-minute barrier in the 1,500 freestyle, accomplishing the feat when he was 16 years old.

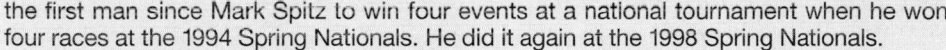

WORLD CHAMPIONSHIP RESULTS — MEN

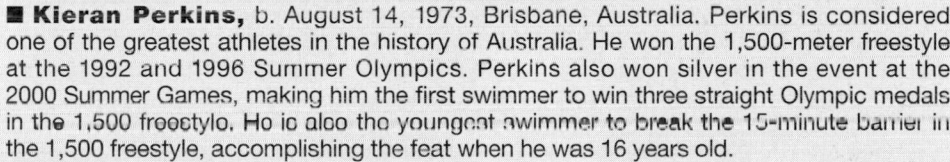

50-METER FREESTYLE

1973-82	Event not held	
1986	Tom Jager, United States	22.49
1991	Tom Jager, United States	22.16
1994	Alexander Popov, Russia	22.17
1998	Bill Pilczuk, United States	22.29
2001	Anthony Ervin, United States	22.09
2003	Alexander Popov, Russia	21.92

100-METER FREESTYLE

1973	Jim Montgomery, United States	51.70
1975	Andy Coan, United States	51.25
1978	David McCagg, United States	50.24
1982	Jorg Woithe, East Germany	50.18
1986	Matt Biondi, United States	48.94
1991	Matt Biondi, United States	49.18
1994	Alexander Popov, Russia	49.12
1998	Alexander Popov, Russia	48.93
2001	Anthony Ervin, United States	48.33
2003	Alexander Popov, Russia	48.42

200-METER FREESTYLE

1973	Jim Montgomery, United States	1:53.02
1975	Tim Shaw, United States	1:51.04
1978	Billy Forrester, United States	1:51.02
1982	Michael Gross, West Germany	1:49.84

200-METER FREESTYLE (cont.)

1986	Michael Gross, West Germany	1:47.92
1991	Giorgio Lamberti, Italy	1:47.27
1994	Antti Kasvio, Finland	1:47.32
1998	Michael Klim, Australia	1:47.41
2001	Ian Thorpe, Australia	1:44.06
2003	Ian Thorpe, Australia	1:45.14

400-METER FREESTYLE

1973	Rick DeMont, United States	3:58.18
1975	Tim Shaw, United States	3:54.88
1978	Vladimir Salnikov, U.S.S.R.	3:51.94
1982	Vladimir Salnikov, U.S.S.R.	3:51.30
1986	Rainer Henkel, West Germany	3:50.05
1991	Joerg Hoffman, Germany	3:48.04
1994	Kieran Perkins, Australia	3:43.80
1998	Ian Thorpe, Australia	3:46.29
2001	Ian Thorpe, Australia	3:40.17
2003	Ian Thorpe, Australia	3:42.58

800-METER FREESTYLE

1973-98	Event not held	
2001	Ian Thorpe, Australia	7:39.16
2003	Grant Hackett, Australia	7:43.82

SWIMMING

WORLD CHAMPIONSHIP RESULTS — MEN (cont.)

1,500-METER FREESTYLE
1973	Stephen Holland, Australia	15:31.85
1975	Tim Shaw, United States	15:28.92
1978	Vladimir Salnikov, U.S.S.R.	15:03.99
1982	Vladimir Salnikov, U.S.S.R.	15:01.77
1986	Rainer Henkel, West Germany	15:05.31
1991	Joerg Hoffman, Germany	14:50.36
1994	Kieran Perkins, Australia	14:50.52
1998	Grant Hackett, Australia	14:51.70
2001	Grant Hackett, Australia	14:34.56
2003	Grant Hackett, Australia	14:43.14

50-METER BACKSTROKE
1973-98 Event not held
2001	Randall Bal, United States	25.34
2003	Thomas Rupprath, Germany	24.80

100-METER BACKSTROKE
1973	Roland Matthes, East Germany	57.47
1975	Roland Matthes, East Germany	58.15
1978	Bob Jackson, United States	56.36
1982	Dirk Richter, East Germany	55.95
1986	Igor Polianski, U.S.S.R.	55.58
1991	Jeff Rouse, United States	55.23
1994	Martin Zubero, Spain	55.17
1998	Lenny Krayzelburg, United States	55.00
2001	Matt Welsh, Australia	54.31
2003	Aaron Peirsol, United States	53.61

200-METER BACKSTROKE
1973	Roland Matthes, East Germany	2:01.87
1975	Zoltan Varraszto, Hungary	2:05.05
1978	Jesse Vassallo, United States	2:02.16
1982	Rick Carey, United States	2:00.82
1986	Igor Polianski, U.S.S.R.	1:58.78
1991	Martin Zubero, Spain	1:59.52
1994	Vladimir Selkov, Russia	1:57.42
1998	Lenny Krayzelburg, United States	1:58.84
2001	Aaron Peirsol, United States	1:57.13
2003	Aaron Peirsol, United States	1:55.92

50-METER BREASTSTROKE
1973-98 Event not held
2001	Oleg Lisogor, Ukraine	27.52
2003	James Gibson, Great Britain	27.56

100-METER BREASTSTROKE
1973	John Hencken, United States	1:04.02
1975	David Wilkie, Great Britain	1:04.26
1978	Walter Kusch, West Germany	1:03.56
1982	Steve Lundquist, United States	1:02.75
1986	Victor Davis, Canada	1:02.71
1991	Norbert Rozsa, Hungary	1:01.45
1994	Norbert Rozsa, Hungary	1:01.24
1998	Frederik Deburghgraeve, Belgium	1:01.34
2001	Roman Sloudnov, Russia	1:00.16
2003	Kosuke Kitajima, Japan	59.78

200-METER BREASTSTROKE
1973	David Wilkie, Great Britain	2:19.28
1975	David Wilkie, Great Britain	2:18.23
1978	Nick Nevid, United States	2:18.37
1982	Victor Davis, Canada	2:14.77
1986	Jozsef Szabo, Hungary	2:14.27
1991	Mike Barrowman, United States	2:11.23
1994	Norbert Rozsa, Hungary	2:12.81
1998	Kurt Grote, United States	2:13.40
2001	Brendan Hansen, United States	2:10.69
2003	Kosuke Kitajima, Japan	2:09.42

50-METER BUTTERFLY
1973-98 Event not held
2001	Geoff Huegill, Australia	23.50
2003	Matt Welsh, Australia	23.43

100-METER BUTTERFLY
1973	Bruce Robertson, Canada	55.69
1975	Greg Jagenburg, United States	55.63
1978	Joe Bottom, United States	54.30
1982	Matt Gribble, United States	53.88
1986	Pablo Morales, United States	53.54
1991	Anthony Nesty, Suriname	53.29
1994	Rafal Szukala, Poland	53.51
1998	Michael Klim, Australia	52.25
2001	Lars Frolander, Sweden	52.10
2003	Ian Crocker, United States	50.98

200-METER BUTTERFLY
1973	Robin Backhaus, United States	2:03.32
1975	Bill Forrester, United States	2:01.95
1978	Mike Bruner, United States	1:59.38
1982	Michael Gross, West Germany	1:58.85
1986	Michael Gross, West Germany	1:56.53
1991	Melvin Stewart, United States	1:55.69
1994	Denis Pankratov, Russia	1:56.54
1998	Denys Sylantyev, Ukraine	1:56.61
2001	Michael Phelps, United States	1:54.58
2003	Michael Phelps, United States	1:54.35

200-METER INDIVIDUAL MEDLEY
1973	Gunnar Larsson, Sweden	2:08.36
1975	Andras Hargitay, Hungary	2:07.72
1978	Graham Smith, Canada	2:03.65
1982	Aleksandr Sidorenko, U.S.S.R.	2:03.30
1986	Tamás Darnyi, Hungary	2:01.57
1991	Tamás Darnyi, Hungary	1:59.36
1994	Jani Sievin, Finland	1:58.16
1998	Marcel Wouda, Netherlands	2:01.18
2001	Massimiliano Rosolino, Italy	1:59.71
2003	Michael Phelps, United States	1:56.04

400-METER INDIVIDUAL MEDLEY
1973	Andras Hargitay, Hungary	4:31.11
1975	Andras Hargitay, Hungary	4:32.57
1978	Jesse Vassallo, United States	4:20.05
1982	Ricardo Prado, Brazil	4:19.78
1986	Tamás Darnyi, Hungary	4:18.98
1991	Tamás Darnyi, Hungary	4:12.36
1994	Tom Dolan, United States	4:12.30
1998	Tom Dolan, United States	4:14.95
2001	Alessio Boggiatto, Italy	4:13.15
2003	Michael Phelps, United States	4:09.09

400-METER MEDLEY RELAY
1973	United States (Mike Stamm, John Hencken, Joe Bottom, Jim Montgomery)	3:49.49
1975	United States (John Murphy, Rick Colella, Greg Jagenburg, Andy Coan)	3:49.00
1978	United States (Robert Jackson, Nick Nevid, Joe Bottom, David McCagg)	3:44.63
1982	United States (Rick Carey, Steve Lundquist, Matt Gribble, Rowdy Gaines)	3:40.84
1986	United States (Dan Veatch, David Lundberg, Pablo Morales, Matt Biondi)	3:41.25
1991	United States (Jeff Rouse, Eric Wunderlich, Mark Henderson, Matt Biondi)	3:39.66
1994	United States (Jeff Rouse, Eric Wunderlich, Mark Henderson, Gary Hall, Jr.)	3:37.74
1998	Australia (Matt Welsh, Phil Rogers, Michael Klim, Chris Fydler)	3:37.98
2001	Australia (Matt Welsh, Ian Thorpe, Geoff Huegill, Regan Harrison)	3:35.35
2003	United States (Aaron Peirsol, Brendan Hansen, Ian Crocker, Jason Lezak)	3:31.54

400-METER FREESTYLE RELAY

1973	United States (Mel Nash, Joe Bottom, Jim Montgomery, John Murphy)	3:27.18
1975	United States (Bruce Furniss, Jim Montgomery, Andy Coan, John Murphy)	3:24.85
1978	United States (Jack Babashoff, Rowdy Gaines, Jim Montgomery, David McCagg)	3:19.74
1982	United States (Chris Cavanaugh, Robin Leamy, David McCagg, Rowdy Gaines)	3:19.26
1986	United States (Tom Jager, Mike Heath, Paul Wallace, Matt Biondi)	3:19.59
1991	United States (Tom Jager, Brent Lang, Doug Gjertsen, Matt Biondi)	3:17.15
1994	United States (Jon Olsen, Josh Davis, Ugur Taner, Gary Hall)	3:16.90
1998	United States (Scott Tucker, Jon Olsen, Neil Walker, Gary Hall)	3:16.69
2001	Australia (Michael Klim, Ian Thorpe, Todd Pearson, Ashley Callus)	3:14.10
2003	Russia (Andrei Kapralov, Ivan Usov, Denis Pimankov, Alexander Popov)	3.14.06

800-METER FREESTYLE RELAY

1973	United States (Kurt Krumpholz, Robin Backhaus, Rick Klatt, Jim Montgomery)	7:33.22
1975	West Germany (Klaus Steinbach, Werner Lampe, Hans Joachim Geisler, Peter Nocke)	7:39.44
1978	United States (Bruce Furniss, Billy Forrester, Bobby Hackett, Rowdy Gaines)	7:20.82
1982	United States (Rich Saeger, Jeff Float, Kyle Miller, Rowdy Gaines)	7:21.09
1986	East Germany (Lars Hinneburg, Thomas Flemming, Dirk Richter, Sven Lodziewski)	7:15.91
1991	Germany (Peter Sitt, Steffen Zesner, Stefan Pfeiffer, Michael Gross)	7:13.50
1994	Sweden (Christer Waller, Tommy Werner, Lars Frolander, Anders Holmertz)	7:17.74
1998	Australia (Daniel Kowalski, Grant Hackett, Ian Thorpe, Michael Klim)	7:12.48
2001	Australia (Michael Klim, Ian Thorpe, William Kirby, Grant Hackett)	7:04.66
2003	Australia (Grant Hackett, Craig Stevens, Nicholas Sprenger, Ian Thorpe)	7:08.58

TODAY'S STARS

Larsen Jensen holds American records in the 800-meter and 1,500-meter freestyle.

DAVID EULITT/KRT/ISCA

■ **Larsen Jensen,** b. September 1, 1985, Bakersfield, California. Jensen is one of the world's best distance swimmers. He was a silver medalist in the 1,500-meter freestyle at the 2004 Summer Olympics, breaking the U.S. record by more than 11 seconds. He finished fourth in the 400-meter freestyle. Jensen also holds U.S. records in the 800-meter freestyle and the mile. He is one of the youngest members of the U.S. National Team. He swam his first full collegiate season for Southern California as a sophomore in 2004-05.

■ **Leisel Jones,** b. August 30, 1985, Katherine, Australia. A breaststroke specialist, "Lethal Leisel" competed in two Olympics before her 19th birthday. At the 2000 Summer Games, she won silver medals in the 100-meter breaststroke and the 400-meter medley relay. At the 2004 Summer Olympics, Jones won silver in the 200-meter breaststroke and bronze in the 100-meter breaststroke. She won her first Olympic gold medal as part of the world-record-breaking 400-meter medley relay team. Jones is the world-record holder in the 100-meter breaststroke. She set the mark at the 2003 World Championships.

■ **Amanda Beard,** b. October 29, 1981, Irvine, California. Beard is one of the world's top breaststrokers. She became the second-youngest medalist (age 14) in U.S. swimming history when she won silver medals in the 100-meter and 200-meter breaststroke and a gold in the 400-meter medley relay at the 1996 Summer Olympics. Beard holds the world record in the 200-meter breaststroke. At the 2004 Summer Games, she won gold in that event in Olympic-record time. Beard also added a silver medal in the 200-meter individual medley.

SWIMMING

WORLD CHAMPIONSHIP RESULTS — WOMEN

50-METER FREESTYLE

1973-82	Event not held	
1986	Tamara Costache, Romania	25.28
1991	Zhuang Yong, China	25.47
1994	Le Jingyi, China	24.51
1998	Amy Van Dyken, United States	25.15
2001	Inge de Bruijn, Netherlands	24.47
2003	Inge de Bruijn, Netherlands	24.47

100-METER FREESTYLE

1973	Kornelia Ender, East Germany	57.54
1975	Kornelia Ender, East Germany	56.50
1978	Barbara Krause, East Germany	55.68
1982	Birgit Meineke, East Germany	55.79
1986	Kristin Otto, East Germany	55.05
1991	Nicole Haislett, United States	55.17
1994	Le Jingyi, China	54.01
1998	Jenny Thompson, United States	54.95
2001	Inge de Bruijn, Netherlands	54.18
2003	Hanna-Maria Seppala, Finland	54.37

200-METER FREESTYLE

1973	Keena Rothhammer, United States	2:04.99
1975	Shirley Babashoff, United States	2:02.50
1978	Cynthia Woodhead, United States	1:58.53
1982	Annemarie Verstappen, Netherlands	1:59.53
1986	Heike Friedrich, East Germany	1:58.26
1991	Hayley Lewis, Australia	2:00.48
1994	Franziska Van Almsick, Germany	1:56.78
1998	Claudia Poll, Costa Rica	1:58.90
2001	Giaan Rooney, Australia	1:58.57
2003	Alena Popchanka, Belarus	1:58.32

400-METER FREESTYLE

1973	Heather Greenwood, United States	4:20.28
1975	Shirley Babashoff, United States	4:16.87
1978	Tracey Wickham, Australia	4:06.28
1982	Carmela Schmidt, East Germany	4:08.98
1986	Heike Friedrich, East Germany	4:07.45
1991	Janet Evans, United States	4:08.63
1994	Yang Aihua, China	4:09.64
1998	Chen Yan, China	4:06.72
2001	Yana Klochkova, Ukraine	4:07.30
2003	Hannah Stockbauer, Germany	4:06.75

800-METER FREESTYLE

1973	Novella Calligaris, Italy	8:52.97
1975	Jenny Turrall, Australia	8:44.75
1978	Tracey Wickham, Australia	8:24.94
1982	Kim Linehan, United States	8:27.48
1986	Astrid Strauss, East Germany	8:28.24
1991	Janet Evans, United States	8:24.05
1994	Janet Evans, United States	8:29.85
1998	Brooke Bennett, United States	8:28.71
2001	Hannah Stockbauer, Germany	8:24.66
2003	Hannah Stockbauer, Germany	8:23.66

1,500-METER FREESTYLE

1973-98	Event not held	
2001	Hannah Stockbauer, Germany	16:01.02
2003	Hannah Stockbauer, Germany	16:00.18

50-METER BACKSTROKE

1973-98	Event not held	
2001	Haley Cope, United States	28.51
2003	Nina Zhivanevskaya, Spain	28.48

100-METER BACKSTROKE

1973	Ulrike Richter, East Germany	1:05.42
1975	Ulrike Richter, East Germany	1:03.30
1978	Linda Jezek, United States	1:02.55
1982	Kristin Otto, East Germany	1:01.30
1986	Betsy Mitchell, United States	1:01.74
1991	Krisztina Egerszegi, Hungary	1:01.78
1994	He Cihong, China	1:00.57
1998	Lea Maurer, United States	1:01.16
2001	Natalie Coughlin, United States	1:00.37
2003	Antje Buschschulte, Germany	1:00.50

200-METER BACKSTROKE

1973	Melissa Belote, United States	2:20.52
1975	Birgit Treiber, East Germany	2:15.46
1978	Linda Jezek, United States	2:11.93
1982	Cornelia Sirch, East Germany	2:09.91
1986	Cornelia Sirch, East Germany	2:11.37
1991	Krisztina Egerszegi, Hungary	2:09.15
1994	He Cihong, China	2:07.40
1998	Roxanna Maracineanu, France	2:11.26
2001	Diana Mocanu, Romania	2:09.94
2003	Katy Sexton, Great Britain	2:08.74

50-METER BREASTSTROKE

1973-98	Event not held	
2001	Xuejuan Luo, China	30.84
2003	Xuejuan Luo, China	30.67

100-METER BREASTSTROKE

1973	Renate Vogel, East Germany	1:13.74
1975	Hannalore Anke, East Germany	1:12.72
1978	Julia Bogdanova, U.S.S.R.	1:10.31
1982	Ute Geweniger, East Germany	1:09.14
1986	Sylvia Gerasch, East Germany	1:08.11
1991	Linley Frame, Australia	1:08.81
1994	Samantha Riley, Australia	1:07.96
1998	Kristy Kowal, United States	1:08.42
2001	Xuejuan Luo, China	1:07.18
2003	Xuejuan Luo, China	1:06.80

200-METER BREASTSTROKE

1973	Renate Vogel, East Germany	2:40.01
1975	Hannalore Anke, East Germany	2:37.25
1978	Lina Kachushite, U.S.S.R.	2:31.42
1982	Svetlana Varganova, U.S.S.R.	2:28.82
1986	Silke Hoerner, East Germany	2:27.40
1991	Elena Volkova, U.S.S.R.	2:29.53
1994	Samantha Riley, Australia	2:26.87
1998	Agnes Kovacs, Hungary	2:25.45
2001	Agnes Kovacs, Hungary	2:24.90
2003	Amanda Beard, United States	2:22.99

50-METER BUTTERFLY

1973-98	Event not held	
2001	Inge de Bruijn, Netherlands	25.90
2003	Inge de Bruijn, Netherlands	25.84

100-METER BUTTERFLY

1973	Kornelia Ender, East Germany	1:02.53
1975	Kornelia Ender, East Germany	1:01.24
1978	Joan Pennington, United States	1:00.20
1982	Mary T. Meagher, United States	59.41
1986	Kornelia Gressler, East Germany	59.51
1991	Qian Hong, China	59.68
1994	Liu Limin, China	58.98
1998	Jenny Thompson, United States	58.46
2001	Petria Thomas, Australia	58.27
2003	Jenny Thompson, United States	57.96

200-METER BUTTERFLY

1973	Rosemarie Kother, East Germany	2:13.76
1975	Rosemarie Kother, East Germany	2:13.82
1978	Tracy Caulkins, United States	2:09.87
1982	Ines Geissler, East Germany	2:08.66
1986	Mary T. Meagher, United States	2:08.41
1991	Summer Sanders, United States	2:09.24
1994	Liu Limin, China	2:07.25
1998	Susie O'Neill, Australia	2:07.93
2001	Petria Thomas, Australia	2:06.73
2003	Otylia Jedrzejczak, Poland	2:07.56

200-METER INDIVIDUAL MEDLEY

1973	Andrea Huebner, East Germany	2:20.51
1975	Kathy Heddy, United States	2:19.80
1978	Tracy Caulkins, United States	2:14.07
1982	Petra Schneider, East Germany	2:11.79
1986	Kristin Otto, East Germany	2:15.56
1991	Li Lin, China	2:13.40
1994	Lu Bin, China	2:12.34
1998	Wu Yanyan, China	2:10.88
2001	Martha Bowen, United States	2:11.93
2003	Yana Klochkova, Ukraine	2.10.75

400-METER INDIVIDUAL MEDLEY

1973	Gudrun Wegner, East Germany	4:57.71
1975	Ulrike Tauber, East Germany	4:52.76
1978	Tracy Caulkins, United States	4:40.83
1982	Petra Schneider, East Germany	4:36.10
1986	Kathleen Nord, East Germany	4:43.75
1991	Li Lin, China	4:41.45
1994	Dai Guohong, China	4:39.14
1998	Chen Yan, China	4:36.66
2001	Yana Klochkova, Ukraine	4:36.98
2003	Yana Klochkova, Ukraine	4:36.74

400-METER MEDLEY RELAY

1973	East Germany (Ulrike Richter, Renate Vogel, Rosemarie Kother, Kornelia Ender)	4:16.84
1975	East Germany (Ulrike Richter, Hannelore Anke, Rosemarie Kother, Kornelia Ender)	4:14.74
1978	United States (Linda Jezek, Tracy Caulkins, Joan Pennington, Cynthia Woodhead)	4:08.21
1982	East Germany (Kristin Otto, Ute Gewinger, Ines Geissler, Birgit Meineke)	4:05.80
1986	East Germany (Kathrin Zimmermann, Sylvia Gerasch, Kornelia Gressler, Kristin Otto)	4:04.82
1991	United States (Janie Wagstaff, Tracey McFarlane, Crissy Ahmann-Leighton, Nicole Haislett)	4:06.51
1994	China (He Cihong, Dai Guohong, Liu Limin, Lu Bin)	4:01.67
1998	United States (Kristy Kowal, Lea Maurer, Jenny Thompson, Amy Van Dyken)	4:01.93
2001	Australia (Dyana Calub, Sarah Ryan, Petria Thomas, Leisel Jones)	4:01.50
2003	China (Shu Zhan, Xuejuan Luo, Yafei Zhou, Yu Yang)	3:59.89

* Because of timing malfunctions and an overturned disqualification of the U.S., gold medals were awarded to Great Britain and the U.S.

400-METER FREESTYLE RELAY

1973	East Germany (Kornelia Ender, Andrea Eife, Andrea Huebner, Sylvia Eichner)	3:52.45
1975	East Germany (Kornelia Ender, Barbara Krause, Claudia Hempel, Ute Bruckner)	3:49.37
1978	United States (Tracy Caulkins, Stephanie Elkins, Jill Sterkel, Cynthia Woodhead)	3:43.43
1982	East Germany (Birgit Meineke, Susanne Link, Kristin Otto, Caren Metschuk)	3:43.97
1986	East Germany (Kristin Otto, Manuela Stellmach, Sabine Schulze, Heike Friedrich)	3:40.57
1991	United States (Nicole Haislett, Julie Cooper, Whitney Hedgepeth, Jenny Thompson)	3:43.26
1994	China (Le Jingyi, Ying Shan, Le Ying, Lu Bin)	3:37.91
1998	United States (Catherine Fox, Lindsey Farella, Melanie Valerio, B.J. Bedford)	3:42.11
2001	Germany (Petra Dallman, Antje Buschschulter, Katrin Meissner, Sandra Volker)	3.39.58
2003	United States (Natalie Coughlin, Lindsay Benko, Rhi Jeffrey, Jenny Thompson)	3:38.09

800-METER FREESTYLE RELAY

1973–82	Event not held	
1986	East Germany (Manuela Stellmach, Astrid Strauss, Nadja Bergknecht, Heike Friedrich)	7:59.33
1991	Germany (Kerstin Kielgass, Manuela Stellmach, Dagmar Hase, Stephanie Ortwig)	8:02.56
1994	China (Le Ying, Yang Aihua, Zhou Guabin, Lu Bin)	7:57.96
1998	Germany (Silvia Szalai, Antje Buschschulte, Janina Goetz, Franziska Van Almsick)	8:01.46
2001	Great Britain (Nicola Jackson, Janine Belton, Karen Legg, Karen Pickering)/United States (Natalie Coughlin, Cristina Teuscher, Julie Hardt, Diana Munz)*	7:56.53
2003	United States (Lindsay Benko, Rachel Komisarz, Rhi Jeffrey, Diana Munz)	7:55.70

> ■ **Fast Fact:** At the 2004 Summer Games, Tara and Dana Kirk of the United States became the first sisters to swim on the same Olympic team.

TRACK and FIELD

A new generation of track-and-field athletes took center stage in 2004 and early 2005. Distance runner Kenenisa Bekele of Ethiopia made the biggest impact. After setting an indoor world record in the 5,000 meters in February 2004, the 22-year-old set outdoor world records in the 5,000 and 10,000 meters in May and June 2005, respectively. Bekele also won the short- and long-course races at the 2005 World Cross Country Championships for the fourth straight year.

Women's pole vaulter Yelena Isinbayeva of Russia continued to take her event to new heights. Isinbayeva, age 22, broke the world record eight times in 2004 — five times outdoors and three times indoors.

Sprinter Jeremy Wariner of the United States went from being a college star to an Olympic star. The 20-year-old dominated the college season while running the 400 meters for Baylor University, winning both the indoor and outdoor NCAA titles in the event. Wariner then led an American sweep of the 400 at the 2004 Summer Olympics. He became the youngest runner to win the Olympic gold medal in the event since 1988.

Another young American sprinter, Justin Gatlin, age 22, earned the title of World's Fastest Man when he won the 100 meters at the 2004 Summer Games.

Allyson Felix, at 18 the youngest member of the U.S. national team, won the 200 meters at the 2004 U.S. Olympic Trials. She won a silver medal in the event at the Olympics, breaking the world junior record with a time of 22.18 seconds.

While young stars were making headlines, several veterans continued to make their marks. Gail Devers of the U.S. won her 10th national championship in the 100-meter hurdles and tied a record by competing in her fifth Olympics. Distance runner Hicham El Guerrouj of Morocco became the first man in 80 years to win Olympic gold in the 1,500 and 5,000 meters in the same year.

Paula Radcliffe of Great Britain established herself as the world's best woman

At age 18, Allyson Felix won a silver medal in the 200 meters at the 2004 Summer Olympics.

JAMIE SQUIRE/GETTY IMAGES

marathon runner even after a nightmarish experience at the 2004 Summer Olympics. Favored to win the gold medal, she had to drop out of the race after 22 miles because of illness and a leg injury. Two months later, Radcliffe came back to win the New York City Marathon. In April 2005, she won the London Marathon in 2:17:42, just two minutes off her world record.

Paula Radcliffe of Great Britain (center) won the 2004 New York City and 2005 London marathons.

■ **Fast Fact:** Lynn Jennings has won a record nine U.S. Cross Country Championships. She has also won three straight world titles.

2004 U.S. OLYMPIC TEAM TRIALS

JULY 9–18, 2004, SACRAMENTO, CALIFORNIA

Men's 100 Meters

ATHLETE	TEAM	TIME
Maurice Green	adidas	9.91
Justin Gatlin	Nike	9.92
Shawn Crawford	Nike	9.93

Women's 100 Meters

ATHLETE	TEAM	TIME
LaTasha Colander	Nike	10.97
Torri Edwards	adidas	11.02
Lauryn Williams	Miami	11.10

Men's 200 Meters

ATHLETE	TEAM	TIME
Shawn Crawford	Nike	19.99
Justin Gatlin	Nike	20.01
Bernard Williams	Nike	20.30

Women's 200 Meters

ATHLETE	TEAM	TIME
Allyson Felix	adidas	22.28
Muna Lee	Nike	22.36
Torri Edwards	adidas	22.39

Men's 400 Meters

ATHLETE	TEAM	TIME
Jeremy Wariner	Baylor	44.37
Otis Harris	Nike	44.67
Derrick Brew	Nike	44.69

Women's 400 Meters

ATHLETE	TEAM	TIME
Monique Hennagan	Unattached	49.56
Sanya Richards	Nike	49.89
DeeDee Trotter	Tennessee	50.28

Men's 800 Meters

ATHLETE	TEAM	TIME
Jonathan Johnson	Texas Tech	1:44.77
Khadevis Robinson	Nike	1:44.91
Derrick Peterson	adidas	1:45.08

Women's 800 Meters

ATHLETE	TEAM	TIME
Jearl Miles-Clark	New Balance	1:59.06
Nicole Teter	Nike	2:00.25
Hazel Clark	Nike	2:00.37

Men's 1,500 Meters

ATHLETE	TEAM	TIME
Alan Webb	Nike	3:36.13
Charlie Gruber	Nike	3:38.45
Rob Myers	Unattached	3:38.93

Women's 1,500 Meters

ATHLETE	TEAM	TIME
Carrie Tollefson	adidas	4:08.32
Jennifer Toomey	Nike	4:08.43
Amy Rudolph	adidas	4:08.57

Men's 5,000 Meters

ATHLETE	TEAM	TIME
Tim Broe	adidas	13:27.36
Jonathon Riley	Nike	13:30.85
Bolota Asmerom	Nike	13:32.77

Women's 5,000 Meters

ATHLETE	TEAM	TIME
Shayne Culpepper	adidas	15:07.41
Marla Runyan	Nike	15:07.48
Shalane Flanagan	Nike	15:10.52

Men's 10,000 Meters

ATHLETE	TEAM	TIME
Meb Keflezighi	Nike	27:36.49
Abdi Abdirahman	Nike	27:55.00
Daniel Browne	Nike	28:07.47

TRACK and FIELD

Women's 10,000 Meters

ATHLETE	TEAM	TIME
Deena Kastor	Asics	31:09.65
Elva Dryer	Nike	31:58.14
Kate O'Neill	Nike	32:07.25

Men's 110-Meter Hurdles

ATHLETE	TEAM	TIME
Terrence Trammell	Mizuno	13.09
Duane Ross	Nike	13.21
Allen Johnson	Nike	13.25

Women's 100-Meter Hurdles

ATHLETE	TEAM	TIME
Gail Devers	Nike	12.547
Joanna Hayes	Nike	12.549
Melissa Morrison	adidas	12.61

Men's 400-Meter Hurdles

ATHLETE	TEAM	TIME
James Carter	Nike	47.68
Angelo Taylor	Nike	48.03
Benny Brazell	LSU	48.05

Women's 400-Meter Hurdles

ATHLETE	TEAM	TIME
Sheena Johnson	Nike	52.95
Brenda Taylor	Nike	53.36
Lashinda Demus	South Carolina	53.43

Men's 3,000-Meter Steeplechase

ATHLETE	TEAM	TIME
Daniel Lincoln	Nike	8:15.02
Anthony Famiglietti	adidas	8:17.91
Robert Gary	adidas	8:19.46

Women's 3,000-Meter Steeplechase

ATHLETE	TEAM	TIME
Ann Gaffigan	Nebraska	9:39.35 (A)
Kathryn Andersen	Brigham Young	9:45.52
Carrie Messner	Asics	9:50.70

Men's 20,000-Meter Race Walk

ATHLETE	TEAM	TIME
Tim Seaman	NYAC	1:25:40
John Nunn	U.S. Army	1:26:23
Kevin Eastler	U.S. Air Force	1:28:49

Women's 20,000-Meter Race Walk

ATHLETE	TEAM	TIME
Teresa Vaill	Walk USA	1:35:57
Joanne Dow	adidas	1:38:42
Bobbi Chapman	Unattached	1:39:01

Men's High Jump

ATHLETE	TEAM	HEIGHT
Jamie Nieto	Nike	2.33
Matt Hemingway	adidas	2.30
Tora Harris	Nike	2.27

Women's High Jump

ATHLETE	TEAM	HEIGHT
Tisha Waller	Nike	1.98
Chaunte Howard	Georgia Tech	1.95
Amy Acuff	Asics	1.95

Men's Pole Vault

ATHLETE	TEAM	HEIGHT
Timothy Mack	Nike	5.90
Toby Stevenson	Nike	5.85
Derek Miles	Nike	5.80

Women's Pole Vault

ATHLETE	TEAM	HEIGHT
Stacy Dragila	Nike	4.75
Jillian Schwartz	Nike	4.55
Kellie Suttle	Nike	4.55

Men's Long Jump

ATHLETE	TEAM	DISTANCE
Dwight Phillips	Nike	8.28
Tony Allmond	Unattached	8.10
John Moffitt	Nike	8.07

Women's Long Jump

ATHLETE	TEAM	DISTANCE
Marion Jones	Nike	7.11
Grace Upshaw	Nike	6.83
Akiba McKinney	Unattached	6.57

Men's Triple Jump

ATHLETE	TEAM	DISTANCE
Melvin Lister	Unattached	17.78
Walter Davis	Nike	17.63
Kenta Bell	Nike	17.58

Women's Triple Jump

ATHLETE	TEAM	DISTANCE
Tiombe Hurd	Nike	14.45 (A)
Shakeema Walker	Unattached	14.06
Vanitta Kinard	Nike	13.73

Men's Shot Put

ATHLETE	TEAM	DISTANCE
Adam Nelson	Nike	21.64
Reese Hoffa	NYAC	21.14
John Godina	adidas	21.08

Women's Shot Put

ATHLETE	TEAM	DISTANCE
Laura Gerraughty	North Carolina	18.50
Kristin Heaston	Nike	18.10
Jillian Camarena	Stanford	17.73

Men's Discus

ATHLETE	TEAM	DISTANCE
Jarred Rome	Unattached	65.77
Ian Waltz	Unattached	64.69
Casey Malone	Nike	64.47

Women's Discus

ATHLETE	TEAM	DISTANCE
Aretha Hill	Nike	63.55
Stephanie Brown	Moreno Trenching	61.90
Seilala Sua	Nike	61.60

Men's Hammer Throw

ATHLETE	TEAM	DISTANCE
James Parker	U.S. Air Force	77.58
A.G. Kruger	Ashland Elite	76.02
Travis Nutter	Pacific Bay Track Club	72.46

(A)=American record. *Note:* Height and distance measured in meters.

2004 U.S. OLYMPIC TEAM TRIALS (cont.)

Women's Hammer Throw

ATHLETE	TEAM	DISTANCE
Erin Gilreath	NYAC	70.42
Anna Mahon	Nike	69.23
Amber Campbell	Coastal Carolina	65.98

Men's Javelin

ATHLETE	TEAM	DISTANCE
Breaux Greer	adidas	82.39
Brian Chaput	Penn	79.81
Leigh Smith	Tennessee	76.38

Women's Javelin

ATHLETE	TEAM	DISTANCE
Kim Kreiner	Nike	55.65
Sarah Malone	Oregon	54.22
Denise O'Connell	Unattached	54.05

Decathlon

ATHLETE	TEAM	POINTS
Bryan Clay	Nike	8,660
Tom Pappas	Nike	8,517
Paul Terek	World's Greatest Athlete Decathlete Club	8,312

Heptathlon

ATHLETE	TEAM	POINTS
Shelia Burrell	Nike	6,194
Tiffany Lott-Hogan	Unattached	6,159
Michelle Perry	Nike	6,126

LEGENDS

Michael Johnson holds world records in the 200 meters, 400 meters, and 4 x 400-meter relay.

SIMON BRUTY/SPORTS ILLUSTRATED

■ **Michael Johnson, sprinter,** b. September 13, 1967, Dallas, Texas. Johnson made history at the 1996 Summer Olympics by becoming the first man to win gold medals in the 200 and 400 meters. Johnson's time in the 200 (19.32 seconds) set a world record that still stood as of the middle of 2005. He also held the world record in the 400 (43.18 seconds), set at the 1999 world track-and-field championships. At the 2000 Summer Olympics, Johnson became the first man to defend his gold medal in the 400. His nine world championship gold medals are more than anyone else has earned in track-and-field history.

■ **Daley Thompson, decathlete,** b. July 30, 1958, London, England. Thompson is considered one of the greatest British athletes of all time. He is one of only two athletes to win the gold medal in the Olympic decathlon twice (1980 and 1984). Thompson defended his Olympic title at the 1984 Summer Games with 8,797 points, one point shy of the world record. A scoring error was found a year later, and he was given 50 more points and the world record. Thompson is also the only athlete to hold the world, Olympic, Commonwealth, and European titles as well as the decathlon world record at the same time.

■ **Joan Benoit, marathoner,** b. May 16, 1957, Freeport, Maine. Benoit was a pioneer in women's marathon running. The women's marathon was a first-time event at the 1984 Summer Olympics. Benoit had qualified for the event at the U.S. Olympic Trials less than three weeks after having arthroscopic surgery on her knee. At the Olympics, she won the gold medal by defeating rival Grete Waitz of Norway by 400 meters. Benoit also won the Boston Marathon twice (1979 and 1983). She set a world record (2 hours, 22 minutes, and 43 seconds) when she won it in 1983.

2005 U.S. INDOOR TRACK AND FIELD CHAMPIONSHIPS

FEBRUARY 25-27, 2005
BOSTON, MASSACHUSETTS

VICTAH SAILER/PHOTO RUN

Angela Daigle, 60 meters

Men's 800 Meters

ATHLETE	TEAM	TIME
Kevin Hicks	Florida A&M	1:48.73
Richard Smith	Unattached	1:48.80
Joel Legare	Unattached	1:48.86

Women's 1,500 Meters

ATHLETE	TEAM	TIME
Jen Toomey	Nike	4:13.25
Treniere Clement	Nike	4:14.20
Christin Wurth	Nike	4:14.74

Men's 1,500 Meters

ATHLETE	TEAM	TIME
Scott McGowan	New Balance	3:44.06
Rob Myers	Reebok	3:45.18
Charlie Gruber	Nike	3:46.11

Women's 3,000 Meters

ATHLETE	TEAM	TIME
Shayne Culpepper	Nike	8:55.57
Amy Rudolph	adidas	8:57.42
Lauren Fleshman	Nike	8:59.93

Shayne Culpepper, 3,000 meters

VICTAH SAILER/PHOTO RUN

Women's 60 Meters

ATHLETE	TEAM	TIME
Angela Daigle	Nike	7.09
Muna Lee	Nike	7.11
Me'Lisa Barber	Unattached	7.18

Men's 60 Meters

ATHLETE	TEAM	TIME
Mardy Scales	Nike	6.61
Joshua Norman	Unattached	6.62
Aaron Armstrong	Nike	6.64

Women's 400 Meters

ATHLETE	TEAM	TIME
DeeDee Trotter	adidas	52.01
Mary Danner	Unattached	53.25
Maisha Pinkard	Hampton University	54.35

Men's 400 Meters

ATHLETE	TEAM	TIME
Bershawn Jackson	Nike	46.05
James Davis	Unattached	46.75
Ashton Collins	Unattached	47.26

Women's 800 Meters

ATHLETE	TEAM	TIME
Hazel Clark	Nike	2:01.98
Alice Schmidt	Unattached	2:02.32
Kameisha Bennett	Nike	2:02.77

Men's 3,000 Meters

ATHLETE	TEAM	TIME
Jonathon Riley	Nike	7:53.73
Bolota Asmerom	Nike	7:53.81
Luke Watson	adidas	7:57.23

Women's 60-Meter Hurdles

ATHLETE	TEAM	TIME
Danielle Carruthers	Nike	7.95
Sheena Johnson	Nike	8.14
Hyleas Fountain	Nike	8.22

Men's 60-Meter Hurdles

ATHLETE	TEAM	TIME
Joel Brown	Nike	7.60
Anwar Moore	Nike	7.63
David Payne	Unattached	7.64

Women's 3,000-Meter Race Walk

ATHLETE	TEAM	TIME
Amber Antonia	NYAC	12:55.69
Joanne Dow	adidas	13:09.62
Deborah Huberty	NYAC	13:26.03

Men's 5,000-Meter Race Walk

ATHLETE	TEAM	TIME
Tim Seaman	NYAC	19:56.41
Curt Clausen	NYAC	20:41.33
Benjamin Shorey	Unattached	21:48.56

Women's High Jump

ATHLETE	TEAM	HEIGHT
Gwen Wentland	Nike	1.88
Kaylene Wagner	California Polytechnic	1.85
Sharon Day	California Polytechnic	1.82

Men's High Jump

ATHLETE	TEAM	HEIGHT
Tora Harris	Shore AC	2.27
Jamie Nieto	Nike	2.24
Adam Shunk	Unattached	2.24

Women's Pole Vault

ATHLETE	TEAM	HEIGHT
Jennifer Stuczynski	Roberts Weslyan	4.35
Becky Holliday	Unattached	4.30
Mary Sauer	Asics	4.30
Erica Bartolina	Unattached	4.30

Men's Pole Vault

ATHLETE	TEAM	HEIGHT
Brad Walker	Nike	5.65
Tommy Skipper	Oregon	5.55
Paul Litchfield	Unattached	5.45

Women's Long Jump

ATHLETE	TEAM	DISTANCE
Rose Richmond	Unattached	6.44
Hyleas Fountain	Nike	6.29
Ola Sesay	Unattached	6.26

Men's Long Jump

ATHLETE	TEAM	DISTANCE
Brian Johnson	Holyfield International	7.89
Tony Allmond	Unattached	7.76
Juaune Armon	Unattached	7.73

Women's Triple Jump

ATHLETE	TEAM	DISTANCE
Shani Marks	Unattached	13.65
Nicole Whitman	Unattached	13.23
Simidele Adeagbo	Team XO	13.19

Walter Davis, triple jump

JESSICA RINALDI/REUTERS

Men's Triple Jump

ATHLETE	TEAM	DISTANCE
Walter Davis	Nike	17.31
Kenta Bell	Nike	16.86
Chris Hercules	Unattached	16.83

Women's Shot Put

ATHLETE	TEAM	DISTANCE
Jillian Camarena	Unattached	17.31
Janae Strickland	Unattached	16.35
Leann Boerema	Unattached	16.00

Men's Shot Put

ATHLETE	TEAM	DISTANCE
John Godina	adidas	21.83
Reese Hoffa	NYAC/Nike	21.74
Adam Nelson	Unattached	21.59

John Godina, shot put

KIRBY LEE/WIREIMAGE.COM

Women's Weight Throw

ATHLETE	TEAM	DISTANCE
Erin Gilreath	NYAC	24.46 (W)
Amber Campbell	Mjolnir TC	23.99
LaQuanda Cotten	Unattached	21.42

Men's Weight Throw

ATHLETE	TEAM	DISTANCE
A.G. Kruger	Ashland Elite	23.47
Jake Freeman	Unattached	23.16
Kibwe Johnson	Unattached	22.27

(W)=world record

TODAY'S STARS

Meb Keflezighi won the silver medal in the marathon at the 2004 Summer Olympics.

LAURENT REBOURS/AP

■ **Mebrahtom Keflezighi, marathoner,** b. May 5, 1975, Asmara, Eritrea. Keflezighi has become the top American distance runner. He grew up in a village in Eritrea, a small nation in Africa. His family moved to San Diego, California, in 1987. Keflezighi became an American citizen in 1998 after graduating from UCLA. At the 2004 Olympic Games, he won a silver medal in the marathon, becoming the first American man since 1976 to medal in the event. Two months later, Keflezighi finished second in the New York City Marathon.

■ **Lauryn Williams, sprinter,** b. September 11, 1983, Pittsburgh, Pennsylvania. Williams is one of the world's top young sprinters. She was the 2004 NCAA champion in the 100 meters, running for the University of Miami. She won a silver medal in the same event at the 2004 Summer Olympics. Williams had a breakout performance at the 2003 Pan American Games. She won gold in the 100 meters in an event-record 11.12 seconds. She added another gold as part of the 4 x 100-meter relay team. Williams holds her high school's records for the 100 meters, 200 meters, long jump, and 4 x 100-meter relay.

■ **Jeremy Wariner, sprinter,** b. January 31, 1984, Irving, Texas. At the 2004 Summer Olympics, Wariner won the biggest race of his life, taking the gold medal in the 400 meters. He became the youngest athlete to win gold in the event since 1988 and led the first U.S. sweep of the event since 1988. Wariner added another gold as part of the 4 x 400-meter relay team. While attending Baylor University, he was coached by Clyde Hart, who also coached track legend Michael Johnson. Wariner holds the school record in the 400 and was part of the 4 x 400 relay team that won NCAA indoor and outdoor titles and set the NCAA indoor record in 2004. Wariner is also the only man to win NCAA titles in the 400 and 4 x 400 indoors and outdoors in the same season (2004).

2005 WORLD CROSS COUNTRY CHAMPIONSHIPS

MARCH 19–20, 2005
SAINT-GALMIER, FRANCE

Long Race — Men

ATHLETE	TEAM	TIME
Kenenisa Bekele	Ethiopia	35:06
Zersenay Tadesse	Eritrea	35:20
Abdullah Ahmad Hassan	Qatar	35:34

Long Race — Women

ATHLETE	TEAM	TIME
Tirunesh Dibaba	Ethiopia	26:34
Alice Timbilili	Kenya	26:37
Werknesh Kidane	Ethiopia	26:37

Short Race — Men

ATHLETE	TEAM	TIME
Kenenisa Bekele	Ethiopia	11:33
Abraham Chebii	Kenya	11:38
Isaac Kiprono Songok	Kenya	11:39

Short Race — Women

ATHLETE	TEAM	TIME
Tirunesh Dibaba	Ethiopia	13:15
Werknesh Kidane	Ethiopia	13:16
Isabella Ochichi	Kenya	13:21

DID YOU KNOW?

Ulrike Meyfarth of West Germany is the youngest individual gold medalist in Olympic track and field history. Meyfarth won the high jump at the 1972 Summer Olympics at age 16.

2004-05 MARATHONS

Chicago Marathon
OCTOBER 10, 2004

MEN	COUNTRY	TIME
Evans Rutto	Kenya	2:06:16
Daniel Njenga	Kenya	2:07:44
Toshinari Takaoka	Japan	2:07:50

WOMEN	COUNTRY	TIME
Constantina Tomescu-Dita	Romania	2:23:45
Nuta Olaru	Romania	2:24:33
Svetlana Zakharova	Russia	2:25:01

London Marathon
APRIL 17, 2005

MEN	COUNTRY	TIME
Martin Lel	Kenya	2:07:26
Jaouad Gharib	Morocco	2:07:49
Hendrik Ramaala	South Africa	2:08:32

WOMEN	COUNTRY	TIME
Paula Radcliffe	Great Britain	2:17:42
Constantina Tomescu-Dita	Romania	2:22:50
Susan Chepkemei	Kenya	2:24:00

New York City Marathon
NOVEMBER 7, 2004

MEN	COUNTRY	TIME
Hendrik Ramaala	South Africa	2:09:28
Meb Keflezighi	United States	2:09:53
Timothy Cherigat	Kenya	2:10:00

WOMEN	COUNTRY	TIME
Paula Radcliffe	Great Britain	2:23:10
Susan Chepkemei	Kenya	2:23:14
Lyubov Denisova	Russia	2:25:18

Boston Marathon
APRIL 18, 2005

MEN	COUNTRY	TIME
Hailu Negussie	Ethiopia	2:11:45
Wilson Onsare	Kenya	2:12:21
Benson Cherono	Kenya	2:12:48

WOMEN	COUNTRY	TIME
Catherine Ndereba	Kenya	2:25:13
Elfenesh Alemu	Ethiopia	2:27:03
Bruna Genovese	Italy	2:29:51

WORLD RECORDS — MEN

EVENT	MARK	RECORD HOLDER	DATE	SITE
100 Meters	9.77	Asafa Powell, Jamaica	6-14-05	Athens, Greece
200 Meters	19.32	Michael Johnson, United States	8-1-96	Atlanta, Georgia
400 Meters	43.18	Michael Johnson, United States	8-26-99	Ceville, Ojain
800 Meters	1:41.11	Wilson Kipketer, Denmark	8-24-97	Cologne, Germany
1,000 Meters	2:11.96	Noah Ngeny, Kenya	9-5-99	Rieti, Italy
1,500 Meters	3:26.00	Hicham El Guerrouj, Morocco	7-14-98	Rome, Italy
Mile	3:43.13	Hicham El Guerrouj, Morocco	7-7-99	Rome, Italy
2,000 Meters	4:44.79	Hicham El Guerrouj, Morocco	9-7-99	Berlin, Germany
3,000 Meters	7:20.67	Daniel Komen, Kenya	9-1-96	Rieti, Italy
Steeplechase	7:53.63	Saif Saaeed Shaheen, Qatar	9-3-04	Brussels, Belgium
5,000 Meters	12:37.35	Kenenisa Bekele, Ethiopia	5-31-04	Hengelo, Netherlands
10,000 Meters	26:20.31	Kenenisa Bekele, Ethiopia	6-8-04	Ostrava, Czech Republic
20,000 Meters	56:55.6	Arturo Barrios, Mexico	3-30-91	La Flache, France
Hour	21,101 meters	Arturo Barrios, Mexico	3-30-91	La Flache, France
25,000 Meters	1:13.55.8	Toshihiko Seko, Japan	3-22-81	Christchurch, New Zealand
30,000 Meters	1:29:18.8	Toshihiko Seko, Japan	3-22-81	Christchurch, New Zealand
Marathon	2:04:55.0	Paul Tergat, Kenya	9-28-03	Berlin, Germany
*110-Meter Hurdles	12.91	Colin Jackson, Great Britain	8-20-93	Stuttgart, Germany
	12.91	Xiang Liu, China	8-27-04	Athens, Greece
400-Meter Hurdles	46.78	Kevin Young, United States	8-6-92	Barcelona, Spain
20-Kilometer Walk	1:17:21.0	Jefferson Perez, Ecuador	8-23-03	Paris, France
30-Kilometer Walk	2:01:44.1	Maurizio Damilano, Italy	10-3-92	Cuneo, Italy
50-Kilometer Walk	3:36:03	Robert Korzeniowski, Poland	8-27-03	Paris, France
*4 x 100-Meter Relay	37.40*	United States (Mike Marsh, Leroy Burrell, Dennis Mitchell, Carl Lewis)	8-8-92	Barcelona, Spain
		United States (Jon Drummond, Andre Cason, Dennis Mitchell, Leroy Burrell)	8-21-93	Stuttgart, Germany

*Shared record

Kenenisa
Bekele,
Ethiopia

■ **Fast Fact:** British medical student Roger Bannister was the first man to break the four-minute barrier in the mile. He ran a time of 3:59.4 on May 6, 1954, at the Iffley Road track in Oxford, England.

WORLD RECORDS — MEN (cont.)

EVENT	MARK	RECORD HOLDER	DATE	SITE
4 x 200-Meter Relay	1:18.68	Santa Monica TC (Mike Marsh, Leroy Burrell, Floyd Heard, Carl Lewis)	4-17-94	Walnut, California
4 x 400-Meter Relay	2:54.20	United States (Jerome Young, Antonio Pettigrew, Tyree Washington, Michael Johnson)	7-22-98	New York, New York
4 x 800-Meter Relay	7:03.89	Great Britain (Peter Elliott, Garry Cook, Steve Cram, Sebastian Coe)	8-30-82	London, England
4 x 1,500-Meter Relay	14:38.8	West Germany (Thomas Wessinghage, Harald Hudak, Michael Lederer, Karl Fleschen)	8-17-77	Cologne, Germany
High Jump	8 ft ½ in	Javier Sotomayor, Cuba	7-27-93	Salamanca, Spain
Pole Vault	20 ft 1¾ in	Sergei Bubka, Ukraine	7-31-94	Sestriere, Italy
Long Jump	29 ft 4½ in	Mike Powell, United States	8-30-91	Tokyo, Japan
Triple Jump	60 ft ¼ in	Jonathan Edwards, Great Britain	8-7-95	Goteborg, Sweden
Shot Put	75 ft 10¼ in	Randy Barnes, United States	5-20-90	Westwood, California
Discus Throw	243 ft	Jurgen Schult, East Germany	6-6-86	Neubrandenburg, Germany
Hammer Throw	284 ft 7 in	Yuri Syedikh, U.S.S.R.	8-30-86	Stuttgart, Germany
Javelin Throw	323 ft 1 in	Jan Zelezny, Czech Republic	5-25-96	Jena, Germany
Decathlon	9,026 pts	Roman Sebrle, Czech Republic	5-27-01	Gotzis, Austria

Roman Sebrle, Czech Republic

STU FORSTER/GETTY IMAGES

DID YOU KNOW?

In the 1904 Olympic marathon, Fred Lorz of the U.S. finished first in 3 hours, 13 minutes. But Lorz was disqualified when officials discovered he had hitched a ride in the pace car for 11 of the 26 miles.

WORLD RECORDS — WOMEN

EVENT	MARK	RECORD HOLDER	DATE	SITE
100 Meters	10.49	Florence Griffith Joyner, United States	7-16-88	Indianapolis, Indiana
200 Meters	21.34	Florence Griffith Joyner, United States	9-29-88	Seoul, Korea
400 Meters	47.60	Marita Koch, East Germany	10-6-85	Canberra, Australia
800 Meters	1:53.28	Jarmila Kratochvílová, Czechoslovakia	7-26-83	Munich, Germany
1,000 Meters	2:28.98	Svetlana Masterkova, Russia	8-23-96	Brussels, Belgium
1,500 Meters	3:50.46	Qu Yunxia, China	9-11-93	Beijing, China
Mile	4:12.56	Svetlana Masterkova, Russia	8-14-96	Zurich, Switzerland
2,000 Meters	5:25.36	Sonia O'Sullivan, Ireland	7-8-94	Edinburgh, Scotland
3,000 Meters	8:06.11	Wang Junxia, China	9-13-93	Beijing, China
Steeplechase	9:08.33	Gulnara Samitova, Russia	8-10-03	Tula, Russia
5,000 Meters	14:24.68	Elvan Abeylegesse, Turkey	6-11-04	Bergen, Norway
10,000 Meters	29:31.78	Wang Junxia, China	9-8-93	Beijing, China
Hour	18,340 meters	Tegla Loroupe, Kenya	8-8-98	Borgholzhausen, Germany
20,000 Meters	1:05:26.6	Tegla Loroupe, Kenya	9-3-00	Borgholzhausen, Germany
25,000 Meters	1:27:05.9	Tegla Loroupe, Kenya	9-21-02	Mengerskirchen, Germany
30,000 Meters	1:45:50.0	Tegla Loroupe, Kenya	6-6-03	Warstein, Germany
Marathon	2:15:25.0	Paula Radclifffe, Great Britain	4-13-03	London, England
100-Meter Hurdles	12.21	Yordanka Donkova, Bulgaria	8-20-88	Stara Zgora, Bulgaria
400-Meter Hurdles	52.34	Yuliya Pechenkina, Russia	8-8-03	Tula, Russia
5-Kilometer Walk	20:02.60	Gillian O'Sullivan, Ireland	7-13-02	Dublin, Ireland
10-Kilometer Walk	41:56.23	Nadezhda Ryashkina, Russia	7-24-90	Seattle, Washington
4 x 100-Meter Relay	41.37	East Germany (Silke Gladisch, Sabine Reiger, Ingrid Auerswald, Marlies Gohr)	10-6-85	Canberra, Australia

WORLD RECORDS — WOMEN (cont.)

EVENT	MARK	RECORD HOLDER	DATE	SITE
4 x 200-Meter Relay	1:27.46	United States (LaTasha Jenkins, LaTasha Colander-Richardson, Nanceen Perry, Marion Jones)	4-29-00	Philadelphia, Pennsylvania
4 x 400-Meter Relay	3:15.17	U.S.S.R. (Tatyana Ledovskaya, Olga Nazarova, Maria Pinigina, Olga Bryzgina)	10-1-88	Seoul, Korea
4 x 800-Meter Relay	7:50.17	U.S.S.R. (Nadezhda Olizarenko, Lyubov Gurina, Lyudmila Borisova, Irina Podyalovskaya)	8-5-84	Moscow, Russia
High Jump	6 ft 10¼ in	Stefka Kostadinova, Bulgaria	8-30-87	Rome, Italy
Pole Vault	16 ft 5¼ in	Yelena Isinbayeva, Russia	8-12-05	Helsinki, Finland
Long Jump	24 ft 8¼ in	Galina Chistyakova, U.S.S.R.	6 11-88	Leningrad, Russia
Triple Jump	50 ft 10¼ in	Inessa Kravets, Ukraine	8 10 05	Goteborg, Sweden
Shot Put	74 ft 3 in	Natalya Lisovskaya, U.S.S.R.	6-7-87	Moscow, Russia
Discus Throw	252 ft	Gabriele Reinsch, East Germany	7-9-88	Neubrandenburg, Germany
Hammer Throw	247 ft 3 in	Mihaela Melinte, Romania	8-29-99	Rudlingen, Switzerland
Javelin Throw	235 ft 3 in	Osleidys Menéndez, Cuba	8-14-05	Helsinki, Finland
Heptathlon	7,291 pts	Jackie Joyner-Kersee, United States	9-23-88/9-24-88	Seoul, Korea

Yelena Isinbayeva, Russia

KAY NIETFELD/EPA

TRIVIA CHALLENGE

Who are the only two U.S. athletes to win four track-and-field gold medals at one Olympics?

Jesse Owens (1936) and Carl Lewis (1984).

2004-05 TIME LINE

■ **June 11, 2004:** Elvan Abeylegesse of Turkey breaks the women's world record in the 5,000 meters (14:24.68) at the Bislett Games in Bergen, Norway. She is Turkey's first world-record holder in track and field.

■ **June 19, 2004:** Alan Webb runs the fastest mile by an American on U.S. soil (3:50.85) at the Prefontaine Classic in Eugene, Oregon.

■ **August 23, 2004:** Jeremy Wariner of the U.S. wins the gold medal in the 400 meters at the 2004 Summer Olympics. The United States sweeps the event as Otis Harris wins the silver and Derrick Brew takes the bronze.

■ **August 28, 2004:** Hicham El Guerrouj of Morocco wins the Olympic gold medal in the 5,000 meters. He becomes the first man since 1924 to win the 1,500 and 5,000 meters at the same Olympics.

■ **November 7, 2004:** Paula Radcliffe wins the New York City Marathon by just four seconds over Susan Chepkemei of Kenya.

■ **February 26, 2005:** Yelena Isinbayeva of Russia breaks the world indoor record in the pole vault (16' ½") for the third consecutive meet.

■ **March 20, 2005:** One day after he wins the short-course race, Kenenisa Bekele of Ethiopia wins the long-course race at the World Cross Country championships. It is the fourth straight year that Bekele has won both races.

SUMMER OLYMPICS

More than 11,000 athletes from 202 countries competed in 28 sports at the XXVIII Summer Olympics in Athens, Greece. The United States led the medal haul with 103. Russia was second (92), and China was third (63).

The story of the Games was U.S. swimmer Michael Phelps. He set one world and one U.S. record while winning eight medals, tying the record held by gymnast Aleksandr Dityatin of Russia, who won eight in 1980. Six of Phelps's medals were gold. Gymnast Paul Hamm won the first Olympic individual all-around gold medal by a U.S. man, and Carly Patterson won the second by a U.S. woman. In team sports, the U.S. women's softball and basketball teams went undefeated to earn gold. The U.S. women's soccer team also won gold. The U.S. men's hoops team settled for bronze.

The next Summer Games will be held in Beijing, China, in 2008. After its successful showing in 2004, the host country could dominate the gold medal count.

The 2004 Summer Olympics were held in Athens, Greece.

ATHENS 2004 MEDAL COUNT* — NATION

NATION	GOLD	SILVER	BRONZE	TOTAL
1. UNITED STATES OF AMERICA	35	39	29	103
2. RUSSIA	27	27	38	92
3. PEOPLE'S REPUBLIC OF CHINA	32	17	14	63
4. AUSTRALIA	17	16	16	49
5. GERMANY	14	16	18	48
6. JAPAN	16	9	12	37
7. FRANCE	11	9	13	33
8. ITALY	10	11	11	32
9. SOUTH KOREA	9	12	9	30
10. GREAT BRITAIN	9	9	12	30
11. CUBA	9	7	11	27
12. UKRAINE	9	5	9	23
13. THE NETHERLANDS	4	9	9	22
14. ROMANIA	8	5	6	19
15. SPAIN	3	11	5	19
16. HUNGARY	8	6	3	17
17. GREECE	6	6	4	16
18. BELARUS	2	6	7	15
19. CANADA	3	6	3	12
19. BULGARIA	2	1	9	12
21. BRAZIL	4	3	3	10
21. TURKEY	3	3	4	10
21. POLAND	3	2	5	10
24. THAILAND	3	1	4	8
24. DENMARK	2	0	6	8
24. KAZAKHSTAN	1	4	3	8
24. CZECH REPUBLIC	1	3	4	8

*Top 24 nations listed

2004 SPORT-BY-SPORT RESULTS

ARCHERY

■ Individual
GOLD – Sung Hyun Park, South Korea
SILVER – Sung Jin Lee, South Korea
BRONZE – Alison Williamson, Great Britain
■ Team
GOLD – South Korea
SILVER – China
BRONZE – Taiwan
MEN
■ Individual
GOLD – Marco Galiazzo, Italy
SILVER – Hiroshi Yamamoto, Japan
BRONZE – Tim Cuddihy, Australia
■ Team
GOLD – South Korea
SILVER – Taiwan
BRONZE – Ukraine

BADMINTON

WOMEN
■ Singles
GOLD – Ning Zhang, China
SILVER – Mia Audina, Netherlands
BRONZE – Mi Zhou, China
■ Doubles
GOLD – China
SILVER – China
BRONZE – South Korea
MEN
■ Singles
GOLD – Taufik Hidayat, Indonesia
SILVER – Seung Mo Shon, South Korea
BRONZE – Soni Dwi Kuncoro, Indonesia
■ Doubles
GOLD – South Korea
SILVER – South Korea
BRONZE – Indonesia
■ Mixed Doubles
GOLD – China
SILVER – Great Britain
BRONZE – Denmark

BASEBALL
GOLD – Cuba
SILVER – Australia
BRONZE – Japan

BASKETBALL
WOMEN
GOLD – USA
SILVER – Australia
BRONZE – Russia

Dawn Staley,
United States

MEN
GOLD – Argentina
SILVER – Italy
BRONZE – USA

BEACH VOLLEYBALL
WOMEN
GOLD – Misty May
and Kerri Walsh, USA
SILVER – Shelda Bede and
Adriana Behar, Brazil
BRONZE – Holly McPeak and
Elaine Youngs, USA
MEN
GOLD – Ricardo Alex Santos and
Emanuel Rego, Brazil
SILVER – Javier Bosma and Pablo Herrera, Spain
BRONZE – Patrick Heuscher and
Stefan Kobel, Switzerland

BOXING
■ Light Flyweight
GOLD – Yan Bhartelemy Varela, Cuba
SILVER – Atagun Yalcinkaya, Turkey
BRONZE – Shimming Zou, China; and Sergey Kazakov,
Russia
■ Flyweight
GOLD – Yuriorkis Gamboa Toledano, Cuba
SILVER – Jerome Thomas, France
BRONZE – Fuad Aslanov, Azerbaijan; and Rustamhodaa
Rahimov, Germany
■ Bantamweight
GOLD – Guillermo Rigondeaux Ortiz, Cuba
SILVER – Worapoj Petchkoom, Thailand
BRONZE – Bahodirjon Sooltonov, Uzbekistan; and
Aghasi Mammadov, Azerbaijan
■ Featherweight
GOLD – Alexei Tichtchenko, Russia
SILVER – Song Guk Kim, North Korea
BRONZE – Seok Hwan Jo, South Korea; and Vitali
Tajbert, Germany
■ Lightweight
GOLD – Mario Cesar Kindelan Mesa, Cuba
SILVER – Amir Khan, Great Britain
BRONZE – Murat Khrachev, Russia; and Serik Yeleuov,
Kazakhstan
■ Light Welterweight
GOLD – Manus Boonjumnong, Thailand
SILVER – Yudel Johnson Cedeno, Cuba
BRONZE – Boris Georgiev, Bulgaria; and Ionut Gheorghe,
Romania
■ Welterweight
GOLD – Bakhtiyar Artayev, Kazakhstan
SILVER – Lorenzo Aragon Armenteros, Cuba
BRONZE – Oleg Saitov, Russia; and Jung Joo Kim,
South Korea

2004 SPORT-BY-SPORT RESULTS (cont.)

BOXING (cont.)

■ **Middleweight**
GOLD – Gaydarbek Gaydarbekov, Russia
SILVER – Gennadiy Golovkin, Kazakhstan
BRONZE – Suriya Prasathinphimai, Thailand;
and Andre Dirrell, USA

■ **Light Heavyweight**
GOLD – Andre Ward, USA
SILVER – Magomed Aripgadjiev, Belarus
BRONZE – Utkirbek Haydarov, Uzbekistan;
and Ahmed Ismail, Egypt

■ **Heavyweight**
GOLD – Odlanier Solis Fonte, Cuba
SILVER – Viktar Zuyev, Belarus
BRONZE – Mohamed Elsayed, Egypt;
and Naser Al Shami, Syria

■ **Super Heavyweight**
GOLD – Alexander Povetkin, Russia
SILVER – Mohamed Aly, Egypt
BRONZE – Roberto Cammarelle, Italy;
and Michel Lopez Nunez, Cuba

CANOE/KAYAK SLALOM RACING

WOMEN

■ **K1 Kayak Single**
GOLD – Elena Kaliska, Slovakia
SILVER – Rebecca Giddens, USA
BRONZE – Helen Reeves, Great Britain

MEN

■ **K1 Kayak Single**
GOLD – Benoit Peschier,
France
SILVER – Campbell Walsh,
Great Britain
BRONZE – Fabien Lefevre,
France

■ **C1 Canoe Single**
GOLD – Tony Estanguet, France
SILVER – Michal Martikan, Slovakia
BRONZE – Stefan Pfannmoeller, Germany

■ **C2 Canoe Double**
GOLD – Slovakia
SILVER – Germany
BRONZE – Czech Republic

CANOE/KAYAK FLATWATER RACING

WOMEN

■ **K1 500 meters**
GOLD – Natasa Janics, Hungary
SILVER – Josefa Idem, Italy
BRONZE – Caroline Brunet, Canada

■ **K2 500 meters**
GOLD – Hungary
SILVER – Germany
BRONZE – Poland

■ **K4 500 meters**
GOLD – Germany
SILVER – Hungary
BRONZE – Ukraine

*Natasa Janics,
Hungary*

MEN

■ **K1 500 meters**
GOLD – Adam van Koeverden, Canada
SILVER – Nathan Baggaley, Australia
BRONZE – Ian Wynne, Great Britain

■ **K1 1,000 meters**
GOLD – Eirik Veraas Larsen, Norway
SILVER – Ben Fouhy, New Zealand
BRONZE – Adam van Koeverden, Canada

■ **K2 500 meters**
GOLD – Germany
SILVER – Australia
BRONZE – Belarus

■ **K2 1,000 meters**
GOLD – Sweden
SILVER – Italy
BRONZE – Norway

■ **K4 1,000 meters**
GOLD – Hungary
SILVER – Germany
BRONZE – Slovakia

■ **C1 500 meters**
GOLD – Andreas Dittmer, Germany
SILVER – David Cal, Spain
BRONZE – Maxim Opalev, Russia

■ **C1 1,000 meters**
GOLD – David Cal, Spain
SILVER – Andreas Dittmer, Germany
BRONZE – Attila Vajda, Hungary

■ **C2 500 meters**
GOLD – China
SILVER – Cuba
BRONZE – Russia

■ **C2 1,000 meters**
GOLD – Germany
SILVER – Russia
BRONZE – Hungary

CYCLING (ROAD)

WOMEN

■ **Road Race**
GOLD – Sara Carrigan, Australia
SILVER – Judith Arndt, Germany
BRONZE – Olga Slyusareva, Russia

■ **Individual Time Trial**
GOLD – Leontien Zijlaard-van Moorsel, Netherlands
SILVER – Dede Demet-Barry, USA
BRONZE – Karin Thuerig, Switzerland

MEN

■ **Road Race**
GOLD – Paolo Bettini, Italy
SILVER – Sergio Paulinho, Portugal
BRONZE – Axel Merckx, Belgium

■ **Individual Time Trial**
GOLD – Tyler Hamilton, USA
SILVER – Viatcheslav Ekimov, Russia
BRONZE – Bobby Julich, USA

DID YOU KNOW?

At the 1956 Summer Olympics in Melbourne, Australia, athletes entered the stadium together for the first time during the Closing Ceremony as a symbol of global unity.

LEGENDS

Karch Kiraly is the only Olympic volleyball player to win a gold medal three times.

■ **Karch Kiraly, volleyball player,** b. November 3, 1960, Jackson, Mississippi. At the 1996 Summer Olympics, Kiraly and teammate Kent Steffes won the first Olympic gold medal in beach volleyball. Kiraly was the captain of the U.S. men's Olympic indoor volleyball team that won the gold medal at the 1984 and 1988 Games. He was the youngest player on the 1984 team (age 23) and played in all 19 matches, more than any other player on the team.

■ **Bob Beamon, long jumper,** b. August 29, 1946, Jamaica, New York. At the 1968 Summer Olympics, Beamon shattered the long jump world record by almost two feet. His 29' 2½" leap stood as the world record for 23 years. (Mike Powell of the U.S. broke the record by two inches in 1991.) Beamon was inducted into the U.S. Olympic Hall of Fame in 1983.

■ **John Smith, wrestler,** b. August 9, 1965, Oklahoma City, Oklahoma. Smith is considered one of the greatest wrestlers of all time. He is the only U.S. wrestler to win six world championships in a row (1987-92). Smith won gold medals in the 136.5-pound division at the 1988 and 1992 Summer Olympics. He returned to the Olympics in 2000 as coach of the U.S. men's freestyle team, which earned one gold, one silver, and two bronze medals.

2004 SPORT-BY-SPORT RESULTS (cont.)

CYCLING (TRACK)

Sarah Ulmer, New Zealand

WOMEN

■ **500-meter Time Trial**
GOLD – Anna Meares, Australia
SILVER – Yonghua Jiang, China
BRONZE – Natallia Tsylinskaya, Belarus

■ **3,000-meter Individual Pursuit**
GOLD – Sarah Ulmer, New Zealand
SILVER – Katie Mactier, Australia
BRONZE – Leontien Zijlaard-van Moorsel, Netherlands

■ **Sprint**
GOLD – Lori-Ann Muenzer, Canada
SILVER – Tamilla Abassova, Russia
BRONZE – Anna Meares, Australia

■ **Points Race**
GOLD – Olga Slyusareva, Russia
SILVER – Belem Guerrero Mendez, Mexico
BRONZE – Erin Mirabella, USA

MEN

■ **1-kilometer Time Trial**
GOLD – Chris Hoy, Great Britain
SILVER – Arnaud Tournant, France
BRONZE – Stefan Nimke, Germany

■ **4,000-meter Individual Pursuit**
GOLD – Bradley Wiggins, Great Britain
SILVER – Brad McGee, Australia
BRONZE – Sergi Escobar, Spain

■ **Team Sprint**
GOLD – Germany
SILVER – Japan
BRONZE – France

■ **4,000-meter Team Pursuit**
GOLD – Australia
SILVER – Great Britain
BRONZE – Spain

■ **Points Race**
GOLD – Mikhail Ignatyev, Russia
SILVER – Joan Llaneras, Spain
BRONZE – Guido Fulst, Germany

2004 SPORT-BY-SPORT RESULTS (cont.)

CYCLING (TRACK) (cont.)

MEN

■ **Sprint**
GOLD – Ryan Bayley, Australia
SILVER – Theo Bos, Netherlands
BRONZE – Rene Wolff, Germany

■ **Madison**
GOLD – Australia
SILVER – Switzerland
BRONZE – Great Britain

■ **Keirin**
GOLD – Ryan Bayley, Australia
SILVER – Jose Escuredo, Spain
BRONZE – Shane Kelly, Australia

CYCLING (MOUNTAIN BIKE)

WOMEN
GOLD – Gunn-Rita Dahle, Norway
SILVER – Marie-Helene Premont, Canada
BRONZE – Sabine Spitz, Germany

MEN
GOLD – Julien Absalon, France
SILVER – Jose Antonio Hermida, Spain
BRONZE – Bart Brentjens, Netherlands

DIVING

WOMEN

■ **3-meter Springboard**
GOLD – Jingjing Guo, China
SILVER – Minxia Wu, China
BRONZE – Yulia Pakhalina, Russia

■ **10-meter Platform**
GOLD – Chantelle Newbery, Australia
SILVER – Lishi Lao, China
BRONZE – Loudy Tourky, Australia

■ **Synchronized 3-meter Springboard**
GOLD – Minxia Wu and Jingjing Guo, China
SILVER – Vera Ilyina and Yulia Pakhalina, Russia
BRONZE – Irina Lashko and
Chantelle Newbery, Australia

■ **Synchronized 10-meter Platform**
GOLD – Lishi Lao and Ting Li, China
SILVER – Natalia Goncharova and Yulia Koltunova,
Russia
BRONZE – Blythe Hartley and Emilie Heymans, Canada

MEN

■ **3-meter Springboard**
GOLD – Bo Peng, China
SILVER – Alexandre Despatie, Canada
BRONZE – Dmitri Sautin, Russia

■ **10-meter Platform**
GOLD – Jia Hu, China
SILVER – Mathew Helm, Australia
BRONZE – Liang Tian, China

Bo Peng, China

> ■ ***Fast Fact:*** Women's sabre made its debut at
> the 2004 Summer Olympics. Mariel Zagunis of the
> U.S. earned the gold medal, the first Olympic gold
> medal in U.S. fencing history.

■ **Synchronized 3-meter Springboard**
GOLD – Nikolaos Siranidis and Thomas Bimis, Greece
SILVER – Andreas Wels and
Tobias Schellenberg, Germany
BRONZE – Robert Newbery and
Steven Barnett, Australia

■ **Synchronized 10-meter Platform**
GOLD – Liang Tian and Jinghui Yang, China
SILVER – Peter Waterfield and Leon Taylor, Great Britain
BRONZE – Mathew Helm and
Robert Newbery, Australia

EQUESTRIAN

■ **Individual Eventing**
GOLD – Leslie Law, Great Britain
SILVER – Kimberly Severson, USA
BRONZE – Philippa Funnell, Great Britain

■ **Team Eventing**
GOLD – France
SILVER – Great Britain
BRONZE – USA

■ **Individual Dressage**
GOLD – Anky van Grunsven, Netherlands
SILVER – Ulla Salzgeber, Germany
BRONZE – Beatriz Ferrer-Salat, Spain

■ **Team Dressage**
GOLD – Germany
SILVER – Spain
BRONZE – USA

■ **Individual Jumping**
GOLD – Rodrigo Pessoa, Brazil
SILVER – Chris Kappler, USA
BRONZE – Marco Kutscher, Germany

■ **Team Jumping**
GOLD – USA
SILVER – Sweden
BRONZE – Germany

FENCING

WOMEN

■ **Individual Sabre**
GOLD – Mariel Zagunis, USA
SILVER – Xue Tan, China
BRONZE – Sada Jacobson, USA

■ **Individual Épée**
GOLD – Timea Nagy, Hungary
SILVER – Laura Flessel-Colovic, France
BRONZE – Maureen Nisima, France

■ **Individual Foil**
GOLD – Valentina Vezzali, Italy
SILVER – Giovanna Trillini, Italy
BRONZE – Sylwia Gruchala, Poland

■ **Team Épée**
GOLD – Russia
SILVER – Germany
BRONZE – France

FENCING (cont.)

MEN

■ **Individual Sabre**
GOLD – Aldo Montano, Italy
SILVER – Zsolt Nemcsik, Hungary
BRONZE – Vladislav Tretiak, Ukraine

■ **Individual Épée**
GOLD – Marcel Fischer, Switzerland
SILVER – Lei Wang, China
BRONZE – Pavel Kolobkov, Russia

■ **Individual Foil**
GOLD – Brice Guyart, France
SILVER – Salvatore Sanzo, Italy
BRONZE – Andrea Cassara, Italy

■ **Team Sabre**
GOLD – France
SILVER – Italy
BRONZE – Russia

■ **Team Épée**
GOLD – France
SILVER – Hungary
BRONZE – Germany

■ **Team Foil**
GOLD – Italy
SILVER – China
BRONZE – Russia

FIELD HOCKEY

WOMEN
GOLD – Germany
SILVER – Netherlands
BRONZE – Argentina

MEN
GOLD – Australia
SILVER – Netherlands
BRONZE – Germany

GYMNASTICS

WOMEN

■ **Team**
GOLD – Romania
SILVER – USA
BRONZE – Russia

■ **Individual All-Around**
GOLD – Carly Patterson, USA
SILVER – Svetlana Khorkina, Russia
BRONZE – Nan Zhang, China

■ **Vault**
GOLD – Monica Rosu, Romania
SILVER – Annia Hatch, USA
BRONZE – Anna Pavlova, Russia

■ **Uneven Bars**
GOLD – Emilie Lepennec, France
SILVER – Terin Humphrey, USA
BRONZE – Courtney Kupets, USA

Carly Patterson, United States

■ **Balance Beam**
GOLD – Catalina Ponor, Romania
SILVER – Carly Patterson, USA
BRONZE – Alexandra Georgiana Eremia, Romania

■ **Floor Exercise**
GOLD – Catalina Ponor, Romania
SILVER – Nicoleta Daniela Sofronie, Romania
BRONZE – Patricia Moreno, Spain

■ **Trampoline**
GOLD – Anna Dogonadze, Germany
SILVER – Karen Cockburn, Canada
BRONZE – Shanshan Huang, China

MEN

■ **Team**
GOLD – Japan
SILVER – USA
BRONZE – Romania

■ **Individual All-Around**
GOLD – Paul Hamm, USA
SILVER – Dae Eun Kim, South Korea
BRONZE – Tae Young Yang, South Korea

■ **Floor Exercise**
GOLD – Kyle Shewfelt, Canada
SILVER – Marian Dragulescu, Romania
BRONZE – Jordan Jovtchev, Bulgaria

■ **Pommel Horse**
GOLD – Haibin Teng, China
SILVER – Marius Daniel Urzica, Romania
BRONZE – Takehiro Kashima, Japan

■ **Rings**
GOLD – Dimosthenis Tampakos, Greece
SILVER – Jordan Jovtchev, Bulgaria
BRONZE – Yuri Chechi, Italy

■ **Vault**
GOLD – Gervasio Deferr, Spain
SILVER – Evgeni Sapronenko, Latvia
BRONZE – Marian Dragulescu, Romania

■ **Parallel Bars**
GOLD – Valeri Goncharov, Ukraine
SILVER – Hiroyuki Tomita, Japan
BRONZE – Xiaopeng Li, China

■ **Horizontal Bar**
GOLD – Igor Cassina, Italy
SILVER – Paul Hamm, USA
BRONZE – Isao Yoneda, Japan

■ **Trampoline**
GOLD – Yuri Nikitin, Ukraine
SILVER – Alexander Moskalenko, Russia
BRONZE – Henrik Stehlik, Germany

HANDBALL

WOMEN
GOLD – Denmark
SILVER – South Korea
BRONZE – Ukraine

2004 SPORT-BY-SPORT RESULTS (cont.)

HANDBALL (cont.)
MEN
GOLD – Croatia
SILVER – Germany
BRONZE – Russia

JUDO
WOMEN
■ **48 kg**
GOLD – Ryoko Tani, Japan
SILVER – Frederique Jossinet, France
BRONZE – Julia Matijass, Germany; and Fen Gao, China

■ **52 kg**
GOLD – Dongmei Xian, China
SILVER – Yuki Yokosawa, Japan
BRONZE – Amarilys Savon, Cuba; and Ilse Heylen, Belgium

■ **57 kg**
GOLD – Yvonne Boenisch, Germany
SILVER – Sun Hui Kye, North Korea
BRONZE – Deborah Gravenstijn, Netherlands; and Yurisleidy Lupetey, Cuba

■ **63 kg**
GOLD – Ayumi Tanimoto, Japan
SILVER – Claudia Heill, Austria
BRONZE – Urska Zolnir, Slovenia; and Driulys Gonzalez, Cuba

■ **70 kg**
GOLD – Masae Ueno, Japan
SILVER – Edith Bosch, Netherlands
BRONZE – Annett Boehm, Germany; and Dongya Qin, China

■ **78 kg**
GOLD – Noriko Anno, Japan
SILVER – Xia Liu, China
BRONZE – Lucia Morico, Italy; and Yurisel Laborde, Cuba

■ **+78 kg**
GOLD – Maki Tsukada, Japan
SILVER – Dayma Beltran, Cuba
BRONZE – Tea Donguzashvili, Russia; and Fuming Sun, China

MEN
■ **60 kg**
GOLD – Tadahiro Nomura, Japan
SILVER – Nestor Khergiani, Georgia
BRONZE – Min Ho Choi, South Korea; and Khashbaatar Tsagaanbaatar, Mongolia

■ **66 kg**
GOLD – Masato Uchishiba, Japan
SILVER – Jozef Krnac, Slovakia
BRONZE – Georgi Georgiev, Bulgaria; and Yordanis Arencibia, Cuba

■ **73 kg**
GOLD – Won Hee Lee, South Korea
SILVER – Vitaliy Makarov, Russia
BRONZE – Leandro Guilheiro, Brazil; and James Pedro, USA

■ **81 kg**
GOLD – Ilias Iliadis, Greece
SILVER – Roman Gontyuk, Ukraine
BRONZE – Dmitri Nossov, Russia; and Flavio Canto, Brazil

■ **90 kg**
GOLD – Zurab Zviadauri, Georgia
SILVER – Hiroshi Izumi, Japan
BRONZE – Mark Huizinga, Netherlands; and Khasanbi Taov, Russia

■ **100 kg**
GOLD – Ihar Makarau, Belarus
SILVER – Sung Ho Jang, South Korea
BRONZE – Ariel Zeevi, Israel; and Michael Jurack, Germany

■ **+100 kg**
GOLD – Keiji Suzuki, Japan
SILVER – Tamerlan Tmenov, Russia
BRONZE – Indrek Pertelson, Estonia; and Dennis van Der Geest, Netherlands

MODERN PENTATHLON
WOMEN
GOLD – Zsuzsanna Voros, Hungary
SILVER – Jelena Rublevska, Latvia
BRONZE – Georgina Harland, Great Britain
MEN
GOLD – Andrey Moiseev, Russia
SILVER – Andrejus Zadneprovskis, Lithuania
BRONZE – Libor Capalini, Czech Republic

RHYTHMIC GYMNASTICS
■ **Team**
GOLD – Russia
SILVER – Italy
BRONZE – Bulgaria

■ **Individual All-Around**
GOLD – Alina Kabaeva, Russia
SILVER – Irina Tchachina, Russia
BRONZE – Anna Bessonova, Ukraine

ROWING
WOMEN
■ **Single Sculls**
GOLD – Katrin Rutschow-Stomporowski, Germany
SILVER – Ekaterina Karsten-Khodotovitch, Belarus
BRONZE – Rumyana Neykova, Bulgaria

■ **Double Sculls**
GOLD – New Zealand
SILVER – Germany
BRONZE – Great Britain

■ **Lightweight Double Sculls**
GOLD – Romania
SILVER – Germany
BRONZE – Netherlands

Ryoko Tani, Japan

CHARLES PLATIAU/REUTERS

ROWING (cont.)

WOMEN

Quadruple Sculls
GOLD – Germany
SILVER – Great Britain
BRONZE – Australia

Pair
GOLD – Romania
SILVER – Great Britain
BRONZE – Belarus

Eight
GOLD – Romania
SILVER – USA
BRONZE – Netherlands

MEN

Single Sculls
GOLD – Olaf Tufte, Norway
SILVER – Jueri Jaanson, Estonia
BRONZE – Ivo Yanaklev, Bulgaria

Double Sculls
GOLD – France
SILVER – Slovenia
BRONZE – Italy

Lightweight Double Sculls
GOLD – Poland
SILVER – France
BRONZE – Greece

Quadruple Sculls
GOLD – Russia
SILVER – Czech Republic
BRONZE – Ukraine

Pair
GOLD – Australia
SILVER – Croatia
BRONZE – South Africa

Four
GOLD – Great Britain
SILVER – Canada
BRONZE – Italy

Lightweight Four
GOLD – Denmark
SILVER – Australia
BRONZE – Italy

Eight
GOLD – USA
SILVER – Netherlands
BRONZE – Australia

SAILING

WOMEN

Keelboat: Yngling Class
GOLD – Great Britain
SILVER – Ukraine
BRONZE – Denmark

Double-handed Dinghy: 470 Class
GOLD – Greece
SILVER – Spain
BRONZE – Sweden

Single-handed Dinghy: Europe Class
GOLD – Siren Sundby, Norway
SILVER – Lenka Smidova, Czech Republic
BRONZE – Signe Livbjerg, Denmark

Windsurfing
GOLD – Faustine Merret, France
SILVER – Jian Yin, China
BRONZE – Alessandra Sensini, Italy

MEN

Double-handed Dinghy: 470 Class
GOLD – USA
SILVER – Great Britain
BRONZE – Japan

Single-handed Dinghy: Finn Class
GOLD – Ben Ainslie, Great Britain
SILVER – Rafael Trujillo, Spain
BRONZE – Mateusz Kusznierewicz, Poland

Keelboat: Star Class
GOLD – Brazil
SILVER – Canada
BRONZE – France

Open Single-handed Dinghy: Laser Class
GOLD – Robert Scheidt, Brazil
SILVER – Andreas Geritzer, Austria
BRONZE – Vasilij Zbogar, Slovenia

Open Double-handed Dinghy: 49er Class
GOLD – Spain
SILVER – Ukraine
BRONZE – Great Britain

Open Multihull: Tornado Class
GOLD – Austria
SILVER – USA
BRONZE – Argentina

Windsurfing
GOLD – Gal Fridman, Israel
SILVER – Nikolaos Kaklamanakis, Greece
BRONZE – Nick Dempsey, Great Britain

SHOOTING

WOMEN

10-meter Air Pistol
GOLD – Olena Kostevych, Ukraine
SILVER – Jasna Sekaric, Serbia-Montenegro
BRONZE – Maria Grozdeva, Bulgaria

10-meter Air Rifle
GOLD – Li Du, China
SILVER – Lioubov Galkina, Russia
BRONZE – Katerina Kurkova, Czech Republic

*Gal Fridman,
Israel*

CLIVE MASON/GETTY IMAGES

2004 SPORT-BY-SPORT RESULTS (cont.)

SHOOTING (cont.)

WOMEN

■ **25-meter Pistol**
GOLD – Maria Grozdeva, Bulgaria
SILVER – Lenka Hykova, Czech Republic
BRONZE – Irada Ashumova, Azerbaijan

■ **50-meter Rifle 3 Position**
GOLD – Lioubov Galkina, Russia
SILVER – Valentina Turisini, Italy
BRONZE – Chengyi Wang, China

■ **Trap**
GOLD – Suzanne Balogh, Australia
SILVER – Maria Quintanal, Spain
BRONZE – Bo Na Lee, South Korea

■ **Double Trap**
GOLD – Kim Rhode, USA
SILVER – Bo Na Lee, South Korea
BRONZE – E Gao, China

■ **Skeet**
GOLD – Diana Igaly, Hungary
SILVER – Ning Wei, China
BRONZE – Zemfira Meftakhetdinova,
Azerbaijan

MEN

■ **10-meter Air Pistol**
GOLD – Yifu Wang, China
SILVER – Mikhail Nestruev, Russia
BRONZE – Vladimir Isakov, Russia

■ **10-meter Air Rifle**
GOLD – Qinan Zhu, China
SILVER – Jie Li, China
BRONZE – Jozef Gonci, Slovakia

■ **10-meter Running Target**
GOLD – Manfred Kurzer, Germany
SILVER – Alexander Blinov, Russia
BRONZE – Dimitri Lykin, Russia

■ **25-meter Rapid-fire Pistol**
GOLD – Ralf Schumann, Germany
SILVER – Sergei Poliakov, Russia
BRONZE – Sergei Alifirenko, Russia

■ **50-meter Pistol**
GOLD – Mikhail Nestruev, Russia
SILVER – Jong Oh Jin, South Korea
BRONZE – Jong Su Kim,
North Korea

■ **50-meter Rifle 3 Position**
GOLD – Zhanbo Jia, China
SILVER – Michael Anti, USA
BRONZE – Christian Planer, Austria

■ **50-meter Rifle Prone**
GOLD – Matthew Emmons, USA
SILVER – Christian Lusch, Germany
BRONZE – Sergei Martinov, Belarus

■ **Trap**
GOLD – Alexei Alipov, Russia
SILVER – Giovanni Pellielo, Italy
BRONZE – Adam Vella, Australia

■ **Double Trap**
GOLD – Ahmed Almaktoum, United Arab Emirates
SILVER – Rajyavardhan S. Rathore, India
BRONZE – Zheng Wang, China

■ **Skeet**
GOLD – Andrea Benelli, Italy
SILVER – Marko Kemppainen, Finland
BRONZE – Juan Miguel Rodriguez, Cuba

SOCCER

WOMEN
GOLD – USA
SILVER – Brazil
BRONZE – Germany

MEN
GOLD – Argentina
SILVER – Paraguay
BRONZE – Italy

SOFTBALL
GOLD – USA
SILVER – Australia
BRONZE – Japan

SWIMMING

WOMEN

■ **50-meter Freestyle**
GOLD – Inge de Bruijn, Netherlands
SILVER – Malia Metella, France
BRONZE – Lisbeth Lenton, Australia

■ **100-meter Freestyle**
GOLD – Jodie Henry, Australia
SILVER – Inge de Bruijn, Netherlands
BRONZE – Natalie Coughlin, USA

■ **200-meter Freestyle**
GOLD – Camelia Potec, Romania
SILVER – Federica Pellegrini, Italy
BRONZE – Solenne Figues, France

■ **400-meter Freestyle**
GOLD – Laure Manaudou, France
SILVER – Otylia Jedrzejczak, Poland
BRONZE – Kaitlin Sandeno, USA

■ **800-meter Freestyle**
GOLD – Ai Shibata, Japan
SILVER – Laure Manaudou, France
BRONZE – Diana Munz, USA

■ **100-meter Backstroke**
GOLD – Natalie Coughlin, USA
SILVER – Kirsty Coventry, Zimbabwe
BRONZE – Laure Manaudou, France

■ **200-meter Backstroke**
GOLD – Kirsty Coventry, Zimbabwe
SILVER – Stanislava Komarova, Russia
BRONZE – Reiko Nakamura, Japan; and Antje
Buschschulte, Germany

*Abby Wambach,
United States*

*Laure Manaudou,
France*

SWIMMING (cont.)

WOMEN

100-meter Breaststroke
GOLD – Xuejuan Luo, China
SILVER – Brooke Hanson, Australia
BRONZE – Leisel Jones, Australia

200-meter Breaststroke
GOLD – Amanda Beard, USA
SILVER – Leisel Jones, Australia
BRONZE – Anne Poleska, Germany

100-meter Butterfly
GOLD – Petria Thomas, Australia
SILVER – Otylia Jedrzejczak, Poland
BRONZE – Inge de Bruijn, Netherlands

200-meter Butterfly
GOLD – Otylia Jedrzejczak, Poland
SILVER – Petria Thomas, Australia
BRONZE – Yuko Nakanishi, Japan

200-meter Individual Medley
GOLD – Yana Klochkova, Ukraine
SILVER – Amanda Beard, USA
BRONZE – Kirsty Coventry, Zimbabwe

400-meter Individual Medley
GOLD – Yana Klochkova, Ukraine
SILVER – Kaitlin Sandeno, USA
BRONZE – Georgina Bardach, Argentina

400-meter Medley Relay
GOLD – Australia
SILVER – USA
BRONZE – Germany

400-meter Freestyle Relay
GOLD – Australia
SILVER – USA
BRONZE – Netherlands

800-meter Freestyle Relay
GOLD – USA
SILVER – China
BRONZE – Germany

MEN

50-meter Freestyle
GOLD – Gary Hall, Jr., USA
SILVER – Duje Draganja, Croatia
BRONZE – Roland Mark Schoeman,
   South Africa

100-meter Freestyle
GOLD – Pieter van den Hoogenband, Netherlands
SILVER – Roland Mark Schoeman, South Africa
BRONZE – Ian Thorpe, Australia

200-meter Freestyle
GOLD – Ian Thorpe, Australia
SILVER – Pieter van den
   Hoogenband, Netherlands
BRONZE – Michael Phelps, USA

400-meter Freestyle
GOLD – Ian Thorpe, Australia
SILVER – Grant Hackett, Australia
BRONZE – Klete Keller, USA

Ian Thorpe,
Australia

1,500-meter Freestyle
GOLD – Grant Hackett, Australia
SILVER – Larsen Jensen, USA
BRONZE – David Davies, Great Britain

100-meter Backstroke
GOLD – Aaron Peirsol, USA
SILVER – Markus Rogan, Austria
BRONZE – Tomomi Morita, Japan

200-meter Backstroke
GOLD – Aaron Peirsol, USA
SILVER – Markus Rogan, Austria
BRONZE – Razvan Florea, Romania

100-meter Breaststroke
GOLD – Kosuke Kitajima, Japan
SILVER – Brendan Hansen, USA
BRONZE – Hugues Duboscq, France

200-meter Breaststroke
GOLD – Kosuke Kitajima, Japan
SILVER – Daniel Gyurta, Hungary
BRONZE – Brendan Hansen, USA

100-meter Butterfly
GOLD – Michael Phelps, USA
SILVER – Ian Crocker, USA
BRONZE – Andriy Serdinov, Ukraine

200-meter Butterfly
GOLD – Michael Phelps, USA
SILVER – Takashi Yamamoto, Japan
BRONZE – Stephen Parry, Great Britain

200-meter Individual Medley
GOLD – Michael Phelps, USA
SILVER – Ryan Lochte, USA
BRONZE – George Bovell, Trinidad and Tobago

400-meter Individual Medley
GOLD – Michael Phelps, USA
SILVER – Erik Vendt, USA
BRONZE – Laszlo Cseh, Hungary

400-meter Medley Relay
GOLD – USA
SILVER – Germany
BRONZE – Japan

400-meter Freestyle Relay
GOLD – South Africa
SILVER – Netherlands
BRONZE – USA

800-meter Freestyle Relay
GOLD – USA
SILVER – Australia
BRONZE – Italy

SYNCHRONIZED SWIMMING

Duet
GOLD – Russia
SILVER – Japan
BRONZE – USA

Team
GOLD – Russia
SILVER – Japan
BRONZE – USA

Kosuke
Kitajima,
Japan

Michael Phelps,
United States

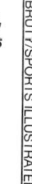

2004 SPORT-BY-SPORT RESULTS (cont.)

BILL FRAKES/SPORTS ILLUSTRATED

TABLE TENNIS

WOMEN

■ **Singles**
GOLD – Yining Zhang, China
SILVER – Hyang Mi Kim, North Korea
BRONZE – Kyung Ah Kim, South Korea

■ **Doubles**
GOLD – China
SILVER – South Korea
BRONZE – China

MEN

■ **Singles**
GOLD – Seung Min Ryu, South Korea
SILVER – Hao Wang, China
BRONZE – Liqin Wang, China

■ **Doubles**
GOLD – China
SILVER – Hong Kong
BRONZE – Denmark

TAEKWONDO

WOMEN

■ **Under 49 kg**
GOLD – Shih Hsin Chen, Taiwan
SILVER – Yanelis Yuliet Labrada Diaz, Cuba
BRONZE – Yaowapa Boorapolchai, Thailand

■ **Under 57 kg**
GOLD – Ji Won Jang, South Korea
SILVER – Nia Abdallah, USA
BRONZE – Iridia Salazar Blanco, Mexico

■ **Under 67 kg**
GOLD – Wei Luo, China
SILVER – Elisavet Mystakidou, Greece
BRONZE – Kyung Sun Hwang, South Korea

■ **Over 67 kg**
GOLD – Zhong Chen, China
SILVER – Myriam Baverel, France
BRONZE – Adriana Carmona, Venezuela

MEN

■ **Under 58 kg**
GOLD – Mu Yen Chu, Taiwan
SILVER – Oscar Francisco Salazar Blanco, Mexico
BRONZE – Tamer Bayoumi, Egypt

■ **Under 68 kg**
GOLD – Hadi Saei Bonehkohal, Iran
SILVER – Chih Hsiung Huang, Taiwan
BRONZE – Myeong Seob Song, South Korea

■ **Under 80 kg**
GOLD – Steven Lopez, USA
SILVER – Bahri Tanrikulu, Turkey
BRONZE – Yossef Karami, Iran

■ **Over 80 kg**
GOLD – Dae Sung Moon, South Korea
SILVER – Alexandros Nikolaidis, Greece
BRONZE – Pascal Gentil, France

Steven Lopez, United States

TENNIS

WOMEN

■ **Singles**
GOLD – Justine Henin-Hardenne, Belgium
SILVER – Amélie Mauresmo, France
BRONZE – Alicia Molik, Australia

■ **Doubles**
GOLD – China
SILVER – Spain
BRONZE – Argentina

MEN

■ **Singles**
GOLD – Nicolas Massu, Chile
SILVER – Mardy Fish, USA
BRONZE – Fernando Gonzalez, Chile

■ **Doubles**
GOLD – Chile
SILVER – Germany
BRONZE – Croatia

TRACK AND FIELD

WOMEN

■ **100 meters**
GOLD – Yuliya Nesterenko, Belarus
SILVER – Lauryn Williams, USA
BRONZE – Veronica Campbell, Jamaica

■ **200 meters**
GOLD – Veronica Campbell, Jamaica
SILVER – Allyson Felix, USA
BRONZE – Debbie Ferguson, Bahamas

■ **400 meters**
GOLD – Tonique Williams-Darling, Bahamas
SILVER – Ana Guevara, Mexico
BRONZE – Natalya Antyukh, Russia

■ **800 meters**
GOLD – Kelly Holmes, Great Britain
SILVER – Hasna Benhassi, Morocco
BRONZE – Jolanda Ceplak, Slovenia

■ **1,500 meters**
GOLD – Kelly Holmes, Great Britain
SILVER – Tatyana Tomashova, Russia
BRONZE – Maria Cioncan, Romania

■ **5,000 meters**
GOLD – Meseret Defar, Ethiopia
SILVER – Isabella Ochichi, Kenya
BRONZE – Tirunesh Dibaba, Ethiopia

■ **10,000 meters**
GOLD – Huina Xing, China
SILVER – Ejegayehu Dibaba, Ethiopia
BRONZE – Derartu Tulu, Ethiopia

■ **20-kilometer Walk**
GOLD – Athanasia Tsoumeleka, Greece
SILVER – Olimpiada Ivanova, Russia
BRONZE – Jane Saville, Australia

■ **100-meter Hurdles**
GOLD – Joanna Hayes, USA
SILVER – Olena Krasovska, Ukraine
BRONZE – Melissa Morrison, USA

Kelly Holmes, Great Britain

STUART HANNAGAN/GETTY IMAGES

TRACK AND FIELD (cont.)

WOMEN

■ 400-meter Hurdles
GOLD – Fani Halkia, Greece
SILVER – Ionela Tirlea-Manolache, Romania
BRONZE – Tetiana Tereshchuk-Antipova, Ukraine

■ High Jump
GOLD – Yelena Slesarenko, Russia
SILVER – Hestrie Cloete, South Africa
BRONZE – Viktoriya Styopina, Ukraine

■ Pole Vault
GOLD – Yelena Isinbayeva, Russia
SILVER – Svetlana Feofanova, Russia
BRONZE – Anna Rogowska, Poland

■ Long Jump
GOLD – Tatyana Lebedeva, Russia
SILVER – Irina Simagina, Russia
BRONZE – Tatyana Kotova, Russia

■ Triple Jump
GOLD – Francoise Mbango Etone,
Cameroon
SILVER – Hrysopiyi Devetzi, Greece
BRONZE – Tatyana Lebedeva, Russia

■ Shot Put
GOLD – Yumileidi Cumba, Cuba
SILVER – Nadine Kleinert, Germany
BRONZE – Svetlana Krivelyova, Russia

■ Discus Throw
GOLD – Natalya Sadova, Russia
SILVER – Anastasia Kelesidou, Greece
BRONZE – Irina Yatchenko, Belarus

■ Javelin Throw
GOLD – Osleidys Menendez, Cuba
SILVER – Steffi Nerius, Germany
BRONZE – Mirela Manjani, Greece

■ Hammer Throw
GOLD – Olga Kuzenkova, Russia
SILVER – Yipsi Moreno, Cuba
BRONZE – Yunaika Crawford, Cuba

■ 4 x 100-meter Relay
GOLD – Jamaica
SILVER – Russia
BRONZE – France

■ 4 x 400-meter Relay
GOLD – USA
SILVER – Russia
BRONZE – Jamaica

■ Heptathlon
GOLD – Carolina Kluft, Sweden
SILVER – Austra Skujyte, Lithuania
BRONZE – Kelly Sotherton, Great Britain

■ Marathon
GOLD – Mizuki Noguchi, Japan
SILVER – Catherine Ndereba, Kenya
BRONZE – Deena Kastor, USA

MEN

■ 100 meters
GOLD – Justin Gatlin, USA
SILVER – Francis Obikwelu, Portugal
BRONZE – Maurice Greene, USA

■ 200 meters
GOLD – Shawn Crawford, USA
SILVER – Bernard Williams, USA
BRONZE – Justin Gatlin, USA

■ 400 meters
GOLD – Jeremy Wariner, USA
SILVER – Otis Harris, USA
BRONZE – Derrick Brew, USA

■ 800 meters
GOLD – Yuriy Borzakovskiy, Russia
SILVER – Mbulaeni Mulaudzi, South Africa
BRONZE – Wilson Kipketer, Denmark

■ 1,500 meters
GOLD – Hicham El Guerrouj, Morocco
SILVER – Bernard Lagat, Kenya
BRONZE – Rui Silva, Portugal

■ 3,000-meter Steeplechase
GOLD – Ezekiel Kemboi, Kenya
SILVER – Brimin Kipruto, Kenya
BRONZE – Paul Kipsiele Koech, Kenya

■ 5,000 meters
GOLD – Hicham El Guerrouj, Morocco
SILVER – Kenenisa Bekele, Ethiopia
BRONZE – Eliud Kipchoge, Kenya

■ 10,000 meters
GOLD – Kenenisa Bekele, Ethiopia
SILVER – Sileshi Sihine, Ethiopia
BRONZE – Zersenay Tadesse, Eritrea

■ 20-kilometer Walk
GOLD – Ivano Brugnetti, Italy
SILVER – Francisco Javier Fernández, Spain
BRONZE – Nathan Deakes, Australia

■ 50-kilometer Walk
GOLD – Robert Korzeniowski, Poland
SILVER – Denis Nizhegorodov, Russia
BRONZE – Aleksey Voyevodin, Russia

■ 110-meter Hurdles
GOLD – Xiang Liu, China
SILVER – Terrence Trammell, USA
BRONZE – Anier Garcia, Cuba

■ 400-meter Hurdles
GOLD – Felix Sanchez, Dominican Republic
SILVER – Danny McFarlane, Jamaica
BRONZE – Naman Keita, France

■ High Jump
GOLD – Stefan Holm, Sweden
SILVER – Matt Hemingway, USA
BRONZE – Jaroslav Baba, Czech Republic

■ Pole Vault
GOLD – Timothy Mack, USA
SILVER – Toby Stevenson, USA
BRONZE – Giuseppe Gibilisco, Italy

*Jeremy Wariner,
United States*

*Xiang Liu,
China*

2004 SPORT-BY-SPORT RESULTS (cont.)

TRACK AND FIELD (cont.)

MEN

■ **Long Jump**
GOLD – Dwight Phillips, USA
SILVER – John Moffitt, USA
BRONZE – Joan Lino Martinez, Spain

■ **Triple Jump**
GOLD – Christian Olsson, Sweden
SILVER – Marian Oprea, Romania
BRONZE – Danila Burkenya, Russia

■ **Shot Put**
GOLD – Yuriy Bilonog, Ukraine
SILVER – Adam Nelson, USA
BRONZE – Joachim Olsen, Denmark

■ **Discus Throw**
GOLD – Virgilijus Alekna, Lithuania
SILVER – Zoltan Kovago, Hungary
BRONZE – Aleksander Tammert, Estonia

■ **Javelin Throw**
GOLD – Andreas Thorkildsen, Norway
SILVER – Vadims Vasilevskis, Latvia
BRONZE – Sergey Makarov, Russia

■ **Hammer Throw**
GOLD – Koji Murofushi, Japan
SILVER – Ivan Tikhon, Belarus
BRONZE – Esref Apak, Turkey

■ **4 x 100-meter Relay**
GOLD – Great Britain
SILVER – USA
BRONZE – Nigeria

■ **4 x 400-meter Relay**
GOLD – USA
SILVER – Australia
BRONZE – Nigeria

■ **Decathlon**
GOLD – Roman Sebrle, Czech Republic
SILVER – Bryan Clay, USA
BRONZE – Dmitriy Karpov, Kazakhstan

■ **Marathon**
GOLD – Stefano Baldini, Italy
SILVER – Mebrahtom Keflezighi, USA
BRONZE – Vanderlei de Lima, Brazil

TRIATHLON

WOMEN
GOLD – Kate Allen, Austria
SILVER – Loretta Harrop, Australia
BRONZE – Susan Williams, USA

MEN
GOLD – Hamish Carter, New Zealand
SILVER – Bevan Docherty, New Zealand
BRONZE – Sven Riederer, Switzerland

VOLLEYBALL

WOMEN
GOLD – China
SILVER – Russia
BRONZE – Cuba

MEN
GOLD – Brazil
SILVER – Italy
BRONZE – Russia

WATER POLO

WOMEN
GOLD – Italy
SILVER – Greece
BRONZE – USA

MEN
GOLD – Hungary
SILVER – Serbia-Montenegro
BRONZE – Russia

WEIGHTLIFTING

WOMEN

■ **48 kg**
GOLD – Nurcan Taylan, Turkey
SILVER – Zhuo Li, China
BRONZE – Aree Wiratthaworn, Thailand

■ **53 kg**
GOLD – Udomporn Polsak, Thailand
SILVER – Raema Lisa Rumbewas, Indonesia
BRONZE – Mabel Mosquera, Colombia

■ **58 kg**
GOLD – Yanqing Chen, China
SILVER – Song Hui Ri, North Korea
BRONZE – Wandee Kameaim, Thailand

■ **63 kg**
GOLD – Nataliya Skakun, Ukraine
SILVER – Hanna Batsiushka, Belarus
BRONZE – Tatsiana Stukalava, Belarus

■ **69 kg**
GOLD – Chunhong Liu, China
SILVER – Eszter Krutzler, Hungary
BRONZE – Zarema Kasaeva, Russia

■ **75 kg**
GOLD – Pawina Thongsuk, Thailand
SILVER – Natalia Zabolotnaia, Russia
BRONZE – Valentina Popova, Russia

■ **+75 kg**
GOLD – Tang Gonghong, China
SILVER – Mi Ran Jang, South Korea
BRONZE – Agata Wrobel, Poland

MEN

■ **56 kg**
GOLD – Halil Mutlu, Turkey
SILVER – Meijin Wu, China
BRONZE – Sedat Artuc, Turkey

■ **62 kg**
GOLD – Zhiyong Shi, China
SILVER – Maosheng Le, China
BRONZE – Israel Jose Rubio, Venezuela

■ **69 kg**
GOLD – Guozheng Zhang, China
SILVER – Bae Young Lee, South Korea
BRONZE – Nikolay Pechalov, Croatia

Yanqing Chen, China

NEIL TINGLE/ACTION PLUS/ICON SMI

Stefano Baldini, Italy

LAURENT REBOURS/AP

WEIGHTLIFTING (cont.)

MEN

■ 77 kg
GOLD – Taner Sagir, Turkey
SILVER – Sergey Filimonov, Kazakhstan
BRONZE – Oleg Perepetchenov, Russia

■ 85 kg
GOLD – George Asanidze, Georgia
SILVER – Andrei Rybakou, Belarus
BRONZE – Pyrros Dimas, Greece

■ 94 kg
GOLD – Milen Dobrev, Bulgaria
SILVER – Khadjimourad Akkaev, Russia
BRONZE – Eduard Tjukin, Russia

■ 105 kg
GOLD – Dmitry Berestov, Russia
SILVER – Igor Razoronov, Ukraine
BRONZE – Gleb Pisarevskly, Russia

■ +105 kg
GOLD – Hossein Reza Zadeh, Iran
SILVER – Viktors Scerbatihs, Latvia
BRONZE – Velichko Cholakov, Bulgaria

WRESTLING (FREESTYLE)

WOMEN

■ 48 kg
GOLD – Irini Merleni, Ukraine
SILVER – Chiharu Icho, Japan
BRONZE – Patricia Miranda, USA

■ 55 kg
GOLD – Saori Yoshida, Japan
SILVER – Tonya Verbeek, Canada
BRONZE – Anna Gomis, France

■ 63 kg
GOLD – Kaori Icho, Japan
SILVER – Sara McMann, USA
BRONZE – Lise Legrand, France

■ 72 kg
GOLD – Xu Wang, China
SILVER – Gouzel Maniourova, Russia
BRONZE – Kyoko Hamaguchi, Japan

MEN

■ 55 kg
GOLD – Mavlet Batirov, Russia
SILVER – Stephen Abas, USA
BRONZE – Chikara Tanabe, Japan

■ 60 kg
GOLD – Yandro Miguel Quintana, Cuba
SILVER – Masuod Jokar, Iran
BRONZE – Kenji Inoue, Japan

■ 66 kg
GOLD – Elbrus Tedeyev, Ukraine
SILVER – Jamill Kelly, USA
BRONZE – Makhach Murtazaliev, Russia

■ 74 kg
GOLD – Buvaysa Saytiev, Russia
SILVER – Gennadiy Laliyev, Kazakhstan
BRONZE – Ivan Fundora, Cuba

■ 84 kg
GOLD – Cael Sanderson, USA
SILVER – Eui Jae Moon, South Korea
BRONZE – Sazhid Sazhidov, Russia

■ 96 kg
GOLD – Khadjimourat Gatsalov, Russia
SILVER – Magomed Ibragimov, Uzbekistan
BRONZE – Alireza Heidari, Iran

■ 120 kg
GOLD – Artur Taymazov, Uzbekistan
SILVER – Alireza Rezaei, Iran
BRONZE – Aydin Polatci, Turkey

WRESTLING (GRECO-ROMAN)

MEN

■ 55 kg
GOLD – Istvan Majoros, Hungary
SILVER – Gueidar Mamedaliev, Russia
BRONZE – Artiom Kiouregkian, Greece

■ 60 kg
GOLD – Ji Hyun Jung, South Korea
SILVER – Roberto Monzon, Cuba
BRONZE – Armen Nazarian, Bulgaria

■ 66 kg
GOLD – Farid Mansurov, Azerbaijan
SILVER – Seref Eroglu, Turkey
BRONZE – Mkkhitar Manukyan, Kazakhstan

■ 74 kg
GOLD – Alexandr Dokturishvili, Uzbekistan
SILVER – Marko Yli-Hannuksela, Finland
BRONZE – Varteres Samourgachev, Russia

■ 84 kg
GOLD – Alexei Michine, Russia
SILVER – Ara Abrahamian, Sweden
BRONZE – Viachaslau Makaranka, Belarus

■ 96 kg
GOLD – Karam Ibrahim, Egypt
SILVER – Ramaz Nozadze, Georgia
BRONZE – Mehmet Ozal, Turkey

■ 120 kg
GOLD – Khasan Baroev, Russia
SILVER – Georgiy Tsurtsumia, Kazakhstan
BRONZE – Rulon Gardner, USA

Cael Sanderson,
United States

MATTHEW STOCKMAN/GETTY IMAGES

DID YOU KNOW?

China had its most successful Olympics ever at the 2004 Games. Chinese athletes won 63 medals, including 32 gold medals. The wins came in 14 sports and included first-time gold medals in tennis, men's track and field, wrestling, and canoeing.

TODAY'S STARS

■ **Paul Hamm, gymnast,** b. September 24, 1982, Washburn, Wisconsin. Hamm won the first U.S. men's all-around gymnastics title at the 2004 Summer Olympics. He also won silver medals in the team competition and the high bar. Hamm was the first U.S. men's world champion in 2003. He and his twin brother, Morgan, made history at the 2000 Summer Games: They were the first twins to compete in the same Olympic gymnastics competition.

■ **Xiang Liu, hurdler,** b. July 13, 1983, Shanghai, China. Liu tied the world record (12.91 seconds) in the 110-meter hurdles at the 2004 Summer Olympics. He became the first Chinese athlete to win a gold medal in a short-distance track event. Liu's time broke the previous Olympic record of 12.95 seconds set in 1996. He was third in the hurdles at the 2003 World Championships and set a junior world record in the event in 2002.

Paul Hamm won one gold and two silver medals at the 2004 Summer Olympics.

BILL FRAKES/SPORTS ILLUSTRATED

■ **Deena Kastor, marathoner,** b. February 14, 1973, Waltham, Massachusetts. Kastor won the bronze medal in the marathon at the 2004 Summer Olympics. It was just the second women's Olympic marathon medal for the United States. Kastor ran a remarkable race, moving up from 28th place after 3 miles to 6th place after 21 miles to 3rd at the finish. She is also the 2004 U.S. champion in the 10,000 meters.

■ *Fast Fact:* The U.S. women's 800-meter freestyle relay team broke swimming's oldest world record at the 2004 Summer Olympics. The foursome of Natalie Coughlin, Carly Piper, Dana Vollmer, and Kaitlin Sandeno smashed the 17-year-old record previously held by East Germany by 2½ seconds (7:53.42).

TRIVIA CHALLENGE

Who is the only athlete to win a Summer and Winter Olympic medal in the same year?

Christa Luding-Rothenburger of Germany. She earned a silver medal in cycling at the 1988 Summer Games in Seoul, South Korea. Seven months earlier, Luding-Rothenburger won one gold medal and one silver medal in speed skating at the 1988 Winter Games in Calgary, Alberta, Canada.

PAST SUMMER OLYMPIC HOSTS

YEAR		HOST	DATES	MEN	WOMEN	NATIONS
XXVIII	2004	ATHENS, GREECE	August 13-29	11,099 (total)		202
XXVII	2000	SYDNEY, AUSTRALIA	September 15-October 1	6,582	4,069	199
XXVI	1996	ATLANTA, GEORGIA, USA	July 19-August 4	6,806	3,512	197
XXV	1992	BARCELONA, SPAIN	July 25-August 9	6,652	2,704	169
XXIV	1988	SEOUL, KOREA	September 17-October 2	6,197	2,194	159
XXIII	1984	LOS ANGELES, CALIFORNIA, USA	July 28-August 12	5,263	1,566	140
XXII	1980	MOSCOW, U.S.S.R.	July 19-August 3	4,064	1,115	80
XXI	1976	MONTREAL, QUEBEC, CANADA	July 17-August 1	4,824	1,260	92
XX	1972	MUNICH, WEST GERMANY	August 26-September 11	6,075	1,059	121
XIX	1968	MEXICO CITY, MEXICO	October 12-27	4,735	781	112
XVIII	1964	TOKYO, JAPAN	October 10-24	4,473	678	93
XVII	1960	ROME, ITALY	August 25-September 11	4,727	611	83
XVI	1956	MELBOURNE, AUSTRALIA	November 22-December 8	2,938	376	72
XV	1952	HELSINKI, FINLAND	July 19-August 3	4,436	519	69
XIV	1948	LONDON, GREAT BRITAIN	July 29-August 14	3,714	390	59
XIII	1944	LONDON, GREAT BRITAIN	Canceled because of World War II			
XII	1940	TOKYO, JAPAN	Canceled because of World War II			
XI	1936	BERLIN, GERMANY	August 1-16	3,632	331	49
X	1932	LOS ANGELES, CALIFORNIA, USA	July 30-August 14	1,206	126	37
IX	1928	AMSTERDAM, THE NETHERLANDS	May 17-August 12	2,606	277	46
VIII	1924	PARIS, FRANCE	May 4-July 27	2,954	135	44
VII	1920	ANTWERP, BELGIUM	April 20-September 12	2,561	65	29
VI	1916	BERLIN, GERMANY	Canceled because of World War I			
V	1912	STOCKHOLM, SWEDEN	May 5-July 27	2,359	48	28
IV	1908	LONDON, GREAT BRITAIN	April 27-October 31	1,971	37	22
—	1906	ATHENS, GREECE	April 22-May 28	77	7	20
III	1904	ST. LOUIS, MISSOURI, USA	July 1-November 23	645	6	12
II	1900	PARIS, FRANCE	May 14-October 28	975	22	24
I	1896	ATHENS, GREECE	April 6-15	241	0	14

SUMMER OLYMPICS

ALL-TIME SUMMER OLYMPIC MEDAL COUNT — NATION

NATION	GOLD	SILVER	BRONZE	TOTAL
UNITED STATES	907	697	615	2,219
SOVIET UNION (1952-88)	395	319	296	1,010
GREAT BRITAIN	189	242	237	668
FRANCE	199	202	230	631
ITALY	189	154	168	511
GERMANY (1896-1936, 1992-present)	151	154	178	483
SWEDEN	140	157	179	476
HUNGARY	158	141	161	460
EAST GERMANY (1956-88)	159	150	136	445
AUSTRALIA	119	126	154	399
JAPAN	113	106	114	333
WEST GERMANY (1952-88)	77	104	120	301
FINLAND	101	83	114	298
CHINA	112	96	78	286
ROMANIA	82	88	114	284
POLAND	59	74	118	251
RUSSIA	85	79	84	248
CANADA	54	87	101	242
THE NETHERLANDS	65	76	94	235

ALL-TIME SUMMER OLYMPIC MEDAL COUNT — MEN

ATHLETE, Nation	SPORT	GOLD	SILVER	BRONZE	TOTAL
NIKOLAI ANDRIANOV, U.S.S.R.	Gymnastics	7	5	3	15
BORIS SHAKHLIN, U.S.S.R.	Gymnastics	7	4	2	13
EDOARDO MANGIAROTTI, Italy	Fencing	6	5	2	13
TAKASHI ONO, Japan	Gymnastics	5	4	4	13
PAAVO NURMI, Finland	Track	9	3	0	12
SAWAO KATO, Japan	Gymnastics	8	3	1	12
ALEXEI NEMOV, Russia	Gymnastics	4	2	6	12
MARK SPITZ, United States	Swimming	9	1	1	11
MATT BIONDI, United States	Swimming	8	2	1	11
VIKTOR CHUKARIN, U.S.S.R.	Gymnastics	7	3	1	11
CARL OSBURN, United States	Shooting	5	4	2	11

Six tied with 10.

ALL-TIME SUMMER OLYMPIC MEDAL COUNT — WOMEN

ATHLETE, Nation	SPORT	GOLD	SILVER	BRONZE	TOTAL
LARISSA LATYNINA, U.S.S.R.	Gymnastics	9	5	4	18
BIRGIT FISCHER, Germany	Canoe/Kayak	8	4	0	12
JENNY THOMPSON, United States	Swimming	8	3	1	12
VERA CASLAVSKA, Czechoslovakia	Gymnastics	7	4	0	11
AGNES KELETI, Hungary	Gymnastics	5	3	2	10
POLINA ASTAKNOVA, U.S.S.R.	Gymnastics	5	2	3	10
NADIA COMANECI, Romania	Gymnastics	5	3	1	9
LYUDMILA TOURISCHEVA, U.S.S.R.	Gymnastics	4	3	2	9
DARA TORRES, United States	Swimming	4	1	4	9
KORNELIA ENDER, East Germany	Swimming	4	4	0	8
DAWN FRASER, Australia	Swimming	4	4	0	8
INGE DE BRUIJN, The Netherlands	Swimming	4	2	2	8
SHIRLEY BABASHOFF, United States	Swimming	2	6	0	8
SOFIA MURATOVA, U.S.S.R.	Gymnastics	2	2	4	8

Eight tied with 7.

ALL-TIME SUMMER OLYMPIC GOLD MEDALISTS

MEN

RAY EWRY, United States	10
PAAVO NURMI, Finland	9
CARL LEWIS, United States	9
MARK SPITZ, United States	9
SAWAO KATO, Japan	8
MATT BIONDI, United States	8
NIKOLAI ANDRIANOV, U.S.S.R.	7
BORIS SHAKHLIN, U.S.S.R.	7
VIKTOR CHUKARIN, U.S.S.R.	7
ALADAR GEREVICH, Hungary	7

WOMEN

LARISSA LATYNINA, U.S.S.R.	9
BIRGIT FISCHER, Germany	8
JENNY THOMPSON, United States	8
KRISTIN OTTO, East Germany	6
AGNES KELETI, Hungary	5
NADIA COMANECI, Romania	5
POLINA ASTAKNOVA, U.S.S.R.	5
KRISZTINA EGERSZEGI, Hungary	5
AMY VAN DYKEN, United States	5
KORNELIA ENDER, East Germany	4
DAWN FRASER, Australia	4
LARISSA LAZUTINA, United Team/Russia	4
LYUDMILA TOURISCHEVA, U.S.S.R.	4
EVELYN ASHFORD, United States	4
JANET EVANS, United States	4
FANNY BLANKERS-KOEN, The Netherlands	4
BETTY CUTHBERT, Australia	4
PAT MCCORMICK, United States	4
BARBEL ECKERT WOCKEL, East Germany	4
INGE DE BRUIJN, The Netherlands	4
YANA KLOCHKOVA, Ukraine	4
DARA TORRES, United States	4

WINTER OLYMPICS

The XX Winter Olympics will be held from February 10-26, 2006, in Turin, Italy. More than 2,500 athletes from 85 countries will compete in eight sports: biathlon, bobsled, curling, ice hockey, luge, skating, skiing, and snowboarding.

Four-time European men's figure-skating champion Evgeny Plushenko of Russia, World Cup overall moguls champion Jeremy Bloom of the U.S., and X Games snowboard champion Hannah Teter of the U.S. are among the athletes expected to compete.

Turin, Italy, will host the 2006 Winter Olympics.

ANSA-FILES/AFP

2006 WINTER OLYMPICS SCHEDULE *

■ **OPENING CEREMONY**

SATURDAY, FEBRUARY 11

■ **BIATHLON**
M 20 kilometer

■ **NORDIC COMBINED**
M 15-kilometer individual

■ **LONG-TRACK SPEED SKATING**
M 5,000 meters

■ **FREESTYLE SKIING**
W Moguls

SUNDAY, FEBRUARY 12

■ **LONG-TRACK SPEED SKATING**
W 3,000 meters

■ **SHORT-TRACK SPEED SKATING**
M 1,500 meters

■ **SKI JUMPING**
M Normal hill individual

■ **CROSS-COUNTRY SKIING**
W 7.5-kilometer pursuit
M 15-kilometer pursuit

■ **ALPINE SKIING**
M Downhill

■ **LUGE**
M Singles

■ **SNOWBOARDING**
M Halfpipe

MONDAY, FEBRUARY 13

■ **LONG-TRACK SPEED SKATING**
M 500 meters

■ **FIGURE SKATING**
Pairs

■ **BIATHLON**
W 15 kilometer

■ **SNOWBOARDING**
W Halfpipe

*Finals listed; M=men; W=women

TUESDAY, FEBRUARY 14

■ **LONG-TRACK SPEED SKATING**
W 500 meters

■ **CROSS-COUNTRY SKIING**
M, W Team sprint

■ **ALPINE SKIING**
M Combined

Bode Miller,
United States

■ **BIATHLON**
M 10-kilometer sprint

■ **LUGE**
W Singles

WEDNESDAY, FEBRUARY 15

■ **SHORT-TRACK SPEED SKATING**
W 500 meters

■ **NORDIC COMBINED**
M Team

■ **ALPINE SKIING**
W Downhill

■ **LUGE**
M Doubles

■ **FREESTYLE SKIING**
M Moguls

THURSDAY, FEBRUARY 16

■ **LONG-TRACK SPEED SKATING**
M, W Team pursuit

■ **FIGURE SKATING**
M Singles

■ **CROSS-COUNTRY SKIING**
W 10 kilometer

■ **BIATHLON**
W 7.5 kilometer

■ **SKELETON**
W Singles

■ **SNOWBOARDING**
M Snowboard cross

FRIDAY, FEBRUARY 17

■ **CROSS-COUNTRY SKIING**
M 15 kilometers

■ **ALPINE SKIING**
W Combined

■ **SKELETON**
M Singles

■ **SNOWBOARDING**
W Snowboard cross

SATURDAY, FEBRUARY 18

■ **LONG-TRACK SPEED SKATING**
M 1,000 meters

■ **SHORT-TRACK SPEED SKATING**
W 1,500 meters
M 1,000 meters

■ **SKI JUMPING**
M Large hill individual

■ **CROSS-COUNTRY SKIING**
W 4 x 5-kilometer relay

■ **ALPINE SKIING**
M Super-G

■ **BIATHLON**
W 10-kilometer pursuit
M 12.5-kilometer pursuit

SUNDAY, FEBRUARY 19

■ **LONG-TRACK SPEED SKATING**
W 1,000 meters

■ **CROSS-COUNTRY SKIING**
M 4 x 10-kilometer relay

■ **ALPINE SKIING**
W Super-G

■ **BOBSLED**
M Two-man

MONDAY, FEBRUARY 20

■ **ICE HOCKEY**
W

■ **FIGURE SKATING**
Ice dancing

■ **SKI JUMPING**
M Large hill team

■ **ALPINE SKIING**
M Giant slalom

**Noelle Pikus-Pace,
United States**

DID YOU KNOW?

Snowboard Cross will be a first-time event at the 2006 Winter Games. In the preliminary heats, snowboarders will ride individually down a course of jumps, snow banks, and obstacles to advance to the next round. In the finals, four riders will race at the same time to determine the winner.

2006 WINTER OLYMPICS SCHEDULE (cont.)

Shani Davis,
United States

YURI KADOBNOV/AFP/GETTY IMAGES

TUESDAY, FEBRUARY 21

LONG-TRACK SPEED SKATING
M 1,500 meters

NORDIC COMBINED
M Sprint

BIATHLON
M 4 x 7.5-kilometer relay

BOBSLED
W Two-man

WEDNESDAY, FEBRUARY 22

LONG-TRACK SPEED SKATING
W 1,500 meters

SHORT-TRACK SPEED SKATING
W 3,000-meter relay

CROSS-COUNTRY SKIING
M, W Sprint

ALPINE SKIING
W Slalom

FREESTYLE SKIING
W Aerials

SNOWBOARDING
M Giant slalom

THURSDAY, FEBRUARY 23

FIGURE SKATING
W Singles

CURLING
W

BIATHLON
W 4 x 6-kilometer relay

FREESTYLE SKIING
M Aerials

SNOWBOARDING
W Giant slalom

FRIDAY, FEBRUARY 24

LONG-TRACK SPEED SKATING
M 10,000 meters

CURLING
M

CROSS-COUNTRY SKIING
W 30-kilometer mass start

ALPINE SKIING
W Giant slalom

SATURDAY, FEBRUARY 25

LONG-TRACK SPEED SKATING
W 5,000 meters

SHORT-TRACK SPEED SKATING
M 500 meters
W 1,000 meters
M 5,000-meter relay

ALPINE SKIING
M Slalom

BIATHLON
W 12.5-kilometer mass start
M 15-kilometer mass start

BOBSLED
M Four-man

SUNDAY, FEBRUARY 26

ICE HOCKEY
M

CROSS-COUNTRY SKIING
M 50-kilometer mass start

CLOSING CEREMONY

Joe Pack,
United States

PETER READ MILLER/SPORTS ILLUSTRATED

Fast Fact: Finnish ski jumpers showed off a new aerodynamic technique at the 1956 Winter Games. They held their arms flat to their sides while jumping instead of overhead in a diving position. The new style was successful. The Finns won a gold and a silver medal in the individual large hill event. That jumping technique is still used today.

PAST WINTER OLYMPIC HOSTS

YEAR		HOST	DATES	MEN	WOMEN	NATIONS
XIX	2002	SALT LAKE CITY, UTAH, USA	February 8-24	1,513	886	77
XVIII	1998	NAGANO, JAPAN	February 7-22	1,389	787	72
XVII	1994	LILLEHAMMER, NORWAY	February 12-27	1,215	522	67
XVI	1992	ALBERTVILLE, FRANCE	February 8-23	1,313	488	64
XV	1988	CALGARY, ALBERTA, CANADA	February 13-28	1,122	301	57
XIV	1984	SARAJEVO, YUGOSLAVIA	February 8-19	998	274	49
XIII	1980	LAKE PLACID, NEW YORK, USA	February 13-24	840	232	37
XII	1976	INNSBRUCK, AUSTRIA	February 4-15	892	231	37
XI	1972	SAPPORO, JAPAN	February 3-13	801	205	35
X	1968	GRENOBLE, FRANCE	February 6-18	947	211	37
IX	1964	INNSBRUCK, AUSTRIA	January 29-February 9	892	199	36
VIII	1960	SQUAW VALLEY, CALIFORNIA, USA	February 18-28	521	144	30
VII	1956	CORTINA d'AMPEZZO, ITALY	January 26-February 5	687	134	32
VI	1952	OSLO, NORWAY	February 14-25	585	109	30
V	1948	ST. MORITZ, SWITZERLAND	January 30-February 8	592	77	28
--	1944	CORTINA d'AMPEZZO, ITALY	Canceled because of World War II			
--	1940	GARMISCH-PARTENKIRCHEN, GERMANY	Canceled because of World War II			
IV	1936	GARMISCH-PARTENKIRCHEN, GERMANY	February 6-16	566	80	28
III	1932	LAKE PLACID, NEW YORK, USA	February 4-15	231	21	17
II	1928	ST. MORITZ, SWITZERLAND	February 11-19	438	26	25
I	1924	CHAMONIX, FRANCE	January 25-February 5	247	11	16

TRIVIA CHALLENGE

Who is the youngest male athlete to win a gold medal at a Winter Games?

Ski jumper Toni Nieminen of Finland was 16 years, 259 days old when he won the gold medal in the K120 team event at the 1992 Winter Games. Two days later, he won another gold in the K120 individual event.

TODAY'S STARS

■ **Lindsey Kildow, Alpine skier,** b. October 18, 1984, St. Paul, Minnesota. Kildow is a threat in all five skiing events (downhill, slalom, giant slalom, combined, and Super-G). She finished sixth overall in the World Cup standings in 2005. In 2004, Kildow won her first World Cup downhill race and won two medals at the junior world championships. She made the 2002 U.S. Olympic team at age 17 and came in sixth in the combined, the highest finish by an American woman in the history of the event.

■ **Apolo Ohno, speed skater,** b. May 22, 1982, Seattle, Washington. Ohno won the World Cup overall short-track speed skating championship in 2004-05. He also won individual titles in the 1,000-meter and 1,500-meter events. Ohno won the World Cup overall title and was champion in the 1,000 meters in 2003. At the 2002 Winter Olympics, he won a gold medal in the 1,500 meters and a silver in the 1,000 meters, even after crashing on the final turn in that race.

■ **Jeremy Bloom, freestyle skier,** b. April 2, 1982, Fort Collins, Colorado. Bloom won a record-tying six straight World Cup events to become the overall moguls champion in 2005. He reached the World Cup podium five times in 2004, including one win. At the 2003 World Championships, Bloom won a gold medal in duals and a silver in moguls. He finished ninth in moguls at the 2002 Winter Olympics. Bloom was a talented football receiver and punt returner at the University of Colorado from 2002-03. He gave up the sport to concentrate on training for the 2006 Olympics.

SIMON BRUTY/SPORTS ILLUSTRATED

Lindsey Kildow is skilled in all five skiing events: downhill, slalom, giant slalom, combined, and Super-G.

■ **Fast Fact:** At the 2002 Winter Olympics, skier Janica Kostelic of Croatia won gold medals in the combined, the slalom, and giant slalom. She also won a silver medal in the Super-G, becoming the first woman skier to win four medals at one Games.

ALL-TIME WINTER OLYMPIC MEDAL COUNT — NATION

NATION	GOLD	SILVER	BRONZE	TOTAL
NORWAY	94	93	73	260
SOVIET UNION (1956-88)	78	56	59	193
UNITED STATES	70	70	51	191
AUSTRIA	41	57	65	163
GERMANY (1992-present)	54	51	37	142
FINLAND	41	51	49	141
EAST GERMANY (1956-88)	39	37	35	111
SWEDEN	36	28	38	102
SWITZERLAND	32	33	36	101
CANADA	30	20	37	95

ALL-TIME WINTER OLYMPIC MEDAL COUNT — MEN

ATHLETE, Nation	SPORT	GOLD	SILVER	BRONZE	TOTAL
BJORN DAEHLIE, Norway	Nordic Skiing	8	4	0	12
SIXTEN JERNBERG, Sweden	Nordic Skiing	4	3	2	9
A. CLAS THUNBERG, Finland	Speed Skating	5	1	1	7
IVAR BALLANGRUD, Norway	Speed Skating	4	2	1	7
RICCO GROSS, Germany	Biathlon	3	3	1	7
VEIKKO HAKULINEN, Finland	Nordic Skiing	3	3	1	7
KJETIL ANDRE AAMODT, Norway	Alpine Skiing	3	2	2	7
EERO MANTYRANTA, Finland	Nordic Skiing	3	2	2	7
BOGDAN MUSIOL, East Germany/Germany	Bobsled	1	5	1	7
OLE EINAR BJOERNDALEN, Norway	Biathlon	5	1	0	6
THOMAS ALSGAARD, Norway	Nordic Skiing	4	2	0	6
GUNDE SVAN, Sweden	Nordic Skiing	4	1	1	6
VEGARD ULVANG, Norway	Nordic Skiing	3	2	1	6
JOHAN GROTTUMSBRATEN, Norway	Nordic Skiing	3	1	2	6
WOLFGANG HOPPE, East Germany/Germany	Bobsled	2	3	1	6
EUGENIO MONTI, Italy	Bobsled	2	2	2	6
VLADIMIR SMIRNOV, U.S.S.R./ United Team/Kazakhstan	Nordic Skiing	1	4	1	6
MIKA MYLLYLAE, Finland	Nordic Skiing	1	1	4	6
ROALD LARSEN, Norway	Speed Skating	0	2	4	6
HARRI KIRVESNIEMI, Finland	Nordic Skiing	0	0	6	6

ALL-TIME WINTER OLYMPIC MEDAL COUNT — WOMEN

ATHLETE, Nation	SPORT	GOLD	SILVER	BRONZE	TOTAL
RAISA SMETANINA, U.S.S.R./United Team	Nordic Skiing	4	5	1	10
LYUBOV EGOROVA, United Team/Russia	Nordic Skiing	6	3	0	9
LARISSA LAZUTINA, United Team/Russia	Nordic Skiing	5	3	1	9
STEFANIA BELMONDO, Italy	Nordic Skiing	2	3	4	9
GALINA KULAKOVA, U.S.S.R.	Nordic Skiing	4	2	2	8
KARIN KANIA, East Germany	Speed Skating	3	4	1	8
GUNDA NEIMANN-STIRNEMANN, Germany	Speed Skating	3	4	1	8
URSULA DISL, Germany	Biathlon	2	4	2	8
CLAUDIA PECHSTEIN, Germany	Speed Skating	4	1	2	7
MARJA-LIISA KIRVESNIEMI, Finland	Nordic Skiing	3	0	4	7
ELENA VALBE, United Team/Russia	Nordic Skiing	3	0	4	7
ANDREA EHRIG, East Germany	Speed Skating	1	5	1	7
LYDIA SKOBLIKOVA, U.S.S.R.	Speed Skating	6	0	0	6
BONNIE BLAIR, United States	Speed Skating	5	0	1	6
MANUELA DI CENTA, Italy	Nordic Skiing	2	2	2	6

Raisa Smetanina, U.S.S.R.

DOMINIQUE FAGET/AFP/GETTY IMAGES

ALL-TIME INDIVIDUAL OLYMPIC GOLD MEDALISTS

MEN

BJORN DAEHLIE, Norway	8
OLE EINAR BJOERNDALEN, Norway	5
ERIC HEIDEN, United States	5
A. CLAS THUNBERG, Finland	5

Ten tied with 4.

WOMEN

LYUBOV EGOROVA, United Team/Russia	6
LYDIA SKOBLIKOVA, U.S.S.R.	6
BONNIE BLAIR, United States	5
LARISSA LAZUTINA, United Team/Russia	5

Four tied with 4.

ATHLETES WITH WINTER AND SUMMER MEDALS

EDDIE EAGAN, United States — boxing gold medal (1920) and bobsled gold medal (1932)

JACOB TULLIN THAMS, Norway — ski jumping gold medal (1924) and yachting silver medal (1936)

CHRISTA LUDING-ROTHENBURGER, East Germany — speed skating gold medals (1984 and 1988), silver medal (1988), and bronze medal (1992), and cycling silver medal (1988)

CLARA HUGHES, Canada — two cycling bronze medals (1996) and speed skating bronze medal (2002)

TRIVIA CHALLENGE

When was the first time professional players from the National Hockey League participated in the Olympics?

The 1998 Winter Olympics in Nagano, Japan

LEGENDS

Bonnie Blair won a total of six medals at four Winter Olympics (1984, 1988, 1992, and 1994).

■ **Bonnie Blair, speed skater,** b. March 18, 1964, Cornwall, New York. Blair won more Winter Olympic gold medals (5) than any U.S. woman. She won gold medals in the 500-meter and 1,000-meter events at both the 1992 and 1994 Winter Games. Blair also won a gold medal in the 500 meters and a bronze in the 1,000 meters at the 1988 Winter Games. She is the only U.S. Olympian to win a gold medal in the same individual event (500 meters) at three straight Olympics.

■ **Bjorn Daehlie, cross country skier,** b. June 19, 1967, Elverum, Norway. Daehlie is the greatest cross-country skier in the history of the sport. He holds Winter Olympic records for the most overall medals won (12) and the most gold medals won (8). Daehlie has 46 World Cup victories, six overall World Cup titles, and nine World Championship gold medals.

■ **Michelle Kwan, figure skater,** b. July 7, 1980, Torrance, California. Kwan is the most decorated figure skater in U.S. history. In January 2005, she won her ninth U.S. women's championship, tying Maribel Vinson Owen, who won nine titles in the 1920's and 1930's. Kwan has won five world championships (1996, 1998, 2000, 2001, and 2003) and two Olympic medals (silver in 1998 and bronze in 2002). She has received 53 perfect 6.0 marks in major competitions and has been awarded at least one 6.0 in each of the last five U.S. championships, a U.S. record. Kwan is expected to compete at the 2006 Winter Games and try to win her first Olympic gold medal.

DID YOU KNOW?

Officials at the 1960 Winter Games were unsure if a skier had missed a gate in the men's slalom race. They asked CBS, which was televising the Games, if they could look at a videotape of the race. The idea of "instant replay" was born.

sikids.com

Visit our website for the latest stats and sports info.

SPORTS DIRECTORY

BASEBALL

Major League Baseball
245 Park Avenue
New York, NY 10167
(212) 931-7800

Arizona Diamondbacks
Bank One Ballpark
401 East Jefferson Street
Phoenix, AZ 85004
(602) 462-6500

Atlanta Braves
Turner Field
755 Hank Aaron Drive
Atlanta, GA 30315
(404) 522-7630

Baltimore Orioles
Oriole Park at Camden Yards
333 W. Camden Street
Baltimore, MD 21201
(410) 685-9800

Boston Red Sox
Fenway Park
4 Yawkey Way
Boston, MA 02215
(617) 267-9440

Chicago Cubs
Wrigley Field
1060 West Addison Street
Chicago, IL 60613
(773) 404-2827

Chicago White Sox
U.S. Cellular Field
333 West 35th Street
Chicago, IL 60616
(312) 674-1000

Cincinnati Reds
Great American Ball Park
100 Main Street
Cincinnati, OH 45202
(513) 765-7000

Cleveland Indians
Jacobs Field
2401 Ontario Street
Cleveland, OH 44115
(216) 420-4200

Colorado Rockies
Coors Field
2001 Blake Street
Denver, CO 80205
(303) 292-0200

Detroit Tigers
Comerica Park
2100 Woodward Avenue
Detroit, MI 48201
(313) 471-2000

Florida Marlins
Dolphins Stadium
2267 Dan Marino Boulevard
Miami, FL 33056
(305) 626-7400

Houston Astros
Minute Maid Park
501 Crawford Street
Houston, TX 77002
(713) 259-8000

Kansas City Royals
Kauffman Stadium
One Royal Way
Kansas City, MO 64129
(816) 921-8000

Los Angeles Angels of Anaheim
Angel Stadium of Anaheim
2000 Gene Autry Way
Anaheim, CA 92806
(714) 940-2000

Los Angeles Dodgers
Dodger Stadium
1000 Elysian Park Avenue
Los Angeles, CA 90012
(323) 224-1500

Milwaukee Brewers
Miller Park
One Brewers Way
Milwaukee, WI 53214
(414) 902-4400

Minnesota Twins
Metrodome
34 Kirby Puckett Place
Minneapolis, MN 55415
(612) 375-1366

New York Mets
Shea Stadium
123-01 Roosevelt Avenue
Flushing, NY 11368
(718) 507-6387

New York Yankees
Yankee Stadium
161st Street and River Avenue
Bronx, NY 10451
(718) 293-4300

Oakland Athletics
McAfee Coliseum
7000 Coliseum Way
Oakland, CA 94621
(510) 638-4900

Philadelphia Phillies
Citizens Bank Park
One Citizens Bank Way
Philadelphia, PA 19148
(215) 463-6000

Pittsburgh Pirates
PNC Park
115 Federal Street
Pittsburgh, PA 15212
(412) 323-5000

San Diego Padres
PETCO Park
100 Park Boulevard
San Diego, CA 92101
(619) 881-6500

San Francisco Giants
SBC Park
24 Willie Mays Plaza
San Francisco, CA 94107
(415) 972-2000

Seattle Mariners
Safeco Field
1250 First Avenue S.
Seattle, WA 98134
(206) 346-4000

St. Louis Cardinals
Busch Stadium
250 Stadium Plaza
St. Louis, MO 63102
(314) 421-3060

Tampa Bay Devil Rays
Tropicana Field
One Tropicana Drive
St. Petersburg, FL 33705
(727) 825-3137

Texas Rangers
Ameriquest Field in Arlington
1000 Ballpark Way
Arlington, TX 76011
(817) 273-5222

Toronto Blue Jays
Rogers Centre
1 Blue Jays Way
Suite 3200
Toronto, Ontario M5V 1J1
 Canada
(416) 341-1000

Washington Nationals
RFK Stadium
2400 E. Capitol Street, SE
Washington, D.C. 20003
(202) 675-6287

PRO FOOTBALL

National Football League
280 Park Avenue
New York, NY 10017
(212) 450-2000

Arizona Cardinals
8701 South Hardy Drive
Tempe, AZ 85284
(602) 379-0101

Atlanta Falcons
4400 Falcon Parkway
Flowery Branch, GA 30542
(770) 965-3115

Baltimore Ravens
1 Winning Drive
Owings Mills, MD 21117
(410) 701-4000

Buffalo Bills
One Bills Drive
Orchard Park, NY 14127
(716) 648-1800

Carolina Panthers
Bank of America Stadium
800 South Mint Street
Charlotte, NC 28202
(704) 358-7000

Chicago Bears
1000 Football Drive
Lake Forest, IL 60045
(847) 295-6600

Cincinnati Bengals
One Paul Brown Stadium
Cincinnati, OH 45202
(513) 621-3550

Cleveland Browns
76 Lou Groza Boulevard
Berea, OH 44017
(440) 891-5000

Dallas Cowboys
Cowboys Center
One Cowboys Parkway
Irving, TX 75063
(972) 556-9900

Denver Broncos
13655 Broncos Parkway
Englewood, CO 00112
(303) 649-9000

Detroit Lions
222 Republic Drive
Allen Park, MI 48101
(313) 216-4000

Green Bay Packers
Lambeau Field
1265 Lombardi Avenue
Green Bay, WI 54304
(920) 569-7500

Houston Texans
Reliant Stadium
Two Reliant Park
Houston, TX 77054
(832) 667-2000

Indianapolis Colts
7001 W. 56th Street
Indianapolis, IN 46254
(317) 297-2658

Jacksonville Jaguars
One ALLTEL Stadium Place
Jacksonville, FL 32202
(904) 633-6000

Kansas City Chiefs
One Arrowhead Drive
Kansas City, MO 64129
(816) 920-9300

Miami Dolphins
7500 S.W. 30th Street
Davie, FL 33314
(954) 452-7000

Minnesota Vikings
9520 Viking Drive
Eden Prairie, MN 55344
(952) 828-6500

New England Patriots
Gillette Stadium
One Patriot Place
Foxboro, MA 02035
(508) 543-8200

New Orleans Saints
5800 Airline Drive
Metairie, LA 70003
(504) 733-0255

New York Giants
Giants Stadium
East Rutherford, NJ 07073
(201) 935 8111

New York Jets
1000 Fulton Avenue
Hempstead, NY 11550
(516) 560-8100

Oakland Raiders
1220 Harbor Bay Parkway
Alameda, CA 94502
(510) 864-5000

Philadelphia Eagles
NovaCare Complex
One NovaCare Way
Philadelphia, PA 19145
(215) 463-2500

Pittsburgh Steelers
3400 South Water Street
Pittsburgh, PA 15203
(412) 432-7800

San Diego Chargers
Qualcomm Stadium
4020 Murphy Canyon Road
San Diego, CA 92123
(858) 874-4500

San Francisco 49ers
4949 Centennial Boulevard
Santa Clara, CA 95054
(408) 562-4949

Seattle Seahawks
11220 N.E. 53rd Street
Kirkland, WA 98033
(425) 827-9777

St. Louis Rams
One Rams Way
St. Louis, MO 63045
(314) 982-7267

Tampa Bay Buccaneers
One Buccaneer Place
Tampa, FL 33607
(813) 870-2700

Tennessee Titans
460 Great Circle Road
Nashville, TN 37228
(615) 565-4000

Washington Redskins
21300 Redskin Park Drive
Ashburn, VA 20147
(703) 726-7000

OTHER LEAGUES

Canadian Football League
50 Wellington Street East
3rd Floor
Toronto, Ontario M5E 1C8
 Canada
(416) 322-9650

NFL Europe
280 Park Avenue
New York, NY 10017
(212) 450-2000

PRO BASKETBALL

National Basketball Association
645 Fifth Avenue
New York, NY 10022
(212) 407-8000

Atlanta Hawks
Centennial Tower
101 Marietta Street, N.W.
Suite 1900
Atlanta, GA 30303
(404) 827-3800

Boston Celtics
151 Merrimac Street
Boston, MA 02114
(617) 854-8000

Charlotte Bobcats
129 W. Trade Street
Suite 700
Charlotte, NC 28202
(704) 424-4120

Chicago Bulls
1901 W. Madison Street
Chicago, IL 60612
(312) 455-4000

Cleveland Cavaliers
One Center Court
Cleveland, OH 44115
(216) 420-2000

Dallas Mavericks
2500 Victory Avenue
Dallas, TX 75219
(214) 665-4600

Denver Nuggets
1000 Chopper Circle
Denver, CO 80204
(303) 405-1100

Detroit Pistons
Four Championship Drive
Auburn Hills, MI 48326
(248) 377-0100

Golden State Warriors
1011 Broadway
Oakland, CA 94607
(510) 986-2200

Houston Rockets
1510 Polk Street
Houston, TX 77002
(713) 758-7200

Indiana Pacers
125 South Pennsylvania Street
Indianapolis, IN 46204
(317) 917-2500

Los Angeles Clippers
1111 South Figueroa Street
Suite 1100
Los Angeles, CA 90015
(213) 742-7500

Los Angeles Lakers
555 North Nash Street
El Segundo, CA 90245
(310) 426-6000

Memphis Grizzlies
191 Beale Street
Memphis, TN 38103
(901) 205-1234

Miami Heat
601 Biscayne Boulevard
Miami, FL 33132
(786) 777-4328

Milwaukee Bucks
1001 North Fourth Street
Milwaukee, WI 53203
(414) 227-0500

Minnesota Timberwolves
600 First Avenue North
Minneapolis, MN 55403
(612) 673-1600

New Jersey Nets
390 Murray Hill Parkway
East Rutherford, NJ 07073
(201) 935-8888

New Orleans Hornets
1501 Girod Street
New Orleans, LA 70113
(504) 301-4000

New York Knicks
Two Pennsylvania Plaza
14th Floor
New York, NY 10121
(212) 465-5867

Orlando Magic
8701 Maitland Summit
 Boulevard
Orlando, FL 32810
(407) 916-2400

Philadelphia 76ers
3601 South Broad Street
Philadelphia, PA 19148
(215) 339-7600

Phoenix Suns
201 East Jefferson Street
Phoenix, AZ 85004
(602) 379-7900

Portland Trail Blazers
One Center Court
Suite 200
Portland, OR 97227
(503) 234-9291

Sacramento Kings
One Sports Parkway
Sacramento, CA 95834
(916) 928-0000

San Antonio Spurs
One SBC Center
San Antonio, TX 78219
(210) 444-5000

Seattle SuperSonics
351 Elliott Avenue West
Suite 500
Seattle, WA 98119
(206) 281-5800

Toronto Raptors
40 Bay Street
Suite 400
Toronto, Ontario M5J 2X2
Canada
(416) 815-5600

Utah Jazz
301 West South Temple
Salt Lake City, UT 84101
(801) 325-2500

Washington Wizards
601 F Street, NW
Washington, D.C. 20004
(202) 661-5000

WOMEN'S NATIONAL BASKETBALL ASSOCIATION

WNBA
645 Fifth Avenue
New York, NY 10022
(212) 688-9622

Charlotte Sting
129 W. Trade Street
Suite 700
Charlotte, NC 28202
(704) 357-0252

Connecticut Sun
1 Mohegan Sun Boulevard
Uncasville, CT 06382
(860) 862-4000

Detroit Shock
Four Championship Drive
Auburn Hills, MI 48326
(248) 377-0100

Houston Comets
1510 Polk Street
Houston, TX 77002
(713) 627-9622

Indiana Fever
125 S. Pennsylvania Street
Indianapolis, IN 46204
(317) 917-2500

Los Angeles Sparks
2151 East Grand Avenue
Suite 100
El Segundo, CA 90245
(310) 341-1000

Minnesota Lynx
600 First Avenue North
Minneapolis, MN 55403
(612) 673-1600

New York Liberty
Two Pennsylvania Plaza
New York, NY 10121
(212) 564-9622

Phoenix Mercury
201 East Jefferson Street
Phoenix, AZ 85004
(602) 514-8333

Sacramento Monarchs
One Sports Parkway
Sacramento, CA 95834
(916) 928-0000

San Antonio Silver Stars
One SBC Center
San Antonio, TX 78219
(210) 444-5050

Seattle Storm
351 Elliott Avenue West
Suite 500
Seattle, WA 98119
(206) 281-5800

Washington Mystics
MCI Center
601 F Street, NW
Washington, D.C. 20004
(202) 661-5000

HOCKEY

National Hockey League
1251 Avenue of the Americas
47th Floor
New York, NY 10020
(212) 789-2000

Mighty Ducks of Anaheim
Arrowhead Pond of Anaheim
2695 Katella Avenue
Anaheim, CA 92806
(714) 940-2900

Atlanta Thrashers
Centennial Tower
101 Marietta Street, N.W.
Suite 1900
Atlanta, GA 30303
(404) 827-5300

Boston Bruins
TD Banknorth Garden
One FleetCenter
Suite 250
Boston, MA 02114-1303
(617) 624-1900

Buffalo Sabres
HSBC Arena
One Seymour H. Knox III
 Plaza
Buffalo, NY 14203
(716) 855-4100

Calgary Flames
Pengrowth Saddledome
P.O. Box 1540
Station M
Calgary, Alberta T2P 3B9
 Canada
(403) 777-4636

Carolina Hurricanes
RBC Center
1400 Edwards Mill Road
Raleigh, NC 27607
(919) 467-7825

Chicago Blackhawks
United Center
1901 W. Madison Street
Chicago, IL 60612
(312) 455-7000

Colorado Avalanche
Pepsi Center
1000 Chopper Circle
Denver, CO 80204
(303) 405-1100

Columbus Blue Jackets
Nationwide Arena
200 West Nationwide
 Boulevard
Columbus, OH 43215
(614) 246-4625

Dallas Stars
Dr Pepper StarCenter
2601 Avenue of the Stars
Frisco, TX 75034
(214) 387-5500

Detroit Red Wings
Joe Louis Arena
600 Civic Center Drive
Detroit, MI 48226
(313) 396-7544

Edmonton Oilers
Skyreach Centre
11230-110th Street
Edmonton, Alberta T5G 3H7
  Canada
(780) 414-4000

Florida Panthers
Office Depot Center
One Panther Parkway
Sunrise, FL 33323
(954) 835-7000

Los Angeles Kings
HealthSouth Training Center
555 N. Nash Street
El Segundo, CA 90245
(310) 535-4500

Minnesota Wild
317 Washington Street
St. Paul, MN 55102
(651) 602-6000

Montreal Canadiens
Bell Centre
1260 de la Gauchetière West
Montreal, Quebec H3B 5E8
  Canada
(514) 932-2582

Nashville Predators
Gaylord Entertainment Center
501 Broadway
Nashville, TN 37203
(615) 770-2300

New Jersey Devils
Continental Airlines Arena
P.O. Box 504
East Rutherford, NJ 07073
(201) 935-6050

New York Islanders
1535 Old Country Road
Plainview, NY 11803
(516) 501-6700

New York Rangers
Madison Square Garden
Two Pennsylvania Plaza
14th Floor
New York, NY 10121
(212) 465-6486

Ottawa Senators
Corel Centre
1000 Palladium Drive
Kanata, Ontario K2V 1A5
  Canada
(613) 599-0250

Philadelphia Flyers
Wachovia Center
3601 South Broad Street
Philadelphia, PA 19148
(215) 465-4500

Phoenix Coyotes
5800 W. Glenn Drive
Suite 350
Glendale, AZ 85301
(623) 463-8800

Pittsburgh Penguins
Mellon Arena
66 Mario Lemieux Place
Pittsburgh, PA 15219
(412) 642-1300

San Jose Sharks
HP Pavilion at San Jose
525 West Santa Clara Street
San Jose, CA 95113
(408) 287-7070

St. Louis Blues
Savvis Center
1401 Clark Avenue
St. Louis, MO 63103
(314) 622-2500

Tampa Bay Lightning
St. Pete Times Forum
401 Channelside Drive
Tampa, FL 33602
(813) 301-6500

Toronto Maple Leafs
Air Canada Centre
40 Bay Street
Suite 400
Toronto, Ontario M5J 2X2
  Canada
(416) 815-5700

Vancouver Canucks
General Motors Place
800 Griffiths Way
Vancouver, British Columbia
  V6B 6G1
  Canada
(604) 899-4600

Washington Capitals
401 Ninth Street, NW
Suite 750
Washington, D.C. 20004
(202) 266-2200

COLLEGE SPORTS

National Collegiate Athletic Association (NCAA)
700 W. Washington Street
P.O. Box 6222
Indianapolis, IN 46206-6222
(317) 917-6222

Atlantic Coast Conference
P.O. Drawer ACC
Greensboro, NC 27417-6724
(336) 854-8787

Big East Conference
222 Richmond Street
Suite 110
Providence, RI 02903
(401) 272-9108

Big Ten Conference
1500 West Higgins Road
Park Ridge, IL 60068-6300
(847) 696-1010

Big 12 Conference
2201 Stemmons Freeway
28th Floor
Dallas, TX 75207
(214) 742-1212

Big West Conference
2 Corporate Park
Irvine, CA 92606
(949) 261-2525

Conference USA
5201 North O'Connor Blvd.
Suite 300
Irving, TX 75039
(214) 774-1300

Ivy League
228 Alexander Street
2nd Floor
Princeton, NJ 08544
(609) 258-6426

Mid-American Conference
24 Public Square
15th Floor
Cleveland, OH 44113
(216) 566-4622

Pacific-10 Conference
800 S. Broadway
Suite 400
Walnut Creek, CA 94596
(925) 932-4411

Southeastern Conference
2201 Richard Arrington
Boulevard North
Birmingham, AL 35203
(205) 458-3000

Western Athletic Conference
9250 East Cootilla Avenue
Suite 300
Englewood, CO 80112
(303) 799-9221

OTHER SPORTS

Association of Tennis Professionals Tour (ATP)
201 ATP Boulevard
Ponte Vedra Beach, FL 32082
(904) 285-8000

Championship Auto Racing Teams (CART)
5350 West Lakeview Parkway
South Drive
Indianapolis, IN 46268
(317) 715-4100

Indy Racing League
4565 West 16th Street
Indianapolis, IN 46222
(317) 484-6526

Ladies Professional Golf Association (LPGA)
100 International Golf Drive
Daytona Beach, FL 32124
(386) 274-6200

Major League Soccer (MLS)
110 East 42nd Street
10th Floor
New York, NY 10017
(212) 450-1200

National Association for Stock Car Auto Racing (NASCAR)
1801 W. International
Speedway Boulevard
Daytona Beach, FL 32114-1243
(386) 253-0611

PGA Tour
112 PGA Tour Boulevard
Ponte Vedra Beach, FL 32082
(904) 285-3700

United Soccer Leagues
14497 North Dale Mabry
Highway
Suite 201
Tampa, Fl 33618
(813) 963-3909

United States Olympic Training Center
One Olympic Plaza
Colorado Springs, CO 80909
(719) 632-5551

USA Basketball
5465 Mark Dabling Boulevard
Colorado Springs, CO 80918
(719) 590-4800

USA Cycling
One Olympic Plaza
Colorado Springs, CO 80909
(719) 866-4581

USA Hockey
1775 Bob Johnson Drive
Colorado Springs, CO 80906
(719) 576-8724

USA Luge
57 Church Street
Lake Placid, NY 12946
(518) 523-2071

USA Swimming
One Olympic Plaza
Colorado Springs, CO 80909
(719) 866-4578

USA Track & Field
1 RCA Dome
Suite 140
Indianapolis, IN 46225
(317) 261-0500

USA Water Polo, Inc.
1631 Mesa Avenue
Suite A-1
Colorado Springs, CO 80906
(719) 634-0699

U.S. Bobsled and Skeleton Federation
P.O. Box 828
Lake Placid, NY 12946
(518) 523-1842

U.S. Figure Skating Association
20 First Street
Colorado Springs, CO 80906
(719) 635-5200

U.S. Ski and Snowboard Association
P.O. Box 100
Park City, UT 84060
(435) 649-9090

U.S. Soccer Federation
1801 South Prairie Avenue
Chicago, IL 60616
(312) 808-1300

U.S. Speedskating
P.O. Box 450639
Westlake, OH 44145
(440) 899-0128

Women's Tennis Association (WTA)
One Progress Plaza
Suite 1500
St. Petersburg, FL 33701
(727) 895-5000